W9-ATT-404

Successful Direct Marketing Methods

Fifth Edition

Bob Stone

Chairman Emeritus, Stone & Adler, Inc.

NTC Business Books

NTC a division of *NTC Publishing Group* • Lincolnwood, Illinois USA

Library of Congress Cataloging-in-Publication Data

Stone, Bob,
     Successful direct marketing methods / Bob Stone. — 5th ed.
       p.   cm.
     ISBN 0-8442-3510-5
     1. Direct marketing.   I. Title.
    HF5415 . 126 . S757
    658 . 8 ' 4—dc20

93–5716
CIP

Published by NTC Business Books, a division of NTC Publishing Group
4255 West Touhy Avenue,
Lincolnwood (Chicago), Illinois 60646-1975, U.S.A.
© 1994 by Bob Stone. All rights reserved.
No part of this book may be reproduced, stored in a retrieval system,
or transmitted in any form or by any means,
electronic, mechanical, photocopying, recording or otherwise,
without the prior permission of NTC Publishing Group.
Manufactured in the United States of America.

3 4 5 6 7 8 9 AG 9 8 7 6 5 4 3 2 1

Contents

SECTION II

Choosing Media for Your Message

CHAPTER FOURTEEN

Telemarketing   323

S E C T I O N   III

Creating and Producing Direct Marketing

CHAPTER FIFTEEN

Techniques of Creating Direct Mail Packages   362

CHAPTER TWENTY-ONE

Research for Direct Marketers

About the Author

Bob Stone

Position
Chairman Emeritus of Stone & Adler, Inc.

Articles
Author of more than 200 articles on direct marketing, which have appeared in *Advertising Age* magazine since 1967.

Awards
Six-time winner of the Direct Marketing Association's Best of Industry Award. The firm he cofounded, Stone & Adler, has received the Direct Marketing Association's highest honors, including the Silver and Gold Echo Awards as well as the International Direct Marketing & Mail Order Symposium's Bronze Carrier Pigeon Award. Member of the Direct Marketing Hall of Fame. Recipient of the Edward N. Mayer, Jr., Award for contributions to direct marketing education, the Charles S. Downes Award for direct marketing contributions, and the John Caples Award for copy excellence.

Affiliations
Former director of the Direct Marketing Association
Former president of the Chicago Association of Direct Marketing
Former membership chairman of the Direct Marketing Association
Former president of the Associated Third Class Mail Users
Board member of the Direct Marketing Educational Foundation
Adjunct Professor at the University of Missouri
Adjunct Professor at Northwestern University

Foreword

When my good friend and author of this book, Bob Stone, told me that the fifth edition of *Successful Direct Marketing Methods* would be the largest yet, I was not surprised. Such has been the growth of direct marketing itself: the philosophy, the discipline, the tools, the techniques. Indeed the four prior editions, and Bob Stone himself, have played a major role in educating students and professionals in this growing discipline. This new edition continues, enhances, and updates that educational process.

There are many, practitioners and academics alike, who have come to view Bob Stone as a direct marketing "guru." *Successful Direct Marketing Methods* itself has been called the "bible" of direct marketing ever since its first edition. Both of these accolades are not without cause. Yet, twenty years prior to the first edition of *this* text in 1975, Bob had already reached best-seller status with eight printings of his earlier book, *Successful Direct Mail Advertising and Selling*. (My own copy of *that* volume was personally inscribed and dated by Bob on 6/27/55!)

Certainly few, if any, can match Bob Stone's track record as an author, educator, long-time practitioner, and then co-founder of Stone & Adler, Inc., the legendary advertising agency which was the first to devote itself to direct response.

The contents of the twenty-one chapters that follow confirm the fact that the tenets of direct marketing are now multidisciplinary. There is more here than just direct response advertising; more than simply measurement and accountability; more even than the all-important database—all of these characteristics which have been said to distinguish "direct" from traditional marketing. We now find that direct marketing is an attitude, a belief, a way of doing things. Bob Stone aptly deals with the totality of direct marketing by transferring to it knowledge from a variety of disciplines and honing those many skills necessary for success in its practice.

From the first chapter devoted to an overview of the scope of direct marketing through the final chapters devoted to its management, *Successful Direct Marketing Methods* takes you through all of the discipline's media and message aspects. The text is full of cases, experiences, and illustrations presented in the clear writing style typical of Bob Stone.

Marketing today must be directed and targeted. Offers must be both relevant and benefit-oriented. While the tools and techniques of modern direct marketing have long been used by mail-order firms for remote transactions, these same tools and techniques are today being applied to retail traffic-building and business-to-business lead generation for personal or telephone

sales follow-up. They are being applied with equal fervor by product *and* service enterprises; by consumer *and* industrial companies; by for-profit *and* non-profit organizations; by fund-raising agencies *and* political action groups. *Successful Direct Marketing Methods* is a text for all reasons.

Martin Baier
Director
Center for Direct Marketing Education and Research
University of Missouri-Kansas City

Preface

Before 1975 there were a number of books written about letter writing and mail order advertising. But, strange as it may seem, never before had there been a book written about the totality of direct marketing. *Successful Direct Marketing Methods* was the very first.

It has been said that timing is everything. This certainly proved to be true in my case, for a quiet revolution was taking place—not only in the United States, but around the world. Direct marketing was, at last, becoming recognized as a major discipline, a discipline that was more measurable than any other.

Direct marketing agencies sprang up everywhere. Fortune 500 companies embraced the concept. Direct marketing seminars sold out to capacity audiences. The Direct Marketing Association attracted thousands instead of hundreds to its annual conventions. And the Direct Marketing Educational Foundation was on its way towards getting direct marketing taught in college classrooms. Direct marketing had truly arrived.

Direct marketing grew at such a rapid rate that revised, updated editions of *Successful Direct Marketing Methods* were published in 1979, 1984, and 1988. Now we have the 1993 edition.

The world of direct marketing is a vastly different world than it was in 1975. All of the intervening years have been evolutionary. The driving force of evolutionary changes has been refinement and sophistication of data bases, the ability to target market as never before.

But the changes have not been restricted to mechanical techniques. Perhaps even more evolutionary is the way we think about direct marketing today. Where back in the '70s and '80s traditional marketers thought of direct marketing as a stand-alone discipline, they now embrace it as a part of their total marketing mix.

The evolution has brought us from a stand-alone discipline to becoming an integral part of integrated communications. Direct marketing integrated with general advertising, sales promotion, and public relations is the latest trend. Will the evolution stop here? Probably not.

A peek into the future, as envisioned by some of our leaders, might foretell future developments. In the year-end issue of *The DeLay Letter*, Bob DeLay, former president of the Direct Marketing Association, provides these quotes from Harris Gordon, partner, Deloitte & Touche, and Jeffrey Steinberg, senior consultant, Deloitte & Touche:

"The impact of advanced technology on direct marketing will accelerate in the next 5–10 years as households, as well as businesses, 'plug' into more

xvi SUCCESSFUL DIRECT MARKETING METHODS

advanced, interactive technologies that provide better targeting, increased media choices, and quicker response time. The enabling technologies will be: CDIs (interactive CDs) and photo CDs used with home computers and entertainment systems; large scale cable TV channels; and interactive TV. The increase in cable channels will be based on fiber optic cable or current cable technology augmented with advanced data compression techniques.

"Interactive CDs and photo CDs will allow direct marketers to build personalized disks that show pictures of the offer on a TV or computer screen. L.L. Bean is now testing such a system. A click of a button will show a sweater from a catalog page in the color you desire. Future revisions of the software might allow the consumer to enter an order and credit card number saving time and order entry.

"With the advent of hundreds of cable TV channels and the like conversion of the phone system to fiber optic delivery, *there will be an explosion of choices*. Where we now have two primary home shopping channels, there may be 50—fashion, electronics, collectibles, etc. Combined with interactive TV, viewers will be able to electronically request promotional material and products without using the telephone.

"While all this sounds fancy and grandiose, it is not going to happen next year. Probably in the next five years on a limited scale. And, definitely in the next ten years. What does this coming convergence of technology mean for you today? It means that *you will need to start planning to become a rapid response organization*. Your firm will need to be able to select merchandise, develop offers, fulfill orders, and analyze back-end performance much faster than you do today. Processes that took weeks will need to be done in days or even hours since a new catalog or promotion will be airing every day. This capability will require leading-edge information and database marketing systems, a flexible management structure, technological savvy, and an overall low-cost infrastructure. As a result, the leading direct marketers in the coming interactive age are going to be the ones who can make decisions quicker and react to a large quantity of electronic orders."

Richard C. Anderson, vice chairman/CEO of Lands End, Inc., said this about the future:

"The mere promise of change has elected a new American president. Hopefully the most formidable achievement lies just ahead: taking a sharp axe to the federal deficit strangling not only the American economy, but disturbing the world community as well.

"If we begin to see this happen, I firmly believe those of us in the specialty catalog business can realistically envision a very positive future, for three commanding reasons.

"First, our very special segment of the marketplace—highly educated, professionally active, yet family-oriented customers, with incomes to match their professionalism—is growing faster than any other group.

"Second, their impatience with the time-consuming rigors of shopping, crowded malls with clogged parking lots, and stores with fewer and more indifferent clerks is also growing.

"And finally, in these more realistic times, they are becoming more and more insistent on high-quality products that deliver genuine value, not adulterated by the customary middlemen markups they encounter in the general retail environment."

Yes—direct marketing is in the forefront of new evolutions and new revolutions yet to come. The best of success to you in the exciting world of direct marketing!

Acknowledgments

As with all editions of *Successful Direct Marketing Methods*, the materials in this fifth edition in no way reflect the sole thinking of the author. Instead, this book is a reflection of all that is happening in direct marketing, with generous contributions from a host of people and organizations.

Thanks to the Direct Marketing Association for the statistics it has provided. To Pete Hoke, publisher of *Direct Marketing*, for his contributions. To Rose Harper, president of the Kleid Co., Inc., for her input on mailing lists. To Stan Rapp and Tom Collins, cofounders of Rapp & Collins, for their contributions on magazines and the techniques of creating print advertising.

And my thanks go likewise to Jack Schmid, president of J. Schmid & Associates, Inc., for his input on catalogs. To Vic Hunter, president of Hunter Business Direct, for his contributions on business-to-business direct marketing. To Martin Baier, director of the University of Missouri Center for Direct Marketing, for his contributions on data bases. And to Bob Kestnbaum, president of Kestnbaum & Company, for his input on the mathematics of direct marketing.

Numerous present and former staff members of Stone & Adler contributed to this book. Special thanks go to Jerry Wood for his contributions on strategic planning. To Don Kanter for his input on creating mail packages. And to Vince Copp for his contributions on direct marketing research.

Thanks also go to Frank Daniels for his input on idea development. And finally—a special thank you to Aaron Adler, cofounder of Stone & Adler, for lending his wisdom to the chapter on selecting and selling merchandise.

The World of Direct Marketing

CHAPTER ONE

The Scope of Direct Marketing

The scope of direct marketing has continued to expand for decades, and new applications have been numerous. Long trumpeted as a stand-alone discipline, direct marketing has matured and is rapidly taking its place as a key component in the total marketing mix.

A Rich Legacy

To explore where we are, we must look back to where we've been. The chronicle of direct marketing has been enriched by pioneers who were both visionary and innovative, and the number of technical breakthroughs boggles the mind.

We start in the early 1900s when Richard Sears, a young railroad station-master, was stuck with a shipment of gold watches. He asked a logical question of himself: "Who absolutely positively has to know the correct time at all times?" "Other railroad station agents" was the obvious deduction. He got a list, mailed, and sold out. Thus niche marketing was born.

Having separately discovered the wonders of mail order, he and Aaron Montgomery Ward launched the first mail-order catalogs.

By 1910 Sears realized that if his mail-order business was to sustain rapid growth he'd have to allow credit to his prime market—farmers—so they could make purchases between harvests. With the issuance of the first Sears credit card, sales boomed.

It wasn't until the 1950s that Diners Club and American Express were introduced. Visa and MasterCard came a few decades later, followed by the Discover Card.

The father of the "lead" generation was John Patterson, founder of the National Cash Register Co. He discovered back in the 1880s that his derby-topped salesmen could sell more of his newfangled cash registers if he provided them with qualified leads.

It's only a little over 50 years ago that the Book-of-the-Month Club was launched. It spread selling cost over a number of titles instead of applying it to one at a time. This innovative concept led to scores of "of-the-month clubs," including records, tapes, and CDs.

In the late 1950s direct response print began to boom due to a single publishing development—regional editions. For the first time, direct response advertisers could test mass circulation magazines at a fraction of total circulation costs. And in the same decade, bind-in cards were introduced, increasing response over on-page coupons up to 600 percent.

In 1965 newspaper inserts arrived on the scene, making it possible for the first time to enjoy the same quality of printing in a newspaper as in direct mail.

Just one year later, in 1966, toll-free phone service was introduced, spawning a whole new industry—telemarketing.

Only one year after that, in 1967, ZIP codes became mandatory. First viewed as a financial burden, ZIP codes were later considered a dynamic marketing tool, bringing segmentation, with overlays, to new heights.

Through all these exciting decades America's love affair with catalogs continued to grow. Neiman-Marcus is credited with introducing the first upscale catalog. But a deluge of upscale catalogs was started in 1972 by Roger Horchow with his Horchow Collection catalog. Previously Mr. Horchow was in charge of the famous Neiman-Marcus catalog.

The 1980s were marked by more breakthroughs. Videocassettes became a direct response medium, cable joined regular television as a dynamic direct response medium, Fax came into its own, and home-shopping shows proliferated, selling billions in merchandise. Personal computers became interactive mediums. On-line information services such as Comp-U-Serve and Prodigy became a way of life for a computer generation.

The 30 Timeless Direct Marketing Principles

From the rich history of direct marketing certain timeless principles have emerged. There are 30 principles that, when applied consistently and creatively with the tools now available, lead to direct marketing success.

1. *All customers are not created equal*. Give or take a few percentage points, 80 percent of repeat business for goods and services will come from 20 percent of your customer base.

2. The most important order you ever get from a customer is the *second order*. Why? Because a two-time buyer is at least twice as likely to buy again as a one-time buyer.

3. Maximizing direct mail success depends first upon the *lists you use*, second upon the *offers you make*, and third upon the *copy and graphics you create*.

4. If, on a given list, *"hotline" names don't work*, the other list categories offer little opportunity for success.

5. *Merge/purge names*—those that appear on two or more lists—will outpull any single list from which these names have been extracted.

6. *Direct response lists* will most always outpull compiled lists.

7. *Overlays on lists* (enhancements), such as lifestyle characteristics, income, education, age, marital status, and propensity to respond by mail or phone, will always improve response.

8. A *follow-up* to the same list within 30 days will pull 40 percent to 50 percent of the first mailing.

9. *"Yes/No" offers* consistently produce more orders than offers that don't request "no" responses.

10. The *"take rate"* for negative option offers will always outpull positive option offers at least two to one.

11. Credit card privileges will *outperform cash* with order at least two to one.

12. Credit card privileges will *increase the size* of the average catalog order by 20 percent or more.

13. *Time limit offers*, particularly those which give a specific date, outpull offers with no time limit practically every time.

14. *Free-gift offers*, particularly where the gift appeals to self-interest, outpull discount offers consistently.

15. *Sweepstakes*, particularly in conjunction with impulse purchases, will increase order volume 35 percent or more.

16. You will collect far more money in a fund-raising effort if you ask for a *specific amount* from a purchaser. Likewise, you will collect more money if the appeal is tied to a specific project.

17. People buy *benefits*, not features.

18. The *longer* you can keep someone reading your copy, the better your chances of success.

19. The *timing and frequency* of renewal letters is vital. But I can report nothing but failure over a period of 40 years in attempts to hype renewals with "improved copy." I've concluded that the product—the magazine, for example—is *the factor* in making a renewal decision.

20. Self-mailers are cheaper to produce, but they practically never outpull *envelope-enclosed* letter mailings.

21. A *preprint* of a forthcoming ad, accompanied by a letter and response form, will outpull a postprint mailing package by 50 percent or more.

22. It is easier to increase the *average dollar amount* of an order than it is to increase percent of response.

23. You will get far more new catalog customers if you put your proven winners in the *front pages* of your catalog.

24. Assuming items of similar appeal, you will always get a higher response rate from a *32-page catalog* than from a 24-page catalog.

25. A *new* catalog to a catalog customer base will outpull cold lists by 400 percent to 800 percent.

26. A print ad with a *bind-in card* will outpull the same ad without a bind-in up to 600 percent.

27. A *direct response*, direct sale TV commercial of 120 seconds will outpull a 60-second direct response commercial better than two to one.

28. A *TV support commercial* will increase response from a newspaper insert up to 50 percent.

29. The *closure rate* from qualified leads can be from two to four times as effective as cold calls.

30. *Telephone-generated leads* are likely to close four to six times greater than mail-generated leads.

Direct Marketing Defined

The definition of direct marketing has evolved over time. The current "official" definition given by the Direct Marketing Association is:

> Direct marketing is an interactive system of marketing which uses one or more advertising media to effect a measurable response and/or transaction at any location.

There are those who make a case that, with continuing growth and development in the field, a standard definition is no longer valid. There are those who would drop the term *direct marketing* in favor of such terms as *directed marketing*, or *relationship marketing*, or *action advertising*, or *integrated marketing*. Where the debate will end no one knows.

Nevertheless, it is important to have a thorough understanding of the current official definition. Let us dissect the definition.

- *Interactive*: Interaction—one-on-one communication between marketer and prospect/customer—is an important key.

- *One or more advertising media*: Direct marketing is not restricted to any one medium. Indeed, direct marketers have discovered there is synergism among the media. A combination of media often is far more productive than any single medium.

- *Measurable response*: Measurability is a hallmark of direct marketing. Everything in the field, with rare exceptions, is measurable. Direct marketers know what they spend, and they know what they get back.

- *Transaction at any location*: The world is direct marketing's oyster—transactions can take place by telephone, at a kiosk, by mail, at home, at a store.

An overall view of the media from which direct marketers can choose is given in the direct marketing flowchart presented in Exhibit 1–1. Interspersed with the media in the flowchart are the disciplines involved in a successful direct marketing operation.

Exhibit 1–1. Direct Marketing Flow Chart

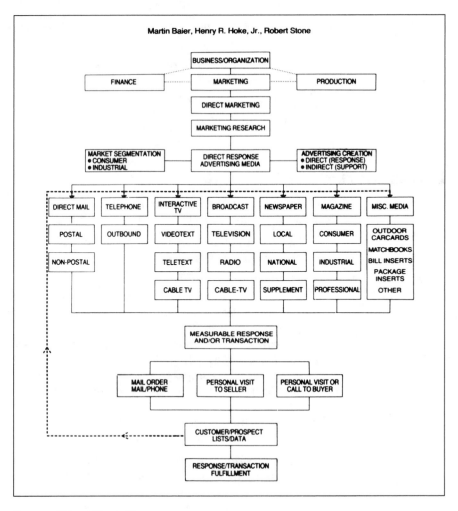

Source: *Direct Marketing*.

Integrated Communications

As direct marketing continues to expand in scope and to mature as a discipline, a trend seems to be developing to include direct marketing in a total loop along with general advertising, sales promotion, and public relations. Hence the term *integrated communications*.

The concept makes a lot of sense. But if integrated communications is to be the bright future for direct marketing, as many predict, then both advertising agencies and direct marketers must begin to look at direct marketing in a different way.

The boom years of direct marketing—from the late 1950s to the 1980s—saw direct marketing enjoy fantastic growth as a stand-alone discipline and as a separate profit center. Integrated communications dictates integrated budgets, a concept contrary to the way direct marketing units are set up in most general advertising agencies. There is a problem with most national advertisers too: Direct marketing units, for the most part, are separate and apart from general advertising, sales promotion, and public relations budgets. This situation leads to turf battles, direct marketing being the Orphan Annie in the fight for budget dollars in many cases.

There are two notable exceptions to these turf battles: Leo Burnett USA, which does not operate direct marketing as a separate profit center, and IBM, which has integrated all forms of communication and has assigned a "policeman" to allocate budget dollars according to the marketing needs for the implementation of each given program (see Exhibit 1–2).

Integrated Communications Defined

Recognizing the trend toward integrated communications, the American Association of Advertising Agencies has settled on the following definition:

> *Integrated communications:* A concept of marketing communications planning that recognizes the added value in a program that integrates a variety of strategic disciplines, e.g., general advertising, direct response, sales promotion and public relations—and combines these disciplines to provide clarity, consistency and maximum communications impact.

Jerry Reitman, executive vice president of Leo Burnett, paraphrases the definition by stating: "Campaigns should have the same tonality, the same creative direction . . . and, more importantly, the same strategic direction."

The case for integrated communications is thoroughly explored in a recent book, *Integrated Marketing Communications*, written by three prominent university professors.[1] In describing the content of the book, the publisher states:

> *Integrated Marketing Communications* challenges business to confront a fundamental dilemma in today's marketing—the fact that

---

[1] *Integrated Marketing Communications*, Don E. Schultz, Stanley I. Tannenbaum, and Robert F. Lauterborn, Lincolnwood, IL: NTC Business Books, 1993.

Exhibit 1–2.   **IBM Integrated Marketing Communications Model**

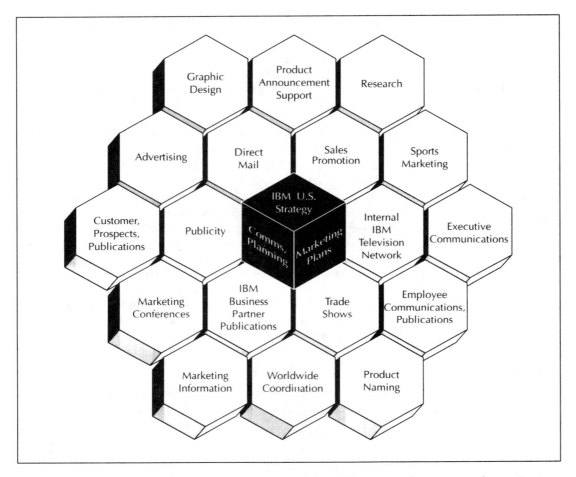

IBM's U.S. marketing communications disciplines are integrated into a single group, Marketing Services and Communications (MS&C), pictured here as a honeycomb of interlinked cells. Each represents a specialty with a defined role to play in achieving the larger marketing communications objectives of IBM United States.

Source: Association of National Advertisers, *The Advertiser*, Fall 1991.

mass media advertising *no longer works*. This landmark book reveals that strategies long used to deliver selling messages to a mass culture through a single medium are obsolete—and shows marketers how to get back on track.

The answer lies in database-driven marketing, a key planning tool that can—in today's diverse, fragmented marketplace, create a complete picture of the lifestyles, attitudes, and motivations of distinct buyer groups.

In the text the authors identify the database as the linchpin necessary for the effective functioning of an integrated marketing communications program. Exhibit 1–3 illustrates the ideal planning model for such a program. Commenting on the planning model, the authors state:

> As can be seen, we start with a database of information on both customers and prospects. While the database should be as complete as possible, we recognize that many companies, particularly those that market through retail channels, often have only limited information about their actual customers. This is especially true of large, high-penetration, fast-moving consumer products. Yet this type of information is critical to the future success of an integrated marketing communications program.
>
> The planning model that we illustrate is idealized, that is, it represents the best of all worlds. Few organizations have reached this point as yet in database development. There are some, however, who have been gathering data about their users for several years.
>
> Tobacco companies, for example, have very complete databases on their users. Automobile companies are also building detailed databases on ownership and histories of purchase patterns. Direct marketers such as American Express, Visa, MasterCard, and financial organizations also have detailed information on their customers and prospects. In our experience, service organizations and business-to-business marketers are generally far ahead of consumer product companies in developing usable databases for integrated marketing communications.
>
> As shown, the database should contain at a minimum such hard data as demographics, psychographics, and purchase history. In addition, attitudinal information such as the customer's category network and how consumers associate the products they use is vital for a solid integrated marketing communications approach. (Note: The planning form we have illustrated was developed for a consumer product. The database for a service organization would likely be quite different as would that for a business-to-business organization.)
>
> The integrated marketing communications process begins with a business problem, does not assume an advertising solution, takes the time necessary to research and develop an integrated strategy, puts all elements in place before pulling the trigger, measures everything, and accepts accountability.
>
> These are the new criteria of business success—if not survival—as the millennium dawns.

For an understanding of how the concept of integrated marketing communications is implemented, let us look at how two integrated communications programs were recently executed.

Exhibit 1–3.   **Ideal Planning Model**

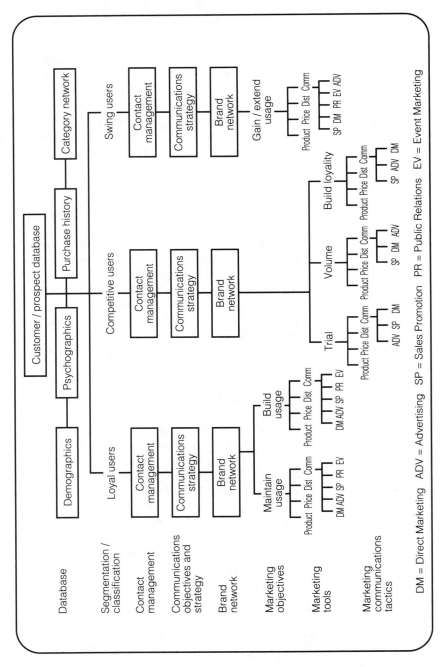

Source: Don E. Schultz, Stanley I. Tannenbaum, and Robert F. Lauterborn,
Integrated Marketing Communications, Lincolnwood, IL: NTC Business
Books, 1993.

Leo Burnett: Heinz Pet Products' Amore Cat Food

Market Conditions

The ultra-gourmet 3 oz. segment of the canned cat food category has been one of the primary driving forces behind the growth of the overall canned category. On a 52-week basis (most recent period ending 3/24/90), the ultra-gourmet 3 oz. segment accounts for approximately 14.2 percent of total canned cat food volume, up almost 8 percent vs. year-ago. More significantly, by virtue of its incredible price premium, this segment accounts for approximately 28 percent of total canned category sales.

Given the relatively high profit margins attainable (operating income roughly 18 percent to 20 percent of gross sales), the ultra-gourmet 3 oz. segment has experienced a tremendous influx of new entrants within the past 20 months, including Sheba (Mars Company), Fresh Catch (Carnation), 9-Lives 3 oz., Alpo 3 oz., and Whiskas Select Entrees (Mars Company). Additionally, the media spending allocated in support of these introductions has been significant, and is expected to increase through calendar 1990.

As a result of the increasingly competitive ultra-gourmet 3 oz. environment, innovative and effective media vehicles have become an essential marketing ingredient for success. Given the tremendously indulgent and involving nature of cat owners who serve ultra-gourmet 3 oz. canned cat food, and the ability to isolate a significant number of these potential purchasers, use of direct marketing evolved as a critical component of Amore's overall advertising effort.

Amore Direct-to-Consumer Background

Purchasers of ultra-gourmet 3 oz. canned cat food tend to be incredibly indulgent individuals who disregard the 100 percent price premium (of 3 oz. canned cat food) in order to serve their cats the best cat food available.

Through a Dunham and Marcus research study fielded in the summer of 1989, two salient findings were uncovered which suggested the use of a direct-to-consumer program for Amore:

1. *Finding*:
   Eighteen percent of the purchasers of 3 oz. canned cat food account for 62 percent of total 3 oz. volume. There are approximately 1.5 million of these individuals in the United States.
   Implication:
   A significant, identifiable, and isolatable target audience could be reached.

2. *Finding*:
   These heavy purchasers of 3 oz. canned cat food were incredibly indulgent, involving cat owners.
   Implication:
   Amore's emotional, involving positioning could be effectively communicated to this target audience via a warm, personalized direct-to-consumer approach.

Target Audience

- *Demographic*: Women 35–64. Tend to be employed, with slightly higher income (skew $50 thousand and over) and small household size (2 people, on average). As mentioned, these heavy purchasers (although only 18 percent of total purchasers) account for roughly 62 percent of total 3 oz. volume.

- *Purchase Motivation*: These women are *heavy* purchasers of 3 oz. canned cat food. They are indulgent cat owners committed to doing the best they can for their cat. The relationship they enjoy with their cats is a fundamental component of their lives.

Direct-to-Consumer Objectives

Overall, the purpose of Amore's Direct program is to increase usage of Amore. The objectives of Amore's Direct-to-Consumer program are as follows:

- Compel targeted individuals to purchase more Amore (including incremental consumption among loyal users as well as trial among competitive users).

- Enhance Amore's image among indulgent cat owners.

- Support and enhance communication of Amore's emotional, involving positioning against the target of indulgent, heavy users of 3 oz. canned cat food: "By serving Amore, you will feel like a more loving cat owner. . . ."

Strategies

The strategic initiatives for Amore's Direct-to-Consumer program are as follows:

- Initiate relevant dialog with heavy 3 oz. purchasers, via personal letters from Barbara Chapman (sponsored by Amore), an involved cat owner who is employed by Heinz Pet Products.

- Provide compelling trial purchase incentives, as well as response incentives.

- Provide compelling continuity premium offer through which brand-loyal purchase behavior can be generated by extending the impact of the Direct-to-Consumer program beyond its three-mailing scope.

Program Structure/Creative Material

The Amore Direct-to-Consumer program is in the form of Amore-sponsored letters from Barbara Chapman, an employee of Heinz Pet Products who is an avid Amore purchaser. Barbara's letters are intended to initiate a dialog between her and consumers, primarily focused on cat-owner relationships. Consumers will become involved in the program by responding to the *Crazy About Cats* survey, asking cat owners about how their cats behave as well as the various ways in which they interact with their cats.

Consumers will feel a sense of affiliation with Barbara and with other cat owners involved in the program. The intention is to make the consumer feel positive about Amore through the communication from Barbara Chapman, and ultimately consider Amore an important component of the fundamental relationship between cat and owner.

The program consists of three mailings, as follows:

- *Mailing 1*: Mailed nationally to 500,000 heavy purchasers of 3 oz. canned cat food, the initial mailing includes the following components:

    —Outer folding piece, with teaser copy enticing recipients to open the mail
    —Letter from Barbara Chapman (see Exhibit 1–4)
    —*Crazy About Cats* survey (see Exhibit 1–5)
    —Buy 2, get 1 free coupon
    —Business reply envelope (with postage paid), for ease in returning the survey

- The initial mailing is designed to accomplish the following objectives:

    —Introduce the program.
    —Communicate why Barbara Chapman is writing, and why the recipient should be interested in the program.
    —Request and elicit response to the survey. The survey includes both open-ended and close-ended questions, through which responders can convey usage information as well as discuss various aspects of their relationship with their cat.
    —Deliver promise of a free gift (cat poster) and survey results.

- *Mailing 2*: This mailing includes two versions:

    Responder mailing: Sent to all individuals who respond to the survey, it consists of the following:
    —Thank-you note from Barbara Chapman
    —Cat poster (free gift promised in initial mailing)
    —Buy 2, get 1 free coupon
    —Promise of survey results by Thanksgiving

    Nonresponder mailing: Sent to all individuals who do not respond to the survey distributed in the initial mailing, this mailing consists of the following:

    —Letter from Barbara Chapman
    —Buy 2, get 1 free coupon
    —*Crazy About Cats* survey
    —Business reply envelope (postage paid)
    —Promise of survey results by Thanksgiving

Exhibit 1–4. Two-Page Letter and Manufacturer's Coupon Included in Mailing 1

Barbara Chapman/P.O. Box 609/Bellwood, Illinois 60104

9999-999

Dear Sample A. Sample:

You're on a luxury cruise liner in the Caribbean. A wave smashes over the deck, washing your husband and your cat overboard.

Who would you save, you either thought about it for a minute, or chose the cat right off. Because you know, as well as I do, that the love between you and your cat is as strong and as real as any other kind of love in the world.

Maybe even stronger.

Sure, many people love their cats. But there are those, such as myself, that go even a step further. We're _crazy_ about them.

That's why I'm writing with your cat. Why? Because more about your relationship with the most amazing relationships of my life with my cat, Mischief. For the past 14 years, I've had one Mischief.

He watches for me to come home every day, faithfully perched on the windowsill overlooking my street. He becomes extraordinarily attentive and affectionate when I am upset -- he knows when I need him most.

Mischief is so much a part of my life that, even when I'm away from him, I spend hours just talking about him, what he does, and how he makes me feel. And I've found that other people who love their cats enjoy sharing the same stories and exploits of their most significant "others."

That's what brought me to Amoré. I've been working for them for the past few years. And when they found out more about my relationship with Mischief, they wanted to know more about it. The more I shared with them, the more they wanted to know about the loving relationships others share with their cats. (After all, the name "Amoré" means

"love" in Italian. That's why they put such care into making Amoré cat food.)

So they helped devise this Crazy About Cats Survey. It's fun to do, and will help you discover just how much you really love your cat, and how much your cat really loves you. Are we crazy? Or just crazy about our cats? That's what's in store with these 21 fun questions.

Then, you'll get a chance to learn how other cat lovers feel. Once you're done, send the finished survey back to me. I'll compile them all and send you the results in time for the holidays this December, sharing the fun and feelings from all over the country.

Everyone who sends in their survey by June 30 will receive the results, plus the folks at Amoré will send you a terrific gift.* You've already received a coupon for a free can of Amoré, just for taking the time to read this letter. You can use the coupon to buy your cat's favorite flavor (Mischief likes Ocean Whitefish and Tuna).

So what are you waiting for? Curl up with your better half, and let me know how you feel about your cat. Mischief and I will be waiting impatiently!

In the meantime, I wanted to leave you with a thought. The last time I went on a business trip, I left extra food and water for Mischief. I was only gone a day, but when I came home, he wasn't waiting for me. He wasn't talking to me. In fact, he wouldn't even acknowledge my presence. Oh, about dinner time he began to forgive me, and that's when I started to realize something. If he didn't care, he wouldn't be angry. So why give someone who cares enough to be mad anything less than Amoré? Isn't he worth it? I think so!

Sincerely,

Barbara and Mischief

*You'll have to allow 4 to 6 weeks for delivery of the gift, and the offer's _only_ good while supplies last! So hurry! © 1990 Heinz Pet Products

Exhibit 1–4 *(Continued)*. **Two-Page Letter and Manufacturer's Coupon Included in Mailing 1**

Exhibit 1–5.   Twenty-one Question Survey Included in Mailing 1

Exhibit 1–5 (*Continued*).   **Twenty-one Question Survey Included in Mailing 1**

Name _____   (____)
Area Code   Phone Number

Address _____   City _____   State _____   Zip _____

What type of cat(s) do you have? _____

What is/are your cat's name(s) _____   Cat's Birthday

AMORÉ CRAZY ABOUT CATS SURVEY
(Check appropriate box. Write in your own comments where necessary.)

1. Which best describes the personality of your cat?
   - ☐ *Mother—he/she takes care of me*   ☐ *Shy—hides from strangers*
   - ☐ *Teenager—always bouncing off the walls*   ☐ *Lover—attentive and demanding*
   - ☐ *Other_____*

2. Does your cat get jealous?
   - ☐ *Yes*   ☐ *No*

3. If so, of whom?
   - ☐ *Boyfriend/Girlfriend*   ☐ *Family Members*   ☐ *Other_____*
   - ☐ *Husband/Wife*   ☐ *Other Pets*

4. When I'm sad or down, my cat comforts me. Does your cat comfort you?
   - ☐ *Yes*   ☐ *No*

5. If so, how does he or she go about doing it? _____
_____

6. When your cat gets angry, does he/she:
   - ☐ *Hide*   ☐ *Ignore you*   ☐ *Knock things over*
   - ☐ *Other_____*

7. Has your cat ever made you cry?
   - ☐ *Yes*   ☐ *No*

(Continued)

Exhibit 1–5 (*Continued*). **Twenty-one Question Survey Included in Mailing 1**

8. If yes, tell us how it happened: _____

_____

_____

9. If your cat is like mine, he or she loves gourmet cat food. Which, if any, do you serve your cat?

Serve (*Check all that apply.*)	Most often (*Check one.*)
☐ *Amoré*	☐
☐ *Fancy Feast*	☐
☐ *Sheba*	☐
☐ *Fresh Catch*	☐
☐ *Other (specify)*_____	☐

10. What does your cat like to play with most?
   ☐ *Yarn balls*   ☐ *Cat toys (Which types?)* _____
   ☐ *Scratching posts* ☐ *Other*_____

11. When you have to leave town, do you:
   ☐ *Put your cat in a kennel*   ☐ *Leave your cat with a friend*
   ☐ *Hire cat sitters to come in*   ☐ *Take your cat with you*
                ☐ *Other*_____

12. Pretend that you were offered a job overseas, but found you couldn't take your cat. Which best describes your considerations?
   ☐ *You'd never go*   ☐ *You'd think about it, but still not go*
         ☐ *You'd go only if your best friend kept your cat*

13. What do you think your cat does when you're away from home? _____

_____

(over)

Exhibit 1–5 *(Continued)*.   **Twenty-one Question Survey Included in Mailing 1**

14. Mischief sleeps curled up next to me. Where does your cat sleep?
    ☐ *In your bed*   ☐ *In his/her bed*   ☐ *On the couch*   ☐ *On the floor*
    ☐ *Other* _____

15. Cats love to hide. Where is your cat's favorite hiding place?
    ☐ *Underneath furniture*   ☐ *In the kitchen*
    ☐ *Behind the bed*   ☐ *Other* _____

16. Mischief loves to play, and I love to play with him! What are your cat's favorite games or activities which you share with your cat? _____
_____

17. Does your cat snub his/her food if it's not fresh?
    ☐ *Yes*   ☐ *No*

18. How often would you say you serve three-ounce cans of cat food?
    ☐ *Daily*   ☐ *2–6 times a week*   ☐ *Once a week, for a treat*

19. Does your cat talk to you?
    ☐ *Yes*   ☐ *No*

20. Every cat communicates in their own special way. How does your cat tell you when he or she is hungry? _____
_____

How about when he or she is happy? _____
_____

21. Does your cat kiss you?
    ☐ *Yes*   ☐ *No*

0369-002   201137577   © 1990 Heinz Pet Products

- *Mailing 3*: Mailed to all program responders, this mailing consists of the following:

  —Survey results
  —Letter from Barbara Chapman
  —Premium gift offer

  (See Exhibit 1–6.)

Incentives/Offers

Consumers were provided with several purchase incentives and rewards:

- Buy 2, get 1 free coupon (1 million to be distributed during the course of the program)

- Free cat poster, for responding to the survey (distributed in the second mailing to all initial mailing responders)

- Premium offer (distributed to all responders in the third mailing)

- Survey results (distributed to all responders in the third mailing)

Media

Strategically, Amore's Direct-to-Consumer program works synergistically with Amore's television and print creative campaigns. Each of these campaigns is focused around the theme "Isn't He/She Worth It?," emphasizing the special relationship between cat and owner. Additionally, Amore's print and television media flighting was tailored to enhance the potential impact of Amore's Direct program, by running/airing simultaneously with the projected receipt of Amore's initial Direct-to-Consumer mailing. Perhaps most significantly, *Cat Fancy* magazine was used not only as a source of list names for receipt of the Direct program, but also as the primary vehicle for Amore's print advertising.

Executionally, Amore's print campaign is perfectly synergistic with Amore's Direct-to-Consumer campaign, utilizing identical creative material in an effort to enhance the overall impact of Amore's advertising. Similarly, one of Amore's three television executions visually depicts Amore's Direct creative material, also in an effort to enhance the impact of Amore's Direct-to-Consumer advertising by stimulating survey response. (See Exhibit 1–7).

In total, Amore's Direct-to-Consumer, print, and television campaigns work in strategic and executional harmony in an effort to enhance the overall impact of Amore's advertising campaign.

List Name Sources

Amore's 500,000 targeted individuals were derived from three sources, in order of priority as follows:

- Select and Save (heavy users of canned cat food)

Exhibit 1–6.   **Two Components of Mailing 3**

Barbara Chapman/P.O. Box 609/Bellwood, Illinois 60104   001-238

Dear Sample:

If you fell in love with the stationery I used on the letters, notes, and surveys (which many of you did, judging from the number of requests and questions I received about the custom-made letterhead), then here is something especially for you.

Amoré is offering a custom-made "Crazy About Cats" stationery kit, just like the one in the picture, for only $9.99 and 10 Amoré proofs of purchase. (If Bijou enjoys Amoré as much as Mischief, that won't take too long to collect!)

Just send your check or money order along with 10 Amoré UPCs (those funny-looking straight lines on the label) in the enclosed envelope for each kit, and you'll receive the complete Amoré stationery kit(s) in four to six weeks. (Wouldn't it be a great holiday gift?)

Our lawyers told me to tell you that the offer is void where prohibited, and that the kits are only available until January 31, 1991, or while supplies last, so hurry!

Sincerely,

Barbara and Mischief

Send me _____ Stationery Kit(s) at $9.99 each (shipping and handling included).

Amount enclosed: _____.

UPCs enclosed: _____.
(10 Amore UPCs per each kit).

Please make check or money order payable to AMORE, and send along with UPCs to:
Barbara Chapman, P.O. Box 659, Bellwood, Ill. 60104. Do not enclose cash.

name

address

city   state   zip

123456789

Mailing 3 was composed of another letter offering a handsome stationery kit and a note offering the opportunity to provide the names of fellow cat lovers. Not shown is the booklet containing the results of the survey.

(Continued)

Exhibit 1–6 (*Continued*).   Two Components of Mailing 3

A Note from Barbara:

Many of you wrote to tell me of friends or relatives who were as "Crazy about Cats" as you and I. And they wanted to share in the fun. Well, here's their chance.

If you know anyone who would like to be included in our feline fun, just jot their name and address down on this note. Or, just give this form to any interested cat lover and they can request to be included themselves.

Use the enclosed envelope to send this back to me. You can put it in with your stationery order form, or just send it by itself.

NAME			CAT'S NAME	
ADDRESS	CITY		STATE	ZIP

NAME			CAT'S NAME	
ADDRESS	CITY		STATE	ZIP

NAME			CAT'S NAME	
ADDRESS	CITY		STATE	ZIP

NAME			CAT'S NAME	
ADDRESS	CITY		STATE	ZIP

Exhibit 1–7.   **Thirty-Second TV Commercial Visually Depicting Amore's Mailing 1 Creative Material**

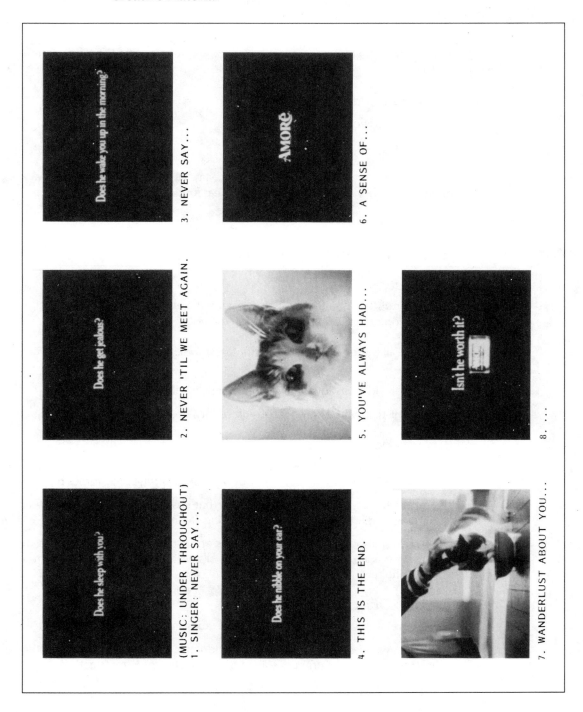

- *Cat Fancy* subscriber list
- Amore promotion sweepstakes responders

Timing

Amore's three Direct-to-Consumer mailings were scheduled for distribution as follows:

Mailing 1: w/o May 15

Mailing 2: w/o July 15

Mailing 3: w/o October 22

Amore's initial mailing was distributed on May 15 to 487,000 targeted heavy purchasers of ultra-gourmet 3 oz. canned cat food.

Allstate Insurance Company: Life Campaign

Introduction

In support of the Allstate agency force, an integrated life insurance campaign was developed in 1991. This promotion included:

- An overall theme: *I want to be your agent for Life* (a sort of implied double entendre)
- National and local advertising support utilizing the Life theme
- An agent-paid and company-subsidized targeted lead-generation mailing

Background

The 1991 annual sales promotion was geared to increasing the number of Life sales in the Allstate agent's current book of business/customer base.

Research has shown that Allstate's current customer base was virtually an untapped market in terms of cross-selling life insurance.

Research also indicated that there was an increase in property and casualty insurance retention if there was Allstate life insurance present in a household.

Program Objectives

- Promote Allstate's financial strength/and rating in the life insurance business.
- Create awareness of Allstate's Life products and promote agents as the prospect/customer's primary source of contact for more information.
- Increase Life sales within agent's own customer base.

- Meet or exceed the Life Company's 1991 premium plan.
- Increase retention through cross-selling life insurance.

Program Strategies

- Develop a comprehensive communication plan integrating all marketing efforts.
- Increase life insurance cross-line sales through lead-generation mailings and co-op advertising.
- Provide national advertising support for the Life Campaign.
- Create employee awareness of the Life Campaign.

Target Audience

- Current customers with and without life insurance.

Program Components

- National advertising campaign: television, radio, print
- Local advertising (agent and company participation in cost)
- Lead-generation mailing program (agent and company participation in cost)
- Sales support material
- Billing messages
- Employee awareness
- Agent communication

Results

Life Company year-end premium plan was exceeded (102 percent) and promotion results were 40 percent over the prior year's.

Putting together an integrated campaign calls for a sophisticated planning process. Here is how advertising support was orchestrated.

Advertising Support

The advertising message was twofold: (1) Allstate agents can take care of their customers' life insurance needs and (2) a long-term relationship with an Allstate agent is important.

NATIONAL ADVERTISING
Television
- Messages used the ongoing, distinctive campaign currently airing that included the highly successful combination of live action with animation and capitalized on one of Allstate's best-recognized assets, the "Good Hands."

- Advertising messages ran throughout the promotion period on programs that supported Allstate's objectives of product awareness and agent support.

- Two 15-second executions were utilized that emphasized the "I want to be your agent for Life" message. These executions highlighted the lead lines (auto/home) as a transition into the life insurance sale.

Radio

- National radio advertising via Paul Harvey supported the product message during the promotion period.

- Radio scripts were developed that focused on the life insurance product message and were aired where appropriate.

- National radio schedules were integrated with television air dates.

Print

- Print ads featured the same look and message as the television messages.

- Print ads lent topspin to the promotion effort and provided merchandising consideration to agents.

- Print ads were featured in national magazine publications.

- National print schedules were integrated with television and radio schedules.

LOCAL ADVERTISING

A portfolio of new Life Co-op advertising materials was developed for Allstate agents' individual use. It focused on the same theme as the national advertising message: "I want to be your agent for Life."

Television Two 30-second Life Co-op television commercials were developed based on the national messages; they included a 15-second tag for agent personalization.

Radio A 30-second live-read radio script was developed that could be personalized for each agent's use.

Print Two versions of a Life print ad were developed that focused on the "I want to be your agent for Life" message and incorporated a new concept that allowed agents to personalize the ad with their signature.

Telephone (Office Support) Life product scripts for agent offices' use with customer-on-hold phone systems were developed.

With advertising support in place, the next step was to create lead-generation support for those Allstate agents involved in the total campaign.

Mailing/Lead-Generation Support

MAILING PACKAGE

Letter emphasizes the agent-customer relationship and makes an offer to review the customer's current insurance portfolio to make certain existing coverage is keeping pace with current lifestyle.

Features

- Professionally written and designed mailing package

- Business card with the agent's name, address, and phone number

- "I want to be your agent for Life" theme printed on business card

- Multiline reply device offering various life products

- Business reply envelope

List Selections: Agents had the choice of mailing to several targeted lists.
- Auto customers with homeowners

- Auto customers with property

- Property customers

- Auto customers

- Life customers

- Customers without Life

- Other line customers

Special Offer: To encourage agents to order the lead-generation mailings, the company subsidized 50 percent of the mailing cost for letters sent to the agent's customers.

FOLLOW-UP

As with any lead-generation effort, follow-up is critical for success. Agents received an extensive follow-up list for each of their mailings. The list included:
- Customer name

- Customer address

- Customer phone number

- Description of mailing package

- Date that the mailing package was sent

Sales Support Materials

Agents were provided with an array of product support materials:

- Brochures

- Counter cards

- Buttons, banners
- Letters, mailing kits, postcards
- The words "Your Allstate agent wants to be your agent for Life" were even printed on the policy-billing envelope.

Internal Support

- A comprehensive *Administrative Guide*, which gave a clear picture of what the Life Campaign was all about, was produced and distributed to field managers so they could review the program details with their agents.

- The internal theme "Jazz up your Life" contained various award levels that were appropriately named for famous jazz musicians. To win one of the awards, an agent needed to sell a specified amount of life insurance.

- Agent support was also provided through internal communications—desk-toppers and letters touting the theme "I want to be your agent for Life."

- "Jump Start Your Market"—a starter kit consisting of actual samples and ordering information on all of the marketing materials available—was provided for all agents.

The Life Campaign was a remarkable program from the standpoint of planning and execution. Exhibit 1–8 presents representative executions. Exhibit 1–9 is one of two Life co-op television commercials that included a 15-second tag for agent personalization.

Six Big Keys to Direct Marketing Success

The expanded scope of direct marketing begs the question, "What does make direct marketing successful?" An oversimplified answer might be: *Offering the right products or services via the right media, with the most enticing propositions, presented with the most effective formats, proved successful as a result of the right tests.*

Sounds pretty simple. But, of course, it isn't! Let's explore the six big keys to direct marketing success and some basic questions relating to them.

1. *Right products or services.* Success in any endeavor starts with the product. No matter what the selling medium, no business can long survive unless the product is *right.* Time was when direct sale of products via mail, print, or broadcast advertising was looked upon as a means of "dumping" merchandise that did not sell well through retail channels. Time was when off-brand merchandise, which couldn't get shelf space in retail stores, was offered direct to the consumer. That's all changed today. Successful direct marketers offer quality merchandise of good value.

Exhibit 1–8. **Ad Campaign Mailings**

Lead-Generation Mailing

Co-op Mailing

Agent-Support Materials

Employee Awareness

Exhibit 1–9. Life Co-op Television Commercial

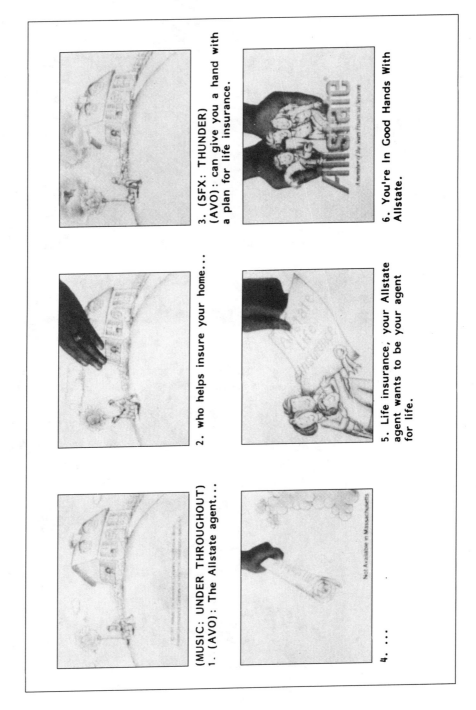

2. *Right media*. Some authorities give half or more of the credit for the success of a mailing to the lists that are used. You can't prove the figure. But you can bet on this: One of the most important keys to success is lists! Likewise, selection of the publications used for print ads and the stations used for broadcast are vital keys to success. (Chapters Nine through Fourteen cover each major medium in depth.)

3. *Right offer*. There is no key to success more important than the offer. You can have the right product, the right mailing lists, the right print and broadcast media. But you still won't make it big if you don't have the right offer. You've got to overcome human inertia, whatever the medium. (Chapter Four covers offers designed to overcome human inertia.)

4. *Right formats*. The number of formats for presenting offers is almost endless. This is particularly true of direct mail, where there are few restrictions on format. The marketer can use anything from a simple postcard to a 9" × 12" mailing package that could include a giant four-color brochure, a letter, a giant order card, tokens, stamps, pop-ups, and so on.

   Restrictions on print and broadcast advertising are, of course, more stringent, because of controls by the publishers and the stations. But the important point is that there is a *right* format for a given mailing package, a given ad, and a given commercial. Depending on the format selected, the results can range from disastrous to sensational.

5. *Right tests*. With literally thousands of chances to do the wrong thing, the way to achieve direct marketing success is to test to determine the *right* thing. Indeed, direct marketing is the most *measurable* type of marketing there is.

   Mailing packages can be tested scientifically to determine such vital factors as best offer, best format, best lists, best copy, best postage, and the like.

   The print medium, with the advent of regional editions, has also made an endless variety of tests possible. Direct marketers now test by regions. They test for size and color. They test for position. They test bind-in cards and bingo cards. They test special- against general-interest magazines. Newspapers can be tested to learn all you have to know.

   It is also possible to test the efficiency of broadcast on a control basis. Testing is likewise possible when the telephone is used as a selling medium. (Chapter Twenty clearly spells out the techniques that enable you to test for the right answers.)

6. *Right analyses*. The final element essential to a successful direct marketing program is right analyses. Direct marketers live by figures, but misinterpretation of figures often leads to erroneous conclusions. Fortunes have been lost by counting *trial orders* instead of counting *paid-ups*. Fortunes have been lost by *averaging* response, by not really knowing

break-even points, by never determining the value of a customer, by never preparing cash-flow charts.

Chapter Nineteen is devoted to applying the mathematics of direct marketing properly.

Checklist for Applying the Six Big Keys to Direct Marketing Success

1. The product or service you offer
   - ☐ Is it a real value for the price asked?
   - ☐ How does it stack up against competition?
   - ☐ Do you have exclusive features?
   - ☐ Does your packaging create a good first impression?
   - ☐ Is the market broad enough to support a going organization?
   - ☐ Is your product cost low enough to warrant a mail-order markup?
   - ☐ Does your product or service lend itself to repeat business?

2. The media you use
   Customer lists
   - ☐ Is your customer list cleaned on a regular basis?
   - ☐ Do you keep a second copy of your list in a secure place to avoid loss?
   - ☐ Have you developed a profile of your customer list, giving you all the important demographic and psychographic characteristics?
   - ☐ Have you coded your customer list by recency of purchase?
   - ☐ Have you worked your customer list by the classic mail-order formula: recency—frequency—monetary?
   - ☐ Have you thought of what other products or services may appeal to your customer list?
   - ☐ Do you mail your customer list often enough to capitalize on the investment?

   Prospect lists
   - ☐ Do you freely provide facts and figures to one or more competent mailing-list brokers, enabling them to unearth productive lists for you?
   - ☐ Have you worked with competent list compilers in selecting names of prospects who match the profile of those on your customer list?
   - ☐ Do you test meaningful, measurable, projectable quantities?
   - ☐ Have you measured the true results of prospect lists, computing for each list the number of inquiries, the quantity of returned goods, net cash receipts per thousand mailed, and repeat business?
   - ☐ Have you determined how often you can successfuly mail to the same prospect lists?

   Print
   - ☐ Have you matched your offers with your markets and used print publications with good direct response track records?

☐ Have you measured the true results of print media, computing for each newspaper or magazine the number of inquiries, the amount of returned goods, net cash receipts per insertion, and repeat business?

☐ Have you determined how often you can successfully use the same print media?

Broadcast

☐ Have you selected broadcast media that best fit your objective: (a) to get inquiries or orders, (b) to support other advertising media?

☐ Have you measured the true results of broadcast media, computing for each station the number of inquiries, the amount of returned goods, net cash receipts per broadcast schedule, and repeat business?

☐ Have you determined the proper times and frequency for broadcast schedules?

3. The offers you make

☐ Are you making the most enticing offers you can within the realm of good business?

☐ Does your offer lend itself to the use of any or all of these incentives for response: free gift, contest, free trial offer, installment terms, price savings, money-back guarantee?

☐ Does your offer lend itself to the development of an "automatic" repeat business cycle?

☐ Does your offer lend itself to a "get-a-friend" program?

☐ Have you determined the ideal introductory period or quantity for your offer?

☐ Have you determined the ideal introductory price for your offer?

☐ Have you determined the possibility of multiple sales for your offer?

4. The formats you use

Direct mail

☐ Are you mailing packages in character with your product or services and the markets you are reaching?

☐ Have you developed the ideal format for your mailing packages, with particular emphasis on mailing envelope, letter, circular, response form, and reply envelope?

☐ Do you work with one or more creative envelope manufacturers?

☐ Are your sales letters in character with your offers?

☐ Are your circulars graphic, descriptive, and in tune with the complete mailing package?

☐ Does your response form contain the complete offer? Is it attractive enough to grab attention and impel action?

Print

☐ Are your ads in character with your product and services and the markets you are reaching?

☐ Have you explored newspaper inserts, magazine inserts, bind-in cards, tip-on cards, Dutch-door newspaper inserts, plastic records?

Broadcast
- ☐ Are your commercials in character with your products and services and the markets you are reaching?
- ☐ Have you determined the efficiency of stand-up announcer commercials vs. staged commercials?
- ☐ Have you explored the efficiency of noted personality endorsements?

5. The tests you make
- ☐ Do you consistently test the big things: products, media, offers, and formats?
- ☐ Have you tested to determine the best timing for your offers, the best frequency?
- ☐ Have you determined the most responsive geographic areas?
- ☐ Do you consistently test new direct mail packages against control packages, new ads against control ads, new commercials against control commercials?
- ☐ Do you use adequate test quantities?
- ☐ Do you follow your test figures through to conclusion, using net revenue per thousand as the key criterion?
- ☐ Do you interpret your test figures in the light of the effect on the image and future profits of your company?

6. The right analyses
- ☐ Do you track results by source, computing front-end and back-end response, returned-goods factors, and bad-debt factors for each source?
- ☐ Do you analyze results by ZIP codes, by demographics, and by psychographics?
- ☐ Do you compute the level of repeat business by original source?

Self-Quiz

1. How did Richard Sears get into the mail-order business? _____

_____

_____

_____

2. In order of effectiveness, maximizing direct mail success depends on:

a. _____

b. _____

c. _____

3. Credit card privileges will outperform cash with order at least ____ to ____.

4. People buy _____, not _____.

5. Telephone-generated leads are likely to close ____ to ____ times more often than mail-generated leads.

6. Define *direct marketing*. _____

_____

_____

7. Define *integrated communications*: _____

_____

_____

_____

_____

8. Complete this list of the six big keys to direct marketing success:
   a. Right products or services
   b. Right media
   c. Right offer
   d. Right tests

   e. _____

   f. _____

9. Describe the profile of a customer list. _____

_____

_____

_____

10. Describe some of the incentives you can use to make an offer more enticing. _____

_____

_____

_____

Pilot Project

You are the catalog manager of a women's apparel catalog. You discover that 80 percent of your business is coming from 20 percent of your customer base.

Your assignment is to come up with a program to maintain the loyalty of that important 20 percent of the customer base. Develop an outline of incentives you would employ to retain the loyalty of your best customers.

CHAPTER TWO

Database Marketing

If there is one thing that truly distinguishes direct marketing from other marketing disciplines, it is that direct marketing is database-driven. Knowing who the best customers are, what they buy, and how often they buy provides a "secret weapon."

Sophistication in database marketing continues to grow. But if we were to trace the history of database marketing growth, the proper starting point might well be an article that appeared in the January-February 1967 issue of *Harvard Business Review*. In this article, titled "ZIP Code—New Tool for Marketers," the author, Martin Baier, identified ZIP codes as a segmentation tool that divides consumers into homogeneous groups. Baier, director of the Center for Direct Marketing , Kansas City, Missouri, and long-time executive vice president for marketing at Old American Insurance Company, has been a key player in database-marketing development for almost three decades. We are indebted to Mr. Baier for his contributions to this chapter.

Developing a Database

As the concept of marketing has matured and as its technology has become increasingly powerful, and as marketing has become directed or targeted, databases have emerged as a characteristic and a requirement of direct marketing.

Any organization with a list of "customers"—mail-order buyers, association members, salesperson-sold prospects, retail store shoppers, charitable contributors, or political supporters—and with data on the actions taken by those customers and with information about them as individuals or organizations, can increase its market efficiency and effectiveness.

What to Include

In the preparation of a marketing database, the first and obvious requirement is the recording of accurate names and mailing addresses. It is then necessary to determine what other useful data, in terms of the qualification of

individuals and organizations on the list, must be collected and recorded and in what form for what purpose.

As a guideline in the development of a database, this question should be asked: "What data will be needed in order to carry on a meaningful dialog with customers by mail, by phone, or in person?" While database requirements will vary greatly within consumer or industrial markets, as well as by category of business enterprise, there are base data such as the following that probably should go into any customer database:

Name of individual and/or organization

Mailing address, including Zip code

Telephone number

Source of inquiry or order

Date and purchase details of first inquiry or order

Recency/frequency/monetary purchase history

  By date

  By dollar amounts of purchases (cumulative)

  By product or product lines purchased

Credit history and rating (scoring)

Relevant demographic data for individual consumers: age, gender, marital status, family data, education, income, occupation

Relevant organizational data for industrial buyers: Standard Industrial Classification (SIC) code, size of firm, revenues, number of employees.

Format

An example of a customer database record is shown in Exhibit 2–1. This record registers the customer name and mailing address as well as the initial and most recent order dates. Other data captured on this record are customer source (media) and the order and payment characteristics. Demographics of the individual customer, if relevant, could also be included, as could relevant information about the industrial customer.

Keeping Current

A database is a perishable commodity. Not only does the degree of activity (or inactivity) fluctuate, but also the individuals and organizations contained on database records are far from static. Their demographics change. Their attitudes and preferences change. They move—to new homes or to new jobs. In one year an average customer list could change by as much as 20 percent in address updates alone. Thus on-going maintenance of a database is vital!

Exhibit 2–1.   Database/Record Format of a Customer's History File

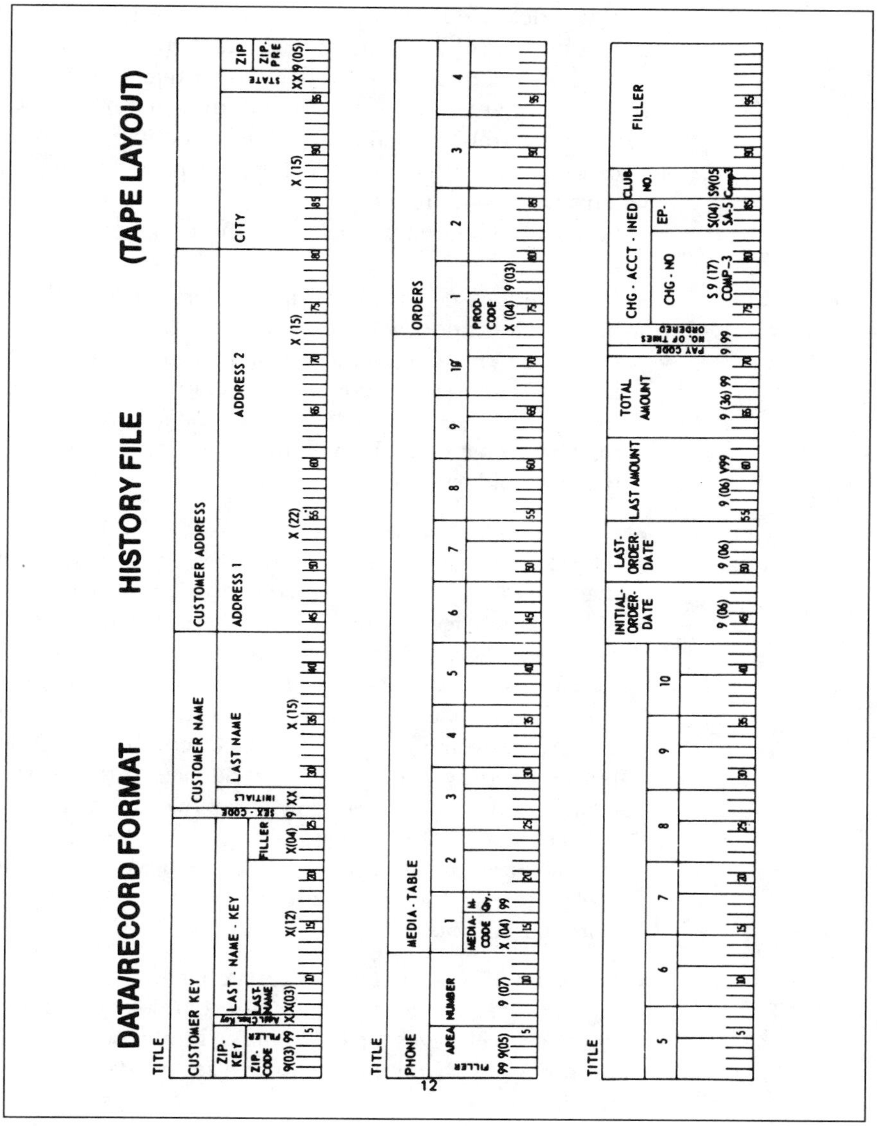

Such maintenance applies not only to address correction but also to
continual updating of the transactions and/or demographic data carried in
each customer's record. Should a phone number be in a customer record,
for example, if there is to be no mechanism for keeping that number up to
date? The cost of updating phone numbers should be considered relative to
the time and expense of calling a wrong number when soliciting additional

sales. Above all, direct marketers do not want to distribute their response advertising indiscriminately. They want to ensure that their messyages are not only delivered but that they are delivered to the right prospects. That is a key objective of direct marketing aided and abetted by a database.

An initial requirement for the proper maintenance of a database is that it be compiled and developed in a uniform manner. Only when such uniformity exists in a computerized database is it possible, for example, to identify duplication of records within and between lists or to spot identical buyers when several lists are merged.

Database maintenance falls into three categories:

- *Nixie removal*: The term nixie refers to mail that has been returned because it is undeliverable as addressed. There might be a simple error in the name or street address, or possibly in the ZIP code, that can be identified and corrected. Or the person to whom the piece is addressed may be deceased, may have moved and left no forwarding address, or may have changed jobs within the firm or left the organization where the piece was addressed.

- *Change of address*: If the addressed person does not provide timely address correction, it is often possible to obtain this through various maintenance services provided by the U.S. Postal Service. Letter-type mail is forwarded for a specific time period without payment of additional postage if the addressee so requests.

  However, advertising mail is forwarded only if arrangements to prepay postage are made in advance by either the sender or the addressee. In any event, even if the piece is forwarded, the new address must ultimately be provided by either the Postal Service or the addressee. In the case of customer databases especially, it behooves direct marketers to encourage addressees to inform them of any change of address or of status within an organization. If incorrect addresses result in misdirected promotions, the cost is twofold: (1) that of the wasted contact and (2) the sacrifice of potential response.

- *Record status*: In maintaining databases, it is important that the record status of customers be kept up to date. New orders from customers or any status changes of customers should be entered into the database promptly. Such record keeping also avoids unnecessary duplication of mailings or phone calls to customers who either already have the product or service or have no need for it.

Keeping databases up to date at all times is essential for direct marketers. And since data are collected for future use, a retrieval mechanism needs to be anticipated. How will individual customer name/and address records be qualified and selected? One of the best ways to qualify and select names is to use the R-F-M formula.

The R-F-M Formula

In the R-F-M (recency, frequency, monetary) formula, best customers, and therefore those most likely to buy again, are identified as those who bought most recently, those who bought most frequently within a specified period, and those who spent specified amounts.

Through testing, the large mail-order catalog firms learned that these three criteria—recency, frequency, monetary—are the basis for maximizing profits. Indeed, these firms soon found it possible to develop pro-forma statements that enabled them to predict with deadly accuracy what their profits would be based upon which customers they selected to receive their current catalog and which customers they excluded from their current circulation.

In its simplest form, the R-F-M formula calls for the establishment of a point system with purchases broken down by quarter-years. A typical formula might be as follows:

- *Recency points*:
    24 points—current quarter
    12 points—last 6 months
    6 points—last 9 months
    3 points—last 12 months

- *Frequency points*: Number of purchases × 4 points.

- *Monetary points*: 10 percent of dollar purchase with a ceiling of 9 points. (The ceiling avoids distortion by an unusually large purchase.)

The number of points allotted varies among those using R-F-M formulas, but the principle is the same. Once the system is established and point values are assigned, the opportunities for maximizing profits are enormous. Some sophisticated systems have scores of categories with profit figures ranging from $50 per 1,000 catalogs mailed to $1,500 and more. Under the system, each account is isolated from all other accounts. Buying habits dictate how frequently an account is solicited.

Once the R-F-M point system is computer-programmed, producing a monthly update is a simple matter. Table 2–1 shows what a hypothetical partial printout might look like for a representative group of accounts. The table shows the activity of five accounts for December 1992. Account number 16,441 bought twice in September and once in December. Recency points were computed in relation to the time interval since each purchase.

Frequency points were computed by multiplying the number of purchases by 4. Monetary points were computed by multiplying the dollar amount of purchases by 10 percent. Note that under "Cumulative Total Points" this marketer had carried over 16 accumulated points from the previous calendar year, indicating that his customer first bought in calendar year 1991.

Table 2–1.   Analysis of Accounts by Recency, Frequency, and Monetary Points—December 1992

Account Number	Month	Recency Points	No. of Purchases	Frequency Points	Dollar Purchases	Monetary Points	Total Points	Cumulative Total Points
16,441	9	12	2	8	32.17	3.21	23	39
16,441	12	24	1	4	46.10	4.61	32	71
16,521	1	3	3	12	87.09	8.71	23	23
16,608	7	12	1	4	21.00	2.10	18	28
16,708	4	6	1	4	33.60	3.36	13	18
16,708	8	12	2	8	71.00	7.10	27	45
16,708	11	24	1	4	206.00	9.00	37	82
16,921								68

In reviewing the list of accounts, note that account number 16,708 spent $206 in November but was given only 9 monetary points. This reflects the arbitrary decision of the marketer to give no more than 9 monetary points regardless of amount of purchase. Finally, note that account number 16,921 shows no activity for calendar year 1992 but has a total of 68 points for 1991.

The opportunities for manipulating a database under R-F-M system are numerous. And, of course, the system need not be restricted to catalog firms. It is clearly applicable to telemarketing.

The R-F-M Formula Expanded

Robert Kestnbaum, a noted authority on database management, has altered and added to the R-F-M formula. He has found for his clients—those engaged in direct marketing and in telemarketing as well—that profits are maximized even further by employing his altered formula, which is identified by the acronym FRAT.

F stands for frequency of purchase within a specified period. (Kestnbaum gives the greatest weight to frequency.) This factor is followed by R, recency of purchase. Then comes A, amount of purchase, followed by T, type of merchandise or service purchased. The T is an important addition to the R-F-M formula, for what a person buys currently serves as a statement about what else that person is likely to buy in the future. For example, subsequent purchases made by a woman who just bought support hose are likely to be quite different from subsequent purchases made by a woman who just bought jogging shoes.

Being given a database that provides almost unlimited information fires the imagination. Think of the demands that can be made of the computer on behalf of a telemarketing center.

- Give me a list of all of our customers who have bought two or more times in the last 6 months.

- Give me a list of all of our customers who first bought within the last 3 months.

- Give me the names of those who have bought Product X in the last 12 months. I want to phone them about preference treatment in testing our new model.

- Let me have a list of everyone who bought a personal computer from us in the last year. I want to mount a mail campaign to sell our new software program.

If you've got the database, the computer will give you whatever you ask for, and give it to you fast.

Information: Cost vs. Value

In developing a database, it is important to consider what will be done in the future with the collected data. The collection of information costs money and must therefore produce benefits at least equal to that cost. Questions such as these are pertinent: "Does such cost exceed the value of lost opportunity of future sales?" "Will the data be used for analysis and evaluation that will either lower future costs or increase future revenues?"

Utilizing a Database

A database provides the means for an organization, through both continuity selling and cross-selling, to maximize the value of its relationship with its acquired customers. In addition, it provides the profiles needed to define likely prospects and thus facilitate the acquisition of new customers similar to those the organization already has.

Market Segmentation

Market segmentation—dividing the heterogeneous total marketplace into homogeneous subgroups—is vital in direct marketing. Customers, whether they be consumer or industrial, can best be served by organizations that know the characteristics of their present buyers. Databases provide that knowledge.

Since all customers are not alike, they need to be placed into groups, or segments, according to geographic (area), demographic (individual), and psychographic (lifestyle) factors. These segments, which are defined from customer databases, then become focal points for positioning and product differentiation.

Similarly, business-to-business direct marketers can analyze their databases of industrial buyers to determine market penetration in terms of SIC codes, revenues, number of employees, and even the socioeconomic and demographic characteristics of the business communities in which their customers are located.

Both consumer and business-to-business direct marketers can refer to databases for "action taken," or prior-purchase behavior, by individuals,

households, or industrial buyers. Just what do these respondents order, inquire about, subscribe to, attend, raise funds for, visit, or shop for? Do they have an "affinity" for a particular credit card or a veterans' organization or a type of publication or a particular catalog or retailer?

Continuity Selling

Direct marketers are concerned with creating, caring for, and keeping customers. The objective of profitable direct marketing is not a single response or transaction, but rather the acquisition of a customer who will remain active for an extended period of time.

Continuity selling is a hallmark of direct marketers. In the sale of an insurance policy, for example, the process of continuity involves renewing that policy periodically, increasing the initial coverage, or simply keeping the policy in force. This is not unlike the renewal of a magazine subscription or of a book or record club membership, the purchase of additional merchandise from a series of catalogs, repeat contributions from prior donors, or voting again for the same political candidate.

All too frequently, unfortunately, some direct marketers do not cultivate their present customers as vigorously as they seek new ones. Even if they recognize the importance of continuity selling, they often do not seek cross-selling opportunities.

Cross-Selling

Like continuity selling, cross-selling is an important attribute of direct marketing. Through the use of this technique, new or related products, or even unrelated ones, are offered to existing customers. For example, a purchaser of books or records might be offered other books or records, or possibly an insurance policy or even a home power tool.

When a magazine such as *Time* renews the subscriptions it has already acquired, it engages in continuity selling. When *Time* offers its present customers the opportunity to also receive one or more of the other magazines it publishes—*People, Money, Fortune, Sports Illustrated*—it engages in cross-selling. Each of these cross-selling opportunities, then, becomes its own continuity sale. Beyond the magazines it publishes is an endless array of Time-Life Books' continuity series. There's even Home Box Office or possibly the promotion of a movie produced by Warner.

As another example, consider banks. The computer can easily segment out of all of the accounts in a bank's database certain products:

Savings accounts

Personal checking accounts

Commercial checking accounts

Home mortgages

Commerical real estate loans

Inventory loans

Accounts receivable loans

Car loans

Home improvement loans

Trust accounts

Pinpointing accounts by products or class and/or dollar amount leads to cross-selling opportunities. Holders of commercial checking accounts, for example, are prime prospects for inventory loans. Holders of savings accounts are prime prospects for car loans. Those who have paid down or paid off home mortgages are prime prospects for home equity loans. Opportunities for cross-selling abound.

Insurance companies have also mastered the art of cross-selling, and they have the databases to make it happen. They know about their policyholders: gender, marital status, number of children and their ages. And they know what insurance coverage each policyholder has with them at the present time. These insurance companies can get a tabulation any time they want of families with preschool children; the cross-selling opportunity here would be an educational insurance program. The database manipulation opportunities for insurance companies are practically endless: cross-sell hospital insurance to accident insurance policyholders, cross-sell cancer insurance to hospital insurance policyholders, cross-sell homeowner's insurance to mortgage insurance policyholders, and on and on.

Certainly one of the most exciting potentials for direct marketing is in the area of cross-selling. When you know, through a database, what every customer buys, it's a simple matter to cross-sell. Most important for successful cross-selling, however, is the way in which the customers view the direct marketer in terms of reputation, integrity, reliability, and overall image.

Cumulatively, each customer transaction adds to the value of that customer. It is because of both continuity selling and cross-selling that new customers have value well beyond their initial acquisition cost.

Market Value of the Going Business

Direct marketers typically are in business for the long run. Much of the image they build through the products they sell and the services they provide—some call it *goodwill*—is concerned with the long-range aspect of both continuity selling (repeat purchasing) and cross-selling (offering both related and non-related products to existing customers).

Virtually all businesses capitalize and treat as a balance-sheet asset their plant, equipment, and inventory—all essential to the enterprise, but they

almost never capitalize what is probably their most valuable asset of all—their customers, their means of generating future revenues and ongoing profits.

A well-developed database provides the means for a firm to determine both the present and future value of its most important asset—the customer list. The firm will know precisely what its investment is in each new customer, as well as what it should be in terms of its budget for advertising to initially acquire new customers.

The company will know the dates and amounts of purchases for each customer and exactly what each customer bought, thereby allowing trends to be measured and future sales to be predicted. It will have a running profit and loss statement for each customer. And ultimately it will be able to measure the lifetime value (LTV) of a customer. In effect, this becomes the market valuation of the going business at any point in time. (See Chapter Nineteen, "The Mathematics of Direct Marketing.")

Enhancing the Database

As we saw earlier in this chapter, a database is enhanced when we incorporate in it more than simply a name, an address, and possibly a telephone number. It is enhanced when we incorporate demographic and lifestyle data about individuals or firms and information about the type and extent of actions these customers have taken.

A database is also enhanced, as we will see in the next section of this chapter, when we augment such data about individuals or firms with environmental data, similar to that derived from demographics and lifestyles, relating to geographic units (ZIP code areas, for example) in which individuals reside or firms are located and do business or to standard industrial classification codes.

Database Overlays

Mass databases and their enhancements are leading the way to refined target marketing. Such target marketing makes it possible to increase response dramatically. Going beyond individual or firm and environmental enhancements within an organization's own database, another technique for enhancement is the use of database overlays. (Similarly, using targeted segments of mailing lists—such as products purchased or recency of response—the direct marketer can expand the number of lists or list segments that will produce a satisfactory response. For a thorough discussion of mailing lists, see Chapter Nine.)

Today, sophisticated computer systems enable the matching and merging of separate and diverse databases as well as the transference of key indicators from one database to another. In its simplest form, such a process can identify "multibuyers"—those names that appear simultaneously on more than one list. Also, it can identify the "hotline" names of those who

have responded most recently.

From mass compilations such as those of drivers' licenses issued or of telephone directory listings, public record information such as age (from the former) and length of residence (from the latter) can be affixed to an organization's own customer database. Sometimes, as with credit experience overlaid from other databases, this information can serve as a negative screen, i.e., "do not solicit."

Here is an application example. The Catholic Guild for the Blind in Chicago obviously has its strongest appeal among Catholics. The Guild knows from experience that its best response comes from Catholic donor lists. To build its donor base, however, it is dependent, for the most part, on using lists of donors from philanthropic organizations that do not appeal to any particular religious group.

The Guild achieved a major breakthrough when it was able to apply a Catholic overlay to some major donor lists. The overlay identified ZIP code areas that have a high concentration of Catholics, such as certain areas of Boston and Chicago. By mailing only to these selected ZIP codes, the Guild essentially doubled its response rate. It is also conceivable that having determined its likely prospects to be older persons, the Guild's database could be further enhanced by the addition of age to each record through the use of a driver's license overlay.

Another example of using overlays to better target prospects comes from a business-to-business direct marketer. The database application is by a manufacturer of aircraft selling through dealers. Because the details of this highly sophisticated overlay of up to eight separate databases are proprietary, this example has been generalized and is presented solely as food for thought.

The overlay process started with a major business list compilation such as Dun & Bradstreet, American Business Information, or Database America, all of which provided key data on up to 10 million organizations, including standard industrial classification, size, sales revenues, number of employees, and the like. Another database then identified those organizations that currently operate jet aircraft, and still another identified those that operate piston aircraft. To this body of data was added aircraft serial numbers by year of manufacture, provided by yet another major database. Fortune 500 and INC 500 companies were identified, as were Value Line's top 50 growth industries. Through a process of telephone qualification, key persons in the decision process of each company were identified: CEO, CFO, chief pilot, among others. When all of these data had been put together, record by record, each record was sent for validation and verification to a local dealer.

The outcome: Lead-generating direct mail consisting of personalized, versioned letters was sent, with the local dealer's concurrence, to each category of decision maker. Also, different versions were sent to (1) organizations now owning that manufacturer's product, (2) organizations now owning a competitor's product, and (3) organizations not owning aircraft at the present time but otherwise qualified.

These two diverse examples point up the value of databases and the opportunity to maximize profits that their proper application presents. It's small wonder that the database is often referred to as direct marketing's secret weapon.

Other Sources of Database Enhancement

National Demographics & Lifestyles (NDL) of Denver, Colorado, is in the forefront of providing large, highly responsive lists of consumers with precise selections of demographics and lifestyles. Jock Bickert, former chairman of NDL, illustrates the importance of enhanced demographics and lifestyle data by comparing two men who live in the same city and who are the same age and have the same income and same marital status, but who exhibit major differences in other demographics and in their lifestyles.

David Day—Bloomington, Minnesota		Nick Night—Bloomington, Minnesota	
Demographics		*Demographics*	
Sex	Male	Sex	Male
Household income	$40,000	Income	$40,000
Age	34	Age	34
Marital status	Married	Marital status	Married
Occupation	Sales/marketing	Occupation	Professional/technical
Spouse occupation	Clerical	Spouse occupation	Homemaker
Home ownership	Single family home	Home ownership	Single family home
Length of residence	Eight years	Length of residence	Four years
Children at home	Two, ages four and one	Children at home	One, age five
Lifestyle Activities		*Lifestyle Activities*	
Golfing		Fishing	
Foreign travel		Working on automobiles	
Physical fitness exercise		Camping	
Investing in stocks and bonds		Watching sports on TV	
Home workshop		Personal computing	

Looking at the accompanying profiles of David Day and Nick Night, we find that their "differences" are readily apparent: Day is in sales/marketing; Night is a professional/technical person. Day's wife works at a clerical job; Night's wife is a homemaker. But the really significant differences are in the men's lifestyle activities.

Day is a golfer; Night likes to fish. Day is interested in foreign travel; Night likes to work on automobiles. Day is a physical fitness devotee; Night likes to camp. Day is a serious investor in stocks and bonds; Night, on the other

hand, devotes a lot of time to watching sports on TV. Day devotes free time to his home workshop, while Night works on his personal computer.

It is through the selection of lifestyle criteria that direct marketers can match prospects to customer profiles. Let's look at the profiles of David Day and Nick Night and translate them to prospecting opportunities.

David Day:

- Golfing—golf equipment, golf magazines, golf books, golf trips, golf club memberships
- Foreign travel—tours, travel books, travel magazines
- Physical fitness—jogging apparel, physical fitness magazines, physical fitness equipment
- Stocks and bonds—investment services, brokerage houses, investment books and publications
- Home workshop—workshop equipment, do-it-yourself books and magazines

Nick Night:

- Fishing—fishing equipment, fishing trips, books and magazines on fishing
- Working on automobiles—auto repair manuals, auto equipment catalogs, auto books and publications
- Camping—campsite directories, camping equipment, camping apparel, camping books and publications
- Sports on TV—subscription to cable sports networks, sports books and publications
- Personal computer—computer programs, PC equipment, PC books and publications

NDL maintains a "lifestyle inventory" of approximately 60 activities and interests based upon data compiled from responses to consumer questionnaires. Over 18 million questionnaires are returned each year. Its master list is appropriately called The Lifestyle Selector®. The massive database size also permits NDL to accurately profile small geographic areas—even down to the postal carrier route level.

Successful use of The Lifestyle Selector® is very much dependent upon a marketer's ability to obtain a precise definition of the demographic and lifestyle characteristics of its target markets. Most marketers, however, don't have much access to such precise definitions.

So NDL provides a number of analytic services by which mailers can determine the precise demographic and lifestyle characteristics of their target markets. The process is relatively simple. NDL compares the mailer's customer file (or subsegments of the file, such as "high ticket" buyers, new

subscribers, etc.) to The Lifestyle Selector database, identifies the matches between both of the comparison files, and then profiles and/or scores the matches. NDL conducts over 1,000 such analyses each year.

These profiles can be used to describe the mailer's entire file. With a match rate that consistently falls between 15 and 25 percent, the analysis is highly reliable. Another way of viewing the process is that it represents a customer survey that generates an average response rate of 20 percent.

The large match sample sizes that ensue (e.g. 200,000 for a million-name customer file) not only ensure reliability, but also allow NDL to apply so-phistiticated multivariate analytic techniques that are precluded with small samples. Those multivariate analyses lead to the identification of important secondary and tertiary markets, which may be very different from the ob-vious, primary market.

Once the analysis is complete, NDL applies the criteria to the remaining noncustomer portion of "The Lifestyle Selector"® database and supplies the mailer with the names of likely prospective customers—customer "twins."

While NDL has been a pioneer in database enhancement, dating back some 16 years, many other enhancement systems have emerged in the in-terim. Prominent in the consumer field are TRW, Equifax, Axciom, Metromail, Donnelley, and R.L. Polk. Prominent in the business-to-business field are American Business Information, Database America, and Dun & Bradstreet.

Predictive Modeling with Databases

Market segmentation, a natural outgrowth of the marketing concept, has been enhanced by the combination of the direct marketing concept and database technology. Customers can be served best by organizations that know the characteristics of both their customers and their customers' buying environments. Since all buyers are not alike, they are placed into groups (or clusters), called market segments, according to geographic, demographic, and psychographic (lifestyle) factors. Such market segments then become the focal points of both product differentiation and positioning.

In market segmentation the idea is to zero in on homogeneous groups, those likely to show an interest in a product/service and to respond to an offer of it. It is also desirable to eliminate those who are not likely to respond. Otherwise, the marketer is not only spending more money in marketing than is necessary but is also reducing the chances for marketing success. Direct marketing thus always embraces a measurement of results as well as accountability for costs, together with a reliance on databases.

Databased Market Segmentation

Databased market segmentation (DMS) has evolved from these principles of direct marketing. It is a highly sophisticated system brought to fruition by today's computer capabilities for storing massive relational databases and for accessing and analyzing these efficiently.

DMS utilizes three advanced mutivariate techniques—cluster analysis, factor analysis, and regression and correlation analysis—to measure and identify market segments having the most (or the least) relevance to a particular organization's offering. It has the capability both to predict and to explain marketing effectiveness. Instead of using an arbitrary scheme of pre-clustering, applicable to all organizations, DMS couples data about individual customers and prospects with custom data about the buying environment of an individual organization.

Although it was applied initially and extensively for maximizing the results from direct response advertising used by mail-order organizations, DMS has also been effective in generating leads, in fund raising, and in building retail traffic. Recent applications have also extended to site location, product differentiation, and the development of promotion strategies for specific organizations.

The Nature of ZIP Code Areas

Many direct marketers view ZIP code areas as ideal units for describing the environment of market segments in both geographic and psychographic (lifestyle) terms. Such description, of course, necessarily augments what is known about each of the individuals within the segments.

Not only do ZIP code areas have a ready numerical identification with an individual customer/prospect, but homogeneity resulting from their structure, coupled with accepted concepts of the interdependence of consumer behavior, causes them to be environmentally measurable.

Databased market segmentation was initially oriented to ZIP code areas and identified and measured data about the residents of such areas. However, the model has been used for such other geodemographic areas as census tracts and block groups. Two requirements for this use are (1) that such units be identified for each customer or prospect, and (2) that the units be culturally, sociologically, and economically homogenous. For statistically significant measurement, smaller areas must be clustered before valid measurement can be accomplished.

Conceptual Bases of the DMS Model

In addition to the ideas of market segmentation itself and of the interdependence of consumer behavior (conspicuous consumption, "keeping up with the Joneses") and the consequent suitability of ZIP code areas as units of observation, the following conceptual bases of the DMS model should be considered:

- ZIP code areas have become well established as marketing units that are readily identifiable and in which a relative homogeneity of consumer behavior makes possible the measurement of the characteristics of areas, often in concert with those of individuals.

- The ability to buy is not the same thing as the proneness to spend—a fact already well established.

- Environmental measurement is more valid than absolute measurement; that is, an absolute of income earned in a rural area of Mississippi, for example, would provide relatively more spending power than would that same absolute amount of income in New York City.

- Lifestyle can often be described through the measurement of the interaction of a variety of independent variables—income interacting with educational level or automobile value, for example.

Modeling Requirements

The principal assumption in the DMS model is that direct marketing effectiveness is somehow related to a degree of presence or absence of certain demographic variables, either individually or in combination. If penetration of a potential market segment can be related to these variables, then the model can attain its specified objectives. The model thus requires:

- That the marketing unit (cluster of ZIP code areas) be large enough to make measurement statistically reliable.

- That the cluster be sufficiently homogeneous to make possible the detection of distinct demographic profiles.

- That the cluster be readily identifiable with a customer's location (as are ZIP code areas).

A second assumption in the DMS model is that vast amounts of data can be utilized for analysis in a manageable form. Factor analysis is used to combine independent variables that appear together in an area; cluster analysis is used to combine individual areas having similar characteristics; and regression and correlation analysis is used to provide a customer profile and prediction of results.

Stages in the DMS Model

The five stages in the DMS model are: (1) potential of the market, (2) penetration of the market, (3) market segmentation, (4) retrieval of market segments, and (5) validation of retrieval.

Stage 1: Potential of the Market   In this stage ZIP code areas relevant to a particular marketer (initially categorized as either urban or rural areas) are combined, through cluster analysis, into homogeneous groupings for subsequent measurement using numbers of observations sufficient to ensure statistically valid predictions.

The clustering process can be visualized by imagining each of about 40,000 ZIP code areas as a centroid with 25 rays, the length of each of which describes the presence (or absence) of an independent variable. Cluster analysis involves the simultaneous comparison of the length of each of these 25 rays, pairwise, among all of the 40,000 ZIP code areas, and it brings together, as the clustering proceeds, those areas that are most alike on all 25 dimensions!

Certain of the data for ZIP code area clusters are indexed to some larger contiguous area such as a sectional center (the first three digits of the five-digit number) or a state (such as Mississippi or New York). This makes possible environmental (as opposed to absolute) measurement of each area's characteristics.

In addition to clustering similar ZIP code areas, many of which involve relatively small numbers of observations, information is needed on as many as 100 independent variables. This is necessary because at the outset it is not known which variable might be relevant for a particular organization. Also, the interaction between and among these variables must be observed and measured. To simplify and to explain, factor analysis is used. The resultant groupings of manifest variables, called factors, are then analyzed subjectively in order to determine what latent dimensions they seem to have in common. These latent dimensions can describe aspects of lifestyles: affluence, poverty, senior citizens, settled singles, and so on.

Stage 2: Penetration of the Market Utilization of the DMS model presupposes a list: (1) responses recorded from a mailing list and measuring penetration, e.g., percentage response from a direct mail offering; (2) a customer list, presuming equal effort over time and measuring penetration of a benchmark universe, e.g., percentage of potential households; (3) survey or responses obtained at traffic locations such as retail stores, e.g., penetration by ZIP code categorization. Table 2–2 provides an example of such penetration measurement.

Table 2–2. Penetration Measurement

Zip Code Cluster	Total Mailed	Total Responses	Percent Responses Mailed
A	5,793	60	1.04%
B	2,735	33	1.21
C	6,731	138	2.05
D	4,341	119	2.79

The measurement of penetration of market segments thus goes beyond the simple definition of these segments on the basis of product preferences and/or usages. The key question for an organization is: "What is *my* profile?" Such profiles, even within organizations, will likely vary according to the enterprise's product line(s) or within groupings according to the characteristics of customers or the nature of their transactions.

Penetration (within a cluster) is the ratio of items of interest (responses, customers, survey answers) to some base count (mailings, households, survey distribution). Penetration is the dependent variable whose variation over all of the ZIP code area clusters is explained by one or more independent variables defining these clusters.

Calculation of penetration is a relatively simple arithmetic process. When significant differences of penetration are observed between clusters, then the need for explanation becomes apparent, as does the desire to be able to predict future results. In Stage 3 is achieved a statistically reliable prediction coupled with a plausible explanation that can be validated through experimentation in the marketplace.

Stage 3: Market Segmentation   The statistical technique used in this stage of the DMS model is stepwise multivariate correlation regression analysis. Table 2–3 presents an abbreviated example of such statistical analysis.

Table 2–3.   Stepwise Multivariate Regression Analysis

```
STEP  #1
    VARIABLE ENTERING            X– 5
R  = 0.583959         R  SQ. = 0.341008
    F  LEVEL  =         23.8036
    STANDARD ERROR OF Y   =       0.06341
    CONSTANT TERM  =        0.27470726
```

VARIABLE NO.	COEFFICIENT	STD ERR OF COEFF
X– 5	−0.28683022E–01	0.00594

```
STEP  #2
    VARIABLE ENTERING            X– 2
R  = 0.717396         R  SQ. = 0.514658
    F  LEVEL  =        16.1004
    STANDARD ERROR OF Y   =       0.05504
    CONSTANT TERM  =        0.25037676
```

VARIABLE NO.	COEFFICIENT	STD ERR OF COEFF
X– 2	0.11710477	0.02951
X– 5	−0.25006641E–01	0.00524

```
STEP  #3
    VARIABLE ENTERING            X– 16
R  = 0.814453         R  SQ. = 0.663334
    F  LEVEL  =        19.4310
    STANDARD ERROR OF Y   =       0.04637
    CONSTANT TERM  =        0.17120540
```

VARIABLE NO.	COEFFICIENT	STD ERR OF COEFF
X– 2	0.12946498	0.02503
X– 5	−0.21160301E–01	0.00450
X– 16	0.10500204E–01	0.00241

STEP #4
    VARIABLE ENTERING   X– 14
R = 0.831825   R SQ. = 0.691934
    F LEVEL =   3.9919
    STANDARD ERROR OF Y   =   0.04488
    CONSTANT TERM =   0.11676645

VARIABLE NO.	COEFFICIENT	STD ERR OF COEFF
X– 2	0.12659431	0.02427
X– 5	–0.18140811E–01	0.00462
X– 14	0.27103789E–01	0.01373
X– 16	0.99606328E–02	0.00235

⋮

STEP #10
    VARIABLE ENTERING   X– 22
R = 0.896520   R SQ. = 0.803748
    F LEVEL =   2.8542
    STANDARD ERROR OF Y   =   0.03766
    CONSTANT TERM =   0.39812356

VARIABLE NO.	COEFFICIENT	STD ERR OF COEFF
X– 2	0.13928533	0.02095
X– 9	–0.20301903E–02	0.00064
X– 10	–0.87198131E–02	0.00257
X– 14	0.69082797E–01	0.01875
X– 15	0.13623666E–01	0.00421
X– 16	0.22368859E–01	0.00380
X– 22	–0.15226589E–02	0.00091
X– 23	–0.21373443E–02	0.00081

Even if the process isn't always clearly understood, the results can be: a rank ordering of predicted penetration attributable to each ZIP code area contained within statistically measurable clusters, as shown in Table 2–4. (Note that the prediction for the cluster is for each ZIP code area within that cluster.) The researcher decides how big a market segment is needed and then determines, from the rank ordering, what the overall penetration would be. Or the minimum marketing requirement (either average or marginal) is set and the size of the resultant market segment is determined.

Explanation of variances is provided through evaluation of the independent variables entering the regression equation and thus accounting for the rank ordering. For a particular organization or even for a particular product line, which of these variables is most highly correlated, singly and/ or in combination, with the dependent variable—penetration?

Stage 4: Retrieval of the Market Segments

When the statistical profile has been developed (as in Stages 1 and 2 of the DMS model) and the measurement has been evaluated (as in Stage 3), there follows the selection

Table 2–4. Rank Ordering of ZIP Code Area Clusters According to Predicted Penetration

CLUSTER #	ZIP #	PENETRATION ACTUAL	PERCENTAGES **		***** BASECOUNTS ****	
			PRED	CUM PRED	ZIP ONLY	CUMULATIVE
39	32009	.00	.0449	.0449	89	89
	32265	.00	.0449	.0449	4	93
	32560	.1070	.0449	.0449	93	186
	32563	.00	.0449	.0449	6	192
	32710	.00	.0449	.0449	37	229
	32732	.00	.0449	.0449	200	429
	32740	.00	.0449	.0449	42	471
	32766	.1500	.0449	.0449	200	671
	33070	.0460	.0449	.0449	651	1322
	33470	.00	.0449	.0449	132	1454
	33527	.00	.0449	.0449	716	2170
	33534	.0590	.0449	.0449	505	2675
	33550	.00	.0449	.0449	194	2869
	33556	.0750	.0449	.0449	528	3397
	33569	.0480	.0449	.0449	1637	5034
	33584	.0390	.0449	.0449	1001	6035
	33586	.00	.0449	.0449	62	6097
	33592	.0770	.0449	.0449	518	6615
	33600	.0750	.0449	.0449	398	7013
	33943	.00	.0449	.0449	139	7152
3	32600	.0420	.0342	.0363	28855	36007
11	32301	.0560	.0327	.0360	3533	39540
	32304	.0230	.0327	.0358	2532	42072
	32500	.0360	.0327	.0355	4873	46945
	32570	.0120	.0327	.0354	2312	49257
	32601	.0330	.0327	.0350	7826	57083
⋮	33030	.0120	.0327	.0348	5564	62647
13	32211	.0240	.0246	.0291	6134	222185
	32303	.0160	.0246	.0290	4243	226428
	32561	.0330	.0246	.0289	1203	227631
	32701	.0140	.0246	.0289	2038	229669
	32751	.0140	.0246	.0288	3379	233048
	32786	.00	.0246	.0288	229	233277
	32789	.0170	.0246	.0287	7543	240820
⋮	33511	.0370	.0246	.0287	2115	242935
10 ⋮	33900	.0210	.0206	.0255	53503	511276
37	33062	.0170	.0111	.0198	6834	1234153
	33140	.00	.0111	.0198	56	1234209
	33154	.0060	.0111	.0198	3120	1237329
	33160	.0130	.0111	.0197	16354	1253683
	33306	.0100	.0111	.0197	986	1254669
30	33064	.0210	.0076	.0196	8201	1262870
	33516	.00	.0076	.0195	11202	1274072
	33570	.0090	.0076	.0195	3190	1277262

of the best clusters of ZIP code areas (market segments) and/or the elimination of those areas in which a poor or undesirable response is predicted. Refer to Table 2–4 for an example of the rank ordering of ZIP code area clusters derived from stepwise multivariate regression analysis. If the findings from the measurement (prediction) and then the identification (explanation) procedures can't be practically applied to retrieve the most desirable market segments—for mail-order offerings, for site locations, for follow-up by a salesperson—then the wisdom of the process thus far can and should be questioned.

It is a relatively simple matter to select and mail only to those ZIP code areas that have the characteristics desired. However, the DMS model is not limited to direct response applications.

A knowledge of market segments affording an organization its greatest potential for penetration is a prerequisite for any marketer. Such knowledge enables the optimal location of dealer outlets, franchises, and salespeople. It pinpoints the distribution of advertising—direct mail as well as print and broadcast—or other promotional efforts. It aids and abets product development and helps direct differentiated products to relevant market segments.

A market segment, in the sense illustrated here, is a cluster, or a combination of clusters, of ZIP code areas with lifestyle attributes relevant for the marketing organization. The DMS model, however, is additive in that it cuts across other known characteristics of the individuals/organizations that compose lists.

Stage 5: Validation of Retrieval   There must be validation to confirm whether the lifestyles identified as important in the DMS model are really relevant. It is in this stage that some models break down, either because they are not validated or because there is no means of validation. For example, a dealer is established at a particular site, but there is no control of what would have happened if that dealer were not there.

One way to validate findings is to mail to a rank-ordered list. Another is to survey store traffic with some response mechanism such as a coupon redemption. Still another is to set up an experiment with a differentiated product either tested against a control offered to a selected market segment or tested in two comparable sites.

An example of an actual rank-ordered mailing and validation is presented in Table 2–5. Here the validation mailing occurred three months after the initial mailing with the only variance being the timing. As expected, the overall response rate dropped 50 percent but an index of quintiled response rates validated the differences initially seen in the rank ordering.

Table 2–5. **Indexed Response**

Quintile	Number of Pieces Mailed	First Effort Response Percentage	First Effort Response Index	Second Effort Response Percentage	Second Effort Response Index
1	242,935	2.87	147	1.36	143
2	268,341	2.26	116	1.08	111
3	230,592	1.94	99	.96	99
4	290,001	1.54	79	.81	84
5	245,393	1.19	61	.67	67

Mastering database marketing isn't child's play, but the payoff more than rewards the effort!

Self-Quiz

1. Name six pieces of basic data that should be included in a database.

   a. _____

   b. _____

   c. _____

   d. _____

   e. _____

   f. _____

2. Define the R-F-M formula.

   R _____

   F _____

   M _____

3. Define FRAT.

   F _____

   R _____

   A _____

   T _____

4. If you are a bank, for example, and have a large group of savings account customers, what type of additional account would you attempt to sell them?

   _____

5. What is perhaps the most valuable asset for any business?

   _____

6. What is the advantage of a database overlay?

   _____

   _____

   _____

7. To maximize results from a list, it's essential that a marketer know not only the demographics of his list but the _____ as well.

8. Databased market segmentation employs three multivariate techniques. Two are listed below. Name the third.

   a. Cluster analysis

   b. Factor analysis

   c. _____ and _____ analysis.

9. The ability to buy is not the same as the _____ to buy.

10. There are five stages of databased market segmentation. The first four are listed below. Name the fifth.

   a. Potential of the market

   b. Penetration of the market

   c. Market segmentation

   d. Retrieval of market segments

   e. _____

Pilot Project   You are the marketing director of a chain of men's clothing stores. You have a customer base of 100,000 customers, dating back 3 years. The only segmentation in the list at this time is a record of when each customer last bought.

   List the data you must accumulate to develop a meaningful database.

CHAPTER THREE

Strategic Business Planning

With the new professionalism that has come to direct marketing, the discipline is being treated more and more as a "business." And with this new viewpoint the need for strategic business planning has emerged. Major traditional marketers who have established direct marketing units as separate profit centers have insisted upon strategic business planning for these centers just as they do for their traditional operations. But strategic business planning is quite foreign to those who have built businesses based solely upon direct marketing methods. Yet the rewards that can come from strategic business planning can be as great proportionately for the entrepreneur as for the giant corporation.

When facing the reality that large- and medium-size companies have been the stimulus for recent growth, it behooves today's direct marketers to take heed of the signals and make sure that their approaches are as contemporary as their potential targets. Since accountability is one of the key elements in direct marketing programs, it is necessary for us to ensure that we remain on track with our own marketing plans, that we are up to date with the emerging technologies, and, finally, that we optimize our own organization's resources.

Strategic Business Planning Defined

First of all, let's define our terms. *Strategic business planning* is a formal method to consider alternatives related to the growth, development, or other options of an enterprise, organization, or business. It has application for large and small companies in direct marketing, ranging from fund raising to lead generation to product sales. When properly developed, a strategic business plan should provide:

- A comprehensive review of the current business

- A description of the problems and opportunities that must be dealt with in the short term

- Clear direction

- A practical action plan

A strategic business plan is *not* a marketing plan. It is much broader in scope, but it does address marketing issues related to a business or company. A well-designed plan will permit much greater control over one's business, enabling the individual to deal with critical situations in a proactive rather than a reactive manner.

Direct marketers have countered the strategic planning issue with a number of comments such as:

- "It's expensive and time-consuming."

- "My plan is based on past experience and current expectations."

- "We don't have the availability of talent in our organization to make planning work."

These comments seem valid, especially for smaller firms. Many are hard pressed to look out further than three months at a time. However, when the following questions are asked, companies of all sizes are likely to agree on the impact:

- Has your company felt the impact of new or revised federal regulations over the past few years?

- Is the current economic environment having an impact on profitablility?

- Are sales increasing at the rate you forecasted?

- Are you comfortable with your organization's ability to adapt to change?

These questions, and many more like them, apply to virtually every business endeavor. Managing these responses and affiliated actions are the key to success in direct marketing today.

How to Develop a Plan

After disposing of the questions on what strategic business planning entails and how it applies to direct marketers, the next step is to develop a plan and determine what should be included. Let's agree on one more fact. There are countless methods used for developing strategic business plans. They range from the efforts of a single, specially trained planning executive to extensive committee approaches. The range of the information developed is equally broad. A plan in some industries may dictate a company's action for a ten-year period, whereas in other cases it may suggest very specific actions for a

twelve-month period. Depending upon the purpose and expectations, any approach may benefit an organization.

There does not seem to be any evidence that better results are achieved through any one methodology. However, for direct marketers, I feel that a more simplified and practical approach will yield the most actionable information. Further, while it would be nice to be able to project, with infinite wisdom, what will happen to our industry and organization or company over the next five years, it is next to impossible. Just review recent growth, technological change, and new applications of direct marketing and you will understand the difficulty of accurate long-term planning. Also, the array of information to be included in a strategic business plan should be subject to the criterion of what is absolutely necessary, rather than what you would like to include. The simpler the plan and the process for developing it, the higher the likelihood of success.

To provide a clearer understanding of a business plan, look at the planning model in Exhibit 3–1. It has proven successful with a number of direct marketing operations. Initial examination of the model suggests a planning time span of three years. However, the meat of the plan is in the annual action plan that covers a twelve-month time frame. As stated, a twelve-month planning horizon seems to provide more than enough opportunity to manage change.

Lets' examine each of the components of the model in detail.

Exhibit 3–1. **A Model for Strategic Business Planning**

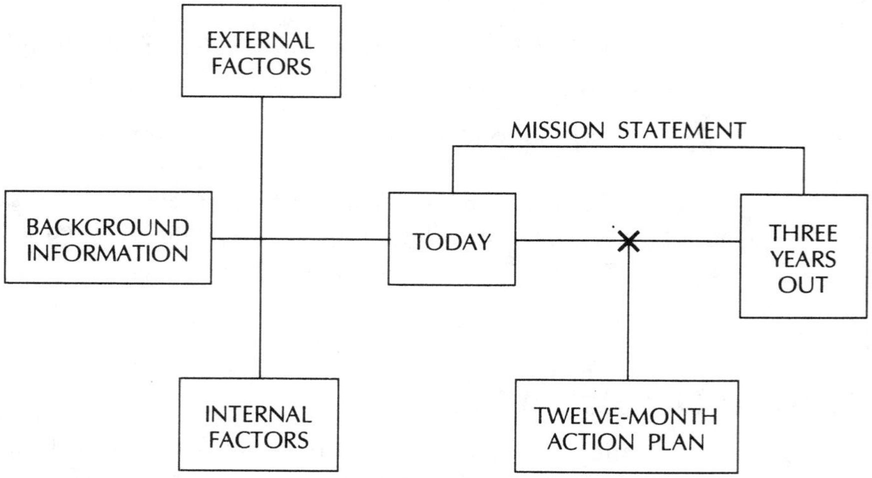

Background Information

In order to develop a strategic business plan, it is necessary to carefully and thoroughly investigate a company's performance. In effect, you are trying to take a "snapshot" of activities covering the current situation and extending

back two or three years. As this is done, you can separate data into two categories: (1) financial and marketing/sales and (2) organizational data.

In the first case, you are looking for the following types of information:

- Growth

- Market share

- Expenditures in specific categories

- Seasonality of sales

- Profit levels

- Product/service line

- Financial resources

- Allocation of resources

- How you rate against your competition

In the second case, you must review how the organization and staff conduct the business. You must determine how the organization works rather than how it looks on the formal organization chart. You must get a "fix" on the company's personality.

For example, is the good work being accomplished on a daily basis spread evenly across the staff, or is it really accomplished by a core of dedicated people? Or, do the key employees understand what the business is trying to accomplish, rather than just reporting the "party line"? This case is every bit as important as knowing the financial operations of the business. However, it is the one most often overlooked in business planning.

After collecting the raw data on business, marketing, and organizational issues, we are ready to proceed to the next step in the model.

External Factors

Simply stated, *external factors*, sometimes referred to as *exogenous factors*, are all of those activities and actions that have an impact on your business but are out of your immediate control. You might quickly say, "If we cannot exert any control over these factors, why include them at all?" The answer to that is twofold: positioning and contingency.

Examples of external factors are:

- Current economy

- Federal regulation

- Competition

- Availability of resources

- Postal rates

- Technology

If we examine one external factor, you will get a clearer understanding of why it is important to determine what these factors are and how they impact your business.

Current Economy   We certainly cannot control this complex and far-reaching factor. However, consider for a moment some of the actions we might take to optimize our position:

- Better manage cash flow

- Reduce inventory

- Tighten receivables

By taking one or more of these actions, we can reduce some of the impact of this external factor on our business.

In the development of a list of external factors, two considerations are important:

1. Limit the list to the most important factors—ten or fewer for many companies. There is nothing more frustrating or less rewarding than considering all of the perils outside of your control and never getting to the major issues that affect your firm directly.

2. As you discuss and decide on each major external factor, be specific in defining what impact it has on your business. If this is impossible, discard the factor.

After looking outside your company or business and sifting through the relevant information, it is time to move to the next phase of plan development.

Internal Factors

Internal factors are those you have control and influence over. Such factors are probably best described as the strengths and weaknesses of your company. These strengths and weaknesses are often referred to as the "building blocks" of a sound strategic business plan. Experience has indicated it is easier and more productive to start with the positive aspects—the strengths.

Basically, strengths include those activities that you consistently complete extremely well—the things that give you an edge on your competition. They can include but are not limited to:

- Technology
- Product
- Marketing
- Process
- Service

- Systems
- People
- Organization
- Attitude

- Flexibility
- Management
- Communication
- Leadership

For example, in direct marketing, a company might refer to its preeminence in product development, production innovations, back-end service and performance, and so forth. All of these are significant attributes and must be defined. This will allow for leveraging real strengths against stated goals. One note of caution: Make sure your description of a strength is accurate. Often the definition of these considerations is completed in a cavalier manner, and what is described by some as being a strength turns out to be of less value than previously reported.

The next move in the development of internal factors is defining weaknesses. Actually, this is the toughest part in developing a strategic business plan. However, this part of the inspection will yield the greatest return. It is difficult to elaborate on the shortfalls of a business. In this case, we are often getting at subpar performance levels. How many executives really want to define what's wrong with the operation, the staff, or even their direction of them? Weaknesses can be described as what a company does poorly and can include the following:

- Technology
- Product
- Marketing
- Process
- Service

- Systems
- People
- Organization
- Attitude

- Flexibility
- Management
- Communication
- Leadership

A comprehensive review of internal factors will provide an accurate picture of the company as it is today. More often than not, when completed objectively, it is quite revealing. In content alone, it can include a number of documents and summary sheets. Gathering the data is only one step. The next is to condense those data into an accurate, readable document. And this brings us to the next component of the planning model.

Mission Statement

The *mission statement* is a condensation of what the company is today and what we want (expect) it to be tomorrow. Let's separate the mission statement into those parts and describe each individually.

Mission Statement—Today   The purpose of this statement is to accurately define in business shorthand the position of the company as it now exists. It is derived from the microscopic review discussed earlier. It usually is restructured in length to one or two typewritten pages. If it is honest, it will probably sound somewhat pessimistic. But that's acceptable, for more often than not, where the company is today is not where it wants to be tomorrow.

Let's take a look at a mission statement. After considerable discussion, one direct marketing company, which for the sake of this discussion we'll call Leisure Time Activities, developed this statement of where it is today:

LEISURE TIME ACTIVITIES Today—1992

Today we are an established mail order company operating in the U.S. and Canada with a preeminent niche in the leisure activities market. In 1987, we had sales of $17 million and an embarrassing shortfall of $1.5 million in profits. Our recent growth has been sluggish and has not met our expectations. We have limited information on the market, but we do know we have a dominant share of the hobby segment. We have not extended this strength into the larger market of sporting goods.

The competition is intensifying, especially for sporting goods. Major companies have an edge and they are expanding the market. This is all taking place in a market where there is little current product innovation. We feel technological change is coming, but don't know when. As a company, we have moved from a leadership position to a company that follows.

Although we have good products and a good customer base, we have become complacent. We have not leveraged our small size and financial strength to the best advantage. Our marketing approach is lackluster. We have experienced a breakdown in leadership, management, and communications. This has confused our direction and has had a negative impact on company spirit and teamwork; and as a result, we have had a breakdown in company performance in several areas.

Although we perceive our company and organization to be in a growth mode, we have not taken effective actions to make it happen. We have discussed an appetite for change and have developed a consensus on the major issues that must be resolved.

In summary, we are at a turning point. We must leverage our good name and products which have enabled us to become a major force in this industry, develop innovative marketing plans, and move in one direction, collectively.

Mission Statement—Tomorrow   The purpose of this statement is to define reasonable goals to be achieved within a specific period. The length of time to cover for this type of statement varies. A three-year period for goal setting is often an agreeable compromise.

But let's take a look at Leisure Time Activities again—where does the company see itself in three years?

LEISURE TIME ACTIVITIES Three Years Out

By the end of 1995 we will be recognized as an aggressive, multiline direct marketing company. We will have demonstrated state-of-the-art marketing programs, a collective winning attitude, and financial results in line with written plans. We will have a sales volume of $20 million with a minimum of 25 percent R.O.I. And we will generate a profit on sales of 10 percent.

Our growth will be carefully planned. We will have expanded our capabilities and increased our share of the sporting goods market. Our product lines will include, but not be limited to, equipment and supplies, clothing, and related gift items, and will tend to have more proprietary products.

Our management has become a cohesive team which is directing a qualified, experienced, and motivated staff. This collective effort has provided a competitive edge and the flexibility to use our strengths in the best possible way.

Our financial performance has enabled the company to easily secure capital for further investment opportunities.

In summary, we have turned Leisure Time Activities around. This has been recognized by our stockholders, our employees, and the industry. We have replaced our former complacency with a demonstrated winning attitude.

If you manage to plan correctly, you will revisit these goals on an annual basis to make sure you remain on track and that changing conditions are updated. Remember, a plan is not a document that is put on the shelf and dusted off each December. In developing this section of the mission statement, you may wish to include:

- Sales/income
- Markets
- Technology
- Organization/size
- New products
- Position in market

The checklist in Exhibit 3–2 is provided to assist in structuring your mission statement.

You are now at a critical point in the planning model—you have developed:

What You Are Today—What You Want to Be in Three Years

The next step is to deal with the "gaps" in the mission statement, the differences between your strengths/weaknesses now and your expected position in three years.

Exhibit 3–2.   **Mission Statement**

General Information	Today	Three Years Out
Volume		
Profit		
Growth		
Market position		
External Factors		
Competition		
Industry factors		
Geography		
Internal Factors		
Strengths		
Weaknesses		
Product		
Summary		

Action Plans

The fundamental output from any good strategic business plan is the identification of those actions or activities that must be accomplished in order to reach your intended position. These actions or activities spring forth from your examination of internal and external factors and are summarized in the today section of the mission statement.

The question is, how do you prepare an action plan that guarantees progress toward your stated goals? There may be several ways to develop this kind of plan. However, there are a few fundamentals to success:

- Top management endorsement
- Clearly stated tasks
- Complete understanding by those who must implement the plan
- Realistic and attainable actions

If the above criteria can be met, the likelihood of success is greatly increased. Now, let's move on to the development of an action plan. An *action plan* defines the "must-do" tasks for completion, usually over a twelve-month

period. These are the problems or opportunities that must be handled in order to achieve planning goals. They must be specific and precisely worded to ensure that those responsible for achievement have a clear understanding of the tasks to be accomplished. Participants must know *what* is to be accomplished, *how* it will be accomplished, by *whom*, and *within what time frame*. Anything short of these conditions will negatively impact performance against the plan.

There are some guidelines for developing objectives and strategies that detail the action plan. Let's start by clearly defining these terms:

- *Objective*: A statement that accurately describes *what* is to be accomplished over the next twelve months. In almost all cases, it is a must-do task.

- *Strategies*: A listing of methods, events, and the like that describe *how* an objective will be achieved. Completed strategies always list who is responsible, for what, and when.

To simplify the discussion, let's divide it into two parts:

- How to develop good objectives
- How to develop effective strategies

How to Develop Good Objectives

The first step in moving toward the development of action plan objectives is to review any notes taken during the strengths and weaknesses identification. Determine the problems (not the symptoms) and then review the problems and define them as clearly as possible. It is necessary at this stage to move from the general to the specific. It is easier to reduce a general concept by listing all situations or actions relating to the problem prior to specifically pinpointing it. Perhaps the following example will make this clear.

Example 1. Let's take a look at the Leisure Time Activities company again. In the general area, one of the problems is the need to increase profits.

"There is a definite need to increase profit."

If we dig deeper, we can expand this problem to include:

1. We need a 10 percent profit on all sales made in 1992–1993.

2. We must improve our marketing approach.

3. We must regain our leadership position.

4. We lack specific controls—financial, purchasing, inventory, marketing programs.

5. We need to develop systems to accurately project our financial future.

6. We need a minimum of 25 percent R.O.I.

While all of the above statements are valid, they do not relate directly to the same specific problem: No. 1 gets at the heart of the problem—how much and when. It further describes the scope of what is to be done. The others, Nos. 2–6, may either be strategies (how to do it) or be related to another problem.

It is necessary to use this process for all problem areas so that accurate descriptions of the problems are developed.

The next step is to take the refined list for each problem and write an objective. As this is done, consider whether the problem or task is realistic and achievable. If you should feel that nothing can practically be done in a given situation, why continue working on it? While this situation doesn't happen very often, it should be acknowledged. Let's assume that the problem can be dealt with. You must now put it in a clear statement that describes what is to be accomplished. We have found that there are three integral parts in defining problems:

1. A clear, concise statement of the *task*

2. The *purpose* for completing the task

3. Reasonable *time* measurement(s)

Further, we have found that when these factors are included, the probability of successful completion is greatly increased.

The outline method seems to be the easiest approach in applying the factors. Here's an example:

Task	Purpose	Time
• What do we want to do?	• Why are we doing it?	• When do we want it completed, or what interim time checks should we use?

Referring to an earlier situation, we can develop an objective that meets the criteria. (For sake of discussion, we have stated the real problem as the need to increase profits through planning.)

Task	Purpose	Time
• Achieve a sales volume of $20 million with a minimum 25 percent R.O.I.	• Increase profits	• Within next twelve months
• Develop short- and long-term plans	• Regain leadership position	• By December 1993
		• Monitor progress quarterly

Using this information, we can develop an objective statement that clearly reflects our intention:

By December 1993,   we must develop short- and long-term plans
TIME   TASK
to achieve a sales volume of $20 million with a minimum 25 percent R.O.I.
PURPOSE
and regain a leadership position in our market. Progress on this will be *formally monitored on a quarterly basis.*
ADDITIONAL MEASUREMENTS

At this point you may ask the question: Is all this really necessary? The best answer is simply this: If you do not take the time to clearly select and write the plan objectives, not much will happen. One other example might help to clarify this.

Example 2.   Managers at Leisure Time Activities found that after a comprehensive assessment there were a number of internal problems related to morale and communications. As they focused on the problem, it seemed that improved communications would really clear up the situation. After thrashing out problems, they then developed this objective:

"We must improve company internal communications."

From this point, they further identified five strategies that would be necessary to achieve the objective. After additional discussion, they felt that even if all of the strategies were implemented, they would, at best, achieve only a partial solution to the problem. In reanalyzing the objective, they found these critical flaws:

1. Only part of the task was identified.

2. The purpose of the action was not specified.

3. There were no time measurements or checkpoints.

They went back to discuss the objectives. The following revision makes the point quite well:

Within six months, we will improve the interchange of information and ideas throughout the company about plans and activities affecting operations and policies, in order to encourage feedback and involvement of all employees.

You will notice, when we move into strategy development, that a clear objective reduces the difficulty of strategy selection.

How to Develop Effective Strategies

Now that you know what must be done, we will discuss approaches and methods to describe *how* it should be done. Strategies are events, methods, and the like that crisply define the kinds of actions that should be taken to solve a problem, that is, to complete an objective. If an objective has been clearly written, the strategies are easily developed.

One way to look at strategies is to think of an action plan. What kind of actions should you take to rectify this problem or improve that situation? At this point, you are not trying to get down to details. Rather, you are looking for a logical sequence of activity that will outline actions for the next twelve months or so (though some strategies may extend beyond a twelve-month period). To get a better fix, let's continue with the objective discussed in Example 2 above:

> Within six months, we will improve throughout the company the interchange of information and ideas about plans and activities affecting operations and policies, in order to encourage feedback and involvement of all employees.

While this objective may be typical of any number of companies, the methods used to achieve it may vary considerably. A group must consider all of the problems, resources, and other considerations. Let's list some facts that seem apparent:

1. We know when we want to accomplish it.

2. We know the type of communication we want to disseminate (plans and activities).

3. We know what areas it will affect (operations and policies).

4. We know we need to encourage feedback and involvement.

What seems to emerge is that Leisure Time Activities management needs to improve interchange of information on a companywide basis. It now knows what it wants to do and needs to develop how it is going to do it. In discussing the matter further, it came up with the following action recommendations:

- Set up a departmental activities program.

- Set up an Operations Improvement Committee to answer questions and get employee feedback.

- Provide a forum for departmental information interchange.

- Meet informally with employees.

- Deliver a "State of the Company" message.

- Provide feedback on progress of plans and activities.

These were refined and expanded as shown in Exhibit 3–3.

Exhibit 3–3.   **Executing Strategies**

Strategies	Responsibility	Due Date
1. Company orientation to department activities: set up program and schedule.	Personnel and division managers	Monthly
2. Operations Improvement Committee set up to answer questions and obtain feedback from employees.	A representative from each department	5/15
3. Management Committee to be the forum for interchange of departmental information and in turn inform their departments and get feedback.	Management Committee	3/23
4. "State of the Company" message: where we are, how we are doing, etc.	President	4/1 and annual
5. Informal meeting of all employees.	Executive Committee	6/1 and 12/1 and semiannual
6. Memo from Executive Committee to employees on how we are doing.	Executive Committee	Monthly
7. Staff luncheons with informal meetings— opportunity for employees to ask questions.	Management Committee	When necessary
8. New-employee orientation.	Personnel and department peer level	5/1

9. Social/athletic activities:
  a. Set up program
  b. Schedule an "activity day"
	Personnel
	Personnel Management Committee
		5/1
		4/15

As you can see, the group went from the general to the specific. When approaching it in this manner, you can see where the plan stands at all times. This company turned a normal problem into a reasonable and practical opportunity.

How to Manage the Plan

Once a strategic business plan is written, there is a tendency to forget about it and to return to the normal everyday grind. This happens in spite of the fact that the objectives that were developed during the process were *must-do* tasks. To ensure that must-do tasks are acted upon and to make certain the plan functions as a road map, proceed as follows:

1. Set up a small planning coordination function (one to two persons). This function is responsible for managing the plan from the meeting to back on the job. The function should:
   a. Coordinate with each person responsible for an objective and make sure that the assigned objective is in final form with realistic due dates, strategy assignments, and so forth. (During the planning meeting, appoint one or two persons to be responsible for each objective developed.)
   b. Consolidate all objectives and review background data (developed in the meeting).
   c. Submit it for management approval.
   d. Develop a short typewritten overview of the planning meeting that describes the highlights of the plan (no confidential information) for all employees. After the management's approval, this should be discussed with all employees as appropriate.
   e. Stay on top of the plan. The coordination group should establish a practical method to evaluate progress against strategies. This should be put into a two-page report and presented to management on a quarterly basis.

2. A number of other practical approaches can be utilized. These range from getting lower-level organizational participation on strategies to individual departmental plans.

   In summary, strategic business planning is a management tool that enables an organization to focus on problems and opportunities, on current position and future direction, and, finally, on what to do next. Participating in the development of a strategic business plan is only one phase. Making it work is another.

Self-Quiz

1. Define *strategic business planning*.

_____

_____

_____

_____

2. What are the two types of data required for background information pertinent to developing a strategic business plan?

a. _____

b. _____

3. List six external factors that can have an impact on a direct marketing operation but cannot be directly controlled.

a. _____   d. _____

b. _____   e. _____

c. _____   f. _____

4. List six internal factors over which a direct marketing operation can exercise control.

a. _____   d. _____

b. _____   e. _____

c. _____   f. _____

5. Define *mission statement*.

_____

_____

_____

_____

6. What are the four fundamentals in making an action plan work?

a. _____

b. _____

c. _____

d. _____

7. Define *objective* as it relates to a business plan.

_____

_____

_____

_____

8. Define *strategy* as it relates to a business plan.

_____

_____

_____

_____

9. In moving toward the development of action plan objectives, one should determine the _____, not the _____.

10. What are the three integral parts involved in defining a problem?

a. _____

b. _____

c. _____

Pilot Project

For three years your company has had a mail order catalog that offers ladies' apparel, home furnishings, and gift items. You are no match for competitors like Horchow and Neiman-Marcus. Your resources, both personnel and financial, are limited. As you are now positioned, it is obvious that you are fighting a losing battle.

Your objective is to change direction and establish a clearly defined niche in the marketplace, changing your merchandise mix to items not generally available from your competition.

Your assignment is to develop strategies and an action plan that will reposition your catalog in the marketplace over the next twelve months. (Among the strategies you might consider are: positioning your catalog as the *source* for apparel, home furnishings, and gifts for the career woman; or positioning your catalog as the *source* for apparel and gift items for those engaged in outdoor activities.)

Importance of the Offer

The propositions you make to customers—more often referred to as *offers*—can mean the difference between success and failure. Depending on the offer, differences in response of 25, 50, or 100 percent and more are commonplace.

Not only is the offer you make the key to success or failure, but the manner in which the offer is presented can have a dramatic effect. For example, here are three ways to state the same offer:

1. Half price!

2. Buy one—get one *free!*

3. 50 percent off!

Each statement conveys the same offer, but No. 2 pulled 40 percent better than No. 1 or No. 3. Consumers perceived No. 2 to be the most attractive offer.

Offers with Multiple Appeals

Exhibit 4–1 illustrates what appears to be a very innocent order card. But the multiple appeals used are certain to have a strong effect on front-end response. And the "conditions" for accepting are certain to have an immediate and long-term effect on how well the publisher does both front-end and back-end.

Let's examine the appeals and conditions. "Please send me, free, the Premier issue of GEO." That's strong; You can't beat the appeal of something free. But note the slight condition ". . . and reserve a money-saving Charter Subscription in my name."

The first appeal is followed by another appeal and a condition: "At the end of thirty days, if I have not instructed you to cancel my reservation, you

Exhibit 4–1.   **Offers with Multiple Appeals and Conditions**

FREE PREMIER ISSUE/CHARTER SUBSCRIPTION RESERVATION

Please send me, free, the Premier Issue of GEO, and reserve a money-saving Charter Subscription in my name. At the end of thirty days, if I have not instructed you to cancel my reservation, you may enter my subscription at the Charter Rate of $36 for one year (12 more monthly issues)—a savings of $12 off the annual cover price of $4 per issue.

As a Charter Subscriber, I am entitled to renew annually at savings of 25% off the newsstand price. Please bill me automatically each year. If at any time, for any reason, I elect to cancel my subscription, I will receive a full refund on all un-mailed issues. The Premier Issue is mine to keep in any case.

In addition, when I pay for my Charter Subscription, as a special gift I will receive a limited-edition copy of the GEO Premier Issue Cover Poster.

Please make any necessary corrections in your name or address. Return this reservation form in the postage-paid reply envelope enclosed.

H-PF-R   P.O. BOX 2552, BOULDER, COLORADO 80322

may enter my subscription at the Charter Rate of $36 for one year (12 more monthly issues)—a savings of $12 off the annual cover price of $4 per issue."

So the *basic* offer breaks out like this: First issue free (appeal); right to cancel at the end of thirty days (appeal); enter twelve-month subscription at $36 unless instructed otherwise (condition); save $12 off the annual cover price (appeal).

But the offer doesn't end there. "As a Charter Subscriber, I am entitled to renew annually at savings of 25% off the newstand price" (appeal). "Please bill me automatically each year" (condition). "If at any time, for any reason, I elect to cancel my subscription, I will receive a full refund on all unmailed issues. The Premier issue is mine to keep in any case" (appeal).

Finally, "In addition, when I pay for my Charter Subscription, as a special gift I will receive a limited-edition copy of the GEO Premier Issue Cover Poster" (both a condition and an appeal). In total, a brilliantly conceived and well-thought-through offer.

The Effects

This offer, one of many tested by *Geo* in the process of introducing the international magazine, can have a tremendous effect on immediate and long-term results.

Geo and its agency know that offering the premier issue free will almost certainly bring a greater response than "tighter" offers that don't allow for cancellation after the first issue. But it also knows that, historically, its "loose" offer can result in cancellations of as high as 65 percent. So, to be determined is whether the superb quality of the magazine will overcome the historically poor conversion rate of this type of offer.

Guaranteeing in perpetuity a renewal rate of 25 percent off the newsstand price is a "safe" offer in that it is a more or less standard discount for the publishing industry. There should be no long-term problems with that offer.

But "Please bill me automatically each year" could be a problem, or it could be a bonanza. This condition allows *Geo* to bill automatically without employing a renewal series, often six to eight efforts. Yet to be determined, however, is whether (1) the cancellation rate will be the same, better, or worse than when a renewal series is used and (2) whether the pay-ups will be the same, better, or worse than when a renewal series is used.

The sign-off offer—"In addition, when I pay for my Charter Subscription, as a special gift I will receive a limited-edition copy of the Premier Issue Cover Poster"—is smartly conceived. It is clear recognition on the part of *Geo* and its agency that not only do "loose" offers like this one historically result in a low conversion rate, but that pay-ups for those who don't cancel tend to be lower than for "tighter" offers. To be learned is whether the lure of the free cover poster upon payment will increase the conversion rate and the payment rate.

So this "innocent" offer is loaded with immediate and long-term implications. And so it is with all direct response offers. That's why no direct response person worth his salt would consider starting creative until offers are clearly thought through.

Factors to Consider

Basically, there are ten factors to consider when creating an offer:

1. *Price*. This is a toughie. Does the price you settle upon allow for a sufficient markup? If you have competition, is the price competitive? Is the price you settle upon perceived by the consumer to be the right price for the value received?

   If you want to sell your item for $7.95 each, how about two for $15.90 (same price, but you get twice the average sale)? How about selling the first for $11.95 and the second for $3.95 (same total dollars if you sell two units—and if you don't sell two units you get a higher price for a single unit)?

   Pricing—there's nothing more important. Testing to determine the best price is vital to maximizing long-term payoff.

2. *Shipping and handling*. Where applicable (and it's usually not applicable when selling a publication or service), shipping and handling charges can be an important factor in pricing. It's important to know how much you can add to a base price without adversely affecting sales.

Many merchandisers follow a rule of thumb that shipping and handling charges should not exceed 10 percent of the basic selling price. But again, testing is advisable.

3. *Unit of sale*. Will your product or service be offered "each"? "Two for"? "Set of X?" Obviously, the more units you can move per sale, the better off you are likely to be. But if your prime objective is to build a large customer list fast, would you be better off to offer single units if you got twice the response over a "two for" offer?

In the case of *Geo*, suppose it had offered six months for $18? Would it be better off long term?

4. *Optional features*. Optional features include such things as special colors, odd sizes, special binding for books, personalization, and the like.

Optional features often increase the dollar amount of the average order. For example, when the publisher of a dictionary offered thumb indexing at $2 extra, 25 percent of total purchasers opted for this added feature.

5. *Future obligation*. Subscribers to *Geo*, returning the illustrated order card, have agreed to automatic billing, if they don't elect to cancel.

More common are book and record offers that commit the purchaser to future obligation. ("Take ten records for $1 and agree to buy six more in the coming twelve months.") A continuity program offer might state: "Get Volume 1 free—others will be sent at regular intervals."

Future obligation offers, when successful, enable the marketer to "pay" a substantial price for the first order, knowing there will be a long-term payout.

6. *Credit options*. Many marketers believe that a major factor in the direct marketing explosion during the past decade was the proliferation of credit cards. It's rare today to receive a catalog that does not contain one or more of these options: "Charge to American Express, Diners Club, Carte Blanche, VISA, MasterCard, Discover." It pays: The average order is usually at least 15 percent larger than a cash order.

Some major direct marketers offer credit for thirty days (*Geo* did this), and others offer installment credit with interest added (oil companies are a good example). Whether it be commercial credit cards or house credit, history says credit options increase revenue.

7. *Incentives*. Incentives include free gifts, discounts, and sweepstakes. (*Geo* offered two incentives, the premier issue free with a conditional subscription and a free poster upon payment.)

Toll-free ordering privilege is likewise an incentive—ease of ordering. Not unlike credit options, toll-free ordering privileges tend to increase the average order 15 percent and more.

But incentives must be tested front-end and back-end. Are people "buying" the free gift or sweeps? Will they be as good repeat customers as those who bought in the first instance without incentive?

8. *Time limits.* Time limits add urgency to an offer. (*Geo*, for example, could have applied a time limit to its charter offer—with good logic.)

One word of caution: If you establish a time limit, stick to it!

9. *Quantity limits.* One of the major proponents of quantity limits is the collectibles field. ("Only 5,000 will be minted. Then the molds will be destroyed.") There is something in the human psyche that says, "If it's in short supply, I want it!" Even "Limit—two to a customer" often outperforms no limit.

But if you set a limit, stick to it.

10. *Guarantees.* Of the ten factors to be considered in structuring an offer, there is one that should never be passed up—the *guarantee*. *Geo* has two guarantees: Cancel the subscription if not pleased with the free premier issue and "if at any time, for any reason, I elect to cancel my subscription, I will receive a full refund on all unmailed issues."

Hundreds of millions of people have ordered by phone or mail over the decades with the assurance their satisfaction is guaranteed. Don't make an offer without a guarantee!

Nothing should happen in the creative process until you have structured an offer, or offers, that will make the creative process work. But remember this—what you offer is what you live with!

Checklist of Basic Offers

The following checklist briefly describes basic offers that may be used singly or in various combinations, depending on the marketer's objectives. Variations on some of these basic offers are illustrated in Exhibits 4–2 through 4–6.

1. *Free information.* This is often the most effective offer, particularly when getting leads for salespeople is the prime objective or when nonprospects must be screened out at low cost before expensive literature is sent to prime prospects.

2. *Samples.* A sample of a product or service is often a very effective sales tool. If a sample can be enclosed in a mailing package, results often more than warrant the extra cost. Consideration should be given to charging a nominal price for a sample. The recipient's investment in a sample promotes trying it, and this usually results in a substantial increase in sales.

Exhibit 4–2.   **Involvement Device**

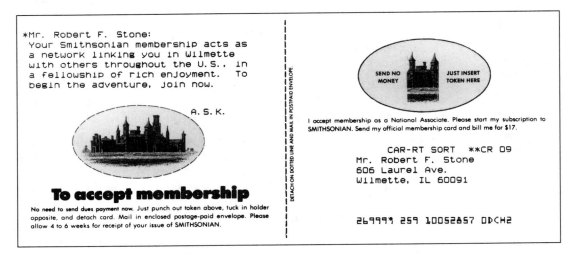

Order form, with personal message from Smithsonian, includes involvement device.

3. *Free trial.* This is the bellwether of mail order. Free trial melts away human inertia. Consider fitting the length of the trial period to the nature of the product or service, rather than the standard 15 days.

4. *Conditional sale.* This prearranges the possibility of long-term acceptance based on a sample. Example: "Please send me, free, the premier issue of *Geo*, and reserve a money-saving Charter Subscription in my name. At the end of the thirty days, if I have not instructed you to cancel my reservation, you may enter my subscription at the Charter Rate of $36 for one year (twelve more monthly issues)—a savings of $12 off the annual cover price of $4 per issue."

5. *Till forbid.* This prearranges continuing shipments on a specified basis. The customer has the option to forbid future shipments at any specified time. Works well for business-service offers and continuity book programs.

6. *Yes–no.* This is an involvement offer. The prospect is asked to respond, usually through a token or stamp, indicating acceptance or rejection of the offer. Historically, more favorable responses are received with this offer than when no rejection option is provided.

7. *Time limit.* Setting a time limit on a given offer *forces* action, either positive or negative. Usually it is more effective to name a specific date rather than a time period. It is important to test for the most effective time limit because a short period may not allow sufficient time for deliberation. Too long a period, on the other hand, may promote inertia.

Exhibit 4–3.   **Postcard Mailing with Multiple Devices**

SAVE 75% WITH NEWSWEEK'S GOLDEN ANNIVERSARY SUBSCRIPTION OFFER!

Dear Mr. Stone,
No big sales pitch. Subscribe to Newsweek now and take
advantage of our special 50th Anniversary Offer -- the
lowest rate available -- a full 75% off the cover price and
50% off the basic subscription rate. Act now!

Mr. Robert Stone
606 Laurel Ave
☐ **I do**   Wilmette, Il. 60091
☐ **I do not**
34471215   Offer ends 7/15/82

accept this special invitation to receive **26 weeks** of Newsweek for **$9.75** (only 37.5¢ a copy)—75% off the $1.50 cover price,
50% off the 75¢ basic subscription rate. I prefer this alternate term ☐ **52 weeks** for **$19.50** (I still pay only 37.5¢ a copy).

Please check one: ☐ Bill me ☐ Payment enclosed   ☐ Charge ☐ American Express   ☐ Diners
(put form in envelope)   (put form in envelope) ☐ VISA ☐ Master Card
1159714485

Card # _____   Expires _____

Interbank # (Master Card) _____   Signature _____
Good only in the 50 states of the U.S.A.

Newsweek

P.O. BOX 411 • LIVINGSTON, N.J. 07039
Tell us, Mr. Stone,
whether you will
accept this special
HALF-PRICE OFFER!

USA 12¢
FREEDOM OF CONSCIENCE

FIRST CLASS PRESORTED

SPECIAL
ANNIVERSARY
OFFER!
NEWSWEEK
AT
37 ½ ¢
A Copy

Mr. Robert Stone
606 Laurel Ave
Wilmette, Il. 60091

Simple postcard mailing from Newsweek includes sales message, yes-no offer, discount offer, and subscription card.

8. *Get-a-friend*. Based on the axiom that the best source for new customers is one's present list of satisfied customers. Many get-a-friend offers get new customers in a large volume at low acquisition cost. The best response for a get-a-friend offer usually results from limiting the number of friends' names requested and offering a reward for providing names or securing new customers.

9. *Contests*. These create attention and excitement. Stringent FTC rules apply. Contests are highly effective in conjunction with magazine subscription offers and popular merchandise offers.

Exhibit 4–4.   **Three-Tier Offer**

FREE SOCIAL SECURITY FACT KIT

Here is what you get in your FREE Fact Kit:

50-page Handbook tells you all about your rights, benefits, and privileges under Social Security. It even explains how to collect the money you're entitled to.

Benefits Computer makes it easy to calculate the approximate monthly benefits you'll collect.

Official Social Security Request Form Send it in, and the government reports directly to you on the Social Security earnings credited to your account for each of your working years. It's important to check this report for accuracy, since there's a 3-year time limit for correcting any errors.

1982 GUIDE TO SOCIAL SECURITY

SOCIAL SECURITY FACT KIT

As a free gift to you, Old American invites you to accept a 3-piece Social Security Fact Kit. To receive this no-obligation gift, place Label A here.

BOX A
AFFIX LABEL A HERE

TRIP-AID ACCIDENT POLICY CERTIFICATE

APPLICATION

☐ **YES** Send me your policy. I have enclosed 10¢ with my application.

Date of Birth _____
Month   Date   Year

Beneficiary _____
First Name   Middle Initial   Last Name

Relationship of Beneficiary _____

To the best of my knowledge and belief, I am sound mentally and physically. I understand that the policy (Series ID3077) becomes effective when issued.

Signature X _____
First Name   Middle Initial   Last Name

Licensed Resident Agent, if applicable
ID2000   Old American Ins. Co. • 4900 Oak • PO Box 573 • K.C., MO 64141

BOX B
AFFIX LABEL B HERE

Indicate any change to name and/or address by crossing out and inserting correct information.

OLD AMERICAN TRIP-AID ACCIDENT POLICY

For persons 40 to 85 years of age
30 DAYS COVERAGE FOR 10¢
(Regular premium is $5.40 monthly)

TRIP-AID ACCIDENT POLICY CERTIFICATE

APPLICATION

☐ **YES**. Send me your policy. I have enclosed 10¢ with my application.

Date of Birth _____
Month   Date   Year

Beneficiary _____
First Name   Middle Initial   Last Name

Relationship of Beneficiary _____

To the best of my knowledge and belief, I am sound mentally and physically. I understand that the policy (Series ID3077) becomes effective when issued.

Signature X _____
First Name   Middle Initial   Last Name

Licensed Resident Agent, if applicable
ID2000   Old American Ins. Co. • 4900 Oak • PO Box 573 • K.C., MO 64141

THIS APPLICATION FOR USE BY SPOUSE OR OTHER FAMILY MEMBER, AGE 40 TO 85, WHO ALSO WISHES TO APPLY

Name _____
Please Print

Address _____

City _____

State _____ **Zip** _____

DP:AP1082:25T

Three-tier offer from Old American Insurance Company offers: (1) a free Social Security Fact Kit, (2) an opportunity for the mail recipient to accept a 10-cent introductory offer for a Trip-Aid Accident Policy, and (3) the same opportunity for a spouse or other family member.

Exhibit 4–5.   Get-a-Friend Offer

Get-a-friend offer from the Literary Guild: Member encourages a friend to fill in new application. Member fills in the balance of the card, indicating bonus desired as a reward for acquiring a new member.

The Literary Guild   231-3

New Applicant: Choose 4 books for $1 with membership!

Please accept my application for membership in The Literary Guild. Send me the 4 books indicated and bill me just $1, plus shipping and handling. I agree to the membership plan described in the enclosed circular and understand that I need buy only 4 more books at the regular low club prices whenever I want them. After buying 4 more books I may resign or remain a member for as long as I wish without further obligation to purchase books.
SATISFACTION GUARANTEED: If not completely satisfied with your Introductory package, return all four books within ten days. Your membership will be canceled and you'll owe nothing.

Write in code numbers of your 4 books here

Mr.
Mrs.
Miss
Ms.
(please print)
Address   Apt.
City   State   Zip

Present Member: Take 2 books FREE for each friend who becomes a member!

Write in code numbers of your 2 books here:

SPECIAL BONUS: Take one of these gifts free for each friend you introduce to The Literary Guild. Check one box for each friend:
☐ 88278 "Foot Notes" Memo Board
☐ 81075 The Literary Guild Book Jacket
☐ 85597 The Literary Guild Mini-Bag

81075
88278
85597

PRESENT MEMBER: In addition to your 2 FREE books, take one of these gifts free for each member recruited.

IMPORTANT: To avoid delay, please enter your current book club account number.

Name
(please print)
Address   Apt.
City   State   Zip

53   Order cannot be processed unless this card is filled in by both Present Member and New Applicant   FG033

10. *Discounts.* A discount is a never-ending lure to consumers as well as businesspeople. Discounts are particularly effective where the value of a product or service is well established. Three types of discounts are widely offered: (a) for cash, (b) for an introductory order, and (c) for volume purchase.

Discounts for volume purchases are often tied to levels of purchase. For example, "5 percent discount on orders up to $25; 10 percent discount on orders from $25 to $50; 15 percent discount on orders of $50 and over."

Another play on basic discount offers is what is commonly referred to as *multiple time-dated discount offers*. The objective here is to get the customer into the habit of using your product or service. (Exhibit 4–7 is a good example of this technique.)

Exhibit 4–6. Use of Token with Free Offer

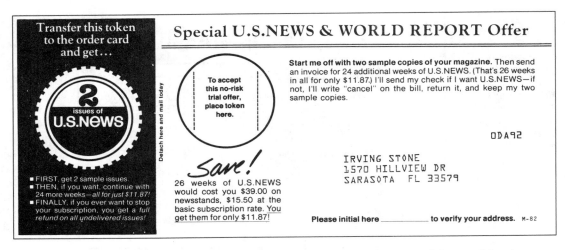

U.S. News and World Report offers the first two issues free, with the right to cancel the conditional subscription for 24 additional issues. Token dramatizes the free offer.

11. *Negative Option*. This offer, in popular use by book and record clubs, prearranges for shipment if the customer doesn't abort the shipment by mailing the rejection form prior to deadline date. FTC guidelines must be followed carefully.

12. *Positive Option*. Every shipment is based on a *direct action* by the club member, rather than a *nonaction* as exemplified by the negative option feature of most book and record clubs. Front-end response to a positive option is likely to be lower, but long-pull sales are likely to be greater.

13. *Lifetime membership*. Under this plan, the member pays one fee, $5, for instance, at the time of becoming a member. In return, the member is guaranteed substantial reduction from established retail prices. There is no requirement that the respondent make a specified number of purchases. But the safeguard to the marketer is that the member is more likely to make purchases because of his front-end investment.

14. *Load-ups*. This proposition is a favorite of publishers of continuity series. Example: The publisher offers a set of 12 books, one to be released each month. After the purchaser has received and paid for the first three books, the publisher invites him to receive the remaining nine, all in one shipment, with the understanding that payments can continue to be made monthly. This load-up offer invariably results in more *complete sets* of books being sold.

15. *Free gift*. Most direct response advertisers have increased response through free-gift offers. For best results, you should test several gifts to determine the most appealing. There's no set criterion for the cost of a

Exhibit 4–7.   Multiple Time-Dated Discount Offer

gift as related to selling cost. The most important criteria are: (a) appropriateness of the gift, (b) its effect on repeat business, and (c) net profit per thousand circulation or distribution including cost of the gift.

16. *Secret gift*. Lester Wunderman, chairman of Wunderman Worldwide, invented the secret-gift offer, commonly known as the "Gold Box offer." Conceived to measure the impact of TV upon the pull of a newspaper or magazine insert, the viewer was told that there was a secret gold box on the insert order form and that by filling in the box the prospect would receive an extra free gift over and above the regular free-gift offer.

17. *Cash-up free gift*. Used primarily by publishers, cash-up offers stimulate cash with order. Incentives for advance cash payment usually involve one or two extra issues of a publication, or a special report not available to charge subscribers.

18. *Add-on offers*. One of the most innovative offers ever developed for increasing the unit of sale was first used, I believe, by the "Horchow Collection." The offer was directed to catalog buyers about to place a phone order, toll-free. The direction was, "When you place your phone order, ask about our Special-of-the-Month." The special was always a discount on a catalog item. One catalog marketer adapted this idea and consistently sold the "special" to 10 percent to 15 percent of phone-order inquirers.

19. *Deluxe alternative*. Related to the famous Sears tradition of *good, better, best* are offers for deluxe alternatives. A classic example would be a dictionary offered in a regular edition or in a thumb-indexed edition for $2 more. By giving the prospect the choice, the advertiser often increases total response and total dollars.

20. *Charters*. A charter offer, by its very nature, denotes something special. The offer plays on the human trait that many people want to be among the first to see, try, and use something new. The most successful charter offers include special rewards or concessions for early support.

21. *Guaranteed buy-back*. "Satisfaction guaranteed" ·is the heart of mail order selling. But the guaranteed buy-back offer goes much further. This guarantee pledges to buy back the product (if the customer so requests) at the original price for a period of time after original purchase.

22. *Multiproduct*. Multiproduct offers may take the form of a series of postcards or a collection of individual sheets, each with a separate order form. Each product presentation is structured to stand on its own.

23. *Piggybacks*. These are "add-on" offers that ride along with major offers at no additional postage cost. The unit of sale is usually much smaller than the major offer. Testing is advocated to determine whether piggybacks add to or steal from sales of the major offer.

24. *Bounce-backs*. Bounce-back offers succeed on the premise that "the best time to sell a person is right after you have sold him." Bounce-back order forms are usually included in shipments or with invoices or statements. Bounce-backs may offer (a) more of the same, (b) related items, or (c) items totally different from those originally purchased.

25. *Good-better-best*. The essence of this offer is to give the prospect a choice between something and something. Example: For their State of the Union series, the Franklin Mint gave the prospect three choices: 24k gold on sterling at $72.50 monthly, solid sterling silver at $43.75 monthly, and solid bronze at $17.50 monthly.

26. *Optional terms*. The technique here is to give the prospect the option of choosing terms at varying rates. The bigger the commitment, the better the buy.

27. *Flexible terms*. A derivative of optional terms is flexible terms. The potential subscriber to a magazine is offered a bargain weekly rate of, say, 25 cents a week for a minimum period of 16 weeks. But the subscriber may choose to enter the subscription for any number of weeks beyond the minimum at the same bargain rate.

28. *Exclusive* rights. This is an offer made by publishers of syndicated newsletters. Under the term of such an offer, the first to order—an insurance broker, for example—has exclusive rights for his trading area so long as he remains a subscriber.

29. *Upgrade offers*. Upgrade offers are particularly effective when applied to a customer base. Insurance companies are very adept at applying this technique: "Double the daily benefits on your cancer policy for a small additional premium" is typical of upgrade offers by insurance companies. A response rate of 25 percent to 30 percent isn't unusual.

   Credit card companies have done a remarkable job of upgrading members based upon their activities with existing card membership. American Express is a classic example, starting with its Green Card and moving up to its Gold and Platinum Cards.

30. *Promotional videocassettes*. Direct marketers have been among the first to see the promotional opportunities through the medium of advertising videocassettes. It is estimated that by the end of this decade 66 percent of television households will be equipped with a VCR. This gives the direct marketer the opportunity to use the demonstration power of TV without TV's time restraints.

   An offer to send a videocassette, either free or for a small charge, gives the marketer a unique opportunity for a professional, "live," indepth, presentation of a product or service. Cruise lines, exercise equipment manufacturers, art galleries, and luxury apartment complexes are among business categories benefiting from videocassette offers.

Merchandising the Offer

Each of the offers we have just reviewed has wide application. As a matter of fact, many of the offers can be used successfully in combination. However, as powerful as many of these offers are, one must keep in mind that to maximize success the *offers must be merchandised properly to target markets.*

Anatomy of an Upgrade Offer

We are indebted to Jim Schmidt, former senior vice president and creative director of McCann Direct, New York City, for a fascinating case history of an *upgrade offer* that illustrates concisely the degree of thinking and quality of execution that must be applied to make an offer truly successful.

American Express: The Platinum Card

Background and Specific Opportunity

American Express decided to develop a "super premium" charge card that would serve to:

- Reinforce the American Express franchise among the most important card member segment—heavy billers.

- Retain leadership in the top-end charge card category.

- Act as an additional revenue-generating product for American Express Travel-Related Services Inc.

Target Prospects

Based on research and judgment, the criteria for solicitation were established as:

- Existing American Express Personal and Gold Card members

- Achievement of a minimum of two years tenure as an American Express Card member

- Expenditures totaling a minimum of $10,000 on their American Express Card(s) annually

- Maintenance of an impeccable payment history with American Express

Product Strategy

To offer a new "exclusive" charge card to a select group of American Express Card members who entertain and travel extensively.

The customized array of benefits and services afforded these Platinum Card prospects meets the criteria of their lifestyles, and it also appeals to their need for recognition and prestige.

Research

A study was conducted among American Express Card members to gauge interest in the Platinum Card concept. Fifteen percent of all qualified responders indicated an interest in holding this "super premium" card. In addition, psychographic profiling was executed to define more clearly the primary target segments to aid in product positioning and communications development.

The cost of the product was set at $250 per Platinum Card.

Communications Strategy

The target market was relatively small and was clearly defined by American Express membership criteria. Information on these potential customers was available in American Express's own database.

Therefore, the exclusive utilization of direct mail—with the support of a public relations effort to hype awareness for this initial launch—was determined to be the most efficient method for extending the offer. This direct mail effort was sent to a random selection of American Express Gold Card members who met the qualification criteria.

Executional Points

- Utilize a "preapproved" and "best customer" message.

- Incorporate a "by-invitation-only" approach to reinforce the highly personalized nature of the product.

- Issue only one offer per year per qualifier to reinforce the unique positioning and limited availability of the Platinum Card.

- Extend the offer from the president of the Consumer Card Division to establish a sense of recognition from American Express.

- Use of personalization (closed-face outer envelope, letter, acceptance form, reference to the card member's date of original membership) to differentiate the offer as unique and reinforce the product positioning as an exclusive payment instrument for a small group of American Express Card members.

Format

- Outer envelope (personalized by a computer-driven word-processing system)

- Letter (personalized by a computer-driven word-processing system)

- Brochure—a simple, straightforward presentation of Platinum Card benefits (in keeping with the "invitational" concept, graphics were not used)

- Acceptance form (personalized by a computer-driven word-processing system, thus requiring only the card member's signature for enrollment)

- Business reply envelope
- Personal "invitation" from the president of the Consumer Card Division enclosed in an envelope

Note that particular attention was paid to the tone and look of each element of the package in order to reflect the positioning of the Platinum Card itself and increase appeal to this select market. All elements, except the brochure, were silver foil embossed on textured stock.

Test

Three different tests were executed for the letter copy only. All other elements remained the same.

Results

The initial test mailing generated an outstanding response, which was five times the response projected. The "sharing important news" letter (Exhibit 4–8) slightly outperformed the other two test cells.

In addition, annual card member spending substantially increased post-purchase of the Platinum Card, thus meeting the initial business objective.

Additional Offer Considerations

The American Express case history is a classic example of all the elements involved in conceiving, targeting, and executing an offer. But there are still other considerations, particularly as they relate to *free-gift offers* and *get-a-friend offers*.

Free-Gift Offers

Giving free gifts for inquiring, for trying, and for buying is as old an incentive as trading stamps. It is not at all unusual for the right gift to increase response by 25 percent and more. On the other hand, a free-gift offer can actually reduce response or have no favorable effect on the basic offer. This is particularly true where the unit of sale or amount of sale consideration overshadows the appeal of the free gift.

What's more, there is a tremendous variance in the appeal of free gifts. For example, the Airline Passengers Association tested two free gifts along with a membership offer: an airline guide and a carry-on suit bag. The suit bag did 50 percent better than the guide.

A fund-raising organization selling to schools tested three different gifts: a set of children's books, a camera, and a thirty-cup coffee maker. The coffee maker won by a wide margin; the children's books came in a poor third.

Testing for the most appealing gifts is essential because of the great differences in pull. In selecting gifts for testing purposes, follow this good

Exhibit 4–8. The "Sharing the Important News" Letter

The Platinum Card^{SM}

James F. Calvano
President
Payment Systems Division

Mr. H. L. Clark
123 Main Street
Anywhere, USA 12345

Dear Mr. Clark:

I would like to share with you some important news about a Card from American Express that is planned for introduction in August of this year.

This new Card is and will continue to be beyond the aspirations and reach of all but a few of our Card members. Appropriately called The Platinum Card, it is reserved solely for those whose long association with American Express and annual volume of travel and entertainment charges indicate that they require and deserve to command the best.

Receipt of this Invitation certifies that you are among them.

As you would expect, the new Platinum Card^{sm} will continue to secure Card member services to which you are already accustomed. Worldwide charge privileges. Assured Reservations. No pre-set spending limit. Duplicate receipts. Emergency card replacement. Emergency check cashing at hotels, motels, airline counters. Travel Accident Insurance. And Express Cash.

What distinguishes The Platinum Card and sets its possessor on a new plateau of recognition, service and convenience are the newly customized services it will provide.

First and foremost, it will command immediate recognition and respect at the finest hotels, restaurants and selected private clubs worldwide.

Secondly, The Platinum Card Personalized Travel Service will also assure customized attention to your travel needs and arrangements

AMERICAN EXPRESS TRAVEL RELATED SERVICES COMPANY, INC.   POST OFFICE BOX ONE, BOWLING GREEN STATION, NEW YORK, NEW YORK 10274

(Continued)

Exhibit 4–8 (*Continued*).   The "Sharing the Important News" Letter

24 hours a day. We'll keep a record of your travel preferences --
what hotels, airlines, and ground transportation (limousines and
car rentals) you like to use -- so many of the bothersome travel
details are easily taken care of in advance. And we'll be happy to
make en route changes to the original itinerary we booked for you
should you have a change in plans.

What's more, in keeping with The Platinum Card level of
service, you will have increased Travel Accident Insurance
protection -- to a full $500,000 -- every time you charge your
common carrier travel tickets to The Platinum Card. And should
the need arise, you will now be able to cash your personal check for
up to $10,000 at participating American Express(R) Travel Service
Offices worldwide.

You will also be able to obtain up to $10,000 in Travelers
Cheques from our network of automated dispensers and up to $1,000
in cash from automated teller machines at participating U.S.
financial institutions.

Arrangements for billing are similarly customized:

o   You may choose the billing time most convenient for you --
    the beginning, middle or end of the month.

o   And at year end, you may receive a customized summary of
    all charges itemized by category of expense: retail, hotel,
    restaurants, and the like.

Should you have questions or problems concerning Card
membership and its services, you will have a Customer Service
Representative available any hour of the day or night via an
exclusive toll-free 800 telephone number reserved for Platinum
Card members only. You will also have access to a special number
you can call collect when outside the U.S. You are assured prompt,
one-stop personal attention to all your inquiries.

Please read the enclosed brochure which more fully explains
the privileges and benefits of the new Platinum Card.

You've earned The Platinum Card and we recognize that. To
obtain one in your name, simply complete and return the enclosed
request by July 31, 1984. Assuming your American Express account

Exhibit 4–8 (*Continued*).   **The "Sharing the Important News" Letter**

has remained in good standing, The Platinum Card will be mailed to you in August, 1984 and the annual fee of $250 will then be billed to your account.   Along with The Platinum Card, we'll give you instructions for canceling your present account if you wish to do so.

I look forward to hearing from you soon, and including you in the privileged company of Platinum Card members.

Cordially,

James F. Calvano

James F. Calvano

PS.   One further thought -- lest it be a matter of concern.   Let me assure you that your original Membership Date will remain intact and will be shown on the new Platinum Card.

rule of thumb: Gifts that are suited to personal use tend to have considerably more appeal than those that aren't.

There is yet another consideration about free gifts: Is it more effective to offer a selection of free gifts of comparable value than to offer only one gift? The answer is that offering a selection of gifts of comparable value usually reduces response. This is perhaps explained by the inability of many people to make a choice.

Adopting the one-gift method (after testing for the one with the most appeal) should not be confused with offering gifts of varying value for orders of varying amounts. This is quite a different situation. A multiple-gift proposition might be a free travel clock for orders up to $25, a free transistor radio for orders from $25 to $50, and a free Polaroid camera for orders over $50.

Offering gifts of varying value for orders of varying amounts is logical to the consumer. The advertiser can afford a more expensive gift in conjunction with a larger order. His prime objective is accomplished by increasing his average order over and above what it would be if there were no extra incentive.

The multiple-gift plan works for many, but it can also boomerang. This usually happens when the top gift calls for a purchase over and above what most people can use or afford. The effect can also be negative if the gift offered for the price most people can afford is of little value or consequence. The multiple-gift plan tied to order value has good potential advantages, but careful tests must be conducted. An adaptation of the multiple-gift plan is a gift, often called a "keeper," for trying (free trial), plus a gift for keeping (paying for the purchase). Under this plan the prospect is told he or she can keep the gift offered for trying even if the product being offered for sale is returned. However, if the product being offered is retained, the prospect also keeps a second gift of greater value than the first.

Still another possibility with gift offers is giving more than one gift for either trying or buying. If the budget for the incentive is $1, for example, the advertiser can offer one gift costing $1, two gifts combined, costing $1, or even three gifts totaling $1. From a sales strategy standpoint, some advertisers spell out what one or two of the gifts are and offer an additional "mystery gift" for prompt response. Fingerhut Corporation of Minneapolis is a strong proponent of multiple gifts and "mystery gifts".

Free gifts are a tricky business, to be sure. Gift selection and gift tie-ins to offers require careful testing for best results. The $64 question always is: "How much can I afford to spend for a gift?" Aaron Adler, cofounder of Stone & Adler, maintains that most marketers make an erroneous arbitrary decision in advance, such as "I can afford to spend 5 percent of selling price." He maintains that a far more logical approach is to select the most appealing gift possible, without being restricted by an arbitrary cost figure, rather than to be guided by the net profit figures resulting from tests. For example, Table 4–1 shows a comparison of net profits for two promotions, one with a gift costing $1.00 and the other with a gift costing $2.00 on a $29.95 offer, given a 50 percent better pull with the $2.00 premium.

Table 4–1.   Comparison of Profits from Promotions with Free Gifts of Different Costs

Item	$1 Gift	$2 Gift
Net pull of promotion	1%	1.5%
Sales per thousand pieces	$299.50	$449.25
Less		
Mailing cost	120.00	120.00
Merchandise cost (45%)	134.98	202.16
Administrative cost (10%)	30.00	44.93
Premium cost	10.00	30.00
Total costs	$294.98	$397.09
Profit per thousand pieces	$ 4.52	$ 52.16

It is interesting to note that, in this example, when the $1.00 gift was offered, the mailing just about broke even. But when the cost of the gift was doubled, the profit jumped from $4.52 to $52.16 per thousand mailed.

Another advantage of offering more attractive gifts (which naturally cost more) is to offer gifts of substantial value tied to cumulative purchases. This plan can prove particularly effective when the products or services being offered produce consistent repeat orders. A typical offer under a cumulative purchase plan might be: "When your total purchases of our custom-made cigars reach $150, you receive a power saw absolutely free."

Get-a-Friend Offers

Perhaps one of the most overlooked and yet most profitable of all offers is the get-a-friend offer. If you have a list of satisfied customers, it is quite natural for them to want to let their friends in on a good thing.

The basic technique for get-a-friend offers is to offer an incentive in appreciation for a favor. Nominal gifts are often given to a customer for the simple act of providing friends' names, with more substantial gifts awarded to the customer for friends who become customers.

Based on experience, here is what you can expect in using the get-a-friend approach: You will get a larger number of friends' names if the customers are guaranteed that their names will not be used in soliciting their friends. Response from friends, however, will be consistently better if you are allowed to refer to the party who supplied their names.

To get the best of two worlds, therefore, you should allow customers to indicate whether their names may be used in soliciting their friends. For example: "You may use my name when writing my friends" or "Do not use my name when writing my friends."

Response from friends decreases in proportion to the number of names provided by a customer. One can expect the response from three names provided by one person to be greater than the total response from six names provided by another person. The reason is that it is natural to list the names in order of likelihood of interest.

Two safeguards may be applied to getting the maximum response from friends' names: (1) Limit the number of names to be provided, for example, to three or four, and (2) promote names provided in order of listing, such as all names provided first as one group, all names provided second as another group, and so forth. Those who have mastered the technique of getting friends' names from satisfied customers have found that, with very few exceptions, such lists are more responsive than most lists they can rent or buy.

Short- and Long-Term Effects of Offers

A major consideration in structuring offers is the effect a given offer will have on your objective.

- Is it your objective to get a *maximum* number of new customers for a given product or service as quickly as possible?

- Is it your objective to determine the *repeat business factor* as quickly as possible?

- Is it your objective to break even or make a profit in the shortest possible period?

So, the key question to ask when designing an offer is: "How will this offer help to accomplish my objective?"

Offers Relate to Objectives

Say you are introducing a new hobby magazine. You have the choice of making a short-term offer (three months, for instance) or a long-term offer (say twelve months). Since you want to determine acceptances as quickly as possible (your objective), you would rightly decide on a short-term offer. Under the short-term offer, after three months you will be getting a picture of renewal percentages. If you have made an initial offer of twelve-month subscriptions, you would have to wait a year to determine the publication renewal rate. In the interim, you would be missing vital information important to your magazine's success.

If the three-month trial subscriptions are renewed at a satisfactory rate, you can then safely proceed to develop offers designed to get initial long-term subscriptions. It is axiomatic in the publishing field that the longer the initial term of subscription, the higher the renewal rate is likely to be. Professional circulation men know from experience that if they are getting, say, a 35 percent conversion on a three-month trial, they can expect a conversion of 50 percent or more on twelve-month initial subscriptions. This knowledge, therefore, can be extrapolated from the short-term objective to the long-term objective.

Sol Blumenfeld, a prominent direct marketing consultant, when addressing a Direct Mail/Marketing Association convention, made some pertinent remarks about the dangers of looking only at front-end response. Blumenfeld stated, "Many people still cling to the CPA (cost per application) or CPI (cost per inquiry) response syndromes. In their eagerness to sell now, they frequently foul up their chances to sell later."

He then asks, "Can the practice of those who concern themselves only with front-end response at least partially explain book club conversions of only 50 to 60 percent? Magazine renewal rates of only 30 percent? Correspondence school attrition factors of as much as 40 percent?"

Blumenfeld gives us a case in point. A control for the Britannica Home Study Library Service (a division of Encyclopaedia Britannica) was run against several test ads developed by the agency. Control ads offered free the first volume of *Compton's Encyclopedia*. Major emphasis was placed on sending for the free volume; small emphasis was placed on the idea of ultimately purchasing the balance of the 24-volume set. Front-end response was excellent; the rate of conversion to full 24-volume sets was poor. Profitability was unacceptable.

Against the control ad, the agency tested several new ads that offered Volume 1 free but also revealed the cost of the complete set—right in the headline. Here's what happened: The cost per coupon for the new ads was 20 percent higher than for the control ad, but conversions to full sets improved a full 350 percent!

Ways to Hype Response

Once you have decided on your most appealing offer, either arbitrarily or by testing, you should ask a very specific question: How can I hype my offer to make it even more appealing? There are several ways.

Terms of Payment

Where a direct sale is involved, the terms of payment you require can hype or depress response. A given product or service can have tremendous appeal, but if payment terms are too stringent—beyond the means of a potential buyer—the offer will surely be a failure. Five general categories of payment terms may be offered: (1) cash with order, (2) C.O.D., (3) open account, (4) installment terms, and (5) revolving credit.

If a five-way split test were made among these categories, it is almost certain that response would be in inverse ratio to the listing of the five categories. Revolving credit would be the most attractive and cash with order the least attractive terms. With each loosening of terms, the appeal of the offer is hyped. In a four-way split test on a merchandise offer, here's how four terms actually ranked (the least appealing terms have a 100 percent ranking): cash with order, 100 percent; cash with order—free gift for trying,

144 percent; bill-me offer (open account), 177 percent; and, bill-me offer (open account) and free gift, 233 percent.

As the figures disclose, the most attractive terms (bill-me offer and free gift) were almost two and one-half times more appealing than the least attractive terms (cash with order).

While C.O.D. terms are generally more attractive than cash-with-order requirements, the hazard of C.O.D. terms is refusal on delivery. It is not unusual to sustain an 8 percent refusal rate when C.O.D. terms are offered. (Many C.O.D. orders are placed emotionally, and emotion cools off when the delivery man or letter carrier calls and requests payment.)

When merchandise or services are offered on open account, payment is customarily requested in 15 or 30 days. Such terms are naturally more appealing than cash with order or C.O.D. Open-account terms are customary when selling to business firms. When used in selling to the consumer, however, such terms, while appealing, can result in a high percentage of bad debts, unless carefully selected credit-checked lists are used.

The best appeals lie in installment terms and revolving credit terms. Both mechanisms require substantial financing facilities and a sophisticated credit collection system. Installment selling in the consumer field is virtually essential for the successful sale of "big ticket" merchandise—items selling for $69.95 and up.

One can have the best of two worlds—most appealing terms and no credit risk—by making credit arrangements through a sales finance firm or commercial credit card operations, such as American Express, Diners Club, Discover, or one of the bank cards—Visa or MasterCard.

Banks cards and travel-and-entertainment cards have proved a boon to mail-order operations, especially catalog operations. It is not unusual to hype the average order from a catalog by 15 percent when bank card privileges or travel-and-entertainment card privileges are offered. Not only do these privileges tend to increase the amount of the average order, they also tend to increase the total response.

When arrangements are made through commercial credit card operations, any member may charge purchases to his or her card. The credit of all members in good standing is ensured by the respective credit card operations. The advertiser is paid by the agency for the total sales charged less a discount charge, usually about 1 to 3 percent for bank cards and 3 to 7 percent for travel-and-entertainment cards.

Sweepstakes

Perhaps the most dramatic hype available to direct marketers is sweepstakes. (See Exhibit 4–9.) A sweeps overlaid on an offer adds excitement and interest. Two major direct marketers who have used sweepstakes through the 1960s and on into the 1990s are *Reader's Digest* and Publishers Clearing House. The techniques they use are the ultimate in sophistication.

Exhibit 4–9.   Sweepstakes Offer

Playboy Great Escape Sweepstakes offers a $72,235 grand prize and an array of lesser prizes on the front cover of a four-page folder and provides personalized entry coupons for the same group of prizes.

Both *Reader's Digest* (RD) and Publishers Clearing House (PCH) use TV support as an integral part of their sweepstakes promotions. Success depends upon (1) heavy market penetration of the printed materials, (2) time-controlled delivery of the printed offer to coincide with TV support, and (3) sufficient TV impact to excite interest in the printed promotion. Careful testing is required to determine the most cost-efficient amount of TV laid over the print offer. "Keep TV commercials simple," cautions Publishers Clearing House. Current PCH commercials prove they practice what they preach: They feature the sweepstakes, using past winners to carry the message, leaving the magazine savings story to the mailing package.

Astute direct marketers like RD and PCH know incentives for prompt response tend to increase total response. Each has built incentives for prompt response into its sweepstakes contests. RD, for example, has offered the following bonus award incentive: "$1,000 a day for every day your entry beats the deadline of January 31." This means that, if the grand prize is $50,000 and your entry is postmarked before January 21, you, as the grand prize winner, will win an extra $10,000. Another technique is reader involvement. "Seven Chances to Be a Winner," PCH announced in promoting a $400,000 sweepstakes. The entrant was given seven prize numbers.

Umbrella Sweepstakes

A big sweepstakes requires a bushel of money for prizes and administration. Direct marketers, bottom-line people that they are, have found ways to overlay a major sweeps on more than one proposition. *Reader's Digest*, for example, can overlay the same sweeps on a magazine subscription offer, a book club offer, and a tape offer—each falling under the umbrella of one prize budget.

D.L. Blair, the largest sweepstakes judging agency in the country, points out that there are many questions to be answered for anyone contemplating a sweepstakes. Here are questions D.L. Blair has answered for us.

Q. Currently, what are the most popular prize structures?

A. Cash, automobiles, travel, and home entertainment appliances—in that order—continue to be the most appealing and popular prize structures. According to our most recent research, apparel (fur coats, designer dresses) has virtually no appeal. As for other merchandise, we generally prefer to eschew the use of merchandise prizes except when we have conclusive research indicating greater consumer preference for the prize item than for its equivalent cash value.

Q. When a sweeps is tested against a nonsweeps, what range of increase might be expected for a magazine subscription offer or catalog offer?

A. Using a sweepstakes overlay, we have never seen less than a 15 percent increase in orders for either a catalog or a magazine subscription. The

greatest increase we have ever seen is 350 percent. Generally, the increment falls between 30 and 100 percent.

Q. Can a low-budget sweeps be successful?

A. Though it is generally true that the success levels of any sweepstakes are importantly impacted by the prize budget, we have seen low-budget programs work extremely well when directed at special-interest groups. Thus, while a $3,500-value grand prize would provide little or no motivation to most broad audience segments, a $3,500 home flight simulator would be highly appealing to an audience comprised solely of private pilots; a $3,500 hunting carbine would be highly appealing to NRA members; a $3,500 one-of-a-kind Wedgwood bud vase would be extremely appealing to Wedgwood collectors.

Q. From a legal standpoint, must all prizes be awarded in a sweepstakes offer?

A. Speaking solely from the narrow area of what is strictly legal, it is only necessary to award prizes to those who have submitted entry numbers that the judges have preselected as winning numbers. There are, however, very compelling business and ethical reasons that strongly suggest that any direct marketer would be ill-advised to consider awarding fewer than the full number of prizes that it has advertised.

Q. Is the average order from a catalog, for example, likely to be smaller with a sweeps entry?

A. It depends on whether the order is from a former buyer or a new customer. The average order from former buyers tends to be larger. We're seen a sweepstakes increase the value of each catalog order by more than 40 percent. New-customer orders, on the other hand, tend to be lower than average, probably because these are fringe buyers coming in as a result of the sweepstakes overlay.

Q. Having acquired a new customer with a sweepstakes contest, would you say that repeat business is likely to depend on additional sweepstakes contests?

A. Yes, to some degree it is true that continuing sweepstakes promotions might be necessary to maintain a normal level of repeat business. (See Exhibit 4–10.) I would say this is true to the same extent that a customer first acquired with incentives such as price-off coupons, free gifts, discount offers, and the like would be conditioned to such offers in the future.

Q. What is the profile of sweepstakes entrants these days?

A. It's becoming broader with more geographic, economic, and educational homogeneity. This "flattening" process extends to the sex of respondents: men account for almost 47 percent of sweepstakes entrants.

Exhibit 4–10. Devices to Hype Response

Read this only if you've decided to say "no".
D.R.

Dear Friend,

Before you decide not to subscribe to PLAYBOY, please take one more minute to reconsider. Why? Because there are at least three good reasons to say "YES" instead.

(1.) PLAYBOY'S EDITORIAL. PLAYBOY is recognized as the world's best forum for male entertainment.

(2.) PLAYBOY'S GREAT HALF-PRICE OFFER. You can have 12 issues of PLAYBOY delivered to your door for just $15.50. That's half the $31.00 newsstand rate -- you save $15.50.

(3.) PLAYBOY'S NO-RISK GUARANTEE. If at any time you aren't delighted with PLAYBOY, you can cancel your subscription. We'll send you a full refund for all remaining issues -- no questions asked.

If you think about all the benefits, you really have nothing to lose by saying "YES." And you have PLAYBOY to gain. So insert your 6 YES Sweepstakes Certificates into the Official Entry Envelope and return them to us today.

Thank you. And good luck in The $165,000.00 Great Escape Sweepstakes.

Doug Robinson

Doug Robinson

DR/bl

"EARLY BIRD" BONUS
$5,000.00

To qualify for the "Early Bird" Bonus Prize Drawing, detach your 6 YES or 6 NO Certificates—whichever you choose—and return them in the preaddressed reply envelope before March 9th.

TO ENTER, ACT BEFORE MARCH 9, 1982

If you're the lucky winner, you will receive a check for $5,000.00 . . . and you'll still be eligible to win any one of the other prizes to be awarded in . . .

THE PLAYBOY $165,000.00 GREAT ESCAPE SWEEPSTAKES

4025

Included in the Playboy Great Escape Sweepstakes mailing package are two devices: a "Pulisher's Letter" and an "Early Bird" bonus offer.

Q. Is the appeal of sweepstakes to direct marketing customers increasing, declining, or holding flat?

A. Almost without exception, our direct mail marketing clients are reporting greater new-customer and current-buyer penetration from their sweepstakes programs. Since we are seeing comparable response increases in programs run by our package-goods clients, it would appear that there is significantly more customer interest in sweepstakes than has ever been the case before.

Telephone

Toll-free telephone response (800 numbers) offers the opportunity to hype the response from just about any offer, particularly offers involving free information or the sale of merchandise. (See Chapter Fourteen, "Telemarketing.")

Publisher's Letter

Another innovative device that has been developed for hyping responses during the past decade is an extra mailing enclosure known as the "publisher's letter." It gets its name from its first usage—a short letter from a magazine publisher enclosed in the basic mailing package.

The publisher's letter usually carries a headline: "If you have decided not to respond, read this letter." The letter copy typically reinforces the offer

made in the basic mailing packages, assures the reader it is valid, and guarantees the terms. This extra enclosure often increases response by 10 percent and more. While the publisher's letter was originated for subscription letters, this device was soon adopted by other direct marketers selling goods and services. Results have been equally productive.

The Guarantee

No matter what the terms or basic offer may be, a strong guarantee is essential when selling products or services direct. For more than 95 years, Sears, Roebuck and Company has guaranteed satisfaction for every article offered (Exhibit 4–11). Over the years, no one else has ever succeeded in mail-order operations without duplicating the Sears guarantee or offering a similar assurance.

Exhibit 4–11.   **Sears Guarantee**

SEARS GUARANTEE

Your satisfaction is guaranteed or your money back.

We guarantee that every article in this catalog is accurately described and illustrated.

If, for any reason whatever, you are not satisfied with any article purchased from us, we want you to return it to us at our expense.

We will exchange it for exactly what you want, or will return your money, including any transportation charges you have paid.

SEARS, ROEBUCK AND CO.

The importance of the guarantee is perhaps best understood by recognizing a negative fact of life. It is this. Over 95 years after Sears first established its ironclad guarantee, it is still a fact of human nature that one is hesitant to send for merchandise unless one knows that the product may be returned for full credit if it does not meet expectations. Guaranteed satisfaction should be a part of any offer soliciting a direct sale.

Many marketers have developed unique guarantees that go beyond the trial period. Madison House, for instance, advertised a new fishing lure in a March issue of *Family Weekly*. The company knew, of course, that in northern areas, lakes were frozen over and that there would be no opportunity to test and use this lure before spring. Madison House overcame the problem beautifully by urging the fishing buff to send for the lure *now*, with

the proviso that the lure could be returned any time within six months for a full cash refund. This guarantee had two advantages: It assured the fishing buff that, even though he was ordering the lure out of season, he could return it after he tried it in season; and it enabled Madison House to advertise and get business out of season.

One of the most successful manuals ever produced at National Research Bureau was the 428-page *Retail Advertising Sales Promotion Manual*. It was offered on a 10-day free-trial basis with the guarantee: "If this manual isn't all we say it is, you may return it any time within 12 months for full refund." National Research Bureau sold over 20,000 manuals at $19.95. It is significant that, after several years, no one has ever asked for a refund!

Many marketers reinforce their own guarantees with a third-party guarantee. "Approved by Underwriters Laboratory" can make the difference where electrical appliances are concerned. The *Good Housekeeping* Seal of Approval has long been accepted as a guarantee of validity of claim.

Publishers Clearing House has made this statement: "In addition to the publisher's own warranties, Publishers Clearing House makes you this unconditioned guarantee: You may have a full cash refund at any time, or for any reason, on the unused part of any subscription ordered through the clearing house. This guarantee has no time limit. It is your assurance that you can order from Publishers Clearing House with complete confidence."

In direct sales, the right proposition and the right terms of payment are only two-thirds of the impetus. A clear, strong guarantee completes the trio.

Danger of Overkill

The power of an offer cannot be overestimated. But there's such a thing as too much of a good thing—offers that sound too good to be true or that produce a great front-end response but make for poor pay-ups or few repeat customers. Here are two thought-provoking examples:

A comprehensive test was structured for a fund-raising organization to determine whether response would best be maximized by (1) offering a free gift as an incentive for an order, (2) offering a combination of free gift plus a cash bonus for completing a sale, or (3) offering a cash bonus only. The combination of free gift plus cash bonus pulled the lowest response by far; · the free-gift proposition far outpulled the cash-bonus proposition.

The second example: A $200 piece of electronic equipment was offered for 15-day free trial. This was the basic proposition. But half the people on the list also were invited to enter a sweepstakes contest. Those on the portion of the list not invited to enter a sweepstakes responded 25 percent better than those on the portion invited to enter.

In both these examples, the more generous offer proved to be "too much." One must be most careful not to make the offer so overwhelming that it overshadows the product or service being offered. Another important

consideration in structuring offers is the axiom, "As you make your bed, so shall you lie in it." Here's what we mean. If you obtain thousands of new customers by offering free gifts as incentives, don't expect a maximum degree of repeat business unless you continue to offer free gifts. Similarly, if you build a big list of installment credit buyers, don't expect these buyers to respond well to cash-basis offers, and vice versa.

Certain offers attract certain types of customers. Make sure these are the types you really want. Here is an illustration of our axiom. A firm selling to businesses built a large customer list based on a series of soft-sell offers. The firm then went into another product line, offering products to its customers and to cold-prospect lists. Three offers were tested: (1) a free gift for ordering, (2) a discount for ordering, and (3) no incentive. The results of the three offers against cold lists and against the customer list are provided in Table 4–2.

Table 4–2.   Results of Testing Three Types of Offers with Both Cold-Prospect and Customer Lists

	Results (in Percent)	
	Cold-Prospect Lists	Customer Lists
Free gift	2.2	3.2
Discount	5.2	3.1
No incentive	2.5	3.9

Note the dramatic differences in response between cold-prospect lists and the customer list. The discount offer was more than twice as attractive to cold-prospect lists. But, to the customer list, not nurtured in this manner, the discount offer was the least attractive. Note also that the offer with no extra incentive was the most attractive to the customer list.

Effect on Bad Debts

It is rarely mentioned that a misleading offer can have a devastating effect on bad debts. A misleading offer causes the consumer, without consciously thinking about it, to feel that he has been rooked and often leads him to conclude, "They can whistle for their money." The justice, if it may be called that, is that those who would mislead usually end up paying dearly for their misdeeds.

The fact that it is poor business to make misleading offers is underscored by the following true story. For many years two large publishers exchanged mailing lists—each making noncompeting offers to the list of the other. The two publishers exchanged bad-debt lists. Time after time, the publisher

known for its misleading offers would send the other publisher a list of customers with whom it had bad-debt experience. When the names were compared, it was found that, in over 80 percent of the cases where both publishers had the same customers, the publisher who practiced forth-rightness had no bad-debt experience with the identical customers. Honesty does pay.

Making It Easy to Order

The structure of an offer should not be taken lightly. The impact an offer can have on immediate and long-term results can be tremendous. It is sad but true that some of the most brilliant offers fail not because the offers aren't appealing, but because they are poorly presented verbally, graphically, or both. The greatest sins of execution are to be found in coupon space ads.

Tony Antin, who directed creative services for *Reader's Digest*, laid down this mandate for coupon order forms: "A coupon (order form) should be—*must be*—an artistic cliché. Rectangular. Surrounded by dash lines. Not even dotted lines. Because one connects dots. One cuts along dashes. Moreover, the coupon should be where it belongs, at the lower outside. The coupon should stand out from the rest of the ad."

So, construction of offers boils down to this: Your primary job is to overcome human inertia. Your offers should relate to objectives. Consider the short- and long-term effects. And, by all means, make it easy to order!

Self-Quiz

1. An ad, a TV or radio commercial, or a direct mail piece can't be regarded as direct marketing unless there is an offer. ☐ True   ☐ False

2. List the ten basic factors to consider when creating an offer.

   a. _____   f. _____

   b. _____   g. _____

   c. _____   h. _____

   d. _____   i. _____

   e. _____   j. _____

3. Of the ten factors above, which one should *always* be applied to a direct sale offer?

   _____

4. What is a "till forbid" offer?

_____

_____

_____

5. What is the difference between a *negative option* and a *positive option*?

_____

_____

_____

6. What is the basic rule to follow in testing a variety of free gifts to determine which is most appealing?

_____

_____

_____

7. Here are five terms of payment: (1) cash with order, (2) C.O.D., (3) open account, (4) installment terms, and (5) revolving credit. Which is likely to have the most appeal?

_____

8. Define *umbrella sweepstakes*.

_____

_____

_____

9. Currently, what are the most popular prize structures for sweepstakes?

_____

_____

_____

10. Define *publisher's letter*.

_____

_____

_____

11. Why is the guarantee in direct sale offers so essential?

_____

_____

_____

12. What is a third-party guarantee?

_____

_____

_____

13. Under what conditions can an offer be too attractive?

_____

_____

_____

14. Check the requirements for an effective coupon (order form):
Coupons should be ☐ rectangular   ☐ oval and should be surrounded
by ☐ dotted lines   ☐ dash lines.

Pilot Project

You have been given an important assignment: to launch a new publication called *Prime Time* for the over-50 market.

This is to be a monthly publication carrying a cover price of $2.50, with a mail subscription rate of $24 a year. The publisher is anxious to: (1) reach a subscription base of 100,000 subscribers before the first issue appears and (2) determine the renewal rate as quickly as possible. There will be no newstand distribution.

Keeping the publisher's objectives in mind, develop three different offers that might be tested.

CHAPTER FIVE

Selecting and Selling Merchandise and Services

The urge to enter the mail-order businesss is an urge that just won't go away for thousands of entrepreneurs. Yet most who enter the arena fail—miserably. The reasons for failure are multitudinous: A false belief one can get rich quick. Lack of intuitive feelings about mail-order products. No sense of the required ratio of cost to selling price. Failure to test properly. A dearth of knowledge about appropriate media. Poor merchandise sources. Insufficient capital. And on and on and on.

How then does one find hot mail-order items? Where do you go? What do you look for? What should you avoid? How do you start?

There is no greater authority to answer these questions than Len Carlson of Los Angeles, who pioneered and marketed about 10,000 mail-order items over the past 30 years. His sage advice could pay the cost of this book hundreds of times over.

The first tip from Len Carlson is that you should look for items whose benefits you can demonstrate with photos, graphics, and copy that dramatize the end use.

And where do you find such items? They are rarely found in general merchandise stores. More often they are found in boutiques—off-beat stores that offer the unusual—in this country and particularly in boutiques abroad.

Then there are the trade shows, the Housewares Show in Chicago, the hardware and stationery shows, the premium shows. And the foreign trade shows, too. Mr. Carlson calls his escapades "treasure hunts."

He doesn't just look. He asks questions: "What items are you selling to mail-order companies now?" "Can you add this feature?" "What are the requirements for getting an exclusive on this item?" "What kind of a backup inventory can you guarantee?"

Most manufacturer's representatives are startled when he asks, "What do you have in your big briefcase that doesn't sell well?" Often he finds items that bombed out on retail shelves that he can bring to life in catalogs and promote with demonstrable benefits.

Along the same line, he recommends resurrection of oldies but goodies, taking them out of mothballs for new generation of buyers. An analogy he gives is a technique Walt Disney employed to bring back his successful kid movies every seven years.

The tips for finding mail-order items continue. "You have to become a great reader, subscribing to jillions of consumer and trade magazines," says Mr. Carlson. "Not only United States magazines, but foreign magazines as well." Many of the magazines are available in libraries. Then there is what he calls "the rule of two." Here's how that works. You religiously accumulate mail-order catalogs. When you see a new item, you record it as a test. If you see the same item in a subsequent catalog, you assume the test worked and your interest should be piqued. If you don't see the item a second time, you can assume the item bombed.

One of the top mail-order secrets Mr. Carlson learned years ago is the appeal of personalization. Few stores personalize. So a mail-order operation can take a standard stock item, personalize it, and change the appeal from "ho-hum" to "exciting." Such mundane items as dog and cat dishes, floor mats, and paper napkins are good examples.

But there is one rule he uses for selecting hot mail-order items that is my favorite: Show all new items to your wife. If she says "no"—go with them! Gloria Carlson, based upon years of experiences, agrees with her husband.

The checklist that follows summarizes the sources for discovering viable mail-order items.

Where to Discover Mail-Order Items

1. Study competitive catalogs and solo offers.

2. Read consumer magazines.

3. Subscribe to pertinent trade journals.

4. Cover United States trade shows.

5. Browse retail stores constantly.

6. Write to manufacturers listed in directories.

7. Talk to manufacturers' representatives.

8. Periodically visit book stores and libraries.

9. Attend foreign trade fairs; shop stores that carry foreign goods.

10. Read foreign magazines and catalogs.

11. Contact foreign commercial attachés.

12. Revive your old successes.

13. Set up and refer to your "idea file" frequently.

14. Add on features to existing items.

15. Personalize if pertinent to product.

- Use your instincts!

- Keep your eyes open!

- Hustle! Work!

- Innovate!

- Think MERCHANDISE—all the time!

- *The search never ends!*

One of the most invaluable checklists developed by Mr. Carlson is the following list of 34 factors to consider when selecting mail-order items.

Thirty-Four Factors to Consider When Selecting Mail-Order Items

1. Is there a perceived need for the product?

2. Is it practical?

3. Is it unique?

4. Is the price right for my customer or prospect?

5. Is it good value?

6. Is the markup sufficient to assure profit?

7. Is the market large enough? Does it have broad appeal?

8. Are there specific smaller segments of my list that have a strong desire for the product?

9. Is it new? Or will my customers perceive it to be new?

10. Will it photograph/illustrate interestingly?

11. Are there sufficient unusual selling features to make the copy exciting?

12. Is it economical to ship? Too fragile? Odd-shaped? Too heavy? Too big?

13. Can it be personalized?

14. Are there any legal problems to overcome?

15. Is it safe to use?

16. Is the supplier reputable?

17. Will backup merchandise be available for fast shipment on reorders?

18. Might returns be too huge?

19. Will refurbishing of returned merchandise be practical?

20. Is it, or can it be, packaged attractively?

21. Are usage instructions clear?

22. How does it compare to competitive products?

23. Will it have exclusivity?

24. Will it lend itself to repeat business?

25. Is it consumable (for repeat orders)?

26. Is it faddy? Too short-lived?

27. Is it too seasonal for mail-order selling?

28. Can an add-on to the product make it more distinctive and salable?

29. Will the number of stock-keeping units (sizes and colors) create inventory problems?

30. Does it lend itself to multiple pricing?

31. Is it too readily available in stores?

32. Is it like an old, hot item that guarantees its success?

33. Is it doomed because similar items have failed before?

34. Does my mother/wife/brother/husband like it? (If so, it probably should be discarded!)

Let's take No. 6, for example: Is the markup sufficient to assure profit? On this Mr. Carlson says, "The books say you need four or five times cost in order to sell profitably. I don't think that's necessarily true. Certainly you need to more than double the cost of an item to come out."

On No, 24: Will it lend itself to repeat business? Here is what he says: "You should search for items that lend themselves to repeat business. Otherwise you've got to keep coming up with new items for repeat business. Consumable items are the idea."

Knowing how to evaluate products is a key to mail-order success. But not the only key. Finding a niche for yourself in the marketplace is at the top of the list.

"Your first question," say Mr. Carlson, "should be: 'What's missing from the market?'" When he launched Sunset House, he perceived a void in the marketplace that could be filled by bringing hundreds of gadgets together in one catalog. A multi-million-dollar business grew from the recognition of this void.

Years later another entrepreneur perceived there was no one place in the market where one could buy hard-to-find tools. Thus the highly successful Brookstone Catalog operation was born.

Finding a void and the right items to fill that void are key. But even these steps are short of achieving success. The entrepreneur, in particular, must be a total businessperson. The final checklist from Len Carlson is the coup de grâce. It's the "moment of truth" for would-be mail-order millionaires. Careful study of this comprehensive checklist could lead many to conclude "mail-order is not for me." And that could be good!

Checklist for Mail-Order Operation
Merchandise Selection and Product Development

1. Set marketing objective.

2. Select products.

3. Perform market research.

4. Evaluate potentials.

Media Selection

1. Make budget decisions.

2. Decide on direct mail circulation.

3. Select appropriate house list segments.

4. Arrange rental/compilation of outside lists (list brokers).

5. Decide timing of campaign.

6. Buy space/time (ad agencies, reps, media).

7. Arrange for inserts/co-ops/package inserts/other media.

8. Consider phone selling.

Creative Decisions

1. Develop the offers and formats.

2. Get copy prepared.

3. Arrange for photography/illustrations.

4. Determine typography, design, and layout.

5. Schedule production operations.

6. Set up printing and mailing program.

7. Buy envelopes.

8. Work with creative consultants.

Testing Projects

1. Offers

2. Prices

3. Lists

4. Geographic areas

5. Formats

Buying Procedures

1. Negotiate with vendors and purchase products.

2. Follow up vendors for delivery.

3. Re-buy.

4. Maintain inventory control.

5. Control inspection of incoming merchandise.

6. Dispose of inventory overstock.

Management Functions

1. Estimate costs, potentials, and profitability.

2. Analyze response and sales.

3. Check legal aspects of merchandising.

4. Double-check record-keeping and data-capture activity.

5. Decide if credit/credit cards are to be offered.

6. Decide if telephone orders should be accepted.

7. Determine if foreign sales are possible.

8. Sell house products, wholesale, to others.

9. Maintain liaison with fulfillment, accounting, and customer service departments.

An Entrepreneurial Success Story

With caution hopefully well established, it's time to give living proof that entrepreneurs can succeed in spite of the hazards involved. Let me tell you about a beautiful, intelligent, and charming young lady by the name of Annie Hurlbut. She is a classic example of getting into mail order by serendipity. A neophyte in every sense, she has performed as if she wrote Len Carlson's checklists!

Annie Hurlbut is an anthropologist who, when she was at Yale, spent her sophomore summer working at an archeological dig in Peru. There she encountered the alpaca, a cameloid animal related to the vicuna and the llama. Although the alpaca has an unpleasant disposition (it spits at people, she says), it is the mainstay of the economy of the Andes, serving as food and, along with the llama, as beast of burden. (The alpaca can carry up to a 50-pound load. "Put 51 pounds on it and it balks," Ms. Hurlbut says.) But the alpaca is raised mainly for its extraordinary wool, which is light-weight, warm, and grows naturally in a variety of colors, from white to beige, brown, and gray.

Ms. Hurlbut returned to Peru again as a graduate student in anthropology, but this time for her thesis research on women who sell in primitive markets. Among their wares were handloomed alpaca garments, which were warm and practical but not exactly stylish.

So, Annie Hurlbut turned designer. She worked with the Peruvians to design sweaters with more flair so they would be more acceptable to North American women. With her first stock, she returned to the Hurlbut farm in Tonganoxie, Kansas, and started a mail-order catalog business, called "The Peruvian Connection," with her mother as a partner. They produced a catalog and did some ads. And with this, Annie Hurlbut was in the mail-order business.

Some of Annie's early ads were primitive. And the first "catalog" was really no more than an amateurish flyer. But the first ads and catalogs sold enough merchandise to pay the bills with some left over to reinvest. Clearly, alpaca styled by Peruvians overcame any lack of sophistication in mail-order techniques. Annie Hurlbut's sense of style, plus alpaca's uniqueness, worked. Annie learned quickly that the secret to building a mail-order business was in developing a customer file as quickly as possible, and then to offer those customers other items.

The Peruvian Connection's first offering outside of apparel was pure alpaca blankets. (See Exhibit 5–1.)

There are a couple of other noteworthy tried-and-true mail-order techniques that Annie Hurlbut used in conjunction with this mailing. Enclosing a swatch of the blanket was a brilliant stroke. (I couldn't resist running my fingers over the swatch—it is really soft!) Also, Annie encouraged ordering by phone and charging to a credit card.

Would you like to guess what the pull was from the customer list? Five percent? No. Ten percent? No. Twenty-five percent? No. It pulled 43 percent —a pull the professionals would give up their birthright to get.

Exhibit 5–1.   **The Peruvian Connection**

Dear Special Customer:

   In early December, on a trip to Peru for Christmas orders,
I stumbled across some extraordinary 100% alpaca blankets, a
swatch of which I'm enclosing in this envelope. I was aston-
ished by the quality of the fibre used and impressed with the
workmanship, even to the blanket-stitched edges. When I heard
the prices (under half of what we pay for the $250 Mon Repos
blankets we import), I called the States to consult with my
partner, and bought up every one. A few hours later The Peruvian Connection was launched into the market of luxury blankets.
As far as I know, we are the first and only U.S. importers
of 100% alpaca blankets, although they have been exported to
Europe for some time.

   Our plan is to sell these blankets at direct-importer
WHOLESALE prices in order to compete with the $75 to $95 prices
of the 50% alpaca/50% sheep's wool blankets currently available
in stores and through catalogues such as Gumps, Brookstone,
Shopping International and others. These half alpaca blankets
are beautiful, warm and sturdy. We know, we've been importing
them for years. But for weightless warmth and silky softness,
no natural fibre-- not mohair, not angora, not even cashmere--
competes with pure alpaca. The secret lies in the high lanolin
content of this wool from the Andes.

   The reason you rarely see 100% alpaca blankets in this country
is simple: Alpacas, which live almost exclusively in the Andes,
produce a limited amount of wool (they are sheared only once
every two years during the rainy season). The global demand for
scarce alpaca fibre, however, is insatiable. In the four years

distributed in the united states by
canaan farm tonganoxie kansas 66086 (913) 845-2750

*Two-page letter gets attention at the outset, and quickly establishes value through
the technique of favorable comparison.*

Exhibit 5–1 (*Continued*).   **The Peruvian Connection**

of our import business, the Peruvian market price of alpaca has more than quadrupled.

Since Inca times, when by law only nobility could wear clothing of fine alpaca, alpaca has been valued over the hair of its coarser cousin, the llama. Now even lesser quality llama sells for astounding prices. In the December, '79 issue of Smithsonian, the domestic price of llama was quoted at $32 a pound, compared to the 75¢ a pound price quoted for sheep's wool. The article didn't mention alpaca, probably because even in Andean marketplaces, the latter sells for considerably more than the highest grade of llama. Predictions are that the price of this once royal fibre will continue to climb. Alpaca is, in effect, Peru's golden fleece.

The small number of blankets I brought back in December were bought just ahead of a substantial mid-December price rise. As a test market, between now and January 31st, we are offering 64 of these blankets at prices well below our own Wholesale prices. Because our supply at this price is limited, we are offering this special discount to only a fraction of our mailing list, most of whom are old customers. You are one of 100 people in on this sneak preview.

If you love alpaca, don't wait for the price rise to buy one of these blankets. As are all of our exotic exclusives from Peru, our new 100% alpaca blankets are fully guaranteed.

We at the Peruvian Connection send you our warmest, softest wishes for a Happy New Year.

WHOLESALE PRICES FOR 100% ALPACA BLANKETS:

SPECIAL PRICE THROUGH JAN 31st

Blanket (86"x65") .... $140.00 $125.
(pictured, in natural alpaca stripes)

Throw Blanket (75"x57") $103.50 $92.50
(pictured, in natural alpaca stripes)

Lap robe (or child's blanket) (43"x35")...... $42.00 $37.50
(not pictured, in solid color soft brown)

(Continued)

Exhibit 5–1 (*Continued*).   The Peruvian Connection

Four-color circular was included with two-page letter

Expanding Existing Mail-Order Operations

It has been said, with considerable validity: "No mail-order item or mail-order line is forever." It is certainly a truism that every mail-order item—not unlike items sold through traditional channels—is subject to product life cycles. (See Exhibit 5–2.) Hence there is the ever-present need to come up with new products and services. How does one do that?

Exhibit 5–2.   Concept of the Product Life Cycle

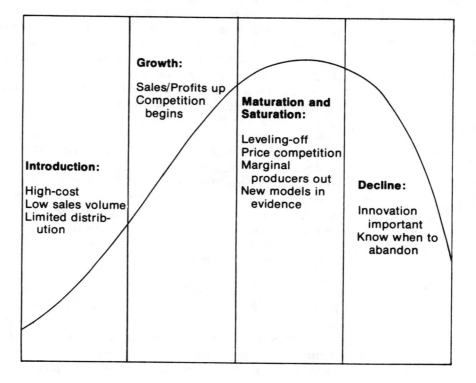

Growth:

Sales/Profits up
Competition
   begins

**Maturation and
Saturation:**

Leveling-off
Price competition
Marginal
   producers out
New models in
   evidence

Introduction:

High-cost
Low sales volume
Limited distrib-
   ution

Decline:

Innovation
   important
Know when to
   abandon

When someone inquires of Aaron Adler, cofounder of Stone & Adler, how to determine what new product or service to offer, he asks, "What business are you in?" Nine times out of ten, the person will say, "Oh, I'm in the catalog business," or, "I sell collectibles," or, "I sell books," or something similar. That type of answer is true, of course, so far as it goes. But it probably doesn't go far enough if you really want to explore all the possibilities of your operation. Executives of companies who think of themselves as being in the "catalog business" or in the "record business" limit their options severely. Their thinking is confined so narrowly that it becomes difficult to come up with new offers for customers. On the other hand, if they give

serious thought to the total character of their business, new avenues of possibility are opened, perhaps leading to the development and promotion of a wider range of products and services.

To illustrate: Is a mail-order insurance company merely in the business of selling insurance? Not at all. It is really in the business of helping to provide financial security to its policyholders and prospects. From that perspective, management of an insurance company can think of offering not only other kinds of insurance policies but also financial planning services, loans, and the sale of mutual funds, assuming, of course, there is no conflict with insurance or investment laws and regulations.

More and more successful mail-order companies have adopted this kind of thinking. A classic example is the Franklin Mint, whose management recognized that the company was not simply in the business of selling limited-edition medallions. The Franklin Mint was actually in the business of producing fine art objects on a limited-edition basis for those who enjoy the pleasure and status provided by owning handsome objects not available to the majority of the general public. In addition, the possibility existed that the value of these objects would increase as time went on. As a result, the company has successfully offered limited-edition art prints, books, glassware, porcelain, and a myriad of other items. (See Exhibit 5–3.)

Another example is Baldwin Cooke Company. This firm for many years had offered an executive planner (desk diary) that businesspeople found made an excellent Christmas gift for their clients and friends. Then came the realization that the company was not simply in the business of selling desk diaries, but rather was in the business of selling executive gifts. This led to the development of a broad line of successful new products. The company's gift catalog today runs to 32 pages with a circulation of more than 1 million.

An outstanding example of this broad-based thinking is the Meredith Publishing Company, publishers of *Better Homes and Gardens*, among other publications. Recognizing that the company was not simply in the magazine-publishing business, but rather in the business of disseminating useful, helpful information to large segments of middle America, management moved into such product areas as geographic atlases, world globes, gardening books, cookbooks, and a whole range of similar materials.

Therefore, if you are looking for new products or services to offer your customers or to reach new prospects, think about what kind of business you are really in. When you make that determination, you'll find that many new areas will open up for you.

For the moment, let's pursue the idea that you are in direct marketing, that you have a list of customers built by offering products or services that they have found eminently satisfactory, and that you would like to expand your sales to those customers with new offerings. Let's also assume that you have answered the question of what business you are really in and have concluded that there are broader areas of endeavor available than you had previously realized. What then?

Exhibit 5–3. **Expanding the Product Line**

Ad from Franklin Porcelain typifies new-product expansion program.

The renowned illustrator of "Little Women" creates her first porcelain sculptures . . .

Amy by Tasha Tudor

Inaugurating Tasha Tudor's first collection of porcelain sculptures. Individually crafted, hand-painted and issued in limited edition. Art of enchanting beauty, at the very attractive price of $75.

In today's world of fine book illustrators, there is one name that stands out among the rest—Tasha Tudor. An artist who, for almost fifty years, has been capturing the hearts of millions with art that is happy, innocent and filled with old-fashioned charm. With delicate use of colors and a wealth of detail, her illustrations create a magical world of make-believe with characters as loveable as they are unforgettable.

Now, to celebrate the 150th anniversary of author Louisa May Alcott's birth, Tasha Tudor has created her very first works in porcelain. A collection of limited edition "Little Women" sculptures that are sure to be of exceptional interest to collectors.

"Amy", portraying Louisa May Alcott's charming, blue-eyed beauty, inaugurates the collection. Crafted in fine, hand-painted porcelain, it is a thoroughly delightful work of art. And it will be issued at the very modest price of just $75—which may itself be paid in convenient monthly installments.

The figure that Tasha Tudor has designed is so vivid, so alive, it's as if "Amy" had invited you into the pages of "Little Women" to come pay a special visit. There she sits with dreamy eyes fixed on the sketchpad in her lap. From her cascading golden curls, to the ruffled pinafore she wears as an artist's smock—she's the very vision of loveliness. A captivating and compelling sculpture as charming and full of grace as Louisa May Alcott's young artist.

To ensure that every small detail of Tasha Tudor's art—every nuance of expression—is faithfully captured, each sculpture will be individually crafted by master porcelain artisans in Japan. Each sculpture will be hand-cast . . . hand-assembled . . . and hand-painted with uncompromising care.

In the tradition of classic works in fine porcelain, "Amy" will be issued in a single limited edition, reserved exclusively for those who order from the collection by November 29, 1982—the 150th anniversary of Louisa May Alcott's birth. When all valid orders from these individuals have been filled, the edition will be closed.

"Amy" will bring her own personality and charm to your home and any room in which you choose to display her. And in time to come, this engaging work of art is likely to become a treasured family heirloom, lovingly passed on from mother to daughter.

To acquire your own hand-painted fine porcelain sculpture of "Amy" by Tasha Tudor, it is important to act promptly. Please be sure to mail the accompanying advance reservation application by May 31, 1982.

Figure shown actual size.

- - - - - - - ADVANCE RESERVATION APPLICATION - - - - - - -

Amy by Tasha Tudor

Valid only if postmarked by May 31, 1982 · Limit: One sculpture per person.

Franklin Porcelain
Franklin Center, Pennsylvania 19091

Please accept my reservation for "Amy" by Tasha Tudor, to be handcrafted for me in fine, hand-painted porcelain.

I understand that I need send no money now. I will be billed in four equal monthly installments of $18.75* plus 75¢ for shipping and handling, with the first payment due in advance of shipment.

*Plus my state sales tax

Signature _____

Mr.
Mrs.
Miss._____

Address _____

City _____

State, Zip _____

3165

What Are Your Capabilities?

First, review your capabilities and those of your organization and, again, try to think in the broadest possible terms.

For example, the G.R.I. Corporation, which originally launched the World of Beauty Club, decided to utilize the ability it had developed in working with cosmetic manufacturers to set up a similar arrangement of sampling with a group of food manufacturers. In this case the market consisted of large numbers of people who wanted to sample new foods and save money on a regular basis.

Other companies that have looked at their own expertise and facilities to determine what new products and services they could develop range all the

way from the Donnelley Company, which utilized its co-op mailings to include the sale of its own products, to Time-Life, which used its editorial and photographic expertise to produce probably the most successful series of continuity books in the publishing industry.

So along with determining the business you're in, probably the second most important factor to investigate is your company's capabilities. As you can see, determining the business you're in and examining your capabilities go hand in hand in helping you pinpoint new merchandise or service opportunities. There are significant differences between these areas, however, and they must be considered individually. By doing so, you will be able to broaden your horizons even more.

What Is Your Image with Your Customers?

A third area to consider in the process of expansion is one that, paradoxically, instead of expanding your horizons, is more likely to limit them, or at least put some boundaries on them. Unlike the first two considerations—determining the business you're in and examining your capabilities—this third area requires you to carefully analyze the image that customers have of your company. (See Exhibit 5–4.)

Every customer has an image of the company he or she deals with. This image may differ from customer to customer (and probably does in degree if not in kind), based on the relationship each customer has had with that company. If one customer has had nothing but satisfactory dealings with a company, that customer's image would differ from that of one who may have had an unsatisfactory experience, regardless of the cause. But the company's basic image will vary only slightly from customer to customer and will be essentially the same for all customers.

For example, General Motors has a particular image with most Americans. That image exists even for those who have never owned a GM car. The buyer of a GM car who was not happy with his or her purchase may have a somewhat different image of that company based on how his or her complaints were treated. But, in general, the American public believes that General Motors is a responsible, reputable company selling various forms of transportation among which are cars they enjoy using and driving.

Another example in an entirely different field is International Business Machines. Here is a company with which, I dare say, the majority of Americans have never had direct contact. But the image of IBM with most people is probably that of a major American, multinational corporation with unsurpassed technical and scientific skill in the development of the most advanced computers. As in the case of Henry Ford of an earlier day, IBM is probably regarded by most Americans as the developer and the most advanced proponent of a particular technology. In the case of IBM, this technology is concerned with sophisticated computers and with office equipment such as word processors.

Exhibit 5–4.   **The Importance of Image**

This classic McGraw-Hill ad, directed to prospects for business publication advertising, applies with equal force to those who would enter the mail-order field.

I don't know who you are.

I don't know your company.

I don't know your company's product.

I don't know what your company stands for.

I don't know your company's customers.

I don't know your company's record.

I don't know your company's reputation.

Now—what was it you wanted to sell me?''

MORAL: Sales start **before** your salesman calls—with business publication advertising.

McGRAW-HILL MAGAZINES
BUSINESS•PROFESSIONAL•TECHNICAL

While the perceived images of GM and IBM have stood the tests of time, it should be acknowledged that both images have become tainted in the past few years in particular: GM for the quality of its cars; IBM for failure to recognize the changing needs of computer users. This is fair warning to the rest of us that our images are subject to decay if we are not sensitive to consumer needs.

This perceived image is a vitally important factor when you are considering what new products or services to offer your customers or your prospects, if your company is sufficiently well known. It has been proved over and over in direct marketing as well as in other distribution channels that a company has great difficulty selling merchandise or services that do not fit the public's preconceived image of that company. This can be illustrated in the case of one company that built its customer list on the sale of power tools and then failed dismally in an offer of books of general interest to the same audience.

Let's take the case of the Minnesota-based Fingerhut Company. This firm has built a fine reputation by offering good values in medium-to low-priced merchandise ranging from power tools to tableware. While the company was able successfully to sell medium- to low-priced men's and women's wear to the same audience, it is highly doubtful that it could as successfully sell fine bound books or Yves St. Laurent clothing. This is true not only because the demographics of the Fingerhut list probably are not suited to the higher-priced category, but also because the Fingerhut image does not conform to that high-priced merchandise.

Unless your customers or prospects are willing to believe that you are a qualified source for the products you are offering, they are unlikely to buy. But if those prospects *expect* certain products from you, because they fit your company image, your chances of success are vastly enhanced.

Thus it is extremely important that you fully recognize the image you present to your customers and that you select offerings that are appropriate to that image. This recognition, as mentioned earlier, narrows your choices. But it narrows them to your ultimate advantage if it keeps you from going so far afield that what you offer will stand little chance of success.

At this point we might discuss the kinds of factors that tend to create a company's image. The combination of such factors consists of approximately equal parts of the following:

- The products or services offered in the past

- The style and quality of the new product itself

- The price level

- The presentation of the product, whether it is an ad, a commercial, or a mailing piece. The "sound" of the copy and the appearance of the graphics send a definite message to the prospect

- The "look" of the merchandise package received by the customer

- The "sound" and appearance of any other communication with your customer, for example, the invoice, the way complaints are handled, and the way telephone communications are conducted

- The "tone" of any publicity your company receives

An excellent example of the difference a company's image can make can be given in a comparison of two companies featuring outdoor products: L.L. Bean of Maine and Norm Thompson of Seattle, Washington. Just as they are at opposite ends of the country, both companies successfully present different, yet equally acceptable, images. L.L. Bean's image is that of an old-line, conservative company with the Yankee habit of underplaying its product, a company featuring timeless styles that appeal primarily to a mature audience. Norm Thompson, on the other hand, shows an image of a company that appeals to men and women with a more youthful lifestyle. The company prides itself on its ability to come up with interesting, often exotic new products from abroad.

What Are the Characteristics of Your Customer List?

Another most important "mine" to explore for products or services is your own customer list. Study your list from a number of different perspectives, such as:

- How your list was developed

- How your customers have been "educated"

- What they are buying, if you give them choices

- The demographics and psychographics of your customers

- The "product experience" of your list

Let's start with the first point—how your list was developed. What type of merchandise have your customers been buying? At what prices? How have they paid—cash, charge, time payment? These may appear to be obvious questions, but it is surprising how often they are overlooked when new product planning is under consideration.

Your customers are constantly "telling" you what they like and are interested in every time they make a purchase. Catalog companies are following this rule every time they analyze each product in their catalog for profitability. By doing this, they automatically determine which products are most popular and, as a corollary, which new products they should add to their line and at what prices.

If you are successfully selling a vacuum cleaner through direct marketing, it is likely your customers would be logical prospects for such products as sets of dishes, tableware, glassware, and similar items. If you are selling clothing through the mail, as do the Haband Company and New Process,

your customers might well be tempted by offerings of economical house-wares, luggage, towel sets, and the like.

Moreover, the price levels of your merchandise are standards by which to judge any new offering. There is one proviso: You should be constantly testing higher price levels to determine the upper pricing limits of your customer list. Just a 10 to 15 percent increase in the price level your customers will accept may suggest many more profitable products or services for you to offer.

This, of course, raises the question of the methods of payment used by your customers. If they pay in cash or by credit card, they will probably prefer to continue to purchase on that basis. This will probably add to the difficulty of introducing a new item that requires a higher purchase price. On the other hand, if your customers are used to paying on the installment plan, they more likely will be willing to purchase higher-priced merchandise, especially if you can increase the number of installments. Customers who prefer to pay for their merchandise on a monthly basis are, generally speaking, more likely to be concerned with the amount of the individual payment rather than with the total price of the product.

The second point is: "How have your customers been educated?" The way in which you first got your customers has an important influence on what they expect of you in future offers. An example of the power of this "educating" process is the Fingerhut Company, whose customers have been conditioned to expect a host of free gifts with every purchase. It is unlikely that Fingerhut would be successful with a new offering that did not include such free gifts.

The Grolier Corporation has built a large list of book customers by offering free the first volume of a set of books, whether or not the prospect decides to continue with the series. Again, an offering to these customers of a new series without the free volume would probably fail. At the same time, Time-Life Books has been extremely successful in a program of selling books with an offer that only permits the prospect to examine a new volume for a limited time, without getting it free.

Especially if you are just starting in business, give serious thought to your front-end offer. Be sure you are clear on how you want your customers "educated." The way you start out is probably the way you will have to continue. If you'd rather not adopt the pattern of free gifts, free volumes, and sweepstakes, you probably ought not to start with such offers.

What Are the Lifestyles of Your Customers?

Now we get to your customers themselves. What kind of a lifestyle do they have? If you haven't already, you should do a comprehensive analysis to develop a "profile" of your "typical customer."

More and more we are finding that the demographic profiles of customers combined with their psychographic (lifestyle) profiles give many clues to successful new-product development and sales.

With such a profile, you will find all kinds of "road signs" to new products or services. How your customers live, the kinds of vacations they take, the type of entertainment they enjoy, whether they prefer books to movies, as well as their income level, education, size of family, whether they live in a house or apartment, and other demographic characteristics—all are hints as to the new products or services they might be interested in.

Obviously, people who live in an apartment are less likely to be prospects for a set of power tools than people who live in a house. Similarly, people who prefer movies to books are not very good prospects for a best-seller.

What New Products Are People Buying?

When you want to determine whether an offering will work in direct marketing, review the products that people are currently buying at retail. Examples are costume jewelry and paperback books.

Formerly, direct marketers tended to shy away from products available at retail. But that is no longer true. A wide variety of products ranging from Polaroid cameras to General Electric toasters have been and are being sold in increasing volume through the direct response method. Only a few years ago the Quality Paperback Book Club was started, successfully, on a direct response basis, to take advantage of the tremendous popularity of paperbacks. When you consider that paperbacks are sold in virtually every drugstore, cigar shop, candy store, railroad station, and airport—as well as every bookstore—QPB's success can be seen as a tribute to the convenience and acceptance of direct marketing.

Look at the New Lifestyles

American lifestyles seem to be changing more rapidly all the time. A few years ago the women's liberation movement initiated a continuing change in the lifestyles of many women that influences the lifestyles of a great many men as well. Over half of all women in America now work outside the home. Obviously employed women have different needs from those who don't work outside the home—more convenient food preparation products, for instance. The number of unmarried women who head households also keeps growing. Their needs, too, are different. Their need for financial advice, for example, is certainly different from that of married women. For many years senior citizens have constituted a growing segment of United States society. Older people have many needs that differ from those of younger age groups. An example of how one group is addressing those needs is the American Association of Retired Persons. The association offers people over 55 years of age a wide variety of services ranging from travel opportunities to insurance. Membership is in the multimillions. All of these groups have particular needs that frequently can be met by the perceptive direct marketer.

Price/Value Relationships

Once you have selected your product or service, you are faced with the problem of pricing it. How much can you get for it? Whatever price you select, it must appear to the prospect to be the "right" price for that item. He or she must perceive your price as being a value. And that perception depends on the item and the person to whom you are appealing.

A person earning $250 per week has one set of price/value relationships. Another earning $750 per week has a different set. To the first person, a $10 tie may have just the right price/value relationship. To the second, the tie may seem "cheap".

A piece of merchandise in itself has a perceived price/value relationship with the customer. One expects a set of cookware to cost less than a set of bone china dishes. A price of $49 for a set of cookware might sound just right. But $49 for a bone china dinnerware set sounds suspiciously inexpensive.

As an example of how people establish a price/value relationship for a product, here's a test conducted by a direct marketer selling a set of four kitchen knives. Five offers were tested, with the results indicated.

- Offer 1—four knives at $19.95 plus $1.00 shipping and handling. Pull: 1.3 percent.

- Offer 2—four knives at $19.95, plus hanging board at $1.50 (optional), plus $1.00 shipping and handling. Pull: 1.3 percent; 80 percent took the hanging board.

- Offer 3—four knives, plus hanging board, plus shipping and handling at $24.95. Pull: 0.9 percent.

- Offer 4—three knives at $19.95, plus $1.00 shipping and handling. Pull: 0.8 percent.

- Offer 5—five knives at $29.95, plus hanging board at $1.50, plus $1.00 shipping and handling. Pull: 0.7 percent.

As you can see, the prospects saw Offer 2 as the best in terms of price and value, far better than Offer 3, which was only $2.50 more. We have been through this time after time, and we have found that the assumption that there is a right price for every item invariably holds true. Certain cookware sets can only be sold at $39.95. Certain clock radios can only be sold at $49.95. Certain sets of stainless tableware can only be sold at $24.95.

Conversely, we have also found that the customer will, in some cases, accept a higher price than you would have chosen as the proper price/value relationship. For example, a paint gun was tested at both $49.95 and $59.95, and sales at the $59.95 price were better. So although you may think you have a good idea what the right price for an item should be, you should test that price and also test at a higher and a lower price. You may be pleasantly surprised.

Price/value relationships change, too. Inflation has an effect on them. So does competition. And the relative popularity of the item is important. The same paint gun that sold successfully at $59.95 a few years ago now sells for $89.95 in about the same quantities as it did at the lower price. Remember when Sharp came out with the first electronic calculator? It was only a four-function model, but American Express sold thousands at $300. Today you'd be lucky to get $15 for it.

Others Areas to Consider

Finally, let's consider several other marketing factors apart from the product or service itself. These are such factors as the offer, the advertising medium to be used, and how to use research in reaching your decisions.

The Offer

The offer should be regarded as an opportunity to say to the prospect, "Here is a special reason for acting now rather than waiting to order at a future date." The best offers flow from the product or service being offered. A good example is the original Franklin Mint five-year buy-back guarantee, an offer that corresponded perfectly with the firm's assumption that its products might increase in value. Book club and record club offers of X number of books or records for as little as ten cents are other examples. Free-gift offers, limited time or quantity offers, free-trial periods, and a wide variety of other offers can be useful. Try to develop an offer that relates to the general character of your merchandise. It can pay big dividends.

Determining the Media

When deciding which advertising medium to use, a number of basic factors must be considered. Generally speaking, if the product doesn't carry at least a $15.00 profit at a $29.95 retail price, you probably won't be successful in a solo mailing, unless the pull is really sensational.

A further consideration in your decision about whether to use the direct mail system is the amount of copy and illustration you need. The more of both you require, the more likely it is that your product belongs in the mail. If your item is suited to a visual demonstration, television becomes a likely medium, especially if the item's price is under $29.95.

Newspaper inserts should not be overlooked as a viable medium today. Inserts have brought a new dimension that offers as much copy space as needed with a wide variety of interesting formats, plus a return envelope, quality reproduction, and, often, market segmentation. Newspaper inserts have opened opportunities for a wide range of offers—from insurance to limited-edition commemoratives and free credit cards.

The Use of Research

In recent years, an activity that has been receiving more attention in determining product selection is market research. For many years, direct marketers believed that the only way to determine the appeal of a product or service was to put it in the mail or run an ad and see if it sold. Today, sophisticated direct marketers are more and more frequently turning to research as a means of helping to determine whether an item stands a chance of success. (See Chapter Twenty-One.)

Consider the various research techniques available to help in selecting your product or service to increase your prospects for success. Research such as focus group testing can give you valuable insights into the appeal (or lack thereof) of your offering. It can also help you determine which one or two or more items have the strongest appeal. Often this procedure can even help you add to the appeal of your product or service by suggesting benefits to be added.

Reliable Sources

Everything we've said so far presupposes that you have a dependable source of supplying your product or that you will have a supplier once you determine what you are going to sell. Seasoned direct marketers always make certain they are ready to deliver when they put a promotion in the mail, or advertise in a magazine, or offer the item via broadcast. A cardinal point to remember is: The product must be on hand before you start your promotion. Once you have mailed or placed your ad, you have committed yourself fully. You can't recall the mailing or magazine. And in the direct response business, if you can't deliver in a reasonable length of time, you will lose a large percentage of your orders. You will create much expensive, time-consuming correspondence. You will engender a lot of ill-will and undoubtedly lose the bulk of your investment.

Mining Your Customer Base

Direct marketers must be on a relentless, continuous search for new products and services. Nevertheless, there is the ever-present danger that the excitement of new-product development will take attention from the product or products that built the business in the first place. Established direct marketers cannot afford to overlook this danger, because their customer bases are the lifeblood of their businesses.

Promoting Services as "Products"

When one considers the idea of mail order, one thinks of products—merchandise, if you will. But the fact is that thousands of services are also sold via mail-order methods.

The tenets that apply to products also apply to services. Indeed, most of the 34 factors to consider when selecting mail-order items, which we discussed earlier in this chapter, are appropriate when considering services —perceived need, uniqueness, sufficient markup, large enough market, and so on. To illustrate how services might be sold using mail-order procedures, let us examine a marketing program involving subscriptions to a course on what it takes to become a millionaire. The mailing package was created by Joan Throckmorton, author of *Winning Direct Response Advertising*, published by Prentice-Hall, and one of the most creative writers in the world. The components of the mailing were:

- A 9" × 12" mailing envelope with teaser copy on both sides
- An eight-page letter (Who says people don't read long copy?)
- A four-page bulletin on tax reform and inflation
- A "buck slip" offering "The Hume Tax Bulletins" free
- A "lift" letter from a multimillionaire physician
- A folder containing the biographics of noted contributors to the course
- A subscription form
- A postage-free business reply envelope

Shown are the mailing envelope (Exhibit 5–5), the eight-page letter (Exhibit 5–6), and both sides of the subscription form (Exhibit 5–7).

Mailing Results

This mailing package for "Successful Investment and Money Management" beat the former control mailing by a wide margin. The question is: Why was this mailing so successful? For the answers, I went to the creator of the package—Joan Throckmorton. Her answers are fascinating.

Why do I feel this beat the control? Well, first the outer. How could you ignore that question?

Everyone wants to know what it takes to become a millionaire. It's the great, elusive American dream.

Notice that Question 5 does not appear on the outer envelope. Instead, there's a teaser to pull you inside. The teaser on the back also works to pull you in. (Using both sides of the outer envelope is like chicken soup. It can't hurt and it sure may help.)

So, this gets them inside, which is half the battle.

The letter (which repeats the questions) introduces the writer (Mr. Hume himself) with a picture, then launches into an impassioned, convincing discussion directed to and about the reader.

The copy is heavy with big benefits and appeals strongly to the prospect's perceived self-image. In a very complimentary way, Hume

Exhibit 5–5.   Mailing Envelope

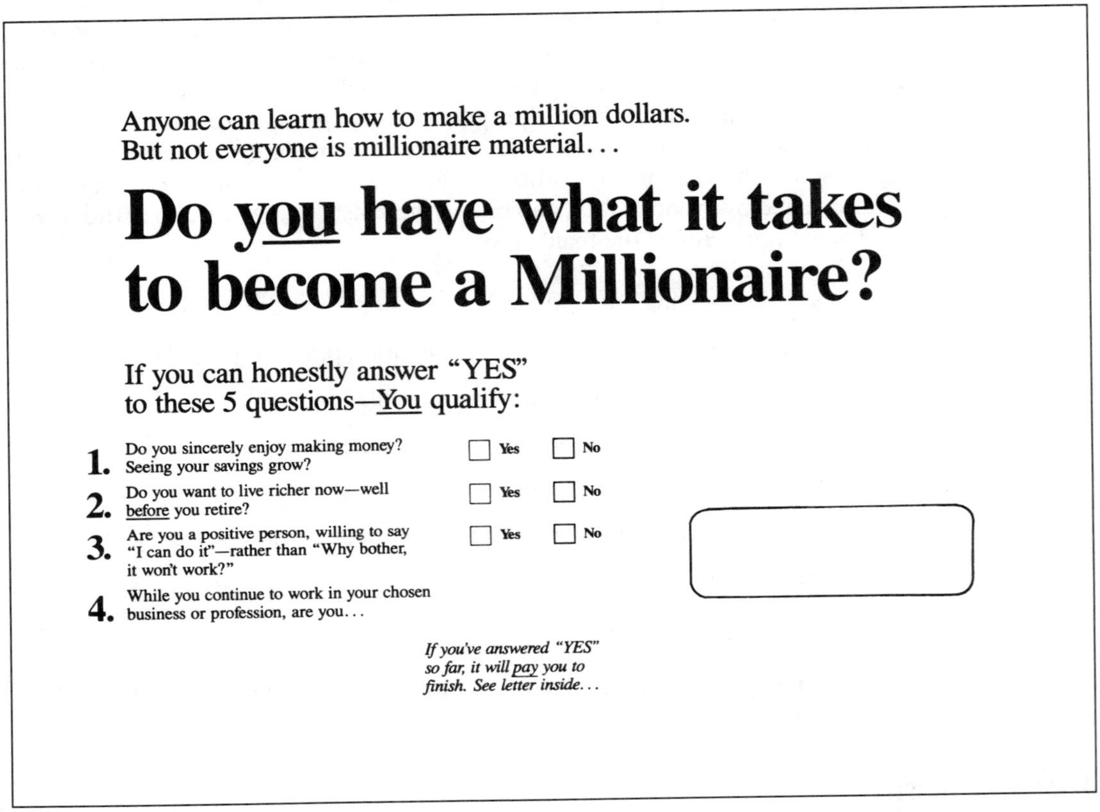

Anyone can learn how to make a million dollars.
But not everyone is millionaire material. . .

Do you have what it takes to become a Millionaire?

If you can honestly answer "YES"
to these 5 questions—You qualify:

1. Do you sincerely enjoy making money? Seeing your savings grow? ☐ Yes ☐ No

2. Do you want to live richer now—well before you retire? ☐ Yes ☐ No

3. Are you a positive person, willing to say "I can do it"—rather than "Why bother, it won't work?" ☐ Yes ☐ No

4. While you continue to work in your chosen business or profession, are you. . .

If you've answered "YES" so far, it will pay you to finish. See letter inside. . .

A 9" × 12" mailing envelope, with teaser copy on both sides.

proceeds to challenge the reader, encourage him and involve him. (I heard Ron Hume as a football coach pep-talking his team.)

Since this is a financial, self-help service, testimonials (the strongest I could get) abound. They always help with credibility. (Notice the footnote that accompanies them to also enhance credibility.)

The offer is described as totally reasonable and honest. It's "good for both of us."

I used the four inner yellow pages as sort of a break in Hume's pep talk. It gives the letter immediacy—introducing current financial news and urging the prospect to take advantage of new aspects of financial planning and investment (in this case, the 1986 tax reforms). I saw this as a segment that could be easily updated in the future as economic changes create shifts in investment strategies.

And, again, I felt the lift letter and little second salesman with his self-made millionaire's point-of-view was another reinforcing element.

Exhibit 5–6.   Eight-Page Letter (partial)

Ronald C. Hume
Founder
HUME PUBLISHING
Atlanta • Los Angeles • Toronto
Publishers of Financial Educational
Materials since 1974

Anyone Can Learn How to Make a Million.
But Not Everyone is Millionaire Material...

Do <u>you</u> have what it takes to become a Millionaire?

If You Can Honestly Answer "**YES**" to These 5 Questions—<u>You</u> Qualify:

1. Do you sincerely enjoy making money? Seeing your savings grow?   ☐ Yes   ☐ No

2. Do you want to live richer now—well <u>before</u> you retire?   ☐ Yes   ☐ No

3. Are you a positive person, willing to say "I can do it"—rather than "Why bother, it won't work?"   ☐ Yes   ☐ No

4. While you continue to work in your chosen business or profession, are you willing to give some of your leisure time to making money—<u>and</u> keep at it as your money grows?   ☐ Yes   ☐ No

5. Do you want to <u>try first</u> before you commit, because you prefer to judge and decide for yourself?   ☐ Yes   ☐ No

If you can say "Yes" to these five questions—good. You'll find this letter of great importance—as a matter of fact, it could change your life!

Dear Reader:

There are <u>two basic requirements</u> for every self-made millionaire. I believe you may already have one of them.

This first requirement is <u>the right attitude</u>. If you've got it, you're halfway there. And if you answered "Yes" to the 5 questions, it's likely you do.

The second requirement is <u>knowledge</u>. This is something I can give you. Actually, it's something a group of self-made millionaires can give you because I've brought them together in an exceptional

(Continued)

Exhibit 5–6 *(Continued)*.   **Eight-Page Letter (partial)**

wishing and start winning. Cut yourself in.

America is still the land of opportunity <u>for those who know how</u> <u>to take advantage of that opportunity</u>. Come join us.

Sincerely,

Ronald C. Hume
Founder

RCH:sjt

P.S.   A smart investor right now is probably asking what all of this costs. You're going to be surprised when you learn how little it is.

Each lesson is $10 (plus a small shipping and handling charge). There are two free lessons plus 27 lessons that you pay for, sent to you two at a time. And you're not committed to accept any set number.

Why don't we charge more? We don't want qualified prospects to be put off by the price or by terms that create obligations to continue purchasing.

We want as many as possible to try our program, then continue with us solely because of "satisfaction received." It's the best way that we know to run a business.

Here is what other smart investors tell us about *Successful Investing & Money Management*...

"Successful Investing & Money Management is exactly what I needed to help myself start controlling, monitoring and maximizing my finances permanently. The course had immediate benefits: When I enrolled last May, I owned a 5-year-old Japanese subcompact car and owed well over $6,000. I even had a negative net worth! Today I drive a new BMW and have no installment debt at all. And my net worth is growing fast. But the course not only has immediate benefits, it also provides basic, in-depth principles that last over time. Having completed all the lessons, I'm now using the materials as the start of my own 'library' of financial references and information. Thank you *very* much!"

N. E. T., Bellevue, Washington

"This is a comprehensive, results-getting course! Your commitment to produce 'the best' training possible is, in fact, as you advertise it. What a refreshing experience!! Thanks!"

J. R., St. Louis, Missouri

"Successful Investing & Money Management has helped me to learn more about investing and money management than I could have ever imagined. I have already put to work what I have learned and am now well on my way to becoming a self-made millionaire."

B. E. E., Chicago, Illinois

"Successful Investing & Money Management is informative and complete. It gave me an excellent background on many types of investments and strategies that I knew little or nothing about. I was able to make use of much of the covered information shortly after completing the lessons. The course was most enjoyable and practical. It will also serve as an excellent reference for years to come."

D. F. L., Benicia, California

"Successful Investing & Money Management gave me an immediate working knowledge of the art of successful investing. The program is very well designed and is easy to follow and understand—and to put into immediate profitable use. The editors are top-notch professionals in the field and the material is up-to-date and thoroughly informative. I would highly recommend this course as a *must* for the seasoned serious investor, as well as for the novice."

W. M. M., Montgomery, Alabama

These comments are selected from our files. Naturally, everyone who participates in the Successful Investing & Money Management program will not have the same sort of experience...but I do guarantee that if you are not 100% satisfied with *your own rate of success*, you may drop out of the program at any time.

R. C. Hume
Founder, Hume Publishing

Exhibit 5–7.   Both Sides of the Subscription Form

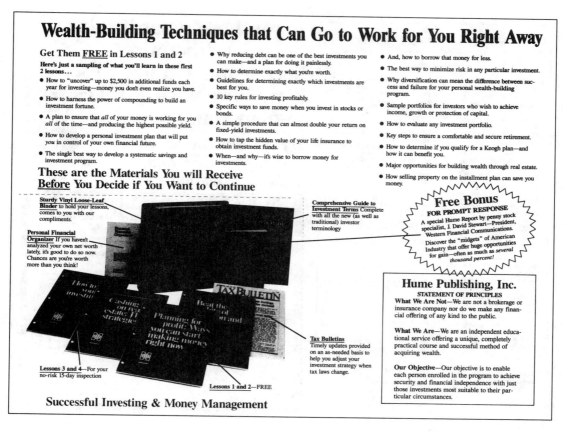

Wealth-Building Techniques that Can Go to Work for You Right Away

Get Them FREE in Lessons 1 and 2

Here's just a sampling of what you'll learn in these first 2 lessons...

- How to "uncover" up to $2,500 in additional funds each year for investing—money you don't even realize you have.
- How to harness the power of compounding to build an investment fortune.
- A plan to ensure that *all* of your money is working for you *all* of the time—and producing the highest possible yield.
- How to develop a personal investment plan that will put *you* in control of your own financial future.
- The single best way to develop a systematic savings and investment program.

- Why reducing debt can be one of the best investments you can make—and a plan for doing it painlessly.
- How to determine exactly what you're worth.
- Guidelines for determining exactly which investments are best for you.
- 10 key rules for investing profitably.
- Specific ways to save money when you invest in stocks or bonds.
- A simple procedure that can almost double your return on fixed-yield investments.
- How to tap the hidden value of your life insurance to obtain investment funds.
- When—and why—it's wise to borrow money for investments.

- And, how to borrow that money for less.
- The best way to minimize risk in any particular investment.
- Why diversification can mean the difference between success and failure for your personal wealth-building program.
- Sample portfolios for investors who wish to achieve income, growth or protection of capital.
- How to evaluate any investment portfolio.
- Key steps to ensure a comfortable and secure retirement.
- How to determine if you qualify for a Keogh plan—and how it can benefit you.
- Major opportunities for building wealth through real estate.
- How selling property on the installment plan can save you money.

These are the Materials You will Receive Before You Decide if You Want to Continue

Sturdy Vinyl Loose-Leaf Binder to hold your lessons, comes to you with our compliments.

Personal Financial Organizer If you haven't analyzed your own net worth lately, it's good to do so now. Chances are you're worth more than you think!

Comprehensive Guide to Investment Terms Complete with all the new (as well as traditional) investor terminology

Tax Bulletins Timely updates provided on an as-needed basis to help you adjust your investment strategy when tax laws change.

Lessons 3 and 4—For your no-risk 15-day inspection

Lessons 1 and 2—FREE

Free Bonus
FOR PROMPT RESPONSE
A special Hume Report by penny stock specialist, J. David Stewart—President, Western Financial Communications. Discover the "midgets" of American Industry that offer huge opportunities for gain—often as much as *several thousand percent!*

Hume Publishing, Inc.
STATEMENT OF PRINCIPLES
What We Are Not—We are not a brokerage or insurance company nor do we make any financial offering of any kind to the public.

What We Are—We are an independent educational service offering a unique, completely practical course and successful method of acquiring wealth.

Our Objective—Our objective is to enable each person enrolled in the program to achieve security and financial independence with just those investments most suitable to their particular circumstances.

Successful Investing & Money Management

(Continued)

(I could just "hear" Schulman and Hume speaking together to convince our prospect.)

Assuming that the letter did its job, I economized and let the order card do double duty.

You'll notice that the order card carries a lot of the "brochure" work on the back. It shows all components of the product; gives good teaser samplings of compelling financial advice to come. On the front is a full nuts-and-bolts wrap-up of the offer plus guarantee.

I felt, and still do, that if the outer, letter (and even the little lift) did their jobs, the order card was a good place for the rest.

Exhibit 5–7 (*Continued*).   Both Sides of the Subscription Form

Here's Exactly What Happens When You Return the Enrollment Card— *I Guarantee It!*

- Send in your $5 Registration Fee along with your enrollment form today—and we'll send you:

LESSONS 1 AND 2 OF SUCCESSFUL INVESTING & MONEY MANAGEMENT. YOURS TO *KEEP*—FREE OF CHARGE, WHATEVER HAPPENS.

Special Bonus
Reply promptly and also receive **Free**, with our compliments: *"What You Should Know About Playing the Penny Stock Markets"*—J. David Stewart, newspaper columnist, financial commentator and well-known financial specialist in penny stocks, explains the thrills and excitement of buying low and selling high in America's most volatile market—stocks priced below $10 a share.

- When your first two lessons arrive, start right in. Don't wait. Let the information alone convince you that we're going to travel the road to riches together. Because—

- Shortly afterwards, we'll also send you Lessons 3 and 4. You will then have an additional 15 days to decide. (That's 15 days to evaluate and apply the information and guidance in the first 4 lessons of *Successful Investing & Money Management* absolutely *risk free*.)

- *Then* decide.

If **"No"**—Simply mail back Lessons 3 and 4—*at our expense* (within 15 days of receiving them). When we get these lessons, a refund check for

your $5 Registration Fee goes out to you *by return mail*. No questions asked. And no other obligations on your part. Your copy of "What You Should Know About Playing the Penny Stock Markets" and Lessons 1 and 2 are yours to keep.

If **"Yes"**—We'll send you the remaining lessons at the leisurely rate of 2 lessons every three weeks. We'll bill you only $10 plus shipping and handling for each of the 27 lessons and you aren't expected to pay until you've examined each shipment for a full 15 days.

- You'll also receive a variety of totally free benefits as you move ahead, starting with

  - *Your Personal Financial Organizer*, then
  - *Two Sturdy Vinyl Binders* to hold Course Material,
  - *A Comprehensive Guide to Investment Terms*, and
  - *The Hume Tax Bulletin*.

- Of course, you can cancel at any time along the way. And that will be that. No questions asked. And no salesman will ever bother you.

I guarantee it.

Ron Hume

Important: This liberal, risk-free offer is made possible because so many individuals realize an immediate payout from Lessons 1 and 2—often enough to offset more than the cost of the entire course. These enthusiastic builders then go on to reap even greater rewards.

If <u>you</u> have what it takes to be a millionaire— here's your chance to see if we have what it takes to help you.

Try the first two lessons absolutely FREE and without obligation

Respond Promptly and Get Your Free Copy

NO-RISK ENROLLMENT FORM
Successful Investing & Money Management

<u>YES.</u> I accept your invitation to evaluate *Successful Investing & Money Management* for myself without risk or obligation to continue. Please send me Lessons 1 and 2 and "What You Should Know About Playing the Penny Stock Markets" free of charge according to the terms described at the left.

Tax-Deductible Tuition
All payments may be tax deductible if the program is used to make investment or business decisions, depending on your personal tax situation.

This enrollment form is non-transferable. Please make any necessary corrections in the address shown here.

☐ My $5 Registration Fee is enclosed. (Please make check payable to Hume Financial Education Services.)

☐ I prefer to use my
☐ VISA   ☐ American Express
☐ MasterCard   ☐ Diners Club

Account No. _____ Expiration Date _____

Signature (Credit Card users only)

California and Georgia residents: State sales tax will be charged as applicable.

Hume Financial Education Services
835 Franklin Court • Box 105627 • Atlanta, Georgia 30348

9321 SJT

Self-Quiz

1. The first tip in selecting mail-order items is that you should select items whose benefits you can _____ with photos and graphics.

2. List ten sources for discovering mail-order items:

a. _____   f. _____

b. _____   g. _____

c. _____   h. _____

d. _____   i. _____

e. _____   j. _____

3. List ten factors to consider when selecting mail-order items:

a. _____   f. _____

b. _____   g. _____

c. _____   h. _____

d. _____   i. _____

e. _____   j. _____

4. What are the four phases of the product life cycle?

a. _____   c. _____

b. _____   d. _____

5. In attempting to expand your business with new products or services, what is the first question you should ask yourself?

_____

_____

6. How does the image of your company influence your selection of products?

_____

_____

7. In determining what other products you might offer your customers, you should look at your house list from five different angles. They are:

a. _____

b. _____

c. _____

d. _____

e. _____

8. Define price/value relationships.

_____

_____

_____

_____

9. The more copy and illustration you need to adequately present your product, the more likely it is that:
☐ Space is your best medium.
☐ Direct mail is your best medium.

10. A major source of gaining new customers is _____.

Pilot Project

You are Annie Hurlbut. You have developed a customer base of 50,000 women who have purchased hand-loomed alpaca garments made in Peru.
    The question you face is: "What else might I offer to my customer list?" Make a list of ten products you think would be most attractive to this customer base.

CHAPTER SIX

Business-to-Business Direct Marketing

I've often commented to my students at Northwestern University that if I were to start my career over, I'm quite certain I would specialize in business-to-business direct marketing. The opportunities are so great— opportunities to get qualified leads, opportunities to screen leads and to sell by telephone, opportunities to create catalogs and sales support material.

One man I know who has done it all is Vic Hunter, founder and president of Hunter Business Direct Inc., Milwaukee, Wisconsin. Mr. Hunter has consistently developed complete business and marketing programs for Fortune 500 companies that have proved hugely successful. One of the keys to his success has been the ability of his organization to develop highly automated computerized process and reporting systems for his company's clients.

I asked Mr. Hunter to contribute his wisdom and experience to this chapter, and he has graciously complied.

Definition

Business-to-business direct marketing is a special type of direct marketing in which the response to value-based contacts is made by an individual on behalf of a company, institution, or professional organization. This includes the individual end users, buyers, influencers, and reseller contacts for whom information is captured in a database for the purpose of sustaining a long-term relationship and supporting all channels of distribution.

A special case exists when business direct marketing becomes a channel (i.e., catalog sales, solo mailing, fax ordering, and the like). The driving force and the foundation for successful business-to-business direct marketing is the concurrent improvement of sales productivity and customer relationships.

To achieve these objectives, we must strive for the optimal mix of value-based contacts in an integrated campaign of mail, phone, and field sales. The economics of these contact strategies and the monitoring of customer relations creates a process that must be tested continually.

Philosophy

Business-to-business direct marketing is a highly personal form of marketing that respects and recognizes the unique needs of individuals within a business environment. A properly designed and maintained database provides information about individuals within the account. The communications derived from these data can be of genuine value to the customer or prospect, and the resulting direct marketing programs are characterized by solid relationships, high retention rates, and increased profitability.

Direct marketing programs should arise from the business plan and should implement the business unit's strategic objectives. Business objectives are incorporated into the targeting process through the marketing plan on one of two distinct platforms: acquisition of new customers (investment) and cultivation of existing customers (profit). Although each of these platforms requires a differentiated approach and measurement, together they must integrate contact media in order to achieve increased sales at a lower overall cost.

Business-to-business direct marketing combines value-based contacts into a highly personal form of marketing whose heart is the database and whose soul is a sensitivity to people, relationships, and applications. When a value-based contact is properly executed, the communication has high perceived personal value.

The fundamental concepts supporting this philosophy are:

- You market to individuals, not corporations.

- You address unique sets of needs.

- Individuals are clustered around common sets of needs.

- All contacts must be of value to the customer or prospect.

- The best technology is transparent (i.e., not obvious to the customer).

- Planning is critical.

- Testing is mandatory.

- Integration is the means by which program excellence is most economically achieved.

- Properly executed, integrated direct marketing is a continuous improvement process capable of profitably implementing business strategy.

Reason for Growth

The continued growth and profitability of direct marketing is fueled by a two-pronged driving force from business management: (1) retention of customers and (2) focus on increased sales productivity.

Retention of Customers

Let's first look at retention of customers. Management has discovered that retaining customers is the foundation for profitablility in the 1990s. This is contrary to our experience in the 1970s and early 1980s, when many markets were growing and the primary focus was on acquisition of new customers. Market position was determined more by keeping up with the growth in the market than by taking away market share from others. Profitability came through economical management of this customer acquisition.

That situation has changed. Business now finds a need to focus on retention of its customers as a strategy to protect the investment it has made in building a customer base and to leverage the higher acquisition costs of flat or declining markets.

Retention of customers means a new focus on the end user as an individual, the identification and satisfaction of customer needs, ownership of the customer relationship, and the necessity of finding new ways of continuing the customer partnership. Customer retention is improved through increased frequency of contact with the customer and management of all contact mediums so that those contacts with individuals become value-based communications in an integrated and disciplined strategy. Key performance measures are reorder rate, related product purchase, and referrals.

Critical to customer retention is getting the customer to complain. Complaints spotlight problems, and problem grading can lead to corrective action. This process requires a new ease of doing business with the manufacturer or product/service provider and an assurance of no risk—even of enthusiasm—arising from being able to identify and solve these problems. There is a need to focus on new and easier ways for the customer to do business. It is an attitude as much as it is a process or a matter of having the right tools. (See Exhibit 6–1.)

Examples of successful customer-retention programs are the customer information centers and customer service centers being developed in corporations as an integration of contact media, providing a new effectiveness for the field salespeople and directly supporting the end users.

The typical customer retention program is based on delivery of value-based contacts and is focused on building a stronger customer partnership. The frequency of contact is of greater importance than the contact medium, and the recognition of value-based contacts as the foundation for customer retention becomes more important in the planning process. These integrated direct marketing systems have caused exponential growth in the use of mail and phone contacts.

Exhibit 6–1. **Effective Communication**

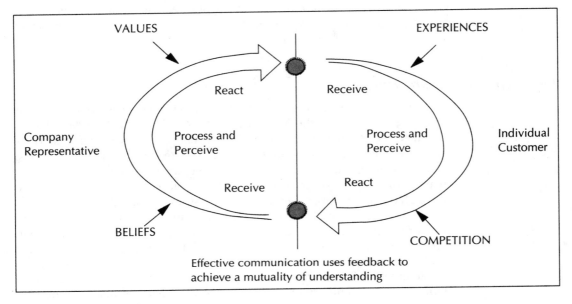

Effective communication uses feedback to
achieve a mutuality of understanding

Source: © Hunter Business Direct Inc.

Increased Sales Productivity

The second aspect of the two-pronged driving force for profits is management's concern for increased sales productivity. Two key performance
measures are (1) revenue per field sales rep and (2) revenue per total sales
and marketing expense for sales productivity. In the 1970s, manufacturing
productivity improved through utilization of tools such as shop floor control
and just-in-time inventory systems. With the advent of systems integrators as
technical facilitators to provide increased manufacturing efficiency, businesses saw new processes leverage production.

We now find that these same concepts for processes, systems, and integration are applicable to sales and marketing. As management finds it more
difficult to compete and to differentiate its products and services, as margins
decline and the cost of the field sales contact continues to increase, new,
more efficient and effective sales processes must be developed to leverage
the face-to-face field contact. Essential to leveraging sales is the existence of
a documented sales process. If there is not a sales process, it must be
created before productivity programs can be implemented.

Some markets may be economically forced to replace the field sales
contact with an integrated set of mail and phone contacts. It is preferable and
usually cost effective, however, to integrate mail and phone contacts with
the field sales team; such contacts should not serve as a replacement for the
team or to segment customers serviced by phone sales from field sales.

When successful, such integrated programs are given enthusiastic support by the sales force.

Economically, increases in sales productivity result from the integration of field contacts with more frequent, lower-cost phone and mail contacts. The increased frequency of value-based contacts between the customer and salesperson will strengthen the partnership. Sales productivity produces geometric increases in phone and mail contacts, serving as a more frequent and less costly leverage of sales activity.

Both of these sources of growth in business-to-business direct marketing require a fundamental modification in the role of the sales rep. This change reflects the higher annual cost of a field sales contact, an increased focus on the end-user/customer, a sharing of account responsibilities, and a discipline in acquiring and updating information.

Although difficult to implement, business-to-business direct marketing is achieving a growing acceptance as a credible, effective, and efficient sales and marketing tool supporting the field sales effort in an integrated, seamless process.

Another reason for growth in the 1990s is an increased concern for the accountability and measurability of results from the sales and marketing budget. There is also a strong continuing need for better identification of market niches and adequate defense of those niches.

The product life cycle is continuing to shorten as industry emphasizes the importance of market share and customer satisfaction. Sales management is finding economically and organizationally stressful the rising number of contacts needed per order, the increased cost of sales training, and the complexity associated with training around these shorter product cycles.

Businesses continue to migrate out of highly centralized business centers. Sales and marketing management is continually being forced to find new and more cost-effective ways of taking products and services to market and managing relationships with the customers. There is no question that direct marketing will continue to grow in importance.

Planning and Organizational Impact
Planning

Because successful integrated direct marketing campaigns implement business strategy, it is necessary to define strategic needs before defining program tactics. Information acquired through the direct marketing process provides a reliable knowledge base for planning the business strategy. This strategy, in turn, is implemented through tactical direct marketing programs that are evaluated against the strategic objectives. This approach is intended not to discount the importance of tactical application, but rather to stress that no amount of tactical excellence can rectify a poor or inappropriate strategy.

Focusing first on strategy is a statement of sequence, not priority. Excellent tactical execution is mandatory if the difficulties inherent in implementing an integrated direct marketing program are to be successfully resolved.

Continuous Improvement Direct marketing's inherent quantifiable nature provides an excellent foundation for testing, piloting, and expanding programs with confidence. It is not coincidental that the 1990s find that leading businesses accept direct marketing as a proven, mature, and often preferred form of marketing. Like the quality movement of earlier decades, direct marketing uses the latest technology to conduct research, measure results, and increase the productivity of a firm's marketing and sales efforts. Thus continuous improvement is a hallmark of business-to-business direct marketing.

Integration Direct marketing's strengths can be further enhanced by integrating contact media into an effective process. It is not enough to focus on maximizing the performance of one form of contact. As with any group of interrelated components, optimization of any single element seldom results in an optimal system. For example, the overall effectiveness of a campaign that carefully integrates mail, phone, and field contacts and measures the total effort will generally be greater than that of a campaign that attempts to maximize the performance of each of the contact media separately.

Personalization Business-to-business direct marketing is most effective when it uses cutting-edge technology to address individuals with the personalization of simpler times. Direct marketing contacts should be personal and of value to the recipients, the resulting relationships should be genuine, and the technology that makes this possible should be transparent and subordinate.

Planning begins with the understanding that direct marketing is a process (See Exhibit 6–2.) It applies tools that create measurable responses to improve sales productivity. It engages the contact in a value-based communication—a contact perceived as having value by the customer/prospect.

The planning process must begin with a clear understanding of the customer. The attributes attached to the individual, buyer group, or account are used to select targeted markets that have common sets of needs. A formalized market intelligence system must provide the positioning of the product or service in relation to that of its major competitors.

Those customer needs that are unfulfilled and that can be satisfied best by the product/service become the unique beneficiaries of the marketing campaign. Using selected attributes to cluster individuals with common sets of unfulfilled needs permits the targeting of the campaign message.

Next, the operational and administrative support of the campaign must be considered. Once documented, the economic model for the campaign

Exhibit 6–2. **Direct Marketing Business Plan**

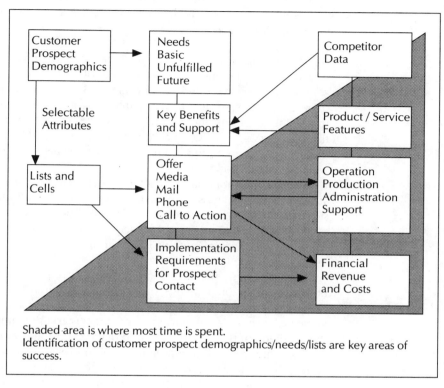

Shaded area is where most time is spent.
Identification of customer prospect demographics/needs/lists are key areas of success.

Source: © Hunter Business Direct Inc.

can then be generated. This economic model produces quantifiable measurement for campaign justification, measurement of success, and continued improvement.

The planning process integrates functions, allowing process control and quality control procedures to be coordinated with sales and marketing. The planning focuses on an orderly way to achieve the desired result.

Organizational Impact

The core of successful business-to-business direct marketing is understanding the customer, particularly in regard to work applications and needs. The typical organization begins with a product or service to take to market. Herein exists a fundamental conflict between organizational structures that are product/service-focused and the direct marketing organizational objectives that are customer-focused.

Direct marketing organizational planning can be initiated by identifying the key objectives of the product-based organization. Seldom is an analysis

of these organizational objectives as effective as when it is supported by a customer-based organization. A practical problem that often exists in moving to this customer focus is the lack of direct marketing functional skills and the supporting infrastructure that is needed to allow them to be utilized effectively.

This initial transition from product-based to functional organizational structure often begins with the creation of a direct marketing competency center and a formal education program. Businesses concurrently establish pilot or prototype direct marketing programs and look to outsourcing marketing functions, including the database. This phase focuses on learning through the use of direct marketing tools, and not the creation of the tools themselves. The emerging direct marketing skills are acquired by applying what has been shown to work.

The subsequent transition from functional to customer organizational structure often begins with a baseline customer satisfaction survey. This survey and ongoing customer contact must begin to focus on the acquisition of individual, buyer group, and account attributes so that the individual customer/prospect needs and applications can be selected and clustered into target markets.

Pilot programs begin to focus more on campaigns to achieve business objectives than on mailings or telephone programs to beat the control. Testing is still important, but the incremental value of a program test is not as great as the value of integration of the direct marketing media into campaigns that implement the overall sales and marketing strategy of the marketer.

Customer-focused organizations typically form vertical market teams. SIC code, job title, and size of company are often chosen as selects for individuals and their companies. Some creative companies may find unique clusters of customers based on common needs but not grouped in a traditional market segment approach. Effective segmentation and targeting finds individuals with common sets of needs and behaviors. The goal is acquisition and retention of customers through a more focused approach to their needs. (See Exhibit 6–3.)

Direct Response Media

In considering direct response media for business-to-business direct marketing, we must first stress the uniqueness of each of the contact media— trade paper advertising, mail, phone, and traditional field sales contact. Each contact medium has a significantly different cost. These cost levels are not contiguous, and in fact exist at quantum levels where activity within each medium, for the most part, does not have a cost/contact that intersects or overlaps the activity cost in one of the other media. (See Exhibit 6–4.)

What this means is that the integration and leveraging of contact media are required to achieve the lowest cost for a selling process. This integration obviously also applies to the information necessary to link lower-cost

Exhibit 6–3.   **Organizational Impact**

	Organizational Objectives	Organization Focus		
		Product	Functional	Customer
E A R L Y	Product development	●	◑	◑
	Manufacturing	◑	●	○
	Product distribution	○	●	○
	Low-cost/low-risk sales	○	●	◑
L A T E R	Ease of doing business for customers	○	◑	●
	Understand customer needs	◑	○	●
	Take new products / services to existing customers	◑	◑	●
	Protect customer base	○	◑	●

● = Very good fit   ◑ = Somewhat a fit   ○ = Not a good fit

Source: © Hunter Business Direct Inc.

Exhibit 6–4.   **Marketing Integration**

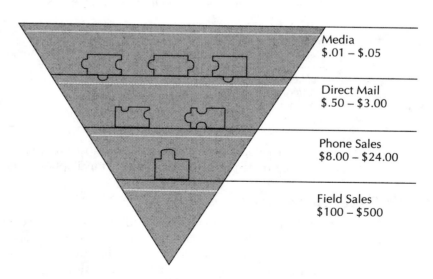

Media
$.01 – $.05

Direct Mail
$.50 – $3.00

Phone Sales
$8.00 – $24.00

Field Sales
$100 – $500

Contact media have discrete costs levels and must be integrated for optional marketing campaign performance. Greater value is gained through integrating contact media than through optimizing marketing results within one medium.

Source: © Hunter Business Direct Inc.

contacts with the more powerful face-to-face contacts. The appropriate contact media and frequency of contact are defined by the customer and justified by the customer's potential contribution.

The optimal performance for a sales campaign is achieved through the integration of contact media and the measurement of the effectiveness of various contacts within each medium as they support the effectiveness of higher-cost media. This means that evaluating a mail program performance apart from its impact on the phone contacts in a mail and phone campaign may produce very strong direct mail results, but it may actually decrease the overall profitability of the mail/phone effort. Lower-cost contacts must leverage higher-cost contacts. Direct mail programs may not produce the highest revenue to cost when integrating phone follow-up into a mail/phone campaign unless they leverage the phone contact.

For example, higher-cost phone contacts are replaced by mail lead generation or written follow-ups to phone calls. The same logic and economics apply to leveraging field sales contacts (e.g., replacing 20 percent of the annual field contacts at an account with regularly scheduled, high-frequency, lower-cost phone and mail contacts). It is critical to remember, therefore, that the integration of contact media and the measurement of performance across all contacts produce the desired responses for a lower cost than does the optimization of marketing results within any one contact medium. Table 6–1 presents the different advantages and limitations offered by the various media.

Table 6–1. Dimensions of Direct Response Media

	Trade Paper Advertising	Direct Mail	Phone	Field Sales
Market reach	Broad	Targeted	Focused	Narrow
Cost/contact	Lowest	Empowering	Restrictive	High
Communication	One-way	One-way	Dialog	Sight and sound

Four categories of contact media most often used as direct marketing tools are trade paper advertising, direct mail, phone, and field sales.

Trade Paper Advertising

Trade paper advertising has traditionally been used in direct marketing because of its broad reach into the marketplace. It also provides the lowest cost per exposure unit (often 1/100 the cost of a mail contact or 1/1000 the cost of a phone contact). Trade paper advertising is limited in the visual and graphic messages that can be brought to the reader, and it is, for the most part, a one-way communication based on a single bold benefit and/or call to action. It is important to differentiate direct response media that cause a response and trade media that manage perceptions and anchor reference points.

Direct Mail

Direct mail has the advantage of being targeted to selected individuals based on responses, to buyer groups based on functional titles or applications, or to specific locations based on mailing addresses or corporate account attributes. These kinds of selects require the acquisition and management of information about applications, number of employees, annual revenue, SIC codes, and the like, that are attached to the specific buyer group, location, or account. Note that these attributes are different from the contact transactions that are always attached to the individual—mail, phone, and field sales contacts with that individual; orders, inquiries, customer service problems, collection contacts, attendance at trade shows, quote activity, and similar points of customer contact.

Targeted direct mail communications can be utilized at one-tenth to one-fiftieth the cost of a phone contact and therefore have an extensive economic foundation in today's business-to-business direct marketing campaigns. Direct mail also has the advantage of offering a broad visual and graphic platform for messaging and personalization, although it is limited, as is trade paper advertising, to one-way communication that depends on persuasive copy.

Phone

The next most costly contact medium is the phone. Phone contact activity can be divided into three functional categories: (1) customer service, or the solving of customer problems; (2) inbound order taking, inquiry handling, and inquiry management; and (3) telemarketing, or the outbound proactive building and management of relationships, making of offers, and closing of sales.

These three categories have developed from a need for unique key performance measurements and a realization that there are three distinct behavioral profiles associated with these different functional skills. Although some success can be attained with skill training across these three categories, experience indicates that long-term satisfaction and optimal performance are achieved when the individual is matched with one of these three phone functions. This has caused considerable stress in some human resource departments because they do not focus on the function performed but rather on the contact medium used—the phone.

The primary advantage of the phone is that it provides the lowest-cost two-way dialog with the customer/prospect, a dialog permitting an exchange and sharing of information. Effective phone communications not only engage the individual, but they also modify the presentation of the product or service while gathering individual attribute information.

The phone contact medium is a targeted, broad-based, selectable medium. It functions at one-tenth to one-hundredth the cost of a field sales contact, and therefore in an integrated direct marketing campaign it offers high frequency of contact in support of the field sales rep. The primary

disadvantage of the phone contact medium is its lack of visual graphic and text prompts. However, tight integration with direct mail through measurement of deliverability and retention as well as concurrent faxing of material can improve the overall performance of the phone program. New industries developing around video conferencing and video phones will further enhance the performance of the phone contact medium.

Field Sales

The field sales contact is the most expensive contact medium. It has unique and unduplicated roles in the overall sales process. Certain aspects of interaction with customers—building trust and confidence, training, and on-site audits of activities—are much more difficult over the phone or through direct mail than they are in a face-to-face relationship. Also, independent observations that one can make when on site often elude the telemarketer. It is therefore economically imperative that the field sales contact focus on those value-based communications that have the highest perceived values as defined by the customer.

Applications of the integration of direct response media are given in the following two models. The first is a customer acquisition model used for acquiring and managing new customers (See Exhibit 6–5.) The second is a cultivation model used primarily for optimizing the sales and marketing expenditures necessary for the profitable retention of customers.

Customer Acquisition Model   The customer acquisition model assumes and requires that all leads are funneled together and that each have attached a source code indicating the ad, mailing, or other medium that generated the lead. This usually means that all leads are received and processed centrally, for consistency of lead handling and acquisition of attribute information. The economics of the qualification process also prompt lead generation over the phone so that the qualification process can begin while the inquirer is on the phone, making unnecessary the multiple callbacks otherwise required to establish contact with the inquirer. An incoming inquiry can be captured and profiled for $5 to $8, whereas an outbound phone contact may average three or four dialings per qualified lead at a cost two or three times higher.

Once a mail inquirer is registered in the database, phone contact is most appropriate before sending literature. This phone contact adds value to the customer by determining the appropriate literature to be sent, allowing for personalization of the cover letter with references to specific applications from the phone call, and reminding the prospect of the next scheduled follow-up call. This process improves both deliverability and retention of qualification material, which are the key performance measurements of the qualified-lead mailing response.

Exhibit 6–5. **Lead-Management System**

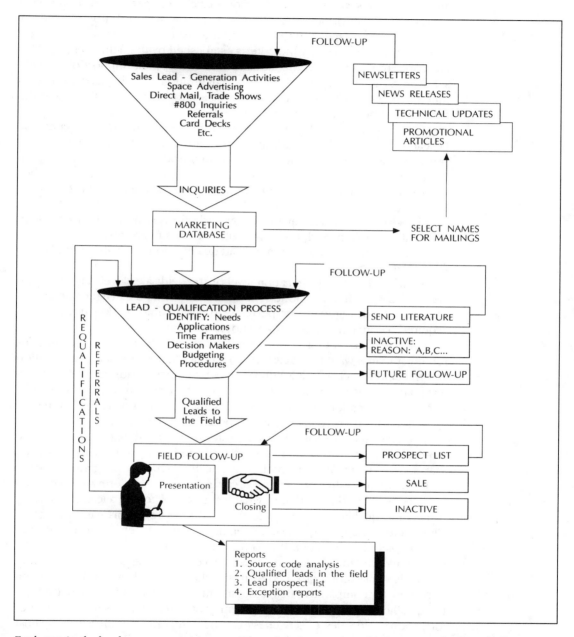

Each step in the lead-management process is based on interaction of information from multiple contact media.

Source: © Hunter Business Direct Inc.

The lead-qualification process, which includes the identification of needs and applications, time frames, decision makers, budgeting, and purchasing procedure, is performed over the phone and is supported by product or service literature, specification sheets, and testimonials. This qualification process must be driven by the criteria established by the field sales rep. This requirement is derived from a need for the enthusiastic support of the field sales representative as well as from the realization that the sales process is fundamentally a narrowing of the funnel around criteria that leverage the field sales effort to close the order.

The customer often has a preference for the sequence of contact media. Research and experience indicate that when being introduced to a new product, many persons prefer to receive an introductory mailing with application information relating to their work. Also, before a field sales visit, they like to talk on the phone and further determine the benefits of the product or service.

The closing of a sale can be accomplished over the phone or through the mail contact. Indeed, the entire sales process might take place within a direct marketing channel, although lead qualification is usually kept discrete from telephone sales.

At either the lead-qualification level or the field sales level, a lead may be requalified by mail and phone. The time line for action may not be appropriate for field follow-up, or perhaps additional information needs to be acquired before field sales contact should continue.

In the lead-generation contact plan, the expected qualified leads per sales rep must match what the sales rep can handle. At both the lead-qualification and the field sales levels, it is appropriate to make the leads inactive. This determination is accompanied by a reason for the inactivity as well as valuable attribute information. The inactive leads are now "turbo-charged" targeted prospects for other types of products or different time frames.

The closing of the sale allows the information on the actual value of the inquiry to revert to the original source of the inquiry and thereby validate that source as an ongoing part of the lead-generation program. An early indicator of the value of sources is calculated by considering the cost per qualified lead by source. That is, what is the cost of getting a lead (by source) to become qualified and to go to the field sales rep? This early indication allows initial fine tuning of lead-generation programs before the actual sales are completed in the field. It also provides an early confirmation of the assumptions used in the planning process to estimate the cost of acquisition.

Leads consistently qualified against field-generated qualification criteria also allow for comparative field assessments. Since all leads passing through the qualification process have a uniformity of potential and similar time lines for action, field sales effectiveness can be comparatively measured against group or national norms.

The evaluation of the sources of leads, the ability to qualify leads, and the measurement of the effectiveness of field sales closure are based on integrated information from several contact media.

Cultivation Model   The cultivation model (See Exhibit 6–6) optimizes the sales and marketing expenditures necessary for retention of customers. It determines the optimal mix of contact media to support different grades of existing customers. Experience shows that because of the wide range of costs per contact medium, traditional grading of accounts in an 80/20 split or A/B/C model is not sufficient to allow the optimal management of contact frequency in each medium. The model shown uses five grades to separate 1,000 buyer groups based on expected sales.

Exhibit 6–6.   **Customer Cultivation Requires a Contact Plan**

Grade/Sales ($000)	1,000=Buyer Groups	Mail Count	Phone Count	Field Count	Sales Cost ($000)	Percent of Sales
AA $60+	50	75 (3,750)	50 (2,500)	20 (1,000)	469	13.4
A $40 – $60	150	75 (11,250)	40 (6,000)	15 (2,250)	1,076	14.4
B $20 – $40	250	50 (12,500)	25 (6,250)	8 (2,000)	988	13.2
C $10 – $20	250	25 (6,250)	12 (3,000)	4 (1,000)	491	13.1
D < $10	300	25 (7,500)	10 (3,000)	1 (300)	218	14.5
Total contacts	68,550 =	41,250	+20,750	+6,550		
Average cost each	$47.28	$5.00	$20.00	$400.00		
Total cost ($000)	$3,241	$206	$415	$2,620		13.6

B Grade = $20,000–$40,000 expected sales
    = 250 accounts
    = 50 planned mailings = 12,500 for all B accounts
    = 25 planned phone accounts = 6,250 for all B accounts
    = 8 planned field contacts = 2,000 for all B accounts
    = $988,000 sales cost for B accounts (as above)
    = 13.2% of expected revenue for all B accounts

Source: © Hunter Business Direct Inc.

The cultivation model recognizes that selling and servicing a customer consists of a continuous stream of value-based contacts and that these contacts are traditionally made through direct mail, phone, or field rep presence. Furthermore, it recognizes that in each medium a disciplined approach in managing the frequency of contact to leverage higher-cost contacts, together with integration of all other contacts in a value-based campaign of supporting existing customers, will produce an optimal mix delivering the highest perceived value for the budgeted expense within each customer grade.

The higher frequency of lower-cost contacts, when related to higher perceived levels of service and increased revenue, can exist concurrently with lower overall cost of selling each customer grade. Note that the customer's

higher perceived level of service is more a function of frequency of contact than of type of contact.

The cultivation model delivers the highest value to each grade through the integration of response media and managing the frequency of contact within each medium so that the overall sales expense as a percentage of expected revenue is balanced across all grades of customers.

Business-to-Business Direct Marketing Objectives and Applications

In considering the primary applications for business-to-business direct marketing, we find there are seven categories of activities into which most marketing campaigns and marketing programs can be classified: (1) research, (2) using low-cost communication to target markets, (3) managing leads for sales reps and resellers, (4) closing sales, (5) directly leveraging the effectiveness of the sales rep, (6) cultivating accounts, and (7) retaining customers. These categories should be viewed not as mutually exclusive, but rather as vague groupings used for broadening the range for potential applications of direct marketing tools.

Research

There are three applications of research imbedded into the business-to-business direct marketing processes: (1) acquisition of attribute information necessary for target marketing; (2) customer satisfaction surveys, including both baseline and follow-up surveys focusing on customer retention and (3) identification of individual needs for the purpose of clustering prospects and developing successful offers.

Attribute Research   Attribute research deals with the acquisition and management of selectable data that can be attached to individuals, buyer groups, locations, or accounts. Since these attributes are captured for analysis or as selects, they must be tightly formatted and attached in an architecture that supports selection as well as the practical updating and maintenance of customer/prospect records.

Customer Satisfaction Research   Customer satisfaction research normally begins with a baseline survey indicating how well the company and its competitors are performing, in the eyes of its customers or prospects, against the company's primary drivers of business. The primary drivers of business are basic to the sustainable competitive advantage attempting to be established in the marketplace. The drivers are also critical to the customer in the differentiation of service providers.

The periodic resurveying of these business drivers gives continual feedback from the marketplace on the acceptability and effectiveness of the company's efforts in establishing differentiation. Recent quantitative research done by the TARP Association has indicated that customer satisfaction surveys can be very misleading and often are not tied directly to retention of customers long term. It is therefore critical that customer satisfaction surveys be designed appropriately and tied to the behavioral results desired in the marketplace. Goals must be developed to create profits through retention of customers, structured satisfaction surveys, use of economic models focusing on reorders, related products purchased, and referrals.

Need Assessment The third application of research is in need assessment. Here one is looking for an opportunity to identify unfulfilled needs of the customer/prospect universe. Those unfilled needs, when attached to individuals, allow for the clustering of those individuals into target markets where personalized and compelling offers can be constructed. The effectiveness of the compelling offer is based on the ability of the offer to meet unfulfilled needs as well as to produce a related risk of not acting. Targeting of the offer is directly related to the clarity of the need assessment research and the ability to cluster individuals with similar needs.

Using Low-Cost Communication to Target Markets

There are three groups of activities in this category: (1) education, (2) building traffic flow, and (3) generating leads. Obviously, the first two are often used in generating leads, but let's explore each separately.

Education To educate means to create goodwill, awareness, positioning, and understanding. In direct marketing, education adds value by providing knowledge to help individuals make informed decisions or reduce uncertainty. Although it is difficult to measure in a direct marketing process, education can provide a valuable foundation, predisposition, and differentiation leading to acceptance of the offer.

Building Traffic Flow Building traffic flow at exhibits, trade shows, seminars, and the like often leverages the presence of field salespeople. It is a very natural use of integrated direct mail and phone contacts to find prospects most likely to be interested in the event message and then to document a clearer understanding of the attendees' needs and perception of the products and services. This information is also often valuable in market research. Ideally, we would like to get the right people to come to a specific event. Once we have identified who will be attending, we can focus on pinpointing their needs and aligning the event and messages to meet those needs.

If possible, we would like to understand attendees' needs with enough clarity that we can collect background material and plan face-to-face meetings with individuals at the event. This type of pre-event contact can often lead to increased effectiveness of the event as well as to increased foot traffic.

Direct marketing also plays a very important role in event follow-up. A limited number of contacts will be prequalified and justify immediate field sales follow-up. Typically, the remaining attendees drop through the cracks. A majority of the attendees should be sorted into active or inactive status. Those active attendees are qualified over a period of time to determine whether they are in fact appropriate for future field follow-up. It is economically appropriate that specific communications, including literature and samples, be managed through a direct mail and phone follow-up system as additional qualification steps.

Both education and building traffic flow often are a part of a successful lead-generation program.

Generating Leads   The low-cost lead-generation activity is designed to have a broad reach in the marketplace, pulling together those people who may be predisposed to a product or service but who may not be in a position to buy. They may be collecting information and defining the requirements for a future purchase.

Low-cost lead-generation programs allow the creation of a database of both potential future customers and a more tightly defined group of qualified leads that will become sales opportunities in the short term. In successful lead-generation lead-management programs, each lead has a source code identifying the unique event that generated that lead. Thus each trade advertising insert, for example, has a unique key code associated with each publication date, and each lead-generation mailing has a unique key code by date of mailing. Source tracking then allows for economically fine-tuning the lead-generation process by tracking costs and revenues to their respective key codes.

Lead-generating activities are often used to reach deeply into a prospect universe for leads, build a direct marketing database, and create the foundation for customer acquisition.

Managing Leads for Sales Rep and Resellers

Managing leads using direct mail and phone contact is an economical way of collecting meaningful data for use in the sales process, sorting out those leads that are not economically justifiable for field sales contact, and then arming the sales rep with information to reduce the number of nonproductive accounts to be visited.

Being provided with qualified leads allows the sales rep to close sales with fewer contacts involved per account and in shorter periods of time. The quantity of qualified leads must be tied to the rate of flow for leads through the sales funnel.

The primary value of marketing programs in the lead-management category is in the economic assessment of lead sources and provision for comparative performance evaluations of field sales activity. Successful lead-management systems provide a sales funnel that helps to project sales volume and provide a higher quality of leads to the field.

As we will show later, acquiring the right type of customer (not just any customer) is critical to successful retention. Lead qualification helps in sorting out the *right* customer for a specific marketing program.

Many lead-management systems provide a closed-loop process in which all leads that come into the company go through the same funnel, are given a source code, and are evaluated in terms of the overall cost of generating a qualified lead that then goes on to the field.

Most companies realize that the effort required to close the loop in the field is simply neither practical nor economically justifiable. These companies have gone to sampling techniques whereby field closure is monitored through surveying specific qualified leads and/or matching order activity against a lead-qualification file.

Marketing programs in the lead-management category increase the productivity of the field sales effort by gathering meaningful account information for immediate closure of sales as well as for future selects and suppress files. Lead management provides a valuable quantifiable performance measurement of field performance and various sources of leads.

Closing Sales

A special application of direct marketing tools is the formation of a direct marketing sales channel. This is a channel of distribution in which the trade paper, direct mail, or phone contact is used to actually close the sale. This stand-alone sales channel has become more popular as economic pressures force manufacturers and distributors to find lower-cost methods of supporting marginal customers or penetrating new markets.

Within this group of activities are found direct marketing catalogs, solo mailings, fax ordering, and many other applications of direct marketing media tailored to the ordering process. Although this is only one of the seven major applications of direct marketing, it is becoming more popular because of its low cost, measurability, and easy order option.

These special low-cost stand-alone offers will continue to figure importantly in the overall business marketing strategy. Nevertheless, because they represent an end point in the cost continuum of integrated sales campaigns, these offers represent only one of many opportunities for the application of direct marketing tools to increasing sales productivity.

Directly Leveraging the Effectiveness of the Sales Rep

Business-to-business direct marketing has an opportunity to directly leverage the effectiveness of the field sales rep in his or her daily tasks and in following up on routine activities. Direct mail and phone contacts often

improve the effectiveness of appointment scheduling. Phone contacts prior to a field visit can often eliminate, manage, or resolve customer service and accounting problems, thereby providing a stronger foundation for the sales offer or strengthening the customer relationship by providing more timely resolution and recording of customer concerns.

A sales rep supported by an integrated sales process will realize that many follow-ups to a successful field visit can be completed through mail and phone contact initiated by other members of the sales team. This integrated follow-up and further cultivation of the relationship leads to even greater productivity and lower cost associated with the overall servicing of the account. Also, because of the team approach and easier access to the company, the customer is better satisfied.

An additional activity in support of leveraging the field sales rep is the carefully planned and well-supervised introduction of new sales reps. An integrated sales process will have created the complete contact record for each individual within an account, and this is managed in the marketing database. Since the contact history for each individual is a combination of mailings, phone contacts, and field contacts made with that individual, this history represents a shared responsibility in servicing and developing the account.

A new sales rep stepping into this environment finds that he has an immediate partner on the phone to assist in introductions. A wealth of database information relating to past contacts in specific accounts and with the individuals in those accounts can help prioritize new field sales calls and give more value to initial contacts. The ability to access relevant personal information about the individual customer helps to speed the assimilation of the new sales rep into his territory.

Tracking the amount of time it takes for a new sales rep to become effective in his territory can be difficult. It's often helpful to look at the number of field contacts per customer that are required to initiate new orders or to achieve a targeted order volume. It is then easy to determine that the elimination of one field sales contact per account and the subscription of a reasonable amount of phone and direct mail contact would be economically justified.

Using lower-cost phone and direct mail contacts to leverage higher-cost field sales contacts is at the heart of sales force productivity gains for the 1990s.

Cultivating Accounts

The process of cultivating accounts is aimed at increasing the value of those accounts. Each account, or corporate buying unit, can have multiple locations. Each location is identified by a street address, and each location potentially has multiple buyer groups or groupings of individuals with the same functional requirements.

A specific buyer group may be in sales, customer service, research, accounting, purchasing, or maintenance, for example, or it may be related to

a new product, production line, market, or technology. Each buyer group is made up of various individuals. An integrated marketing and sales program, then, cultivates accounts at multiple locations around purchases that are being made at any one of those locations. It also identifies the opportunity to sell products and services across different buyer groups located at the same street address. This cross-selling is often facilitated by referrals from existing customers and by specific application briefs that tell how products and services are being used to solve problems. (See Exhibit 6–7.)

An economic model can also be built by looking at increasing the recency and frequency of purchase by an individual or by a group within an account, and then leveraging that purchasing activity to new buyer groups and new locations within a corporate account.

Key performance measurements for this group of programs focus on the number of individuals at each street address who are buying, as well as on the breadth of product lines purchased by street address and the frequency of purchase.

Obviously, the integration of lower-cost phone and direct mail contacts into the overall sales process requires that the sales process be a documentable (in writing) process made up of value-based communications that are clearly understood and confirmed by the customer and delivered through the appropriate contact medium to provide the highest economic value for the least cost.

Another application of account cultivation is the servicing of the after-market in major product sales. This program usually involves selling supplies or services to support major equipment. Because of the direct tie to a large order, the low dollar value per transaction, and the frequency of purchase, these kinds of orders are naturals for direct order taking over the phone or through the mail.

Strong account-cultivation programs usually provide growth in revenue at lower cost than does acquisition of new accounts, and they also protect your account base from predators.

Retaining Customers

The primary demand for products and services that surged in the 1970s and 1980s was driven by the needs of the Baby Boomers. Those steep demand curves are now flattening out, and the market is defining new rules for profitability that are based on the retention of customers.

The TARP Association, in studying and analyzing direct marketing activities in the 1990s, focuses on profitability through retention of customers. Its work reveals that there are three primary quantifiable indicators that positively correlate to retention of customers: customer reorder, related purchase, and customer referral. To make the concept operational, we often work with individuals within buyer groups to focus on the group's overall behavior.

Exhibit 6–7.   **The Account Cube**

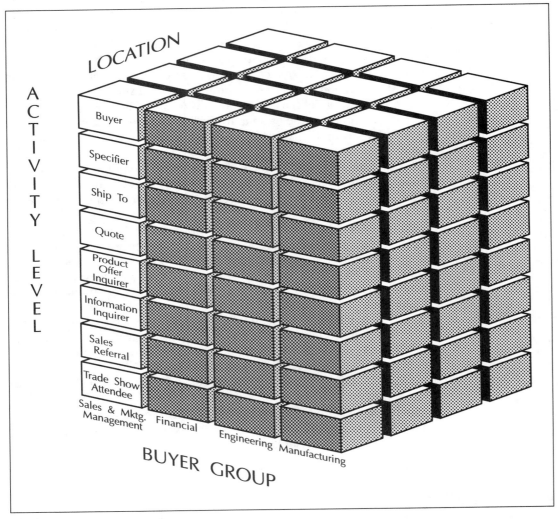

Account information architecture—individual within buyer group within location within account.

Source: © Hunter Business Direct Inc.

The TARP research further defines the economic value of retention of customers by using models based on identifying why customers become inactive. This modeling around the frequency and severity of each occurrence quantifies the impact on the three primary drivers of retention mentioned above. It is therefore possible to look at the economic impact of making various tactical changes in the relationship with the customer. These changes are most often brought about by disciplined targeted communications

executed through mail and phone contact, and supported by field sales presence when appropriate.

It is important to note that because retention management has profound effects on the lifetime value of a customer, it replaces control of acquisition costs as the key factor in customer profitablility.

The management of the customer relationship and in particular the embracing of customer problems offer opportunities to identify weaknesses in the retention strategy and areas in which perceived value might be enhanced. It is becoming increasingly important to maintain a positive relationship with the end-users, and purchasers of the products and services being sold.

It is no longer appropriate or possible for the successful manufacturer or provider of services to be isolated from the end-users by any channel partner. It is also critical that the reseller benefit from the sharing of end-user information.

The profitable retention of customers involves new types of channel partnering based on redefined roles and responsibilities of the manufacturer and the distributor. It will also call for a compelling respect for different customers' desires to purchase products, and to be served through various marketing arrangements. Successful marketing programs will modify their channel relationship to support the individual needs of the customer, recognizing that even within a single location individual purchasers and buyer groups may have requirements for different products and services.

An uncompromising and unselfish respect for the customer's needs will properly align the channel interest to service the customer and ultimately provide the highest profitability for all who are involved in the sale.

The optimal channel strategy for the retention of customers will extend the need for integration of information from manufacturing and primary service providers to channel partners, and it will share that information in a way that will support ongoing sales in a seamless relationship with the customer. (See Exhibits 6–8 and 6–9.)

Note that while customers do not have channel conflict, they have channel preferences and will behave accordingly. Successful service providers will focus on their customers' needs and adjust their channel strategies.

Amoco Tire Program

Situation

Although Amoco supplied an Atlas brand tire to its independent dealers (gas stations), many of these dealers chose to buy other national brands and/or purchase locally. Of the 2,900 stations with service bays and serviced directly by Amoco, 770 did not buy Atlas tires from Amoco. Field sales contacts were too costly to permit a national program. Penetration of the tire market was declining despite seasonal promotions, a major new tire line introduction, and annual volume discounts.

Exhibit 6–8.   **Why Annual Profits Increase throughout Customer Life**

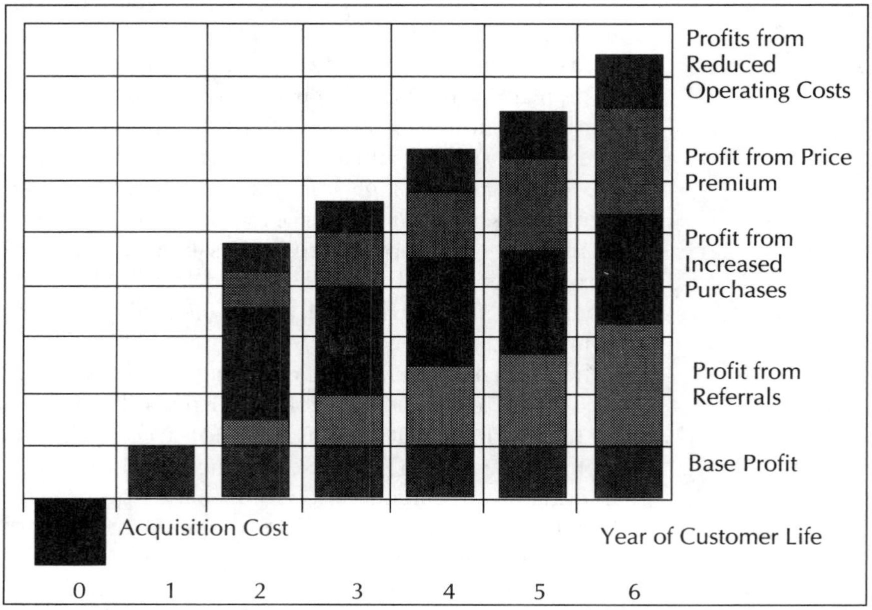

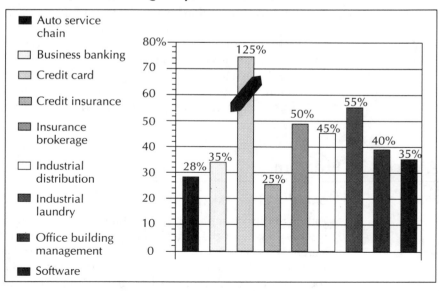

Source: Baines, © Hunter Business Direct Inc.

Exhibit 6–9.   **Service Quality**

Profit Impact of a 5 percent Retention Rate Increase.

Source: Baines, © Hunter Business Direct Inc.

Objective

The objective of the program was to place Atlas tires from Amoco with 50 new dealers, and to roll these new dealers over into active tire dealers in subsequent years.

Program

A "New Tire Dealer" program was designed with special introductory pricing and point-of-purchase support. The offer was mailed to the 770 stations not active in Atlas tires, extending an invitation to respond by calling an 800 number. A second mailing was made to nonrespondents in 14 days, making the same offer and mentioning that a tele-sales rep would call and talk with the dealer the following week. Tele-sales reps called all targeted dealers, answered questions, generated and qualified leads, sold the "New Tire Dealer" package, and scheduled the field sales rep for deal closing (if required) and on-site training. Newly acquired dealers were graded based on expected revenue, and the frequency was set for integrated direct mail, phone, and field contacts.

Measurements

	Goal	Actual
New Dealer	50	115
Program dollars sold		
First full-year revenue		
Cost		

Conclusion

A customer information center can provide the operational support for these integrated marketing campaigns. A new focus on the customer and ease of doing business lead to higher levels of customer involvement in new opportunities to deliver value and profit. (See Exhibit 6–10.)

In summary, business-to-business direct marketing, once undisciplined and unmeasured, is emerging into a database-driven discipline that focuses on the customer and supports all channels of distribution.

Exhibit 6–10.   **Customer Information Center**

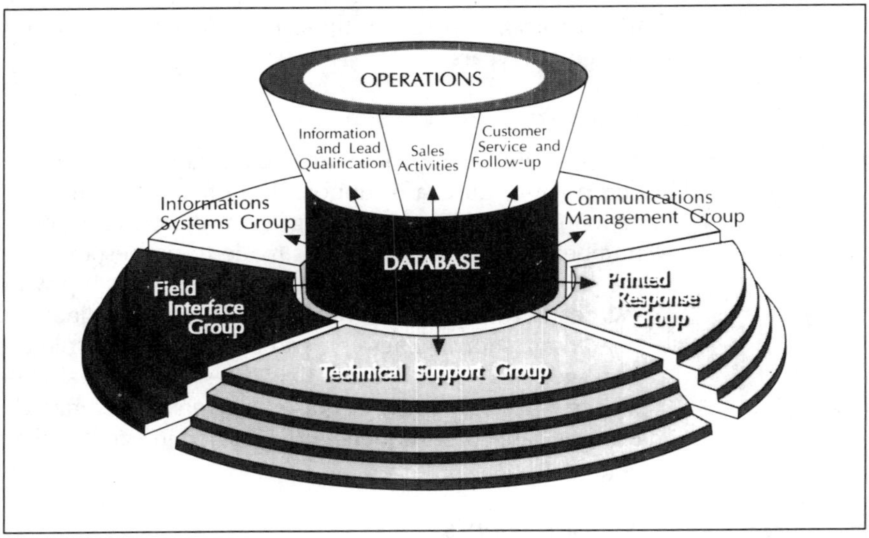

Source: © Hunter Business Direct Inc.

Self-Quiz

1. Business-to-business direct marketing addresses its offer to:
   ☐ Corporations   ☐ Locations   ☐ Individuals

2. The two primary drivers for growth of business-to-business direct marketing in the 1990s are:

   a. _____

   b. _____

3. Integrated direct marketing refers to the integration of trade paper advertising, _____, _____, and field sales.

4. Direct marketing objectives are best met by the following organizational structure:
   ☐ Product   ☐ Function   ☐ Customer

5. The lowest-cost direct response medium for dialog is _____.

6. All direct marketing applications fall into two categories:

   a. Customer _____

   b. Customer _____

7. There are seven basic applications of business-to business direct marketing:

a. _____

b. _____

c. _____

d. _____

e. _____

f. _____

g. _____

8. Which of the applications in No. 7 will be most closely linked to profitability in the 1990s?

_____

9. The customer information center can provide _____ _____ for integrated marketing campaigns.

Pilot Project

You work for a national marketer of high-powered desktop computers. Through your strategic alliances with software manufacturers, you have developed and installed many specialty application packages. Product differentiation is becoming more difficult and margins are declining.

The president of the company invites you to a management briefing to explain specific applications of direct marketing to your business. She also wants to know where you would begin implementation. Your presentation should include answers to the following questions:

- What is business-to-business direct marketing ?
- Why is it growing?
- We have always been a product-focused company. Is this a problem?
- Why integrate direct marketing with field sales?
- For our company, what are examples of direct marketing programs or campaigns for each of the seven basic applications?
- What do we need to do first, and why?

CHAPTER SEVEN

Fund-raising for Worthy Causes

Few people associate fund-raising with direct marketing. But the fact is that fund-raising is a major part of the total scope of direct marketing. Estimates are that well over $40 billion is raised each year for philanthropic organizations alone. This staggering figure does not include multimillions raised for worthy business-related causes.

Corporate America is sympathetic to worthy causes, both philanthropic and business-related. As a matter of fact, scores of major corporations insist that their top executives become actively engaged in local and national causes.

The contributions that executives with direct marketing know-how can make to fund-raising efforts can be phenomenal. Facing the sad fact that most fund-raising efforts are inept in the hands of well-intentioned amateurs increases the importance of applying direct marketing know-how.

Fund-raising Basics

The classic way to raise funds for a worthy cause is to take a three-step approach:

1. Form a committee of influentials with the charge to make face-to-face contacts with potential large contributors, establishing a targeted contribution amount for each potential donor.

2. Mount a direct mail campaign to an identified prospect list (database) of potential contributors.

3. Organize a phone campaign either in support of the direct mail campaign and/or directed to those who have not responded to the direct mail campaign.

This is the classic three-step approach, but the following basic facts are also in order:

1. Direct mail is now the primary fund-raising method used by nonprofit organizations, accounting for about one-third of all dollars contributed.

2. The highest percentage of response in a fund-raising effort comes from previous contributors.

3. The cost of direct mail in ratio to dollars raised can range from a very low percentage—3 percent to 5 percent, for example—for mailings to a select list of previous donors to 100 percent and more for mailings to people who have never contributed before.

4. Favorable response to phone solicitations usually can be enhanced when calls are made by people of stature in a community or in an industry.

5. It generally is agreed that people respond best to emotional appeals when they are backed by a rationale for giving.

6. People tend to respond more readily to appeals for specific projects rather than to appeals for general needs. Example: "Will you help us to raise $92,000 so we can give Braille books to the blind?"

7. When pledges are made by phone, it can be expected that 75 percent to 80 percent of the pledges will be collected, if they are properly followed up.

8. When a phone campaign is handled properly using selected lists, the pledge rate can be as much as 10 to 12 times that of direct mail.

9. The average contribution tends to increase when specific contribution amounts are suggested. Example: "You contributed $20 last year. May we suggest you contribute $25 this year to help our expanded needs."

10. Total amount pledged tends to be greater when a multipayment plan is offered.

11. Setting a specific date for meeting a fund-raising goal tends to increase response and total contributions.

The Mathematics of Fund-raising

The uninitiated in fund-raising often criticize philanthrophic organizations for spending a major portion of their money received from contributions on mailing efforts to get new donors. In most instances this criticism reflects sincere ignorance about the mathematics of fund-raising. Investing in new donors, when done right, produces a substantial return on investment.

In a remarkable book entitled *Billions by Mail*[1], Francis S. Andrews, chairman of American Fund Raising Services Inc., Waltham, Massachusetts, provides all the evidence one would need to prove the validity of investing in new donors. Here, from his book, is what "Andy" Andrews has to say about investing in new donors.

Investment Method of Fund-raising

Just as an investor is interested in the net income he will receive over the useful life of his asset, an institution measures its return on donor investment by the amount of net income it receives over the life of a donor.

Investment portfolio managers can invest an institution's funds in a broad-based list of stocks and bonds, with a substantial element of risk, and secure annual yields ranging from 5% to 20%.

Fund-raising managers can invest an institution's funds in a broad-based list of contributors, with *no* risk, and secure annual yields ranging from 50% to 200%.

An investment in new donors is self-financing. Within 90 to 120 days, often earlier, the total "investment" needed to establish a donor list will be returned to the bank.

Investing in a large donor base is one of the fastest and surest ways of pyramiding capital.

The donor investment process calls for a systematic screening of "mass" mailing lists in search of those families who are willing to support an organization with a continuing series of annual and special gifts.

Donor acquisition carries a high initial commitment of cash or credit. Only a small fraction of all families solicited can be attracted as donors in one year. These percentages range from 1% to 5%, depending on the popularity of the institution or cause. However, over a period of 5 to 10 years, total penetration can grow to 10% or 20% of the total family universe.

The degree of possible penetration is dependent on the socioeconomic mix of the population and the duration and intensity of the fund-raising effort.

The economic justification for direct mail donor investment rests on the premise that a new donor is an investment in future income. Otherwise, such an investment would be classified as an unwarranted churning of institutional dollars.

A lifetime of philanthropy adds up to an impressive return on original investment. If this were not the case, there would be little justification for soliciting new donors or members at costs which sometimes exceed the value of the first friendship gift.

[1] Published by Tabor Oaks, P.O. Box 637, Lincoln, MA 01773, 1987.

Annual giving and membership programs are analogous to a business investment. They are made not for today but for the future. And, since donor income is reliable and predictable, this puts donor investment way ahead of the vagaries of Wall Street.

Lifetime Cumulative Gift

Donors acquired by mail, cultivated by mail, and renewed by mail will contribute in a consistent pattern over a long period of years.

A donor base represents a significant source of income for a nonprofit organization.

The long-term value of a donor was first verified by a ten-year computerized research study conducted by American Fund Raising Services for the Massachusetts General Hospital.

The MGH, one of the major research–teaching hospitals, agreed to cooperate in a decade-long project to document the giving habits of donors.

A computerized fund-raising system, the first for hospitals, was designed and programmed. The system made it possible to retrieve information such as year of first gifts, annual gift, cumulative gift, and mail code. Lost or deceased donors were assigned bypass codes and retained in the system to keep all original donor groups intact for the period of the study.

Changes of address were carefully handled and an intensive investigation of each "loss" was made to assure that all records were maintained perfectly during the life of the study.

Contributors of $500 or more were removed from the general file and set up on a major donor list for special development and tracking.

The results of this *10-Year History of Annual Giving, Massachusetts General Hospital, 1963–1973*, are shown on page 172.

Separate records were kept for each year's donor group. The example shown in this book is for donors acquired in the 1963–64 fund-raising year. That first year, 3,396 new donors contributed a total of $85,806, with an average gift of $25.27.

At the end of ten years, the "class of 63–64" had contributed $831,761. This total was for annual giving only. The hospital estimated, based on its own tracking of major gifts and bequests, that more than $1 million also came in from special gifts.

No investment portfolio would have returned an equal annual income or appreciation of original capital.

Over the ten-year period, a base of more than 175,000 donors was built from annual mailings to Massachusetts families. At the peak of the program, more than $1,000,000 in net income was received annually.

The table reveals some interesting facts about donor renewal rates in the 1960s. First, there is a sizeable drop-off in the renewal rate— from 100% to 56.1%. Second, once the initial drop has taken place,

normal attrition takes over. Third, the average gift tends to increase over the years, cancelling out the decline in rate.

If 44% of the original donor base did not repeat in the first renewal year, does this mean that these donors were lost forever?

The *Study of Lifetime Contributing Patterns, Massachusetts General Hospital—1962–1972*, shown on page 173 answers this question.

This study reveals a remarkable degree of donor loyalty. Eleven years after acquisition, only 6 percent of the original donor group had given just one gift. Forty-three percent had given nine or more gifts and 52 percent had given eight or more gifts.

Massachusetts General Hospital
10-Year History of Annual Giving
1963–1973

Research Project

Officers and directors of the Massachusetts General Hospital, embarking on a major direct mail program which involved a considerable investment in the building of a donor base, wished to confirm the fact that such an investment was a prudent use of funds. American Fund Raising Services was engaged to conduct a long-term project to document the long-term value of new donor acquisitions. The table below traces the contributing records of donors whose first gift was received in 1963 and for nine years thereafter.

Research Results

Year	Number of Donors	Renewal Percentage	Yearly Contributions	Cumulative Gift Totals
1963–64	3,396	100	$ 85,806	—
1964–65	1,905	56.1	78,252	$164,058
1965–66	1,927	56.7	107,095	217,153
1966–67	1,847	54.4	92,388	363,541
1967–68	1,790	52.7	96,656	460,197
1968–69	1,708	50.2	94,697	554,894
1969–70	1,482	43.6	96,380	651,274
1970–71	1,214	35.7	65,411	716,685
1971–72	1,177	34.7	69,272	785,957
1972–73	1,040	30.6	45,804	831,761

Conclusion

More than 175,000 donors were included in the 10-year research project which established the wisdom of investing in a base of donors whose annual

gifts equaled the return on a multimillion dollar endowment. The tabulation shows the performance of only one donor group—those acquired in 1963–64. A similar tabulation, with similar results, was maintained for all new donors. Here, the small group of only 3,396 new donors, contributing $85,806 in their first renewal year, eventually contributed $831,761 to annual giving campaigns over 10 years.

Massachusetts General Hospital Study of Lifetime Contributing Patterns 1962–1972

Research Project

Proof of donor loyalty had not been documented in 1962 when the Massachusetts General Hospital commissioned American Fund Raising Services to conduct a computerized study of long-term donor contributing patterns. This study was a by-product of the *10-Year History of Annual Giving*. The necessity for a donor loyalty study was the unsettling contention among some that half of all new donors are lost in the first renewal year, presumably forever. This study, conducted under strict research standards, would confirm or deny this alleged high loss among new donors.

Research Results

First Gift	One Gift	Two Gift	Three Gift	Four Gift	Five Gift	Six Gift	Seven Gift	Eight Gift	Nine Gift	Ten Gift	Eleven Gift
1972	100%										
1971	54	46%									
1970	39	26	35%								
1969	33	20	18	29%							
1968	29	19	16	15	21%						
1967	28	18	14	12	16	12%					
1966	25	16	13	13	10	11	12%				
1965	23	16	12	11	10	9	9	9%			
1964	20	13	11	11	10	8	8	8	11%		
1963	16	10	9	9	8	9	9	9	9	12%	
1962	6	5	6	7	7	8	9	9	11	14	18%

Conclusion

This research project established the fact that the first-year "drop-off" of approximately 50 percent does not represent a permanent loss of support. On the contrary, the study proved the exceptional loyalty of newly acquired donors. Ten years after acquisition, only six percent of the original donor

group had given one gift only. Unlike membership groups where a non-renewing member cuts his ties with a group, contributors to annual appeals give on an irregular basis.

Educational Foundation Campaign

More often than not, business executives get involved in a fund-raising program when their trade association identifies a worthy industry effort for which funds are required over and above funds normally generated from members.

Such was the case a few years ago with the Direct Mail/Marketing Educational Foundation. Annual income from members covered the cost of bringing college students—all expenses paid—to the Lewis Kleid Institute twice each year. But the foundation had a much larger goal: to establish direct marketing degree programs at three major universities.

For this goal, the foundation had no funds. And it was calculated that it would be necessary to raise a capital fund of $1.2 million to underwrite the program—a tremendous task.

How did the foundation organize to reach its ambitious goal? It followed the classic three-step approach.

1. It formed a committee of influential people to make person-to-person approaches with major organizations having a vested interest in direct marketing, organizations capable of pledging $15,000 to $30,000 and more over three years.
2. It developed a mailing package to go to the 2,400 members of the Direct Marketing Association, all of whom also had a vested interest in the future of direct marketing.
3. It made arrangements with CCI, a leading telemarketing agency, to phone all members who did not pledge as a result of person-to-person contact or as a result of the direct-mail effort.

The letter—a six-pager—and pledge card are shown in Exhibit 7–1. Much of the story behind the fund-raising effort is told in the letter, as you will see.

A couple of comments about the letter and pledge card before we talk about the telephone campaign: First, most neophytes would be aghast at a five-page letter; but the fact is that no letter is too long if written to the interest of the reader.

Second, the letter encouraged pledges by telling what the reader's peer group had already pledged, confirming the acceptance of the worthy goal. And finally, the letter had a sense of urgency—"We must decide very soon upon the first university to establish a Direct Marketing Center."

The pledge card employed two fund-raising principles: (1) Pledges will be larger if they are spread over time (three years in this case), and (2)

Exhibit 7–1. **Educational Foundation Mailing**

STONE & ADLER INC.

150 NORTH WACKER DRIVE
CHICAGO, ILLINOIS 60606
(312) 346-6100

Mr. Jerry Greenberg
The Finals
149 Mercer Street
New York, New York 10012

Dear Mr. Greenberg,

Remember when you were a kid. A "dreamer" was put down as someone who would never amount to anything—destined to be a "non-achiever" for life.

What a myth!

Let me tell you about some "dreamers" who became super achievers in direct marketing. They succeeded beyond their wildest dreams.

There's the thrilling story of L. L. Bean in Maine. For years they ran a successful mail order business...catering to outdoorsmen.

But Leon Gorman dreamed of new horizons...a new world out there of men and women who never fished or hunted—dressed the way outdoors people dress. A pipe dream? Hardly, Leon Gorman turned dream to reality. Sales—plateaued at the $50 million level—boomed past the $100 million level in a few short years.

What about the legendary "kitchen table" people? Len Carlson, out in California, is a part of the legend.

(Continued)

Exhibit 7–1 (*Continued*). **Educational Foundation Mailing**

Len and his wife Gloria shared a dream. They dreamed they
could put together a catalog of hard-to-find gadgets that
would appeal to the masses. Thus Sunset House was born.

Fifteen years and a customer base of 6.5 million names
later, the press announced Sunset House had been acquired
by a major corporation for a price reported to be in the
millions.

The most remarkable dream story on the agency side is that
of Lester Wunderman. Les was an account person with the
Max Sackheim agency. He dreamed of having his own agency.

But an agency that would apply sophisticated direct response
techniques to all media—including a "new" medium called
television. Today his firm—Wunderman, Ricotta & Kline—
has billings in excess of $100 million, with offices in New
York and 12 foreign countries.

As you read of these dreams-come-true I hope you are recall-
ing your own. The dreams you have had which have helped you
to get to where you are today.

> But of all the dreams-come-true which I have
> witnessed over the years there is one which
> supersedes all others. A dream-come-true
> which has touched all our lives, a dream
> which will live on beyond our lifetimes.

The year was 1965. Lewis Kleid, a leading list broker in
his day, was a close friend of Edward N. Mayer, Jr., known
around the world as "Mr. Direct Mail."

Lew made a proposition to Ed. He said, "Ed—if you will
devote time to teaching the rudiments of direct marketing to
college kids, I'll provide the seed money to make it happen."

Thus, with the simplicity that was a trademark of Ed Mayer,
the Lewis Kleid Institute was launched. Today, almost 17
years later, The Direct Mail/Marketing Educational
Foundation, a non-profit organization which sponsors Kleid
Institutes, continues in the Ed Mayer image.

Exhibit 7–1 (*Continued*).   **Educational Foundation Mailing**

Over the past 17 years over 1,000 bright college students have taken the 5-day intensive course, sponsored by the Foundation ...all expenses paid. It is estimated that over 50% of these students have entered into a direct marketing career.

As one of the privileged few who has had the honor of lecturing each new group of candidates over many years—I only wish you could witness, as I have, the excitement that comes to each as they are introduced to the wonders of direct marketing disciplines.

"I learned more in five days than in my four years as a marketing major," is a somewhat typical statement from one of these exuberant students.

But let me give you just a few quotes from hundreds in file.

"I learned so very much—the week just set my spark for direct marketing into a big roaring fire!"

> Marilee Gibson
> Yorchak
> New Mexico State
> University

"The Institute has greatly increased my awareness and understanding of direct marketing, and furthered my career interest."

> Tim Harrison
> University of North
> Carolina

"If one of your objectives was to stimulate young, ambitious people to enter your field, you succeeded with me."

> Paula Miante
> College of William and
> Mary

(*Continued*)

Exhibit 7–1 (*Continued*).   Educational Foundation Mailing

I guess from all of this one would have to conclude our dream
has truly come true. Well—not exactly.

None of us ever dreamed that direct marketing would have the
explosive growth we have all experienced. (As an aside—
when I wrote my first book I trumpeted that total sales of
goods and services via the direct marketing method had reached
the staggering figure of $300 million. The estimated figure
for 1981 is $120 *billion!*)

So now we realize that if our true dream is to be realized—
growing our own at the college level to people our future
growth—we are going to have to raise our sights beyond the
far horizon.

Where we are bringing the gifted student to the Institute—
only one each from about 35 colleges twice each year—we've
got to get Direct Marketing taught on the college campus in
full semester courses. Not to three score and ten for five
days. Instead—to hundreds for full semesters.

Is this "The Impossible Dream"? No!

I'm going to tell you about what some regard to be an
emerging "miracle," which is in the process of happening as
I pen this letter.

At a Board of Directors meeting a few months ago in the
offices of The Direct Mail/Marketing Educational Foundation,
Richard L. Montesi, President, made a startling proposal.
A proposal which he stated would make our ultimate dream
come true.

The ultimate dream, as he expressed it, is to establish a
Chair for a Direct Marketing Center in three major universities: one in the Middle West; one in the East; and one in the West.

The full-scale curriculums will be structured to earn a
degree in Direct Marketing for each graduate, carrying with
them a stature similar to that enjoyed by a graduate from
the Wharton School of Business or Harvard Business School.

Exhibit 7–1 (*Continued*).   **Educational Foundation Mailing**

"An exciting idea," we said. "But how are we going to fund these centers?" "From a capital fund of $1.2 million," Dick said. "$1.2 million. Good God!" was the reaction.

Well then the miracle started happening. Andy Andrews, one of the directors, said—"Why don't we go around the table right now and see how much commitment we can get over the next three years from the small group of directors at this table?"

Would you believe we raised $120,000.00—10% of our goal—within five minutes!

When we left that day a few of us agreed to write some letters and make some phone calls. And what happened as a result surpasses anything in my experience.

Remember those "dreamers" I talked about earlier? Well let me tell you what happened with some of them.

Remember Leon Gorman of L. L. Bean? He's committed $15,000 over three years. And Len Carlson—another $15,000. And Les Wunderman—$15,000. They're putting their money where their dreams are.

The list goes on. "Dusty" Loo of Looart Press—a major commitment. John Flieder of Allstate Insurance—"Count us in." Kiplinger Washington Editors. The Kleid Company. Jim Kobs of Kobs & Brady—"Absolutely!" Publishers Clearing House. Grolier. Colonial Penn. Rodale Press. Spiegel. American Express.

John Yeck of Yeck Brothers Group—"You can count on us." Eddie Bauer. Rapp & Collins. Ogilvy & Mather. Alan Drey. The DR Group. Hanover House. And on and on.

> To this moment, these people and some others we have contacted bring total commitments to $725,000. So we have reached 60% of our goal!

Exhibit 7–1 (*Continued*).   **Educational Foundation Mailing**

This is exciting in itself, but equally exciting is the
fact that we have two formal proposals from two major
universities detailing how a Chair would be established
for Direct Marketing. And the cost.

One proposal is from UMKC—University of Missouri, where
Martin Baier of Old American has taught Direct Marketing
classes for a number of years. The other proposal is from
New York University. Both universities are ready when we are.

So we are this close to bringing off a 20th Century miracle!

Now we come to you to ask you to share in this dream of
dreams. There is a pledge card inside of the enclosed envelope. The amount suggested is just that. A suggestion. You
are the best judge of what your company should pledge against
the future.

I have asked for and have gotten approval to have your
response come back to me personally. I'd like to hear from
you even if there is some unforeseen circumstance under which
you cannot make a pledge.

We must decide very soon upon the first university to
establish a Direct Marketing Center. Therefore I will
appreciate it if you will reply within the next 10 days.
Thank you so very much.

Sincerely,

Bob Stone

P.S. It is my fondest dream that you and I will be
there to witness the commencement exercises of
the first graduating class with a degree in
Direct Marketing.

Exhibit 7–1 (*Continued*).   **Educational Foundation Mailing**

"A Margin of Excellence"

THE DIRECT MAIL/MARKETING EDUCATIONAL FOUNDATION
CAPITAL FUND RAISING PROGRAM

Our organization wishes to participate in the DMMEF Capital Fund Raising Program. Our 3-YEAR PLEDGE is indicated to the right.

Company _____

Officer Name _____

Address _____

Signature _____

YOUR TAX DEDUCTIBLE GIFT WILL MAKE A DIFFERENCE

Contribution Category		Payment Schedule
☐ Leadership Gift $10,000 annually $_____		payable by July 15
☐ Major Gift $5,000 annually $_____		payable by
☐ Special Gift $2,500 annually $_____		payable by
☐ Supporting Gift $1,000 annually		

Pledges are for three years only and are nonbinding commitments. Reminders will be mailed thirty days prior to the payment dates indicated above.

---

suggesting a specific amount (amounts suggested were in ratio to the dues a member paid) improves the chances of a pledge in that amount.

The mailing package was a huge success. Only a handful of those who responded favorably pledged less than the requested amount. But the foundation was still short of its goal. And this is where telemarketing techniques put the campaign over the top.

The Telemarketing Program

The strategy for the telephone effort was developed by the late Murray Roman, founder of Campaign Communications Institute, a pioneer in telemarketing. He first reviewed the membership prospect list, eliminating those who had already pledged, and then selected from those remaining the ones he considered most likely for phone solicitation.

This list agreed upon, he then prepared a script for a taped message from Bob DeLay, president of the Direct Marketing Association, and Bob Stone, chairman of Stone & Adler Inc. The taping completed, his agency started making calls within a few days.

The procedure was for the CCI phone communicator to ask the prospect permission to play a taped message from Bob DeLay and Bob Stone. The taped message follows:

> BOB DE LAY: This is Bob De Lay. I am asking that you take a few minutes to hear Bob Stone and me talk about an industry opportunity

that depends so much on your good will and support. We are talking to you on tape via telephone to be sure you personally get our message and because we like to reach our members as quickly as possible while there is still time for decision making. But here is Bob Stone to tell you more about that opportunity.

BOB STONE: Thanks, Bob. I really appreciate your kindness in allowing me time to bring you up to date on the progress that has been made in the Educational Foundation fund-raising drive. One word that I think describes the progress best is *terrific*!

It's amazing to me that in the most trying of times direct marketers of all sizes across the nation have responded so favorably. This has convinced me that our objective of growing our own talent is absolutely right. I have seen many pledges come through for $15,000, many for $7,500, and scores for $3,000. On the other hand, one company contributed $30,000 and another $52,000.

These major contributions are great but some of the smaller pledges have thrilled me the most. One was from a 24-year old by the name of Michael Gersen who said, "At age 24, recently experiencing the lack of specialization in our university system, I feel your dreams and the steps you have taken are of the utmost importance. I am not in a position to commit an annual gift; however, I would very much like to show my support with the enclosed contribution." And enclosed was his personal check in the amount of $50. Isn't that great?

So here's where we are at this point in time. We are approaching the $900,000 mark with a little over $300,000 to go. To fall short of our goal now, to fail to educate the talent we will need in the future would be tragic.

As I said in my letter to you, the amount of the pledge suggested was just that—a suggestion. I am going to ask the telephone communicator to repeat the suggested pledge for you in a moment.

Let me say, whatever amount you consider adequate from your standpoint will be a profitable investment in the future. And what a great day it will be for you and me and everyone else in direct marketing when we see bright young talent graduating with B.A.s and M.B.A.s in direct marketing. Then our futures will indeed be secure. Thank you for listening.

Upon completing the playing of the taped messages, the CCI phone communicator came back on the line and asked for a three-year pledge in the exact amount suggested in the mailing piece. Results were astounding: 18 percent of those called made a pledge. The campaign went over the top.

So here is a classic example of putting the three-step approach into practice. The person-to-person phase raised $725,000; the direct mail/phone phase raised $505,000. Grand total: $1,230,000—all from 2,400 prospects!

Fund-raising Campaign of the Light Opera Works

There are literally thousands of struggling theater groups and performing arts groups in the United States that are faced with a common problem: The comparatively modest prices they charge for tickets is not sufficient to cover the total costs of producing plays, musicals, and operas.

The Light Opera Works of Evanston, Illinois, is no exception: Its ticket sales cover only about 65 percent of its total costs. How does the organization raise the difference? Through professional fund-raising.

The Light Opera Works is fortunate to have a very generous patron— G. Todd Hunt, who is president of his own direct marketing agency. His efforts have made the Light Opera Works a thriving group.

Commenting on his work for the Light Opera Works, Todd states:

> For Light Opera Works, an opera company in suburban Chicago, fund-raising is closely tied in with ticket sales.
>
> That's because people who are most likely to contribute are those who attend the productions (ticket buyers).
>
> And the most committed ticket buyers are the *subscribers*, who purchase the entire three-show season package in advance.
>
> Therefore, most fund-raising energy and budget is directed at this target.

The most important effort is the renewal package, which urges existing subscribers to renew their season tickets for another year. It also emphasizes the need for additional contributions above and beyond the ticket price. (See Exhibit 7–2.)

The second most effective appeal is the preseason appeal. This appeal is sent to subscribers two weeks before the season's opening production. Copy is tailored to three segments:

1. Subscribers who have already given at least once in the current year.

2. Subscribers who have given in past years but who have not yet contributed in the current year.

3. Subscribers who have never given.

The mailing consists of an outer envelope, a reply card (with suggested contribution amounts tailored to each person's contribution history), a letter from the managing director, a brochure detailing the perks for various gift amounts, and a reply envelope. (Exhibit 7–3 presents the letter and reply card.)

These fund-raising efforts are obviously professional. But were they successful? Yes. Total contributions came to $39,372. Expenses were $7,148. Therefore the contribution/expense ratio was 548 percent.

Exhibit 7–2.   **Subscribers Renewal Mailing**

Fill out your enclosed pink SUBSCRIBER RENEWAL INVOICE and mail it now to get your subscriber savings and priority ...

ADVISORY BOARD

The Honorable Joan Barr
Mayor, City of Evanston
Honorary Chairman, Advisory Board

Richard Alderson
Professor of Voice and Opera,
Northwestern University

Margaret Hillis
Director, Chicago Symphony Chorus

Joseph Lederleitner
General Counsel

Tom Peck
Director, Grant Park Symphony Chorus
St. Louis Symphony Chorus

Marty Robinson
Chief Announcer, WTTW Channel 11

William R.T. Smith
W.R.T. Smith & Co.

Thomas C. Willis
Concert Manager,
Northwestern University
Former Music Critic,
Chicago Tribune

BOARD OF DIRECTORS

John Auwaerter
Harry Clamor
Lawrence E. Freeman
Jonathan Geen
Philip A. Kraus
Estelle Kriv
Bridget McDonough

STAFF

Philip A. Kraus
ARTISTIC DIRECTOR

Bridget McDonough
MANAGING DIRECTOR

Tim Pleiman
BUSINESS MANAGER

Dear Subscriber,

I'm so happy to share with you the exciting plans for LIGHT OPERA WORKS' 12th season in 1992.

But before I do, let's take a quick review of our season just ending...

<u>Bitter Sweet</u> (June 1991), our first Noël Coward piece, was well received by lovers of Viennese operetta and Broadway musicals alike. (Will you ever get "I'll See You Again" out of your mind?)

<u>The Beggar Student</u> (August 1991) was our first operetta by Millöcker. And judging from your favorable comments, we will definitely look at other works by this master in the future.

<u>The Red Mill</u> began rehearsals this week, and I'm happy to report that guest director M. Seth Reines is putting together an old-fashioned smash! You'll love the old vaudeville routines and, of course, those wonderful songs.

NOW FOR THE 1992 SEASON.   AND WHAT A SEASON!

We'll begin in June with a jewel by Oscar Straus,

        A WALTZ DREAM

This Viennese confection is from the pen of the man who wrote <u>The Chocolate Soldier</u>, one of our greatest successes in 1987. You can be sure there won't be a ticket to be had once this show opens.

Then in August you will see the rarely-produced Gilbert and Sullivan work,

        THE GRAND DUKE

We call it Monty Python meets G&S, because it's a wild plot that almost defies description. Read the

LIGHT OPERA WORKS
Illinois' only professional light opera company
A not-for-profit organization

927 Noyes Street • Evanston, Illinois 60201-2799 • (708) 869-6300

Two-page letter to existing subscribers as part of mailing package soliciting renewals and additional contributions above and beyond the ticket price.

Exhibit 7–2 (*Continued*).   **Subscribers Renewal Mailing**

enclosed brochure and you'll see what we mean.

Finally, on New Year's weekend 1992, you'll enjoy that
Broadway chestnut by Kurt Weill,

     KNICKERBOCKER HOLIDAY

This is the show that gave us "September Song," in a score
filled with wit and sophistication.

Quite a line-up, isn't it?

And tickets will be harder than ever to come by -- except
for subscribers (our very favorite people!).

When you renew your subscription now, you are <u>guaranteed</u>
your same seats and series. And if you want to <u>upgrade</u> or
make other changes, you will receive priority <u>as long as
you renew before February 14</u>.

> Your pink SUBSCRIBER RENEWAL INVOICE enclosed
> lists the seats and series you had for 1991.
> If you want everything the same for 1992,
> just check <u>Box 1</u>.
>
> If you'd like to make changes, check <u>Box 2</u>
> and fill in the appropriate information.

See the enclosed card for renewal priorities, then mail your pink form now.

But please, do it <u>now</u> and mail in the enclosed envelope.
Before the hustle and bustle of the holidays.

All performances will be in Evanston's Cahn Auditorium.
All with full cast and orchestra, just as you expect from
LIGHT OPERA WORKS.

> As a subscriber, you know that ticket sales
> alone do not cover the full cost of producing
> these operettas. That's why we're hoping you
> will add a contribution to your renewal order
> (even if you've already given in 1991).

$50, $75, $100 — every dollar helps. And your gift is tax deductible.

Thank you so much for your support. Because of you, LIGHT
OPERA WORKS has flourished, during a time when other arts
organizations are struggling just to stay alive.

Sincerely,

Philip A. Kraus

Philip A. Kraus
Artistic Director

P.S. We'll see you at <u>The Red Mill</u> soon.
     In the meantime, don't forget to renew!

Exhibit 7–3. **Subscribers Update Mailing**

Great news about BITTER SWEET...

ADVISORY BOARD

The Honorable Joan Barr
Mayor, City of Evanston
Honorary Chairman, Advisory Board

Richard Alderson
Professor of Voice and Opera,
Northwestern University

Margaret Hillis
Director, Chicago Symphony Chorus

Joseph Lederleitner
General Counsel

Tom Peck
Director, Grant Park Symphony Chorus
St. Louis Symphony Chorus

Marty Robinson
Chief Announcer, WTTW Channel 11

William R.T. Smith
W.R.T. Smith & Co.

Thomas C. Willis
Concert Manager,
Northwestern University
Former Music Critic,
Chicago Tribune

BOARD OF DIRECTORS

John Auwaerter
Harry Clamor
Lawrence E. Freeman
Jonathan Geen
Philip A. Kraus
Estelle Kriv
Bridget McDonough

STAFF

Philip A. Kraus
ARTISTIC DIRECTOR

Bridget McDonough
MANAGING DIRECTOR

Tim Pleiman
BUSINESS MANAGER

Dear Subscriber,

I just came from a dress rehearsal of
BITTER SWEET and wanted to give you a quick
update before our opening next week.

<u>You'll love the show</u>!

Director Philip Kraus has done his usual
stellar job pulling together singers, orchestra,
sets, costumes and everything else that makes the
magic of light opera come alive.

I guarantee you'll be humming <u>I'll See You
Again</u> and those other great Noël Coward melodies
long after you leave the theater.

As the excitement of opening night builds,
we have to stop for a moment and reflect
on who makes it all possible. <u>You</u>.

Reaching an 11th season is no small feat
for an arts organization, particularly in today's
economy. But you've proven -- by subscribing and
through your financial gifts -- that LIGHT OPERA
WORKS is here for the long haul. For that we thank
you.

<u>You</u> know, perhaps more than anyone else,
how important money is to our company.

The sold-out houses we regularly enjoy
simply do not pay the full costs of running
LIGHT OPERA WORKS.

And it gets more challenging every year.
For example, the Illinois Arts Council just
announced a <u>10 percent cut</u> in funding for 1991.
So that's even more money we must raise from
friends like you.

That's why I'm hoping you'll
send a special <u>"Kick-Off" gift</u> --
to help start our 1991 season on
sound financial footing.

See your green card enclosed

Here are some of the things your contribution

LIGHT OPERA WORKS
Illinois' only professional light opera company
A not-for-profit organization

927 Noyes Street • Evanston, Illinois 60201-2799 • (708) 869-6300

2

*Two-page letter (with reply card) to subscribers who have given in the past but who
have not yet contributed in the current year.*

Exhibit 7–3 (*Continued*).   **Subscribers Update Mailing**

will help pay for:

- THE BEGGAR STUDENT orchestra.
  This lavish production requires 34 musicians in the pit,
  more than any other this season. And at LIGHT OPERA WORKS,
  when the score calls for violins, you get violins -- not
  synthesizers or other electronic gizmos!

- THE RED MILL scenery.
  I don't want to give away the plot, but the climactic
  scene has the leading character make a daring escape
  out of the windmill on one of the real revolving arms.
  You just can't do that with a painted backdrop!

That's only a sampling, of course. I promise your money
will be well spent. We don't waste a penny. Because we plan to
be around next year, and the year after, and the year after...

Did you know that LIGHT OPERA WORKS is not
affiliated with Northwestern University?

Although we use Cahn Auditorium, we get no funding from the
school. In fact, as tenants, we pay Northwestern rent. I wanted
to clarify that because some people were under the impression
that we are subsidized by Northwestern, which we aren't.

And speaking of Cahn Auditorium, we have forwarded your
concern over the limited washrooms, and Northwestern has been
very sympathetic. It now looks like some remodeling may be on
the horizon. No guarantees yet, but we'll keep you posted.

So that's my update. We're looking forward to seeing you
at BITTER SWEET next week. In the meantime, won't you please
send a special 11th Season "Kick-Off" gift?

Just fill out and mail the enclosed   *Your gift is*
green card now, with your contribution.   *tax-deductible!*

Thank you for your support.

Sincerely,

Bridget McDonough

Bridget McDonough
Managing Director

Light Opera Works

Thank you!

YES, I want to support LIGHT OPERA WORKS by making a
tax-deductible **11th Season "Kick-Off"** contribution of:

☐ $30   ☐ $50   ☐ $75   ☐ $ _____

Your gift of $30 or more entitles you to the
benefits described in the enclosed brochure

Mr. Herbert T. Bauer
299 N. Dunton #509
Arlington Heights IL 60004

Please mark any corrections to your name/address above

☐ Check enclosed, payable to LIGHT OPERA WORKS
☐ Charge ☐ American Express ☐ VISA
          ☐ MasterCard   ☐ Discover

Card # _____ Expires _____

Signature_____

Mail this card now in the enclosed envelope to:
LIGHT OPERA WORKS, 927 Noyes, Evanston, IL 60201-2799

In summation, Mr. Hunt attributed the success to:

1. Isolating a small segment of most likely givers.
2. Mailing repeated solicitations.
3. Positioning the company as a successful, well-managed business. Contributors are asked to "buy in" to this success, rather than "give to charity."

National Parks Membership Drive

One of America's major concerns these days is its environment. The stated purpose of the National Parks and Conservation Association of Washington, D.C., is to protect and enhance our environment as it relates to our national park system. Most Americans think that our national park are protected by the federal government from development and other threats. But this isn't always true.

It is the task of the National Parks and Conservation Association to convince consumers that to protect their priceless heritage they should contribute to the cause. Thanks to a magnificent package created by Donna Baier Stein—a talented free-lance writer who resides in Lexington, Massachusetts—consumers are contributing to the association in record numbers.

The mailing consists of:

1. A window mailing envelope with teaser copy stating, "You have been selected to participate in an important national survey on America's National Parks."
2. A four-page, tightly written letter.
3. An insert that details member benefits and offers a free gift for joining.
4. A window decal of the National Parks and Conservation Association logo.
5. A survey questionnaire including check-off boxes to apply for a $15 active membership plus a gift of $10 to $100 or more.
6. A postage-free business reply envelope.

The creative strategies employed are notable. The key element, without a doubt, is the national survey form. Through a series of 12 carefully worded questions the reader is taken by the hand and gently guided to a favorable conclusion as requested in Question 12:

> Would you be willing to make a financial contribution if it could help prevent a full-scale crisis in our National Park System—like the poaching of wildlife or the destruction of priceless cultural resources?
>
> ☐ Yes   ☐ No

The membership and contribution form follows in logical sequence—a brilliant strategy. (Exhibit 7–4 presents the four-page letter, and Exhibit 7–5 the survey form.)

Exhibit 7–4. **Membership and Contribution Letter**

National Parks and Conservation Association

1015 31st Street • Washington, D.C. 20007 • (202) 944-8530

> **You may never have another chance like this one.**
>
> **If you want to see America's National Park System survive, it is *extremely* important you complete and return the enclosed National Survey to the National Parks and Conservation Association *immediately*.**

Dear Friend,

If you've visited a National Park recently, you may not be surprised by the severity of my warning!

Our country's National Park System -- the first and finest in the world -- is in real trouble right now.

Yellowstone ... Yosemite ... Mount Rainier ... Denali ... the Grand Canyon -- wilderness and wildlife in all these magnificent parks are being destroyed by neighboring mining activities, poaching, overcrowding, forest clear-cutting, oil and gas exploration and other damaging development.

Threats like these -- plus a lack of public knowledge that it must be private citizens like you who must act to save these parks -- can be deadly.

> That's why I now ask you to participate in a remarkable new national plan to help save our 80-million acre National Park System. To be a conservator as well as a user of America's most beautiful wild lands and most meaningful historic heritage.

The National Park System touches all parts of our great country -- embracing 355 parks, monuments, historic sites and other recreation areas, preserving places and events that reflect the majestic sweep of American land, life and history.

Gettysburg. The Statue of Liberty. Dinosaur National Monument. The striking cliff ruins of Mesa Verde and the beloved grizzlies, moose and Old Faithful of Yellowstone.

Like a living library, the National Park System makes it possible for you to stand on a Civil War battlefield, to walk through a centuries-old forest, to float on a sparkling river that still runs free.

(over, please)

🔁 *Printed on recycled paper*

(Continued)

Exhibit 7–4 (*Continued*).   Membership and Contribution Letter

-2-

Today, the National Parks and Conservation Association (NPCA) is the only private, citizen-funded
organization dedicated to protecting, promoting and
improving our National Parks.

For more than 70 years, we have fought and won battles on behalf of our
parks:

• BLOCKING pressure from the National Rifle Association to open parks
  to hunting and trapping;
• PREVENTING a nuclear waste dump next to Canyonlands National Park;
• WINNING a lawsuit that rid Mammoth Cave National Park of a source of
  serious pollution;
• PRESERVING the Manassas National Battlefield Park from a plan to
  build a giant shopping mall on adjacent land;
• PROTECTING the mountain lion in New Mexico and grizzly bear in
  Wyoming and Montana;

As a result of these and many other efforts, we have won a reputation
among government officials, the media and the American public for
thoughtful, responsible and effective leadership.

All across our country, NPCA stands at the forefront of national
efforts to preserve important wilderness areas, archeological sites,
historic buildings, battlefields and monuments -- unique records of
America's historic, natural and cultural heritage.

In fact, a group of nearly 70 of the nation's top conservation groups
has selected an NPCA staff member #1 for his conservation programming
efforts, for three years in a row.

But we cannot rest on our laurels now.

Not when Great Smoky Mountains and Shenandoah National Parks are being
heavily, perhaps irreversibly, damaged by acid rain. When increased mining
and petroleum exploration proposals threaten Denali and other parks. When
off-road vehicles damage beaches at Assateague and vandals loot
archeological sites in America's southwest parks.

Not when poachers are threatening the last grizzly bears in the
contiguous United States. And certainly not when power plants and other
sources of pollution make it impossible to see clearly across the Grand
Canyon 100 days each year!

To combat these and many other threats, NPCA has recently developed a
comprehensive National Park System Plan -- a rational, workable program for
park protection, administration, conservation and use. A plan I'd like YOU
to take part in.

The Plan is the first true long-range agenda ever produced to guide our National Parks into the future ...
to guarantee our National Parks will be there for the
children and grandchildren who will follow us.

(next page, please)

Exhibit 7–4 (*Continued*).   **Membership and Contribution Letter**

-3-

Our Plan recommends bold ideas like:

1. Establishing the National Park Service as an agency responsible to the President and Congress rather than Interior Department bureaucrats and appointees.
2. Setting more realistic boundaries for nearly 175 of the 355 park units -- boundaries that will take in all of the resources each park needs (like critical water sources and wildlife habitat).
3. Placing adequately-funded science, historic preservation and conservation programs high among National Park Service priorities.
4. Improving resource management, visitor facilities, education, and interpretive programs.

One of the most far-reaching conservation plans our nation has ever considered, this Plan needs backing from you and many other citizens if it is to succeed.

Right now, NPCA is promoting its Plan to the current Administration ... and fighting for a number of conservation bills like the Clean Air Act that will also determine the future of America's vulnerable park lands.

We are lobbying to protect public lands in the California desert. To support national acid rain control. To save Civil War battlefields and add land to Big Thicket National Preserve.

As you can tell, our programs are many and varied:

... <u>Budget & Land Acquisition</u>

During the last fiscal year, NPCA worked with Congress to substantially increase the administration's funding request for the National Park Service. In particular, land acquisition, maintenance, and construction received these vital increases. NPCA also persuaded Congress to fund studies for Colorado National Monument and the proposed Anasazi National Monument.

... <u>Park Additions and Expansions</u>

We fought for and won the Great Basin National Park, the establishment of Petroglyphs National Monument and the boundary expansion at Everglades National Park. And we are working to authorize additions to Big Thicket National Preserve in Texas, and Death Valley and Joshua Tree Monuments in California.

Eight new areas added to our National Park System, during the past 18 months, were on the list of 86 priority parks published in NPCA's National Park System Plan.

We recently helped lead the fight to add 146,000 acres in Big Cypress to help preserve the endangered Florida panther and the entire Everglades ecosystem.

(over, please)

(Continued)

Exhibit 7–4 (*Continued*).   **Membership and Contribution Letter**

-4-

... <u>Wildlife Protection</u>

In addition to our efforts to protect the Florida panther, we are
helping to save threatened and endangered species like the grizzly,
bald eagle, mountain lion, wolf, sea otters and others through habitat
protection and expansion, species reintroduction and recovery programs,
and legislative lobbying.

... <u>Education</u>

If you've been to a National Park, you've probably seen and used one
of our publications. We develop school programs and educate Americans
of all ages in how to use, enjoy and care for their parks.

Right now, we're alerting people to the problem of poaching in national
parks -- the undetected and illegal slaughter that is robbing the parks
of their most majestic wildlife.

... <u>Grassroots Organizing</u>

NPCA gets individual citizens involved through our National Park Action
Program and Park Contact Program that encourages citizens to write
letters to Congress. With more than 150,000 members nationwide, NPCA is
a strong and effective voice in protecting our parks. Your added voice
can make us even more so.

In 1872, Congress created the National Park System for all Americans to
enjoy for all time.

Without quick action from us now, you'll be lucky to visit, and
recognize, many of them 20 years from now. Please -- join the National
Parks and Conservation Association <u>today</u>.

Sincerely,

Paul C. Pritchard
President

P.S. When you join NPCA now at our low introductory rate of $15 --
     $10 off regular annual dues of $25 -- you will receive a
     subscription to our award-winning, full-color <u>National Parks</u>
     magazine; information on our valuable PARK-PAK with guides, maps,
     and Rand McNally Road Atlas and Travel Guide; plus many other
     benefits. And -- as a special bonus for joining now -- a handsome
     fanny pack to use on your recreational outings. Please see the
     enclosed form for details.

Exhibit 7–5.   **Survey Form**

National Parks and Conservation Association

NATIONAL SURVEY

To be completed by:

Survey Respondent No.

56439-1023

Instructions: After you have read the enclosed letter, please indicate your answers with a check mark in the appropriate box. Then, return this form in the enclosed postage-paid envelope. Your name, address and responses will remain confidential when referendum results are tabulated.

---

1. Which of these park activities do you enjoy?

   ☐ hiking   ☐ riding   ☐ birding or other nature activity
   ☐ camping   ☐ boating   ☐ visiting historical sites
   ☐ fishing   ☐ photography or sightseeing   ☐ other _____

---

2. Most Americans think that our national parks are protected from development and other threats by the federal government. Before reading this mailing, did you know that this isn't always true?

   ☐ Yes   ☐ No

---

3. Americans enjoy the world's first and finest national park system — a role model for park systems in 120 countries around the globe. Do you know if there is a National Park in your home state?

   ☐ Yes   ☐ No

---

4. Yellowstone is one of America's most endangered National Parks. Have you ever visited there?

   ☐ Yes   ☐ No

---

5. The U.S. Forest Service has subsidized timber-cutting in the National Forest around Yellowstone and is now considering opening land around the park to oil and gas leasing.
   Do you support or oppose this?

   ☐ Support   ☐ Oppose   ☐ Need more information

---

6. Many Americans felt the Reagan Administration may have been the most insensitive in history on the issue of national parks — promoting maximum exploitation of public lands and adding less acreage to the park system than any other President in recent years.
   Do you think the Bush administration should endorse NPCA's National Park System Plan to preserve park resources and acquire land for new parks?

   ☐ Yes   ☐ No

♻ *printed on recycled paper*   *Over please . . .*

(Continued)

Exhibit 7–5 (*Continued*).   **Survey Form**

7. Together with the Park Service, NPCA developed the first curriculum on biological diversity for 4th – 6th graders in America. Do you support education efforts to alert today's young people to tomorrow's park problems?

   ☐ Yes   ☐ No

8. One of the biggest legislative battles now facing park conservationists is amending and strengthening the Clean Air Act. Do you support federal controls to ensure cleaner air and clearer views of our nation's scenic wonders?

   ☐ Yes   ☐ No

9. Great Smoky Mountain and Shenandoah National Parks are being heavily, perhaps irreversibly, damaged by acid rain. Do you favor current legislation requiring federal controls on acid rain?

   ☐ Yes   ☐ No

10. Do you agree that National Parks should be closed to hunting and trapping?

    ☐ Yes   ☐ No

11. Currently, about 1 million acres of wilderness land and open space are lost each year. A bill in Congress supporting creation of the American Heritage Trust would secure funds for local communities, as well as state and federal agencies, to preserve land and historic sites rather than see them be lost to development. Would you support such legislation?

    ☐ Yes   ☐ No

12. Would you be willing to make a financial contribution if it could help prevent a full-scale crisis in our National Park System — like the poaching of wildlife or the destruction of priceless cultural resources?

    ☐ Yes   ☐ No

☐ ***Yes,*** I'll gladly do my share to help protect America's National Parks. Please enroll me as a new member of the National Parks and Conservation Association and send my *free* fanny pack, my first issue of *National Parks* magazine, information on PARK-PAK, and many other member benefits.

Enclosed is my tax-deductible check for:

   ☐ $15 Active Membership —1st year introductory rate *(Save $10!)*

To help NPCA even more, I'm enclosing an additional gift of:

   ☐ $10   ☐ $15   ☐ $50   ☐ $100   ☐ Other $ _____

☐ I prefer to charge my dues to: ☐ VISA   ☐ MasterCard

Account No._____   Exp. Date _____

Signature _____

   ☐ Active Membership   ☐ Additional Gift $_____

Please make your check payable to NPCA and return with this form in the reply envelope provided.
All but $7 of your annual dues are tax-deductible to the extent allowed by law.

Yours Free...
as a new member of NPCA

National Parks and Conservation Association • 1015 31st Street, N.W. • Washington, D.C. 20007

NP C 09

The results reflect the success of the strategies employed. When this package was first used, membership stood at 60,000. In the first year, the package brought in 150,000 new members, representing a 233 percent growth in membership. The cost per $17 order, including contributions, was $12, resulting in a net profit of $750,000. The package pulled a full percent over the previous control and raised more than $2.5 million in revenue.

Applying Business Thinking to Worthy Causes

Most philanthropic organizations have two things in common: a severe shortage of funds and a distinguished board of directors to whom they look for guidance. Fund-raising expertise among directors rarely exists, however.

A case in point is the Guild for the Blind in Chicago. They are always pressed for funds to provide the many services they want to perform. Although they have a fine board of directors, I am the only board member with some direct mail fund-raising experience.

Applying the problem-solution technique, which is typical of a business-person's approach, I asked this question of myself: How can we get an extremely high response with practically no investment on the part of the Guild? The solution seemed to be—ask each director to send a fund-raising letter to 50 friends and acquaintances.

To test the idea, I decided to be the guinea pig. I compiled a list of 50 likely prospects and wrote a two-page letter to be processed on my personal letterhead (Exhibit 7–6). Enclosed with the letter was a folder describing activities of the Guild and a donor form recommending contributions of varying amounts, tied to specific projects. In addition, a stamped return envelope was enclosed; the return address was my home.

There were several strategies employed in this mailing:

1. Instead of using the Guild for the Blind letterhead, I opted to use my letterhead because I felt it would be more personal.

2. Since I was trading on friendship, I strategized that the best approach was to admit it, without shame, in the very first paragraph.

3. Using one of the tenets of successful fund-raising, I selected one program —the Mobility Program—as the focus of my appeal.

4. Finally, instead of asking my friends to send their contribution directly to the Guild, I decided that a stamped return envelope with my home address would have more impact.

Those were the strategies. Now the results: Response rate was 64 percent, with the average contribution in excess of $75. Hallelujah!

Exhibit 7–6.   **Guild for the Blind Mailing**

BOB STONE, INC.

1630 SHERIDAN ROAD #8G • WILMETTE, ILLINOIS 60091

Mr. and Mrs. Pat Cunningham
205 9th
Wilmette, Illinois 60091

Dear Mick and Pat:

Frankly this is an appeal for help. And I'll admit without shame that
I am, in effect, trading on our friendship in making this appeal to you.

To get right to the point, I'm proud to be a board member of The Guild
For The Blind, the most unique organization I have ever served. I say
unique because this wonderful organization is showing the blind people
the way to dignity, self respect and a life of fulfillment.

The goal of the Guild is best explained in the words of Stephen Benson,
Assistant Director.

> "I am blind and it is likely that I will remain blind for the
> rest of my life. It seems to me that blind people have at
> least two life options:

> "One - to sit and wait for a cure, or for someone to take care
> of them, push and pull them around like a doll, with nothing
> to do with directing their own lives, thus perpetuating all the
> stereotypes of blind people.

> "Two - blind people can be active, contributing human beings,
> loving life, participating in it to the fullest extent. As
> far as I'm concerned option number two is the only one that
> makes sense. Not only does it offer the opportunity to be a
> wholly vital people, it also offers the opportunity to partici-
> pate in changing the public's mind about blindness.

> "I believe this is an obligation each of us must fulfill so
> blind people who follow will have richer, fuller lives."

This program of fulfillment is called the Mobility Program. To teach it
to blind people Steve Benson has prepared a text which will be available
in braille for the totally blind, in large print for those with sight
impairment and a cassette for those who cannot read braille or large print.

In addition, the Guild will provide instructors to teach blind people how
to travel with the ease that you and I take for granted. Instructors will
show students how to travel with the long white cane...a recent development
which allows them to walk with confidence.

Exhibit 7–6 (*Continued*).   **Guild for the Blind Mailing**

So as each student completes the Program walking up or down steps, boarding buses, and trains, even walking on ice or snow will be as natural as for the sighted person. And, most important of all, many of these good people will be able to travel to work, enjoying gainful employment.

But there is just one thing. No Federal funds are available to make the Mobility Program reality. As a matter of fact - no funds whatever. The future of the Program is solely dependent upon the generosity of fortunate people like you and I.

That's why I have had no hesitancy in sending you this urgent appeal. Whatever you can do at this time will be greatly appreciated by the Guild For The Blind, those they serve and yours truly.

Sincerely,

Robert Stone

P.S. Please use the enclosed form and return to me in the stamped, self-addressed envelope. Thank you so much.

Flushed with my "success story," I presented the plan, the findings, and the results to the board. Several agreed to compile a list of 50 friends and to use the mailing package I had created.

Several weeks later the results from mailings made by other directors were in. My bubble burst with a loud thud! Where I had enjoyed a response rate of 64 percent, mailings by other directors pulled 3 to 5 percent. I couldn't believe it. One thing I did know: My friends were no more wealthy or more sensitive to worthy causes than the friends of the other directors.

The reasons for poor response became abundantly clear with further investigation:

1. Most directors opted to use the Guild's letterhead rather than their own, thus taking the heart out of the personal one-on-one approach.

2. Only a couple had the "courage" to use the first paragraph of the letter, a direct appeal for help. Most used an indirect "weasel approach" instead.

3. Likewise, only a couple enclosed a stamped response envelope addressed to their home address. Most opted for the Guild response envelope instead.

There is a real moral to this "good-news bad-news" story. It is this: *If we violate the precepts of sound fund-raising techniques, results are likely to be dismal.*

The Guild's need to raise funds didn't go away. The ability to acquire new donors continued to be severely hampered by a pitifully small amount of money available to invest in an expanded donor base. But there is a happy ending to this story.

Again applying the problem-solution approach, I came up with a new brainstorm. Suppose we were to ask directors to make loans to the Guild, offering to repay them out of proceeds from contributions? To make it a business proposition, we would pay interest on the unpaid balance until the loans were fully repaid. After that, all future revenue would be retained by the Guild.

Knowing I couldn't sell the concept to the directors without proof of practicality, I decided to make the first loan. Based on what "Andy" Andrews said in his book, *Billions by Mail*, I would have my money back in 90–120 days.

As Andy had predicted, the new donor mailing, with subsequent follow-ups, made it possible for the Guild to repay me in full within 120 days. And, happily, the Guild will profit from these new donors for years to come.

Armed with these results, I had no difficulty arranging for loans from other directors. As a matter of fact, loans from directors led to the largest Christmas mailing in the 40-year history of the Guild for the Blind.

Like so many of the ideas presented in this book, the idea of getting seed money from directors to finance new donor mailings has to be viewed as an *adaptable idea*. For philanthropic organizations this particular idea can solve a persistant major problem.

The need to raise funds for worthy causes will never go away. The concept of applying business acumen with direct marketing know-how can make a major difference in the effort.

Self-Quiz

1. Describe the classic three-step approach to raising funds for a worthy cause.

   a. _____

   _____

   _____

   b. _____

   _____

   _____

c. _____

_____

_____

2. The highest percentage of response in a fund-raising effort comes from

_____ contributors.

3. It is generally agreed that people respond best to appeals that are:
☐ rational   ☐ emotional.

4. The total amount pledged for a cause tends to be greater when which
of these types of payment is offered? ☐ single payment
☐ multipayment.

5. Over the years the average gift to a philanthropic organization tends to:
☐ decrease   ☐ increase.

6. If you had a list of donors all of whom originally contributed $10, how
much of an increase would you ask for in your next solicitation?
☐ $5   ☐ $10   ☐ $15   ☐ $20   ☐ $25

7. In structuring a fund-raising letter, which of these appeals is generally
more effective? ☐ selling one particular cause   ☐ selling the many
causes of a philanthropic organization

8. Why is it good business to "invest" in new donors?

_____

_____

_____

9. The highest percentage of response comes from: ☐ new contributors
☐ previous contributors

10. When pledges are made by phone, it can be expected that about

_____ percent of pledges will be collected, if properly followed up.

Pilot Project

You are on the fund-raising committee of your church. The roof is in serious
disrepair. It is estimated that the work will cost $100,000. But the church
does not have the funds to do the necessary work. The contractor is willing
to accept payment over a 3-year period. Therefore you can ask for pledges
over a 36 month period.

   Your assignment is to write a letter to be mailed to 50 of your friends
and acquaintances soliciting pledges.

CHAPTER EIGHT

Retail Direct Marketing

Handbills. Flyers. Catalogs. Newspaper ads soliciting phone orders. Mailings to store credit card holders. Inserts in billing statements. All of these have been the tools of retailers for decades.

But, more often than not, the prime objective of retailers has been to create store traffic. There is nothing wrong with this except that retailers have been hard put to accurately measure the cost effectiveness of traffic-building material. The fact is that a retailer is rarely sure whether a particular promotion brought people into the store or whether the customers were shopping in the store anyway and discovered the promoted merchandise while browsing.

Today, all this is changing. Major retailers are rapidly embracing the sophisticated techniques now available to all who use the direct marketing discipline. And with this new sophistication retailers are discovering what mail-order firms have known for decades: *All customers are not created equal*.

Identifying Heavy Users

The big breakthrough in direct marketing has been the ability to differentiate heavy users of package goods from average users and occasional users. Consider dog food as a category. Some customers may purchase 20 pounds of dog food a week, as contrasted to an average of, say, 2 pounds a week. Good business dictates that the heavy user be cultivated.

Not only is it important to know who the heavy user is, but it is equally important to know which brand or brands the heavy user is buying. For if it is possible to identify heavy users with their names and addresses along with their brand preferences, then it is possible to persuade those customers either to switch brands or to buy more of a preferred brand.

The natural question is: How does one identify the customer by name, address, and brand purchased? That's where the computer comes into play. As a matter of fact, several systems have been developed that enable the package-goods company and/or the retailer to capture the necessary information. One such company is Schlumberger, of Chesapeake, Virginia. Its system is called *The Smart Card*.

Essentially, here is how the system works. Retail chain store customers are provided ID cards. This gives each store the customers' names and addresses. Then bar codes on the packages identify brands purchased and the amount. All of this information is fed into the computer and stored. Thus cumulative purchases are recorded over time, making it possible to calculate average weekly purchases of given brands.

This type of information is invaluable for both the retailers and the package-goods companies, especially from a competitive standpoint. The package-goods company, for example, can send cents-off coupons or free samples to heavy users of competitive brands.

Case Histories

One person in particular has trumpeted the opportunities in direct marketing for retailers. That person is Peter Hoke, publisher of *Direct Marketing* magazine and publisher of a newsletter entitled *Promoting Store Traffic*. The case histories that follow have been gleaned from Hoke's extensive files.

IGA Supermarket Chain

This is the story of a segment of a supermarket chain that had never used direct mail but achieved a 63 percent return on its first mailing! The hero of the story is Orville Roth, who operates 12 IGA supermarkets in Oregon.

Mr. Roth decided to try direct mail, using one of its greatest strengths—testing. But first he had to build a database—a list. He chose one of his stores for the test.

Mr. Roth started to build a list with a sign-up-to-win sweepstakes promotion. The sign-up card included five household questions, so the database was enhanced by family size, ownership of a VCR, and similar information.

The sweepstakes offered four major prizes, but (this is the important part) *everyone* would win something. The number of households signing up was 2,786, creating a brand-new, clean, accurate database. Winners were drawn for the four major prizes; postcards were mailed to the remaining 2,782 people telling them they had also won something.

All the postcard recipients had to do was bring in the card for their free prize—a dozen eggs. The response was terrific: 1,752 people came into the store. This translates into a response rate of 63 percent. Cost per response

was 66 cents. But what really counts is the bottom line; total store sales increased 43 percent the first day the postcards were received.

After these initial results, Mr. Roth made the understatement of the year saying, "I like this direct mail idea." Naturally, other direct mail promotions followed.

One of Mr. Roth's unique promotions was his Leap Year Promotion. This was another fold-over mailer (see Exhibit 8–1). The headline—"A Sale So Great It Only Happens Once Every Four Years"—plus the four coupons formed the heart of this simple mailing. Results: an 18 percent redemption rate, with store sales increasing 17 percent over the same period in the previous year.

Exhibit 8–1.   Leap Year Promotion

Saks Fifth Avenue Proprietary Charge Card

Time was when famous department stores like Neiman-Marcus, Marshall Field's, Macy's, Bloomingdale's, and Sears honored only one credit card— theirs. But that has changed dramatically. Now Visa and MasterCard, in particular, are widely accepted by major department stores that also offer their own credit cards. This case history, however, proves conclusively that the house card customer is more loyal and spends more money.

Saks Fifth Avenue (SFA) uses its proprietary charge card to assess customer purchase habits, target direct mail promotions, and increase lifetime cus- tomer value. According to William Bloom, vice president for credit and services, private cards "give membership in a prestigious retail family. The loyalty generates a lot of business."

SFA found customers who charge purchases exclusively on its card spend an average of $554 annually, compared with $296 for American Express and $166 for bank cards. Among multicard users, the average is a whopping $1,834, remaining above $1,000 where SFA is one of two cards used. But bank card and American Express users spend just $245 on average. "It's the proprietary card that drives business into the store," states Bloom, "because we're in touch with them all the time."

With SFA's reliance on direct mail, Bloom says, "Knowing where customers live is almost as important as knowing what they buy. It enables you to target existing customers and find additional ones with similar characteristics." Bloom says in 1971 SFA realized it had 1.5 million charge customers "who are waiting to hear from you."

"You lose touch with your customers if you can't contact them," he notes. Without SFA's ability to track people, he says it wouldn't do as much repeat business. One recent 600,000-piece SFA mailing to active accounts offering a 10 percent discount on a day's purchases generated $18 million in incremen- tal sales.

Many retailers who develop extensive catalogs do not accept mail orders. Their sole purpose is to excite interest in given products to induce prospects to come into the store to see, feel, and try on. The next case history is about such a retail operation.

When an established retailer with multiple locations recognizes the power of its database and decides it's time to release that static energy into the marketplace, it's opening the door to expansion. Helzberg Diamonds, Kansas City, Missouri, is a prime example of such a retailer.

Helzberg Diamonds

About 10 years ago, the 75-year-old specialty retailer decided to develop and use its customer database. At that time the company operated approximately 30 stores and had a database of about 25,000 names. In 8 years the company

expanded to more than 70 stores while building a sophisticated database of almost 900,000 names.

In 1956 Barnett C. Helzberg, Jr., joined Helzberg Diamonds as the third generation in the family firm. He took the company into mail-order sales of its nonjewelry product lines. In 1963 Mr. Helzberg took command of the 39-store firm.

In was 1967 when Helzberg Diamonds opened its first corner store in a shopping mall. Success in the mall was immediate, and Helzberg continues to open more mall stores every year. In the mid-1970s Helzberg dropped its ancillary product lines and mail-order operation to focus on diamonds, precious gemstones, and karat gold.

Then in 1979 a young journalism school graduate named John Goodman joined the firm. At that time the firm had about 40 stores and the beginnings of a database—some 20,000 to 30,000 names maintained in-house without the benefits of computerization. Mr. Goodman took some direct marketing lessons from Mr. Helzberg and from Martin Baier, who taught at the Center for Direct Marketing, University of Missouri at Kansas City. As vice president of advertising for Helzberg Diamonds and later as founder of Goodman Direct, Mr. Goodman helped Mr. Helzberg harness the power of the firm's database.

Setting Up the Database

Helzberg Diamonds applied many of the same direct marketing principles it used in its mail-order operations of the 1950s to generate store traffic in the 1980s. The major differences in its current mailings are that the prospect cannot order products by mail and that each mailing goes to a specific segment of the database residing within a certain distance of a shopping mall housing a Helzberg Diamonds shop.

The database is organized so that names can be selected by geodemographics, the amount of money a customer spends over a designated period of time, frequency of purchase, or method of payment. The names of proprietary charge card holders may be selected by active cards with no balance, active cards with a balance, or cards that have never been active. Other selections might be house names, seed names, and various rented files. Different selections are made to achieve different goals.

With almost 900,000 names in its database, Helzberg Diamonds uses an outside full-service direct marketing company, Marketing Communications Inc. (MCI), to maintain its database. Each week the 75 Helzberg Diamond shops in 30 markets send MCI data providing the name and address of each purchaser along with the date and amount of purchase.

MCI staffers then input the data into a single computerized marketing database for all Helzberg Diamonds stores. Maintaining all of the firm's data in a single database provides several marketing benefits.

By monitoring and analyzing sales trends evidenced in this universal database, management can determine which markets require more promotional dollars and which markets could support an additional Helzberg Diamonds shop. If the company wants to do a promotional mailing to all customers who

meet a certain criterion—for example, first-time buyers, big spenders, or holiday purchasers—only one database need be accessed to select the appropriate names for all stores' customers. Another benefit of having all stores share a single database is that the addresses of customers who move from one market to another will be corrected during a national change of address (NCOA) pass. These customers will continue to receive mailings directing them to the Helzberg shop nearest their new residence.

According to Larry Hawks, vice president of development for MCI, the Helzberg database receives a thorough cleaning in the fall, just before the holiday mailings begin. The list is periodically passed against NCOA for address corrections. The Helzberg file is continually being cleaned to keep carrier route codes up to date and to eliminate duplications and therefore unnecessary mailings.

Exhibit 8–2 shows the front cover of a Mother's Day catalog, a typical Helzberg Diamonds promotion.

Databases Make the Difference

The success stories we have just reviewed all have one thing in common—enhanced databases. For a retailer to treat all customers as equals is to lose the advantage that direct marketing offers.

Although the case histories reviewed thus far relate to viewing the customer base, opportunities don't end there. The much larger database to be mined is the prospect database. The principle to apply in this instance is: If you know the profile of your customer base, your objective should be to find prospects with the same profile.

In Chapter Two, "Database Marketing," you were introduced to the matching techniques of National Demographics & Lifestyles (NDL) of Denver, Colorado. In a remarkable little book entitled *Adventures in Relevance Marketing*[1], Jack Bickert, former chairman of NDL, includes a number of case histories that dramatize the happy results when you target prospects. A few of these are presented below.

The Automotive Industry (Buick, Chrysler, Alfa Romeo)

Buick used a survey of auto show attendees to develop the prospect characteristics for a showroom traffic-building promotion. By profiling the 68,000 survey respondents, Buick created the income and car-buying demographics of owners of targeted automobiles. From this process Buick created a master

[1] Published by National Demographics and Lifestyles, 1621 Eighteenth Street, Denver, Colorado 80202, 1991.

Exhibit 8–2. **Mother's Day Catalog Cover**

list that was matched against lists of country club members, golf equipment buyers, and subscribers to special-interest golf magazines. The matching process produced a multimillion-name target list that had appropriate car ownership characteristics and demographics and included people with an interest in golf.

The subsequent promotion, known as the Winning Putt Sweepstakes, was designed to generate showroom traffic in conjunction with two Buick-sponsored golf tournaments. Buick estimated that the final response rate was close to 25 percent. The company expected to sell 31,000 automobiles as a result of the promotion, a very handsome return on an $8 million investment.

That same year, Chrysler countered with its own successful $10 million dealer-traffic promotion. Chrysler used sophisticated analytic techniques from R.L. Polk & Co. to identify households with the greatest likelihood of purchasing a new vehicle. The targets for the promotion—the prospects—were identified by predictive modeling techniques that used auto ownership data as well as demographic and lifestyle variables. Chrysler mailed the prospects invitations to a private screening, which was hosted by Lee Iacocca via satellite transmission, at more than 4,000 dealerships.

Foreign auto manufacturers have also benefited from database development and applications. Alfa Romeo initiated its database program by running direct response ads in consumer magazines that appealed to auto enthusiasts, men, or people who live in a particular region. The audience profiles of the selected magazines conformed to Alfa Romeo's target audience profiles of well-educated, affluent males under the age of 55.

Several weeks later, Alfa Romeo ran direct response spots on seven cable networks. All of the advertising featured an 800 number. Respondents were directed to the nearest dealer for a test drive of an Alfa 164S and a gift of a specially designed Alfa Romeo paperweight. The campaign generated nearly 2,000 calls a week.

The Liquor Industry (Seagram)

The use of databases is not new to Seagram. In 1986 the company began collecting data about drinkers and their individual tastes. The information has been collected through promotions for various Seagram brands, as well as from inbound telemarketing, in-package promotions, and magazine surveys. Seagram, unlike many other database builders, has avoided incorporating any names generated by magazine sweepstakes, apprehensive that those names would damage the integrity of its database. Because of Seagram's heavy reliance on surveys, the database is extremely rich in specific category and brand-behavior information.

Because liquor advertising is not permitted on broadcast media, Seagram used the benefits of database marketing. As Ashleigh Groce, formerly of Leo

Burnett, points out, Seagram qualifies as a natural database user because of its broad spectrum of brands. For its Glenlivet single-malt scotch, a fairly complex offer package of gifts, rebates, and cassette tapes was used to increase awareness and brand-attribute recall. Cross-selling mailings were used to stimulate the trial of other Seagram brands.

One objective of a database-driven promotion for Chivas Regal was to overcome the brand's premium-price image and increase its use among scotch drinkers familiar with the brand. One of the techniques Seagram used was to establish a Chivas Class, which, through promotional tie-ins with airlines and hotels, reinforced the first-class image of Chivas. Seagram introduced a campaign for Crown Royal, a Canadian whiskey, to increase brand awareness. The Seagram database effort is given added potency through sophisticated modeling techniques that allow the company to predict likely users of a liquor category with remarkable precision.

Easily the most unusual and provocative database building effort was attempted by Johnnie Walker Red. The company conducted tests in Los Angeles and San Francisco where 18 strategically located billboards featured an attractive woman who urged viewers to fax her at a featured number if they drank Johnnie Walker Red. Respondents were then faxed a provocatively worded reply. The campaign blended two unique media—billboards and fax—to establish a dialog with consumers.

There's no question that retailers have joined the direct marketing party. And they are having a ball!

Self-Quiz

1. What is the prime objective of most retailers? _____

2. Name two techniques you would apply to accurately measure the cost effectiveness of traffic-building material.

   a. _____

   b. _____

3. What lesson have retailers learned that mail-order firms have always known? _____

4. When package-goods companies use direct marketing, their primary objective is to identify _____.

5. Describe how a supermarket might record customer names and what those customers purchase over time. _____

   _____

   _____

   _____

6. If a package-goods company has access to names of heavy users of competitive brands, how might it induce consumers to switch brands?

   _____

   _____

   _____

   _____

7. For a department store, what are the advantages of a house credit card over a bank credit card such as Visa and MasterCard?

   a. _____

   b. _____

8. Why would a retailer send out a catalog but refuse to accept mail orders?

   _____

   _____

   _____

   _____

9. Complete this direct marketing principle: If you know the profile of your customer base, your objective should be _____

   _____

Pilot Project

You work for a chain of four supermarkets. You don't know who your regular customers are by name and address, yet you believe that direct marketing could increase traffic, sales, and profits.

Prepare a letter to your management outlining how you would proceed to build a database, what incentives you would employ to increase store traffic, and what tests you would make.

Choosing Media for Your Message

CHAPTER NINE

Mailing Lists

Chapter Two, "Database Marketing," emphasized the importance of developing and working databases from all media sources. This chapter is devoted solely to mailing lists, the major sources of input for databases.

What is a list? *Random House Dictionary* defines a list as "a series of names or other items written or printed together in meaningful groupings so as to constitute a record." The operative words are *meaningful groupings*. In direct marketing, then, the list is simply a way to organize otherwise random material into market segments.

In general terms, there are three procedures that are both central and indispensable to direct marketing through lists:

1. Identifying the best customers on internal (house) lists

2. Finding more customers through outside lists

3. Selling to customers at a maximum profit with minimum waste

Types of Lists

There are two broad categories of lists: internal (house) lists and external (outside) lists. *Internal lists* are derived from a company's own files and include customers, former customers, subscribers, former subscribers, donors, former donors, inquiries, prospects, and warranty cards. *External lists* include compiled and direct response lists from sources outside the company.

Your best customer is the one you already have. Internal lists, popularly known as house files, should be considered an *information database*.

In every instance, the first expense—and usually the most costly—is the acquisition cost. Over the life of the customer, subscriber, member, or contributor, the acquisition cost isn't really the payoff (the revenue will come from persistency), it's lifetime value. Therefore the database must be structured to serve as a marketing information system. This will enable the marketer to make decisions based on facts.

With certain exceptions, if a product or service can't be sold to your in-house names, it can't be sold anywhere. But even a house file is not effective unless you have the ability to segment it productively and use it selectively.

Internal Lists: House File Segmentation

Let's start with the definition of *segment*—one of the constituent parts into which an entity or quantity is divided as if by natural boundaries.

With lists, then, segmentation works on the theory that parts of a list have more sales potential for a particular product or service than other parts of a list. The art in getting more sales from existing customers is to be able to match offers to the customers' buying preferences. It goes without saying that segmentation is practical in relation to the size of a list. If the list constitutes a few hundred names, segmentation is hardly worthwhile. But if a list runs to as few as 5,000 names, segmentation can prove very worthwhile. And if a list runs into the hundreds of thousands, segmentation becomes essential to maximizing profits. In the classic questions of journalism, each mailer must continually ask:

- *Who* are my customers?
- *What* do they buy from me?
- *Why* do they respond to my mailings?
- *How* do I retain them and increase their purchases?
- *Where* do I find others like them?
- *When* do I sell them more effectively?

The answers to these questions can only be found in careful attention to the specifics of planning. In list utilization, planning encompasses three basic areas: selection, analysis, and budgeting (forecasting).

The first of this vital trio—selection—begins with the internal lists.

Customer value or the determination of a good customer depends on the dynamics of the company. The function of the marketing effort must be geared to converting first-time buyers into loyal, repeat customers. This can be described as target marketing. One approach to target marketing is to use the customer's past history to project future purchases.

If the database is programmed to store certain bits of information about each customer, the database is not just a list of customers—it's a gallery of portraits. The art is to get more sales from existing customers by being able to match offers to their buying preferences. In a sense we're talking about also using the customer information database as a source for product development.

In addition to the behavioral characteristics of R-F-M (recency, frequency, monetary) or FRAT (defined in Chapter Two), other psychodynamic factors that should be included are:

- *Mode of payment*: cash, open account, installments, credit card.

- *Geographics*: not only where the customer lives, but also correlation of recency, frequency, monetary to geographic areas.

- *Type of product purchased*: labeled by product category—household, leisure, recreation, fashion, gourmet, travel, sports, do-it-yourself, and the like.

- *Length of time on the file*: an indication of interest in the specific publication, book club, catalog or other product.

- *Source*: direct mail, radio, TV, space, telephone, cable TV, inserts, co-ops, or other medium. It is important to note that the use of multimedia contributes another lifestyle statistic to the database.

- *Date of last transacton*: includes payment, change of address, correspondence, renewal, and unsolicited contributions.

These are just some of the variables. Others should be determined based on what the company sells. A magazine publisher, for example, will not use the same factors as a catalog company or a fund-raising organization.

Several mathematical regression techniques allow the marketer to relate each element of customer data on the file to other transactional data and thereby to predict customer behavior. It is important to realize that there is no universal equation that applies to all types of regression analysis. Every equation must be custom-designed based on the dynamics of the particular company and must be used, evaluated, and updated on a continuing basis.

Properly structured, this type of research will lead to customer demand analysis and segmentation on the theory that parts of a list have more sales potential (hence more profit) for a particular product than do other parts. The marketer must do everything possible to optimize the segmentation of the customer file for internal use and for list rental to others, because both aspects will contribute substantially to the company's profit picture.

External Lists

Information from the house file can be extended to the use of outside lists. There are two basic kinds of outside, or external, lists: compiled lists (usually by some common interest) and lists of inquiries and/or customers from other companies. With literally thousands of lists to choose from, the dominant characteristics of the internal file will prevail and establish direction for selection of external lists. (See Table 9–1.)

Lists of other companies' customers have an advantage over compiled lists. If those companies sell by direct response. There is a discriminant characteristic: They are direct mail buyers. While compiled lists do not necessarily represent direct response buyers, they do have discriminant characteristics. There are extensive compilations in the business, professional,

Table 9–1. External List: Lifestyle Selector[a]

Selections available by:	
1. *Buyers* (Length on File)	7. *Home ownership*
2. *Income*:	8. *Children at home*
$25,000–$29,999	
$30,000–$34,999	9. *Education*
$35,000–$39,999	
$40,000–$49,999	10. *Selections/M*
$50,000–$59,999	Income $7/M
$60,000–$74,999	State $3.50/M
$75,000–$99,999	SCF $3.50/M
$100,000	Sex $7/M
	Religion $7/M
3. *Age:* 18–24; 24–34; 35–44;	Home ownership $7/M
45–54; 55–64; 65+	Children at home $7/M
	Credit card $7/M
4. *Occupation*	Education $7/M
Professional/technical	
Upper management	11. *Lifestyle selections*
Middle management	Gourmet cooking/fine food
Clerical	Foreign travel enthusiasts
Craftsman/blue collar	Cat owners
Student	Charities/volunteer activities
Homemaker	Cable TV viewers
Retired person	Home video games
Sales/marketing	Home computers
Self-employed/business owner	Craft
Working women	
5. *Marital status*	
6. *Religion*	

[a] List drawn from 28,702,000 buyers.

educational, technical, and agricultural markets, as well as the consumer market. If you want to reach college students, the biggest universe is represented by compiled lists. If you want to reach presidents of firms by number of employees, compiled lists will give you the most complete coverage. If your market is to "new mothers," compiled lists offer the biggest universe, as they do for accountants, engineers, farmers, and scores of other categories.

In the business category (used by business-to-business advertisers, mail-order companies selling to the business community, and business and financial services), these compilations offer the opportunity to reach any segment of United States industry. Selections are available by SIC (Standard Industrial Classification) code, size of company, number of employees, occupational level, individual name, title, and almost any configuration of selection factors required for the particular promotion.

In the professional market, there exists a multitude of choices. For example, doctors (by specialty, age, in private practice, intern, affiliated with hospital practice, hosptial administrator, etc.); lawyers (by size of firm, specialty, one-man firm, senior partner, ABA member, etc.); educators (by discipline, elementary, secondary, college teacher, administrator, pupil enrollment, etc.)

Most business/professional compilations are derived from printed sources: directories, rosters, registrations at trade shows, Dun & Bradstreet. There is a *Directory of Directories* that lists over 5,200 directories of various types. (Note that because lists deteriorate rapidly, it is important to find out when the list was compiled.)

In the consumer market, companies such as Polk, Metromail, and Donnelley, among others, offer the capability of reaching almost every household in the United States with an overlay of census tract statistics. Census tracts are composed of relatively small areas, with the purpose of making each tract as homogeneous as possible. One important use of compiled lists is to match external files against the house list to get a better feel for the demographics of the file for segmentation purposes. For example, one group that can be segmented is super-spot subscribers—those who live in high-income areas. With properly structured tests and in-depth analysis, you can establish a market for your product by demographics such as income, education, number of children in the family, and so on. This type of compilation usually can't be tested with small quantities and/or without carefully structured response analysis. This will be discussed at greater length later in this chapter.

Why do companies rent their lists? Profit. And the recognition that there is no such thing as a captive audience. The fact that a person buys by mail is an indication of a "mail-order buying characteristic." That person is likely to appear on many lists, which is why duplication elimination is an established technique used by most volume mailers.

Let's look at potential profit. Assuming a list of 500,000 names, turned over 20 times per year: 10,000,000 names at a net to list owner of $52 per thousand ($65 per thousand less 20 percent broker's commission) = $520,000. If the list is offered through a List Manager at an additional $10 per thousand, the net to the list owner is $514,800. If you add certain selection charges such as gender, source, state, Zip, and the like, which could add another $10 per thousand (in most cases not subject to commission), you can add back $5,200. At a running cost of about $5 per thousand ($4,000), the income received by the list owner goes right down to the bottom line. Much depends on the size and quality of the list.

How does outside list rental affect internal sales? There have been very carefully structured tests conducted over the years to answer this question. Results show over and over again that there is no effect, or at most a minimal effect, upon internal sales. The number of kinds of lists available for rental boggles the mind. To get a feel for list availability, refer to Table 9–2.

Table 9–2. **Review of List Markets by Category**

Category	1990	
	Number of Lists	Universe (000)
Business and finance	1,123	516,585
New technology	354	49,852
Education/scientific/professional	173	14,697
Fund-raising	202	81,736
Hobbies and special interests	1,154	316,465
Entertainment	457	142,260
Reading	453	102,904
Self-improvement/health/religious	634	285,865
Home interest/family/merchandise	853	613,983
Sub-total:	5,403	2,124,347
Alternate media	267	322,473
Telephone marketing	454	931,040
Compiled	131	268,764
Canadian	483	149,741
Foreign	62	9,202
Total:	6,800	3,805,567

Source: © Rose Harper, The Kleid Company Inc.

Trends

List availability reflects the growth of direct response marketing. It also is a reflection of changing socioeconomic trends. For example, in the consumer market there is money management, hobbies, health, and home interest. In the business market there is business-to-business and new technology. In addition, the expansion of media is evident in the alternate media category, such as package and billing inserts, co-ops and telephone marketing.

ZIP codes, which mailers once feared, have proven to be a boon instead of a burden. They brought list maintenance into the computer age. This step made it possible to identify duplicate names in a mailing and also led to analysis by ZIP codes. It then led to a further refinement in geographic analysis by census tract overlays. Unlike geopolitical districts (cities, counties, states, and even ZIP codes), census tracts are relatively small and homogeneous. Most residents in the census tract exhibit more demographic similarities than differences—age, marital status, income, occupation, education, home ownership, home value, number of children in the household, and so forth. As mentioned previously, this type of analysis can lead to further house file segmentation. In some instances, inferential lifestyle values are added based on the resulting demographics.

Psychographics (Lifestyle)

Veblen's theory of "conspicuous consumption" at one point in time was a sharp behavioral definition. But now we see that consumers, although demographically related, have been showing marked tendencies to spend their discretionary income quite differently. To identify the target market, it is essential to capture lifestyle details. This concept is not new—it has been recognized for a long time that societal changes have influenced demographics.

The significance of these trends can't be ignored. In a highly advanced and rapidly expanding technological environment, we must recognize that socioeconomic changes will come even more rapidly. The only constant we have is change. In marketing, societal change is a subject we can never know enough about.

List Brokers and List Selection

A list broker, as the name implies, serves two sides: the client (mailer) and the list owner. If you (as the client) have a product or service that is to be sold to a vertical market—for example, doctors, lawyers, accountants, or any other pinpointed, highly specialized market—finding the right lists is simple. In almost every field there is a compiler, trade publication, or list owner that has the precise list.

It gets decidedly more complex when you are selling a product that has a broader appeal. Here is where brokers can offer invaluable assistance in suggesting those lists that appear to represent the market you are trying to reach. You get the benefit of experts who make mailing lists their full-time specialization.

A professional relationship doesn't work if you are asked to operate in a vacuum or in abstract terms. You must view the broker as part of the total marketing process. You must specify your needs and objectives well enough in advance to permit the broker to research the list marketplace. (This research is also a valuable tool for the creative people. Working without a clear, complete knowledge of the list market makes it difficult to properly focus the promotional copy.)

In summary, the following factors are necessary to establish a competent working relationship with a list broker:

1. Bring the list broker into the picture at an early stage to help define the market.

2. Give the broker time to do a professional job. Specific, targeted list recommendations take time. Information such as balance counts, selectivity, segmentation, and geographic counts is essential to proper list selection.

3. List-rental orders (accompanied by the mailing piece and a requested specific mail date) must be cleared for approval with the list owner. Allow time for this process (Other list selection strategies are discussed later in this chapter in the sections on list tests and market tests.)

List Managers

In recent years there has been a trend toward list management whereby a list management company takes over the complete management of a list for rental purposes. Under this arrangement, the list manager performs all or almost all of the following functions:

1. Handling contacts with list brokers.

2. Clearing sample mailing piece and mail date with list owner.

3. Processing list-rental orders.

4. Following up on completion of list-rental orders to assure delivery of order within the specified return date.

5. Billing the broker on behalf of the list owner.

6. Collecting payment and remitting it to list owner less broker's commission and list-management fee.

7. Assuming responsibility for all promotions of the list and sales activity, usually without charge (over and above the established fee) to the list owner.

8. If the list owner so desires, assuming responsibility for the maintenance of the list either in-house or with an outside computer service bureau.

9. Providing the list owner with a detailed activity and accounting report, usually on a monthly basis.

The list-rental business is, for some list owners, a part-time activity. Being relieved of the voluminous details involved and the time required to promote the list usually more than warrants the extra compensation the manager receives for the specialized services rendered.

List Information

List brokers and list managers present list information on what is known as a data card. The *data card* shows the price of the list. The rate is quoted on a per-thousand-name (per M) basis. The price range averages $55–$75 per thousand for direct response lists, exclusive of selection charges, with compiled lists having a lower basic rate per thousand. Exhibit 9–1 typifies specific data available to the prospective list renter.

Exhibit 9–1.   **Data Card**

HG   (HOUSE & GARDEN)   20686E

597,982	Subscribers	$90/M
31,500	Paid Hotline (Monthly)	$90/M + $10/M
12,828	Address Changes (Qtly)	$90/M + $10/M
119,221	Expires (Last 4 Months)	$65/M
3,474	Canadian Subscribers	$100/M
**33,056	Business Addresses	$90/M + $10/M
354,275	Women Subscribers	$90/M + $5/M
97,312	Men Subscribers	$90/M + $5/M

(Non-Profit Rate is $10/M less.)

DATA   Published monthly by Conde Nast Publi-
           cations, HG covers the best in interiors,
           furniture, architecture, entertaining &
           fashion for a sophisticated readership.

UNIT $24.00 yearly (12 issues).

PROFILE $74,000 Median Household Income.
           $418,700 Median Net Worth of Household.
           45.9% Median Age. 92.5% Married. 89%
           Attended/Graduated College. 43.4%
           Professional/Managerial. 86% Homeowners
           (Average Value $261,106); 30% Own Second
           Vacation Home.

SEX   Dual audience.
SOURCE   100% Direct Response.

  **BUSINESS ADDRESSES available only to Business-
  to-Business Mailers. Upon request, can omit
  business addresses for consumer mailers.

NOTE: Orders cancelled 5 days prior to or after
original mail date will require full payment. Orders cancelled before mail date are subject to a
$25 flat fee, plus applicable production charges.

List owner requires payment 30 days after mail
date.

                    MINIMUM: 5,000
                    or All Canadian

                    ADDRESSING

            4-up CHESHIRE   N/C
            P/S LABELS $10/M
            MAGTAPE   9T/1600
            NON-RETURN $20/F
            KEYING $2/M
            (to 4 digits)

                    SELECTIONS / M

            Nth NAME   N/C
            STATE/SCF/ZIP $5
            SOURCE $10
            SEX $5

                    Two complete
                    samples required
                    in advance for
                    all new tests and
                    continuations.

            Signed agreement
            form from Mailer
            required for ini-
            tial test order.

            --- NET NAME -----
            (50,000 Minimum)
            85% + $6/M
            with verification.

            UPDATED WEEKLY.

THE
KLEID EXCLUSIVE *LIST MANAGEMENT* DIVISION
COMPANY
INC.
                    CONDE NAST PUBLICATIONS
                    MARGE KELLER
530 FIFTH AVENUE • NEW YORK, NY 10036-5101 • (212) 819-3400 • FAX (212) 719-8769
                    750 MADISON AVENUE/7TH FLOOR
                    NEW YORK, NY 10017
                    (212)-880-8282

List-Rental Procedures

Lists can be ordered directly from a list owner, but most list-rental orders are placed through list brokers. The broker handles all the details with the list owner: clearances, order placement, follow-up for order completion, billing, collecting, and payment to the list owner, less the usual 20 percent commission that accrues to the list broker.

The rental of lists involves the following conditions:

1. The names are rented for *one-time use* only. No copy of the list is to be retained for any purpose whatsoever.

2. Usage must be cleared with the list owner in advance. The mailing piece that is approved is the only one that can be used.

3. The mail date approved by the list owner must be adhered to.

4. List rentals are charged on a per-thousand-name basis.

5. Net name arrangements vary, but most list owners will specify the percentage (of the names supplied) for which the full list rental charge per thousand must be paid plus a specific running cost for the names not used.

6. Most list owners charge extra for selections such as sex, recency, ZIP code, state, unit of sale, or any segmentation available on the particular list. Prices vary.

List Tests

A *test* is the means by which the presence, quality, or genuineness of any-thing is determined; it is a means of trial. As any crossword-puzzle fan knows, a test is an experiment, an attempt to determine by small-scale trial, by *sampling*, whether something will or won't work consistently or universally.

How big should a sample be? The proper sample size is determined by two factors: sampling tolerance (or deviation) and the degree of risk that the user is willing to accept. As long as we have perfect random samples, we can keep the sampling tolerance small by taking large samples. This part of the equation is scientific.

The risk factor is much harder to deal with because it involves subjective judgments. Some mailers can't tolerate much risk.

Some practitioners advocate that the sample size should be based on the number of responses needs. The caution here is that some mailers, particularly on a new product, have what might be termed unreasonable expectations. The higher the price of the product, the lower the response is likely to be. Under these circumstances, a small test quantity will not yield the numbers needed to project with a degree of confidence. If, for example,

you expect three orders per 1,000, you should test 20,000 to give you a sense of response validity.

Others advocate that the ideal sample should be a constant percentage of the entire list. This is impractical and expensive when the list is large. Moreover, sampling tolerance is minimally affected by the size of the list.

List testing, unfortunately, is not conducted under laboratory conditions. For starters, we can't get a true random sampling in most instances. The best we can do is systematic sampling—an nth name sample—and even this is not always executed properly. For example, here are the results from a total mailing of 37,500 pieces, all mailed to the identical list, all mailed the same day, but broken out under five different keys.

Key Code	Quantity	Percentage of Response
91035	7,500	1.48
91036	7,500	1.29
91037	7,500	1.39
91038	7,500	1.48
91039	7,500	1.25

Theoretically, the percentage of response should be identical for all five keys, but actually there is a variation of 18 percent from high to low response. So one way to get a feeling for the validity of a test is to use a checking system whereby you give a separate key to each one-fifth of a test quantity. If the response percentage is identical, there is nothing to worry about. If there are substantial variations within the subsets, you must proceed cautiously.

Another universal practice is reconfirming the test with a larger sample. Actually, this type of sequential sampling is the most schematic because quantities on each successive usage can be scheduled in an orderly fashion and supported by monitored results. Thus risk can be controlled and minimized.

Another important factor to be considered in the "how big" question is the back-end (persistency) factor. If you must track these customers (frequency of purchase, collections, conversions, renewals, average take), you need to test in larger quantities. For example, if each test list is 5,000 names and response is 2 percent, tracking future activity of an average of only 100 respondents from each list can prove unreliable from the standpoint of mathematical analysis. In tracking studies of book, record, and tape clubs, for example, the number of *starts* to be analyzed is critical to the evaluation process.

In general terms, then, based on experience, a 5,000 quantity is usually adequate and more than 10,000 doesn't seem to be worthwhile.

The testing question of "how many" will always be with us. It can't be answered in an absolute way because there are no consistent elements that are universally applicable to every product or service being sold by mail. Actually, continuation mailings rarely yield the same response as the test, because there are variables from test to continuation that cannot be controlled—time

lapse, seasonality, change in list sources, the economy, weather conditions, consumer behavior, increase in costs, and a host of other factors.

Market Tests

If you are introducing a new product, it is essential to use the direct mail test to determine the potential universe for the product. Initial preconceptions about ultimate sales penetration and about target markets are usually restrictive and rarely accurate.

In addition, the initial test mailing is sometimes too small to be projectable to a large continuation mailing. For example, an initial test of 50,000, which usually includes offer and package tests, is not projectable to a continuation mailing of 500,000 or more. Yet in many instances this is the stated objective. It is therefore recommended that no less than a 100,000 quantity and preferably 150,000, be used, particularly if tests, other than the market test, are being conducted.

To identify the market, a test known as a *spectrum test* is recommended. Working with 20 to 30 lists, you construct a ladder of three tests—a sort of X, Y, Z arrangement. Your middle group, the Y of the spectrum, is drawn from lists that appear to be right on target. Your X group is drawn form those that, because of certain affinity factors, could be considered good prospects. The Z group, while it reflects a very different profile, inferentially could have reasons for being interested. This type of spectrum testing yields clues about how deeply you can mail because it is a two-dimensional sample. You are sampling the universe of lists as well as the people on the particular lists chosen.

Then there is always the question of what to do on a test mailing of, say, 150,000. Are you better off testing 30 lists of 5,000 each or 15 lists of 10,000? The answer depends on the growth pattern established in the original forecast plan.

Let's run through, as an example, a magazine called the *Glory of Art*. The first step was an "Overview of List Markets." The intention of this overview is to provide a feel for the potential universe and to decide on the specific lists to be selected from each category. (See Table 9–3.) On the *Glory of Art* it was decided to go with 30 lists, because the market testing was crucial in determining whether or not this was a viable publication in the marketplace. (See Table 9–4.)

Note that, while the schedule is concentrated in the more targeted categories, other categories, such as women's fashions, were explored with an eye toward market evaluation and expansion.

In analyzing by category in the initial stages, it is better to look at the number of lists tested in each category and at the success ratio, rather than averaging response in each category. Averages can be misleading: One list in a particular category that responds dramatically higher or lower than the other lists can influence the overall average.

Table 9–3.   *Glory of Art:* Overview of List Markets

Category	No. of Lists	Potential Universe
Art/antiques/collectibles	31	2,995,900
Up-scale gifts and decorating items	24	2,088,600
Luxury foods and gifts	16	3,316,200
Photography	5	968,900
Women's high fashions	8	843,500
Cultural books and magazines	31	5,232,200
Regional publications	20	2,732,100
Cultural arts	7	485,400
Miscellaneous (credit card)	5	1,732,000
Total	147	20,394,800[a]

[a] Can be reduced by approximately 25 percent due to the duplication factor.
Source: © Rose Harper, The Kleid Company Inc.

Table 9–4.   *Glory of Art:* List Test Schedule 150,000

Category	Universe	Test quantity	No. of Lists
Art/antiques/collectibles	1,215,600	45,000	9
Up-scale gifts and decorating items	383,000	20,000	4
Luxury foods and gifts	1,871,900	25,000	5
Photography	150,000	5,000	1
Women's high fashions	185,000	5,000	1
Cultural books and magazines	876,900	25,000	5
Regional publications	267,000	10,000	2
Cultural arts	245,000	10,000	2
Miscellaneous (credit card)	125,000	5,000	1
Total	5,319,400	150,000	30

Source: © Rose Harper, The Kleid Company Inc.

This type of analysis should be considered directional and not an absolute. In some instances the ratios are reliable, and in some instances they're not. For example, where only one list was tested in a category and proved responsive, that category must be approached more cautiously than the category where five lists were tested and were all responsive. (See Table 9–5.)

The most important element to consider, however, is that the dynamics of each testing situation are dissimilar, particularly the objectives, the time frame, and the financials. These variables must be studied and given consideration in structuring the initial test.

Elimination of Duplication

The advent of ZIP codes in 1967 forced list owners into the computer age. This led to the breakthrough in the ability to remove duplicate names (dupes) within a mailing. The popular term is merge/purge, and what it

Table 9–5. *Glory of Art*: Analysis Success Factor by Category

	No. of Tests	No. of Continuations	Percentage of Success
Y (*of the Spectrum*):			
Art/antiques/collectibles	9	7	77.8
Cultural books and magazines	5	5	100.0
Cultural arts	2	1	50.0
Subtotal	16	13	81.3
X:			
Upscale gifts and decorating items	4	1	25.0
Photography	1	1	100.0
Regional publications	2	2	100.0
Subtotal	7	14	57.1
Z:			
Luxury foods and gifts	5	2	40.0
Women's high fashions	1	1	100.0
Miscellaneous (credit card)	1	—	—
Subtotal	7	3	42.9
Total	30	20	66.6

Source: © Rose Harper, The Kleid Company Inc.

means is the matching of two or more mailing lists by electronic means to remove duplication and to ensure that each addressee receives only one mailing piece. This is accomplished by the use of a match code, which is a series of characters that is extracted on a consistent basis from the name and address and that fully identifies that person to the computer.

Aside from avoiding the irritation to the recipient of receiving several of the same mailings at almost the same time and sending a solicitation to a present customer, there are considerable dollar savings involved. (See Table 9–6.)

Table 9–6. Dollar Saving on Dupe Removal [a]

Percent Duplication	Mailing Quantity			
	1,000,000	2,500,000	5,000,000	10,000,000
5	$ 15,000	$ 37,500	$ 75,000	$ 150,000
10	30,000	75,000	150,000	300,000
15	45,000	112,500	225,000	450,000
20	60,000	150,000	300,000	600,000
25	75,000	187,500	375,000	750,000
30	90,000	225,000	450,000	900,000
35	105,000	262,500	525,000	1,050,000

[a] Savings achieved by eliminating duplicate names from a mailing (based on a mailing cost of $300 per thousand pieces).
Source: © Rose Harper, The Kleid Company Inc.

Another factor that needs to be considered because of merge/purge is the resulting true or actual list cost per thousand. This is essential information in projecting a mailing plan—and an *actual* list cost per order. (See Table 9–7.)

In most instances, the house file (or segment of the house file) is the primary list against which the rental lists are matched. Then all lists are matched against each other. In the process, intralist duplication is also discovered. Since the mailing tape, after the match, is in ZIP code sequence, it provides the opportunity to:

1. Analyze response by ZIP code by matching the tape or response against the mailing tape.

2. Omit all ZIP codes that, from previous experience, have not been responsive or have proven to have a high bad-pay factor.

Table 9–7. Actual List Cost per Thousand after Merge/Purge, Assuming Gross Quantity of 50,000 Names and a 25 Percent Duplication Factor

Gross Qty.	List Cost per M	Running Charges per M	Selection Charges per M	85% on Basic List Rental	Running Costs	Selection Charges	Total Billing	Actual List CPM Assuming 75% Qty. Mailed
50,000	$45.00	$5.00	$0.00	$1,912.50	$37.50	$ 0.00	$1,950.00	$52.00
50,000	45.00	5.00	6.50	1,912.50	37.50	325.00	2,275.00	60.67
50,000	50.00	5.00	0.00	2,125.00	37.50	0.00	2,162.50	57.67
50,000	50.00	5.00	4.50	2,125.00	37.50	225.00	2,387.50	63.67
50,000	55.00	5.00	0.00	2,337.50	37.50	0.00	2,375.00	63.33
50,000	55.00	5.00	7.50	2,337.50	37.50	375.00	2,750.00	73.33
50,000	60.00	5.00	0.00	2,550.00	37.50	0.00	2,587.50	69.00
50,000	60.00	5.00	6.50	2,550.00	37.50	325.00	2,912.50	77.67

Source: © Rose Harper, The Kleid Company Inc.

At what quantity it makes sense to 'merge/purge against the house file is a knotty question. Some managements maintain a strict policy against any duplication of their house file regardless of the quantity of the rental names. In such instances merge/purge is an imperative.

Judgment dictates that the larger your house file becomes, the higher the percentage of duplication you can expect from rented lists. Thus if a direct marketer has a house list of 1,000,000 names, for example, merge/purge is always advisable, no matter what the quantity of rented names. On the other hand, if the house list is, say, only 50,000 names, it hardly makes sense to merge/purge five lists of 5,000 each against the house file because the duplication factor would be very small.

However, the duplication factor should not be the sole consideration in deciding for or against merge/purge. A firm with a house file of 50,000 names might elect to build its house file fast and therefore test 20 lists of 5,000

names simultaneously. The chances of heavy duplication among these 100,000 names could be in the 25 percent range. Therefore merge/purge would make sense even though duplication against the house file would probably be small.

Tape-to-tape matching offers other marketing opportunities. For example, an insurance company had been reaching "golden age" prospects via census tract addressing by using tracts with the highest density of older people. There was waste, however, in reaching everyone in a census tract. By tape-to-tape matching against a list of families with young children in the same areas, it was possible to refine the selections by suppressing the young families.

Tape-to-tape matching also allows for file overlay analysis to take advantage of various types of information available on consumer files. Lifestyle Selector (Denver), for example, through the information it collects on consumer information cards, will overlay its master file on a house file. The names that match are then analyzed to produce a lifestyle profile of the house file—demographically by age, income, occupation, marital status, or home ownership—plus a lifestyle profile including interest and hobby categories such as foreign travel, gardening, cooking, photography, physical fitness, among others. (Refer to Table 9–1.)

Presented below is some of the terminology used in the merge/purge process:

- *Contribution to multibuyers*—names appearing more than once that are transferred to the multibuyer file
- *Quantity ordered*—by the mailer
- *Gross input*—actual quantity processed into the system
- *Unordered names*—involving requested omits such as state, sectional center, ZIP code
- *Edit error*—usually mistakes in addresses (city, state, ZIP code)
- *Net records into merge/purge*—after omitting unordered names and edit errors
- *Internal duplication*—also described as intrafile duplicates that represent names and addresses appearing more than once within one file
- *Pander file matches*—usually from the Direct Marketing Association Mail Preference Service tape; people who have written to the DMA indicating they prefer *not* to get any direct mail
- *Suppression matches*—usually an internal file of customers plus those people who have requested that their name not be used for list-rental purposes, bad-pay file, and the like
- *Unique records*—names that remain on the mailing tape only one time

Scheduling and Analysis of Direct Mail Programs

The attraction of direct mail is its *measurability*. Direct mail is not inexpensive. On a cost-per-thousand exposure, aside from the phone, it is probably the most expensive medium. But unlike most media, the response per thousand is not extrapolated. It is an arithmetical fact.

Let's go back to the *Glory of Art*, where 30 lists were tested in the initial mailing. In order to plan the continuation mailing, there is the need to analyze the test results, which are presented in Table 9–8. Note that the factors considered were also considered on a list-by-list basis.

Table 9–8. *Glory of Art*: Results of Test Mailing

Actual mail quantity	150,040
Gross subscribers	3,256
Gross percentage response	2.17%
Package cost per M	$300
List cost per M	$60
Total cost per M	$360
Total cost	$54,014
Gross cost per subscriber	$16.59
Percent credit	90.40%
Pay percentage	71.90%
Net subscribers	2,341
Net percentage response	1.56%
Net cost per subscriber	$23.07
Total revenue (on net)	$58,408
Net revenue (total revenue minus total cost)	$4,394
Net revenue per subscriber	$1.88

Another important step is to consider the assumptions that need to be applied when projecting the roll-out response. This qualifier is necessary for a variety of reasons: The test quantity was 5,000 in each list, the test mailing was made at a different time (see the discusssion of seasonality later in this chapter), the increase in the merge/purge factor due to the larger mailing quantity.

In the *Glory of Art* case, the following assumptions were used:

1. 12 percent loss through merge/purge

2. 10 percent lift for seasonality

3. 7 percent decrease for test to continuation

4. Credit and bad-pay at actual for each list

These assumptions were applied on a list-by-list basis, with the starting point being previous response. Table 9–9 shows a sampling of the list-by-list analysis.

Now let's look at the summary of the continuation mailing (Table 9–10), using the same factors that were used to analyze the test mailing. You will

Table 9–9.   *Glory of Art*: Continuation Mailing (Art/Antiques/Collectibles)[a]

	Previous		Projected																
List	Mail Quantity	Gross Pct. Response	Mail Qty.	No. Orders	Gross Pct.	Pkg. C.P.M.	List C.P.M.	Total C.P.M.	C.P.O.	Pct. Credit	Pay Pct.	Net Orders	Net Pct. Response	Net C.P.O.	Total Cost	Total Revenue	Net Revenue	Net Rev. per Subscr.
1	5,004	2.90	44,300	1,315	2.97	$300	$45.45	$345.45	$11.64	91.0	72.4	952	2.15	$16.08	$15,303	$23,752	$ 8,449	$ 8.88
2	4,950	3.10	35,250	1,117	3.17	300	63.85	363.85	11.48	88.0	71.9	803	2.28	15.97	12,826	20,035	7,209	8.98
3	5,007	3.00	44,000	1,350	3.07	300	45.47	345.47	11.26	89.0	77.0	1,040	2.36	14.62	15,201	25,948	10,747	10.33
4	5,100	2.90	43,200	1,278	2.96	300	63.66	363.66	12.29	91.0	70.7	904	2.09	17.38	15,710	22,555	6,845	7.57
5	4,999	2.80	43,100	1,232	2.86	300	50.72	350.72	12.27	82.0	79.0	973	2.26	15.54	15,116	24,276	9,160	9.41
6	5,060	3.00	47,600	1,461	3.07	300	63.02	363.02	11.83	85.0	74.0	1,081	2.27	15.98	17,280	26,971	9,691	8.97
7	4,975	3.10	30,800	976	3.17	300	51.13	351.13	11.08	92.0	72.0	703	2.28	15.38	10,815	17,540	6,725	9.57

[a] Sampling of list-by-list evaluation.
Source: © Rose Harper, The Kleid Company Inc.

note that 100,000 in new list tests was included. In order to sustain a continuing and ongoing direct mail program, it is essential that an inventory of profitable lists be developed. Therefore, in most instances, 10 percent of the total mailing should be devoted to list testing.

Table 9–10.   *Glory of Art*: Continuation Mailing

	Continuations	List Tests	Total
Mail quantity	866,702	100,000	966,702
Number of orders	23,759	2,000	25,759
Percentage response	2.74%	2.00%	2.66%
Package C.P.M.	$300.00	$300.00	$300.00
List C.P.M.	$51.73	$45.00	$51.03
Total C.P.M.	$351.73	$345.00	$351.03
C.P.O.	$12.83	$17.25	$13.17
Percentage credit	89.4%	89.3%	89.4%
Pay percentage	73.4%	72.7%	73.4%
Net orders	17,439	1,454	18,893
Net percent response	2.01%	1.45%	1.95%
Net C.P.O.	$17.48	$23.73	$17.96
Total cost	$304,845	$34,500	$339,345
Total revenue	$435,106	$36,277	$471,383
Net revenue	$130,261	$1,777	$132,038
Net revenue per subscriber	$7.47	$1.22	$6.99

Source: © Rose Harper, The Kleid Company Inc.

Remember that mailing plans are budgets or pro-forma profit plans. In direct mail, it all starts with list history. The ability to review the history of a list on an each-time-used basis is critical to structuring a sound mailing plan, because in direct mail the list is the medium.

One of the most helpful evaluation tools is the break-even analysis. This technique measures the response needed for total revenue to meet total promotional cost. At this point, obviously, there is no profit. Each company, then, must add other constants (overhead, cost of money, cost of product, bad-pay, returns, refurbishing, customer lifetime value, and the like) to determine how much it can afford to pay for an order.

There are many variations in the analytical process. The charts refer to magazines, but with some variations they could apply to books or catalogs. It all boils down to the absolute necessity of measuring results within the parameters of the financial dynamics of the particular situation. If direct mail is measurable, then the message must be loud and clear. And it doesn't stop with front-end response.

One precaution: There is a danger in working with averages. The average is a handy mathematical device, but remember that there are several kinds of averages, all different and each revealing a wholly different aspect of the same set of figures. Table 9–11 shows how a group's typical income would differ, using just four of the simpler averaging methods.

Table 9–11.   Averaging Methods for Group Income

Family Income[a]	Income-Averaging Methods
1. $60,000 2. $50,000 3. $40,000 4. $30,000 5. $25,000 6. $20,000 7. $20,000 8. $20,000 9. $20,000 10. $15,000	*Arithmetic Mean*: $30,000[b] The most common kind of average. Computed by taking the sum of all the families divided by the number of families. In this example, three families earn more than the mean and six earn less. *Midrange*: $37,500[b] The richest earns four times more than the poorest. Add the bottom and divide by 2. Three families earn more than the midrange and seven earn less. *Median*: $22,500[b] If you want to represent the group by what a family in the exact middle gets, you must locate the median—the income that will be higher that the incomes of the lower half and lower than the upper half. If there were eleven families, the median income would be the sixth highest. With only ten—no family is in the middle, so you find the dividing line by adding the fifth and sixth and dividing by 2. In this example, the median is less than both the midrange and the mean. *Mode*: $20,000[b] Also called the *norm*. Mode in statistical work equals that value, magnitude, or score which occurs the greatest number of times in a given series of observations. In this example, the modal income is $20,000. If there had been no set of two or more, there would have been no mode.

[a] Total = $300,000.
[b] "Typical" income for group.
Source: © Rose Harper, The Kleid Company Inc.

The use of averages is not being disputed; rather what is being suggested is that the nuances behind averages should be observed. To use a statistical term, there should be an awareness of the "outliers," the freaks, that can influence an average unduly and lead to incorrect interpretation of results.

Seasonality

Seasonality has been a priority subject in direct mail for a long time. Have seasonality patterns been changing? It appears so, from the results of the seasonality study conducted by The Kleid Company that are presented in Table 9–12.

Direct mail marketing is complex. There are many variables that make it difficult to reduce research findings to a common denominator or to an absolute mathematical formula. The external environment and internal environment do not happen on a schedule. Therefore this study should be considered directional. It has inspired multiproduct direct marketers to conduct

Table 9–12. Seasonality Study: Summary by Category Showing Top Three Months

Categories	1989—1990	1990—1991	1991—1992
Business/finance	December May March	December June January	December September August
Cultural reading	December May/June September	December November June	December November January
General reading	December June January	December June May	December June August
Self-improvement	May December March	December March May	December May August
Health	December June September	June December July	December June August
Home interest	September December June	June December January	December June January
Parents and children	September December June	January June Sept/Dec	December June September
Hobbies/related subjects	December June Aug/Sept	December June September	June December September
Entertainment	December January June	December June January	December September August
Educational, technical, professional	July December March	December October July	August December June
Fund-raising	November October February	November October January	November September February

First line = top, second line = second place, third line = third place.
Source: © Rose Harper, The Kleid Company Inc.

their own seasonality studies on a product-by-product basis. As a matter of fact, the reason for some of the seasonal changes and consistencies is that many mailers have monitored their own promotional patterns and have graduated from two mailings per year to four or five mailings.

For results-oriented mailers, it is important to recognize the electricity of direct mail, which impacts "when to mail" as much as "what to mail and to whom."

Statistical and Analytical Techniques

Statistics is a branch of mathematics dealing with the collection, analysis, and interpretation of masses of numerical data. In some instances it is easy, as for example, in descriptive statistics, which represent numbers that yield an efficient summary of some type of information—batting averages, unemployment rates, Dow-Jones averages, and the like.

In direct mail it is essential to segment and define a market. To do this, it becomes necessary to look at the statistical techniques available as aids in analysis and as market research tools.

Multivariate methods are not new, but the proliferation of these techniques in marketing research has been spurred by the ability of the computer to perform enormous numbers of calculations in a short time. Factor analysis, one multivariate method, is based on the proposition that if there is a systematic interdependence among a set of variables, it must be due to something fundamental that created the interdependence. These underlying factors will tend to cluster the variables into categories. The categories are not mutually exclusive. Factor analysis will perform the identification of underlying factors and the grouping of manifest (observed) variables under each factor.

For example, Old American Insurance Company of Kansas City, Missouri, has a unique databank that stores up to 103 bits of manifest data about each ZIP code. The databank lists potential marketing units (ZIP code areas) in terms of their environmental characteristics, which, when combined into factors, provide the inferential dimension of lifestyle and are thus used to predict consumer behavior. Using factor analysis, Old American can mathematically correlate the 103 environmental variables of the ZIP code areas of interest with each other and thus condense them into a dozen or more uncorrelated factors that are much more meaningful and manageable in subsequent analysis.

Regression analysis and correlation analysis enable us to deal with variables that are stated in terms of numerical values rather than qualitative categories. These methods provide the basis for measuring the strength of the relationships among the variables. The term *regression analysis* refers to the methods by which estimates are made of the values of a variable from a knowledge of the values of one or more other variables and to the measurement of the errors involved in this estimation process. The term *correlation analysis* refers to methods for measuring the strength of the associations (correlations) among these variables. Equations are used in both instances to express the relationship among the variables.

There are many variations of these analytical systems. As a direct marketer, you must be aware of the importance of statistical analysis for decision making. To make it worthwhile, you need to establish the marketing concepts or criteria so that the statisticians can decide on the technique to be used to get actionable information—information from the database that will help you manage your other resources better.

Mathematical Modeling

Modeling techniques have been used in direct mail for some time, but today's advanced technology allows for marketing information systems with predictive capabilities. The initial gross cost of acquiring a new customer is not the key to the real value of the order. Back-end performance (pay-ups, conversions, renewal rates) provides the definitive measurement of response. Source evaluation is a method for examining the lifetime value and profitability of a new customer or product through a variety of sources within a particular time frame.

There are also marketing decision models. In general, a model allows the exploration of alternatives by profit ratios, return on investment, and any other pertinent statistics. You can play the "what if" game by making a number of changes to see their effect on the overall plan. This is a simulation technique. And it all starts with information from past experience: pricing, source, response, list markets, gender, repeat business, unit of sales, and so on. The data collection and processing activity is extremely important and will be directional in the selection of the model to be developed.

The heart of every direct marketing operation is the customer file, the database. The degree of success you achieve in the use of direct mail will be measured by your ability to extract the most profitable segments from your database and rental lists.

Self-Quiz

1. What three things are both central and indispensable to direct marketing through lists?

    a. _____

    b. _____

    c. _____

2. The two broad categories of lists are _____ and

    _____.

3. Your best customer is _____.

4. The art of getting more sales from existing customers is to be able to

    match _____ to customer buying _____

    _____.

5. Define the R-F-M formula:

R stands for _____.

F stands for _____.

M stands for_____.

6. Define *super-spot subscribers*.

_____

_____

7. More than _____ of all married women work.

8. List brokers serve two sides: the _____ and the

_____.

9. In testing a new list a quantity of _____ names is usually adequate.

10. If a mailer is testing offers and mailing packages simultaneously, a

quantity of at least _____ names is recommended.

11. Define *spectrum test*.

_____

_____

_____

12. Define *merge/purge*.

_____

_____

_____

13. How does one best establish the seasonality factor of a mailing program?

_____

_____

_____

Pilot Project

You are the circulation director of a consumer magazine. You have agreed to conduct a mailing list seminar for the marketing class of a leading university.

In preparation for this seminar, itemize all aspects of the following outline:

A. Definition of a list

B. The three things central and indispensable to direct marketing through lists

C. Definition of internal and external lists

D. The theory of segmentation

E. Definition of the R-F-M formula

F. Value of census tracts

G. Value of ZIP codes

H. Functions of list brokers

I. Functions of list managers

J. Components of list data cards

K. Purpose of list tests

L. Test quantities

M. Theory of a spectrum test

N. Duplication elimination

O. Break-even analysis

P. Seasonality

Q. Factor analysis

R. Regression and correlation analysis

S. Modeling techniques

CHAPTER TEN

Magazines

Where Do You Go First?

The advertising pages of magazines are to the direct response advertiser what the retail outlet is to the manufacturer selling through the more traditional channels. A magazine that performs consistently well for a variety of direct response advertisers is like a store in a low-rent, high-traffic location. It's far more profitable than a store selling the same merchandise on the wrong side of town.

Such a magazine just seems to have an atmosphere that is more conducive to the mail response customer. The mail order shopping reader traffic is high in relation to the publication's cost per thousand. Magazines in this category (and this is by no means a complete list) are *National Enquirer*, *Parade*, and the mighty *TV Guide*. Women's publications also doing well for mail-order advertisers are *Family Circle, Better Homes and Gardens, Good Housekeeping, Cosmopolitan, Woman's Day, Seventeen*, and *Redbook*. Men's publications include *Home Mechanix, Moose, Playboy*, and *Penthouse*. (For a comprehensive list of magazines that provide a structured mail-order atmosphere, see Table 10–1.)

But just as retail locations come into and go out of favor with each passing decade, so do the trends that determine which publications work well in the mail order marketplace at a particular time. For example, coming into favor right now are *New Yorker, Country Living, Family Circle*, and *Smithsonian*. In the 1960s there was much greater interest in such publications as *McCall's, Ladies' Home Journal, House & Garden, House Beautiful*, and the *National Observer*. And I can remember in the 1950s looking to *Living for Young Homemakers, Harper's/Atlantic*, and *Saturday Review* — and the *Saturday Evening Post* could be counted on for good results.

There are some publications that one might assume at first glance to be perfect for the mail-order advertiser. But close examination of performance figures for many different advertisers in these publications causes a red flag to be raised for the direct marketing advertiser. Here are a few places to go right now at your own risk. *Reader's Digest, National Geographic, New York*, and *Town & Country*. Some of these publications, though, have done well for high-ticket items like collectibles.

Table 10–1. U.S. Consumer Magazines with Mail-Order and/or Shopping Advertising Pages

Class	Publication

A

Class	Publication
10A	A+
33	Absolute Sound, The
23	Accent on Living
8	Across the Board
30A	Adirondack Life
8A	Adventure Magazine
46	Adventure Road
21A	Advocate, The
4	Aero
10A	Ahoy
23	Aimplus
22	Air & Space, Smithsonian
31	Air Force Times
4	Air Line Pilot
4	Air Progress
1	Air Travel Journal
30A	Alaska
1	Alaska Airlines Magazine
9B	Alcalde
46	Aloha
2	American Artist
5	American Baby
18	American Brewer
8	American Business
13	American Cage-Bird Magazine
2	American Collector's Journal
13	American Field
17A	American Film
19	American Handgunner
23	American Health
22	American Heritage
23A	American History Illustrated
21	American Horticulturist
19	American Hunter, The
20	American Legion Auxiliary's National News, The
20A	American Legion Magazine, The
31A	American Motorcyclist
39	American Photographer
19	American Rifleman
21	American Rose Magazine
26	American Scholar, The
19	American Shotgunner, The
41	American Spectator, The
12	American Square Dance Magazine
1	American Way
22	American West
24	Americana
1	Amtrak Express
35	Animal Kingdom
28	Antaeus
10A	Antic
2	Antique Market Report
2	Antique Monthly
2	Antique Trader Weekly, The
2	Antiques Directory
4	AOPA Pilot
25	Appaloosa Journal
25	Appaloosa World
25	Arabian Horse World
25	Arabians
22	Archaeology
19	Archery World
24	Architectural Digest
30A	Arizona Living
31	Army Times
31	Army Times Military Group
2	Art & Antiques
2	Art & Auction
2	Art & Crafts Catalyst
2	Art in America
2	Artist's Magazine, The
2	Artnews
2	Art Now Gallery Guide
2	Art/World
2	Artforum
30A	Atlantic City Magazine
22	Atlantic, The
22	Attenzione
33	Audio
35	Audubon
24	Austin Homes & Gardens
3	Auto Racing Digest
3	Autobuff
3	Automobile Magazine
3	AutoWeek
4	Aviation Digest

B

Class	Publication
20	B'nai B'rith International Jewish Monthly, The
30A	Back Home in Kentucky
8B	Backpacker
25	Backstretch, The
51	Barbie
8	Barron's-National Business and Financial Weekly
45	Baseball Digest
45	Basketball Digest
19	Bassmaster Classic Report
19	Bassmaster Magazine
6	Bay & Delta Yachtsman
23	Bestways
13	Better Beagling
24	Better Homes and Gardens

Table 10–1 (Continued). U.S. Consumer Magazines with Mail-Order and/or Shopping Advertising Pages

24 Better Homes and Gardens All-Time Favorite Recipes	14 Better Homes and Gardens Needlecraft Ideas	8 Business Month
24 Better Homes and Gardens Building Ideas	24 Better Homes and Gardens Remodeling Ideas	8 Business Week
11 Better Homes and Gardens Christmas Ideas	24 Better Homes and Gardens Traditional Home	10A Byte
11 Better Homes and Gardens Country Crafts	24 Better Homes and Gardens Window and Wall Ideas	**C**
24 Better Homes and Gardens Decorating	8 Better Investing	30B Cable Choice
24 Better Homes and Gardens Do-It Yourself Home Improvement and Repair	22 Better Living	30A California
	44 Beverly Hills (213)	45 California Bicyclist
	45 Bicycle Guide	25 California Horse Review
	45 Bicycle Rider	43A California Senior Citizen
	45 Bicycle USA	8B Camping and RV Magazine
21 Better Homes and Gardens Garden Ideas and Outdoor Living	19 Big Three, The	8B Canoe
	45 Billiards Digest	30A Cape Cod Life
	13 Bird Talk	24 Capper's
43A Better Homes and Gardens Grandparents	35 Bird Watcher's Digest	3 Car and Driver
	8 Black Enterprise	3 Car and Driver Buyers Guide
	11 Blade Magazine, The	3 Car Collector/Car Classics
24 Better Homes and Gardens Holiday Cooking	25 Blood-Horse, The	3 Car Craft
	1A Blum's Farmers & Planters Almanac and Turner's Carolina Almanac	46 Caribbean Travel & Life Magazine
11 Better Homes and Gardens Holiday Crafts	45 BMX Action	3 Cars & Parts Magazine
	45 BMX Plus	13 Cat Fancy
	6 Boating	42 Catholic Twin Circle
24 Better Homes and Gardens Home Plan Ideas	6 Boatracing	13 Cats Magazine
	30A Boca Raton	45 Century Sports Network
	45 Body Boarding	16 Change
24 Better Homes and Gardens Kitchen & Bath Ideas	18 Bon Appetit	24 Changing Homes
	30A Boston Magazine	22 Changing Times
	49 Boston Woman	42 Charisma
24 Better Homes and Gardens Low Calorie	30A Bostonia Magazine	6 Chesapeake Bay Magazine
	19 Bowhunter	19 Chevy Outdoors
	45 Bowling	38 Chicago Tribune Magazine Sunday
49 Better Homes and Gardens Microwave Recipes	45 Bowling Digest	49 Child
	51 Boys' Life	18 Chocolatier
	1 Braniff's Destination	42 Christian Century, The
	7 Bride's	42 Christian Herald
	23A British Heritage	42 Christianity Today

(Continued)

Table 10–1 (Continued). **U.S. Consumer Magazines with Mail-Order and/or Shopping Advertising Pages**

25	Chronicle of the Horse, The
42	Church Herald, The
30A	Cincinnati
3	Circle Track
33	Circus Magazine
44	City & Country Club Life
8	City & State
23A	Civil War Times Illustrated
15	Classified, Inc.
30A	Cleveland Magazine
11	Coin World
11	Coins
2	Collector Editions
2	Collectors Mart
2	Collectors News
2	Collectors' Showcase
9B	College Woman
24	Colonial Homes
45	Colorado SportStyles
41	Commonweal
10A	Compute!
10A	Compute!'s Apple Applications Special
10A	Compute!'s Gazette
10A	Computer Digest
10A	Computer Graphic
10A	Computer Living/New York
10A	Computer Shopper
46	Conde Nast's Traveler
30A	Connecticut Magazine
22	Connoisseur, The
22	Consumers Digest
33	Contemporary Christian Music
1	Continental Airlines Magazine
49	Cooking Light
18	Cook's Magazine, The
49	Cosmopolitan
24	Country Home
24	Country Journal
24	Country Living
18	Country Living/Country Cooking
30B	CPI Guide Network, The
11	Craft Art Needlework Digest
11	Crafts 'N Things
11	Crafts Magazine
8	Crain's Chicago Business
8	Crain's New York Business
49	Creative Ideas for Living
41	Crisis, The
45	Cross Country Skier
6	Cruising World
31A	Cycle
31A	Cycle Guide
31A	Cycle News
31A	Cycle World
31A	Cycle World 1987 Annual & Buyer's Guide
45	Cycling U.S.A.
45	Cyclist
	D
30A	D Magazine
24	Dallas-Fort Worth Home & Garden
17A	Dancemagazine
17A	DancScene
39	Darkroom & Creative Camera Techniques
39	Darkroom Photography
11	Dell Puzzle Magazine Group
30A	Denver Magazine
30A	Detroit Monthly
30B	Dial
9B	Directions
31A	Dirt Bike
31A	Dirt Rider Magazine
31A	Dirt Wheels
45	Disc Sports
43	Discover
46	Discovery
20	Discovery YMCA
49	Disney Channel Magazine, The
46	Diversion
13	Dog Fancy
13	Dog World
11	Dolls
9B	Dorm Magazine
33	Down Beat
30A	Down East
11	Dragon
17A	Dramatics
33	Drum Corps World
19	Ducks Unlimited
3	Dune Buggies & Hot VWs
	E
20	Eagle Magazine
24	Earth Shelter Living
22	East West
6	Eastern Boating
25	Eastern Horse World
31A	Easyriders
50	Electricity
20	Elks Magazine, The
50	Elle
46	Endless Vacation
6	Ensign, The
8	Entrepreneur
42	Episcopalian, The
25	Equus
34	Espionage Magazine
30	Esquire
49	Essence
42	Eternity
46	European Travel & Life
16	Exceptional Parent, The

Table 10–1 (Continued). U.S. Consumer Magazines with Mail-Order and/or Shopping Advertising Pages

49 Executive Female, The	18 Food & Wine	18 Gourmet
5 Expecting	45 Football Digest	19 Gray's Sporting Journal
51 Eye, The	8 Forbes	6 Great Lakes Sailor
	41 Foreign Affairs	30A Great Lakes Travel & Living
F	41 Foreign Service Journal	
3 Fabulous Mustangs and Exotic Fords	8 Fortune	30A Greenville Magazine
	3 4WD Action	1A Grier's Almanac
49 Fairfield County Woman	3 4 Wheel & Off-Road	22 Grit
	3 Four Wheeler	42 Group
49 Family Circle	16 4-H Leader—The National Magazine For 4-H	5 Guide for Expectant Parents
49 Family Circle Great Ideas		21A Guide Magazine/Gay Life
24 Family Handyman, The	45 Freestylin'	5 Guide to Your Child's Development
	8 Frequent Flyer	
8A Family Motor Coaching	46 Friendly Exchange	33 Guitar World
	19 Full Cry	19 Gun Dog
21 Farmstead Magazine	19 Fur-Fish-Game	19 Gun Week
34 Fate	8 Futures	30 Gung-Ho
20 Federal Times	22 Futurist, The	19 Guns & Ammo
2 Fiberarts		19 Guns & Ammo Annual 1988
19 Field & Stream	**G**	
43A 50 plus	30 Gallery	19 Guns Magazine
11 FineScale Modeler	20A Gambling Times	
30B Fine Tuning	19 Game & Fish Magazine	**H**
11 Fine Woodworking		20 Hadassah Magazine
19 Fins and Feathers	11 Games	47 Ham Radio Magazine
46 First Class	20A Gaming International Magazine	47 Hands-On Electronics
5 First Year of Life, The		50 Harper's Bazaar
19 Fish Sniffer, The	4 General Aviation News	22 Harper's Magazine
19 Fisherman, The		24 Harrowsmith
19 Fishing & Hunting News	23 Generations	9B Harvard Magazine
	30 Genesis	46 Hawaii
19 Fishing Facts	30 Gentlemen's Quarterly	23 Health
19 Fishing World		3 Hemmings Motor News
19A Flex	7 Getting Married: A Planning Guide	
45 Florida Golfweek		21 Herb Quarterly, The
45 Florida Racquet Journal	50 Glamour	33 High Fidelity
	22 Globe	8 High Technology
19 Florida Sportsman	45 Golf Digest	23A Highlander, The
21 Flower & Garden	45 Golf Illustrated	8 Hispanic Business
4 Flying	45 Gold Magazine	24 Historic Preservation
11 Flying Models	49 Good Food Magazine	45 Hockey Digest
30A Folsom World & Northlake News, The	49 Good Housekeeping	24 Home
	8A Good Sam's Hi-Way Herald	29 Home Mechanix

(Continued)

Table 10–1 (Continued).   U.S. Consumer Magazines with Mail-Order and/or Shopping Advertising Pages

11 Home Shop Machinist, The	**K**	34 Magazine of Fantasy and Science Fiction, The
24 Homeowner, The	8B KOA Directory Road Atlas and Camping Guide	11 Magical Blend
24 Homes International		30A Manhattan
30A Honolulu Magazine	30A KS. Magazine	30A Manhattan Living
25 Hoof Beats		6 Marine and Recreation News
2 Horizon	**L**	
11 Horoscope	30A L.A. Weekly	19 Marlin
25 Horse Digest, The	30A L.A. West	10 Marvel Comics Group
25 Horse Illustrated	1 LACSA'S World	43A Mature Outlook
25 Horseman	1A Ladies Birthday Almanac, The	49 McCall's
25 Horse World		49 McCall's Beauty, Diet & Health Guide
25 Horseman's Service Directory and Desk Reference, The	49 Ladies' Home Journal	49 McCall's Cooking School
	49 Lady's Circle	
	6 Lakeland Boating	14 McCall's Needlework & Crafts
25 Horsemen's Journal	5 Lamaze Parents' Magazine	
25 Horseplay		23 Medical Self-Care
25 Horsetrader, The	11 Lapidary Journal	30 Men's Health
	16 Learning 87	45 Met Golfer, The
I	23 Let's Live	24 Metropolis
44 Illustrated, The	24 Life & Home	30A Metropolitan Detroit
46 In-Fisherman Angling Adventures, The	10A Link-Up	24 Metropolitan Home
	11 Linn's Stamp News	30A Miami Mensual
8 Inc.	11 Live Steam	30A Miami/South Florida Magazine
8 Income Opportunities	42 Living Church, The	
30A Indianapolis Monthly	11 Llewellyn New Times, The	19 Michigan Out-Of-Doors
45 Inside Sports		
16 Instructor	6 Log, The	30A Mid-Atlantic Country
45 International Gymnast	30A Los Angeles Magazine	4 Midwest Flyer Magazine
46 International Travel News	8B Lost Treasure	
	20A Lottery Player's Magazine	24 Midwest Living
46 Islands		19 Midwest Outdoors
24 It's Your Move	42 Lutheran, Standard, The	27 Milwaukee Labor Press AFL-CIO
9B Ivy League Magazines		
	42 Lutheran, The	11 Miniature Collector
J		11 Model Railroader
1A J. Gruber's Almanack	**M**	7 Modern Bride
30A Jacksonville Magazine	30 M	33 Modern Drummer
30A Japanese-American Yellow Pages	42A Macfadden Women's Group	47 Modern Electronics
		43A Modern Maturity
33 Jazziz	10A Macworld	33 Modern Percussionist
33 Jazztimes	50 Mademoiselle	39 Modern Photography
20 Junior League Review	2 Magazine Antiques, The	22 Moneysworth
51 Junior Scholastic		

Table 10–1 (Continued). U.S. Consumer Magazines with Mail-Order and/or Shopping Advertising Pages

22	Mother Earth News	22	Natural History	43A	NRTA/AARP News Bulletins
22	Mother Earth News American Country	31	Navy News	22	Nuestro
22	Mother Jones	31	Navy Times	11	Numismatic News
5	Mothers Today	14	Needle & Thread	11	Nutshell News
5	Mothers Today Sourcebook	14	Needlecraft For Today	51	NYC
31A	Motocross Action	11	Needlepoint News		**O**
6	Motor Boating & Sailing	30A	Nevada Magazine	3	Off-Road
3	Motor Trend	22	New Age	6	Offshore: New England's Boating Magazine
31A	Motorcyclist	30A	New Dominion		
8A	Motorhome	30A	New England Monthly		
46	Motorland	43A	New England Senior Citizen	30A	Ohio Magazine
9B	Moving Up			3	Old Cars Weekly
49	Ms.	24	New Homeowner Guide, The	1A	Old Farmer's Almanac, The
51	Muppet Magazine	6	New Jersey Boater	34	Old West
19A	Muscle & Fitness	19	New Jersey Hunting and Fishing Guide	24	Old-House Journal, The
3	Muscle Car Review				
3	Muscle Cars	30A	New Jersey Monthly	43	Omni
33	Music City News	30A	New Mexico Magazine	3	On Track
	N	30A	New Orleans Magazine	24	1,001 Home Ideas
				3	Open Wheel
30A	Nashville	22	New Realities	30A	Orange Coast
41	Nation, The	41	New Republic, The	30A	Oregon Coast
42	National Catholic Register	49	New Woman	30A	Orlando Magazine
		24	N.Y. Habitat	30	Oui
11	National Doll World	36A	New York Magazine	42	Our Sunday Visitor
3	National Dragster	28	New York Review of Books, The	19	Outdoor America
22	National Examiner			19	Outdoor Life
46	National Geographic Traveler	38	The New York Times Magazine	39	Outdoor Photographer
25	National Horseman, The	30A	New York Woman	19	Outdoor Press, The
		22	New Yorker, The	19	Outdoor Sports & Recreation
11	National Knife Magazine, The	44	Newport Beach (714)		
		38	Newsday Magazine, The	45	Outside
30	National Lampoon			33	Ovation
45	National Masters News	42	Nor'easter	24	Owner Builder, The
		19	North American Hunter		**P**
8	National OTC Stock Journal, The				
		30A	North Shore	25	Pacific Coast Journal
8B	National Parks	30A	Northeast Magazine	30A	Pacific Northwest
45	National Racquetball	8B	Northeast Outdoors	25	Paint Horse Journal
41	National Review	31A	Northeast Riding	44	Palm Beach Social Pictorial
3	National Speed Sport News	35	Not Man Apart		
				45	Parachutist

(Continued)

Table 10–1 (Continued).   **U.S. Consumer Magazines with Mail-Order and/or Shopping Advertising Pages**

22 Parade	4 Private Pilot	34 Rod Serling's The
20 Paraplegia News	51 Progressive Forensics	Twilight Zone
49 Parenting	45 Prorodeo Sports	Magazine
49 Parents	News	49 Rodale's Children
11 Passenger Train	22 Psychic Guide	21 Rodale's Organic
Journal	22 Psychology Today	Gardening
10A PC World	13 Pure-Bred Dogs	33 Rolling Stone
10A PCM, The Personal	American Kennel	9A Rotarian, The
Computer	Gazette	3 Rotary Rocket
Magazine for Tandy	51 Purple Cow	45 Rugby
Computer Users		10A Run
30A Peninsula	**Q**	45 Runner's World
19 Pennsylvania	47 QST	45 Running Times
Sportsman, The	25 Quarter Horse	25 Rural Heritage
25 Performance	Journal, The	
Horseman	25 Quarter Horse News	**S**
8 Personal Investor	25 Quarter Racing	30A Sacramento Magazine
39 Petersen's	Record, The	25 Saddle & Bridle
Photographic	18 Quick & Healthy	25 Saddle Horse Report
Magazine	Cooking	19 Safari
30A Philadelphia		6 Sail
Magazine	**R**	6 Sailboat & Equipment
30A Phoenix Metro	45 Racquet	Directory
11 Pipe Smoker	45 Racquetball in Review	6 Sailing
30A Pittsburgh	47 Radio-Electronics	6 Sailing World
4 Plane & Pilot	11 Raitfan & Railroad	30A St. Louis Magazine
30 Playboy	11 Railroad Model	23 Saint Raphael's Better
30 Players	Craftsman	Health
25 Polo	10A Rainbow, The	6 Salt Water Sportsman
3 Pontiac	46 Rand McNally Road	30A San Francisco Focus
3 Popular Cars	Atlas	30A San Jose Metro
11 Popular Ceramics	17A Rave	47 Satellite Orbit
3 Popular Hot Rodding	22 Reader's Digest	47 Satellite TV Week
29 Popular Mechanics	49 Redbook Magazine	22 Saturday Evening
39 Popular Photography	31 Retired Officer, The	Post, The
29 Popular Science	31A Rider	22 Saturday Review
24 Popular	3 Road & Track	8 Savvy
Woodworking	31A Road Rider	45 Scholastic Coach
6 Power and	22 Robb Report, The	51 Scholastic Magazines
Motoryacht	33 Rock Magazine	High School
6 Powerboat	33 Rocket, The	Network
24 Practical Homeowner	30A Rockford Magazine	20 Scouting
25 Practical Horseman	46 Rocky Mountain	45 Scuba Times
42 Presbyterian Survey	Motorist	6 Sea Magazine
23 Prevention	19 Rod & Reel	30A Seacoast Life

Table 10–1 (Continued). U.S. Consumer Magazines with Mail-Order and/or Shopping Advertising Pages

49	Self	24	Southern Living	24	Texas Homes
43A	Senior American News	30A	Southern Magazine	30A	Texas Monthly
43A	Senior Golfer, The	19	Southern Outdoors	25	Thoroughbred Record, The
49	Seventeen	2	Southwest Art	25	Thoroughbred Times
14	Sew News	3	Special Interest Autos	14	Threads
10A	Sextant	43	Spectrum Magazine, IEEE	31A	3&4 Wheel Action
49	Shape	1	Spirit of Aloha	22	Tiffany
33	Sheet Music Magazine	45	Sport	49	Today's Chicago Woman
19	Shooting Times	4	Sport Aviation	49	Today's Christian Woman
24	Shop-At-Home Directory, The	19	Sport Fishing	11	Tole World
19	Shotgun Sports	19	Sporting Classics	30A	Toledo Metropolitan
39	Shutterbug	36A	Sporting News, The	23	Total Health
2	Shuttle Spindle & Dyepot	45	Sports 'N Spokes	46	Tours & Resorts
35	Sierra	19	Sports Afield	22	Town & Country
14	Simplicity Magazine	19	Sports Afield/Special Publications	45	Track & Field News
51	16 Magazine	3	SportsCar	1A	Trail Blazers' Almanac and Pioneer Guide Book
19	Skeet Shooting Review	3	Sports Car Illustrated		
45	Ski	45	Sports Collectors Digest	8A	Trailblazer
45	Ski America	45	Sports History	6	Trailer Boats
45	Ski X-C	41	Spotlight, The	8A	Trailer Life
45	Skiers Directory	9B	Stanford Magazine, The	11	Trains
1	Skies America	46	State, The	19	Trap & Field
45	Skiing	3	Street Rodder	19	Trapper, The
45	Skin Diver Magazine	30A	Summit	46	Travel & Leisure
16	Skip	24	Sunset	46	Travel/Holiday
45	Skydiving	3	Super Chevy	25A	Travelhost
49	Slimmer	47	Super Television	1	Travelling on Business
6	Small Boat Journal	45	Surfing	8B	Treasure
43C	Snow Week	43B	Swank	11	Tropical Fish Hobbyist
43C	Snowmobile	45	Swimming World-Junior Swimmer	3	Truckin'
49	Soap Opera Digest			34	True West
4	Soaring			3	Turbo
45	Soccer Digest		**T**	19	Turkey
30	Soldier of Fortune	49	Taxi	30A	Twin Cities
6	Soundings	43	Technology Review		
24	South Florida Home & Garden	49	'Teen		**U**
24	Southern Accents	49	Teenage	9B	UCLA Monthly, The
6	Southern Boating	30A	Tempo	4	Ultralight Flying!
17	Southern California Guide	45	Tennis	45	Ultrasport
		9B	Texas College Student	45	Underwater USA
		21	Texas Gardener	24	Unique Homes
				22	USA Today

(Continued)

Table 10–1 (Continued).   U.S. Consumer Magazines with Mail-Order and/or Shopping Advertising Pages

30A Utah Holiday Magazine	17 Welcome to Miami and the Beach	49 Woman's Day Simply Delicious Meals in Minutes
22 Utne Reader	28 West Coast Review of Books	14 Woman's Day 101 Sweater & Craft Ideas
V	6 Western Boatman, The	
20 V.F.W. Magazine	4 Western Flyer	23 Women's Health
30A Valley Magazine	25 Western Horseman	49 Women's Record, The
22 Vanity Fair	19 Western Outdoor News	49 Women's Sports and Fitness
23 Vegetarian Times	46 Westways	29 Wood
45 Velo-News	1 What's Up?	8A Woodall's 1988 RV Buyer's Guide
8 Venture	3 Wheel, The	
3 Vette	23 Whole Life	8B Woodall's 1988 Tenting Directory
43A VFW Auxiliary	35 Wildbird Magazine	
24 Victorian Homes	35 Wilderness	6 WoodenBoat
47 Video	19 Wildfowl	24 Woodheat Woodstove Directory
47 Video Review	22 Wilson Quarterly, The	
47 Videomaker	45 WindRider	
18 Vintage	19 Wing & Shot	20 Woodmen of the World Magazine
30A Virginian, The	45 Winning Bicycle Racing Illustrated	
42 Virtue		11 Woodworker's Journal, The
50 Vogue	11 Winning!	
14 Vogue Patterns	49 Woman's Day	49 Workbasket
45 Volleyball Monthly	49 Woman's Day Special Interest Magazines	24 Workbench
3 VW & Porsche, Etc.		49 Working Mother
3 VW Trends	11 Woman's Day Best Ideas For Christmas	49 Working Mother Digest
W	19A Woman's Day Diet & Fitness	49 Working Parents
49 W		49 Working Woman
25 Walking Horse Report	49 Woman's Day Family Holiday Favorites	4 World Airshow News
19A Walking Magazine, The		22 World Press Review
41 Washington Monthly, The	14 Woman's Day Granny Squares & Crafts	45 World Tennis
38 Washington Post Magazine, The	49 Woman's Day Great Holiday Baking	46 World Traveling
		47 Worldradio
36A Washington Post National Weekly Edition, The	24 Woman's Day Home Decorating Ideas	28 Writer's Digest
	24 Woman's Day Home Improvements	**Y**
49 Washington Woman		
30A Washingtonian Magazine, The	24 Woman's Day Kitchens & Baths	6 Yachting
		6 Yachting's Boat Buyers Guide
45 Water Skier, The	19A Woman's Day 101 Ways to Lose Weight and Stay Healthy	22 Yankee
6 Waterfront		49 YM
36A Weekly, The		23 Yoga Journal
18 Weight Watchers Magazine		

Regional Editions: When Is the Part Bigger than the Whole?

For the buyer of space in magazines today, most publications with circulations of over 1.5 million offer the opportunity to buy a regional portion of the national circulation. But it was not always so.

Although it has been said that the *New Yorker* was the first to publish sectional or regional editions in 1929, it wasn't until the late 1950s that major magazines began selling regional space to all advertisers, not just to those that had distribution limited to a particular section of the circulation area.

The availability of regional editions for everyone opened important opportunities to the mail-order advertiser. Here are a few of the things you can do with regional buys.

1. You don't have to invest in the full national cost of a publication to get some indication of its effectiveness for your proposition. In some cases, such as *Time* or *TV Guide*, by running in a single edition you can determine relative response with an investment at least 20 percent less than what it costs to make a national buy.

2. Some regions traditionally pull better than others for the mail-order advertiser. For many mail-order products or services, nothing does better than the West Coast or worse than the New England region. You can select the best response area for your particular proposition.

    Remember that in most publications you will be paying a premium for the privilege of buying partial circulation. If you are testing a publication, putting your advertising message in the better-pulling region can offset much of this premium charge.

3. Availability of regional editions makes possible multiple copy testing in a single issue of a publication. Some magazines offer A/B split-run copy testing in each of the regional editions published. For example, in *TV Guide* you can test one piece of copy against your control in one edition, another against your control in a second edition, another against your control in a third, and so on. As a result, you can learn as much about different pieces of copy in a single issue of one publication as you could discover in several national A/B copy splits in the same publication over a time span of two years or more.

4. When testing regionally, don't make the mistake of testing too small a circulation quantity. It is essential that you test a large enough circulation segment to provide readable results that can be projected accurately for still larger circulations.

    Warning: Buying regional space is not all fun and games. You will have to pay for the privilege in a number of ways. As mentioned, regional space costs more.

Another factor to keep in mind is the relatively poor position regional ads receive. The regional sections usually appear far back in the magazine or in a "well" or signature of several consecutive pages of advertising with no editorial matter to catch the reader. As you will see later in our discussion of position placement, the poor location of an ad in a magazine can depress results as much as 50 percent below what the same advertisement would pull if it were in the first few pages of the same publication. If you are using regional space for testing, be certain to factor this into your evaluation.

Shown below is an example of how various factors must be weighed in utilizing regional circulation for text purposes.

Regional Test Schedule for XYZ Yarn & Craft Company

REDBOOK

Space:	Full-page four-color insert
Position:	Back of main editorial (regional forms)
Issue:	June 1993
Space cost:	$14,235 (printing cost not included)
Editions used:	New England
	Mid-Atlantic
	South Atlantic
Total test circulation:	1,121,000 (35 percent of total circulation)
Regional premium:	None

FAMILY CIRCLE

Space:	Full-page four-color insert
Position:	Back of main editorial (regional forms)
Issue:	June 1993
Space cost:	$3,800 (printing cost not included)
Editions used:	Los Angeles (383,000)
	San Francisco (209,000)
Total test circulation:	592,000 (15.3 percent of total circulation)
Regional premium:	None

Since full-page four-color inserts have been extremely profitable for some of the large mail-order advertisers, this size unit was tested for the XYZ Yarn & Craft Company to see if such inserts could bring in a lower lead cost than obtained from a black-and-white page and card.

Because women's publications are the most successful media for this advertiser, the company went to two that offered the mechanical capabilities for regional testing of such an insert. Although May and June are not prime mail-order months, it was necessary to test then in order to allow turnaround time for the next season's scheduling. Therefore the following factors would have to be taken into consideration in projecting test results to learn whether this unit would be successful in prime mail-order months with full circulation: (1) regional premium, (2) month of insertion, (3) position in book, and (4) relative value of specific media.

Pilot Publications: The Beacons
of Direct Response Media Scheduling

When planning your direct marketing media schedule, think about the media universe the way you think about the view of the sky in the evening. If you have no familiarity with the stars, the sky appears to be a jumble of blinking lights with no apparent relationship. But as you begin to study the heavens, you are soon able to pick out clusters of stars that have a relationship to one another in constellations.

You will recognize the stars that make up the Big Dipper in the Ursa Major, the Hunter, the Swan, the Bull, and other familiar constellations. If you were to go on to become a professional astronomer, you would eventually recognize 89 distinctly different groups. Once you know the various constellations, a star within a particular grouping inevitably leads your eye to the other related stars.

The magazine universe is no different. There are nearly 400 consumer magazines published with circulations of 100,000 or more. The first step in approaching this vast list is to sort out the universe of magazines into categories. Although this process is somewhat arbitrary, and different experts may not agree entirely as to which magazines fall into which category, we are going to set down a chart of the major publications that you can use like a chart of the skies to map out particular magazine groupings. Once you begin to think of magazines as forming logical groupings within the total magazine universe, you can begin to determine the groupings offering the most likely marketplace for your product or proposition. Table 10–2 is a basic magazine category chart and lists some of the publications currently available for the direct response advertiser.

Within each category there are usually one or more publications that perform particularly well for the direct response advertiser at a lower cost than other publications in the group. We call those magazines the *pilot publications* for the group. If you use the pilot publications and they produce an acceptable cost per response, you can then proceed to explore the possibility of adding other magazines in that category to your media schedule.

In selecting the pilot publications in a category, keep in mind that you are not dealing with a static situation. As indicated earlier, a publication's mail-order advertising viablility changes from year to year, and what is a bellwether publication this season may not be the one to use next year. What is important is that you check your own experience and the experience of others in determining the best places to advertise first in each category, and the next best, and the next best, and so on.

Think of your media-buying program as an ever-widening circle, as illustrated in Exhibit 10–1. At the center is a nucleus of pilot publications. Each successively larger ring would include reruns in all profitable pilot publications plus new test books. In the same way, you can expand from campaign to compaign to cover wider levels of the various media categories until you have reached the widest possible universe.

Table 10–2. Basic Consumer Magazine Categories

Demographic	Category	Sample Publications
Dual audience	General editorial/ entertainment	Grift, National Enquirer, National Geographic, New York Times Magazine, Parade, People, Reader's Digest, TV Guide
	News	Time, Newsweek, Sports Illustrated, U.S. News & World Report
	Special interest	Architectural Digest, Business Week, Elks, Foreign Affairs, High Fidelity, Modern Photography. Natural History, Ski, Travel & Leisure, Wall Street Journal, Yankee
Women	General/service/ shelter (home service)	Better Homes & Gardens, Cosmopolitan, Ebony, Family Circle, Good Housekeeping, House Beautiful, House & Garden, Ladies' Home Journal, McCall's, Redbook, Sunset, Woman's Day
	Fashion	Glamour, Harper's Bazaar, Mademoiselle, Vogue
	Special interest	Brides, MacFadden Women's Group, McCall's Needlework & Crafts, Parents, Working Woman
Men	General/ entertainment/ fashion	Esquire, Gentlemen's Quarterly, Penthouse, Playboy
	Special interest	Field & Stream, Home Mechanix, Outdoor Life, Popular Mechanics, Popular Science, Road & Track, Sports Afield
Youth	Male	Boy's Life
	Female	Teen, YM
	Dual audience	Scholastic Magazines

Bind-In Insert Cards

The reason for the success of the insert card is self-evident. Pick up a magazine, thumb through its pages, and see for yourself how effectively the bound-in-cards flag down the reader. Each time someone picks up the publication, there is the insert card pointing to your message. Another reason is the ease with which the reader can respond. The business reply card eliminates the trouble of addressing an envelope, providing a stamp, and so on.

Before the development of the insert card, the third and fourth covers of a magazine were the prime mail order positions and were sold at a premium.

Exhibit 10–1. **Circle Approach to Media Selection**

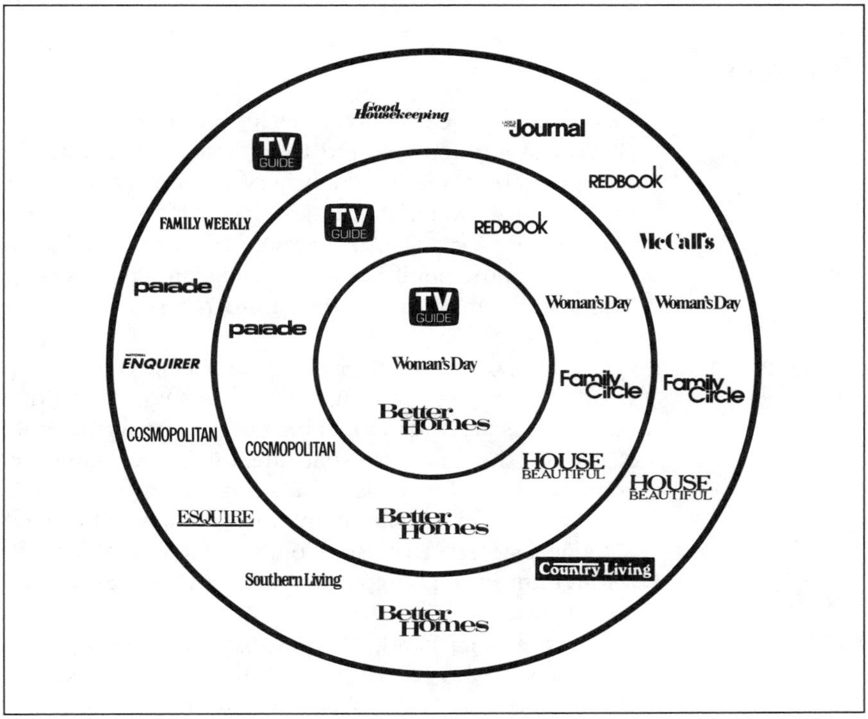

The bind-in insert card has created a world in which three, four, five, or more direct response advertisers can all have the position impact once reserved for the cover advertisers alone.

When you go to purchase space for a page and an accompanying insert card, you must face the fact that the best things in life are not free. Insert card advertising costs more. You must pay a space charge for the page and the card and sometimes a separate binding charge, and you must then add in the cost of printing the cards. How much you pay, of course, depends on the individual publication, the size of the card, and a number of other factors. There is no rule of thumb to follow in estimating the additional cost for an insert card. Space charges alone for a standard business reply card can be as little as 40 percent of the black-and-white page plus additional binding charges.

When the cost of the insert unit adds up to as much as four times the cost of a black-and-white page, you will have to receive four times the response to justify the added expense.

For most direct response advertisers, the response is likely to be six to eight times as great when pulling for an order and as much as six to eight times as great in pulling for inquiries. As a result, you can expect to cut your

cost per response by 50 percent or more with an insert card as opposed to an ordinary on-page coupon ad.

Bingo Cards

Insert cards have a dramatic effect upon response, and so do bingo cards. Bingo cards, often referred to as "information cards," are a unique device developed by magazine publishers, both consumer and business, to make it easy for the reader to request more information. *Bingo card* is really a generic term for any form—a reply card or printed form on a magazine page —on which the publisher prints designated numbers for specified literature. The reader simply circles the number designated for the literature desired. (See Exhibit 10–2.)

Typically, an advertiser placing a specified unit of space in a magazine is entitled to a bingo card in the back of the publication. Ads reference these bingo cards with statements such as "For further information circle Item No. 146." The cards are sent directly to the publisher who, in turn, sends compiled lists of inquiries to participating advertisers. The respective advertisers then send fulfillment literature to all who have requested it.

A neat system, to be sure, but a caveat is in order. "We get tons of requests for literature from bingo cards, but they're not worth anything" is a frequent advertiser complaint.

On the other hand, "Bingo cards can be very productive," states Adolph Auerbacher, who has been publisher of 22 special-interest publications for *Better Homes and Gardens*. Auerbacher points to two prime reasons for poor sales conversions: (1) failure of advertisers to respond to inquiries quickly, and (2) failure of advertisers to qualify prospects properly. Pointing to a survey by *Better Homes and Gardens* among 203 companies to whom they responded, Auerbacher reports the following response times. During the first week 13 percent sent literature. At the end of the first month they had heard from 62 percent. Thirty-eight percent of the companies had not responded a month after the first response was received. And 10 percent were never heard from. (For maximum effectiveness, all advertisers should have responded within two weeks.)

In regard to qualifying prospects properly for a better likelihood of sales conversion. Mr. Auerbacher gives some interesting theories and facts. Responding to the age-old question, "Should the advertiser charge for literature or send it free?" he makes this key point:

> If an air conditioner advertiser, for example, has a literature cost of $1, he has a natural tendency to want to get his dollar back. But he may lose sight of the fact that his real objective is to sell a $500 air conditioner.
>
> Even taking into account that those who pay $1 for the literature might be more qualified, the ratio of free requests to dollar payments may be so overwhelming that more air conditioners in total might be sold to consumers who requested free literature.

Exhibit 10–2. **Bingo Card for** *Better Homes and Gardens*

Information

WORTH WRITING FOR

**Better Homes and Gardens®
REMODELING IDEAS,
Summer 1987 Dept. SURI7
P.O. BOX 2611
CLINTON, IA 52732**

Issue 66

TO ENSURE PROMPT HANDLING OF YOUR ORDER FOLLOW THESE INSTRUCTIONS:

- Circle your choice
- Enclose cash, check, money order for cost of booklets plus $1.00 service charge (no stamps/foreign)

- Send coupon and remittance to address above
- ALLOW 4-6 WEEKS FOR DELIVERY
- Coupon expires July 19

FREE LITERATURE   Circle numbers below corresponding to items in this issue.
Please include $1.00 for handling charge

5.	214.	323.	400.	406.	1321.	1810.
9.	300.	324.	401.	602.	1602.	4056.
55.	301.	330.	402.	613.	1664.	
59.	303.	344.	403.	919.	1666.	
71.	322.	376.	405.	1205.	1668.	

PRICED LITERATURE   Numbers below refer to items on which there is a charge.
Please include proper remittance.

25 .... 35¢	73 ..... 50¢	332 ..... 50¢	762 .... $2.00	1256 .. $10.00	1305 .... $2.95	1679 ..... $2.00
27 .... 25¢	74 ... $3.00	407 ... $1.25	802 .. $14.50	1271 .... $3.95	1306 .... $2.95	1808 ... $1.00
35 .... $3.00	75 ... $1.00	410 ...... 25¢	821 ... $3.00	1272 .... $4.95	1307 .... $2.95	1816 .... 50¢
57 .... $2.00	94 ... $1.99	415 ..... 15¢	827 ... $1.00	1273 .... $5.95	1335 .... $1.00	1824 ... $2.00
60 .... $1.00	95 ... $1.99	420 ..... 75¢	828 ... $1.00	1274 .... $4.95	1359 .... $1.00	4011 ... $1.00
61 .... $1.00	150 ..... 35¢	426 ..... 50¢	844 ..... 25¢	1275 .... $3.95	1361 .. $12.00	4012 ... $1.00
62 .... $1.00	205 ..... 25¢	430 ..... 25¢	855 .... $1.99	1290 .... $9.75	1362 .. $12.00	4013 ... $1.00
63 .... 50¢	217 ... $1.00	437 ... $2.00	902 .. $14.50	1291 .... $8.75	1363 .. $12.00	4014 .... 25¢
67 .... 50¢	310 ..... 25¢	438 ... $1.00	911 ..... 25¢	1293 .... $8.75	1364 .. $12.00	
68 .... $1.00	316 ..... 35¢	612 ... $1.00	1001 ..... 40¢	1294 .... $3.75	1365 .. $12.00	
69 .... 25¢	321 ... $1.00	614 ... $1.00	1005 ..... 40¢	1296 .. $28.00	1604 .... $2.00	
70 .... $1.00	327 ... $1.00	616 ... $1.00	1217 .... $5.00	1303 .... $2.95	1672 .... $2.00	
72 .... $1.00	329 ..... 50¢	744 ... $1.00	1244 .... $5.00	1304 .... $2.95	1673 ..... 25¢	

Name (please print) _____

Address _____

City _____

State_____ Zip Code _____

I AM ENCLOSING:

$_____for priced items

$___1.00___for handling

$_____total remittance

But often it is best to charge for literature as a qualifier. The question is "how much?" Here Mr. Auerbacher provides some hard facts. Citing Table 10–3, he refers to three titles among their stable of special-interest books with the details of response by amount charged for literature. Free-literature requests had the greatest response in every case, as one would expect. But note the differences in response between varying amounts requested. For *Remodeling Ideas*, for example, a 10¢ request pulled 22 percent as many requests as free. But 25¢ pulled more requests than 10¢. And in the case of *Building Ideas*, a 50¢ request pulled as well as a 25¢ request. With the exception of *Decorating Ideas*, both a $1 and a $2 request got a very poor response, perhaps suggesting upper limits of resistance.

Table 10–3. Tabulation of Literature Requests

Price	Median Response	Percentage of Free	High[a]	Low[b]	Ratio H/L[c]
Better Homes and Gardens Remodeling Ideas, Spring					
Free	672		1171	192	6 : 1
10¢	148	22	373	113	3 : 1
25¢	213	32	408	51	8 : 1
50¢	130	19	540	51	10 : 1
$1	82	12	240	3	80 : 1
$2	19	3	129	2	65 : 1
Better Homes and Gardens Building Ideas, Spring					
Free	781		1501	252	6 : 1
10¢	108	14	199	60	3 : 1
25¢	298	38	430	109	4 : 1
50¢	297	38	722	97	7 : 1
$1	95	12	431	3	143 : 1
$2	31	4	164	3	55 : 1
Better Homes and Gardens Decorating Ideas, Spring					
Free	491		1420	21	67 : 1
10¢	62	13	72	49	1.5 : 1
25¢	193	39	400	68	6 : 1
50¢	138	28	646	35	18 : 1
$1	102	21	282	17	16 : 1
$2	79	16	123	19	6 : 1

[a] High means the highest number of requests for the literature of a given advertiser in a particular issue.
[b] Low means the lowest number of requests.
[c] Ratio H/L means the ratio of response of the best puller contrasted to the worst puller.

So, as Mr. Auerbacher points out, success in the use of bingo cards depends, to a major degree, upon rapid fulfillment of literature requests and qualifying prospects in the most cost-efficient way. Two additional factors must be taken into account: (1) The closer the literature offered ties to the special interest of the book, the better the response is likely to be; and (2) advertiser awareness is an important response factor (an Armstrong will most always outpull a Joe Blow).

Magazine Advertising Response Pattern: What Do These Early Results Mean?

There is a remarkable similarity from one insertion to another in the rate of response over time for most magazines. Monthly publications generally have a similar pattern for the rate of response from week to week. However, the pattern of response for publications in different categories can vary. For example, a mass circulation weekly magazine (*TV Guide* or *Parade*) will pull a higher percentage of the total response in the first few weeks than a shelter book (such as *House & Garden* or *Better Homes and Gardens*).

A shelter book has a slower response curve but keeps pulling for a long period of time because it is kept much longer and is not so short-lived as a mass circulation magazine.

Also, subscription circulation will pull faster than newsstand circulation. Subscribers usually receive their copies within a few days, whereas newsstand sales are spread out over an entire month. Consequently, the response pattern is spread out as well.

If you are running an ad calling for direct response from a monthly magazine, here is a general guide to the likely response flow:

After the first week	3–7%	After 2 months	75–85%
After the second week	20–25%	After 3 months	85–92%
After the third week	40–45%	After 4 months	92–95%
After one month	50–55%		

From a weekly publication such as *Time* or *TV Guide*, the curve is entirely different; 50 percent of your response usually comes in the first two weeks.

These expectations, of course, represent the average of many hundreds of response curves for different propositions. You may see variations up or down from the classic curve for any single insertion.

As a general rule for monthlies, you can expect to project the final results within 10 percent accuracy after the third week of counting responses. If you are new to the business, give yourself the experience of entering daily result counts by hand for dozens of ads. Before long you will develop an instinct for projecting how an ad for your particular proposition is doing within the first ten days of measured response.

Timing and Frequency: When Should You Run? How Often Should You Go Back?

Once you determine where you want to run, timing and frequency are the two crucial factors in putting together an effective print schedule.

Of course, there are some propositions that have a time of the year when they do best. For example, novelty items are likely to be purchased in October and November or even as early as late September for Christmas gifts. But for nonseasonal items, you can look forward to two major print advertising seasons for direct response.

The first and by far the most productive for most propositions is the winter season, which begins with the January issue and runs through the February and March issues. The second season begins with the August issue and runs through the November issue.

The best winter months for most people are January and February. The best fall months are October and November. For schools and book continuity propositions, September frequently does as well or better.

If you have a nonseasonal item and you want to do your initial test at the best possible time, use a February issue with a January sale date or a January issue with a late December or early January sale date of whatever publication makes the most sense for your proposition.

How much of a factor is the particular month in which an ad appears? It could make a difference of 40 percent or even more. Here is an example of what the direct response advertiser may expect to experience during the year if the cost per response (C.P.R.) in February were $2; January, $2.05; February, $2; March, $2.20; April, $2.50; May, $2.60; June, $2.80; July, $2.60; August, $2.40; September, $2.60; October, $2.20; November, $2.20; December, $2.40.

These hypothetical relative costs are based on the assumption that the insertion is run one time in any one of the 12 issues of a monthly publication. But, of course, if you are successful, you will want to run your copy more than once. So now you are faced with the other crucial question: What will various rates of frequency do to your response? Should you run once a year? Twice? Three times? Or every other month?

The frequency factor is more difficult to formulate that the timing factor. Optimum frequency cannot be generalized for print media advertising. Some propositions can be run month after month in a publication and show very little difference in cost per response. At one time, Doubleday & Company had worked out optimum frequency curves for some of its book club ads that required a 24-month hiatus between insertions.

How, then, do you go about determining ideal frequency of insertions? Try this procedure: The first time your copy appears in a publication, run it at the most favorable time of the year for your special appeal. If you have a nonseasonal proposition, use January or February issues.

If the cost per response is in an acceptable range or up to 20 percent better than expected, wait six months and follow with a second insertion. If that insertion produces results within an acceptable range, you probably are a twice-a-year advertiser.

If the first insertion pulls well over 20 percent better than the planned order margin, turn around and repeat within a three or four-month period.

If the response to the test insertion in January or February was marginal, it usually makes sense to wait a full year before returning for another try in that publication.

The best gauge of how quickly you can run the next insertion aimed at the same magazine audience is the strength of the response from the last insertion. What you are reading in the results is a measurement of the saturation factor as it relates to that portion of the circulation that is interested in your selling message.

Of course, like all the other factors that affect response, frequency does not operate in a vacuum. The offer of a particularly advantageous position in a particular month or a breakthrough to better results with improved copy can lead you to set aside whatever carefully worked out frequency you had adopted earlier.

Determining Proper Ad Size: How Much Is Too Much?

A crucial factor in obtaining an acceptable cost per response is the size of the advertising unit you select. Ordinarily, the bigger the ad, the better job the creative people can do in presenting the selling message. But there is one catch: Advertising space costs money. And the more you spend, the greater the response you need to get your money back.

What you want to find is the most efficient size for your particular proposition and for the copy approach you have chosen. Just as with frequency, there is no simple rule of thumb here.

Generally speaking, advertising for leads or prospects or to gain inquiries requires less advertising space than copy that is pulling for orders. Many companies seeking inquiries or running a lead item to get names for catalog follow-up make use of advertising units of less than one column. Only a handful of companies looking for prospects can make effective use of full-page space. Going one step further and using a page and insert card to pull for leads runs the risk of being too effective. This until can bring in inquiries at very low cost, but there is always the danger that the quality will be very poor. Find out at your own peril.

For example, if you use a black-and-white page with a tear-off coupon that generates leads at $5 each and that converts at a 10 percent rate, then your advertising cost per sale is $50. Take the same insertion and place it as a page and insert card, and the cost per response may be as low as $3. If the conversion rate held up at 10 percent, the advertising cost per sale would be only $30. But it is more likely that the advertiser would experience a sharp conversion rate drop to perhaps 5 percent, with a resultant $60 cost per sale plus the cost of processing the additional leads.

When a direct sale or a future commitment to buy is sought, the dynamics usually are different from those when inquiries are sought. As a general rule, the higher the unit of sale or dollar volume commitment, the larger the unit of space that can be afforded, right up to the double-page spread with insert card. However, there are a number of additional factors to be considered:

1. The nature of the product presentation may inherently require a particular space unit. For example, in record club and book club advertising, experience has shown that a maximum number of books and records should be displayed for best results. As a consequence, many of these clubs run a two-page spread as their standard advertising unit. And in a small-size publication such as *TV Guide*, they may take six or even eight pages to display the proper number of books and records.

2. Some propositions, such as Time-Life Books in the continuity bookselling field, require four-color advertising in order to present the beautiful color illustrations that are an important feature of the product being sold.

3. Usually full-page ads appear at the front of a publication and small-space ads at the back. So going to a full-page units is often related to the benefits you can expect from a premium, front-of-publication position.

4. If you are successful with a single-page ad with coupon, test using an insert card before you try to add a second page. If the page and insert card work for you, give the spread and card a try.

5. Most mail-order advertising falls into one of three size categories: (a) the spectacular unit—anything from the page and standard card insert to the four-page preprinted insert, (b) the single full-page unit or (c) the small-space unit less than one column in size.

The awkward sizes in pulling for an order appear to be the one-column and two-column units. These inserts seldom work better than their big-brother pages or little-sister 56-line, 42-line, and 21-line units, although a "square third" (2 columns by 70 lines) can be a very efficient space unit.

Always remember that space costs money. The objective is to take the minimum amount of space you need to express your proposition effectively and to return a profit.

Start by having the creative director at your advertising agency express the proposition in the amount of space needed to convey a powerful selling message. Once you have established the cost per response for this basic unit, you can experiment with other size units.

If you have two publications on your schedule that perform about equally well for the basic unit, try testing the same ad approach expressed in a smaller or larger space size in one of those two publications while running the basic control unit in the same month in the other publication.

Four-Color, Two-Color, Black-and-White: How Colorful Should Your Advertising Be?

All magazines charge extra for adding color to your advertising. And remember there will be additional production expense if you go this route.

Usually the cost of adding a second color to a black-and-white page does not return the added costs charged by the publication for the space and the expense of producing the ad. If the copy is right, the words will do their job without getting an appreciable lift from having headlines set in red or blue or green. An exception might be the use of a second-color tint as background to provide special impact to your page.

It is with the use of four-color advertising that the direct response advertiser has an opportunity to profit on an investment in color.

A number of publications (for example, *Esquire, Time, Woman's Day, Ladies' Home Journal*) allow you to run a split of four-color versus black-and-white, in an alternating copy A/B perfect split-run. Test results indicate an increase of anywhere from 30 percent to almost 60 percent where there is appropriate and dramatic utilization of the four-color process.

Given a striking piece of artwork related to the proposition or an inherently colorful product feature to present, you can expect an increase in

response when you use four-color advertising. Since you will need more than a 20 percent increase in most publications to make the use of color profitable, it is wise to pretest the value of this factor before scheduling it across the board. Some products such as insurance simply do not benefit from color.

What can you expect the cost of four-color advertising to be? Table 10–4 shows four-color charges for a representative group of consumer publications.

Table 10–4.   Four-Color Rate Examples

Publication	Black-and-White Page Rate	Four-Color Page Rate	Percentage Increase
Woman's Day	$ 70,435	$ 84,320	19.7%
Family Circle	55,847[a]	66,188[a]	18.5
Ladies' Home Journal	61,800[a]	73,500	18.9
Seventeen	21,840[a]	34,975	60.0
Redbook	52,750	69,755	32.2
McCall's	70,615	83,315	18.0
Good Housekeeping	97,260	122,035	25.5
Glamour	37,800[a]	53,110	40.5
Newsweek	73,620	114,535	56.1
Time	91,000	134,400	47.7
Sports Illustrated	84,260	127,600	51.4
Popular Mechanics	24,755[a]	27,940[a]	12.9
Home Mechanix	14,810[a]	15,645[a]	12.4
Reader's Digest	121,500	141,300	16.3
Esquire	17,905[a]	26,865[a]	50.0

[a] Mail-order rates.

If you plan to use four-color advertising, the increase in publication space cost is only one of the cost factors to be weighed. The cost of the original four-color engravings for a 7" × 10" page runs from $3,000 to $5,000 depending on the copy and artwork being used. This compares with a black-and-white engraving cost that could be from $200 to $300. In addition, any dye transfers or other four-color preparatory work will probably increase mechanical preparation costs by 50 percent or more over a comparable black-and-white insertion.

The Position Factor

Position in life may not be everything, but in direct response it often means the difference between paying out or sudden death. By *position* we mean where your advertisement appears in the publication. There are two rules governing position. First, the closer to the front of the publication an ad is placed, the better the response will be. Second, the more visible the position, the better the response will be.

The first rule defies rational analysis. Yet it is as certain as the sun's rising in the morning. Many magazine publishers have offered elaborate research studies demonstrating to the general advertiser than an ad in the editorial matter far back in a publication gets better readership than an ad placed within the first few pages of the publication. This may well be true for the general or institutional advertiser, but it is not true for the direct response advertiser.

Whatever the explanation may be, the fact remains that decades of measured direct response advertising tell the same story over and over again. A position in the first seven pages of the magazine produces a dramatically better response (all other factors being the same) than if the same insertion appears farther back in the same issue.

How much better? There are as many answers to this question as there are old pros in the business. However, here is about what you might expect the relative response to be from various page positions as measured against the first right-hand page arbitrarily rated at a pull of 100.

First right-hand page	100	Back of the publication	
Second right-hand page	95	(following main body of	
Third right-hand page	90	editorial matter)	50
Fourth right-hand page	85	Back cover	100
Back of front of the publication		Inside third cover	90
(preceding editorial matter)	70	Page facing third cover	85

The second rule is more easily explained. An ad must be seen before it can be read or acted on. Right-hand pages pull better than left-hand pages, frequently by as much as 15 percent. Insert cards open the magazine to the advertiser's message and thereby create their own "cover" position. Of course, the insert card introduces the additional factor of providing a postage-free response vehicle as well. But the response from insert cards is also subject to the influence of how far back in the magazine the insertion appears. Here is what you can expect in most publications (assigning a 100 rating to the first card):

First insert card position	100
Second insert card position	95
Third insert card position	85
Fourth insert card position	75[a]
Fifth insert card position	70[a]

[a] If position follows main editorial matter.

The pull of position is as inexorable as the pull of gravity. Well, almost. There are a few exceptions. In the fashion and the mechanics magazines, card positioning seems to make little or no difference. Another exception may involve the placement of an ad opposite a related column or feature article in a publication (for example, a *Home Handyman's Encyclopedia* ad

opposite the Home Handyman column). Another exception may involve placement of an ad in a high-readership shopping section at the back of a magazine.

How to Buy Space

Because mail-order advertising is always subject to bottom-line analysis, the price you pay for space can mean the difference between profit and loss. Mrs. Florence Peloquin, head of Florence Peloquin Associates, New York City, provides the following basic questions the advertiser should ask the publisher or the publisher's agency before placing space.

1. Is there a special mail-order rate? Mail-order rates are usually 10 percent to 30 percent lower than general rates.

2. Is there a special mail-order section, a shopping section where special mail-order ads are grouped? (This section is usually found in the back of the book.)

3. Does the magazine have remnant space available at substantial discounts? Many publishers offer discounts of up to 50 percent off the regular rate.

4. Is there an insertion frequency discount or a dollar volume discount? Is frequency construed as the number of insertions in a time period or consecutive issues? Many publishers credit more than one insertion in an issue toward frequency.

5. Do corporate discounts apply to mail-order? Sometimes the corporate discount is better than the mail-order discount.

6. Are there seasonal discounts? Some publishers have low-volume advertising months during which they offer substantial discounts.

7. Are there spread discounts when running two pages or more in one issue? The discount can run up to 60 percent on the second page.

8. Is there a publisher's rate? Is this in addition to or in lieu of the mail-order rate? It can be additive.

9. Are per-inquiry (P.I.) deals accepted? In P.I. deals, the advertiser pays the publisher an amount for each inquiry or order, or a minimum flat amount for the space, plus so much per inquiry or order.

10. Are "umbrella contracts" accepted? Some media-buying services and agencies own banks or reserves of space with given publications and can offer discounts even for one-time ads.

11. Is bartering for space allowed? Barter usually involves a combination of cash and merchandise.

When bought properly, tested properly, and used properly, magazine advertising represents a vast universe of sales and profit potential for the direct response advertiser.

Self-Quiz

1. Name five magazines that provide a conducive atmosphere for direct response advertisers.

   a. _____

   b. _____

   c. _____

   d. _____

   e. _____

2. Name the four major advantages of using regional editions of magazines.

   a. _____

   b. _____

   c. _____

   d. _____

3. What are the two negative factors involved in buying regional space?

   a. _____

   b. _____

4. Name five basic consumer magazine categories.

   a. _____

   b. _____

   c. _____

   d. _____

   e. _____

5. Define *pilot publication*.

   _____

   _____

   _____

6. What is the theory of an expanded media-buying program based on an ever-widening circle?

_____

_____

_____

_____

7. What is the principal advantage of an insert card in a magazine?

_____

_____

_____

8. When direct response advertisers use insert cards, the response is likely to be _____ to _____ times as great when pulling for an order and as much as _____ to _____ times as great in pulling for inquiries.

9. What are the two prime reasons for poor sales conversions to bingo cards?

a. _____

b. _____

10. As a general rule, when direct response advertisers use a monthly magazine, they can usually expect to have about 50 percent of their total response after _____ weeks.

11. For weekly publications, 50 percent of total response can be expected after _____ weeks.

12. From a timing standpoint, which is the most productive season for most direct response propositions?

_____

_____

13. Which is the second most productive season?

_____

_____

14. When is the best possible time to test a nonseasonal item?

_____

_____

15. How much is the cost per response (C.P.R.) likely to vary between the best-pulling month and the poorest-pulling month? _____ percent.

16. Provide guidelines for frequency factors in magazine advertising.

    a. If the cost per response is in an acceptable range or up to 20 percent better than expected, wait _____ months and follow up with a second insertion in the second half of the year.

    b. If the first insertion pulls well over 20 percent better than allowed order margin, turn around and repeat within a _____ or_____ month period.

    c. If response to the test insertion in January or February was marginal, it usually makes sense to wait _____ before returning for another try in that publication.

17. Generally speaking, which requires more space for effective direct response advertising?
    ☐ Pulling inquiries   ☐ Pulling orders

18. What is the prime advantage of a full-page ad vs. a small ad in a magazine?

    _____

    _____

19. If a single-page ad with coupon is successful, what is the next logical test?

    _____

    _____

20. What are the three size categories for most mail-order advertising?

    a. _____

    b. _____

    c. _____

21. When four-color versus black-and-white is tested, results indicate an increase of anywhere from _____ percent to almost _____ percent where there is appropriate and dramatic utilization of the four-color process.

22. What are the two rules governing the position factor for the direct response advertiser?

    a. _____

    b. _____

23. Right-hand pages pull better than left-hand pages by as much as _____ percent.

24. If a 100 rating is assigned to a first insert card position in a publication having five insert card positions, the fifth insert card rating would be _____.

25. Mail-order rates are usually _____ percent to _____ percent lower than general rates.

Pilot Project

You are the advertising manager for a publisher of children's books. It is your assignment to test-market a new continuity series of 10 books written for age levels 6 to 10. Each book in the series will sell for $4.95. Outline a plan for test marketing in magazines.

1. What pilot publications would you schedule for testing?

2. Will you use any regional editions? Why or why not?

3. Do a circle approach to media selection indicating what additional publications you will expand to if the pilot publications prove sucessful.

4. Prepare a timing schedule, indicating when your pilot ads will break and when your expanded media-buying program will take place.

5. What ad size will you use? Will the ad be black and white, two colors, or four color?

Newspapers

For sheer circulation in print, there is nothing to compare with the daily and Sunday newspapers. There were 1,586 daily newspapers in the United States with an average daily circulation of about 60 million as of February 1, 1992. Thus the circulation available through newspapers offers an exciting opportunity for direct response advertisers. It is significant that many direct response advertisers spend all or a major portion of their budgets in newspapers.

Newspapers are unique in that they can serve as a vehicle for carrying direct response advertising formats foreign to their regular new pages. Remarkable results have been achieved by using these special formats.

Newspaper Preprints

Use of newspaper preprints by direct response advertisers is a phenomenon of this decade. The Newspaper Advertising Bureau of New York estimates that 71.6 billion preprints circulated in 1991. Preprints became a viable method for direct marketers in 1965. In the first five months of that year there was only one preprint mail-order advertiser (Time-Life Books) in million-circulation newspapers.

Columbia Record & Tape Club followed Time-Life Books in 1965. Wunderman Worldwide, the club's agency, first tested preprints in newspapers in six markets (*Akron Beacon, Dallas Times Herald, Des Moines Register, Minneapolis Tribune, Peoria Journal Star*, and *Seattle Times*). Hundreds of millions of preprints have since been run in newspapers by Columbia. There are two obvious advantages to preprints such as those used by Columbia. First, they provide abundant space for the detailed listing of items available. Second, a perforated postpaid return card may be imprinted, which, because of the weight of the stock used, closely resembles an ordinary postcard and can be mailed easily by the respondent. (See Exhibit 11–1.)

The dramatic impact of preprints in a newspaper must be measured against the greatly increased cost. Comparing a four-page preprint with a fourth cover in a syndicated Sunday supplement, one finds the preprint costs almost four times as much. The tremendous volume of preprints found in

Exhibit 11–1.   **First Page of a Six-Page Newspaper Insert for Columbia House**

the Sunday newspaper is good evidence that the increased cost often is more than warranted.

Printing costs of the inserts must be added to the space cost for them. A breakdown of costs for space, depending on the sizes of preprint, for representative newspapers is given in Table 11–1. Careful note should be taken of the fact that the C.P.M. tends to be lower for large metro papers. Thus, if a direct marketer has a proposition that appeals only to small towns, the chances for successful use of preprints are greatly diminished.

Table 11–1. National Estimated Tabloid Insert Costs For Sunday Newspapers Published within MSA

(MSA) Top	Number of Newspapers	TOTAL CIRC. (000)	COST PER 1,000					
			2 Pgs.	4 Pgs.	8 Pgs.	12 Pgs.	16 Pgs.	24 Pgs.
10	41	15,352	$49.93	$51.72	$59.70	$67.42	$73.52	$84.10
25	79	24,942	49.99	51.87	59.72	67.66	73.86	86.17
50	117	35,160	50.01	52.24	59.90	67.81	74.08	86.53
75	161	41,350	50.05	53.00	60.17	67.97	74.31	87.01
100	202	45,492	50.06	53.15	60.31	68.09	74.45	87.09
150	274	51,266	50.10	53.20	60.75	68.34	74.89	87.74
200	333	54,906	50.16	53.45	61.10	68.58	75.08	87.83
250	384	56,996	50.28	53.75	61.44	68.96	75.34	88.03
320	454	59,527	50.54	54.13	61.78	69.25	75.55	88.18

Note: The national newspaper insert rates shown are based on an insert measuring 10¾" × 13" for distribution on Sunday. Since the basis of the newspapers' insert rates can vary (square inch, lines, flat rate, cost per 1,000, etc.), these rates are not the final cost. They should be used for *estimating purposes only*, subject to confirmation by the newspaper for a specific insertion date. *Inserts must be furnished.*

Sources: Audit Bureau of Circulation; SRDS, February 1991.

Acceptable Size

Size depends on the newspaper's policy and equipment, but, generally speaking, minimum size is 5½" × 8⅛". Maximum size is 10¾" × 14½". These minimum and maximum sizes are folded sizes—unfolded size could be larger. For example, a standard format size of 21½"×14½" printed on heavy stock could fold in half to 10¾" × 14½".

Sunday vs. Weekday Inserts

Figures for 1991 show that weekday preprints constitute about 45.7 percent of total preprint circulation in the United States.

Syndicated Newspaper Supplements

Imagine placing three space insertion orders and buying newspaper circulation of 65 millions plus! This is indeed possible if you place insertion orders in the three major syndicated newspaper supplements: Sunday Magazine Network (Mag/Net), *Parade*, and *USA Weekend*. (See Table 11–2.)

Distribution of the three syndicated supplements breaks down about this way. Sunday Mag/Net is distributed by about 24 member newspapers.

Table 11–2. Summary of Circulation and Rates for Sunday
Newspaper Supplements

Publication	Circulation	Four-Color		Black-and-White	
		Pages	C.P.M.	Pages	C.P.M.
Sunday Magazine					
Network	16,278,800	215,758	$13.25	185,234	$11.37
Parade	36,444,000	488,000	13.39	395,100	10.84
USA Weekend	15,636,950	198,120	12.67	180,180	11.52

Source: *Newspaper Rates and Data,* May 1992.

Those carrying Sunday Mag/Net supplements offer a choice of 26 top metro areas for advertising.

USA Weekend is generally carried by the newspapers with smaller circulations. Table 11–3 gives breakouts by county size.

Table 11–3. Summary of *USA Weekend*'s Circulation By County Size,
Effective August 2, 1992

County Size	HH (000)	Total Newspapers	Circ.	Cov.	Comp.
A County	36,122.4	101	6,678,500	18.5%	41.9%
B County	33,905.9	113	5,621,867	16.6	35.2
C County	12,900.9	134	3,382,033	26.2	21.2
D County	10,192.2	20	271,908	2.7	1.7
Total	93,121.4	368	15,954,308	17.1%	100%

Sources: HH—Nielsen Household Estimates, 9/91 (Continental U.S.)
USA Weekend Based on ABC/Certified Circulation, 3/31/92.

Parade is included in some of the Sunday Mag/Net newspapers, but generally it is more evenly distributed among the top 100 metro areas. Obvious advantages of syndicated supplements are their relatively low cost per thousand circulation and the possibility of reaching top metro areas as well as smaller cities, depending on the supplement used. One thing going for the syndicated supplements is their mail-order atmosphere. *Parade*, for instance, points out that 60 percent of its advertising carries some kind of coupon that enables the advertiser to measure results.

Among the syndicated supplements, *Parade* and *USA Weekend* offer a mail-order booklet inserted on a regular basis. This booklet, commonly called a Dutch door, usually runs 12 pages. Its page size is one-half that of the supplement. Some issues are taken over entirely by one advertiser. Other issues contain a variety of small mail-order ads.

It is obvious that a direct marketer that has not previously placed space in one of the syndicated supplements would not go full run without testing. *Parade*, for example, offers remnant space to mail-order advertisers at 20 percent discount. Remnant space is advertising space left over when package-goods advertisers buy only in those markets where they have distribution. Second to testing in remnant space is testing in regions.

With about 722 Sunday and weekend magazines, both syndicated and locally edited, a direct response advertiser has an incredible amount of distribution available at low cost.

Comics as a Direct Marketing Medium

Perhaps the biggest sleeper as a medium for direct marketers is the comic section of weekend newspapers. Comics are not glamorous, nor are they prestigious. But their total circulation, readership, and demographics constitute an exciting universe for the direct response advertiser. Here are some of the fascinating facts and figures about comics as an advertising medium.

Each week, usually on Sunday, millions of color comics are distributed through nearly 400 different newspapers. These comics literally saturate the major and secondary markets, providing the better coverage in strategic metro markets of the country. The major comics network is Metro-Puck Comics, distributed in 250 newspapers with a total circulation of 46,160,899.

The demographic characteristics of comics readers are quite a surprise to most advertisers, who seem to have ill-conceived ideas about this type of reader. The median age of the adult comics reader is 39 years, slightly younger than the United States median age of 40.2 years.

One of the major misconceptions about comics readership is that the higher one's education, the less likely one is to read the comic pages. The statistics presented in Table 11–4 dispute this.

Table 11–4.   Demographic Characteristics of Readers of Comics

Characteristics	Comics Readers	U.S. Population
Age		
18–24	19.0%	13.9%
25–34	24.7	23.4
35–49	19.2	20.3
50–64	11.4	13.5
65+	25.4	28.7
Sex		
Male	48.5	48.4
Female	51.5	51.6
Education		
Any college	50.6	—
College graduate	24.9	—
College graduate+	9.8	—
High school graduate+	35.1	—
Income		
$50,000+	25.5	24.0
$35,000–$49,999	24.7	23.1
$25,000–$34,999	16.6	17.6
$15,000–$24,999	17.2	18.1
Under $15,000	16.0	17.1

Source: "Serious Business," Belden study for Metro-Puck Comics Network, 1990.

Finally, there is the misconception that the higher one's income, the less likely one is to read comics. Again, the figures refute this.

Among direct response advertisers, the largest users of comic-page advertising in the past have been photo finishers. Huge photo finishing businesses have been started from scratch using comics as a prime advertising medium. The availability of the ad-and-envelope technique in conjunction with comic-page advertising serves a genuine need of photo finishers because they are able to provide an envelope in which the prospect can return completed film rolls. The standard charge for a free-standing envelope or for affixing a card or envelope to the ad averages about $40 per thousand, plus the cost of printing the response vehicle. With ad-and-envelope, the direct response advertiser provides the same impetus to response with a reply card or reply envelope. (See Exhibit 11–2.)

Following the photo finishers with comic-page advertising have been insurance companies and land developers. Opportunities obviously exist for a host of other direct response advertisers seeking mass circulation at low cost. Comic-page advertising traditionally limits advertising to one advertiser per page. Thus full-page advertising is not essential to gain a dominant position. Comics, not unlike syndicated supplements, should be tested before one goes full run. You can test individual papers in the Metro-Puck Comics Network. (For ADI analysis of the Metro-Puck Network, see Table 11–5.)

Table 11–5. Metro-Puck Comics Network: ADI Analysis

Total circulation	47,294,542
Total newspapers covered	245
Total ADIs covered	210
Total ADI households	93,375,500
Total U.S. retail sales	$1,719,542,600

Source: 1991 Circulation:
Retail sales and households—*Sales and Marketing Management, Survey of Buying Power,* June 1990; total circulation—3/31/91 ABC statements; ADI circulation—latest ABC annual audit and date audit; non-ABC newspapers—latest sworn post office statement.

Run-of-Paper Advertising

We have been exploring formats carried by newspapers—preprints, syndicated supplements, and comics. Not to be overlooked, of course, is run-of-paper (R.O.P.) advertising. Generally, direct response advertisers have failed to get the results with R.O.P advertising that they have obtained from newspaper preprints and syndicated newspaper supplements. One obvious reason is that four-color advertising is not generally available for R.O.P. Another is that R.O.P. ads don't drop out for individual attention. But many successes can be cited for small-space R.O.P. ads that have run frequently year after year in hundreds of newspapers. When small-space ads are run over a long period of time with high frequency, the number of reader impressions multiplies rapidly in proportion to the cost.

Exhibit 11–2.   Comic-Page Advertising

Ad calls attention to an envelope inserted loose in newspaper.

Effect of Local News on Results

A major difference between newspaper advertising and all other print media is that the newspaper reader is more likely to be influenced by local news events. All newspaper advertising appears within the atmosphere of the local news for a given day. A major scandal in local politics or a catastrophe such as a tornado in a local area can have a devastating effect on the advertising appearing in a given issue. Magazines, on the other hand, do not tie in closely with local events. Magazines are normally put aside to read during hours not taken up by involvement in local events. Because local events have a strong effect on response, positively or negatively, markets with similar demographics don't always respond in the same manner. All newspaper advertising tends to be *local*, even though a schedule may be national.

Developing a Newspaper Test Program

When direct response advertisers first consider testing newspapers as a medium, they have a myriad of decisions to make. Should they go R.O.P., the newspaper preprint route, local Sunday supplements, syndicated supplements, TV program supplements, comics? What papers should they test? Putting ad size and position aside for the moment, there are two initial considerations: the importance of advertising in a mail-order climate and the demographics of markets selected as they relate to the product or service being offered.

If you had one simple product, say a stamp dispenser, for instance, and a tiny budget, you might place one small ad in one publication. You could run the ad in the mail-order section of the *New York Times Sunday Magazine*. Generally, if you don't make it there, you won't make it anywhere. Running such an ad would give a "feel." If it works, it would be logical to test similar mail-order sections in major cities such as Chicago, Detroit, and Los Angeles. (See Exhibit 11–3.)

Simple items, which are suited to small-space advertising in mail-order sections, greatly simplify the testing procedure. But, more often than not, multicity testing in larger space is required.

Prime direct response test markets in the United States include Atlanta, Buffalo, Cleveland, Dallas-Fort Worth, Denver, Des Moines, Indianapolis, Omaha, and Peoria. In the selection of test markets, you should analyze the newspaper to make certain it has advertising reach and coverage and offers demographics that are suitable to your product. If there are two newspapers in a market, it is worthwhile to evaluate both of them. Let us say that because of budget limitations advertising can be placed in only a limited number of markets. Such criteria as circulation, household penetration, male or female readers, and advertising lineage relating to the product to be advertised should be measured.

A number of sources will provide the data necessary for evaluation. You would begin with SRDS's *Newspaper Rates and Data* for general cost and circulation information. *SRDS Circulation Analysis* would provide information about metro household penetration. *Simmons Total Audience Study* could then be used to isolate male or female readers of a particular age group. Other criteria to be measured are retail lineage in various classifications and spendable income by metro area.

Demographics are a major consideration market by market whether you are going R.O.P. preprints, local supplements, syndicated supplements, or TV program supplements. Once an advertiser develops a test program that closely reflects the demographics for the product or service, expansion to like markets makes possible the rapid acceleration of a full-blown program. But selecting newspapers is tedious, because there are hundreds from which to choose as compared with a relative handful of magazines whose demographics can be more closely related to the proposition. As an example, a test newspaper schedule could be placed in the following markets: Atlanta, preprint; Cleveland, Metro comics; Dallas-Fort Worth, R.O.P.; Denver, preprint; Des Moines, R.O.P.; Indianapolis, preprint; Omaha, Metro comics; and Peoria, *Parade* remnant. If there is more than one newspaper in a test market, the paper with the most promising demographics should be selected.

A test schedule like this would be ambitious in terms of total dollars, but it would have the advantage of simultaneously testing markets and formats. Once a reading has been obtained form the markets and formats, the advertiser can rapidly expand to other markets and will have the advantage of using the most productive formats.

Advertising Seasons

As in direct mail and magazine direct response advertising, there are two major newspaper direct response advertising seasons. The fall mail-order season begins roughly with August and runs through November. (A notable exception is a July insertion, which is often useful especially when using a pretested piece.) The winter season begins with January and runs through March.

Exceptions to the two major direct response seasons occur in the sale of seasonal merchandise. Christmas items are usually promoted from September through the first week of December. A nursery, on the other hand, will start promoting in late December and early January, then again in the early fall. Many nurseries follow the practice of promoting by geographic regions, starting earlier in the south and working up to later promotion in the north.

Exhibit 11–3.   Mail-Order Shopping Guide from the *Chicago Tribune Sunday Magazine*

Timing of Newspaper Insertions

Beyond the seasonal factor of direct response advertising in newspapers, timing is important as it relates to days of the week. According to the *E&P Yearbook, Bureau of Advertising Circulation Analysis*, the number of copies of a newspaper sold per day is remarkably constant month after month—despite such events as summer vacations and Christmas holidays. And people buy the newspaper to read not only the editorial matter but also the ads. According to an *Audits & Surveys Study*, the percentage of people opening an average ad page any weekday, Monday through Friday, varies less than 3 percent, with Tuesday ranking the highest at 88 percent.

There is no question that the local newspaper is an integral part of practically everyone's daily life. While magazines may be set aside for reading at a convenient time, newspapers are read the day they are delivered or purchased or are not read at all. Monday through Thursday are favorite choices of many direct response advertisers for their R.O.P. advertising. Many direct response advertisers judiciously avoid the weekday issue containing grocery advertising.

As we have seen, more and more newspapers are accepting preprints for weekday insertions. This can be a major advantage, considering the larger number of preprints appearing in most metro Sunday newspapers.

Newspaper Response Patterns

Newspapers have the shortest time lapse from closing date to appearance date of all print media. In most cases, ads can appear in the newspaper within 72 hours after placement. Depending on the format used, up to 90 percent or more of responses will be reached for a typical direct response newspaper ad within these time frames: R.O.P., after the second week; preprints, after the third week; syndicated newspaper supplements, after the third week; and comics, after the second week.

Naturally, response patterns vary according to the proposition. Thus it is important for advertisers to develop their own response pattern. But the nature of newspaper advertising permits a quick turnaround. *Dow Theory Forecasts*, for instance, has run ads in hundreds of newspapers. Dow is able to project results, giving the advertiser the option of deciding whether to repeat an ad, within a week after the first orders are received.

Determining Proper Ad Size

In direct response newspaper advertising, as in retail or national newspaper ads, few people dispute the claim that the larger ad generally will get more attention than a smaller one. But whether the full-page ad gets twice the

attention of the half-page ad or four times the attention of the quarter-page ad is debatable. It is cost per response that counts. Just as in magazine advertising, less space is usually indicated for inquiry advertising and more space for a direct order ad.

According to one study conducted by the Bureau of Advertising relating to mail-back newspaper coupons, the size of the space seems to be a factor in reader response only to the extent that it is a factor in initial reader attention. In this study 85 percent of newspaper inserts ran ads of 1,000 lines or more. Only half used fewer than 1,000 lines, with a minimum of 500 lines per ad.

A low-budget advertiser often must choose between a single full-page ad and several small ads over an extended time. The proper guide to follow in determining the initial size of ads is to base the size on the space required to tell the *complete story*.

Trying to sell membership in a record and tape club in a small space would be ludicrous. Experience shows that a wide selection of records must be offered in the ad to get memberships. The same is true for a book club. On the other hand, if you are selling a single item at a low price—say, a cigarette lighter for $4.95—the complete story can be told in a small space. Where small-space advertising can tell the whole story, consistency and repetition often prove to be keys to success.

Aside from the obvious requirement of using a full page or more for a proposition, constant testing of ad sizes will establish the proper size to produce the most efficient cost per inquiry or per order.

The Position Factor

Newspapers and magazines have many similarities in respect to the importance of position in direct response advertising. Research has demonstrated high readership of newspaper ads, whatever the position. However, direct response advertisers still prefer right-hand pages. Generally, such advertisers find that ads are more effective if they appear in the front of the newspaper rather than in the back. Placement of coupon ads in the gutter of any newspaper page is almost always avoided.

All newspapers are printed in sections. Special consideration should be given to the reading habits of men and women as they relate to specific sections of a newspaper. Table 11–6 details the readership habits of men and women, showing that readership by males and females is fairly evenly divided with the exception of four sections—food and cooking, home furnishings, gardening, and sports.

Table 11–6.   Daily Newspaper Pages or Sections Usually Read by Adult
Men and Women

	Adults	Men	Women
Usually Read every page	56%	57%	54%
Read certain pages or sections	44	43	46
Read:			
Business/finance	74	78	71
Classified	72	73	72
Comics	74	74	75
Editorial	76	75	77
Entertainment (movies, theater, etc.)	80	76	84
Food or cooking	75	67	82
General news	91	90	92
Home (furnishings, gardening, etc.)	72	67	76
Sports	75	85	64
TV, radio listings	74	73	75
Base: Average weekday audience (000)	(113,322)	(56,114)	(57,207)

Source: SMRB, *1991 Study of Media & Markets.*

Color vs. Black-and-White

The possibilities of using color in newspaper advertising may be regarded as similar to those for magazine advertising, with one major exception. If you plan to use one or more colors other than black in an R.O.P. ad, you simply can't get the quality that you can in a color magazine ad. This does not mean that R.O.P. color shouldn't be tested. A majority of newspapers that offer color will allow A/B splits of color versus black and white.

Studies have used split runs and the recognition method to test the attention-getting power of both two-color and full-color R.O.P. ads. These studies show increases of 58 percent for two-color ads and 78 percent for full-color ads above the level of results for black-and-white versions of the same ads. Comparable cost differences are 21 percent and 25 percent, respectively.

When Starch "noting score" norms are used to estimate the same attention-getting differential, a different conclusion is reached. The differences are about 10 percent and 30 percent, respectively (when size and product category are held constant). Using norms means comparing a black-and-white ad for one product in another city at another time. These variables inevitably blur the significance of comparisons.

For the direct response advertiser, these studies are interesting. However, you should remember that genuine controlled testing is the only way to get true figures.

Self-Quiz

1. Name the two obvious advantages of preprints.

   a. _____

   b. _____

2. Which is the most popular format for a preprint?
   ☐ Card   ☐ Multipage

3. Name the three major syndicated newspaper supplements.

   a. _____

   b. _____

   c. _____

4. Define *Dutch door*.

   _____

   _____

   _____

   _____

5. What is remnant space?

   _____

   _____

   _____

   _____

6. The higher one's education, the less likely one will read the comic
   pages.   ☐ True   ☐ False

7. The higher one's income, the less likely one will read the comic pages.
   ☐ True   ☐ False

8. What is the advantage of the ad-and-card and ad-and-envelope for
   comic-page advertisers?

   _____

   _____

   _____

9. How many advertisers per page are allowed in comic-page advertising?

   _____

10. What major advantage over R.O.P. advertising is offered to direct response advertisers by preprints and supplements?

   _____

   _____

   _____

11. In regard to potential results, what is the major difference between newspaper advertising and all other print advertising?

   _____

   _____

   _____

12. What are the two initial considerations in the development of a newspaper test program?

   a. _____

   b. _____

13. If you have a single item that is suitable for advertising in a small space and a limited budget for testing, which publication would you test first?

   _____

14. What are the two main seasons for newspaper direct response advertising?

   a. _____

   b. _____

15. Give the preferred weekdays for R.O.P. advertising:

   _____

   _____

16. Depending on the format used, up to 90 percent or more of responses will be reached for a typical direct response newspaper ad within these time frames:

   R.O.P.: after _____ week(s)

   Preprints: after _____ week(s)

   Supplements: after _____ week(s)

   Comics: after _____ week(s)

17. The size of newspaper space seems to be a factor in reader response only to the extent that it is a factor in _____

_____

18. When running R.O.P., direct response advertisers should specify:
    ☐ Left-hand page   ☐ Right-hand page

19. What is the major disadvantage of running color R.O.P.?

_____

_____

_____

_____

Pilot Project

You are the advertising manager of a mail-order operation selling collectibles. You have been successful in magazines offering a series of historic plates. You have never used newspapers, but now you have a $75,000 budget to test the medium.

Outline a newspaper test plan.

1. Select your test cities.

2. Will your tests run in the Sunday edition or the weekday edition, or both?

3. What formats will you test—preprints, supplements, comics, local TV guides, R.O.P.?

4. What size preprints or ads will you test?

5. At what time of the year will you run your tests?

Note: If you use preprints, your total space budget should cover printing costs.

CHAPTER TWELVE

Electronic Media

Broadcast TV, cable TV, AM-FM radio, computer networks, videocassettes, and video discs—these are the major electronic media available to direct response advertisers. To get a quick insight as to how these media are being used, let's take a look at some applications.

Electronic Media Applications
Broadcast TV

The range of TV direct response offers has greatly expanded in recent years. While direct selling of magazines, tapes and records, and innovative products certainly still exists, many different types of direct response offers have surfaced.

Lead-generation commercials for high-ticket products and services such as home mortgages, insurance, and exercise equipment are now common. In addition, many Fortune 500 companies have started incorporating TV direct response into their marketing mix. The diversity of TV direct response offers is evidenced by broadcast direct response agency A. Eicoff & Company's client roster—its accounts include American Express, Time-Life, Beltone Electronics, Rodale Press, and St. Jude Children's Hospital.

A truly unique application of broadcast TV involves White Castle. Hundreds of thousands of Midwesterners were practically raised on White Castle hamburgers. Each year many of those same Midwesterners move to other regions of the country. Even without a White Castle nearby, the taste lingered on.

White Castle solved the availability problem by initiating a unique TV campaign with the theme "White Castle has the taste some people won't live without" (Exhibit 12–1). Outside of the White Castle trading area, commercials ended with this tag line: "Hamburgers to Fly. Call 1-800-W CASTLE." Over 10,000 hamburgers were being sold a week, with a minimum order of 50 hamburgers for $57!

Exhibit 12–1. **White Castle Campaign**

DAUGHTER: I miss you, momma. I miss the city, too.

MOMMA: What if we sent you a little bit of your home town.

DAUGHTER: Now, how are you gonna do that?

White Castle hamburgers from back home! You can't get them out here.

My folks sent them!

ROOMMATE: Hey! Johnson's got White Castles!

GANG: White Castles!

DAUGHTER: You know, on my first date we stopped at a White Castle.

SINGERS: WHITE CASTLE HAS THE TASTE SOME PEOPLE WON'T LIVE WITHOUT.

Cable TV

Broadcast TV, both local and network, has long been a major medium for consumer direct response advertisers, producing inquiries, supporting other media, and selling goods and services to the consumer. But in the last five years, in particular, cable has come on strong.

Cable TV *looks* like broadcast TV, but it is different in many ways. First, the cable TV audience is highly defined. Cable operators know who is tied

into the system—they send them a bill every month. This demographic information, and some psychographic information as well, is available to the advertiser.

With many more channels available than are available for broadcast TV, cable, not unlike the audience selectivity traits of radio and special-interest magazines, provides more special-interest programming. Thus the direct response advertiser can tie offers to predefined audiences who have a pro-clivity toward special interests such as sports, news, and entertainment.

One of the most firmly established special-interest channels is Home Box Office (HBO). Its appeal is to those who have a particular interest in movies, sports, and special events. To be successful, not only must HBO offer supe-rior programming, but it must sell subscriptions for the programs as well. We are indebted to Jim Kobs, chairman of Kobs, Gregory, and Passavant, Chicago, for the case history that follows.

HBO Campaign

When you are the leading cable TV premium channel, and you're selling a visual product, it seems only natural that TV advertising would be an important part of your marketing program. And it is for Home Box Office.

But that wasn't always the case. Until a few years ago, HBO had relied primarily on consumer direct mail to generate leads for the local cable system operators, who serve as distributors for the HBO channel.

TV had been considered prior to that, but it simply wasn't cost efficient. In a typical local media market, most TV households were not wired or eligible to receive cable TV. So TV spots would be wasted on too many viewers who had no opportunity to sign up for the movies, sports, and special events that HBO offered. But as cable's distribution grew (it is now available to over 70 percent of U.S. TV households), and as cable operators saw the benefits of cooperating in areawide promotions, direct response TV became a viable medium for selling cable TV and HBO.

With the help of its direct marketing agency, Kobs, Gregory, and Passavant, HBO began running TV spots in a few small media markets in the early 1980s. The purpose of the spots was to generate leads for the cable companies, which, in turn, followed up with their own pricing and installation details. So HBO felt that 60-second spots were sufficient to put across its message and elicit a response. (Ninety-second spots were later tested, but they didn't pay out as well. Also, they were more likely to be preempted by advertisers paying the full standard rate than the 60-second spots were.)

Leads from the spots were received via telephone, with a separate 800 number assigned to each station for tracking purposes. These leads were then sorted and sent, via overnight or electronic mail, to the appropriate cable com-panies for follow-up. Lead information was also sent to HBO and the agency for evaluation. When a cable company closed a sale, this too was reported.

After a few years of limited activity, enough data had been accumulated both to justify and to implement an expanded direct response TV campaign. By evaluating such factors as number of spots aired, length of flight, type of station (independent or affiliated), cost per spot, and cable penetration, it was determined that a few facts were important for planning future TV efforts:

- *What doesn't work in Week 1 won't work in subsequent weeks.* Traditional direct response television theory holds that advertisers should let a spot air for at least two or three weeks, allowing the frequency of the message to build before making any judgment. HBO, however, has found that if a spot doesn't work in Week 1, it will never work; little or no improvement can be seen in subsequent weeks of airing. Why? HBO is a product that already has high consumer awareness. And there are few details to explain. Thus frequency of message is far less important in generating a lead.

- *The first quarter is consistently the strongest.* The fact that January–March saw the highest response rates of any season should be no surprise to traditional users of direct response TV. But in the broadcast industry, where new programming has been historically introduced in the fall, it *was* a surprise to see another period do so much better.

- *Large urban media markets are more successful than small rural media markets.* Large urban media markets obviously have more potential cable subscribers than smaller ones. But HBO had always had difficulty in reaching them via direct mail because many mailing lists were supplied by cable operators, who found it hard to come by reliable lists of apartment dwellers and new residents. TV, on the other hand, is a mass medium that reaches both these segments very well.

In 1986 HBO's use of direct response spots contributed a significant number of new subscribers to cable TV and HBO, at a lead cost that was most efficient. In addition, this success led to a breakthrough in another important area: the use of support TV.

Like many other direct marketers, HBO had previously used only 30-second TV spots to support its mail and *TV Guide* print campaigns, paying full standard rates for guaranteed time. Upon evaluation of the 60-second direct response spots, however, Kobs, Gregory, and Passavant recommended that HBO begin using 60-second support TV spots as well—even though they would be preemptible—because they could be bought at much lower direct response media rates. Mary Pat Ryan, vice president and management supervisor at the agency, gave the reasons for this recommendation as follows:

First, HBO has a fairly mass audience, with little differentiation based on lifestyle or psychographics. In addition, mail is dropped to almost every household in the cabled area—again, not to demographically or psychographically targeted lists. As a result, targeted support TV buys are not necessary for supporting HBO's mail pieces.

Also, experience had shown that 60-second preemptible spots were not, in fact, preempted often enough to be real problem for HBO. On the contrary, with smart media planning and buying, a large market could be reached at a highly efficient cost.

In addition, everything HBO had done in the media market had proved that prominent display of their product—their movies, sports, and entertainment specials—was crucial. A 60-second spot allowed time enough to both display the HBO product *and* support the mail/print campaign.

Finally, HBO was moving toward integrated campaigns, with every promotion—from mail to TV, from general awareness to direct response—utilizing the same creative themes and graphic looks. The 60-second spot, therefore, became useful in achieving its integration of an overall image and a specific call to action: "Look for this announcement in your mail or *TV Guide*." A good example of this is HBO's 1987 campaign called "Your Summer Entertainer." Both mail and print used similar graphics to dramatize the programming that HBO would bring into the viewer's home. TV support used the same theme, coupled with dramatic aerial graphics, to build expectation for the mailings. (See Exhibit 12.2.)

To sum up, HBO and Kobs, Gregory, and Passavant found that by utilizing 60-second support TV spots at lower-cost preemptible rates, they could get double the air time for about the same cost of 30-second nonpreemptible spots. And they could use this extra time not only to give extra support to their mail campaigns, but also to better tell the whole HBO story.

Today, HBO sends out over 100 million direct mail pieces a year, utilizes four-page inserts in national *TV Guide* runs, and supports both efforts with 60-second spots in over 120 markets three times a year. According to Steve Janas, vice president of direct marketing at HBO, results show that in those media markets where mail and *TV Guide* advertising are supported by TV, subscriber acquisition is over 100 percent higher than in similar media markets using no TV at all!

Home-Shopping Shows

A phenomenon of our times is the home-shopping show on TV. The telephone is integral to its explosive growth. The pioneer was HSN (Home Shopping Network).

A later entrant—QVC Network—has experienced dramatic growth. Revenues for the first quarter of 1990, for example, came to $161.3 million, an increase of 207 percent over the same period in 1989. QVC now reaches around 34 million homes, 3 million of which are satellite-dish owners.

The QVC shopping channel is broadcast live 24 hours a day, 7 days a week. QVC built its huge volume by featuring prescheduled programs, offering products from specific product categories such as jewelry, electronics, and apparel. Under a new policy, customers may order any item presented on QVC at any time that's convenient to them, providing the item is still in stock.

Throughout all TV broadcasts, the QVC toll-free number is flashed constantly. Phone response is almost instantaneous.

Exhibit 12–2.   "Summer Entertainer" Spot

HOME BOX OFFICE

"SUMMER ENTERTAINER"

1. (MUSIC UNDER)
ANNCR: (VO) This summer, some of the greatest names in Hollywood will gather here,

2. and here's your chance to see them.

3. The world's heavyweight championship will be a

4. the nation's top comedians and most exciting events will be seen here,

5. all at great savings if you act now.

6. This summer,

7. one of the major entertainment centers will be your home.

8. With HBO, your summer entertainer.

9. And you can bring HBO into your home by calling this toll-free number.

10. You'll get installation at special savings.

11. Savings that connect you to the blockbusters

12. and show stoppers,

13. crowd thrillers

14. and bone chillers on HBO.

15. Plus on cable TV, the risk takers

16. newsbreakers

17. and music makers 24 hours a day.

18. So call now and you'll get installation for only $9.95.

19. A big saving off the regular price. Call 1-800-346-3000.

20. This is a limited time offer, so call 1-800-346-3000. HBO. We're your summer entertainer.

"Summer Entertainer" theme is used in both response and support spots for HBO.

Exhibit 12–3.   **Cover Panel of Folder Announcing Free Prizes to Cable Viewers**

To promote viewership, QVC mails extensively to cable subscribers, providing them with free memberships in the QVC Shoppers Club and notifying them about free prizes awarded each day. (See Exhibits 12–3 and 12–4.)

Radio

Radio has two things going for it over broadcast TV: (1) program formats to which advertisers can better target, and (2) much lower costs for similar time periods.

Targeting to the right program formats is the key. For example, if an advertiser is soliciting phone-in orders for a rock album or tape, there's no problem running a radio commercial on scores of stations that feature rock music; these listeners are the very audience the advertiser is seeking.

Or if a financial advertiser is soliciting inquiries from potential investors, there are program formats that help the advertiser reach a target audience: "Wall Street Report," for example, or FM stations with a high percentage of upper-income listeners.

This 60-second radio commercial by Merrill Lynch was run in conjunction with program formats with a high percentage of listeners who match its customer profile.

Exhibit 12–4.   **First Page of Two-Page Letter to Cable Subscribers with Free Membership Card for QVC Shoppers Club**

MultiVision
QVC Network
Channel 23

1-800-345-1515   **1-800-345-1515**
QVC MEMBERSHIP NO.   QVC MEMBERSHIP NO.
1449-3828   **1449-3828**

1-800-345-1515   **1-800-345-1515**
QVC MEMBERSHIP NO.   QVC MEMBERSHIP NO.
1449-3828   **1449-3828**

QVC SHOPPERS CLUB

★ MEMBERSHIP CARD ★

MEMBERSHIP
NUMBER   **1449-3828**

Mr. Don Corley
P.O. Box 641
Cambria, IL 62915

QVC - Cable Channel 23

CAR-RT SORT   **B009

Place these stickers on your phones so you'll always have your membership number and QVC phone number handy!

Mr. Don Corley
P.O. Box 641
Cambria, IL 62915

Dear Cable Subscriber:

Because you're a MultiVision cable subscriber, we're pleased to award you a FREE membership in the QVC Shoppers Club!

Your exclusive membership number is valuable. It's your key to winning great prizes on QVC. And you'll have lots of opportunities to win, because QVC GIVES AWAY HUNDREDS OF PRIZES EVERY DAY!

<u>Hourly</u> $25 prizes. <u>Daily</u> $1000 shopping sprees. And <u>weekly</u> grand prizes such as new cars and dream vacations -- all to help introduce cable viewers to QVC, the <u>new</u> way of shopping, on Cable Channel 23.

QVC stands for Quality, Value and Convenience. Tune in to channel 23 <u>anytime,</u> day or night, for a wide variety of high-quality products to help you look your best, beautify your home and make your life easier. You can order any item by phone, with <u>a 30-day money-back guarantee.</u>

However, you don't have to buy <u>anything</u> to win prizes on QVC. Here's just <u>one</u> way you could win:

Tune in for QVC's hourly Lucky Number drawings. Every time the number drawn matches <u>either</u> the first 4 digits <u>or</u> the last 4 digits of your QVC membership number, YOU'RE A WINNER! Just phone QVC before the next Lucky Number is drawn and you'll <u>instantly</u> win $25 credited to your QVC account. Plus, you'll automatically be entered in QVC's DAILY $1000 GRAND PRIZE DRAWING!

Your membership number is 1449-3828, which gives you <u>two</u> opportunities to win during each drawing! Every time 1449 <u>or</u> 3828 is drawn, YOU'RE A WINNER!

Over, please...

(Music up and under)

ANNOUNCER: A word on money management from Merrill Lynch. Today, many banks are trying to copy our revolutionary Cash Management Account financial service. Here's why they can't. Bank money market accounts are simply that: bank accounts. A Merrill Lynch CMA gives you access to the entire *range* of our investment opportunities. Instead of just an account, you get an Account Executive, backed by the top-ranked research team on Wall Street. Idle cash is automatically invested in your choice of *three* CMA money market funds. You enjoy check writing, a special Visa card, automatic variable-rate loans up to the full margin loan value of your securities— at *rates* banks aren't likely to match. So give your money sound management, and *more* to grow on. The all-in-one CMA financial service. *(Music)* From Merrill Lynch. A breed apart.

LOCAL ANNOUNCER: For more complete information and a free prospectus, including sales charges and expenses, call 000-0000. Read it carefully before you invest or send money. That's 000-0000.

Computer Networks

Another electronic medium available to the direct marketer, but not widely used, is the computer network. There are millions of home computers in place in the United States today; most have been purchased by business people who rationalize the cost as an extension of their business activities. Many are connected via telephone lines to central databases such as the Dow Jones News Retrieval Service.

These networks are used essentially for business-to-business purposes; this use does not exclude opportunities to program consumer product information. One of the largest and most successful "programs" available to the computer networker is CompuServe's comparative shopping service.

Various brands of merchandise offered for sale by different merchants can be called up from the database. The user can make an item-by-item, feature-by-feature comparison, including price—all with the calculating aid of the computer. The user can actually order the item he or she wants, via the return leg of the telephone line, for later delivery to home or office. In this sense, we are dealing with an electronic sales directory or catalog. It differs from a printed catalog in that, for the most part, computer networks are limited to text-only displays.

Videocassettes and Video Disks

Today more than half of all TV homes will have one or more VCRs. This could be bad news for movie theaters: Close to $3 billion annually is spent

on movie rentals. The onslaught of VCRs isn't good news for TV networks either: Millions use their TV sets to watch taped movies, sporting events, and special events—*sans commercials.*

But for the direct marketer, VCRs offer an opportunity rather than a threat: Direct marketers have the opportunity to become sponsors of video-cassette programming.

By incorporating commercial messages in the programs, producers can defray the high cost of production and sell their tapes at a lower price. In addition, they may be able to open new distribution outlets. As an example, the hour-long "Mr. Boston Official Video Bartender's Guide," sponsored by Glenmore Distilleries, is available through liquor stores as well as the more usual outlets. Along with the cassette goes an eight-page catalog of each Glenmore product.

With such a catalog, or with specific sales and response information incorporated into a taped presentation, a sponsored videocassette might prove so productive for an advertiser that it could afford to sell the tape cheaply, use it as a self-liquidating premium, or even give the tape to video cassette outlets for low-rate rental. Videocassette catalogs also show potential for high-ticket items that benefit from demonstration.

While video disks haven't attained the popularity of videocassette recorders, they have been gaining ground with consumers in recent years.

For catalogs and for many other types of electronic publishing, the technology of choice may soon be the compact random-access optical video disk. These digitally encoded disks pack an enormous amount of audio and/or video information in a small space. For example: Grolier's 21-volume *Academic American Encyclopedia* was first issued on a single 4.7-inch disk in the fall of 1985. It costs less than half as much as the printed version and it uses only one-fifth of the total capacity of the disk!

Video disks can store sound, still pictures, and moving images as well as computer data. There appear to be limitless commercial applications—from the ultimate catalog to ad-supported cooking courses.

Direct Response TV

Buying and scheduling TV and radio time is best left to the experts—direct marketing agencies and some select buying services. But for a direct marketer to recognize the opportunities and pitfalls of advertising in these media, it is imperative that the basics be understood. The following comments about buying and scheduling TV apply equally to radio.

Ratings

It is important to keep in mind that the cost of a commercial time period is based on its *rating.* This is a measure of its share of the total TV households viewing the show. The more highly rated the show, the higher the cost. One

rating point equals 1 percent of the total households in the market. A show with a 20 rating is being watched by 20 percent of TV households.

When the total ratings of all the time periods in a schedule are combined, the result is called *gross rating points* (or GRPs). Simply stated, if a television schedule has 100 GRPs per week, it is reaching the equivalent of 100 percent of TV households in the market in that week. Obviously, this is a statistical reach with varying degrees of duplication. It does not guarantee 100 percent of the individual homes will be reached.

Commercial Lengths

While 30 seconds is the most common time length for general or image advertising, direct marketers seldom find that adequate to tell their selling story in a persuasive way. Ninety to 120 seconds is usually required for a direct sale commercial, while 60 to 90 seconds is usually required for lead-generation commercials. On the other hand, support commercials with sufficient GRPs prove effective with a combination of 10-second and 30-second commercials. But key outlet marketing usually requires longer lengths.

Of course, with the popularity of 30-second announcements and the premium broadcasters can get for them, it is not always possible to clear longer-length commercials, particularly during periods of high demand.

Reach and Frequency

TV advertisers use two terms in measuring the effectiveness of their television schedules. *Reach* refers to the number of different homes exposed to the message within a given time segment. *Frequency* is a measure of how many times the average viewer will see the message over a given number of weeks. Frequency also can be measured against viewer quintiles (e.g., heaviest viewers, lightest viewers, etc.).

The combination of reach and frequency will tell you what percentage of the audience you are reaching and how often on average they will see your message. Television schedules often are purchased against reach and frequency goals and actual performance measured in postanalysis.

For most direct marketers, reach and frequency are not as important as actual response rates, which represent a true return on the media dollar. But a knowledge of what reach and frequency are is critical when television is used in a supporting role.

Buying Time

Buying time for very specific time periods is the most expensive way to purchase it. You pay a higher price to guarantee your message will run at a precise time within a predetermined program environment. Television time also can be bought less expensively. Stations will sell R.O.S. (run-of-station) time, time available during periods the station has been unable to sell at

regular rates. This is particularly true with independent (non-network) stations, which often have sizable inventories of unsold time. If the station, however, subsequently sells the time to a specific buyer, your commercial will be preempted.

Preemptible time can be an excellent buy for direct response advertisers because of the combination of lower cost and quite respectable response rates. When buying preemptible time, it also is possible to specify the day-parts (daytime, early fringe, late fringe, and so on.) for slightly more than straight R.O.S. rates. This can be important for direct marketers with a specific target audience for their product. Such spots still may be preempted at any time, however.

Television time also may be purchased on the basis of payment per inquiry (or P.I.) and bonus-to-pay-out. P.I. allows the station to run as many commercials as it wishes, whenever it wishes. There is no charge for the time, but the station receives a predetermined sum for every inquiry or sale the advertisement generates for the advertiser. The advertiser is not committed to pay for a spot until it delivers an inquiry or sale and then only in relation to responses.

But there are disadvantages. It is almost impossible to plan methodically for fulfillment. Such programs cannot be coordinated reliably with other efforts or promotion timetables. And, since the station will run the commercials that it feels will perform best for it, your spot may never run and you may not know it until it has jeopardized your entire selling program.

Bonus-to-pay-out involves a special arrangement with the station to deliver a certain number of responses. A schedule is negotiated with the station to guarantee a certain minimum schedule. If at the end of the schedule the response goal has not been reached, the station must continue to run the commercial until it is reached. This method provides a better planning base for the direct marketer.

With television time in high demand, such opportunities are not as available as they once were. But if they can be located, they can be a superb vehicle for direct marketers.

TV Schedules

What kind of broadcast TV schedule is most productive and/or efficient for the direct marketer? It depends on the objective. For direct sale or lead-generation commercials, which require the viewer to get up and take some action within minutes, certain criteria apply. For example, the TV viewing day is divided into various *day-parts*. There are weekday daytime, early evening or fringe, prime time, late night or fringe, and weekend. Each day-part tends to reach one group or combination of viewers better than the others.

It is important to know your primary target group so you can select the most appropriate day-part. Prime time is so called because it reaches the largest audience with the most exciting shows. It is also the most expensive. The more attentive viewers are to the show, the less likely they are to

respond immediately. Therefore, times of lower viewer involvement and attentiveness are better and less expensive for the advertiser who expects a direct response. Reruns, talk shows, old movies, and the like often are the best vehicles for direct response advertising. These tend to run predominantly in daytime, fringe, and late-night time slots.

Similarly, because independent stations tend to run a higher percentage of syndicated reruns and movies, their viewers tend to have a lower level of attentiveness to the programming. But even on independent stations, avoid news shows and other high-interest programming. Check the ratings. They are a good guide.

Seasonality is another factor in direct response TV. The first and third quarters are the best seasons for television response, just as they are for print and mail. Moreover, television time pricing is related to viewing levels, which are seasonal and vary month to month as well as by day-part.

Market Performance

Some geographic locations are good for certain products or offers. Others are simply not receptive. It pays to know ahead of time what a market's propensity is. Previous experience with mail or print can be a reasonably reliable guide.

In any event, it is not necessary to jump in up to your neck. Start with a handful of markets, two to five, say, and test the waters. Try a one- or two-week schedule. As few as ten commercials per week can give you a reading. Monitor your telephone response daily. You'll know within two or three days if it's bust or boom. After a week or so you'll have an even more precise fix on how well your commercial is doing. If it holds up, stay with it—until it starts to taper off. Then stop. Don't try to milk a stone.

Meanwhile, move on to other markets in the same methodical and measured way. You always can return to your most successful markets later in the marketing year after your commercial has had a rest. Or you can come back with a new offer.

Advantages and Disadvantages of Different Types of Stations

Media-buying decisions have become more complex because of the expansion and success of various cable and broadcast stations and programming packages. Let's examine the advantages and disadvantages of the five major options for most TV direct response offers.

Network   The four major networks are ABC (195 affiliated stations), CBS (189 affiliated stations), NBC (186 affiliated stations), and Fox (134 affiliated stations).

The advantage of the network option is that network reaches 95 percent of the potential U.S. TV households with each spot.

The disadvantages are: (1) There are very few if any 120-second spots available, (2) it is generally cost-prohibitive, (3) telemarketing blockage problems would occur in most day-parts, and (4) talent payments could present a problem.

Conclusion: Though once considered prohibitively expensive, with astute planning the network option can be a viable direct response vehicle.

Spot TV   The use of spot TV is a very localized way of making a buy, and it can be done through independent stations and/or affiliates. Whether you buy one or five stations in a spot market, you are reaching only one TV market. Rates vary greatly, depending on the station's ranking in and the size of the market.

The advantages of spot TV are: (1) It is very cost efficient; because of competition within a market, reasonable buys generally can be made. (2) You can maximize efficiencies in the better-performing markets and on the better-performing stations.

The disadvantage is that for a national campaign, it's more labor-intensive to buy each market individually.

Conclusion: Spot TV is the common approach for most direct response television campaigns.

Network Cable   The total cable penetration in the United States is 61 percent. There are 32 advertiser-supported cable networks and 16 regional cable networks.

The advantages of network cable are: (1) It is very cost efficient, (2) it enables targeting an offer to a cable network, and (3) back-end tends to be better on cable than on broadcast TV because cable has a more upscale audience.

The disadvantage is that there are limited availabilities, especially if you have a two-minute spot.

Conclusion: Network cable is especially appropriate if you have a one-minute spot and an offer perfectly matched to a cable network's audience.

Local Cable   Unlike cable network, local cable enables you to buy on a market basis or, in some instances, on a neighborhood basis.

The advantages of local cable are that it allows (1) a very targeted approach that works for products with narrow market segments, and (2) the securing of additional cable time when networks are tight.

The disadvantages are: (1) There are no two-minute breaks, (2) rates aren't particularly cost-efficient, (3) you have to work with five or more cable operators in order to cover one market, and (4) it offers a very fragmented audience.

Conclusion: Local cable is best used for offers that target a narrowly segmented market.

Syndication   Syndication is the sale of a TV program for airing on a market-by-market, station-by-station basis. Though generally associated with re-runs and game shows, syndication can include first-run movies and original, first-run TV shows. Some direct marketing agencies have also been able to buy time within a syndicated program, ensuring that the spot will air every time the show runs.

The advantages of syndication are: (1) It is difficult to preempt a syndicated program, (2) it reaches 80 percent to 90 percent of the country (similar to network), (3) there are no telemarketing headaches because each station airs a particular show at a different time of day or on a different day of the week, and (4) it allows product-to-program matching—a useful targeting tool.

The disadvantages are: (1) It usually accepts only 60-second spots, and (2) for cost efficiency, buyers often have to wait for "distressed" or unsold time within a syndicated program.

Conclusion: Syndication is well-suited to one-minute offers that are matched to a specific program, and it is a good choice for direct marketers having problems with preemptions.

Creating for Direct Response TV and Radio
Creating for TV

In wrestling with concepts for television, remember that it is a visual medium and an action medium. And you are using it in a time of great video literacy. Your concept must be sharp and crisp. It must be designed to jar a lethargic and jaded audience to rapt attention. Your concepts, therefore, require the best and most knowledgeable of talent.

When you have arrived at your concept, it's time to write a script and do a storyboard. The script format is two adjacent columns, one for video descriptions and one for copy and audio directions. The two columns track together so that the apropriate words and sounds are shown opposite the pictures they will accompany. Video descriptions should make it possible to understand the general action in any given scene. It is not necessary at this point to spell out every detail.

Some people prefer to work only with storyboards, while others combine scripts and storyboards. *The storyboard* is a series of artist's drawings of the action and location of each scene. There should be enough individual pictures (called *frames*) to show the flow of the action and provide important visual information. Most concept storyboards run eight to sixteen frames, depending on the length of the commercial, the complexity of the action, and the need to show specific detail.

Novices make two important errors when preparing TV storyboards. One is failure to synchronize the words and the pictures. At no point should the

copy be talking about something different from what the picture is showing, nor should the picture be something that is unrelated to the words.

The second mistake is failure to realize that most people who evaluate a storyboard equate frames with the passage of time. Each frame in an eight-frame storyboard will often be interpreted as one-eighth of commercial time. If some intricate action takes place over five seconds, it could take four or five frames to illustrate. Meanwhile, a simple scene that may run ten seconds can often be illustrated with one or two frames. Imagine the confusion the reviewer of the storyboard faces. Make sure your storyboards show elapsed time. Often an elapsed time indicator next to the picture will do the trick.

Of course, the criteria presented above are only guidelines. They are not rules. Even if they were, the essence of all great advertising, including direct response, is to break the rules to reach people in a way they haven't been reached before. But it is something quite different to violate *principles* that have been developed over years of observation. Do so only at your own peril.

There is a set of rules that relates to the law. Various industry self-regulatory bodies and instruments of the govenment watch over the air-waves. They require that advertising be truthful and not misleading. Don't say (or picture) anything in your commercial that you can't substantiate or replicate in person. And don't make promises your product or service can't deliver.

As you design your direct response commercial, there are some important techniques to keep in mind. If at all possible, integrate your offer with the remainder of your commercial. It will make it easier for the viewer to comprehend and respond. And it will give your offer, and your product or service, the opportunity to reinforce each other in value and impression.

Also, if possible, integrate the 800 toll-free number into the commercial. You should plan to have the telephone number on the screen for at least 25 seconds and more, depending on the length of the commercial. Try to find ways to make it "dance" on the screen. Bring it on visually as it is announced on the sound track.

Once you have developed a television storyboard that you believe is a good representation of what you want to accomplish, it is possible to evaluate it using the following criteria:

1. *Immediacy*. Is there a sense of urgency to "Call this number now"? Does it make viewers feel that an opportunity will be lost if they don't run to the phone?

2. *Clarity*. Is the offer clear? Do people understand exactly what they will receive, or is there room for doubt and ambiguity?

3. *Lack of retail availability*. If the advertised product is not available in any store, make sure that point is communicated to the viewer.

4. *Increased value*. Many tactics can heighten the offer's value, for example, making a "special television offer" and stating "for a limited time only."

5. *Limited options.* If the spot provides viewers with too many choices, they will be confused. Yes-or-no offers usually do better than multiple-choice ones.

6. *Early close.* Ask for the order early and often. If the commercial waits until the final seconds or makes only one request for the viewer to call, it is usually too late.

7. *Less is more.* If you're asking for installment payments, focus the viewers' attention on the installment amount. Do not emphasize the sum total of all the installments.

8. *Show and tell.* It the product does more than one thing, show it. This is the only way viewers will become familiar with the product. Demonstrations work. Make sure the commercial conveys exactly what viewers are getting when they buy the product.

A support television commercial differs from a straight response commercial in ways worthy of note. Since it seeks to reach the largest number of people, it usually runs in time periods when 30 seconds is the prevalent availability. It must have a greatly condensed message, placing a premium on simplicity. As it seeks no immediate response, but directs the viewer elsewhere, such as to a newspaper insert, memorability and a positive attitude about the advertiser become extremely important.

Creating for Radio

In its early days, television was perceived by many copywriters as nothing more than illustrated radio. With the evolution of the medium we learned how limited that vision was. Now, in this age of video, there is a tendency to think of radio as television without the pictures. That perception is equally wrong.

Radio is the "writer's medium" in its purest sense. Words, sounds, music, even silence are woven together by the writer to produce a moving tapestry of thought, image, and persuasion. Connection with the listener is direct, personal, emotional, primal.

In writing for radio, it is important to consider a station's format. The country-and-western station has a different listening audience from the all-news station. Different people listen to classical music vs. talk-back or rock programming. Tailor your message and its style to the format of the station it is running on. That doesn't necessarily mean make it sound exactly like the station's programming. Sometimes it makes sense to break the flow of programming to stand out as a special message, but only within the framework of the format that has attracted the station's listeners.

Remember also that radio is more personal than TV. Radios are carried with the listener—in a car, at the beach, at the office, in the bathroom—and even joggers with their earphones are tuned into the radio cosmos.

Moreover, because the radio listener can supply important elements in the message mosaic, the conclusion drawn from it is likely to be more firmly held than that which the individual has not participated in. Do not fill in all the blanks for your listeners. Let them provide some of the pieces. At the same time, be sure the words you use are clear in their meaning and emotional content. Be sure the sounds are clearly understandable and recognizable. If not, find some way to augment them with narrative or conversation that establishes a setting that is easy to visualize.

Use music whenever you can justify its cost and consumption of commercial time. Music is the emotional common denominator. Its expression of joy, sorrow, excitement, romance, or action is as universally understood as any device available to you. When it comes time to consider music, contact a music production house. There usually are several in every major city. Los Angeles, New York, and Chicago have scores of them. Or consider library music that can be purchased outright at low cost.

Another aspect of radio is its casualness. Whereas television tends to command all of our attention and concentration, radio usually gets only a portion of it. It is important to keep radio commercials simple and stopping. Devices such as special sounds (or silence) can arrest your listener's attention. To hold it, the idea content must be cohesive and uncomplicated. Better to drive one point home than to flail away at many. If many points must be covered, they all should feed to a strong central premise. This advice is appropriate for all advertising. But for radio it is critical.

The length a radio commercial runs is usually 60 seconds. This not only should be adequate for most commercial messages, but it also is the time length listeners have become accustomed to. Thirty-second commercials are available but are not a good buy for direct response purposes.

One other thing that everyone who listens to radio will appreciate is that radio lends itself to humor. For some reason we have become used to hearing humor on radio, and we respond positively to it. The following radio commercial employs humor effectively to address small-business owners while talking to the public at large.

Husband:	How did we get into this anyway?
Wife:	Who knows, we tried to make it work.
Husband:	Well, I guess it's over.
Wife:	We better get on with it.
Husband:	Okay, you get the car.
Wife:	Right.
Husband:	I get the sofa bed. You get the fridge.
Wife:	Right.
Husband:	I get the Bell System Yellow Pages Directory. You get the . . .
Wife:	Hold on—that doesn't mean the Gold Pages Coupon Section, does it?
Husband:	Why, sure it does.

Wife:	I get the Gold Pages Coupons.
Husband:	Well come on—you're getting the bedroom set too.
Wife:	You can have the bedroom set. I want the Gold Pages Coupons good for discounts at local merchants.
Husband:	I'll tell you what.
Wife:	What?
Husband:	I'll throw in the oil painting and the end tables.
Wife:	I want the Gold Pages.
Husband:	Look, you can have everything else. Just let me keep the Gold Pages Coupons.
Wife:	Get off your knees. You really want them that bad?
Husband:	I do absolutely.
Wife:	We could split them.
Husband:	You mean . . . tear them apart?
Wife:	You're right—it won't work.
Husband:	No. Neither will this.
Wife:	It won't work.
Husband:	You mean . . .
Wife:	We'll just have to stay together.
Husband:	Dolores—what a mistake we almost made.
Wife:	Lorraine!
Husband:	Lorraine—what a mistake we almost made.
Wife:	Who's Dolores?

TV in the Multimedia Mix

For decades marketers have regarded electronic media as stand-alone media. But the astute marketers of the 1990s have joined the trend toward integrated communciations. A classic example of this trend was the multimedia campaign for Ryder used trucks, created by Ogilvy & Mather Direct.

Exhibit 12–5 gives a precise description of the campaign. Note that the campaign included direct mail, direct response, TV, print, and radio.

Exhibit 12–6 shows a print ad that appeared in ensuing vertical publications. A vertical publication is one that caters to a specific category of business, such as banking, or a specific interest such as jogging, boating, etc. The headline "Buy a Ryder Road Ready Used Truck and You'll Find One Problem. The Mechnics Hate to See Them Go" carries the campaign theme.

Exhibit 12–7 reveals the 120-second TV commercial. It was tagged as "The Crying Commercial," because it paid off on the theme "The mechanics hate to see them go."

How successful was this multimedia campaign? The combination of direct mail, print, TV, and radio produced a total of 46,046 responses, beating the previous controls by 245 percent.

Exhibit 12–5. **Description of Ryder Campaign**

PRODUCT OR SERVICE

Used vehicle sales, including vans, gas and diesel straight trucks, refrigerated trucks, tractors and trailers. Range in price from $7,000 to $35,000.

TARGET AUDIENCE

- Owners/presidents of small service businesses, small wholesalers/retailers, small trucking companies and light manufacturing companies (cabinetry, auto parts, electronic parts, clothing/candy)
- Owner/operators
- Used truck purchasers in large companies with 10+ vehicle fleet size

MEDIUM/MEDIA USED

Direct Mail—300,000 pieces. Lists included previous customers, Dun & Bradstreet selects (targeted industries; less than 100 employees; transportation titles), Fleet Equipment subscribers, Fleet Owner subscribers, Allied Truck Publication subscribers.

DRTV—   :60 and :120 local television in spot markets. 3–5 stations/market, 10–15 spots/week/station, for 2–4 week flights.

Print—local trade publications (Truck Trader).

Radio—local spot stations.

MARKETING STRATEGY

To remain competitive in its primary business—truck rental and leasing, Ryder needs to keep its truck fleet current. Selling its used vehicles helps Ryder fund the purchase of new vehicles while providing an additional source of revenue.

Problem:
- Increasingly depressed market for Used Vehicle Sales
- Aggressive sales objectives within a more competitive category environment
- Inconsistent awareness that Ryder also sells trucks.

Solution:
- Leverage Ryders' reputation for quality in truck rental and leasing to sell its vehicles at a premium price.
- Establish "Road Ready" as a symbol of reliability, safety and value through a lifetime of maintenance.
- Provide a continuous presence in the marketplace to generate awareness that Ryder sells trucks
- Generate immediate, qualified leads through an offer of a free "How to Buy a Used Truck" booklet.

Exhibit 12–6.   **Print Ad for Ryder Campaign**

Exhibit 12–6 (*Continued*).   **Print Ad for Ryder Campaign**

Exhibit 12–7. **The Crying Commercial**

Ogilvy & Mather Direct

CLIENT: RYDER
PRODUCT: USED TRUCK SALE
TITLE: "CRYING"
COMML No.: RTLR 0111 :120

(SFX-TRUCK HORN) (MUSIC UP-SENTIMENTAL THEME) MECHANIC #1: There goes my baby.

STEVE: Here we go again. I knew it, every time Ryder sells a used truck this happens. (SFX-SOBBING, BLOWING NOSE)

STEVE: Alright, there, there.

You didn't know Ryder sells trucks? They do, they sell them. Excuse me. (SFX-SOBBING)

The same quality trucks they rent and lease to businesses, they also sell to businesses.

Makes these guys fall apart.

MECHANIC #2: We've been caring for them since they were new.

STEVE: See what I mean? They look after these trucks like they were their own.

MECHANIC #3: They've got their whole lives ahead of them.

STEVE: You're going to be okay, don't worry about it. Do you believe these guys?

Ryder sells more kinds of used trucks than anyone. Trucks, vans, tractors, trailers.

Even specialized equipment.

Just call and they'll tell you where to get 'em. They'll even--

MECHANIC #1: (VO) Steve, not the book! STEVE: Eh, I have to do this.

They'll even give you free advice before you look. It's in here: "How to Buy a Used Truck."

You gotta get this. It's the inside story. What to look for, and avoid. Whether you're buying now or just kicking some tires.

Course, with a Ryder used truck you know what you're getting into.

See this tag, "Road Ready." It means this truck has been maintained at the highest standards since it was new.

Ryder has the records to prove it. And a limited warranty to back it. Impressive stuff.

How ya doin'? (MUSIC UP-SENTIMENTAL THEME) MECHANIC #4: Great.

Exhibit 12–7 *(Continued)*. **The Crying Commercial**

STEVE: These guys put their hearts into these trucks. They even fix things before they go wrong.

MECHANIC #4: Brakes. Steering. Engine.

STEVE: You'll love your Road Ready truck as much as they do.

MECHANIC #2: Oh please , I don't want to see you go.

STEVE: Only you'll get to keep yours. So call for the Ryder Road Ready Center near you. Ask about financing.

MECHANIC #1: (VO) Steve! STEVE: It's okay, relax.

MECHANIC #1: Don't give him the number, please.

Just call for the free book: "How to Buy a Used Truck."

Even if you're not buying now, you'll be an expert.

But you gotta call.

MECHANIC #4: Please take good care of them.

STEVE: Don't worry. They'll get more trucks. Sorry, I'm out of tissues.

It's a new jacket, get off me. I'm not kidding!

(SENTIMENTAL MUSIC UP AND OUT)

Self-Quiz

1. Which of these two TV audiences is highly defined?
   ☐ Broadcast TV   ☐ Cable TV

2. HBO is a premium subscription TV channel. It offers subscribers:

   a. Movies

   b. _____

   c. _____

3. HSN is a leading home-shopping show offering, for the most part, liquidated merchandise. QVC, another home-shopping show, features _____ merchandise.

4. Radio has two advantages over broadcast TV:

   a. Program _____.

   b. Lower _____ for similar time periods.

5. How might direct response advertisers benefit from videocassettes and video discs?

   _____

   _____

   _____

   _____

6. Define *gross rating points (GRPs)*.

   _____

   _____

7. Define *reach* and *frequency*.

   Reach: _____

   _____

   Frequency: _____

   _____

8. Within what time frame can a direct response advertiser learn how well a commercial is doing?

   ☐ Within a week

☐ Two to three weeks

☐ A month

9. The day-parts of radio are:

   a. Day

   b. Early evening

   c. Prime

   d. _____

   e. _____

10. If you use a toll-free number as part of your TV commercial, you should plan to have the telephone number on the screen at least:

   ☐ 10 seconds   ☐ 25 seconds   ☐ 60 seconds

11. Name three types of radio program formats:

   a. Country and western

   b. _____

   c. _____

Pilot Project

Your assignment is to sell an album of rock music by a "hot" group for $19.95. The medium you are to use is radio. Prepare a 60-second commercial for a rock station.

CHAPTER THIRTEEN

Co-ops

As advertising costs have continued to spiral over several decades, marketers have sought out ways to reduce their circulation costs. The co-op sharing advertising costs has proved to be one solution.

Package-goods firms, for the most part, disavow direct marketing as a part of their marketing mix. And yet a direct marketing vehicle—the cents-off coupon—is integral to most of their marketing programs.

Cents-off coupons qualify as direct marketing because they meet the three requirements of a direct response proposition: (1) a definite offer (a discount on a specified product), (2) all the information necessary to make a decision (all cents-off coupons contain complete information), (3) a response device (the coupon, when presented at the checkout counter, becomes the transaction device).

Promotions come and go, but cents-off coupons continue to grow. When consumers are asked why they redeem coupons, they give two major reasons:

1. Coupons inform consumers about old-line products and give encouragement to try new products.

2. Coupons reduce the cost of the products consumers buy.

When asked for the reasons why package-goods firms use couponing, Donnelley Marketing, publishers of the Carol Wright co-op, gave these reasons:

- To generate short-term incremental volume

- To reward loyal users

- To counteract competitive-coupon pressure

- To support retail-merchandising events (synergy)

- To build the brand franchise base, attracting new users through the communication of added value

- To generate trial and optimize repeat for a new brand

- To build brand/corporate equity with the retailer/consumer
- To preempt competitive promotional, introductory activity by "protecting" current users

Mass Market Penetration

The Carol Wright mail co-op is distributed to 30 million selected households ten times a year. Selections are made from a consumer database of 87 million identified households.

The program is so sophisticated that through targeting Donnelley can identify a competitive user and also one who buys more of a given product. Similarly, Donnelley can target by product categories such as, for example, household products, nonprescription remedies, beverages, personal care products, and pet products.

Selectivity is further enhanced by demographic profiles (see Tables 13–1 and 13–2.)

Table 13–1. 30 Million Carol Wright Co-op Demographic Profile: 1990–1991 SMRB Database

	Total U.S. Households	Total Co-op	Index	Younger Families	Index	Established Families	Index
Head of Household Education							
Not high school grad	24.1%	12.5%	52	10.5%	44	15.0%	62
High school grad	36.0	35.6	99	37.2	103	33.7	94
Some college/college grad	39.9	51.9	130	52.3	131	51.3	129
Marital Status							
Married	57.2	74.7	131	75.3	132	73.8	129
Children under Age 18							
None	62.6	40.7	65	32.0	51	52.1	83
1	15.0	21.0	140	20.6	137	21.5	143
2	14.2	25.0	176	30.2	213	18.2	128
3 or more	8.2	13.3	162	17.2	210	8.2	100
Average children	.7	1.2	171	1.4	200	.9	129
Presence of Children							
Children under 6	18.1	29.6	164	42.2	233	13.1	72
Children 6–11	18.3	31.7	173	39.2	214	21.9	120
Children 12–17	16.1	23.4	145	17.8	111	30.7	191

Source: Donnelley Marketing Inc.

Table 13–2. 30 Million Carol Wright Co-op Demographic Profile: 1990–1991 SMRB Database

	Total U.S. Households	Total Co-op	Index	Younger Families	Index	Established Families	Index
Household Size							
1–2	56.4%	34.0%	60	29.6%	52	39.9%	71
3 or more	43.6	66.0	151	70.4	161	60.1	138
Average persons	2.6	3.2	123	3.4	131	3.0	115
Head of Household Age							
18–24	5.8	3.1	53	4.7	81	1.1	19
25–34	22.6	31.9	141	48.8	216	9.7	43
35–49	29.7	43.9	148	37.2	125	52.7	177
50–64	20.7	17.9	86	6.5	31	32.9	159
65 and over	21.2	3.2	15	2.8	13	3.6	17
Median age	44.1	38.0	86	33.4	76	45.6	103
Household Income							
$40,000 and over	31.2	48.1	154	44.4	142	52.9	170
$25,000–$39,999	22.8	26.9	118	29.1	128	24.1	106
Under $25,000	46.0	25.0	54	26.5	58	23.0	50
Median income	$27,380	$38,919	142	$37,171	136	$41,858	153
Average income	$34,703	$45,643	132	$42,864	124	$49,278	142

Source: Donnelley Marketing Inc.

Redemption Rates

Table 13–3 shows that redemption rates vary by category and by circulation vehicle. Mail distribution of cents-off coupons, although it is highly effective compared to free-standing inserts, magazines, and newspaper space, has by far the highest per-thousand circulation cost.

Table 13–3. Redemption Rates by Category and by Method Categories

Method	Refrigerated and Frozen	Dry Grocery and Beverage	Health and Beauty Aids	Household Products
Bounce-back	28.9%	23.6%	42.0%	36.8%
Direct mail	5.5	6.5	10.0	5.4
Free-standing insert	2.5	2.5	1.7	2.7
In-ad	0.8	4.0	0.7	1.1
In-pack	6.0	4.9	4.1	3.0
Instant redeemable	21.9	24.3	39.1	29.8
Magazine	0.9	0.6	0.3	1.1
Newspaper R.O.P.	0.8	1.0	0.8	1.0
On-pack	5.5	6.4	4.9	6.8

Traditional Co-ops

While the vast majority of participants in Carol Wright co-ops are package-goods firms, some direct marketers include mail-order offers in their co-ops. However, most direct marketers that use co-ops tend to use those that have a greater number of direct response offers. Types of direct response co-ops available break into the following categories.

1. *Mail order co-ops.* These are arranged by direct marketers that put their own co-ops together. They induce other direct marketers to join forces with them and make combined mailings to their buyer list. The income from other marketers naturally reduces mail circulation cost for the sponsor.

2. *In-house co-ops.* A variation of the commercial co-op is the in-house co-op. In this case the sponsor (marketer) co-ops only products or services that it sells. The advantage is that selling costs are spread over several offers, rather than applied to a single offer.

3. *Vertical co-ops.* Here we are talking about specific groups, such as business people, college students, new mothers, school teachers, accountants, lawyers, engineers, and so forth.

4. *Magazine co-ops.* Many magazines sponsor a co-op of their own, their circulation list serving as the channel of distribution. This service offers two major advantages to the sponsoring magazine: (1) a chance for additional revenue from regular magazine advertisers, and (2) an inducement to prospective advertisers to test the responsiveness of the magazine's market. (See Exhibit 13–1.)

Standard Rate & Data Service (SRDS) has an entire section devoted to co-op mailings in its periodic directory, *Direct Mail List Rates and Data*. The listings contain much valuable information.

Sales/Costs Ratios

Quoting averages is always dangerous but as a rule of thumb response for individual pieces in a co-op is about one-fourth the response of a solo mailing. The cost, however, is similarly about one-fourth. Response rates do vary, of course. A 50 percent discount offer from *Time*—so well known that little explanation is necessary—is likely to pull much better than that for an unknown publication. Also, a new-product offer, because of restricted space in a co-op, is likely to pull far less than one-fourth of a solo mail effort.

Co-op Formats

Direct marketers have two basic formats available to them: postcard and "loose" inserts. (See Exhibit 13–2.) Most postcard publications carry three

Exhibit 13–1. **A Co-op Mailing**

A store redemption coupon and a direct response offer among 43 inserts in a typical Carol Wright co-op.

postcards to the page, the reply card unit size measuring approximately 6" × 3⅝". An advertiser can purchase a single card or two or three adjacent cards (see Exhibit 13–3).

Sponsors determine the size and weight limitations for loose inserts. Typically, the weight limitation is one-quarter ounce, and the size limitation is 5" × 8". If the advertiser exceeds the weight limitation, it is usually subject to a surcharge.

Getting Co-ops Read

Participants in co-ops face fierce readership competition. You can greatly improve your chances for getting your piece read and acted on by knowing the behavior patterns of people who receive co-ops. Phil Dresden, an expert on co-ops, provides a valuable insight:

> I have witnessed a number of focus group research interview sessions through a one-way mirror. Different groups of housewives were brought in and handed co-op envelopes filled with coupons and

Exhibit 13–2. **Three Examples of Participants in** *Advertising Age's* **Loose-Pack Postcard Deck**

SUPER SALESMAN

Need a sales rep who's hard working, loyal, who never gets tired and always delivers your sales message just the way you intended it?

Panasonic's new CT-130V Monitor/VCR is all of these and more. It combines a compact VHS video recorder and big 13" color monitor for **foolproof** delivery of your important sales presentations.

For details, send in this card or call Midwest Visual, Chicago's largest and most respected audio-visual dealer, at (312) 478-1250.

Authorized Dealer
Panasonic

Name _____ Title _____

Company _____ Phone _____

Address _____ City _____ State _____ Zip _____

WIN A VACATION FOR TWO
IN SUNNY SOUTHERN CALIFORNIA!

Yes, I would like the opportunity to win a vacation for two, courtesy of Western Airlines and Disneyland Hotel. Please include my name in the June 14 drawing.

Name _____

Title _____

Company _____

Address _____

City _____ State _____ Zip _____

Daytime Telephone (_____) _____

All entry forms must be received by June 10, 1985. Drawing will be held on June 14, 1985. Reservations for travel and lodging must be completed by December 31, 1985 and are subject to availability. Crain Communications employees, suppliers and their families ineligible to participate.

Disneyland Hotel
OFFICIAL HOTEL OF THE MAGIC KINGDOM
A MOBIL ★★★★ AND AAA ◆◆◆◆ RESORT
ANAHEIM, CALIFORNIA 92802 • A WRATHER HOTEL

Western Airlines
Count on us

Steal this color copier.

Not a sale. Not a bargain. At 29% savings, it's a steal. For only $995 a brand new Savin 7010 gives you:

- One of the smallest personal copiers made.
- Two-sided copying.
- Book copying.
- Letter and legal size copies.
- Faithfully reproduces solids and halftones.
- Copies on label stock and transparencies.
- Fastest 1st copy speed in its class 10 seconds.
- 10 crisp copies per minute.
- Microprocessor controls.
- Fiber optics.
- 100 sheet paper tray.
- Short jamproof paper path.
- Reliability.
- Color copies.

Only $995*
Was $1395 — you save $400.

FOR MORE INFORMATION CALL:
Jim Cook, Sales Manager (312) 640-9595
Or return this card filled out.

savin
The Dependable Decision

NAME _____ TITLE _____

COMPANY _____

ADDRESS _____

CITY _____ STATE _____

ZIP _____ PHONE _____

*Price valid if purchased by phone or demonstrated at Savin sales offices.
® Savin and Savin logotype are registered trademarks of Savin Corporation.
© Copyright 1983 Savin Corporation. Stamford, CT 06904

Exhibit 13–3.   Three Examples of Postcard Advertisers in
Physicians Market Place

New Olympus OSF-2 Flexible Sigmoidoscope now offers

- total immersibility
- automatic water control
- improved resolution

OLYMPUS
SUPERIORITY YOU CAN SEE.

Plus the crystal clear, wide angle optics, narrow distal tip and easy, one-handed operation of the original OSF.

To learn more about the OSF-2, and all the other components of the OSF-2 Flexible Sigmoidoscopy System, return this card today.

☐ Send information   ☐ Arrange for demonstration

Name _____

Specialty _____

Address _____

City _____ State _____ Zip _____

Telephone (_____) _____

Best day to call _____ (____) AM (____) PM

C.M.E. Where & When You Choose

Join more than 20,000 satisfied professionals who continue their education at 33 glorious sun and ski resorts. Money saving custom travel packages are available for most locations.

America's Largest Resort Seminar Sponsor
American Educational Institute, Inc.

Please rush me your schedule of tax-deductible Malpractice & Practice Management Seminars.

Name _____

Address _____

City/State/Zip _____

SEMINARS

Presented Weekly
33 RESORTS

Presented Every Week
at 33 Glorious
Sun and Ski Resorts

Offered to physicians only

THE MEDIFAST® PROGRAM— PROTEIN-SPARING MODIFIED FAST

A comprehensive training program and nutritional supplement—MEDIFAST. Enables you to conduct a *protein-sparing modified fast* in your office. Includes all necessary materials to develop a most valuable addition to your practice.

Over 900,000 patient-weeks experience throughout the United States attest to its safety and efficacy.

Physician supervision is required.

NUTRITION INSTITUTE OF MARYLAND
William J. Vitale, M.D., Medical Director
1840 York Road, Suite H, Baltimore, MD 21093

For free descriptive literature, fill in and mail coupon on the reverse side.
OR CALL TOLL-FREE: 800-638-7867

offers. There was an amazingly consistent behavior pattern. The participants, without exception, sorted each envelope's contents into two piles. Later when they were asked what was the basis for the two piles, they answered: "Interesting–not interesting; like–dislike; value–no value." Your offer must find its way to the right pile during that initial sorting.

The way to get into the first pile is to have a simple message clearly stated with effective graphics. The more alternatives you offer, the less your response will be. In a phrase, don't get sorted out; keep it simple. You only have a few seconds to make an impact. Inserts in direct mail co-ops are more like ads in a magazine than like regular direct mail. If the offer appears to be too much trouble, if it appears that the message is going to take some time and effort to get at, the housewife goes to the next offer.

Before you release your final mechanical to the printer, write two questions down on a piece of paper and see if you can answer them honestly: (1) Have you given the potential respondent an opportunity for dialog with you? (2) What precisely are you asking the potential respondent to believe and to do?

Generally, in co-op direct response advertising, the recipient sees little and remembers less. Any purchase is basically made on impulse, and response levels can be seriously impacted if the potential respondent does not act within a short time span. The products and services should fall into the pattern of something wanted or needed now.

Testing a Co-op

As Phil Dresden points out, testing co-ops is a tricky business. When you test an insert in a co-op, you are doing so with one group of partners; when you "roll out," you are likely to be participating with a different group of partners. So you must live with this variable. Here are a few simple rules for testing co-ops that are based on the Dresden experience:

1. Because testing is a trial for a subsequent major promotion, it is important to ensure that conditions for the major promotion will be as close to those of the original as possible.

2. Know what your break-even point is and test a sample large enough so your result can be acted upon.

3. Test the co-op first and leave the segments for later unless your product clearly suggests a particular segment. For example, if your product is aimed entirely at a female market, test only the female portion of a co-op mailing.

4. Test a cross section of the complete co-op list. If no "*n*th" sample is available, request distribution in several different markets—all widely dispersed.

5. Don't let too much time elapse between your test and your continuation, especially if the item you are testing is of a seasonal nature.

Package Inserts

The never-ending quest for reducing selling costs has led many major direct marketers to offer package insert programs to noncompeting advertisers.

Jack Oldstein, president of Dependable Lists Inc., states, "Package inserts offer immediacy, guaranteed mail-order buyers, with no waste circulation, the understood endorsement by the mailer of your product to his loyal customers, and the names used are fresher than the next update."

The late Virgil D. Angerman, formerly sales promotion manager of Boise Cascade Envelope Division, gave this sage advice about package insert programs: "The planning of a package insert program is much like planning a direct mail campaign. The advertiser should evaluate the type of person who will receive the package insert. The advertiser should ask if he or she is the logical prospect for a particular merchandise or service. The questions should be raised, will the insert do a thorough selling job? Is the offer attractive? Have you made it easy to send an inquiry or order?" Just as with mailing lists, best results are realized when you match your offer to the market. If you are selling insurance to older people, using package inserts with vitamin shipments makes sense. If you are selling sports apparel, using package inserts with shipments going to fishermen and hunters makes sense, and so forth.

Professional mailing-list brokers will provide list cards of firms that accept package inserts just as they supply list cards of direct marketers that make their mailing list available for rental.

Co-op Enhancements

Although card packs dominate co-ops, the following case history details how co-ops can be enhanced. It introduces you to a variety of alternate media that can greatly expand your co-op program.

Hanover House

About ten years ago WEB Specialties Inc., of Wheeling, Illinois, started working with Hanover House, of Hanover, Pennsylvania. Hanover had 21

catalogs at the time, each with a different name and each targeted to a different audience. It needed an alternative to the expensive, time-consuming, two-step catalog process.

The challenge was to develop a low-cost, miniature, four-color catalog with a built-in envelope and coded order form that weighed less than one-third ounce. WEB met the challenge at the budgeted cost with a 3¾" × 5¾" catalog of 16 pages plus envelope and order form. The catalog was dubbed the "mini storybook." (See Exhibit 13–4.)

Exhibit 13–4.   **Mini Storybook Covers**

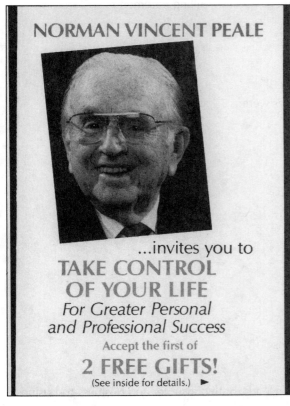

Covers of two mini storybooks typical of those included in co-op programs.

Featuring Hanover's best values and hottest-selling items at a variety of price points, the mini storybook was tested in 100 different package insert programs for a total cost of less than 10 cents each to create, print, insert, and deliver to a targeted audience of proven mail-order buyers.

The program was a big success. On average, across all programs, the profit from the sale of merchandise featured in all of the mini storybooks exceeded

Hanover's total print and media costs. The company actually began to make a profit prospecting for new customers.

Hanover didn't stop with package inserts. Since it weighed only a half-ounce, the mini storybook could ride along with an order acknowledgment, an invoice, a statement, a dun notice, or other customer correspondence.

As for WEB Direct Marketing, with the success of Hanover under its belt, the firm decided, as the saying goes, "We're in business." It went on to develop a business plan that incorporated alternative media and product categories. The alternative media were:

—Card decks	—Magazine bind-ins
—Cable billing statements	—Billing statements
—Package inserts	—Self-mailers
—Co-op mailings	—Take-ones
—Catalog bind-ins	

The prime product categories were:

- Catalog firms
- Office suppliers
- Credit card companies
- Phone companies
- Encyclopedia companies
- Hotels and travel packages
- Hearing-aid firms
- Eye-care programs
- Book publishers
- Major service organizations
- Merchandise clubs
- Sales organizations seeking leads, both consumer and business-to-business

Card Deck Enhancement

With its business plan in hand and a marketing plan to go with it, WEB's major target was card decks for, as partner Joe Kallick pointed out, circulation is huge. There are approximately 950 card decks with circulation in excess of 280 million.

The WEB strategy went beyond being included in a card deck. Instead, WEB told card deck publishers that it wanted to purchase the window position

for its mini storybook clients, it was willing to pay a premium for this position. Kallick's position with the card deck publishers was that WEB's attractive four-color mini storybooks induce the recipient to open the deck and that other participants with one- and two-color cards benefit thereby. The publishers bought into that.

Cable Billing Statements

In its Hanover House program, a second major target for WEB was cable companies. Cable companies combined mail over 50 million statements a month.

After analyzing the cable market and negotiating with cable system operators, WEB developed 574 market selections from a 19 million universe that they could target on a national, regional, or local basis. To further enhance response, WEB overlaid the markets with 29 demographic selections that included age, income, education, housing, and even a special affluence index.

Putting Together a Media Schedule

How does a direct marketer match its profile against the total alternative media available? WEB recognized this problem at the outset and included profiling against media as part of its total service operation.

To illustrate the testing procedure for the mini storybooks, I asked WEB to prepare a test budget for a hypothetical credit card operation using four media alternatives: (1) cable billing statements, (2) card packs, (3) package inserts, and (4) catalog bind-ins. The test budget WEB provided is as follows:

Test Recommendations for Using a Mini Storybook in Alternatvie Media

Mini storybook in cable billing statements	
Circulation 1,000,000 @ $115/M[a]	$115,000
Mini storybook in card packs (10 decks)	
Circulation 1,000,000 @ $110/M	$110,000
Mini storybook in package inserts (20 programs)	
Circulation 1,000,000 @ $120/M	$120,000
Catalog bind-ins (4 catalogs)	
Circulation 1,000,000 @ $100/M	$100,000

[a] The per-thousand prices are based on a combined test circulation of 4 million.

The recommendations are "turnkey in the mail" costs. They include media research, media recommendations, and placement, as well as complete print production, tracking codes, and shipping charges. There are no extras except for creative and film. A three-way perfect split for testing is available.

To zero in on a specific category for the hypothetical credit card company —small-business package insert programs—I asked for insert recommendations. Table 13–4 lists 18 recommendations.

Table 13–4. Overview for Package Insert Media Recommendations

Marketplace/Program Name	Annual Circulation (000)	Distributed
Small-Business—Executives		
1. Drawing Board Business Enclosure Program	475	Monthly
2. Safeguard Business Systems P.I.P.	1,300	Monthly
3. Quill Office Supplies/Equipment P.I.P.	2,600	Monthly
4. Reliable Office Supplies P.I.P.	1,330	Monthly
5. Misco Computer Supplies P.I.P.	130	Monthly
6. Newsweek Movers & Shakers Publ. I.P.	300	Monthly
7. Tools for Business Success P.I.P.	120	Monthly
8. Newbridge Communications Book Club P.I.P.:		
Executive program	215	Monthly
Small computer program	278	Monthly
9. Brooks Brothers P.I.P.	273	Monthly
10. Joseph A. Bank Clothiers P.I.P.	233	Monthly
11. Hanover & Bostonian Shoes P.I.P.	167	Monthly
12. Professional Book Club P.I.P.	600	Monthly
13. Rapidforms P.I.P.	240	Monthly
14. Darby Group P.I.P.	700	Monthly
15. 20th-Century Plastics P.I.P.	242	Monthly
16. Prentice-Hall Bus. Information & Prof. P.I.P.	480	Monthly
17. Fordham Electronics Business Catalog P.I.P.	122	Monthly
18. Histacount Corp. P.I.P.	120	Monthly
18 Programs—Total Annual Circulation:	9,875,000	

Co-ops are a major tool for direct response advertisers when used correctly. They are not suitable for selling a $400 calculator, but they are excellent for getting inquiries about a $400 calculator. Co-ops are highly preferred for in-store coupon redemptions and for scores of direct response offers requiring a minimum of information for a targeted audience.

Self-Quiz

1. Why do cents-off coupons qualify as direct marketing?

_____

_____

_____

2. Heavy users of cents-off coupons skew toward families with:

☐ Annual income under $10,000

☐ Annual income over $25,000

3. Which is the largest distribution channel for cents-off coupons?

☐ Newsapapers   ☐ Magazines   ☐ Direct mail

4. Which medium shows the highest average redemption rate:

☐ Newsapapers   ☐ Magazines   ☐ Direct mail

5. Name four types of traditional co-ops.

a. _____

b. _____

c. _____

d. _____

6. A co-op is likely to pull about one-fourth the response of a solo mailing

at about _____ the cost.

7. What is the difference between "loose" insert co-ops and postcard co-ops?

_____

_____

_____

8. Describe how homemakers tend to sort out the contents of co-op envelopes.

_____

_____

_____

_____

9. What is the one variable you must live with in scheduling the continuation of a co-op you tested previously?

_____

_____

10. Name five advantages of package inserts.

a. _____

b. _____

c. _____

d. _____

e. _____

11. Name two advantages of mini storybooks.

a. _____

b. _____

Pilot Project

You have become promotion director of the *Advertising Age* postcard program, which is distributed several times a year to its 70,000+ subscribers.

As a prelude to developing your promotion program, it is your assignment to develop a list of prospects whose propositions you believe will appeal to advertising agency personnel, marketing executives, advertising managers, advertising research executives, and graphic arts personnel.

Break your prospect categories into two segments: primary and secondary. Expand the list for each to twelve, using the first three as starting points.

Primary	*Secondary*
1. Advertising and marketing books	1. Investment opportunities
2. Premiums	2. Office forms
3. TV production	3. Office equipment
4. _____	4. _____
5. _____	5. _____
6. _____	6. _____
7. _____	7. _____
8. _____	8. _____
9. _____	9. _____
10. _____	10. _____
11. _____	11. _____
12. _____	12. _____

CHAPTER FOURTEEN

Telemarketing

Telemarketing is as much an advertising medium for direct response advertisers as print, broadcast, and direct mail.[1] Telemarketing is particularly powerful when it is integral to other media. The toll-free number in a direct response commercial, a direct response ad, or a direct mail package becomes a major force in overcoming human inertia.

The power of telemarketing begets a responsibility to use the medium with discretion. Intrusive, high-pressure telephone calls at times inconvenient for the consumer are most often counterproductive. Telemarketing is most effective when helpful dialogs are maintained with existing customers and qualified prospects.

Although favorable impact on sales is a given for both consumer marketers and business-to-business marketers, little is known about the major criteria that influence consumers favorably toward proactive telemarketing.

A Landmark Study: The Wyman Survey

The first formal research on the attributes that influence consumers' acceptance of telemarketing when marketers take the initiative (proactive telemarketing) was conducted in 1989 by John Wyman, a former vice president of AT&T.

Methodology

A structured telephone interview was used to obtain information from a statistically valid, nationwide, random sample of 1,000 consumers who have phones. The sample was obtained from the M/A/R/C Inc. Telno telephone database. The database is designed to ensure that virtually all operating phones, listed and unlisted, have an opportunity to be in the sample. The design of the size of this sample enabled inferences to be drawn with a high degree of confidence.

[1] Much of the material in this chapter was previously published in my book, *Successful Telemarketing*, Second Edition, Lincolnwood, IL: NTC Business Books, 1992.

Results

In the survey the consumers were first asked about their experiences with using the phone for information or for purchasing products and services. They were then asked about toll-free 800 service (reactive telemarketing) and finally about receiving proactive telemarketing sales calls.

Telephone Experience
The consumers reported positive experiences in utilizing the phone. Fifty-four percent believed the phone is good for obtaining information or purchasing a product or service. Sixty percent indicated they had made purchases using the phone, and of those, 74 percent were satisfied with phone shopping.

Reactive Telemarketing
The consumers also had had very positive experiences with using a toll-free 800 number. Eighty-three percent of the consumers had used an 800 number. Eighty-nine percent of the consumers who had used an 800 number reported they were satisfied with the experience.

Proactive Telemarketing
Consumers were then asked three questions about their reaction to receiving a proactive telemarketing sales call. An acceptance index (dependent variable) was developed by combining the consumers' answers to the following three questions:

1. How would you rate your acceptance of telephone sales calls made by telephone salespeople who give you information or offer you a wide range of products or services?
2. How likely is it that the information you receive from a telephone sales call will be useful?
3. How likely is it that you would purchase the product or service being offered by a telephone sales call?

While the consumers were clearly not as receptive to receiving proactive telemarketing calls as they were to making reactive telemarketing calls, an initial acceptance rate of 13 percent was achieved.

Calling Attributes
The consumers were then asked to rate the importance of six calling attributes and the likelihood that the six calling attributes existed on telemarketing sales calls that they had received (see Table 14–1). The six calling attributes were originally identified by a focus group of telemarketing experts and further defined through a pilot research study. The consumers found all six calling attributes to be important, and there was a reasonable likelihood that the six calling attributes had existed on telemarketing sales calls that they had received.

Table 14–1.   Telephone Sales Call Attributes

Calling Attributes	Importance		Likelihood	
	Mean	Standard deviation	Mean	Standard deviation
The salesperson is professional and courteous.	5.254	1.409	4.680	1.308
The person calls at a convenient time.	4.892	1.644	3.260	1.677
The company calling has a good reputation.	5.011	1.569	3.680	1.585
You have an interest in the product.	4.679	1.760	2.794	1.595
You have had a good previous experience with the company.	4.537	1.801	2.833	1.719
A person calls rather than a computer.	5.133	1.598	4.307	1.617
All six attributes	4.918		3.592	

On a scale of one to six, with six being very important, the consumers rated the mean of all six attributes at 4.9. On the same scale, with six being very likely to occur, the mean score was 3.6.

The consumers were told to assume that all six calling attributes were present on the telephone sales call they received. They were then asked the same three questions that comprised the original acceptance index. With these six calling attributes present, 34 percent of the consumers shifted from nonacceptance to acceptance. This resulted in a total acceptance of 47 percent.

It is interesting to note that the most important calling attribute is that the salesperson is professional and courteous. It is also rated as the most likely to occur. A person calling, rather than a computer, is second in importance; even with the perception of the increase in electronic calling, the consumers felt a person calling would be highly likely to occur. It was somewhat surprising to see that the consumers' previous positive experience with the company was least important, and having an interest in the product or service was next to last in importance.

Differences between Acceptors and Nonacceptors of Proactive Telemarketing   The consumers were then divided into two groups: acceptors and nonacceptors (acceptors include both initial acceptors and those who shifted to acceptance with the presence of the six calling attributes). The study then determined the differences between the two groups based on the consumers' response to questions in the three categories of previous telemarketing experience, calling attributes, and demographics.

The consumers were asked questions related to 25 independent variables. Nine of these were in reference to telemarketing experience, 6 to calling attributes, and 10 to demographics.

Telemarketing Experience   The consumers were asked if they had ever used the phone to make a purchase. Sixty-five percent of the acceptors had used the phone to make a purchase, compared to 56 percent of the nonacceptors. Those who had made purchases were asked about their satisfaction level when purchasing by phone. The satisfaction level was not significantly different between the acceptors and the nonacceptors.

Consumers were then asked about their experience with using an 800 number. Having previously used an 800 number did not make a difference between the acceptors and the nonacceptors. Since 83 percent of all the consumers had used an 800 number, it would be difficult for this variable to discriminate between the two groups.

Consumers were then asked about their satisfaction with using an 800 number. While 89 percent of the consumers who had used an 800 number reported they were satisfied with the experience, satisfaction with using 800 numbers was not significant in determining acceptance of proactive tele-marketing. The mean score on satisfaction was 5.22 for the acceptors and 5.17 for the nonacceptors, compared to a maximum score of 6. Both groups were very satisfied with using an 800 number.

They were next asked about the number of 800 calls they had made in the preceding three months. The mean number of calls for the preceding three months was 3.62 for the acceptors and 2.91 for the nonacceptors. The means of the two groups are not significantly different (see Table 14–2).

Table 14–2.   Phone Calls Made by respondents to Toll-free Numbers in the Preceding Three Months

Number of Calls	Acceptors	Nonacceptors
0	29.3%	35.9%
1–3	40.1	42.6
4 or more	30.6	21.5

It is concluded that there is no significant difference between acceptance groups based on positive experiences with the use of an 800 number.

The consumers were next asked about their experiences with proactive telemarketing sales calls. The acceptance of proactive telemarketing was significantly lower for consumers who had recently received a large number of telephone sales calls. The mean number of calls received by acceptors during the preceding three months was 4.89, while the nonacceptors had a mean of 8.14 (see Table 14–3). The difference between the two means is statistically significant.

Sixty percent of the acceptors reported receiving three or fewer calls in the preceding three months, compared to 48 percent of the nonacceptors.

It should be noted that the number of calls reported as received by the consumers could involve both an estimation on their part and a perception. There may be a possible correlation between the consumers' attitude about acceptance and their perception of the number of calls received.

Table 14–3. Proactive Telemarketing Phone Calls Received by
Respondents in the Preceding Three Months

Number of Calls	Acceptors	Nonacceptors
Fewer than 3	59.8%	47.7%
4–9	23.0	25.2
4 or more	17.2	27.1

The consumers were also asked to state the number of purchases made from proactive telemarketing calls received within the preceding three months. Fifteen percent of all respondents said they had made a purchase from a call received. The acceptor group reported 23 percent had made purchases in the preceding three months, compared to 8 percent for the nonacceptors. This difference is statistically significant; however, even the percentage of sales to nonacceptors is a relatively successful rate.

Telemarketing Calling Attributes   There was a significant difference between the acceptors and the nonacceptors in terms of their view of the importance of the calling attibutes and the likelihood that the attributes would exist in the telephone sales calls they received. The acceptors found attributes to be very important, with a mean score of 5.3 compared to the nonacceptors' mean score of 4.6. The acceptors also viewed the likelihood of these attributes existing on calls they received to be relatively high, with a mean of 4.0; the nonacceptors had a mean of 3.2.

Demographics   Age plays an important role in understanding the differences between acceptors and nonacceptors of proactive telemarketing. A regression analysis found this variable to be the most significant. In the acceptance group, 21 percent of the respondents were between the ages of 18 and 24 as compared to 10 percent in the nonacceptance group. There is relatively no difference between ages 25 and 44. At age 45 and beyond, 41 percent are nonacceptors, while the acceptors' category is only 30 percent. At age 55 and beyond, 26 percent are nonacceptors, compared to 16 percent for acceptors. There is clearly a greater acceptance of proactive telemarketing by consumers who are younger (see Table 14–4).

Table 14–4. **Ages of Consumers**

Age (in Years)	Acceptors	Nonacceptors
18–24	20.70%	9.52%
25–34	27.89	26.79
35–44	21.57	22.82
45–54	13.94	15.08
55–64	8.06	13.49
65 and over	7.84	12.30

Education is also an important factor in determining acceptance of proactive telemarketing. Forty-six percent of the acceptors had a high school

education or less, while only 29 percent of the nonacceptors were in this category. At the higher end of the education spectrum, 37 percent of the nonacceptors had a college degree or above, while only 21 percent of the acceptors were at that education level. The acceptors of proactive telemarketing are definitely less educated than the nonacceptors (see Table 14–5).

Table 14–5.   Education of Consumers

Education	Acceptors	Nonacceptors
High school or less	46.09%	29.05%
Some College (business or technical)	32.61	33.99
College graduate	15.00	23.12
Postgraduate	6.30	13.83

Total family income is another significant factor in the acceptance of proactive telemarketing. Twenty-six percent of the acceptors have an income of $15,000 or less, while only 15 percent of the nonacceptors are in that income range. The higher-income range of $35,000 a year or above accounts for 44 percent of the nonacceptors and only 26 percent of the acceptors. Acceptors of proactive telemarketing have significantly lower incomes (see Table 14–6).

Table 14–6.   Family Income of Consumers (in Percent)

Income	Acceptors	Nonacceptors
Under $10,000	11.86%	7.43%
$10,000–$15,000	14.53	7.43
$15,000–$25,000	25.92	19.31
$25,000–$35,000	21.79	21.77
$35,000–$50,000	12.83	22.03
$50,000–$75,000	8.23	15.84
$75,000 or more	4.84	6.19

There are important differences between acceptors and nonacceptors based on their demographics—in particular, age, education, and family income.

Listening to the Sales Message   In another effort to determine how strongly consumers felt about receiving a proactive telemarketing call, they were asked "How likely is it that you would hang up or terminate the telephone sales call before the caller was finished?" An extremely high number of consumers, 60 percent initially and 65 percent after the calling attributes were introduced, reported they would not hang up or terminate a sales call before the caller was finished. One may assume that a large number of people considered hanging up or terminating a call to be impolite. It also demonstrates that a high percentage of people, for whatever reason, are willing to listen to the telemarketing sales message.

Calling at a Convenient Time of Day   It had been shown previously that making a telephone sales call to a consumer at a convenient time was an important attribute. The consumers also provided the day of week and time of day that each considered to be the most convenient for them, as displayed in Table 14–7.

Table 14–7.   Most Convenient Time of Day and Day of Week to Receive a Telephone Sales Call

	Weekdays	Saturday	Sunday
Morning	22.2%	10.4%	2.9%
Afternoon	19.5	9.8	3.5
Evening	23.2	3.5	5.0

It is interesting to note the wide distribution of the consumers' preference for receiving a telephone sales call. In particular, only 23 percent of the consumers preferred to receive their call on weekday evenings, while it is estimated that approximately 80 percent of all proactive telemarketing calls to consumers occur on weekday evenings. Since the consumers also stated that calling at a convenient time was an important attribute, there is considerable opportunity to better adapt calling programs to a time preferred by consumers.

Ten demographic variables were analyzed for consumers in each of the nine time-of-day and day-of-week cells to provide insight about the people in each cell.

Some general conclusions can be drawn from the results of this analysis. The consumer groups that prefer receiving phone calls on weekday mornings and afternoons are older, include more females, tend not to be employed outside of the home, include retired and unemployed people, and have a slightly lower level of education and total family income.

The people who prefer to receive their phone calls on weekday evenings or on Saturdays and Sundays have a higher total family income, are employed outside of the home, and have a somewhat higher level of education.

The other demographic variables had relatively the same mean scores across each cell. This information should be useful in developing telemarketing programs that try to contact consumers at a time they find more convenient.

The findings of the Wyman study can be invaluable in catering to consumer preferences, but it should be noted that a similar study for the business-to-business field would undoubtedly produce findings that would be significantly different.

The Spectrum of Telemarketing Applications

One way to explore telemarketing opportunities is to look at a telemarketing sales continuum as a means of identifying applications.

Order taking usually begins with a catalog or other promotion mailed to potential customers. The prospect is encouraged to use the convenience of calling an 800 number to place an order. It is estimated that mature catalog operations like Spiegel receive better than 75 percent of their orders via an 800 number.

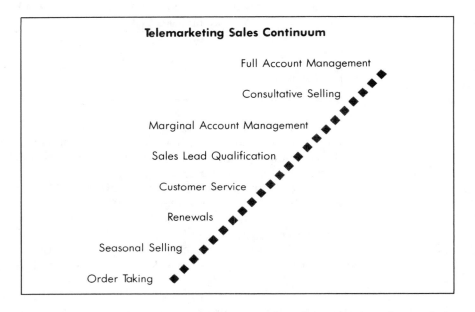

Additionally, an order-taking operation offers the possibility of upgrading by including limited cross-selling, new-product couponing, and even simple marketing research.

Seasonal selling is another telemarketing application. The Swim Shop—a company in Nashville, Tennessee, that supplies gear to summer swim teams —offers an example of how to extend a limited sales season. Since the peak swimming season lasts about 12 weeks—too short a period for the shop to rely on traditional methods to fill orders—it made available an 800 number so orders could be received and filled promptly late in the season. Avoiding the mail stretched out the firm's sales season.

Renewals are another widely used aspect of telemarketing. These applications are now an integral part of a magazine's circulation subscription program. One phone call can produce what it might take several subscription renewal letters to accomplish. The technique has been used successfully also for selling other products—fruit, cheese, even plants.

As a major user of telemarketing for policy renewals, one insurance company's "conservation program" saves about $20,000 per month by using telemarketing to conserve policies about to lapse.

Customer service, another area for improved effectiveness and cost control, is the next step up the telemarketing continuum. Using a unique system,

the 3M Company offers an 800 number to assist their telecommunication equipment customers. The 3M National Service Center, located in St. Paul, Minnesota, is manned 365 days a year, 24 hours a day, with skilled technicians and coordinators. Through systematic questioning and a variety of facsimile, ASCII communication terminals, store-and-forward electronic message distribution terminals, the latest electronic monitoring and testing equipment, and a sophisticated on-line computer system, the staff can pinpoint the failure as an equipment problem or operator error. The 3M center has found that on more than 30 percent of the calls, the equipment failure can be solved in minutes and without dispatching a service technician.

Sales lead qualification is designed to reduce the number of wasted in-person sales visits. With an estimated $205 average for each industrial sales call, companies cannot afford to send salespeople to unqualified prospects. The better qualified a prospect is, the greater the sales call's potential for success. When a prospect is prequalified by phone, telemarketing helps to direct outside salespeople to where the highest sales potential exists.

Reliance Electric, a Cleveland-based manufacturer of electric and mechanical power distribution equipment and weighing scales and systems, uses telemarketing to qualify half of the 125,000 sales leads received annually. Because almost all sales require customized products, Reliance's field sales force of 700 are all highly trained engineers; Reliance utilizes telemarketing to focus its sales team on new business potential.

By incorporating an 800 number into all of its advertising, Reliance generates lead responses into its telemarketing center—called the Marketing Information Center (M.I.C.). Telemarketing specialists qualify these prospects, notifying field sales of the "hot" prospects for follow-up within 24 hours. Reliance also utilizes outbound WATS follow-up to qualify nontelephone-generated leads (i.e., letters, reply cards, trade show contacts, and so on). The M.I.C. system, in its first year of operation, increased quotation activity of field sales by $1 million. In its second year, Reliance expected that figure to further increase by 50 percent.

Marginal account management allows a marketer to capitalize on the revenue potential of smaller accounts without the high cost burden of face-to-face sales visits. Banding together marginal accounts spread over a wide geographic area permits profitable coverage at low cost.

To handle such targeted accounts profitably, Hallmark Cards Inc., the social-expression company, uses telemarketing. Hallmark uses a combination of direct mail and telemarketing to give its remote outlets the same highly personal, current card selection as any large urban card shop or department store.

Consultative selling is a highly personal, involved sales technique. With telemarketing, a customer's needs are probed by a specially trained sales representative. Personalized solutions are designed during the telephone contact, when possible.

Full account management is at the very zenith of the marketing spectrum. It involves order taking, answering questions about order status, inventory

availability, shipment scheduling and billing, credit checking and product consultaton. This full-service operation includes both selling and customer service.

Telemarketing in the Advertising Mix
Direct Mail

Telemarketers learned early on that if you give direct mail recipients the choice of either making a toll-free call or returning a reply card, total response is usually increased. AT&T has found, as have many others, that those who inquire by phone are more likely to order. Exhibit 14–1 is a good example of how long-distance services emphasize their toll-free number in both their letter and reply card. The bottom line is that those who respond by phone prequalify themselves as better prospects. Closure rates are often four to six times greater than mail response.

Of all the advertising applications of the 800 number, none has proved more successful than toll-free phone order privileges for catalog buyers. Catalog director after catalog director reports the average phone order to be 20 percent greater than the average mail order. Thus if a catalog firm gets an average order of $70 by mail, it can expect an average phone order of $84.

The reason for the larger order is easy to explain. A woman ordering a dress by phone, for example, puts the telephone communicator into a natural consultative selling situation. Consider this dialogue:

> Fine, Mrs. Smith. You want size 18 in the royal blue. Have you considered the scarf on page 32, item number 1628? This would really look beautiful with the royal blue . . . . Good. I'll include it with your order. Shipment will go out via UPS tonight. Thank you.

Consultative selling increases the average catalog order. No doubt about it. But here is another unique way to increase the average phone order: Jack Schmid, a catalog consultant in Kansas City, Missouri, came up with this idea when he was catalog manager of Halls, a division of Hallmark.

Mr. Schmid printed the following legend in his catalog—"When you place your order by phone, ask our telephone communicator for the special of the week." Dialog between the customer and the telephone communicator went along these lines:

Customer:	I'd like to order items number 1202 and number 1842. Also I'd like to know what your special of the week is.
Communicator:	Our special of the week is the set of six tumblers on page 21. If you will turn to that page, you will note that the catalog price is $24. Our special price this week is $18.
Customer:	Okay. Add the tumblers to my order.

Exhibit 14–1.   **A Letter from AT&T with a Reply Card**

AT&T

2301 Main Street • P.O. Box 549 • Kansas City, Missouri 64141 • 1 800 821-2121, ext. 626

Dear Executive,

We are pleased to be able to present our special AT&T long distance services in one comprehensive "Business Services Guide."

This gives you the opportunity to review just what the new AT&T is offering. From AT&T Long Distance Service to AT&T Data Services, we bring you the best telecommunications network anywhere.

Our services are designed to help your business grow, and grow with your business, no matter how small or large your company is.

And along with the thorough outline of our services in your enclosed Business Services Guide, we're also offering a free consultation with a professional Consultant, to help you choose the AT&T long distance services that are right for you.

Simply call us toll-free at 1 800 821-2121, ext. 626 to speak to an AT&T Network Consultant.

Our Consultants have worked with businesses of all sizes across the country, so we can help you decide which services make sense for your company. And your Consultant will offer personalized service and advice to help your business use them to cut costs, increase your sales, and help your business grow faster. He or she can even coordinate implementation of the services for you.

So take some time to read through your Business Services Guide. And be sure to contact your Network Consultant at our toll-free number, or mail the enclosed postpaid card, to put these services to work for your business.

Sincerely,

Judy DeVooght

Judy DeVooght
Manager, Network Consultants

FIND OUT HOW YOUR BUSINESS CAN CUT COSTS AND IMPROVE PROFITABILITY WITH AT&T LONG DISTANCE SERVICES

CALL TOLL-FREE

1 800 821-2121, ext. 626

OR MAIL THIS POSTPAID CARD

YES! Please tell me more about AT&T long distance services.

Please fill in Phone Number _____
                              (Area Code)

If address is incorrect, fill out information below

Name Title _____

Company _____

Address _____

City _____ State _____ Zip _____

33U-073

This program was a great success. Depending upon the special of the week, up to 29 percent of those who placed phone orders added the special of the week to their orders.

Print Advertising

It is common today to see in newspapers and magazines ads that feature either a local number or an 800 number to get information or to place an order. Indeed, the 800 number has changed the way many marketers do business.

To illustrate the power of integrating the 800 number into print advertising, let us look at two unique examples:

It's not unusual for consumers to order merchandise by phone in the $10–$100 range. But it's most unusual for consumers to order gold or silver by phone in units of $1,500, $2,500, $5,000, $10,000, and more. And yet they do—in the aggregate of millions of dollars. By phone!

Exhibit 14–2 is typical of the sort of advertisement that Monex International has run consistently in the *Wall Street Journal* and other publications appealing to the serious investor. What is so unique about Monex's use of print and phone is that major purchases of precious metals are consummated entirely by phone.

The second example of a unique application of print and phone involves what is commonly referred to as "dealer-locater advertising." Consider the problem a major marketer with hundreds or thousands of dealers faces when a very special service is offered only through a select number of its dealers. Telemarketing turns out to be the ideal solution.

The Chevron ad in Exhibit 14–3 is a classic example of the solution. Note how Chevron makes it easy for the consumer to learn the name and address of the nearest dealer offering "6-Point Car Service Warranty Protection."

More and more national advertisers are offering a dealer-locater service by providing a toll-free number in their print advertising. It's faster, more economical, and more cost efficient.

TV Advertising

There are few direct response TV commercials these days that do not include an 800 number. The 800 number makes instant response a reality. We have already discussed the impact of the telephone upon TV's home-shopping shows. Millions and millions of dollars in merchandise are being sold via TV with the phone as the catalyst.

But direct response TV, with the toll-free number as an adjunct, goes well beyond the sale of merchandise. Consider, for example, the New York Telephone Company, a major TV advertiser. Among the many services it has offered its customers are information and entertainment services, such as Sports Phone, Dial-A-Joke, and Weather.

Exhibit 14–2. **Monex International Advertisement**

Exhibit 14–4 shows a 30-second commerical promoting Sports Phone. In the short span of 30 seconds, the viewer sees 15 frames with accompanying audio. Note that the phone number is superimposed over four of the frames with the area codes for a call superimposed over two of the frames.

Were these direct response TV commercials successful? And how! In a 12-month period the New York Telephone Company received millions of incremental phone calls.

Exhibit 14–3. Chevron Dealer-Locator Ad

CHEVRON DEALERS SAY... Yes

6-Point Car Service Warranty Protection

While many gas stations are saying no to choices and services, Chevron Dealers say Yes. Yes to a *6-point warranty protection plan* on many car care services at Chevron Hallmark Award Stations.

1. **90 DAYS or 4,000 MILES GUARANTEED**
Whichever comes first. Warranty covers all parts and labor.

2. **PROBLEM SOLVED OR MONEY REFUNDED**
If a problem occurs, either the work will be done over at no cost to you, or the entire cost will be refunded, at the dealer's option.

3. **ADVANCE WRITTEN ESTIMATES**
You'll know the cost before work begins. If additional repairs are needed, your approval will be obtained first.

4. **RETURN OF REPLACED PARTS**
At your request, all replaced parts will be returned for your inspection.

5. **HONORED AT HALLMARK AWARD STATIONS WITH REPAIR FACILITIES**
If a problem occurs, take your car back to the station where the service was performed. If you're more than 50 miles from that station, your warranty will be honored by any Hallmark Award Dealer who performs that type of service.

6. **ON-THE-ROAD HOTLINE**
There are over 1000 Hallmark Award Dealers with service facilities in the U.S. You can call toll-free **(800) 227-1677** for the nearest station which will honor your warranty.
You'll find that all Chevron Hallmark Award Dealers—including those who do not offer car care service—maintain the highest standards of customer service. For the nearest Chevron Hallmark Award Station call:

(800) 227-1677

Chevron

HALLMARK AWARD STATION

Complete Details of Warranty available at your Chevron Hallmark Award Station

Exhibit 14–4. New York Telephone TV Spot

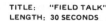

WRK

CLIENT: NEW YORK TELEPHONE CO.   TITLE: "FIELD TALK"   DATE: 4/8
PRODUCT: SPORTS PHONE   LENGTH: 30 SECONDS   CODE NUMBER: AXSP 0333

1. COACH: (OC) Rocky, (SFX: SNAP)

2. go back out there and run the trap reverse.

3. Green T45R

4. wide out set.

5. Got it?

6. ROCKY: Got it.

7. COACH: Now let's call Sports Phone and find out how the competition's doing.

8. It's 976-1313.

9. ROCKY: Got it!

10. COACH: Now run that play boy.

11. ROCKY: (VO FROM FIELD) 976-1313 Hut!

12. COACH: (SFX: GRUNT) ....that's wrong.... ...that's wrong...

13. ANNCR: (VO) It's no more than a dime in these area codes

14. for all the major scores.

15. On Sports Phone.

The Mathematics of Telemarketing

The power of telemarketing is beyond question. Its place in the totality of direct marketing is firmly established. But the mathematics of telemarketing is not clearly understood by many. For starters, we face up to the fact that the telephone is *the most expensive* advertising medium on a per-thousand basis after face-to-face selling. So telemarketing has to be very cost effective to be successful. And for thousands of marketers it is.

To obtain the numbers, we went to Ruby Oetting, president of R.H. Oetting & Associates Inc., a leading telemarketing operation in New York City.

Inbound/Outbound Costs

There are two sets of numbers that are key to estimating telemarketing costs: (1) cost per call for handling *inbound* calls from business firms and consumers, and (2) cost per decision-maker contact in making *outbound* calls to business firms and consumers. Table 14–8 provides the range of costs for each.

Table 14–8.   Per-Call Costs for Inbound and Outbound Calls

Category	Range of Cost
Inbound	
Business	$2.50–$7.00
Consumer	$1.50–$3.00
Outbound	Range of Cost
Business	$6.00–$16.00
Consumer	$1.15–$4.00

The difference in cost range between inbound and outbound calls should be explained. In the case of inbound calls, the initiator is always a prospect or customer: The caller phones at a time of his or her convenience with a view to getting further information or negotiating an order. In the case of outbound calls, the initiator is always the marketer: The call may be made at an inconvenient time for the prospect and the caller may have to generate awareness about a new product or service. Consequently, outbound calls are usually of longer duration and often require more experienced, higher-paid personnel.

The range of costs, whether for inbound or outbound, depends a great deal upon the telemarketing application and the complexity involved for each application. Table 14–9 indicates where ranges of costs are most likely to fall, on average, by application.

Table 14–9. **Range of Costs by Application**[a]

Application	Low range	Mid range	High range
Order processing	X		
Order increase		X	
Customer service		X	
Sales support		X	
Account management			X
Sales			X
Sales promotion	X		

[a] More and more companies are beginning to realize that through the strategy of "customer education and awareness" (helping customers buy), carefully trained and coached inbound representatives using the proper tools and materials can convert sales inquiries to orders and increase the average revenue of an order. There have been recorded differences of as much as $900 per hour betweeen high-end and low-end representatives in the same group, at the same basic cost.

Developing Worksheets

Knowing the average range of costs for inbound and outbound calls is key, but it is just a start. The operation of an in-house telemarketing center requires a full range of personnel. Also, it is subject to taxes, fringe benefit costs, incentive costs, equipment costs, and collateral material costs. To get a true picture of all monthly costs, worksheets are advised.

Mr. Oetting has provided us with two representative worksheets (Exhibits 14–5 and 14–6), one for inbound and one for outbound. It is important to note that the term *phone hour* means workstation time, *not* connect time.

It is easy to see how worksheets lead to capturing all the numbers. The key numbers to explore are (1) cost per phone hour, (2) cost per call, and (3) cost per order (or response). A review of the computations for Exhibit 14–5 (inbound) shows a significant difference in cost, for example, when phone representatives are able to handle 15 incoming calls per phone hour as contrasted to 12 calls per phone hour. And the cost per order drops dramatically if the representative is able to close six orders per phone hour, for example, as contrasted to one order per phone hour.

In Exhibit 14–6 (outbound) similar significant differences are to be noted in costs at different levels relating to total dialings per phone hour, total decision-maker contacts per phone hour, and total orders per phone hour. Such computations provide a realistic approach to determining break-even point.

While these two worksheets relate to the sale of products or services, the same type of arithmetic can be structured to determine likely costs for literature requests, product information, customer service calls, sales support, full account management, or sales promotion. The calls handled or made per phone hour might vary by application, but the principles are the same.

Exhibit 14–5.   **Monthly Expense Statement—Inbound: 9 a.m. to 5 p.m.**

Representative Phone Hours (1235) Direct Expenses	Cost	Cost/Phone Hour
Labor		
Manager ($1/3$ time)	$ 1,250	$ 1.01
Supervisor (full time)	2,750	2.23
Representatives (10 full time)	16,000	12.96
Administration (1 full time)	1,213	.98
Tax and Fringe ($1/3$ of wages)	7,064	5.72
Incentives	2,000	1.62
Subtotal	$30,277	$24.52
Phone		
Equipment and service	1,489	1.21
Lines:		
■ WATS	10,240	8.29
■ MTS (Message Toll Service)	–	–
Subtotal	$11,729	$ 9.50
Automation		
Depreciation	2,500	2.02
Maintenance	750	.61
Subtotal	$ 3,250	$ 2.63
Other		
Lists	–	–
Mail/Catalogs	2,470	2.00
Postage	1,235	1.00
Miscellaneous	1,000	.81
Subtotal	$ 4,705	$ 3.81
Total Direct	49,961	40.45
G&A (15%)	7,494	6.07
Totals	$57,455	$46.52

Exhibit 14–5 (*Continued*).

Basis for Expense Statement

Labor

Manager	Annual—$45,000 × ⅓ allocation—$1,250/month
Supervisor	Annual—$33,000 at full allocation—$2,750/month
Representatives	$9.23/hour × 40 hours/week × 52 weeks full allocation = $1,600/month 6.5 phone hours/day × 19 days/month—123.5 phone hours/month
Administration	$7.00/hour × 40 hours/week × 52 weeks full allocation = $1,213/month
Tax and fringe	33.3% of wages (including contest incentives)
Incentives	Reps only = $2,000/month
Phone *ACD + Sets*	$65,000 depreciated over 5 years plus $4,875 annual maintenance
WATS (800) =	Avg. 40 minutes (69%) per labor hour *WATS* Connect Time: 40 min. × .20/min. avg. cost plus 10 lines access charges
Automation =	$6,000 per workstation for 15 stations (Additional for growth) depreciated over 3 years plus annual maintenance equivalent to 10% of total purchase cost.

Note: The average number of calls handled per rep phone hour is 12 @ 3.1 minutes each. As high as 15 per phone hour during peaks.

Computations
1. @ 12 calls/hour = $3.88/call
2. @ 15 calls/hour = $3.10/call
3. @ 1 Order/rep phone hour = $46.52 per order
4. @ 6 Orders/rep phone hour = $ 7.75 per order

Call Ratios Favor Telemarketing

When comparing outbound sales calls to field sales calls, the pure ratios favor telemarketing. On the average, a field salesperson can make five to six calls a day—25–30 a week; on the average, a telemarketing salesperson can make 25–30 decision-maker contacts a day (DMCs)—125–150 a week.

Put another way, to achieve the same contact level, on average five field salespersons would have to be added for every telemarketing salesperson.

Exhibit 14–6.   **Monthly Expense Statement—Outbound: 9 a.m. to
5 p.m.**

Representative Phone Hours (1235) Direct Expense	Cost	Cost/Phone Hour
Labor		
Manager (¹/₃ time)	$ 1,500	$ 1.21
Supervisor (full time)	3,000	2.43
Representatives (10 full time)	18,000	14.57
Administration (2 full time)	2,426	1.96
Tax and Fringe (¹/₃ of wages)	12,473	10.10
Commissions	12,529	10.14
Subtotal	$49,928	$40.41
Phone		
Equipment and service	350	.28
Lines:		
■ WATS	7,710	6.24
■ MTS (Message Toll Service)	1,297	1.05
Subtotal	$ 9,357	$ 7.57
Automation		
Depreciation	3,542	2.87
Maintenance	1,063	.86
Subtotal	$ 4,605	$ 3.73
Other		
Lists	3,088	2.50
Mail/Catalogs	617	.50
Postage	358	.29
Miscellaneous	1,235	1.00
Subtotal	$ 5,298	$ 4.29
Total Direct	69,188	56.00
G&A (15%)	10,378	8.40
Totals	$79,566	$64.40

The Training Process for Telemarketing

For those who opt for an in-house telemarketing operation, it must be emphasized that there is far more involved than putting a successful sales

Exhibit 14–6 (*Continued*).

Basis for Expense Statement

Labor

Manager	Annual=$54,000 × ⅓ allocation=$1,500/month
Supervisor	Annual=$36,000 at full allocation=$3,000/month
Representatives	$10.38/hour × 40 hours/week × 52 weeks full allocation=$1,799/month 6.5 phone hours/day × 19 days/month=123.5 phone hours/month
Administration	$7.00/hour × 40 hours/week × 52 weeks full allocation=$1,213/month
Tax and fringe	33.3% of wages
Commissions	Reps—40% of Total Remuneration Supervisor—15% of Total Remuneration

Phone

WATS	=	25 minutes per labor hour/Interstate WATS connect time: 25 minutes × .24min. plus 10 lines access charges
MTS (Message Toll Services)	=	5 minutes per labor hour connect time: 5 minutes × .21min.
Automation	=	$8,500 per workstation for 15 stations (Add'l. for growth) depreciated over 3 years plus annual maintenance equivalent to 10% of total purchase cost.

Computations

1. @ 12 TDs (total dialings) per rep phone hour cost per dial=$5.37
2. @ 15 TDs (total dialings) per rep phone hour cost per dial=$4.29
3. @ 5 DMCs (decision-maker contacts) per phone hour cost per DMC=$12.88
4. @ 6 DMCs (decision-maker contacts) per phone hour cost per DMC=$10.74
5. @ 1 Order per rep phone hour cost per order=$64.42
6. @ 3 Orders per rep phone hour cost per order=$21.47

---

person on the phone. As a matter of fact, more often than not, the worst thing one can do is put a successful staff salesperson into a telemarketing center. A field salesperson thrives on face-to-face interaction and resists being desk-bound.

To establish the traits of a successful telemarketing person and to learn what is involved in the on-going training process, we went to the AT&T training center in Cincinnati, Ohio. We are indebted to Nancy Lamberton, staff manager, for sharing her experience with us.

Traits of a Telemarketing Person

Our first question to Nancy Lamberton was: "When recruiting, what traits do you look for?" She listed five traits:

1. Good communication skills, articulate, with a voice quality that is clear and pleasant

2. Persistence and ability to bounce back from rejection

3. Good organization skills

4. Ability to project phone personality—enthusiasm, friendliness

5. Flexibility, ability to adapt to different types of clients and new situations

AT&T has potential applicants for telemarketing sales positions go through 1½-hour telephone assessment process. Applicants are put in several sales situations to determine if they have the dimensions the firm is looking for.

Training for New Hires

AT&T's training program for newly hired personnel covers a period of 18½ days, broken down as follows:

1. *Orientation (4 days)*—Salesperson learns overall structure and goals of AT&T Communications as well as general business functions.

2. *Network services (2½ days)*—Salesperson receives basic knowledge of AT&T Communications products and services. This is what the salesperson will be selling. This course is delivered via computer-based education.

3. *Selling skills (3½ days)*—Salesperson learns sales skills through the interactive video disc, then goes through 4 hours of role playing with an instructor.

4. *Telemarketing (2 days)*—Salesperson learns how to identify client's needs and telemarketing applications. Through casework, the salesperson practices implementing an application for a client.

5. *Account management (3 days)*—Each salesperson has 400 accounts, which means that prioritizing accounts by revenue potential, cycling accounts, and time management are critical.

6. *Advanced account management (3½ days)*—After 3–8 months of experience, the salesperson gets advanced training on how to manage the highest-potential accounts.

The Seven-Step Selling Process

Students are schooled thoroughly in a seven-step selling process, a process developed over time, which leads the salesperson in logical steps from precall planning to the close and wrap-up. The outline below details these steps.

1. Precall Planning
   a. Reviewing client information
   b. Planning objective for the call
   c. Psyching—getting mentally ready for the call

2. Approach/Positioning
   a. Identifying who you are and where you're from
   b. Stating purpose of the call
   c. Making interest-creating statement
   d. Building rapport
   e. Getting the decision maker
   f. Getting through the receptionist/screener

3. Data Gathering
   a. Gaining general understanding of the client's business
   b. Moving from general to specific types of questions
   c. Questioning techniques
   d. Identifying a client's business need

4. Solution Generation
   a. Tailoring communication solution to specific client need
   b. Asking in-depth questions to test the feasibility of the solution
   c. Gathering data for cost/benefit analysis
   d. Preparing client for the recommendation

5. Solution Presentation
   a. Getting client agreement to area of need
   b. Presenting commendation in a clear and concise manner
   c. Explaining benefits of use

6. Close
   a. Timing—when to close
   b. Buying signals
   c. Handling objections
   d. Closing techniques

7. Wrap-up
   a. Implementing issues
   b. Thanking client for the business
   c. Confirming client commitment
   d. Leaving name and number
   e. Positioning next call

Applying the Selling Process   Now let use see how this selling process might be applied outside of the field of communications. For our example, we'll create a wholesaler who specializes in veterinary drugs. The purpose of the call is to introduce a new drug to a regular customer.

1. Precall Planning

    The telemarketer reviews the account file of the Whiteside Veterinary Clinic. He notes that Dr. Sargent ordered her usual drug supplies last month, but that she hasn't tried a new drug that L.L.M. Pharmaceutical has recently introduced via direct mail.

    The telemarketer reviews his introduction briefly, takes a deep breath, and says "Smile!"

2. Approach/Positioning

    "Hello. This is Mark Wiley with L.L.M. Pharmaceutical. Dr. Sargent is usually available about this time. May I speak with her?"

    "Good morning, Dr. Sargent. This is Mark Wiley with L.L.M. How have things been going at your clinic since I last talked to you? (*Pause*) I'm certainly glad to hear that! Dr. Sargent, as a buyer of many of our quality products, I knew you'd be interested in hearing about one of our innovative new drugs. If you have a minute, I'd like to ask you a couple of questions . . . ."

3. Data Gathering

    "Doctor, your practice pretty much covers a suburban area, doesn't it?"

    "Right now when a dog is suffering from hookworm, what drug are you prescribing?"

4. Solution Generation

    "Many vets also used to prescribe that particular drug. Have you had many dogs suffering from various side effects from that drug?"

    "'Would you be interested in prescribing a new drug that has few, if any, side effects?"

5. Solution Presentation

    "L.L.M. has introduced Formula XYZ that not only has fewer side effects, but extensive laboratory tests have shown that the medicine takes effect 24 hours sooner than similar drugs."

6. Close

    "I'm sure that your customers would appreciate faster relief for their pets. Can I add a case of Formula XYZ to your regular order?"

7. Wrap-up

    "I'm sure that you will be pleased with the results, Dr. Sargent. We've gotten excellent comments back from many vets around the country. I'll get that shipment to you by early next week. Thank you for your business. I'll be calling you again the first of next month. Have a good day!"

Role Playing: A Key Teaching Device

AT&T's Ms. Lamberton continued to share her telemarketing-training experience by pointing out that one of the most effective ways to teach proper telemarketing procedures is to get students involved in role playing. Role playing is an excellent way to acclimate the student to the job. By putting students in different selling situations, the learning curve is accelerated. Students make their first mistakes with the instructor rather than the prospect.

Examples   AT&T's instructors put students through role-playing situations and then evaluate their performance. Presented below are examples of a phone dialog, followed by evaluations. (These are abbreviated versions for demonstration purposes.) First we consider a poor example.

Poor Example: Heritage Village Furniture

Sue:	Hello. May I speak to Steve Rooney?
Steve:	This is he.
Sue:	Oh, this is Steve? Well, Steve, this is Sue Jones, your new account executive. I'd like to talk to you about your phone services. Do you have a minute?
Steve:	I didn't catch that company you're with . . . .
Sue:	Oh, gosh, I'm sorry . . . I'm with AT&T.
Steve:	Well, I'm pretty busy today . . . .
Sue:	That's okay, I won't take much of your time. Can I just ask you a few questions about your business?
Steve:	If it only takes a minute . . . .
Sue:	So, are you a furniture retail store?
Steve:	No, actually we manufacture furniture.
Sue:	Do you then sell it to retail furniture stores?
Steve:	Yes, we do.
Sue:	What is your sales volume a year?
Steve:	I don't see what business that is of yours. Anyhow, why are you asking me all these questions? What has it got to do with my phone service?
Sue:	Well, it helps me better understand your company so I can show you how to use telemarketing.

Steve: I'm not interested in telemarketing. The way our business works, you can't sell furniture over the phone.

Sue: A lot of companies are doing it.

Steve: Well, not my company! Maybe you should call me back when you can tell me how to save on my phone bill. I'm really quite busy . . . .

Sue: Can I call you tomorrow, Mr. Rooney?

Steve: Why don't you just send something in the mail? That would be quicker.

Sue: Oh, okay. I'll do that today. Thanks for your time, Mr. Rooney.

The evaluation of this dialog is given in Exhibit 14–7.

Let's consider the same selling opportunity, but with a good example of how it might be handled.

Good Example: Heritage Village Furniture

Sue: Hello. This is Sue Jones with AT&T Communications. May I speak to Steve Rooney?

Steve: This is he.

Sue: Oh, good. How are you doing today, Mr. Rooney?

Steve: Well, actually I'm pretty busy today . . . .

Sue: I understand that you're a busy person. Mr. Rooney, but if I can show you how to get the most out of your communication dollars, would you have a few minutes to discuss some ideas?

Steve: Well, I guess I do have a couple of minutes, but what can AT&T do for me?

Sue: As your account executive, I will be working with you to show you how AT&T long-distance services can be a valuable part of Heritage's profit picture. To see exactly how I can be of service to you, it would be helpful if I understood your business better. Tell me a little about Heritage Village Furniture, if you would . . . .

Steve: We're a manufacturer of traditional home furnishings.

Sue: Whom do you sell to, Mr. Rooney?

Steve: Various retail outlets such as local furniture stores. A lot of it is custom work, special orders.

Sue: Where are these outlets located?

Exhibit 14–7.   Role-playing Evaluation (Poor Example)

ACCOUNT EXECUTIVE
TELEMARKETING SELLING SKILLS
Evaluation Sheets

ROLE PLAY/SKILL PRACTICE

Trainee: _Sue Jones_   Date: _6/16_

Which call (1st, 2nd, etc.) _2ND_   Case—Company name: _Heritage Village_

Instructor/Evaluator: _N. Dambiton_

Skill	ST	SAT	NI	NO	COMMENTS
APPROACH POSITIONING					Sue obviously didn't have a plan going into this call. She confused the client by not explaining who she represented and the purpose of the call. She also didn't get the client's attention.
Managed screener: polite, persistent, used as a resource				✓	
Completed positioning statement: who, where from, why calling			✓		
Made interest-creating opening statement			✓		
Asked for appropriate contact (if no name given prior to call)		✓			The poor introduction set the tone of the entire call — Sue never recovered.
Explained consultative role			✓		
Used listening skills		✓			
DATA GATHERING					Sue assumed Heritage was a retail store, which brought a negative response from the client. A series of close-ended questions then followed. Sue needs to ask more open-ended questions to get the client involved in the conversation.
Made appropriate transition from AP		✓			
Verified existing LD services				✓	
Asked about immediate concerns			✓		
Learned about business operations			✓		
Structured questioning strategy			✓		

Performance rating: ST – Strong; SAT – Satisfactory; NI – Needs Improvement; NO – Not observed.

(Continued)

Exhibit 14–7 (*Continued*).   **Role-playing Evaluation (Poor Example)**

Skill / Performance rating	ST	SAT	NI	NO	COMMENTS
Used open/closed questions appropriately			✓		Her strategy was poor. Before she got the client comfortable, Sue asked about sales volume. At this point, the client's frustration with the call came out.
Questions appeared directed toward objective(s)			✓		
Attempted to build credibility				✓	
Maintained conversational tone		✓			
Maintained control of dialogue			✓		
Demonstrated listening skills: -Probed and clarified -Paid attention to client -Followed client leads -Used silence -Demonstrated empathy -Tied together ideas			✓		
SOLUTION GENERATION/DEVELOPMENT					
Identified relevant/appropriate applications					
Collected appropriate specific data					
Dropped interest-creating hints					
Tailored application(s) to business operations & expressed needs					
SOLUTION PRESENTATION					
Reviewed & got agreement on client's objectives & concerns					
Tailored solution to client					
Focused on relevant benefits					
Demonstrated cost-effectiveness					
Anticipated impact of solution on client's business					

Exhibit 14–7 (*Continued*).   **Role-playing Evaluation (Poor Example)**

Skill	Performance rating ST	SAT	NI	NO	COMMENTS
Made an organized presentation				✓	Sue tried to overcome the objection by talking about telemarketing. Many clients have preconceived notions about telemarketing. Don't throw the firm around — show the client how it can benefit him!
Created interest and continuity in pres'n				✓	
Handled resistance & objections			✓		
Responded to buying signals				✓	
THE CLOSE					
Timed the close right				✓	Sue let the client off the hook, which was probably a good choice considering how the call was going.
Used appropriate technique(s)				✓	
Handled objections successfully				✓	
Gave client time to respond to close				✓	
Got clear commitment/Got an order				✓	
Wrapped up call: -Summarized call -Reinforced close -Arranged for next call -Clarified what client would do -Clarified what AE would do			✓		
FOLLOW-UP (if appropriate)					
Inquired about progress of implementation				✓	
Responded to client concerns				✓	

Steve: Mostly in the eastern part of the country.

Sue: That's a large area. How do you reach all of your customers?

Steve: We have a sales force that visits the stores to keep our name in front
          of them. The salespeople show new samples of fabrics and promote
          sales we have going. The most important thing is that the furniture
          retailer remembers our name when his customer walks in the door.

Sue: Is that because you have a lot of competition?

Steve: You bet. I mean there are all sorts of furniture manufacturers. A lot
          of them with their own stores. We have to rely on the independent
          furniture store to sell our line.

Sue: Let's go back to your sales process. How do you get your orders?

Steve: Well, since most of the work is custom and we can never predict
          when an order will come in, most of the orders are mailed to us by
          the retailer. We have a form in the back of our sample book.

Sue: How long does it take to get that order in from the time it's mailed?

Steve: Oh, probably four days.

Sue: And how long does it take you to get the piece of furniture delivered
          to the customer once you've gotten the order?

Steve: Anywhere from six to eight weeks . . . depends if we have all the
          materials in stock.

Sue: I remember when I ordered a chair recently, that sure seemed like
          a long time. Would you be interested in cutting down that delivery
          time?

Steve: Well, sure, but it takes that long to make the furniture—that can't be
          cut down.

Sue: Oh, I understand, Mr. Rooney. But perhaps we could cut down the
          time it takes you to get the order from the retailer. Would you be
          interested if I could show you a way to shorten those four days to
          just a few minutes to get that valuable order?

Steve: What do you have in mind?

Sue: Instead of using the mail for your orders, you could use a toll free
          number for your retailers to call in their orders. Not only would you
          receive the order immediately, but you could also check on inventory
          while the retailer was on the line. If you were out of a fabric, say, the

retailer could consult his customer to see what they wanted to do. This would save additional time and perhaps even the sale. Don't you think a toll-free number would give you a competitive edge?

Steve: Well, I don't know of anyone else doing that. But what kind of costs are we talking about?

Sue: I think you'll be surprised to see how inexpensive it is to provide this service to your customers. Our 800 toll-free number actually costs less than a regular long-distance phone call. So for a couple of dollars for the phone call, you'll be making a sale worth hundreds of dollars, plus improving your long-term relationship with the retailers. Can I place that order for you today?

Steve: How can I say no? Let's give it a try.

Sue: I'm sure you'll see immediate results. I'll give you a call in a few days to set the installation date. I really appreciate your business, Mr. Rooney. I look forward to working with you on this and perhaps other ideas.

Steve: Sounds good. Be talking to you soon.

Sue: Thanks again, Mr. Rooney. Good-bye

Exhibit 14–8 presents a positive evaluation of this dialog.

900 Number Applications

The 800 toll-free number is the overwhelming choice of marketers, but the place of the 900 number should not be overlooked. Used honestly and properly, the 900 number makes eminent sense.

The 900 numbers make sense to the consumer when products and services being offered can demonstrate perceived value. Leading firms in the service field, such as The Wall Street Journal, are good examples.

Dow Jones & Company, publishers of the Wall Street Journal, utilizes a 900 number to provide current quotes on over 6,500 listed stocks daily, as well as frequently updated news and market reports (see Exhibit 14–9).

Exhibit 14–8. Role-playing Evaluation (Good Example)

ACCOUNT EXECUTIVE
TELEMARKETING SELLING SKILLS
Evaluation Sheets

ROLE PLAY/SKILL PRACTICE

Trainee: _Sue Jones_

Which call (1st, 2nd, etc.) _2nd_   Case-Company name: _Heritage Village_

Instructor/Evaluator: _N. Chamberlin_   Date: _6/16/84_

Skill	Performance rating ST	SAT	NI	NO	COMMENTS
APPROACH POSITIONING					
Managed screener: polite, persistent, used as a resource				✓	Sue got the decision-maker to talk to her by showing some empathy and creating some interest. This was very effective without being too pushy.
Completed positioning statement: who, where from, why calling		✓			
Made interest-creating opening statement	✓				
Asked for appropriate contact (if no name given prior to call)			✓		
Explained consultative role	✓				
Used listening skills	✓				
DATA GATHERING					
Made appropriate transition from AP		✓			Sue built her questions off the client's remarks, although she still kept the focus on her objectives. Some more indepth questions may have been helpful, but Sue identified a business need.
Verified existing LD services				✓	
Asked about immediate concerns		✓			
Learned about business operations	✓				
Structured questioning strategy	✓				

Performance rating   ST - Strong; SAT - Satisfactory; NI - Needs improvement; NO - Not observed.

Exhibit 14–8 (*Continued*). **Role-playing Evaluation (Good Example)**

Skill	Performance rating ST	SAT	NI	NO	COMMENTS
Made an organized presentation	✓				
Created interest and continuity in pres'n	✓				
Handled resistance & objections		✓			
Responded to buying signals		✓			
THE CLOSE					
Timed the close right	✓				*Good timing and aggressiveness.*
Used appropriate technique(s)	✓				*Client's tone indicated that he*
Handled objections successfully		✓			*was interested, but he was*
Gave client time to respond to close		✓			*worried about cost. Sue overcame*
Got clear commitment/Got an order	✓				*the cost issue, and went for*
Wrapped up call: -Summarized call -Reinforced close -Arranged for next call -Clarified what client would do -Clarified what AE would do		✓			*the close. Very effective!*
FOLLOW-UP (if appropriate)					
Inquired about progress of implementation				✓	
Responded to client concerns				✓	

Exhibit 14–8 (*Continued*). **Role-playing Evaluation (Good Example)**

Skill	Performance rating ST	SAT	NI	NO	COMMENTS
Used open/closed questions appropriately		✓			
Questions appeared directed toward objective(s)	✓				
Attempted to build credibility		✓			
Maintained conversational tone	✓				
Maintained control of dialogue		✓			
Demonstrated listening skills: –Probed and clarified –Paid attention to client –Followed client leads –Used silence –Demonstrated empathy –Tied together ideas	✓				
SOLUTION GENERATION/DEVELOPMENT					
Identified relevant/appropriate applications	✓				Overall, Sue did a good job. A few specific facts – like the value of a sale – would have helped build even a stronger case.
Collected appropriate specific data		✓			
Dropped interest-creating hints		✓			
Tailored application(s) to business operations & expressed needs		✓			
SOLUTION PRESENTATION					
Reviewed & got agreement on client's objectives & concerns	✓				Sue used specific benefits to sell the client on the solution. Although she didn't use specific cost figures, her point was well made to the client.
Tailored solution to client		✓			
Focused on relevant benefits	✓				
Demonstrated cost-effectiveness	✓				
Anticipated impact of solution on client's business				✓	

Exhibit 14–9.   The *Wall Street Journal* Provides a Menu of Services through a 900 Number.

THE WALL STREET JOURNAL FRIDAY, APRIL 13, 1990 **C9**

JOURNALPHONE˙ GUIDE

JournalPhone has current quotes on over 6,500 listed stocks, as well as frequently updated news and market reports.

1. CALL 1-900-JOURNAL (1-900-568-7625).
2. Enter any of the four-digit categories below, or 9999 for help. To switch categories at any time, enter the new number.

TRADING UPDATES
1000 Stock Markets
1100 Bond Markets
1200 Foreign Exchange
1300 Foreign Markets
1500 Wall Street Insight
1600 Financial Futures
1800 Commodity Futures
2100 Metals Futures

2200 Petroleum Futures
3000 NYSE Most Actives

MARKETS DIARY
2500 Dow Jones Averages
2600 Key Rates & Prices
2700 Precious Metals Prices
2800 Trading Indexes
2900 Currency Prices—N.Y.

WHAT'S NEWS
4000 Business & Finance
4100 World-Wide
4200 Sports Scoreboard
4300 Sports News
4550 Sports Directory
4500 National Weather
4540 Weather Directory
      for 26 U.S. Cities

FOR JOURNALPHONE QUOTES:

1. Using the chart on the right, translate your stock's ticker symbol into numbers.
2. Enter category 5000.
3. Enter the number of your ticker symbol and press the "∗" key. You'll hear the stock's current price (delayed 15 minutes) and net change from the previous close.
4. By pressing "∗" again, you'll hear that stock's volume and high and low trades. Or, enter another ticker symbol. To return to other JournalPhone categories, press "1" followed by the "∗" key.

A-21	G-41	M-61	S-73	Y-93
B-22	H-42	N-62	T-81	Z-03
C-23	I-43	O-63	U-82	+-11
D-31	J-51	P-71	V-83	.-13
E-32	K-52	Q-01	W-91	∗ Enter
F-33	L-53	R-72	X-92	# Cancel

JournalPhone calls cost 85¢/first minute, 75¢/additional minutes.
For customer assistance, call 1-800-345-NEWS.

JOURNALPHONE 1-900-JOURNAL

© 1989 DOW JONES & COMPANY INC

Summary

Telemarketing is a dynamic medium, without a doubt. When integrated into the total marketing process, it can increase sales efficiency and profits by (1) qualifying leads, (2) increasing response from catalogs, direct mail, print, and broadcast advertising, and (3) maintaining contact with direct marketers' most priceless asset—their customer base.

Self-Quiz

1. In the Wyman study of consumer attitudes about telemarketing, consumers were asked to rate six calling attributes:
   a. The salesperon is professional and courteous.
   b. The person calls at a convenient time.
   c. The company calling has a good reputation.
   d. You have an interest in the product.
   e. You have had a good previous experience with the company.
   f. A person calls rather than a computer.

   Of these attributes, which did consumers rate highest? _____

2. The Wyman survey results disclosed that age is an important factor in being receptive to proactive telemarketing. Which of these groups was more receptive? ☐ 18–24   ☐ 25–34

3. The time of day is a factor in response to proactive calls. Which time period is better when making weekday calls? ☐ Morning ☐ Afternoon   ☐ Evening

4. There are eight major applications of telemarketing. Complete this list:

   a. Order taking   e. _____

   b. Seasonal selling   f. _____

   c. Renewals   g. _____

   d. Customer service   h. _____

5. People who inquire by phone are:

   ☐ more likely to order   ☐ less likely to order

6. What is the function of dealer-locater advertising?

   _____

   _____

   _____

7. Why are outbound calls more expensive than inbound calls?

   _____

   _____

   _____

8. On the average, a field salesperson can make _____ to _____ sales calls a day; a telemarketing salesperson can make _____ to _____ calls a day.

9. Under what conditions is it more appropriate for an organization to test or maintain a telemarketing center in-house?

   _____

   _____

   _____

10. Name two situations in which it makes more sense to use an outside telemarketing organization.

    a. _____

       _____

       _____

    b. _____

       _____

       _____

11. Field salespeople are most likely to succeed at telemarketing.

    ☐ True   ☐ False

12. Name two desirable skills of a successful telephone communicator.

    a. _____

       _____

    b. _____

       _____

13. Complete this list of seven steps involved in the telemarketing selling process.

    a. Precall planning   e. _____

    b. Approach/Positioning   f. _____

    c. Data gathering   g. _____

    d. Solution generation

Pilot Project

You are the marketing director of an envelope company. You have a customer base of 100,000 small-business firms, all secured by direct mail. You have decided to test the efficiency of telemarketing.

Your assignment is to develop a telemarketing test plan. In developing this plan, please answer the following questions:

1. Will you use a commercial organization to structure your test, or will you structure the test in-house? And why?

2. What data, or measures, will you use to estimate when inventories might be depleted for each customer?

3. What information might you request from each customer in the process of making your calls?

4. What special offers might you make in an effort to get repeat business by phone?

Creating and Producing Direct Marketing

CHAPTER FIFTEEN

Techniques of Creating Direct Mail Packages

Direct mail is an expensive advertising medium. It costs 15 to 20 times as much to reach a person with a direct mail package as it does to reach him with a 30-second TV commercial or a full-page ad in a newspaper. But direct mail has certain unique advantages that more than compensate for its higher cost. If you understand what these advantages are and use them properly, you will be able to bring in orders or responses at a cost equal to or below that of space or broadcast. And, as a general rule, customers acquired by direct mail are usually better customers in terms of repeat business than those acquired by space or broadcast advertising.

Advantages of Direct Mail
Selectivity

Through careful list selection and segmentation, direct mail can give you pinpoint selectivity unmatched by any other advertising medium (with the exception of the telephone). You can literally pick out households one by one, mailing only to those that are the best prospects for your offer. The fundamentals of list selection and segmentation are discussed in Chapter Nine. Review these carefully.

Virtually Unlimited Choice of Formats

In direct mail, you are not restricted to 30 seconds of time or a 7" × 10" page. You can use large, lavishly illustrated brochures. You can have any number of inserts. You can use pop-ups, fold-outs, swatches—even enclose a phonograph record. What you can do is limited only by your imagination and budget. For example, one enterprising mailer used a unique response device: He mailed a carrier pigeon to each prospect. The respondent taped

his reply to the pigeon's leg and released the pigeon. The mailer didn't even have to pay a return postage charge!

Personal Character

Even though you mail in the millions, you are still mailing individual pieces to individually addressed human beings. Every recipient knows that an ad or a TV commercial was not created specifically for him or her, but for a mass audience. Direct mail approaches the prospect on a personal level that, with personalized letters, even extends to a greeting by name. As any salesperson will agree, you can sell much better when you are talking to an individual rather than to people en masse.

No Competition

In most advertising media, the advertising is an adjunct, not the main reason the person is watching the TV channel or reading the magazine. In direct mail, advertising arrives all by itself to be opened and read at the recipient's leisure. When it is read, there is nothing to compete with it for your prospect's attention.

Most Testable Medium

With direct mail you can virtually simulate laboratory conditions for testing. You control exactly when the mail is dropped, and you control exactly who gets which test package. Many magazines and newspapers can give you an A/B split, but direct mail will give you as many splits as you care to have.

Unique Capability to Involve the Recipient

Direct mail offers a wide choice of devices that involve the recipient, such as tokens, stamps, questionnaires, and quizzes. And with direct mail, you can literally get the recipients to "talk back" to you—to open a dialog—by asking them questions and giving them space to respond via the reply format.

Selecting the Format

Because direct mail offers an unlimited choice of format, a good place to start is deciding which basic format to use. There are three basic formats to choose from:

The *classic format* utilizes a separate outer or mailing envelope. The size of that envelope, the material from which it is made (paper, plastic, foil), and the number of colors in which it is printed can vary widely. What goes inside that envelope can vary even more widely. Classic formats range from simple, dignified, businesslike letters (Exhibit 15–1) to lavish packages stuffed with brochures, inserts, gift circulars—even pop-ups and phonograph records

Exhibit 15–1. **Classic Direct Mail Format**

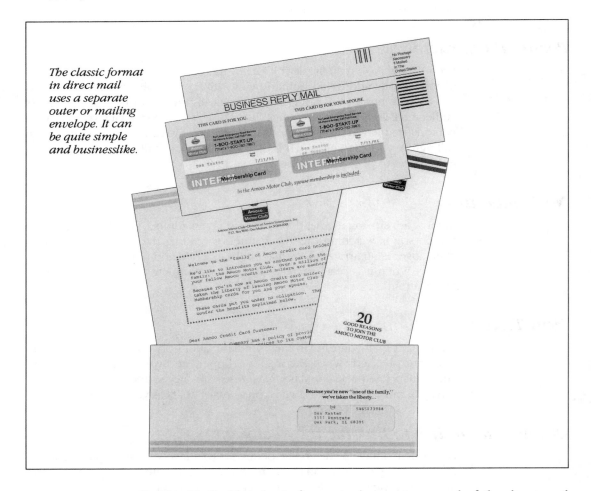

The classic format in direct mail uses a separate outer or mailing envelope. It can be quite simple and businesslike.

(Exhibit 15–2). The classic format is the most personal of the direct mail formats. For this reason, it almost always includes a separate letter, either preprinted or personalized.

The *self-mailer* does not have an outer envelope. These mailers vary from a single sheet of paper folded once for mailing to wonderfully complex pieces with multiple sheets and preformed reply envelopes (Exhibit 15–3). Generally, a self-mailer comes off the press complete, ready to address and mail. As a rule, self-mailers are less expensive than classic mailing packages. There is only one component to produce and no inserting is needed since the piece is completed on-press.

The *catalog* is literally a magazine, with up to many hundreds of pages, stitched, glued, or perfect-bound. Catalogs require a highly specialized format, and their use is subject to many important guidelines. Catalogs are discussed in detail in Chapter Sixteen.

Exhibit 15–1 (*Continued*).   **A Classic Direct Mail Format**

The classic format can also be lavish, exciting, and packed with different pieces, as illustrated by this mailing by American Family Publishers.

Exhibit 15–2. **Expanded Classic Direct Mail Format**

Variety of enclosures enhances interest in the total mailing package.

Exhibit 15–3.   **Self-Mailer**

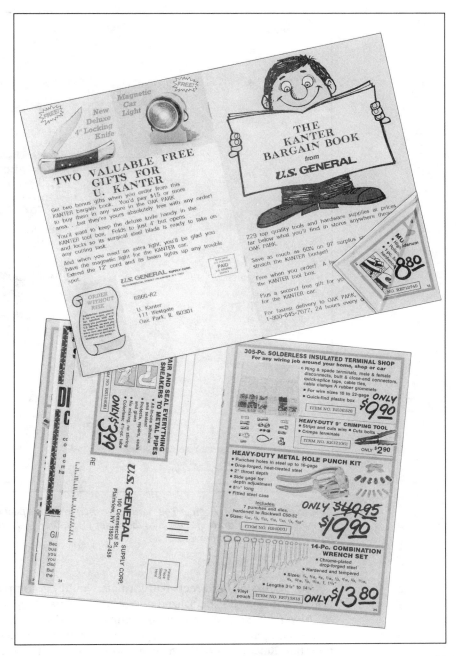

A self-mailer is produced on one pass through the press. When opened, it contains individual, personalized premium (gift) slips, order form, and bound-in 44-page catalog. Even a preformed order envelope is included!

Exhibit 15–4.   **Involvement Device**

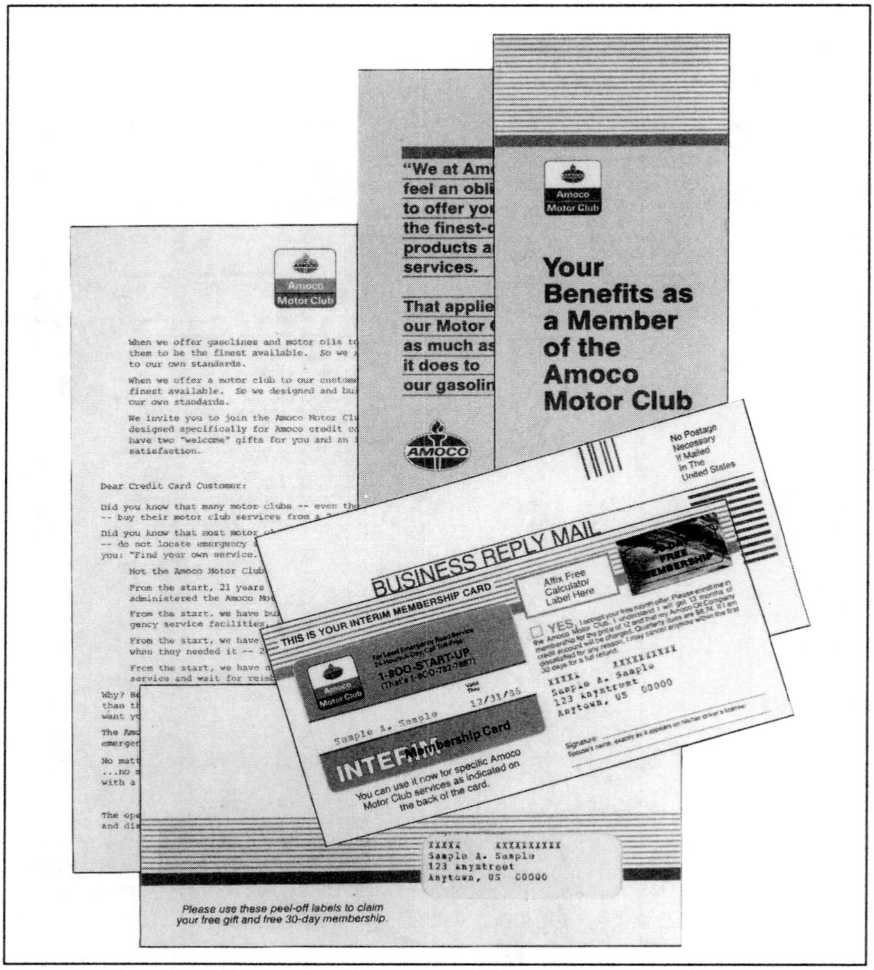

A typical involvement device: The reader is asked to lift the peel-off stickers from the outer envelope and affix them to the order form, thereby "validating" the free gift and free trial membership.

No discussion of direct mail formats would be complete without mentioning some of the specialized devices that are used regularly in direct mail.

Involvement devices include stamps, tokens, rub-offs, sealed envelopes —one company even used a jigsaw puzzle that the recipient had to put together. Regardless of the format you use, reader involvement can make it dramatically more effective. If you get the reader involved with your offer and message, you're well on your way to a sale (Exhibit 15–4). A most effective way to get the reader involved is to include a product sample or

swatch in the mailing. Obviously, this device is not suitable for all types of merchandise, but nothing beats letting somebody touch, feel, and try what you're selling.

Specialized devices include die-cut shapes, tip-ons, and pop-ups. These can be great attention-getters. But be careful: You don't want to let the gimmick take the reader's attention from your basic sales message. One company tested an elaborate (and expensive) pop-up device and found that the mailing actually pulled better without it! The pop-up was stealing attention from the mailer's message.

In connection with formats, there are several tried-and-true variations you should consider for your mailing package.

The *second letter*, or "publisher's letter" (Exhibit 15–5), has become almost a must in direct mail today. Repeated testing indicates that such a letter boosts response 10 percent or more. The letter is either a folded letter or a letter in a separate sealed envelope that warns sternly: "Open this letter *only* if you have decided not to respond to this offer." Of course, everybody opens it immediately. This gives you the chance to do a little extra selling, primarily in reassuring the prospects that they really have nothing to lose and everything to gain in accepting your offer.

The *closed-face envelope* (Exhibit 15–6) has the name and address of the recipient "typed" right on the envelope; there is no window or slot through which the name shows. Inside there are two or three other pieces (letters, applications) on which the recipient's name, address, and other information are also "typed." The mailing looks like it was typed individually, but this is not so: These ingenious mailings are run on computer, then the outer envelope is matched to the pieces inside. Because they look so personal, closed-face packages are rarely discarded without opening.

Invitation formats have been around for a long time (see Exhibit 15–7). They are very effective, especially for publishers, club memberships, and credit card solicitations. The format simulates a formal invitation ("You are invited to accept . . . "). The outside of the invitation usually carries a letter explaining the offer. Naturally, an RSVP—a call to action—is included in the mailing.

The *simulated telegram* is less formal but carries a lot of urgency (see Exhibit 15–8). It's been popular as a follow-up mailing or part of a renewal series and has worked well for credit card solicitation, insurance, and loans-by-mail offers. However, with the decline in the use of real telegrams, the simulated telegram is being used less and less. The simulated telegram is usually printed on yellow stock and, more often than not, is computer-filled. (Caution: the basic telegram format is copyrighted by Western Union. You are not allowed to use it.)

Personalization is common today regardless of what format you use. Personalization is done by computer, by ink-jet imaging, or by laser printing (Exhibit 15–9). Each method has its advantages and its particular requirements. Each method requires specific preparation of materials, so you would be well advised to seek professional production help if you are planning a personalized mailing.

Exhibit 15–5.   Publisher's Letter

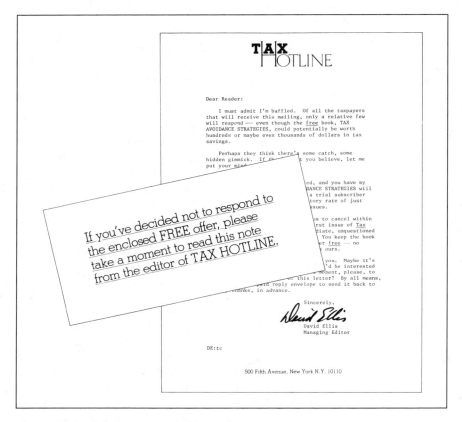

The "publisher's letter" or "second letter" has become a proven results booster in direct mail today.

Exhibit 15–6.   Closed-Face Envelope

The closed-face envelope has no slot or window through which the recipient's name shows. It looks like it was personally typed, but it's actually a computer-generated envelope that is matched to the pieces inside.

Exhibit 15-7.   Invitation Format

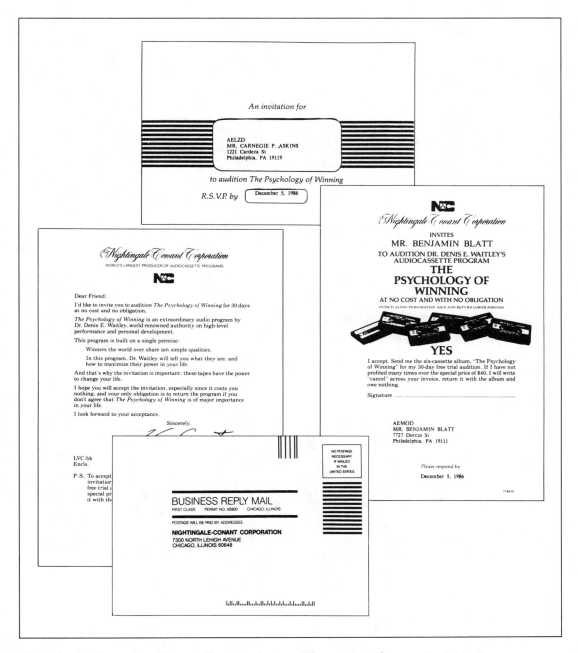

The invitation format remains an effective technique. Who can turn down an invitation?

Exhibit 15–8. **Simulated Telegram**

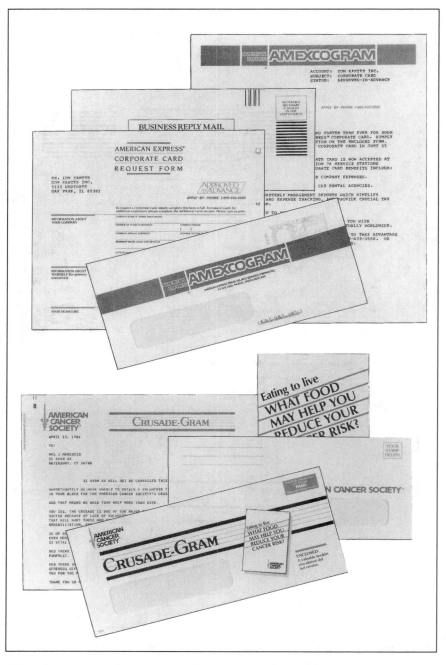

Although not as popular as it was a few years ago, the simulated telegram retains the look—and the urgency—of the real thing.

Exhibit 15–9. Personalized Letters

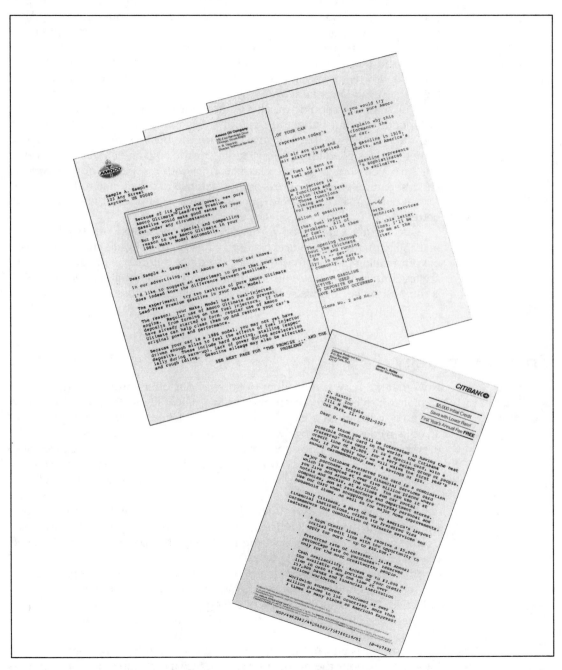

Personalized letters appear to be individually typed. Personalization techniques can vary the size and face of the type, and laser personalization permits economical small-run personalization.

When you run into somebody who tells you that personalized letters "always" outpull nonpersonalized ones, be skeptical. In my experience, personalized letters *usually* outpull nonpersonalized ones, but not always. Also, they have to outpull by enough to pay for the extra cost of personalization. When you use personalization, use all the information you can. But don't scatter the person's name indiscriminately throughout the letter. A good rule to follow is to write a personalized letter as you would write a letter to any person you know fairly well.

Which format should you choose for your mailing piece? That depends. It depends on your budget. It depends on whom you're trying to reach. Do you want a package that will stand out on the businessman's desk? Or is it something designed for leisurely reading by the consumer at home? If you're not sure, you should use the classic format with a separate outer envelope and a separate letter. The great preponderance of direct mail today uses this format, and while it is more expensive than a self-mailer, it will usually pull better.

One further caution on formats: Postal regulations, which govern the mailability of any given piece, change regularly. You should check the layout of your mailing piece with your local post office before you produce it. There are few things in life more disheartening than a phone call that begins: "This is the post office, and we're holding your mailing because . . . ."

Creative Strategy

Now that we have the product or service, our offer (proposition), and our format, we're ready to create the mailing piece. Right? Wrong. And therein lies a basic failing in a lot of direct mail produced today. The writer is too anxious to dash to his typewriter, and the artist is too anxious to get to his drawing board. Why does this occur? Marketing is "work," but creative effort is *fun*, and we all tend to do what we like to do. But unless the creative work is strategically grounded, it is not going to work—or at least, not as well as it should.

As one sage observed: "If you don't know where you're going, any road will take you there." Advertising, general or direct response, has to know exactly where it is going, and the road map that points the way is called *creative strategy*.

Every large advertising agency and virtually every large company has its own creative strategy, under one name or another. They all share a common objective: They focus the efforts of the creative personnel. It is the discipline of creative strategy that prevents advertising from trying to be all things to all people—and, in reality, being nothing to any of them.

Following is an outline for a typical creative strategy that organizes the information about the product or service into a disciplined format. Remember: To be useful, this outline must be *written*.

- *The product*. What it is, what it does, how it works, what it costs, what its features are, what its *benefits* are, what makes it different, what makes it better—even what its weaknesses are.

- *Competitive products*. How they compare with ours in terms of features, benefits, and price.

- *The market*. How big is it and what share of it do we have? Who buys the product today and why? Who else *should* buy it and why? Who are our present customers and future prospects in terms of demographic characteristics, such as age, sex, marital status, income, and education. Who are they in psychographic terms? Are they liberal or conservative, avant-garde, or traditional?

- *The media*. What's going to carry our message? If space or broadcast media are to be used, which ones, how often, and in what space or time units? If direct mail is the only medium, what lists will we be using— specifically or in general? What do we know or assume about quantities, formats, colors?

- *The budget*. What limitations should govern our creative thinking in terms of creative staff time, layout costs, photography, illustrations, production costs?

- *Objective*. As specifically as possible, what are we trying to *do* in terms of overall goals and specific goals, in accordance with the total program, and in line with specific components within the program? Among all possible goals, what are our priorities? Which ones are primary and vital; which are secondary and merely desirable; which are nice but expendable?

- *Creative implementation*. How do we propose to organize what we know or assume about the product, the competition, and the market to achieve our stated objectives? How will we position the product? What relative emphasis will we give to product features and product benefits? What do we anticipate as our central copy theme? How will it be executed visually? And how will it be orchestrated among various elements of the program? Most important of all from a response standpoint, what will our offer be and how will it be dramatized?

How your creative strategy document addresses these questions, the order in which you address them, and the format in which you cast them are all minor matters. They can be varied according to circumstances. When the creative strategy is thoroughly digested by both the writer and the artist, they both have a good idea of what the mailing package should accomplish, how, and why.

Precreative Work

With a creative strategy in place, you're ready to start creative work. Well . . . almost ready.

First, there are some important "precreative" matters to be take care of before one word or copy is written or one piece of the mailing is designed. Listen to Gene Schwartz, a professional direct response writer, as he describes how he listens first with his ears and then with his eyes:

1. Sit down with the owner of the product or service—the man who's hiring you—and pump hell out of him. Put it on a tape recorder and have him talk for three or four hours.

   Ask him where the product comes from, what it does, what are its problems and how he's tried to cure them, why it's better than its competitors, who likes it, who doesn't like it, what proof he's got that it works, what strange uses people have got out of it, what funny stories he has accumulated in regard to its manufacture or use, what problems he was trying to solve when he created it, how he would improve it if he had unlimited money, what causes most of his refunds, who works for him to help him make it, how it is made, how he keeps up the quality, who writes him what about it, etc.

2. Talk to his customers. Do it in person, or on paper. See if they agree with him. If they don't, find out why.

3. Listen to his competitors. They often tell you more about the opportunities they're missing in their ads than the opportunities they're seeing and therefore seizing. Let them write a possible head or two for you—out of the body copy of their ads.

4. Then put all the material down, in one big pile, and underline it. Start blending it together, like you'd make a cake. Give first priority to your head and subheads, then the body claims. And then type it up, preferably adding little of yourself except as selector and condenser.

Direct response creative pros use a variety of techniques for approaching the moment of truth. But they all have one thing in common: They dig, dig, dig. The hack, on the other hand, just sits down to write. Miracle performances don't happen by accident—they're created.

The Copywriter as Salesperson

Listen to Don Kanter, long-time vice president of Stone & Adler, who now owns his own direct response creative service. He has a unique way of describing some copywriters. "The trouble with many copywriters," he says, "is that they think their job is to write copy." Kanter quickly explains this by adding, "That is equivalent to a salesperson saying, 'My job is to talk.' The job is not to 'talk.' For a writer, the job is not to 'write.' For both, the job is to

sell. Selling is the end result; writing is merely the means a copywriter uses to reach that end. This is true of all advertising copywriting; it is especially true of direct response copywriting because the writer is usually the only salesperson with whom the prospect will ever come in contact. If he or she doesn't make the sale, there is nobody else to do it."

The Benefit/Price/Value Equation

To sell effectively, the direct response writer must know why people buy. They buy, essentially, when they consider something to have value. This is often expressed in a simple equation: Benefit divided by price equals value. In other words, every time individuals are confronted with a buying decision, they subconsciously assign a worth to the benefits they perceive. At the same time, they assign a worth to the price they must pay. And subjectively, very subconsciously, they divide one into the other to reach their buying decision. If they believe the benefits outweigh the price, they will buy. If the price outweighs the benefits, they will not buy.

What Is Price?

To most people, *price* is the monetary amount asked for the goods or services being sold: the $29.95, or $39.95, or $5.00 per month, or whatever. But there is more to price than that. There's time. We are asking customers to wait before they can enjoy the benefits of what they buy. There's the factor of buying the product sight unseen (unlike retail purchasing, where customers can see, touch, and often try what they are buying). There's a factor of buying from a company the customers may not know. There's the risk that the product or service may not deliver the benefits that have been promised. In direct marketing, all of these are part of the price that must be paid. While we may not be able to do much about the actual price (the $29.95, or $39.95, or $5.00 a month), we can (and we must) do everything possible to reduce the other factors of price to the minimum.

How? By using the proven techniques that direct marketing has pioneered:

- Testimonials
- Guarantees
- Free-trial offers or cancellation privileges
- Reassurance about the stature and reliability of the selling company

What Is a Benefit?

Let's assume we are selling a stereo system. This system has two three-way speakers, each with a big "woofer" and "tweeter" and a midrange. That's a benefit. Right? Wrong. That's a selling point or product feature. It's a distinc-

tion that every writer must recognize and keep in mind. A benefit is something that affects customers personally. It exists apart from the merchandise or service itself. A selling point or product feature is something in the product or service that makes possible and supports the benefit. Our stereo system with two three-way speaker systems is a selling point. It is a quality in the product itself. That customers can enjoy lifelike, three-dimensional sound is the benefit. It is this benefit that affects them personally. This benefit is made possible by the fact that this stereo system has two three-way speakers. Remember, it is the benefit that customers really wants to have. It is the selling point that proves to them that they can really have it.

Translate Selling Points into Benefits

Before you write any copy, therefore, it is very important to dig out every selling point you can and translate each selling point into a customer benefit. The more benefits customers perceive (i.e., the more benefits you can point out to them), the more likely they will buy. Here's an example: Suppose you're writing copy to sell a portable countertop dishwasher. Below are listed some of the selling points in this merchandise, and alongside each is the benefit that the selling point makes possible:

Selling Point	Benefit
1. A 10-minute operating cycle.	1. Does a load of dishes in 10 minutes; gets you out of the kitchen faster.
2. Measures 18 inches in diameter.	2. Is small enough to fit on a countertop; doesn't take up valuable floor space.
3. Has a transparent plastic top.	3. Lets you watch the washing cycle; you know when the dishes are done.
4. Has a universal hose coupling.	4. Fits any standard kitchen faucet; attaches and detaches in seconds.

Copy Appeals and Basic Human Wants

With your benefits down on paper, you now have to decide on the appeals that will do the best selling job. Creative people refer to this in different ways. Some talk about how you "position" the product in the prospect's mind. Others refer to "coming up with the big idea" behind the copy. What is it about your offer and benefit story that is most appealing? When you stop to think about it, people respond to any given proposition for one of two reasons: to gain something they do not have or to avoid losing something they now possess. As you can see from the accompanying tabulation, basic human wants can be divided into these two categories. Professional copywriters carefully sift and weigh the list of basic human wants to determine the main appeal of their proposition. (In Chapter Seventeen you'll see how the same product can be slanted to employ many different appeals just by changing your headline.)

The Desire to Gain	The Desire to Avoid Loss
To make money	To avoid criticism
To save time	To keep possessions
To avoid effort	To avoid physical pain
To achieve comfort	To avoid loss of reputation
To have health	To avoid loss of money
To be popular	To avoid trouble
To experience pleasure	
To be clean	
To be praised	
To be in style	
To gratify curiosity	
To satisfy an appetite	
To have beautiful possessions	
To attract the opposite sex	
To be an individual	
To emulate others	
To take advantage of opportunities	

Eleven Guidelines to Good Copy

Does your proposition offer the promise of saving time and avoiding hard or disagreeable work? Most people like to avoid work. Saving time is almost a fetish of the American people. Appeal to this basic want, if you can.

Does your proposition help people feel important? People like to keep up with the Joneses. People like to be made to feel that they are a part of a select group. A tremendous number of people are susceptible to snob appeal. Perhaps you can offer a terrific bargain by mail and capitalize on the appeal of saving money. The desire to "get it wholesale" is very strong.

Don Kanter uses these guidelines as checkpoints for good, professional copy:

1. Does the writer know the product? Has he or she dug out every selling point and benefit?

2. Does the writer know his or her market? Is he or she aiming the copy at the most likely prospects rather than at the world in general?

3. Is the writer talking to the prospect in language that the prospect will understand?

4. Does the writer make a promise to the prospect, then prove that he or she can deliver what was promised?

5. Does the writer get to the point at once? Does he or she make that all-important promise right away?

6. Is the copy, especially the headlines and lead paragraphs, germane and specific to the selling proposition?

7. Is the copy concise? There is a great temptation to overwrite, especially in direct mail.

8. Is the copy logical and clear? Does it "flow" from point to point?

9. Is the copy enthusiastic? Does the writer obviously believe in what he or she is selling?

10. Is the copy complete? Are all the questions answered, especially obvious ones like size and color?

11. Is the copy designed to sell? Or is it designed to impress the reader with the writer's ability? If somebody says "that's a great mailing," you've got the wrong reaction. What you want to hear is, "That's a great product (or service). I'd love to have it."

The Changes in Direct Mail

Only a few years ago, direct mail was a "set" medium, with its own rules that you broke at your peril. A direct mail package had—at the minimum—an outer envelope, a reply envelope, a letter (at least two pages and probably more), a brochure, and an order form.

But change is coming. In fact, it's here, according to Don Kanter, who has been doing direct response creative work for 20 years. The changes, he says, are focused on one objective: faster, stronger, more telegraphic communication with the prospect.

Why? Two reasons, Mr. Kanter says. First, "mailbox clutter" is becoming real, just as TV clutter did some years ago. Only a direct mailing that grabs and holds the prospect's attention—from the envelope through every component—has a chance of working. Second, we are now talking to the TV generation, which grew up with visual symbols. Unlike us older folks who grew up reading books, the TV generation is less inclined to stay with you if you don't get your message across very quickly.

Basically, the specific changes are in two areas:

1. *Shorter copy and better copy*: Kanter believes that direct mail historically has been overwritten, because direct mail does not impose the discipline for tight, concise writing that space or broadcast does. Now that discipline is being imposed by outside factors, it means that the direct mail writer must edit and polish copy, making every word justify its existence. A four-page letter (or longer) may still be the best way to go, but it must be a beautifully written, meticulously polished, and lovingly edited four-page letter.

2. *Quicker communication through graphics*. At long last, the designer is becoming an equal partner in the direct mail creative process, as we learn what our brethren in general advertising have always known: Graphics communicate more quickly and more forcefully than words.

An added benefit of the designer's involvement is that we are improving the appearance of direct mail, as well as the level of taste. The old "direct mail look" that was distinguished by type piled up on virtually every component, is slowly disappearing.

Creating the Classic Mailing Package

Now that we've looked at formats and discussed copy, let's turn to the individual pieces in a so-called classic mailing package.

The Outer Envelope

The outer envelope, or carrier envelope (Exhibit 15–10), has one job: to get itself opened. To accomplish this, the envelope can use several techniques:

- It can dazzle recipients with color, with graphics, and with promises of important benefits (including wealth, in the case of sweepstakes offers) if they will only open it.

- It can impress recipients with its simplicity and lead them to believe that the contents must be very important.

- It can tease recipients and so excite their curiosity that they simply must open it.

To help accomplish its purpose, the envelope can be the traditional paper envelope (perhaps with extra cut-outs or "windows"), or it can be made of transparent polyethylene or foil. Whatever it's made of and whatever it says, the outer envelope sets the tone of your mailing. It must harmonize with the materials inside.

The Brochure

As noted, most mailing packages require a good brochure or circular in addition to a letter. It can be a small, two-color affair or a beautiful, giant circular that's almost as big as a tablecloth. But the job it has to do is the same, and it deserves your best creative effort.

One way or another, your circular has to do a complete selling job. To give yourself every chance for success, review the appearance, content, and preparation of your circular. The following is a handy checklist for this purpose.

Appearance

1. Is the circular designed for the market you are trying to reach?

Exhibit 15–10. **Various Envelope Formats**

The outer envelope can be vibrant and exciting . . .

dignified and businesslike . . .

or it can tease the reader.

2. Is the presentation suited to the product or service you are offering?

3. Is the circular consistent with the rest of the mailing package?

Content

4. Is there a big idea behind your circular?

5. Do your headlines stick to the key offer?

6. Is your product or service dramatized to its best advantage by format and/or presentation?

7. Do you show broadly adaptable examples of your product or service in use?

8. Does your entire presentation follow a logical sequence and tell a complete story—including price, offer, and guarantee?

Preparation

9. Can the circular be cut out of standard-size paper stock?

10. Is the quality of paper stock in keeping with the presentation?

11. Is color employed judiciously to show the product or service in its best light?

The Order Form

If Ernest Hemingway had been a direct response writer, he probably would have dubbed the order form "the moment of truth." Many prospects make a final decision on whether to respond after reading it. Some even read the order form before anything else in the envelope, because they know it's the easiest way to find out what's being offered at what price. The best advice I can offer on order forms comes from Henry Cowen, a direct marketing specialist. He says, "There are direct mail manuals around that recommend simple, easy-to-read order forms, but my experience indicates the mailer is far better off with a busy, rather jumbled appearance and plenty of copy. Formal and legal-looking forms that appear valuable, too valuable to throw away, are good." The key words in Cowen's statement are "too valuable to throw away." The order form or reply form that appears valuable induces readership. It impels the reader to do something with it, to take advantage of the offer. High on the list of devices and techniques that make order forms look valuable are certificate borders, safety paper backgrounds, simulated rubber stamps, eagles, blue handwriting, seals, serial numbers, receipt stubs, and so on. And sheet size alone can greatly add to the valuable appearance of a response form (Exhibit 15–11). (You've seen examples of many of these techniques on the order forms shown in Chapter Four.)

Exhibit 15–11.   **Order Form**

The order form (which should never be called an order form) is the moment of truth in a direct mail package. It must look too valuable to throw away.

Above all, don't call your reply device an order form. Call it a Reservation Certificate, Free-Gift Check, Trial Membership Application, or some other benefit heading. It automatically seems more valuable to the reader.

Getting back more inquiry and order forms starts with making them appear too valuable to throw away. But to put frosting on the cake, add the dimension of personal involvement. Give readers something to do with the order form. Ask them to put a token in a "yes" or "no" slot. Get them to affix a gummed stamp. Have them tear off a stub that has your guarantee on it. Once you have prodded the prospect into action, there is a good chance you will receive an order.

Finally, the order form should restate your offer and benefits. If a prospect loses the letter or circular, a good order form should be able to stand alone and do a complete selling job. And if it's designed to be mailed back on its own (without an envelope), it's usually worthwhile to prepay the postage.

Gift Slips and Other Enclosures

In addition to the letter, brochure, and order form, one of the most common enclosures is a free-gift slip. If you have a free-gift offer, you'll normally get much better results by putting that offer on a separate slip rather than building it into your circular (Exhibit 15–12).

If you insert an extra enclosure, make sure it stands out from the rest of the mailing and gets attention. You can often accomplish this by printing the enclosure on a colored stock and making it a different size from the other mailing components. Most free gifts, for example, can be adequately played up on a small slip that's 3½" × 8½" or 5½" × 8½".

Another enclosure that's often used is a business reply envelope. This isn't essential if the order form can be designed as a self-mailer. But if you have an offer that the reader might consider to be of a private nature, an envelope is usually better. Buying a self-improvement book, for example. Or applying for an insurance policy, where the application asks some personal questions. Also, the extra expense of a reply envelope is often justified if you want to encourage more cash-with-order replies.

The Letter—The Key Ingredient of Direct Mail

If any one piece in a direct mail package is key, that piece is the letter. One of the prime advantages of direct mail is its capacity for personal, one-on-one communication, and the letter provides that personal communication. It's no wonder, then, that more has been written about how to create a good direct mail letter than about any other part of the direct mail package.

Seven-Step Formula

Here's a letter-writing formula that has served me well. I believe it follows

Exhibit 15–12. **Free-Gift Offers**

If you have a free gift with your offer, you'll get better results by highlighting it with a separate slip.

a more detailed route than most formulas. And, used wisely, it should not stifle your creativity.

1. *Promise your most important benefit in your headline or first paragraph.* You simply can't go wrong by leading off with the most important benefit to the reader. Some writers believe in the slow buildup. But most experienced writers favor making the important point first. Many writers use the "Johnson Box": short, terse copy that summarizes the main benefits, positioned in a box above the salutation.

2. *Immediately enlarge on your most important benefit.* This step is crucial. Many writers come up with a great lead, then fail to follow through. Or they catch attention with their heading, but then take two or three paragraphs to warm up to their subject. The reader's attention is gone! Try hard to elaborate on your most important benefit right away, and you'll build up interest fast.

3. *Tell readers specifically what they are going to get.* It's amazing how many letters lack details on such basic product features as size, color, weight, and sales terms. Perhaps the writer is so close to the proposition that he or she assumes the readers know all about it. A dangerous

assumption! And when you tell the reader what they are going to get, don't overlook the intangibles that go along with your product or service. For example, they are getting smart appearance in addition to a pair of slacks, knowledge in addition to a 340-page book.

4. *Back up your statements with proof and endorsements.* Most prospects are somewhat skeptical about advertising. They know it sometimes gets a little overenthusiastic about a product. So they accept it with a grain of salt. If you can back up your own statements with third-party testimonials or a list of satisfied users, everything you say becomes more believable.

5. *Tell readers what they might lose if they don't act.* As noted, people respond affirmatively either to gain something they do not possess or to avoid losing something they already have. Here's a good spot in your letter to overcome human inertia—imply what may be lost if action is postponed. People don't like to be left out. A skillful writer can use this human trait as a powerful influence in his or her message.

6. *Rephrase your prominent benefits in your closing offer.* As a good salesperson does, sum up the benefits to the prospect in your closing offer. This is the proper prelude to asking for action. This is where you can intensify the prospect's desire to have the product. The stronger the benefits you can persuade the reader to recall, the easier it will be for him or her to justify an affirmative decision.

7. *Incite action. Now.* This is the spot where you win or lose the battle with inertia. Experienced advertisers know once a letter is put aside or tossed into that file, they're out of luck. So wind up with a call for action and a logical reason for acting now. Too many letters close with a statement like "supplies are limited." That argument lacks credibility. Today's consumer knows you probably have a warehouse full of merchandise. So make your reason a believable one. For example, "It may be many months before we go back to press on this book." Or "Orders are shipped on a first-come basis. The sooner yours is received, the sooner you can be enjoying your new widget." (See Exhibit 15–13.)

Strategic Writing

The seven-step sales letter formula provides a route to follow when constructing a letter. Another way to approach the task is to review the problems you face and then come up with strategic solutions to those problems. Expressed as a formula: Problems ÷ Strategies = Solutions.

A dramatic example of the application of this technique involves the launch of a certificate program in direct marketing at the University of Missouri–Kansas City (UMKC). I accepted the assignment of doing a direct mail package to be tested against a traditional package prepared by a local agency in Kansas City.

Exhibit 15–13.   **The Kiplinger Letter**

STANLEY R. MAYES   *ASSISTANT TO THE PRESIDENT*

THE KIPLINGER WASHINGTON EDITORS, INC.

1729 H STREET, NORTHWEST, WASHINGTON, D. C. 20006   TELEPHONE: 887-6400

THE KIPLINGER WASHINGTON LETTER   THE KIPLINGER TAX LETTER
THE KIPLINGER AGRICULTURAL LETTER   THE KIPLINGER FLORIDA LETTER
THE KIPLINGER CALIFORNIA LETTER   THE KIPLINGER TEXAS LETTER
CHANGING TIMES MAGAZINE

<u>More Growth and Inflation Ahead...</u>
<u>and what YOU can do about it.</u>

The next few years will see business climb to the highest
level this country has ever known. And with it...inflation.

This combination may be hard for you to accept under today's
conditions. But the fact remains that those who do prepare for both
inflation AND growth ahead will reap big dividends for their foresight,
and avoid the blunders others will make.

You'll get the information you need for this type
of planning in the Kiplinger Washington Letter...
and the enclosed form will bring you the next 26
issues of this helpful service on a "Try-out" basis.
The fee: Less than 81¢ per week...<u>only $21 for the</u>
<u>6 months just ahead</u>...and tax deductible for business
or investment purposes.

During the depression, in 1935, the Kiplinger Letter warned
of inflation and told what to do about it. Those who heeded its advice
were ready when prices began to rise.

Again, in January of 1946, the Letter renounced the widely-
held view that a severe post-war depression was inevitable. Instead
it predicted shortages, rising wages and prices, a high level of
business. And again, those who heeded its advice were able to avoid
losses, to cash in on the surging economy of the late '40s, early '50s
and mid '60s. It then kept its clients prepared for the swings of the
'70s, keeping them a step ahead each time.

Now Kiplinger not only foresees expansion ahead, but also
continuing inflation, and in his weekly Letter to clients he points
out profit opportunities in the future...and also dangers.

The Kiplinger Letter not only keeps you informed of present
trends and developments, but also gives you advance notice on the
short & long-range business outlook...inflation forecasts...energy
predictions...housing...federal legislative prospects...politics...
investment trends & pointers...tax outlook & advice...labor, wage
settlement prospects...upcoming gov't rules & regulations...ANYTHING
that will have an effect on you, your business, your personal finances,
your family.

To take advantage of this opportunity to try the Letter and
benefit from its keen judgments and helpful advice during the fast-

(Over, please)

*One of the most famous letters in direct mail, the Kiplinger letter. With minor changes, it beat all
tests against it for almost 40 years! Notice how it follows the seven-step formula for writing sales
letters.*

Exhibit 15–13 *(Continued)*.   **The Kiplinger Letter**

changing months ahead...fill in and return the enclosed form along
with your $21 payment. And do it with this guarantee: That you may
cancel the service and get a prompt refund of the unused part of
your payment any time you feel it is not worth far more to you than
it costs.

I'll start your service as soon as I hear from you, and
you'll have each weekly issue on your desk every Monday morning
thereafter.

Sincerely,

Stanley Mayes
Assistant to the President

SAM:kga

P. S.   More than half of all new subscribers sign up for a full year
at $42. In appreciation, we'll send you FREE five special Kiplinger
Reports on receipt of your payment when you take a full year's service,
too. Details are spelled out on the enclosed slip. Same money-back
guarantee and tax deductibility apply.

Example: The UMKC Certificate Program

In preparing to write the sales letter, I first listed the problems I faced:

1. To enroll, the applicant would have to have a degree from an accredited college or university.

2. The applicant would have to have two or more years' experience as a professional direct marketer.

3. The applicant would have to agree to spend three weeks on campus at UMKC.

4. The student would be subjected to 14-hour days on campus.

5. Each student would be required to take three written examinations as well as participate in team assignments.

6. Each student would be required to complete assignments between intervening on-campus periods.

7. The company sponsoring the applicant had to pay a tuition fee of $4,500.

These problems called for strategic solutions. Here is how each problem was dealt with.

Problem 1:   Will a professional direct marketer accept the word of a college administrator over a professional colleague?
Strategic solution: Write the letter printed on my personal letterhead and use the salutation "Dear Colleague."

Problem 2:   Is it better to bury the stiff requirements in the body of the letter or to get major negatives out of the way in the first paragraph?
Strategic solution: Get the negatives out of the way immediately.

> If you accept this proposal, it will cost your firm $4,500. Not an insignificant sum. And there's more. If you accept this proposal, you or your designate will submit to a series of 14-hour days on campus. So much for the agony: now for the ecstasy!
> The ecstasy paragraph expounded on these benefits:
> If you accept this proposal, you or your designate will be one of 35 nationwide who will be eligible to receive certification as a PROFESSIONAL DIRECT MARKETER (PDM).

Problem 3:   Because most of the prospects probably had attended only one- or two-day seminars they might therefore construe these to be adequate.
Strategic solution: Promote the advantage of the longer time required.

But the lasting impact might be compared to taking a cortisone shot to relieve a current problem as contrasted to a life-long infusion of healthy knowledge. The difference: night and day.

Problem 4:   The prospect might wonder if there is any precedent for education of this nature.

Strategic solution: Put the UMKC program at the same level as similar programs at other prominent universities.

Actually there is strong precedent to recommend the UMKC Professional Direct Marketing Certification Program. It's in exactly the same mode as programs conducted at Harvard, Stanford, and Northwestern's Kellogg School. America's major corporations send their brightest to the on-campus management programs of these distinguished universities.

Problem 5:   There is an unexpected fear of "going back to college." So how can this fear be alleviated?

Strategic solution: Point out the advantages of the professional over the college student—*experience*.

To catch up with professionals, college students would have to attend two classes a week for 15 consecutive weeks.

Problem 6:   If I ask the prospect to return the entrollment form to UMKC, I might break the colleague-to-colleague relationship.

Strategic solution: Have the applicant return the enrollment form to me.

Because I am personally responsible for 17 of the 35 applications, I want to maintain tight control. To accomplish this, I've enclosed a stamped envelope addressed to me at my study at home. I'd appreciate your decision as quickly as possible.

Problem 7:   There is a need to speed up the response process and play upon the one-on-one relationship I've tried to establish.

Strategic solution: Use a postscript to give the prospect an opportunity to contact me directly and engage in a personal conversation.

P.S.: Let me give you my unlisted phone number. It is: 1-708-251-XXXX.

Once the problems had been faced and the strategies for dealing with them had been established, I proceeded to write the six-page proposal letter that is presented in Exhibit 15–14.

Exhibit 15–14. **Six-Page Proposal Letter**

BOB STONE

1630 SHERIDAN ROAD #8G • WILMETTE, ILLINOIS 60091

Dear Colleague:

If you accept this proposal it will cost your firm $4,500. Not an insignificant sum. And there's more. If you accept this proposal you or your designate will commit to a series of 14-hour days on a college campus.

So much for the agony: Now for the ecstasy!

If you accept this proposal you or your designate will be one of 35 nationwide who will be eligible to receive certification as a **PROFESSIONAL DIRECT MARKETER (PDM).** This certification will come from the University of Missouri-Kansas City -- the first university in the nation to establish a Direct Marketing Center.

The significance of being certified probably won't strike home at first. For the opportunity never existed till now. But, to put certification into perspective, it's comparable to an accountant studying for CPA certification. Or, an insurance executive going back to college to become a chartered life underwriter (CLU).

CPA, CLU, PDM. Each certification tells the world the possessor is at the top of a chosen profession.

But you might rightly point out, "I've been to college. That's behind me. And I am a professional." Right on all counts! That's precisely why I'm writing you.

Take college background. If your experience is anything like mine, your major was in marketing. And what did marketing texts teach us about direct marketing? Nothing. Oh, there may have been a page or two about "sales letter writing." Maybe.

Contrast our college background and that of some of your people with collegiate marketing curriculums today. Over 160 colleges and universities teaching one or more courses in direct marketing. Graduate programs at UMKC, Northwestern University, University of Cincinnati, and others. Hundreds are entering the direct marketing

Exhibit 15–14 (*Continued*).   **Six-Page Proposal Letter**

2

profession with foreknowledge we never had.

The first day on the job these "kids" sit down with an incredible body of knowledge.   Databases.   Market segmentation. Socio-economic influences. Positioning. Pricing models. Operations research. Life-time value. Theories   of   productivity.   Statistical   theory. Quantitative methods. Consumer behavior. --- And more.

All these students are computer smart.   Their PC's are to them what our slide rules were to us.

As one who has had the privilege of teaching Direct   Marketing   at   both   UMKC   and Northwestern   University,   I've   seen   the advantages of a combination of academic theory and practical skills. They're inseparable. I've learned, without doubt, that <u>degree of skills is in direct ratio to acquired knowledge.</u>

The bottom line is that after only a few years I'm maintaining   a   lively   correspondence   with   former students.   The letterheads upon which they write speak volumes.   **L. L. Bean, Hewlett-Packard, Spiegel, Allstate, Mayo Clinic, AT&T.** Their acquired knowledge has paid off. Big.

But what about the professionals? You. Me. Our brethren?

What are   our   avenues   of   continuing   education? Chances are, like me, you've attended one-day, two-day seminars.   You may even have enrolled in continuing education programs over several weeks. Most of these programs are excellent.

But the lasting impact might be compared to taking a cortisone shot to relieve a current problem as contrasted to a life-long infusion of healthy knowledge. The difference : night and day.

Now, for the first time, college education is available for the professional. End result: **certification**.

Actually there is strong precedent to recommend the UMKC Professional Direct Marketing Certification Program. It's in exactly the same mode as programs conducted at Harvard, Stanford and Northwestern's   Kellogg   School. America's major   corporations   send

(Continued)

Exhibit 15–14 (*Continued*).   **Six-Page Proposal Letter**

3

their brightest to the on-campus management programs of these distinguished universities.

What the Chief Executive Officers of these leading corporations have learned is that the brightest of people become even brighter and more productive when academic knowledge is melded with practical skills. As one educator put it to me - "An astronaut can have all the technical skills needed, but he can't fly to the moon if he doesn't have the knowledge of the physicist."

So it is with direct marketing. A copywriter, for example, can't become a true wordsmith unless he or she clearly understands consumer behavior. No way. The need for knowledge to implement experience is doubly important for the professional direct marketing manager.

The advantage of the professional: <u>Experience</u>

As bright as these college kids are today, we have an advantage that no <u>magna cum laude</u> can come close to matching - <u>experience.</u> That's why UMKC has developed a concentrated program that will lead to certification in three weeks of on-campus time with several week intervals between each of the three weeks. To catch up with professionals, college students would have to attend two classes a week for 15 consecutive weeks over several semesters!

Here are the specific dates for on-campus course work:

      Week One: **October 30 thru November 3, 1989 (Mon.-Fri.)**

      Week Two: **February 26 thru March 2, 1990 (Mon.-Fri.)**

      Week Three: **April 30 thru May 4, 1990 (Mon.-Fri.)**

Classes will begin each day at 8:00 a.m. and conclude at 10:00 p.m. (Remember, I warned you about those 14-hour days!) But the pros get a break on Fridays: classes conclude at 4:00 p.m.

Over the three one-week periods participants will be graded on three examinations. Plus -- they will be evaluated by their peers for excellence in team assignments. A minimum of 85 percent attendance is

Exhibit 15–14 (*Continued*).   **Six-Page Proposal Letter**

4

<u>mandatory.</u>

There are just two other requirements:

1)To be eligible you or your designate must have two or more years experience as a direct marketer and 2) the enrollee must have completed a degree at an accredited college or university. (Special consideration will be given to applicants not fulfilling the college degree requirement provided they have a minimum of seven years of work experience.) That's it.

A word about UMKC.

     University of Missouri-Kansas City School of Business - world renowned - is enshrined in a beautiful tree-lined campus in the cultural center of Kansas City, Missouri. The number of UMKC students and faculty who have moved on to become Fulbright scholars is legend.

     Classes in the Professional Certification in Direct Marketing program will be held in the magnificent new $8 million Henry W. Bloch School of Business and Public Administration. State-of-the-art in every way, including satellite communication.

     Knowing that the 35 students in residence will all be mature professionals, the administration of UMKC has made some important concessions.

- **Housing.** PDM students won't be subjected to bare-bones college dormitories. Instead they will be housed at the Residence Inn Kitchenette Apartments, just a few blocks off campus. (The group can have their own "beer busts" - if they're up to it!)

- **Breakfast** will be provided with housing. Casual lunches will be provided at the Henry Bloch School.

- **PDM** students will have full access to the famed UMKC library, housing what many believe to be the most complete library of direct marketing books, tapes, videocassettes in the world.

- **And** for exercise buffs, UMKC will provide a <u>free</u> membership in the new multi-million dollar Swinney Recreation Center. The center is just across from the Bloch School.

(*Continued*)

Exhibit 15–14 (*Continued*).   **Six-Page Proposal Letter**

5

About the Curriculum.

The curriculum will enhance all aspects of the direct marketing discipline. Strategy. System. Planning. Communication. Evaluation. There will be independent research, field study and team project development during the intervening time prior to Week Two and Week Three.

For a detailed outline of the on-campus curriculum, see separate sheet enclosed. It's all one could dream of - and more. I guarantee it.

About the faculty.

The UMKC faculty is the priceless ingredient that makes the Professional Direct Marketing certification program possible. The faculty is distinguished.

Among the faculty members who will instruct is **William B. Eddy**, Interim Dean of the business school. Then there's **Richard A. Hamilton**, Associate Professor of Direct Marketing, along with professors of finance, of quantitative analysis, of business operations, of organizational behavior, of operations management. A core of **49** professors in all. And most with a Ph.D. after their names.

This group will be reinforced by direct marketing professionals with extensive teaching experience. **Martin Baier**, for one, who pioneered the Direct Marketing Center at UMKC. And I will complete the faculty by teaching various aspects of direct marketing. (I'm thrilled to be asked.)

Why I am so excited.

Excited really isn't a strong enough word to describe how I feel about the Professional Direct Marketing Program. **Enthralled** comes closer. Enthralled that for the first time in our exciting history full-scale college education is available to professionals. Enthralled that for the first time in history certification (PDM) is available.

Because I believe so strongly in what this program will do for our profession, I made an unusual request of the UMKC administration. I asked if I could be personally responsible for **17** of the **35** students to be accepted nationwide. To my complete delight the response was, **"permission granted!"**

Exhibit 15–14 (*Continued*).   Six-Page Proposal Letter

6

The bottom line is - I want your firm to be one of the 17 accepted.

A challenge to you or your designate.

Because of your experience and stature you may choose to forego the college experience in deference to a designate of your choice. This would be the person in your organization who you single out to be capable of a quantum leap in knowledge and skills.

There is just one thing.   To be accepted, your designate must meet both the academic and experience requirements set forth.   And this person must be personally sponsored by you.

How to lock-up an enrollment.

$500 will lock-up an enrollment. (But as the S&L's put it - "Certain restrictions apply.")   After 35 applications are received, additional applications will be put on a waiting list. Unfortunately there will be no exceptions to the maximum class size of **35**.

Because I am personally responsible for **17** of the **35** applications, I want to maintain tight control. To accomplish this, I've enclosed a stamped envelope addressed to me at my study at home. I'd appreciate having your decision as quickly as possible.

I'll put your application through the moment I receive it.   For sure.   Sending the application in guarantees a once-in-a-lifetime experience that will pay off for decades to come!

Sincerely,

Bob Stone

Bob Stone

P.S. Let me give you my unlisted phone number. It is: **1-312-251-**xxxx . You can reserve by phone, if you wish.

Results This package—six-page letter, application form, and reply envelope—produced some remarkable results. Here are the details:

1. 3,500 packages were mailed to Direct Marketing Association members at a cost of $1 each.

2. Although originally the class was limited to 35 students, response was so strong that the class was expanded to 42 students.

3. Total revenue came to $168,000; promotion cost came to $3,500.

4. This package outpulled by 5 to 1 the traditional package, which consisted of a two-page letter, circular, application form, and reply envelope.

5. All but three of those who responded to this package called the unlisted number to make their reservation.

Choosing the Lead

Whatever formula or philosophy you adopt, the first task is to decide on the lead for the letter. Nothing is more important. Numerous tests have shown that one lead in a letter can pull substantially better than another. Let's look at six of the most common types of leads used in sales letters. To help you compare them, let's take a sample product and write six different leads for that product. The product we'll use is a businessman's self-improvement book, which includes biographical sketches of a dozen prominent business leaders.

1. *News.* If you have a product that is really news, you have the makings of an effective lead. There is nothing more effective than news. If you have a product or service that's been around a while, perhaps you can zero in on one aspect of it that's timely or newsworthy.

   Examples: Now you can discover the same success secrets that helped a dozen famous business leaders reach the top!

2. *How/what/why*: Any beginning newspaper reporter is taught that a good story should start out by answering the main questions that go through a reader's mind—who, what, when, where, why, and how. You can build an effective lead by promising to answer one of these questions and then immediately enlarging on it in your opening paragraphs.

   Examples: How successful people really get ahead; what it takes to survive in the executive jungle; or why some people always get singled out for promotions and salary increases.

3. *Numbered ways.* This is often an effective lead because it sets the stage for an organized selling story. If you use a specific number, it will attract curiosity and usually make the reader want to find out what they are.

   Examples: Seventeen little-known ways to improve your on-the-job performance—and one big way to make it pay off!

4. *Command.* If you can use a lead that will command with authority and without offense, you have taken a big step toward getting the reader to do what you want.

   Examples: Don't let the lack of education hold you back any longer!

5. *Narrative.* This is one of the most difficult types of leads to write, but it can prove to be one of the most effective. It capitalizes on people's interest in stories. To be effective, a narrative lead must lead into the sales story in a natural way and still hold the reader's interest. Ideally, the lead should also give the reader some clue to where the story is going or why he or she should be interested.

   Examples: When he started in the stock room at IBM, nobody ever thought Tom Watson would someday be president of this multibillion dollar corporation.

6. *Question.* If you start with the right type of question, you can immediately put your reader in the proper frame of mind for your message. But be sure the question is provocative. Make it a specific question, promising benefits—one that's sure to be answered in the affirmative.

   Examples: If I can show you a proven way to get a better job, without any obligation on your part—will you give me a few minutes of your time?

It is impossible to put too much emphasis on the importance of working on your leads. The lead is the first thing your reader sees. Usually he or she makes a decision to read or not read at this point. I always write out at least three or four different leads, then choose the one I think will do the best job of appealing to the reader's basic wants.

Make a Letter Look Inviting

Here's a final, very important tip from top professional writers. They try to make their letters look attractive, inviting, and easy to read. (See Exhibit 15–15). The pros keep paragraphs down to six or seven lines. They use subheads and indented paragraphs to break up long copy. They emphasize pertinent thoughts, knowing that many readers will scan indented paragraphs before they decide whether to read a letter clear through. They use underscoring, CAPITAL LETTERS, and a second ink color to make key words and sentences stand out. And they skillfully use leader dots and dashes to break up long sentences.

Scan the two versions of the AMA letter in Exhibit 15–15. Notice how much more inviting the second letter is compared to the original typewritten version. Same copy, but one letter encourages reading and the other doesn't.

Finally, I recommend that you type your letter, or, if you insist on having it typeset, have it set in typewriter type. To me, a letter should *look* like a letter, and "real" letters are done on typewriters.

Exhibit 15–15.   **Effective Letter Design**

This November, you're invited to take an exciting look at what computers can do for you...

...at the landmark course that will give you--as it's given thousands of executives--the confidence and know-how you need to:

* Clear up the mystery and confusion of data processing!
* Make your computer work harder for you!
* Tell your systems people what <u>you</u> want--instead of the other way around!
* Make computers your partner in management

Dear Executive:

If you're baffled by computers...baffaloed when systems people use words like "byte" and "nanosecond"...if you're tired of the data processing department telling <u>you</u> what can be done, because you don't know enough to give the orders...

...it's time you took the American Management Associations' course that's cured thousands of "computer phobia"...

FUNDAMENTALS OF DATA PROCESSING FOR THE NON-DATA PROCESSING EXECUTIVE

Not for programmers or DP professionals...this 3-day course is one of the few computer seminars just for you, the data processing <u>user</u>! One at which you'll take a fascinating look at what computers can do for you...and learn how to utilize them to become a more effective manager...

...And this November, you can attend any of 12 sessions in 10 major cities across the country--<u>including a city near you!</u>

Thousands of managers and executives have attended this landmark course and, without hesitation, many have called it "the best course they've ever taken." <u>Here's what just a few of the recent attendees had to say:</u>

"I got terrific ideas and concepts that I can implement and

(inside...)

American Management Associations · 135 West 50th Street · New York, N.Y. 10020 · (212) 586-8100

Notice how much more inviting the letter on page 401 is, even though the letters have identical copy.

Exhibit 15–15 (*Continued*).   **Effective Letter Design**

```
* * * * * * * * * * * * * * * * * * * * * * * * * * * * * * * * * * *
*                                                                   *
*         This November, you're invited to take an exciting look    *
*                at what computers can do for you...                *
*                                                                   *
*     ...at the landmark course that will give you--as it's given   *
*   thousands of executives--the confidence and know-how you need to:*
*                                                                   *
*      * Clear up the mystery and confusion of data processing!     *
*      * Make your computer work harder for you!                    *
*      * Tell your systems people what you want--instead of the     *
*        other way around!                                          *
*      * Make computers your partner in management                  *
*                                                                   *
* * * * * * * * * * * * * * * * * * * * * * * * * * * * * * * * * * *



Dear Executive:

    If you're baffled by computers...buffaloed when systems people
use words like "byte" and "nanosecond"...if you're tired of the data
processing department telling you what can be done, because you
don't know enough to give the orders...

...it's time you took the American Management Associations' course
that's cured thousands of "computer phobia"...

                 FUNDAMENTALS OF DATA PROCESSING
                 FOR THE NON-DATA PROCESSING EXECUTIVE

              Not for programmers or DP professionals...
              this 3-day course is one of the few computer
              seminars just for you, the data processing
              user! One at which you'll take a fascinating
              look at what computers can do for you...and
              learn how to utilize them to become a more
              effective manager...

              ...And this November, you can attend any of
              12 sessions in 10 major cities across the
              country--including a city near you!

    Thousands of managers and executives have attended this landmark
course and, without hesitation, many have called it "the best course
they've ever taken." Here's what just a few of the recent attendees
had to say:

      "I got terrific ideas and concepts that I can implement and

                                            (inside...)
```

American Management Associations · 135 West 50th Street · New York, N.Y. 10020 · (212)586-8100

Letter Length and the Postscript

"Do people read long copy?" The answer is "Yes!" People will read something for as long as it interests them. An uninteresting one-page letter can be too long. A skillfully woven four-pager can hold the reader until the end. Thus a letter should be long enough to cover the subject adequately and short enough to retain interest. Don't be afraid of long copy. If you have something to say and can say it well, it will probably do better than short copy. After all, the longer you hold a prospect's interest, the more sales points you can get across and the more likely you are to win an order.

Regardless of letter length, however, it usually pays to tack on a postscript. The P.S. is one of the most effective parts of any letter. Many prospects will glance through a letter. The eye will pick up an indented paragraph here, stop on an underlined statement there, and finally come to rest on the P.S. If you can express an important idea in the P.S., the reader may go back and read the whole letter. This makes the P.S. worthy of your best efforts. Use it to restate a key benefit. Or to offer an added inducement, like a free gift. Even when somebody has read the rest of the letter, the P.S. can make the difference between whether or not the prospect places an order. Use the P.S. to close on a strong note, to sign off with the strongest appeal you have.

The Value of Versioned Copy

Suppose, just suppose, that instead of sending exactly the same letter to all your prospects, you could create a number of versions for each major segment of your market. Then rather than talking about all the advantages and benefits of the product, you could simply zero in on those that fit each market segment. Sounds like a logical idea that should increase response, doesn't it?

Yet my own experience with versioned or segmented copy has been mixed. Sometimes I've seen this technique work very effectively; other times it's a bomb. So I suggest that you test it for yourself. If your product story should be substantially different for certain audience segments—and you can identify and select them on the lists you're using—develop special versions of your regular copy and give the technique a try.

One type of versioned copy that generally does pay off is special copy slanted to your *previous* buyers. Customers like to think a firm remembers them and will give them special treatment. In going back to your satisfied buyers, there's less need to resell your company. You can concentrate on the product or the service being offered.

How to Improve a Good Mailing Package

So far we've been talking about how to create a new mailing package. Let's suppose you've done that, and you want to make it better. Or you've got a successful mailing package you've been using for a couple of years (your

control) and you want to beat it. How do you go about it? One of the best ways I know is to come up with an entirely different appeal for your letter. For instance, suppose you're selling an income tax guide and your present letter is built around saving money. That's probably a tough appeal to beat. But to develop a new approach, you might write a letter around a negative appeal, something people want to avoid. Experience with many propositions has proved that a negative appeal is often stronger than a positive one. Yet it's frequently overlooked by copywriters. An appropriate negative copy appeal for our example might be something like, "How to avoid costly mistakes that can get you in trouble with the Internal Revenue Service." Or, "Are you taking advantage of these six commonly overlooked tax deductions?"

Another good technique is to change the type of lead on your letter. Review the examples of six common types of leads given earlier. If you're using a news lead, try one built around the narrative approach. Or develop a provocative question as the lead. Usually a new lead will require you to rewrite the first few paragraphs of copy to fit the lead, but then you can often pick up the balance of the letter from your control copy. A top creative man who has a well-organized approach for coming up with new ideas is Sol Blumenfeld, a veteran direct mail professional. Here are some of the approaches he uses:

The Additive Approach

This approach adds something to a control package that can increase its efficiency in such a way as to justify the extra cost involved. Usually, this entails using inserts. Inserts that can be used to heighten response include testimonial slips, extra discounts, a free gift for cash with order, and a news flash or bulletin. Other additive ideas include building stamps or tokens into the response device. And, if you have a logical reason to justify it, add an expiration date to your offer.

The Extractive Approach

This copy exercise requires a careful review of your existing mailing package copy. You often can find a potential winning lead buried somewhere in the body copy.

The Innovative Approach

Unlike the extractive approach, this approach is designed to produce completely new ideas. If you are testing three or four new copy approaches, at least one of them should represent a potential breakthrough, something that's highly original, perhaps even a little wild. I encourage writers to let themselves go, because we've seen them produce real breakthroughs this way—dramatic new formats, exciting copy approaches, and offers that have really shellacked the old control!

Some Final Tips

When you create your own direct mail, you might check it against the following list of pointers. Remember that these are *guidelines*, not rigid rules, and that when I say "X will usually outpull Y," that means every so often X will not outpull Y.

Mailing Format

- The letter ranks first in importance.

- The most effective mailing package consists of outside envelope, letter, circular, response form, and business reply envelope.

Letters

- Form letters using indented paragraphs usually outpull those in which paragraphs are not indented.

- Underlining important phrases and sentences usually increases results slightly.

- A separate letter with a separate circular generally does better than a combination letter and circular.

- A form letter with an effective running headline ordinarily does as well as a filled-in letter.

- Authentic testimonials in a sales letter ordinarily increase the pull.

- A two-page letter ordinarily outpulls a one-page letter.

Circulars

- A circular that deals specifically with the proposition presented in the letter is more effective than a circular of an institutional character.

- A combination of art and photography usually produces a better circular than one employing either art or photography alone.

- A circular usually proves to be ineffective in selling news magazines and news services.

- In selling big-ticket products, deluxe large-size, color circulars virtually always warrant the extra cost over circulars 11" × 17" or smaller.

Outside Envelopes

- Illustrated envelopes increase response if their message is tied into the offer.

- Variety in types and sizes of envelopes pays, especially in a series of mailings.

Reply Forms

- Reply cards with receipt stubs usually increase response over cards with no stub.
- "Busy" order or request forms that look important usually produce a larger response than neat, clean-looking forms.
- Postage-free business reply cards generally bring more responses than those to which the respondent must affix postage.

Reply Envelopes

- A reply envelope increases cash-with-order response.
- A reply envelope increases responses to collection letters.

Color

- Two-color letters usually outpull one-color letters.
- An order or reply form printed in colored ink or on colored stock usually outpulls one printed in black ink on white stock.
- A two-color circular generally proves to be more effective than a one-color circular.
- Full color is warranted in the promotion of such items as food products, apparel, furniture, and other merchandise if the quality of color reproduction is good.

Postage

- Third-class mail ordinarily pulls as well as first-class mail.
- Postage-metered envelopes usually pull better than affixing postage stamps (and you can meter third-class postage).
- A "designed" printed permit on the envelope usually does as well as postage metered mail.

Self-Quiz

1. What unique advantages permit direct mail to do a better selling job than any other advertising medium?

   a. _____

   b. _____

   c. _____

d. _____

e. _____

2. What are the three basic formats of direct mail?

a. _____

b. _____

c. _____

3. Complete the following true–false quiz:

a. Personalized letters will always outpull nonpersonalized ones. _____

b. A "publisher's letter" will usually boost response 10 percent or more. _____

c. A pop-up device is a sure-fire way to increase response. _____

d. Invitation formats are outmoded. _____

4. Complete this equation for making a sale:

Benefit *divided by* _____ *equals*

_____ .

5. What is the difference between a benefit and a selling point?

_____

_____

_____

_____

6. What are some of the basic wants inherent in most people?

a. _____   f. _____

b. _____   g. _____

c. _____   h. _____

d. _____   i. _____

e. _____   j. _____

7. What do most people want to avoid?

a. _____   d. _____

b. _____   e. _____

c. _____   f. _____

8. Name 11 guidelines for good direct mail copy.

   a. _____   g. _____

   b. _____   h. _____

   c. _____   i. _____

   d. _____   j. _____

   e. _____   k. _____

   f. _____

9. The key objective in preparing an order form is to make order forms

   look _____

   _____.

10. Name four typical involvement devices.

    a. _____

    b. _____

    c. _____

    d. _____

11. Name the six most common types of leads used in sales letters.

    a. _____   d. _____

    b. _____   e. _____

    c. _____   f. _____

12. List the points in the seven-step letter-writing formula in sequence:

    a. _____   e. _____

    b. _____   f. _____

    c. _____   g. _____

    d. _____

13. What are the two best applications of a postscript?

    a. To restate _____

    b. To offer an added _____

14. Define each of these approaches for improving a good mailing package:

a. The additive approach _____

_____

_____.

b. The extractive approach _____

_____

_____.

c. The innovative approach _____

_____

_____.

15. Complete this formula! Problems ÷ Strategies = _____.

Pilot Project

You are the advertising manager of a major national chain store group (e.g., Sears, Wards, J.C. Penney, etc.) Your company wants to get more of its credit cards in the hands of qualified persons. Your assignment is to prepare a direct mail package to "sell" your store's credit card. Use these assumptions:

- The credit card is free; there is no yearly charge or fee for it.

- It is honored in your company's stores from coast to coast for anything sold in those stores.

- In addition to your company's own credit card, your company's stores also accept the two bank credit cards (Visa and MasterCard).

The objective of your direct mail package is to get creditworthy persons to fill out an application for the card. They will be credit-checked, and a certain number of persons will be turned down. Another obvious objective is that, when a person has applied and been approved for the card, you want him or her to *use* it.

Here are some steps to guide you through the decisions you will have to make:

1. Write a creative strategy. Pay particular attention to *competitve products, market,* and *creative implementation*.

2. Which format would you select: classic or self-mailer. Why?

3. Here are some selling points (or product features) of the card. Below each one, list the *customer benefit* made possible by that selling point.

(To get you started, the first one is filled in.) Note: More than one benefit can usually be derived from a single selling point.

a. Lets you charge purchases.
   You don't need to carry cash. _____

b. Card is good nationwide.

   _____

c. Card is good for anything sold at our stores.

   _____

4. What is the "big idea" behind your mailing package? How will you implement this theme in the letter? Circular? Outer envelope? Order form (application)?

5. Are you going to use any additional pieces, such as free-gift slips or a publisher's letter?

6. Write your sales letter. Pay particular attention to the seven-step formula.

7. How could you use versioned copy in your letter?

CHAPTER SIXTEEN

Techniques of Creating and Managing Catalogs

America's longest-standing love affair may well be with the catalog. The reasons for catalog shopping have changed drastically over the past century, but the love affair goes on unabated.

Back in the late 1880s and for decades thereafter, the foremost reason for catalog shopping was to find items not readily available in areas in which millions of Americans lived. But in the World War II period, when shopping centers sprang up even in small towns, two major reasons for catalog shopping emerged: (1) to save time and (2) to find unusual and exclusive items not generally available in retail channels. Business-to-business cataloging also emerged as companies sought new distribution channels and less expensive ways to reach and sell business firms.

The catalogs that succeed today, both customer and business-to-business, rely upon feasibility studies, business planning, niche marketing, customer tracking, product analysis, and all of the other sophisticated tools available to direct marketers in general.

With this sophistication has come a body of catalog specialists who serve mature catalog operations as well as catalog start-ups. The right catalog specialists are worth their weight in gold.

One of the catalog specialists with an outstanding track record is Jack Schmid of Shawnee Mission, Kansas, who heads his own firm, J. Schmid & Associates Inc. He has served such consumer and business-to-business clients as Publishers Clearing House, Hewlett-Packard, Anheuser-Busch, Sara Lee, and Hallmark Cards. We are indebted to Mr. Schmid for the content of this chapter.

The History of Catalogs: 1860–Present

The beginning of cataloging in the United States can be tracked to seed and nursery catalogs published in England by a gardener, William Lucas, with mail-order interest spreading to the colonies in the late 1660s.

The 1770s saw the publishing of a fruit tree catalog by William Prince of Flushing, New York. Both George Washington and Thomas Jefferson were his customers. Around the same time in Philadelphia, Franklin's publishing company produced a catalog of nearly 600 items. As early as 1830 Orvis began selling sporting goods and fishing gear by mail in New England.

Modern cataloging can be credited to Aaron Montgomery Ward, a Midwestern traveling salesman. In the late 1860s he published a catalog sheet for farm families listing 163 items. The catalog grew to 8 pages, then to 72 pages, and by 1884 it had 240 pages presenting over 10,000 items. The catalog carried every conceivable item for farm families, as is illustrated by the following letter that the Montgomery Ward Chicago office reportedly received from a Minnesota woman:

> Do you still sell embalming fluid? I saw it in your old catalog, but not your new one. If you do, send me enough for my husband who is five feet eleven and weighs 160 pounds when in good health. Henry has been laying around the house looking mighty peaked lately and I expect him to kick off any time now. He'd like to have gone last night. When you send the stuff, please send instructions with it. And please rush.

Sears, Roebuck and Company followed Montgomery Ward in the catalog business in 1893, and the two "big books" became an encyclopedia of American family history. Spiegel was founded in 1905, and L.L. Bean started its catalog in 1912.

Cataloging had its foothold in the United States. Although mail order was catching on in the 1950s, it wasn't until the late 1960s and early 1970s that upscale specialty mail-order catalogs such as Horchow, Tiffany, and Talbot's appeared. Other catalogs quickly followed. Today there are thousands of catalogs offering everything from polo shirts to polo mallets.

Key Catalog Trends and Issues

From the early 1980s on, catalog mailings grew dramatically. Table 16–1 and Exhibit 16–1 show how dramatic mail-order growth has been. Sales nearly tripled—and catalogs have been a prime contributor to this growth.

Table 16–1. Sales via Mail (Billions of Dollars)

	Customer	Business to Business	Charitable Contributions
1991	$64.9 products 43.0 services	$54.1	$49.0
1990	57.5 products 40.7 services	53.5	49.0
1989	54.0 products 33.0 services	50.4	45.9
1988	48.0 products 29.0 services	45.6	41.8
1987	43.4	43.6	37.6
1986	29.4	37.6	33.6
1985	27.0	32.4	31.4
1984	24.8	27.5	30.0
1983	22.5	23.1	25.8
1982	41.5	24.4	24.4
1981	31.0	19.5	21.6

Source: Direct Marketing Association, New York, NY.

Trends of the 1990s

One might expect the catalog business to be dominated by huge companies each annually mailing millions of catalogs. But that is not the case. Catalog Age's 1992 annual survey confirms that smaller-sized companies tend to be the norm. (see Exhibit 16–2.)

- 43 percent reported annual sales under $1 million.

- 62 percent reported annual sales under $3 million.

- 84 percent reported annual sales under $10 million.

Another surprise is that the majority of catalog distributors (65 percent) indicate that they each mail fewer than 500,000 catalogs each year. These statistics demonstrate the entrepreneurial nature of cataloging and indicate that its roots have come from small, innovative, niche-driven companies and individuals.

What factors have contributed to the dramatic growth in direct marketing and, in particular, in catalog mailings and sales?

1. A major increase in the number of working women, resulting in a lack of time for women to shop as well as an increase in two-income families with more discretionary income to spend

2. Improved quality of merchandise

3. Improved creative presentation of merchandise

4. Consumers turning away from retail shopping

5. Increased use of credit cards for everyday shopping

6. Increased use of the telephone and fax in the ordering process

Exhibit 16–1.   **Estimated Number of Catalogs Mailed (Billions)**

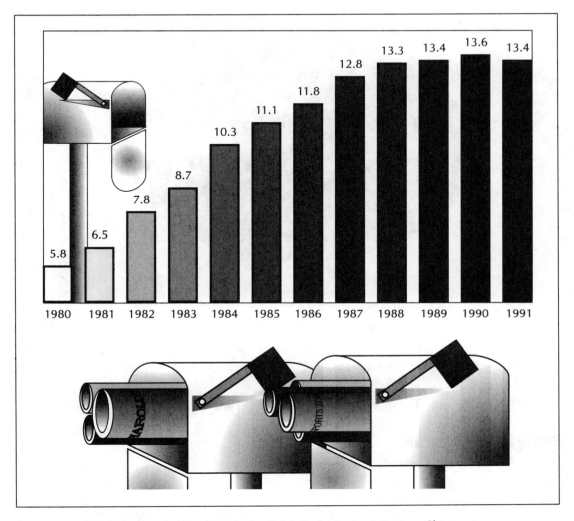

Source: Arnold L. Fishman, *Guide to Mail Order Sales*, Marketing Logistics Inc., Chicago.

7. Increased targeting/specialization of products and markets

8. Improved fulfillment and customer service

9. Better color separations, printing, and paper

10. The computer and its steadily decreasing costs of storing and retrieving information

11. Development of sophisticated customer databases

12. Scarcity of quality salespeople, both retail and business

Exhibit 16–2.   **Small-Firm Sales Figures: 1992**

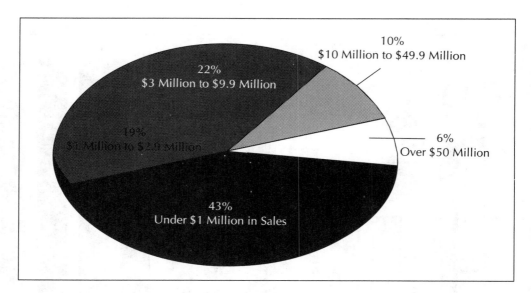

13. High cost of making a sales call

14. Diminished return of cold sales calls

15. New catalog formats such as tabloid size on newsprint, square, oversized, "slim-jim" (under 6-⅛" × 11-½"), unbound multiproduct promotions in an envelope, and the like

16. The demand for measurable and accountable advertising

Issues of the Future

Presented below are a number of issues that will affect cataloging into the next century.

1. *Maturity of the catalog business.* All the signs point to cataloging having reached a level of maturity, at least on the consumer side. The market is not growing at nearly the dramatic rate it did in the past. For years direct marketers have talked about "catalog glut." At the same time only half of the households in the United States regularly use mail-order buying. Business-to-business cataloging, however, remains on a strong growth curve for the future. This is due, in large part, to business catalogs usually being a new marketing channel.

2. *Greater competition.* It's a fact: Consumer, business, and retail catalogs are facing more competition from other mailers. This underscores the importance of *differentiating* one catalog's products and positioning from those of other catalogs.

3. *Niche-driven catalogs.* Greater specialization and narrower niches will be a hallmark of catalogs in the next decade. Much like the magazine industry, which evolved from general to highly targeted editorial content, specialized catalogs are not part of the future—they are here today.

4. *Fewer start-ups.* It is increasingly difficult to launch a new catalog that quickly generates a profit. Unless companies are prepared to look at new start-ups as long-range investments (and have the capital to support them), many new catalogs will die in the planning stages.

5. *Stronger customer service and fulfillment.* It is no longer acceptable to *think about* improving customer service in the future. The industry standard is being set by catalog leaders like Land's End and Reliable, which have superb telephone operations, on-line customer databases and inventory information, and 24-hour turnaround in shipping. These companies have set a standard that customers now expect. If a catalog doesn't meet this standard, it will have a more difficult time staying in business.

6. *New technology.* Catalogers are developing new ways to design, print, and mail catalogs that reduce production costs. Desktop publishing using the Macintosh, Scitex-type color separations, selective binding, personalized ink-jetting of special messages, improved papers (i.e., recycled and recyclable), and improved printing are only a few. It's now possible to reduce creative and prepress costs and ultimately the cost in the mail.

7. *The global village.* One can no longer think about cataloging as just an American phenomenon. U.S. mailers such as L.L. Bean and Sharper Image are mailing into Japan. Canadian markets are being tested by scores of U.S. catalogers, and Canadian catalogers are turning an eye to the United States. International ownership of U.S.-based catalogs is a fact; America's largest cataloger, Spiegel, for example, is owned by Otto Versand of Germany. Japan's interest and investment in catalogs is growing.

8. *Consolidation.* Another development that started in the 1980s and has continued into the 1990s is the consolidation of catalog efforts. Companies like Hanover with over 17 catalogs, CML Group, Spiegel, Arizona Mail Order, Williams Sonoma, Sara Lee, Campbell Soup, and Primerica are all owners of multiple catalogs. They have either acquired existing catalogs or started new ones that complemented their other product offerings and offered seasonal, financial, or recessionary stability.

9. *Greater use of catalogs by nontraditional marketers.* Traditionally, catalogs are thought of as direct-to-the-consumer. But business-to-business cataloging has become very strong in the past two decades. An interesting trend of the 1990s is the use of catalogs by fund raisers, professional

associations, publishers, seminar companies, financial service companies, and even travel companies. Any business that has multiple products or services to sell can do so through cataloging.

10. *Concern for the environment.* There are no direct marketers more visible in the environmental arena than catalogers. With coated paper that is difficult to recycle, packing materials like styrofoam peanuts, and general consumer concern about overuse of paper, catalogers are the target of environmentalists across the country. Smart catalogers are responding to environmental concerns. Many catalog marketers are using biodegradable materials for packaging. Even though it is more expensive, some catalogs are being printed on recycled paper. Some are even using soy-based ink. A new catalog, Seventh Generation, offers only products that are safe for the environment.

11. *Postage and UPS increases.* Today the largest single expense of any catalog mailing is postage. Paper and printing used to be the greatest costs, but rapidly rising postage has become a major concern for catalogers. As a result, alternative delivery that bypasses the postal system has become a hot issue. UPS, which has built a near-monopoly in package delivery, has substantially increased its cost of residential delivery, much to the chagrin of consumer catalogers.

12. *Sales/use taxes.* An issue on which catalog companies are in the forefront is the collection of sales or use taxes. The Supreme Court ruling on National Belles Hess (1967) established "nexus," or physical presence in a state, as the criterion for determining whether a company is required to collect and remit sales taxes to a state. The Quill vs. North Dakota (1992) ruling throws the ball back to Congress, stating that this is an interstate commerce issue. Because so many states are financially strapped and eager to find sources of new revenue, it is unlikely that this issue will go away.

13. *Privacy.* Although privacy may be more of a list or database issue, its concerns will dramatically affect catalogers because of the prevalence of multiple mailings. Consumers object to having corporations know too much about them. Catalogers, on the other hand, want to have every possible piece of information to help them better target their mailings. These two objectives are clearly conflicting.

The Catalog Process and Strategies

The balance of this chapter is devoted to the catalog process and the strategies used to build and manage a winning catalog company. We will consider the key ingredients of catalog success and the strategies smart catalogers are applying in (1) merchandising, (2) positioning of the catalog, (3) building and using the customer database, (4) creative execution, (5) catalog fulfillment, and (6) analysis of results.

Exhibit 16–3.   **The Catalog Process**

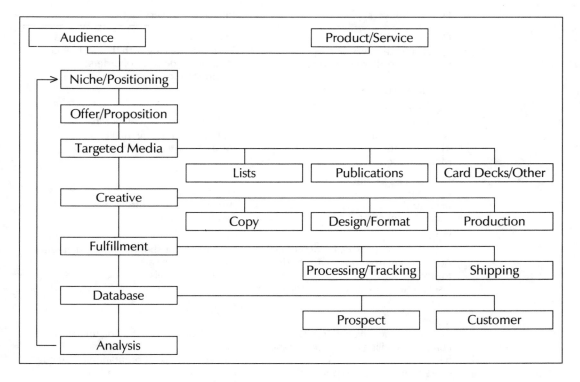

The catalog process chart shown in Exhibit 16–3 identifies the components of a winning catalog. Refer to this chart as you read the rest of this chapter.

Merchandising

Catalogs are a blend of merchandise and audience. The majority of catalogs are "merchandise-driven," that is, they start from a merchandise point of view and address the purchaser of the product. Many of the pioneers in cataloging were first and foremost merchandisers who had a product idea. People like Roger Horchow of the Horchow Collection, Chuck Williams of Williams Sonoma, Manny Fingerhut and Meyer Nemer of Fingerhut, and many others started with a solid product concept and from that concept built a growing business.

Even if a catalog is market- or audience-driven, (that is, if it starts with an audience and then determines what products can be sold), merchandising is of vital importance. The familiar adage "Nothing comes before the product," simply stated, means that if catalogers desire to build repeat buyers—a prime goal for profitability—then they must start with and build a strong merchandising program that will continue to attract customers over time.

Table 16–2. Psychology of the Catalog Buyer

Frequent Buyers	Infrequent Buyers
Convenience	
Quick and easy way to shop	Hassles in dealing with the post office
Comfortable alternative to retail shopping	Waiting for delivery of orders
Way to avoid holiday crowds	Returning merchandise
Merchandise	
Unusual merchandise	Inability to see or feel merchandise
New products and style	Difficulty in judging quality
Ideas for gifts	Problems with fit, color, etc.
Merchandise that fits	
Consumer's Outlook	
Confident	Skeptical
In control	Afraid of losing control
Excited, expectant	Fearful of "rip-offs"
Value	
Lower prices on special promotions	Preference for shopping around at retail
Added value from not having to drive to store	More sales at retail
Use of multiple catalogs to comparison shop	Control over bills
Brand	
Expertise in dealing with direct mail companies selling uncommon brand names	Lack of expertise in buying unknown brands
Trust in direct mail companies	Uncertainty about reputation of catalog companies
Catalog is the brand name	
Need	
Patience in waiting for a number of products	Immediate gratification at time of purchase
Orders placed well in advance of special need	Frustration with waiting for delivery
Overnight delivery option	

Understanding the psychology of the catalog buyer is essential to catalog merchandising (see Table 16–2). If the goal of a catalog is to build repeat buyers, then understanding who those customers are and *why* they come back is of paramount importance. Table 16–2 also differentiates between frequent mail-order buyers and "touch-and-feel shoppers" who prefer to shop in retail stores and who distrust catalog shopping.

Know Thy Customer Know thy customer is the first rule of catalog merchandising. A catalog product buyer understands why and how people use the catalog. A classic mistake made by those who select products for catalogs is putting their own tastes and preferences first and paying little heed to what they know about the ultimate consumers.

How do you get to know your customers? Listed below are a number of techniques used by successful catalogs:

- A demographic survey that rides along in the box shipment to first-time customers.

- Annual demographic surveys to repeat buyers seeking information on who the customers are and what additional products they might like to see in the catalog.

- Phone contact with customers through telemarketing representatives or a phone survey.

- Regular dialog (i.e., taking phone calls or orders) between key people in the company and customers regarding how various aspects of the catalog might be improved.

- Customer focus groups

- Customer advisory boards

The key is to listen to what customers are saying in research surveys and phone conversations.

Build on Your Winners   Issuers of successful catalogs watch what their customers buy and listen to what they say. The worst catalog from a merchandise sales standpoint is the first catalog. With each succeeding mailing, a catalog should build on the merchandise categories and the price points that the customer is buying. Analysis of catalog sales results is essential, especially in the merchandise area.

A favorite example of a company that has listened to its customers is Land's End (Exhibit 16–4). This successful cataloger started in the retail business selling sailing gear. Over several decades it listened and watched as its customers bought more and more soft-sided luggage, sportswear, and nonsailing items. Its merchandise mix evolved into today's men's, women's, and children's clothing, soft goods, and luggage. Could it have experienced outstanding growth to a $600 million public company had it not listened to its customers and built on its winning merchandise?

Other Merchandise Strategies   What other merchandise strategies are smart catalogers using? Listed below are several that have proved to be successful:

1. *Improve product quality while reducing cost.* Customers are concerned about the value of products they buy through a catalog. Value is a price/ quality relationship. Smart catalogers constantly try to improve product quality while improving their margins. Whether through importing,

Exhibit 16–4.   **Land's End Catalog Cover**

buying in larger quantities as the catalog grows, or improving vendor relationships, a catalog's challenge is to buy better and at the same time give the customers more for their money. Surely that will keep them coming back.

2. *Strengthen new-product development efforts.* During recessionary times it is common for companies to cut back or discontinue new-product development. New-product development, however, is the life blood of the catalog. Winning catalogers keep it at the forefront of their minds and budgets at all times.

3. *Strengthen inventory control systems.* A merchandising area that has been a major pitfall for many catalogers is inventory control. One of the major differences between retailing and cataloging is exemplified by the statement: "Retailers sell what they buy, and catalogers buy what they sell." A retailer buys merchandise for an entire season. If a woman comes into a shop to buy an advertised dress and finds her size is unavailable, the shop owner will try to sell her another dress in her size. He is "selling what he bought." A catalog, however, normally will commit for only 40–50 percent of its anticipated needs for a season. Then it will read the selling results early in the season and reorder (they are "buying what they are selling").

It is vital for catalogs to have reliable vendors who can back them up in merchandise and turn around reorders quickly. It is also crucial to have a buying and rebuying staff as well as computer systems that can help forecast product needs down to the last stock-keeping unit (SKU).

Imagine the task of controlling inventory for the women's shoes shown on the catalog page from Bloomingdale's catalog that appears in Exhibit 16–5. One style, the Amalfi pump, comes in 9 colors, 17 shoe lengths, and 5 widths. Guess how many SKUs are involved here? Over 500! And look again—it comes in 3 different heels!

The final aspect of catalog inventory control is disposing of leftover merchandise at the end of a season. There are a number of options:

- Repeating the item in a future catalog
- Special sale pages
- Package inserts of remainder products
- An outlet store
- An annual warehouse sale for local people
- A special sale at the state fair or other event where thousands of people are present
- Telephone specials during the life of the catalog
- Remainder merchants

Exhibit 16–5.   SKUs and Cataloging

BE URBAN AND WISE, YOU CAN'T GO WRONG IF YOU

S H O E S		T O			F I T										
	4	4½	5	5½	6	6½	7	7½	8	8½	9	9½	10	10½	11	11½	12
AAAA					•	•	•	•	•	•	•	•	•	•	•	•
AAA				•	•	•	•	•	•	•	•	•	•	•	•	•
AA			•	•	•	•	•	•	•	•	•	•	•	•
B	•	•	•	•	•	•	•	•	•	•	•	•
C	•	•	•	•	•	•	•	•	•	•

A

A subtle shade of green suggests a softer side to the business suit. The longer length cardigan jacket is embroidered and has a tie back. With snap-in ivory dickie, self covered button. Gored slip skirt has elastic waist. Made in USA for Kwai in olive rayon/acetate for 2 to 16, #57460JH orig. 135.00 **109.98**

B-D

The Amalfi pump, renowned for superior craftsmanship. Great fit in Italian calf leather with leather sole, in every color and every size you'll ever need. In beaver brown(21), black patent(08), old gold(75), black suede(01), taupe(26), red(60), navy(41), bone(11) or black(09). Also in white(10). Monica is also available in black satin(88).
  B. Celeste has a 1″ heel, #46393JH **112.00**
  C. Susan has a 1½″ heel, #46392JH **112.00**
  D. Monica has a 2″ heel, #46389JH **112.00**

order toll-free
800 777 0000
24 ☎ hours

Most successful catalogs have fine-tuned their remainder systems so that they minimize the markdown expense that haunts retail stores.

Positioning the Catalog

As catalog firms strive to set themselves apart from the competition, most seek to define a niche, or a unique positioning, for their catalog. A *niche* is both a unique identity and a special place in the market where there is a void that is not being met by the competition. A catalog can be unique, or set apart from its competition, by its merchandise, creative style or format, offers, and customer service.

Defining the Catalog's Niche
What does a cataloger need to think about before beginning creative execution? Often catalogers, particularly first-time catalogers, jump right into the creative process without first thinking through some very basic issues. Here's a checklist of some key questions that must be answered:

1. Who is the company and the catalog? What products or services does it sell?

2. To whom does it sell? Who are its primary customers, secondary customers, and even tertiary customers?

3. How is the catalog unique? What sets it apart from its competitors? Its products? Its service? Its offers? Its pricing?

4. Who is the competition? What is their niche? What are their strengths? Weaknesses? Do they have a serious void or weakness that can be exploited?

One of the finest ways to articulate the catalog's niche is through a mission statement (see Exhibit 16–6) or a brand identification statement. Presented below are several examples of strong positioning statements.

Brand Identity Statement: Halls Catalog

I am the Halls Catalog. I am feminine and assertive. I'll never tell my age, but you'd guess me to be 25 to 39 (never 40!) years old. I'm contemporary, yet down to earth. I love beautiful, even clever, things around me. Often, I'm quite expensive, but well worth it because my goal in life is to be the single source of only the most special items demanded by those with impeccable taste. Sometimes I'm eccentric, often I'm practical—but always I plan on being the spectacular leader of all my compatriots. I exist because my parents, Hallmark Cards, and Halls retail stores mated with express intent of creating a

Exhibit 16–6.   **Mission Statement**

WE CONSTANTLY STRIVE TO MEET OR BEAT YOUR HIGHEST EXPECTATIONS.

We don't think it's good enough to just sell great items at great prices...we also want to provide an extremely convenient, satisfying buying experience.

Every office product discounter likes to blow their horn about how great their prices are... us included. And when we tell you we have deeply discounted Everyday Low Prices on all 9000 items (not just 150 or so), we really mean it! But what makes Quill truly unique is that you benefit from all the EXTRA customer services provided to you. We've set up the next 4 pages in an easy-to-read, easy-to-understand format that'll describe all the extra benefits Quill offers...real bonuses to you!

We hold these truths to be self-evident...

Our Quill Customers' Bill of Rights states our basic beliefs on how we should run our company. We have followed them from the first day we began doing business 34 years ago.

We first published this Quill Customers' Bill of Rights in the Spring 1970 Catalog, when we had just 32 employees.

Since then, we've published it many times. Now, as we've grown to more than 1100 employees, we wish to restate it for this November '90 through April '91 catalog.

We're certain that following these beliefs has helped us grow to the size we are today.

At this time, we rededicate ourselves to continue following these concepts ...to make Quill the best supplier you have ever had. We take pride in being craftsmen in the craft of running a fine company.

THE QUILL CUSTOMERS'
BILL OF RIGHTS

Restated and approved at Lincolnshire, Illinois, on Thursday the First of November, One Thousand Nine Hundred and Ninety.

The undersigned officers and the more than 1100 employees of Quill Corporation express a desire to clearly state the principles and ideals which guide all of us at Quill in our relationship with our customers.

We feel this unusual step is necessary at this time because we find ourselves, when we are customers...both as individuals and as a company...frequently dissatisfied with the way we are treated. Lack of interest, discourteousness, bad service, late deliveries and just plain bad manners are too common. We can't tell others how to run their businesses (except by not buying from them.) But we can and will run Quill as we feel a business should be run. Therefore, the following is a list of what we consider to be the inalienable rights of our customers. *We expect to be held to account whenever we deny any of these rights to any customer:*

1. As a customer, you are entitled to be treated like a real, individual, feeling human being...with friendliness, honesty and respect.
2. As a customer, you are entitled to full value for your money. When you buy a product, you should feel assured that it was a good buy and that the product is exactly as it was represented to be.
3. As a customer, you are entitled to a *complete* guarantee of satisfaction. This is especially true when you buy the product sight unseen through the mail or over the phone.
4. As a customer, you are entitled to fast delivery. Unless otherwise indicated, the product should be shipped within 24 hours. In the event of a delay, you are entitled to immediate notification, along with an honest estimate of the expected shipping date.
5. As a customer, you are entitled to speedy, courteous, knowledgeable answers on inquiries. You are entitled to all the help we can give in finding exactly the product or information you need.
6. As a customer, you are entitled to the privilege of being an individual and dealing with individuals. If there is a question on your account, you are entitled to talk with or correspond with another individual so the question can be resolved immediately on the most mutually satisfactory basis possible.
7. **AS A CUSTOMER, YOU ARE ENTITLED TO BE TREATED EXACTLY AS WE WANT TO BE TREATED WHEN WE ARE SOMEONE ELSE'S CUSTOMER.**

COPYRIGHT 1970, QUILL CORPORATION

Jack Miller
President

Harvey L. Miller
Secretary

Arnold Miller
Treasurer

(347)

superior individual. And, in that tradition, each Halls Catalog will be better than the last.

Mission Statement: Land's End Direct Merchants—Principles of Doing Business

Principle 1: We do everything we can to make our products better. We improve material, and add back features and construction details that others have taken out over the year. We never reduce the quality of a product to make it cheaper.

Principle 2: We price our products fairly and honestly. We do not, have not, and will not participate in the common retailing practice of inflating mark-ups to set up a phony "sale."

Principle 3: We accept any return for any reason, at any time. Our products are guaranteed. No fine print. No arguments. We mean exactly what we say: GUARANTEED. PERIOD.

Principle 4: We ship faster than anyone we know of. We ship items in stock the day after we receive the order. At the height of the last Christmas season the longest time an order was in the house was 36 hours, excepting monograms, which took another 12 hours.

Principle 5: We believe that what is the best for our customer is best for all of us. Everyone here understands that concept. Our sales and service people are trained to know our products, and to be friendly and helpful. They are urged to take all the time necessary to take care of you. We even pay for your call, for whatever reason you call.

Principle 6: We are able to sell at lower prices because we have eliminated middlemen; because we don't buy branded merchandise with high protected markups; and because we have placed our contracts with manufacturers who have proved that they are cost conscious and efficient.

Principle 7: We are able to sell at lower prices because we operate efficiently. Our people are hard working, intelligent, and share in the success of the company.

Principle 8: We are able to sell at lower prices because we support no fancy emporiums with their high overhead. Our main location is in the middle of a 40-acre cornfield in rural Wisconsin. We still operate our first location in Chicago's Near North tannery district.

Each of these positioning statements is as different as the catalog it was developed for. The key thing is to go through the process of defining the catalog's positioning or niche.

Differentiating the Catalog from the Competition   There are innumerable ways to set a catalog apart. Five variables to consider are given below:

1. *Merchandise*. This is a vital area in which to be different. Perhaps it is acceptable to be No. 2 in the auto rental area, as Avis has shown, but to be No. 2 in a catalog niche and not have a defined difference in product can be financially disastrous.

2. *Pricing or use of credit*. A pricing method can help set a catalog apart. Current Inc.'s catalog is an excellent example. It uses a three-part pricing strategy that basically says to the customer: "The more items you buy, the better the price." Discounters like Damark or Viking are also good at using pricing to help build a unique identity. Fingerhut sells only on credit (its own) and establishes a niche in doing so.

3. *Catalog format and creative presentation*. Besides merchandising, the catalog's creative format, design, and copy can make a tremendous difference in establishing its niche. Examples are catalogs like Patagonia with its unique in-use photography (all supplied by readers and customers); J. Peterman with its unique catalog size, copy, and use of illustrative art; and L.L. Bean with its square shape, cover art, and catalog layout.

4. *Offer*. An offer, or proposition, is what the cataloger is willing to give to customers in return for their response. What catalog has a unique offer that sets it apart? Haverhills consistently offers a special in its catalog: "Buy two items and get a third free." Spiegel offers free UPS pickup on any return. Reliable offers free delivery on any size order.

5. *Customer service/fulfillment*. Here is an ideal way to set a catalog apart: Service so good that it is the envy of every competitor. It starts with the phone people and a database system that allows real-time access to customers' records while they are on the phone. Next is on-line inventory so that customers know before hanging up whether the size and color of the item is in stock and can make a decision about alternatives. Then it's the delivery time of the product. Finally comes the handling of returns and inquiries. Without doubt, customer service can set a catalog apart.

Building and Using the Catalog Customer List

The catalog process chart in Exhibit 16–3 identifies the next series of tasks in building a successful catalog business—targeting media. It is critical for a catalog to build a buyer list—a group of people or companies that will keep coming back and back again to order from it.

To better understand how important this job of building the customer list is, look at Exhibit 16–7.

When a new catalog starts, it has no buyers, and probably it has no affinity names. *Affinity names* are names of potential buyers who have some

Exhibit 16–7.   **Catalog Profitability**

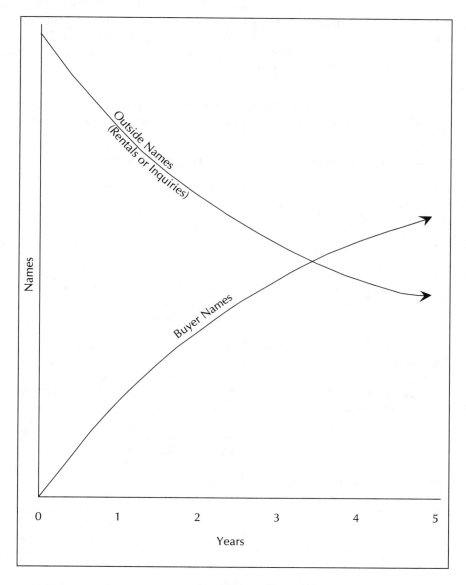

relationship to your company or catalog. For example, Hershey Foods Inc. has well over a million people visit Hershey Chocolate World every year. Some sign up to receive a catalog during the holiday season. Although these are not proven catalog buyers, they represent a list of prospects with whom the company has had some relationship. There is a good chance that a catalog will be received, read, and maybe, if it has the right items, there will be orders.

If a company has no affinity names, then it must rely on building its customer list from list rentals, space ads, and various other media that can be targeted to its audience. It is not unusual for the buyer list to outperform an outside list or nonaffinity names many times over. This is why it usually takes a new catalog three years to break even and about five years to recapture its initial investment.

Front-end/Back-end Marketing A concept well understood by veteran catalogers is front-end and back-end marketing (see Exhibit 16–8).

Exhibit 16–8.   **Front-end/Back-end Concept of Marketing**

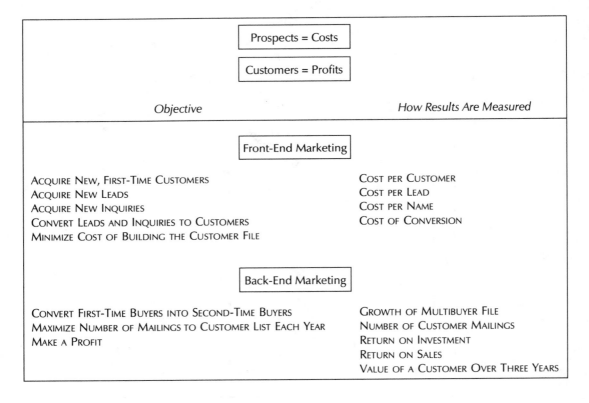

| Prospects = Costs |
| Customers = Profits |

| *Objective* | *How Results Are Measured* |

Front-End Marketing

ACQUIRE NEW, FIRST-TIME CUSTOMERS	COST PER CUSTOMER
ACQUIRE NEW LEADS	COST PER LEAD
ACQUIRE NEW INQUIRIES	COST PER NAME
CONVERT LEADS AND INQUIRIES TO CUSTOMERS	COST OF CONVERSION
MINIMIZE COST OF BUILDING THE CUSTOMER FILE	

Back-End Marketing

CONVERT FIRST-TIME BUYERS INTO SECOND-TIME BUYERS	GROWTH OF MULTIBUYER FILE
MAXIMIZE NUMBER OF MAILINGS TO CUSTOMER LIST EACH YEAR	NUMBER OF CUSTOMER MAILINGS
MAKE A PROFIT	RETURN ON INVESTMENT
	RETURN ON SALES
	VALUE OF A CUSTOMER OVER THREE YEARS

Front-end marketing refers to prospecting or new-customer acquisition. Few catalogers make money on prospecting; it is a cost-related activity. The objectives of front-end marketing are:

- To acquire new first-time customers, or to acquire leads and inquiries that can be converted into first-time buyers
- To acquire the most names at the least cost

Smart catalogers measure precisely what it costs to acquire a new, first-time buyer and are tenacious about tracking where the name came from.

Back-end marketing refers to working the customer list. This is where the profitability for a catalog must come from. The objectives of back-end marketing are:

- To convert first-time buyers into second-time buyers

- To maximize the number of profitable mailings to this list each year

- To determine where the best long-term customers come from so that the catalog can change or modify its front-end media

A winning catalog carefully observes the month-to-month growth of its buyer file, watching especially for buyers who have purchased more than twice.

Large catalogers often divide the marketing functions by front end and back end. The small cataloger must understand and play both roles within the company.

The Hierarchy of a Customer   More than any other type of direct marketer, the cataloger has to understand the hierarchy of a customer (see Exhibit 16–9). Since the primary goal of a catalog is to get repeat orders from its customer list, a successful catalog must build trust, credibility, and confidence. In this process there are three distinct hurdles to be surmounted. The first is converting prospects to first-time buyers. Perhaps these first-time buyers can be called "triers." They are cautious, have a low response rate, have a lower average order size, and expect the catalog to prove itself worthy before ordering again.

What message do buyers give when they purchase a second time? Generally it's this: "You're okay. I like your products, and your service is acceptable." Average order value goes up. A higher response rate develops.

A further step is building the multibuyers into advocates. These buyers will recommend the catalog to others. They will peruse the catalog carefully, and they usually respond at many times the rate of first-time buyers. This phenomenon is what makes a successful, profitable catalog.

New-Customer Acquisition Strategies   Historically, catalogs have relied heavily on rented lists to develop their customer base. But this isn't the only method. Because of rising postal and mailing costs, catalogers are seeking alternative ways to obtain new buyers. Innovation is the name of the prospecting game. Here are 15 options, other than list rentals, that catalogs are using today:

1. *Customer referrals.* These are very good quality names. Ask "advocate" customers for names of friends, relatives, co-workers, and the like.

Exhibit 16–9.   **The Hierarchy of a Customer**

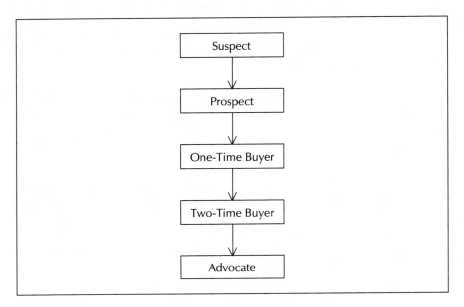

2. *Space advertising.* Many of today's large catalogs built their buyer lists through space advertising. There are many options: for example, small space ads (one-sixth page) vs. large space ads (full page) and the direct sale of a product vs. generating a lead or inquiry.

3. *Magazine catalog sections.* Many consumer and some business magazines publish an annual or a biannual catalog lead-generation section.

4. *Free-standing newspaper inserts (FSIs).*

5. *Package inserts.* These ride along in the box shipment of another mailer. The promotion could be a catalog or a lead-generation flyer.

6. *Co-op mailings.* Carol Wright is an example.

7. *Trade shows* (especially for business catalogs)

8. *Television*

9. *Catalog shoppers.* Today there are several lead-generation publications, such as Shop-at-Home Directory and The Best Catalogs in the World, that exclusively promote catalogs.

10. *Card decks*

11. *Credit card or billing inserts*

12. *Doctor's or dentist's office "take-ones"*

13. *Back panels of cereal boxes*

14. *Public relations*

15. *Gift recipients*

What are the innovative strategies for acquiring new customers that winning catalogs use today? Consider the following list:

1. Aggressively source coding every new-customer acquisition effort and tracking results. Also capturing original source codes on the customer database.

2. Seeking as much publicity (PR) as possbile by creating events such as marathon races sponsored by marketers of health-related products.

3. Measuring the cost of acquiring names by each type of medium. Determining what the catalog can afford to spend for a new customer.

4. Developing customer referral programs such as book clubs use.

5. Carefully watching the seasonality of mailings and concentrating prospecting in the prime season.

6. Targeting, targeting, targeting mailings, especially when using list rentals.

7. Telephoning to prequalify names before mailing a business-to-business catalog. Also sending a postcard before the catalog mails to prequalify the name.

8. Keeping names of old buyers and inquiries that are no longer mailed and putting them into merge-purge.

9. Establishing and maintaining a detailed prospect database of inquiries, gift recipients, people who paid for a catalog, and the like. Also capturing original source codes and dates of inquiry.

10. Getting the catalog to the prospect who requests it as fast as possible. Let the prospect know that "this is the catalog you requested." Maximum turnaround time should be no more than 10–14 days.

11. Correlating back-end customer name value with front-end name source to maximize quality of names over quantity of names.

12. Watching the aging of buyers, inquiries, and catalog requests. People who have not purchased in over 12 months need a special message or incentive to remind them that they asked for the catalogs they receive.

The Customer List—A Catalog's Most Important Asset

Even though few catalogers identify their customer list on the company's balance sheet, it is their most important asset. The buyers are their major source of revenue through sales of merchandise or list rentals. To maximize

the use of this asset, however, the list must be maintained and mailed. Let us further discuss these two factors.

List Maintenance.   Most catalogers will include an "address correction" postal endorsement at least once or twice a year. In this way they can update the names of people or companies that have moved and eliminate catalogs being discarded for insufficient address. The use of the Postal Service's NCOA (National Change of Address) during the merge-purge of the customer list with outside lists is well worth the cost and effort in ensuring better delivery.

Mailing the Customer List.   Mailing catalogs is expensive. Also, too often companies tend to undermail their best customers. During the mid-1970s, for example, Fingerhut was mailing its customer list 20 times a year. By using simple segmentation techniques such as recency, frequency, monetary, and product category, the company was able to test and ultimately increase its mailings to 30 times a year. Most catalogers probably underutilize or undermail their customer list. One reason is that they tend to treat all customers alike. The All Customers Are Not Created Equal chart (Exhibit 16–10) demonstrates the most effective way to identify and test those customer list segments that should get more catalogs. The database will help this segmentation.

Using the Customer List More Effectively   The how-to tips below are suggestions for a more effective and more efficient use of the customer list.

1. The customer list is a catalog's most important asset.
   Track buyers by source.
   Track growth of the customer list on a weekly or monthly basis.

2. Know who the best customers are.
   Survey them.
   Ask them for help.
   Research them.
   Talk to them on the phone.

3. Mail the best customers more often.

4. Build a simple segmentation system to prioritize the buyer file. All customers are not created equal.

5. Keep track of:
   When customers buy.
   What customers buy.
   How customers respond (phone/fax/mail).
   How customers pay (check/cash/credit card/purchase order).
   How and why customers return merchandise.

Exhibit 16–10.   **All Customers Are Not Created Equal**

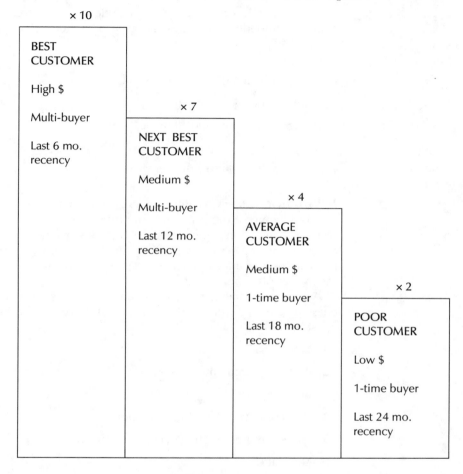

6. Invest in a catalog fulfillment database system that allows tracking, measuring, and segmenting of the customer list.

7. Maintain the list and keep it updated. Remember that 20 percent of the list changes each year.

8. Rent the buyer list for extra income.

9. Reactivate former-year buyers.

10. Treat buyers like good friends.

Circulation Planning   *Circulation* is a word that is very familiar to magazine publishers. It is also a word that is starting to mean more to catalogers. It means: "When are you mailing which catalog and to whom." At a catalog conference, a forum of small catalogers identified circulation as the most important marketing skill for profitable growth.

Catalog Creative Execution

The challenge in catalog creative execution is in differentiating the catalog from its competition. There are six aspects of the creative process:

- Pagination
- Design and layout
- Color as a design element
- Typography as a design element
- Copy
- Photography or illustrative art

Pagination   Many catalog experts think pagination, or planning the overall scheme of the catalog, is the most important aspect of the creative process. Pagination determines the catalog's organization (i.e., by product category, mixing product, product function, theme, color, or price). And pagination determines exactly what product goes where in the catalog. It is the master plan for the catalog.

With a new catalog, there are a number of decisions that have to be made before beginning overall design and layout. Here is a checklist of items to be considered:

1. Catalog size
2. Postal requirements
3. Items per page
4. One-color, two-color, or four-color
5. Space mix among photos, copy, and white space
6. Amount of copy
7. Position of copy
8. Method of layout
9. Method of organization
10. Use of photography and/or illustrative art
11. Type size, type face, use of reverse type in headlines or body copy
12. Color as a design element

The most important thing to keep in mind in pagination is knowing who the customers are and how they will use the catalog. Sound pagination puts the best-selling products in the "hot spots" (see page 439) of the catalog and thereby maximizes sales. Another consideration of pagination is the niche, or positioning, of the catalog. A catalog must provide the ambience that its

audience expects. Pagination ensures that there is "flow" from page to page and from product category to product category.

Design and Layout   If pagination is the master plan, then design and layout is the blueprint that will guide the creative construction process. Unlike many direct mail creative projects that are directed by the copywriter, the catalog is clearly design-driven. Two of the most critical areas of design are covers and page or spread layouts.

Catalog Covers.
The front and back covers have the following roles:

- Attracting the customer's attention
- Telling what the catalog is selling
- Reinforcing the catalog's niche
- Attracting the reader inside the catalog
- Offering a benefit
- Selling products
- Getting the catalog mailed
- Offering service information such as the telephone/fax, guarantee, and credibility information

Preliminary design of a new catalog concentrates a lot of effort on getting the right "feel" on the cover. To illustrate the feel of a catalog cover, note in Exhibit 16–11 how Charles Keith uses a graphic to condition its prospects for its autumn merchandise offerings. In Exhibit 16–12 observe how United Telephone, through photography, alerts prospects to the fact that its catalog is devoted to telecommunications equipment. Compare these covers against the list above. Generally, catalog covers can be most effective in "grabbing" the prospective customer and starting the information/ordering process.

Page or Spread Layouts.   The second critical area of catalog design is page or spread layout. (Most professionals advocate spreads because the eyes tend to scan two facing pages.) Layout options break into five categories:

- Grid layout
- Free form (asymmetrical)
- Single item per page
- Art and copy separation
- Product grouping

Exhibit 16–13 presents a grid layout from a Walter Drake Catalog.

Exhibit 16–11.   **Autumn Merchandising: Charles Keith Catalog
Cover**

Exhibit 16–12.   United Telephone Catalog Cover

Exhibit 16–13.   Grid Layout: Walter Drake catalog.

END RUN-DOWN HEELS! Save expensive shoes, avoid unsightly run-down heels! Self-stick wedges fit inside any shoes . . . help correct weak, rotating ankles that shift weight, running down outside of shoe heel. (Those who wear down inside of heels can switch cushions to opposite shoes.) One pair.

Women's		Men's	
F6062 6-7	$3.49	F6065 8- 9	$3.49
F6063 7-8	$3.49	F6066 9-10	$3.49
F6064 8-9	$3.49	F6067 10-11	$3.49

WELCOME BUNION RELIEF! Designed by an orthopedic surgeon, special appliance urges the big toe toward a more normal position while you sleep. Adjustable tension gently but firmly counteracts the strain which causes discomfort and deformity. Washable. *Please specify* your shoe size, man or woman—right or left foot. Allow 4-6 weeks. Imported.
D1013 Nighttime Bunion Regulator.... $11.99
    Buy 2 or more............only $10.99 each

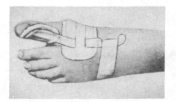

ROTARY NOSE CLIPPERS . . . the safe and sure way to clip hair from nose and ears! Why suffer through the painful tweezing of unwanted hair? With rotary clippers you just squeeze the handles gently and hair is snipped off . . . quickly, simply, safely. The cutting edge is covered and there are no sharp points that might nick or pierce the skin. Surgical steel, 2" long. A grooming aid you won't want to be without!
F2074 Rotary Nose Clippers $3.99

NO MORE ICED-UP WINDOWS when you put Auto Bonnet over the top of your car. Takes just seconds to install—yet keeps off a whole night of ice and snow! Heavy plastic shield fastens to fender and bumper with elastic belts. In the morning, remove shield, and look—windshields and windows are cleared instantly! Specify standard or station wagon size.
H7002 Auto Bonnet, Standard Car $14.99
H7003 Auto Bonnet, Station Wagon ... $16.99

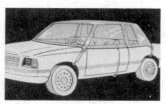

HAPPY HARNESS FOR CATS holds kitty snugly without causing neck strain. He can't slip out, hurt himself or wiggle free! Perfect way to take your cat for a stroll or include him in travel plans. Comfortable 2-strap halter of riveted leather, shiny metal buckles and leash ring. Neck strap adjusts up to 13"; chest strap to 16½". Matching leash snaps on quickly; 47" long with safety loop. Ideal for small dogs, too!
F3154 Kitty Harness $7.49
F3169 Matching Leash $7.49

CONVERT TWIN BEDS INTO KING-SIZE THIS EASY WAY. Span-A-Bed does it! This soft foam insert spans the gap so neatly you'll never know it's there, yet gives you the luxury and comfort of a king-size bed. Can be used for single or double headboard twins. Washable, light, strong polyurethane foam. 72x14".
H2243 Span-A-Bed $7.99

Since the layouts provide the blueprint for copy and photography, it is important that they reinforce the image of the company selling the products. Successful catalogers:

- Make the product the hero. The product is what's being sold, not the models, the props, or the backgrounds.

- Use "hot spots" (front and back covers, inside front cover and inside back cover spreads, the center of a saddle-stitched catalog, the order form, additional spreads in the front of the catalog, i.e., pages 4–5, 6–7) effectively in promoting winning products—those with the best margins.

- Remember their customers and how they will use the catalog.

- Use a logical eye flow within a spread from the right-hand page to the left-hand page and back again to the right-hand page.

- Use the telephone/fax number and other information such as testimonials, technical specifications, and the like as part of the design of the catalog.

- Strive for consistency in layout from catalog to catalog, so that the customer will not be confused.

Color as a Design Element   People react differently to the use of color in catalogs. Red and yellow are strong colors that attract attention. Blue is seldom used with food. Research shows that people prefer the use of white, beige, or gray for backgrounds. Catalog readers like contrast between the product and the background. White space is clearly a design element. Too much of it and layouts appear to have gaping holes; too little and it's confusing. Care in the use of color in cataloging is especially important in page backgrounds, photo backgrounds, headlines, and screens for special sections.

Typography as a Design Element   Everyone learns to read black on white, left to right, left justified columns, top to bottom, with short column length, reasonably sized type, and a serif type face. There needs to be a good reason for an art director to vary from these patterns, otherwise, readability is affected and so is customer response. Attractive type helps readability and ease of catalog use. Unattractive type can actually turn off the reader and result in lost sales. Catalogers must remember their catalog's positioning and target audience in selecting the appropriate type. Art directors should be careful not to overuse reverse type, overprint type on a busy photo, or use all capital letters, extended line length, and type or calligraphy that is difficult to read.

Catalog Copy—Your Salesperson

When we state that a catalog tends to be layout-driven, we do not mean to imply that copy is unimportant. The layout helps to attract and direct the reader's attention, but it is the copy that closes the sale. Catalog copy must perform these functions:

- Reinforce the catalog's niche or positioning
- Inform
- "Grab" the reader with headlines
- Educate
- Entertain
- Give reassurance
- Build credibility and confidence
- Describe the product
- Close the sale

It is not unusual to have a number of writers working on catalog copy. It is therefore important for all of the writers to understand the positioning of the catalog, to know precisely who the target customer is, and to have agreed upon a copy style. Many catalogs have even developed style manuals to achieve consistency. There are many copy styles from which to choose. The right one is selected with the customer in mind.

Photography or Illustrative Art

The catalog is a visual format, and one of the key elements of the design is photography or artwork. Photography helps attract the reader's attention to the product. It also shows product features and color differences. Photography or artwork builds credibility for the product and romances the product. But, most importantly, the photo or illustrative art makes the product the hero.

The photographer, art director, and photo stylist together can make products come alive with effective use of propping, accessorization, lighting, and level of contrast. Whatever the photo style or type of camera and whether or not models are used, photography is a vital part of the catalog creative process. Illustrative art is also used in catalogs to promote greater understanding of hard-to-shoot subjects, to be different from other catalogs, or, sometimes, to effect a cost savings.

Catalog Fulfillment

After the catalog has been targeted, created, and mailed, you are ready to take orders. Fulfillment is an essential element of a profitable catalog. It closes the loop with the customer. During the 1970s there was no urgency to improve catalog customer service, but in the 1980s this function became a "must have" for catalogers. Order entry by phone, mail, and fax; data entry and fulfillment systems; warehousing and pick, pack, and shipping; credit handling; return handling; and customer communications—all have become essential to the fulfillment function. Today's customers demand quality service in every aspect of the catalog operation.

Catalog Database Strategies

The fulfillment function provides information about prospects and customers. Catalogers relish having information about their customers that will help them improve the response percentage, obtain a larger average order, and get customers to buy more frequently. With today's improved computer hardware and software, the arduous task of maintaining critical customer purchase information and demographic data has become very manageable. Computer costs are one of the few costs that have been significantly reduced in the last decade. There are excellent custom-designed PC-based (microcomputer) software packages available. And they are affordable! There is no excuse for a catalog of any size not to have a state-of-the-art fulfillment and database system to track customer activity.

Analysis — The Numbers Side of Cataloging

Closing the loop. Ensuring that every catalog is better than the last one. Making sure that catalog promotions are measurable. This is what analysis is all about. Analysis helps critique each mailing and therefore makes the next one better.

There are few prosperous catalogs that don't devote a lot of effort and manpower to the numbers side of the business. Here is a checklist of the typical analyses that catalogers perform:

1. List/source/media analysis

2. Merchandise analyses:
   Price points
   Square-inch analysis
   Product category analysis
   Sales by catalog page and spread

3. Inventory analyses:
   Product returns
   Cancellations
   Back orders
   Remainders/markdowns of merchandise

4. Analysis of tests such as offers, covers, seasonality, and lists.

5. Mailing plan: actual results vs. projection

6. Profit and loss: actual results vs. plan

7. Name value of customers

The Catalogs of Tomorrow

Will the printed catalog be replaced by a video or computer disk catalog? Probably not, but we will certainly see some inroads by the electronic media.

Catalogs of the twenty-first century will continue to be more and more targeted. They will become more personalized and use more techniques like selective binding to present specialized merchandise to individuals rather than large groups. Catalogs will be easier to produce, with advances continuing in desktop publishing and color separations being made directly from the personal computer. Digitalization of photography will change the way we capture, transmit, and reproduce images.

One thing is certain: The catalog process that we have looked at in this chapter will not go away, even though it will change. Those catalogs that survive and prosper in the 2000s cannot do well some of the tasks mentioned in the catalog process and leave others to chance. Winning catalogs must be able to perform every task well. That's the challenge and the opportunity.

Self-Quiz

1. What two companies can be credited with starting cataloging before 1900?

   _____

2. Name five key factors that have caused the dramatic growth of cataloging since the 1970s.

   a. _____   d. _____

   b. _____   e. _____

   c. _____

3. Based on a *Catalog Age* survey, what percentage of catalogs reported sales under $10 million?

   _____

4. Identify five key issues that catalogers will face in the 1900s.

   a. _____   d. _____

   b. _____   e. _____

   c. _____

5. What are the two primary things the cataloger must consider when starting a new catalog?

   a. _____

   b. _____

6. Name six differences between a frequent catalog buyer and an infrequent catalog buyer.

   a. _____

   b. _____

   c. _____

   d. _____

   e. _____

   f. _____

7. What are three key merchandise strategies that successful catalogs employ?

   a. _____

   b. _____

   c. _____

8. Define *niche* as it applies to a catalog.

   _____

   _____

9. What are several different ways a catalog can set itself apart from the competition?

   _____

   _____

   _____

10. What do catalogers mean by front-end marketing? Back-end marketing?

    _____

    _____

    _____

    _____

11. Identify five different media that catalogs use in prospecting for new customers.

    a. _____   d. _____

    b. _____   e. _____

    c. _____

12. Why is the customer list so important to a cataloger?

_____

_____

13. Identify six vital aspects of the catalog creative process.

a. _____   d. _____

b. _____   e. _____

c. _____   f. _____

14. What are the "hot spots" of a catalog?

_____

_____

15. What type of analyses do catalogers perform, and how is each analysis used?

_____

_____

_____

_____

Pilot Project

You have been asked by a leading brewery to do a feasibility study concerning a new gift catalog. There are two key audiences for the product that the catalog might promote:

Primary audience: Young men and women, age 21–35, who consume more beer than the average American. This audience tends to be middle-American, blue-collar, and with a high school rather than a college education

Secondary audience: Men and women, age 35–60, who are collectors of various beer paraphernalia—beer glasses, steins, mugs, trays, and the like.

With this background, develop a feasibility plan and a strategic business plan that would include answers to the following questions:

1. What might be an appropriate name for the catalog?

2. How could this catalog be unique? What niche could this catalog fill to be successful?

3. Identify 20 items that might be appropriate for this catalog to promote.

4. What mailing lists should the catalog rent for an initial test?

5. What publications might be used to obtain catalog requests and inquiries?

6. How would you treat the front cover of the catalog to maximize the appeal of the first catalog and attract the reader's attention?

Techniques of Creating Print Advertising

Many of the creative techniques needed in creating a successful direct mail package (Chapter Fifteen) are also necessary in creating productive direct response ads in magazines and newspapers. But here the space available for words and pictures is much more severely limited, and most of the gimmicks, gadgets, showmanship, and personal tone of direct mail do not apply. This throws a heavy load of responsibility for the success of the ad on a carefully worded headline, a compelling opening, tightly structured copy, and appropriate visual emphasis.

Before the actual work of creating an ad begins, two important questions should be answered: Who is the prospect? What are the outstanding product advantages or customer benefits?

Often there is no single clear answer, but rather several distinct possibilities. Then the profitable course of action is to prepare ads embodying all your most promising hypotheses and split-test as many of them as your budget permits.

Visualizing the Prospect

Every good mail-order or direct mail piece should attract the most attention from the likeliest prospects, and capable creators of direct response advertising visualize their prospects with varying degrees of precision when they sit down at the typewriter or drawing board.

Good direct response advertising makes its strongest appeal to its best prospects and then gathers in as many additional prospects as possible.

And who are the prospects? They are the ones with the strongest desire for what you're selling. You must look for the common denominators.

For instance, let's say you are selling a book on the American Revolution. Here are some of the relevant common denominators that would be shared by many people in your total audience:

1. An interest in the American Revolution in particular

2. An interest in American history in general

3. A patriotic interest in America

4. An interest in history

5. An interest in big, beautiful coffee table books

6. An interest in impressing friends with historical lore

7. A love of bargains

8. An interest in seeing children in the family become adults with high achievement

Now, out of a total audience of 1,000, some readers would possess all 8 denominators, some would possess some combination of 6, some a different combination of 6, some just one of the 8, and so on.

If you could know the secret hearts of all 1,000 individuals and rank them on a scale of relative desire to buy, you would place at the very top of the list those who possessed all 8 denominators, then just below them those who possessed just 7, and so on down to the bottom of the scale, where you would place those who possessed none.

Obviously, you should make as many sales as possible among your hottest prospects first, for that is where your sales will be easiest. Then you want to reach down the scale to sell as many of the others as you can. By the time you get down to the people possessing only one of the denominators, you will probably find interest so faint that it would be almost impossible to make your sales effort pay unless it were fantastically appealing.

Obvious? Yes, to mail-order professionals who learned the hard way. But to the tenderfoot, it is not so obvious. In an eagerness to sell everybody, he or she may muff the easiest sales by using a curiosity-only appeal that conceals what is really being offered.

On the other hand, the veteran but uninspired pro may gather up all the easy sales lying on the surface but, through lack of creative imagination, fail to reach deeper into the market. For instance, let's say that of 1,000 readers, 50 possess all 8 denominators. A crude omnibus appeal that could scoop up many of them would be something like "At last—for every liberty-loving American family, especially those with children, whose friends are amazed by their understanding of American history, here is a big, beautiful book about the American Revolution you will display with pride—yours for only one-fifth of what you'd expect to pay!" A terrible headline, but at least one that those possessing the denominators of interest would stop to look at and consider. You may get only 5 percent readership, but it will be the right 5 percent.

On the other hand, suppose you want to do something terribly creative to reach a wider market. So you do a beautiful advertising message headed "The Impossible Dream," in which you somehow work your way from that

starting point to what it is you're selling. Again, you may get only 5 percent readership, but these readers will be scattered along the entire length of your scale of interest. Of the 50 people who stopped to read your message, only 2 or 3 may be prime prospects possessing all 8 denominators. Many people really interested in books on the American Revolution, in inspiring their children with patriotic sentiments, and in acquiring big impressive books at big savings will have hurried past unaware.

The point: Don't let prime prospects get away. In mail order you can't afford to. Some people out there don't have to be sold; they already want what you have, and if you tell them that you have it, they will buy it. Alone they may not constitute enough of a market to make your selling effort pay, but without them you haven't got a chance. So, through your clarity and directness, you gather in these prime prospects; then through your creative imagination you reach beyond them to awaken and excite mild prospects as well.

Once the prospect is clearly visualized, a good headline almost writes itself. For example, here is an effective and successful headline from an ad by Quadrangle/New York Times Book Company. It simply defines the prospect so clearly and accurately that the interested reader feels an instant tug:

> For people who are almost (but not quite) satisfied with their house plants . . . and can't figure out what they're doing wrong

A very successful ad for the Washington School of Art, offering a correspondence course, resulted from our bringing the psychographic profile of our prime prospect into sharp focus. We began to confront the fact that the prospect was someone who had been drawing pictures better than the rest of us since the first grade. Such people are filled with a rare combination of pride in their talent and shame at their lack of perfection. And their goal is not necessarily fame or fortune, but simply to become a "real artist," a phrase that has different meanings for different people. The winning headline simply reached out to the right people and offered them the right benefit:

> If you can draw fairly well (but still not good enough), we'll turn you into a real artist

Of course, a good headline does not necessarily present an explicit definition of the prospect, but it is always implied. Here are some classic headlines and the prospects whom the writer undoubtedly visualized:

> Can a man or woman my age become a hotel executive?

The prospect is, probably, a middle-aged man or woman who needs, for whatever reason, an interesting, pleasant, not too technically demanding occupational skill such as hotel management, and is eager for reassurance that you *can* teach an old dog new tricks. Note, however, how wide the net is cast. No one is excluded. Even a person fearing he or she may be too young to be a hotel executive can theoretically read himself into this headline:

Don't envy the plumber—be one

The prospect is a poorly paid worker, probably blue-collar, who is looking for a way to improve his lot and who has looked with both indignation and envy at the plumber, who appears not much more skilled but earns several times as much per hour.

How to stumble upon a fortune in gems

The prospect is everybody, all of us, who all our lives have daydreamed of gaining sudden wealth without extreme sacrifice.

Is your home picture-poor?

The prospect is someone, probably a woman, with a home, who has a number of bare or inadequately decorated walls, and who feels not only a personal lack but also, perhaps more importantly, a vague underlying sense of social shame at this conspicuous cultural "poverty." Whether she appreciates it or not, she recognizes that art, books, and music are regarded as part of the "good life" and are supposed to add a certain richness to life.

Be a "nondegree" engineer

This is really a modern version of "Don't envy the plumber." The prospect is an unskilled or semiskilled factory worker who looks with a mixture of resentment and grudging envy on the aristocracy in his midst, the fair-haired boys who earn much more, dress better, and enjoy special privileges because they are graduate engineers. The prospect would like to enjoy at least some of their job status but is unwilling or unable to go to college and get an engineering degree.

Are you tired of cooking with odds and ends?

The prospect is that Everywoman, or Everyman, who has accumulated over the years an enameled pan here, an aluminum pot there, an iron skillet elsewhere, and to whom a matched set of anything represents neatness, order, and elegance.

Can you call a man a failure at 30?

The prospect is young white-collar worker, 25–32 years old, who is deeply concerned that life isn't turning out the way he dreamed and that he is on the verge of failing to "make it"—permanently.

Selecting Advantages and Benefits

Advantages belong to the product. Benefits belong to the consumer. If the product or service is unique or unfamiliar to the prospect, stressing benefits is important. But if it is simply a new, improved model in a highly competitive field where there already exists an established demand, the product advantage or advantages become important.

When pocket electronic calculators were first introduced, such benefits as *pride*, *power*, and *profit* were important attributes. But as the market became flooded with competing types and brands, product advantages such as the floating decimal became more important.

There are two kinds of benefits, the immediate or obvious benefit and the not-so-obvious ultimate benefit—the real potential meaning for the customer's life of the product or service being sold. (See Exhibit 17–1.) The ultimate benefit often proves to have a greater effect, for it reaches deeper into the prospect's feelings.

Victor Schwab, one of the great mail-order pioneers, was fond of quoting Dr. Samuel Johnson's approach to auctioning off the contents of a brewery: "We are not here to sell boilers and vats, but the potentiality of growing rich beyond the dreams of avarice."

It pays to ask yourself over and over again, "What am I selling? Yes, I know it's a book or a steak knife, or a home study course in upholstering—but what am I *really* selling? What human values are at stake?"

For example, suppose you have the job of selling a correspondence course in advertising. Here is a list of ultimate benefits and the way they may be expressed in headlines for the course. Some of the headlines are patently absurd, but they illustrate the mind-stretching process involved in looking for the ultimate benefit in your product or service.

- *Health*: "Successful ad people are healthier and happier than you think— and now you can be one of them."

- *Money*: "What's your best chance of earning $50,000 a year by the time you are 30?"

- *Security*: "You are always in demand when you can write advertising that sells."

- *Pride*: "Imagine your pride when you can coin a slogan repeated by 50 million people."

- *Approval*: "Did you write that ad? Why, I've seen it everywhere."

- *Enjoyment*: "Get more fun out of your daily job. Become a successful ad writer!"

- *Excitement*: "Imagine working until 4:00 a.m.—and loving every minute of it!"

- *Power*: "The heads of giant corporations will listen to your advice—when you've mastered the secrets of advertising that works." (Just a wee bit of exaggeration there, pehaps.)

- *Fulfillment*: "Are you wasting a natural talent for advertising?"

- *Freedom*: "People who can get million-dollar advertising ideas don't have to worry about punching a time clock."

Exhibit 17–1.   Classic Direct Response Ad

"Can he really play?" a girl whispered.
"Heavens no!" Arthur exclaimed. "He
never played a note in his life."

They Laughed When I Sat Down
At the Piano
But When I Started to Play!~

ARTHUR had just played "The Rosary." The room rang with applause. I decided that this would be a dramatic moment for me to make my debut. To the amazement of all my friends, I strode confidently over to the piano and sat down.

"Jack is up to his old tricks," somebody chuckled. The crowd laughed. They were all certain that I couldn't play a single note.

"Can he really play?" I heard a girl whisper to Arthur.

"Heavens, no!" Arthur exclaimed. "He never played a note in all his life. . . But just you watch him. This is going to be good."

I decided to make the most of the situation. With mock dignity I drew out a silk handkerchief and lightly dusted off the piano keys. Then I rose and gave the revolving piano stool a quarter of a turn, just as I had seen an imitator of Paderewski do in a vaudeville sketch.

"What do you think of his execution?" called a voice from the rear.

"We're in favor of it!" came back the answer, and the crowd rocked with laughter.

Then I Started to Play

Instantly a tense silence fell on the guests. The laughter died on their lips as if by magic. I played through the first few bars of Beethoven's immortal Moonlight Sonata. I heard gasps of amazement. My friends sat breathless — spellbound!

I played on and as I played I forgot the people around me. I forgot the hour, the place, the breathless listeners. The little world I lived in seemed to fade — seemed to grow dim—unreal. Only the music was real. Only the music and visions it brought me. Visions as beautiful and as changing as the wind blown clouds and drifting moonlight that long ago inspired the master composer. It seemed as if the master

musician himself were speaking to me—speaking through the medium of music—not in words but in chords. Not in sentences but in exquisite melodies!

A Complete Triumph!

As the last notes of the Moonlight Sonata died away, the room resounded with a sudden roar of applause. I found myself surrounded by excited faces. How my friends carried on! Men shook my hand—wildly congratulated me—pounded me on the back in their enthusiasm! Everybody was exclaiming with delight—plying me with rapid questions. . . . "Jack! Why didn't you tell us you could play like that?". . . "Where did you learn?"—"How long have you studied?"—"Who was your teacher?"

"I have never even seen my teacher," I replied. "And just a short while ago I couldn't play a note.".

"Quit your kidding," laughed Arthur, himself an accomplished pianist. "You've been studying for years. I can tell."

"I have been studying only a short while," I insisted. "I decided to keep it a secret so that I could surprise all you folks."

Then I told them the whole story.

"Have you ever heard of the U. S. School of Music?" I asked.

A few of my friends nodded. "That's a correspondence school, isn't it?" they exclaimed.

"Exactly," I replied. "They have a new simplified method that can teach you to play any instrument by mail in just a few months."

How I Learned to Play Without a Teacher

And then I explained how for years I had longed to play the piano.

"A few months ago," I continued, "I saw an interesting ad for the U. S. School of Music—a new method of learning to play which only cost a few cents a day! The ad told how a woman had mastered the piano in her spare time at home—and without a teacher! Best of all, the wonderful new method she used, required no laborious scales—no heartless exercises — no tiresome practising. It sounded so convincing that I filled out the coupon requesting the Free Demonstration Lesson.

"The free book arrived promptly and I started in that very night to study the Demonstration Lesson. I was amazed to see how easy it was to play this new way. Then I sent for the course.

"When the course arrived I found it was just as the ad said — as easy as A.B.C.! And, as

the lessons continued they got easier and easier. Before I knew it I was playing all the pieces I liked best. Nothing stopped me. I could play ballads or classical numbers or jazz, all with equal ease! And I never did have any special talent for music!"

Play Any Instrument

You too, can now teach yourself to be an accomplished musician—right at home—in half the usual time. You can't go wrong with this simple new method which has already shown 350,000 people how to play their favorite instruments. Forget that old-fashioned idea that you need special "talent." Just read the list of instruments in the panel, decide which one you want to play and the U. S. School will do the rest. And bear in mind no matter which instrument you choose, the cost in each case will be the same—just a few cents a day. No matter whether you are a mere beginner or already a good performer, you will be interested in learning about this new and wonderful method.

Send for Our Free Booklet and Demonstration Lesson

Thousands of successful students never dreamed they possessed musical ability until it was revealed to them by a remarkable "Musical Ability Test" which we send entirely without cost with our interesting free booklet.

If you are in earnest about wanting to play your favorite instrument—if you really want to gain happiness and increase your popularity—send at once for the free booklet and Demonstration Lesson. No cost — no obligation. Right now we are making a Special offer for a limited number of new students. Sign and send the convenient coupon now — before it's too late to gain the benefits of this offer. Instruments supplied when needed, cash or credit. U. S. School of Music, 1031 Brunswick Bldg., New York City.

Pick Your Instrument

Piano	'Cello
Organ	Harmony and Composition
Violin	Sight Singing
Drums and Traps	Ukulele
Banjo	Guitar
Tenor	Hawaiian
Banjo	Steel Guitar
Mandolin	Harp
Clarinet	Cornet
Flute	Piccolo
Saxophone	Trombone
Voice and Speech Culture	
Automatic Finger Control	
Piano Accordion	

U. S. School of Music,
1031 Brunswick Bldg., New York City.

Please send me your free book, "Music Lessons in Your Own Home", with introduction by Dr. Frank Crane, Demonstration Lesson and particulars of your Special Offer. I am interested in the following course:

....

Have you above instrument?.................

Name..
(Please write plainly)

Address...

City....................... State.................

This ad, written by John Caples, a member of the Direct Marketing Hall of Fame, is considered one of the classics of direct response writing.

- *Identity*: "Join the top advertising professionals who keep the wheels of our economy turning."

- *Relaxation*: "How some people succeed in advertising without getting ulcers."

- *Escape*: "Hate going to work in the morning? Get a job you'll love—in advertising!"

- *Curiosity*: "Now go behind the scenes of America's top advertising agencies—and find out how multimillion dollar campaigns are born!"

- *Possessions*: "I took your course five years ago—today I own two homes, two cars, and a Chris-Craft."

- *Sex*: "Join the people who've made good in the swinging advertising scene"

- *Hunger*: "A really good ad person always knows where his next meal is coming from."

Harnessing the Powers of Semantics

A single word is a whole bundle—a nucleus, you might say—of thoughts and feelings. And when different nuclei are jointed together, the result is nuclear fusion, generating enough power to move the earth.

A whole new semiscience, semantics, has been founded on the unique property of words. The late newspaper columnist Sydney Harris popularized it with his occasional feature, "Antics with Semantics." A typical antic goes something like this: "I am sensible in the face of danger. You are a bit overcautious. He is a coward." The factual content may be the same, but the semantic implications vary widely.

Semantics is the hydrogen bomb of persuasion. In politics, for example, entire election campaigns sometimes hinge on the single word "boss." If one side manages to convince the public that the other side is controlled by a boss or bosses, but that the first side has only "party leaders," the first side will probably win the election.

In direct marketing, clear understanding and skillful use of semantics can make a powerful contribution to ad headlines (Exhibit 17–2). Here are a few examples.

What do you think when you read the word *Europe*? Perhaps there are certain negative connotations—constant military squabbles, lack of Yankee know-how, and so on. But far more important in the psyche of most Americans are the romantic implications—castles, colorful peasants, awesome relics of the past, charming sidewalk cafes, all merging into the lifelong dream of making the Grand Tour of Europe.

Another semantically rich word is *shoestring*. A man is a fool to start a business of his own with inadequate capital. But if he succeeds, he is a

Exhibit 17–2.   The Power of a Strong Headline

At 4½ she's reading 3rd grade books

a child prodigy? not at all! your child, too can be reading one, two or three years beyond his present age level...even if he's a "poor" reader now

Prove it to yourself...with this 10 day free trial!

Reading is fun for Sarah—as it *should be* for every child. At age four and a half, she's already choosing her own books at the San Diego, Cal. library.

She reads books many third graders find "hard going." Yet she won't enter first grade for another year.

Sarah is typical of thousands of children who learned to read with "Listen and Learn with Phonics" — a reading kit that actually makes reading fun.

"Listen and Learn with Phonics" was developed by a reading expert. It has been endorsed, after extensive testing by teachers, schools, and educators.

This practical (and inexpensive) home-learning kit *fascinates* eager young minds from three to ten. The child *hears* the letters or sounds on the phonograph record, *sees* them in his book and repeats them himself. This makes an absorbing *game* of better reading—with amazing results!

FOR EXAMPLE:

● Slow or average readers show sudden, often spectacular improvement in reading, in spelling, in understanding.

● Older children often advance their reading skills several years beyond their age levels.

● Young "pre-schoolers" actually *teach themselves to read* by this simple but startlingly effective phonics method of words, pictures, and records.

6 TEACHING GAMES INCLUDED FREE
Set includes six separate "word building" games. All six are sent with your Listen and Learn Phonics Set FREE of charge!

TEACHERS & PARENTS ACCLAIM RESULTS
"I received your Combination Teaching Set and am positively delighted with it! . . . your marvelous approach to reading is just what we need."
Mrs. Rogavin, Central High School, Snyder, N.Y.

"We purchased 'Listen and Learn With Phonics' . . . for our nine year old son...within two weeks his reading had improved 100%."
Mrs. Gregory Knight, San Leandro, Cal.

4-MONTH UNCONDITIONAL GUARANTEE
If not delighted with the progress shown by your child—just return the set for complete refund.

These "Learning Tools" Simple to Use!
You don't need special teaching skills to use this program. Nor do you need any special knowledge of phonics.

In fact, your child needs no special supervision on your part. This set is so simple, so fascinating, he can learn "on his own" *without help.*

10-DAY FREE TRIAL—PLUS 4-MONTH MONEY-BACK GUARANTEE!
Results are so dramatic, the publishers will make the complete kit available to your child with an equally dramatic FREE trial and guarantee.

Under the terms of this unusual offer you can test the kit free of charge for ten days. Moreover you may use the kit for four months and then return it for *full refund* if you're not completely satisfied with your child's progress!

See for yourself how fast your child can learn to read. Just fill out and mail the coupon below. There's no obligation, and six teaching games are included free—yours to keep whether you buy or not. Americana Interstate, a division of Grolier, Inc., publishers of Book of Knowledge, Mundelein, Ill.

THE RED WORD BOX

THREE UNBREAKABLE 33⅓ RPM RECORDS

LETTER AND WORD STRIPS

Hh   Mm

FOUR ILLUSTRATED WORD BOOKS

TURN-A-WORD GAME

Good Housekeeping GUARANTEE

- MAIL COUPON FOR 10-DAY FREE TRIAL!

CAREER INSTITUTE, MUNDELEIN, ILL. 60060 P2-593

Send me for Free Examination, complete Listen and Learn with Phonics plus Free Educational Games. If not satisfied at the end of 10 days, I may return the $19.95 set and owe nothing. Otherwise, I'll send a first payment of $5.90 and then 3 monthly payments of $5 each which includes shipping and handling.

Name_____

Address_____

City_____State_____Zip_____

Child's Grade Level_____ Your Phone No._____

☐ SAVE! Enclose check or money order for $19.95 and we pay shipping and handling. Same free trial privilege with full immediate refund guaranteed. (Illinois residents add $1.00 Sales Tax.)
This offer available in Canada. Canadian residents mail coupon to Illinois address. Shipment of books and all services will be handled within Canada.

This classic ad, appearing in scores of publications over a period of years, consistently outpulled all ads tested against it. Its success may well be attributed to the major headline's strong appeal to parental pride.

wizard, and his inadequate capital is seen in retrospect as a *shoestring*. Harian Publications got the idea of linking these two words with a couple of modest connectives and achieved verbal nuclear fusion that sold thousands of books on low-cost travel: *Europe on a Shoestring*.

Because there is no copyright on semantic discoveries, Simon & Schuster could capitalize on Harian's discovery and publish its *$1 Complete Guide to Florida*. In fact, it was so successful it broke the mail-order "rule" that a product selling for only $1 cannot be profitably sold in print ads.

For the word *Europe* Simon & Schuster simply substituted another semantically rich word, *Florida*, and came up with another powerful winner. A one-inch advertisement using this headline drew thousands of responses at a profitable cost per order, even when the tiny ad appeared to be completely lost on a 2,400-line page filled with larger ads screaming for attention.

The fascinating thing about this kind of verbal nuclear fusion is that once it has been achieved it can be repeated almost endlessly—not only in the same form but in other forms as well.

For example, a real breakthrough in selling *Motor's Auto Repair Manual* was achieved many years ago with the headline, "Now You Can Lick Any Auto Repair Job." Every single word made a contribution to the power of the headline, as indeed each word always does in an effective headline. *Now* made the ad a news event, even after it has been running for years. *You*, perhaps the sweetest word ever sounded to the ears, made it clear that the benefit included the reader and not just professional auto mechanics. *Can*, another great word, promises power, achievement. *Lick* promises not only sure mastery but sweet triumph. Notice how much richer it is than *do*. *Any* increases the breadth of the promise to the outermost limit. *Auto* selects the prospect and defines the field of interest. *Repair* defines the proposition, and *Job* emphasizes the completeness of its scope.

Once this breakthrough had been achieved, it was possible to make the same statement in many different ways with equal suucess. "Now Any Auto Repair Job Can Be 'Duck Soup' for You." "Now Any Auto Repair Job Can Be Your 'Meat,'" and so on.

Engineer is a rich, many-faceted word. To an artist or a writer, the word may connote a literal-minded square. To an engineer's prospective mother-in-law, it may connote a good provider. To an engineer, it means a degree in engineering and professional standing earned by hard study at college.

But to the manual and semiskilled workers in an electronics plant, our agency reasoned, in developing appeals for the Cleveland Institute of Electronics, the word *engineer* suggests the college-educated wise guy who is the fair-haired boy in the plant—an object both of envy on the part of the worker and of secret derision born of that envy. We couldn't promise "You too can be an engineer," because *engineer* by itself is taken to mean a graduate engineer, and completion of CIE courses doesn't provide college credits or a college degree. However, many of the job titles in our promotion, such as *broadcast engineer*, *field engineer*, or *sales engineer*, have the word *engineer* in them without requiring a college degree. So we were legitimately able

to promise prospective enrollees the prestige and other rewards of being an engineer in an ad headed, "Be a Non-Degree Engineer." (See Exhibit 17–3.)

Semantic considerations like these cause mail-order people to spend hours discussing and tinkering with a single headline or even a single word in the headline. It will pay you to study the mail-order headlines you see used over and over again and try to analyze and apply the semantic secret of their success.

Building In the "Hook"

A successful direct marketing ad must compete fiercely for the reader's time and attention. No matter how great the copy is, it will be wasted if the headline does not compel reading. Most successful headlines have a "hook" to catch the reader and pull him in. The most common hooks are such words as *why, how, new, now, this, what*. They make the reader want to know the answer, *Why* is it? *How* does it? *What* is it?

Consider the flat statement:

Increasing your vocabulary can help you get ahead in life.

This is merely an argumentative, pontifical claim. It doesn't lead anywhere. But notice how the addition of just one word changes the whole meaning and the mood:

How increasing your vocabulary can help you get ahead in life.

This unstylish, uncreative headline, and the copy that followed sold hundreds of thousands of copies of a vocabulary book. It selected the prospects (people who were interested in larger vocabularies), it promised an ultimate benefit (*success*), and it built in a hook (*how*).

Of course, the hook can be merely implied. There is no hook word in the headline. "Be a Non-Degree Engineer." But there is a clear implication that the copy is going to tell you how to achieve this.

Writing the Lead

Perhaps the most troublesome and important part of any piece of mail-order copy is the lead, or opening. A lead that "grabs" readers doesn't guarantee that they will read the rest of the copy. But one that fails to grab them does practically guarantee that they *won't* read the rest.

Always remember in writing or judging a lead that your readers have better things to do than sit around and read your advertising. They don't really want to read your copy—until you make them want to. And your lead has got to make them want to.

Exhibit 17–3.   The Power of Semantics

How to Become a "Non-Degree" Engineer in the Booming World of Electronics

Thousands of real engineering jobs are being filled by men without engineering degrees. The pay is good, the future bright. Here's how to qualify...

By G. O. ALLEN

President, Cleveland Institute of Electronics

THE BIG BOOM IN ELECTRONICS—and the resulting shortage of graduate engineers—has created a new breed of professional man: the "non-degree" engineer. He has an income and prestige few men achieve without going to college. Depending on the branch of electronics he's in, he may "ride herd" over a flock of computers, run a powerful TV transmitter, supervise a service department, or work side by side with distinguished scientists designing and testing new electronic miracles.

According to one recent survey, in military-connected work alone 80% of the civilian field engineers are not college graduates. Yet they enjoy officer status and get generous *per diem* allowances in addition to their excellent salaries.

In TV and radio, you qualify for the key job of Broadcast Engineer if you have an FCC License, whether you've gone to college or not.

Now You Can Learn at Home

To qualify, however, you do need to know more than soldering, testing circuits, and replacing components. You need to really know your electronics theory—and to prove it by getting an FCC Commercial License.

Now you can master electronics theory at home, in your spare time. Over the last 30 years, here at Cleveland Institute of Electronics, we've perfected AUTO-PROGRAMMED™ lessons that make learning at home easy, even if you once had trouble studying. To help you even more, your instructor gives the homework you send in his undivided personal attention—it's like being the only student in his "class." He even mails back his corrections and comments the same day he gets your work, so you hear from him while everything is still fresh in your mind.

Does it work? I'll say! Better than 9 out of 10 CIE men who take the U.S. Government's tough FCC licensing exam *pass it on their very first try.* (Among non-CIE men, 2 out of 3 who take the exam *fail.*) That's why we can promise in writing to refund your tuition in full if you complete one of our FCC courses and fail to pass the licensing exam.

Students who have taken other courses often comment on how much more they learn from us. Says Mark E. Newland of Santa Maria, Calif.:

"Of 11 different correspondence courses I've taken, CIE's was the best prepared, most interesting, and easiest to understand. I passed my 1st Class FCC exam after completing my course, and have increased my earnings by $120 a month."

Mail Coupon for 2 Free Books

Thousands of today's "non-degree" engineers started by reading our 2 free books: (1) Our school catalog "How to Succeed in Electronics," describing opportunities in electronics, our teaching methods, and our courses, and (2) our special booklet, "How to Get a Commercial FCC License." To receive both without cost or obligation, mail coupon below.

CIE Cleveland Institute of Electronics
1776 E. 17th St. Dept. PS-6, Cleveland, Ohio 44114

Cleveland Institute of Electronics
1776 East 17th Street, Dept. PS-6, Cleveland, Ohio 44114

Please send me without cost or obligation:
1. Your 40-page booklet describing the job opportunities in Electronics today, how your courses can prepare me for them, your methods of instruction, and your special student services.
2. Your booklet on "How to Get a Commercial FCC License."

I am especially interested in:
- ☐ Electronics Technology
- ☐ First Class FCC License
- ☐ Broadcast Engineering
- ☐ Electronic Communications
- ☐ Industrial Electronics
- ☐ Advanced Engineering

Name .... Age ......
(Please print)

Address...

City ....State........... Zip........

Present Job Title ....

 Accredited Member National Home Study Council
A Leader in Electronics Training...Since 1934

The power of semantics is shown in this strong headline. It incorporates many favorable connotations in the promise to become a "non-degree engineer."

A common error in writing leads is failure to get to the point immediately —or at least to *point* to the point. Haven't you had the experience of listening to a friend or associate or public speaker who is trying to tell you something but is not able to get to the point? Remember how impatient you felt as you fumed inwardly, "Get to the point!" Your readers feel that same way about copy—and can very easily yawn and turn away. A good roundabout lead is not impossible, but it takes a brilliant writer.

A good principle to follow is that the copy should proceed from the headline. That is, if your headline announces what you are there to talk about, then you should get down to business and talk about it. Although it is true that some successful advertising merely *continues* the message started by the headline or display copy, there is far less danger of confusion if the copy *repeats* and *expands* the headline message, exactly the way a good news item does.

Notice how marvelously these leads from the *Wall Street Journal* news columns form a bridge between the headlines and the rest of the stories:

> New Postage-Stamp Ink to Speed Mail Processing
> New York—U.S. postage stamps will soon be tagged with a special luminescent ink that will permit automatic locating and cancelling of the stamps to speed processing of the mail.

> Affluent Americans Awash in Documents Snap Up Home Safes
> New York—There's a popular new home appliance that won't wash a dish, dry a diaper, or keep a steak on ice. It's a safe. And it's being propelled into prominence by a paperwork explosion.

Notice, too, that although the lead restates the thought of the headline, it does it in a different way, recapping the thought but also advancing the story.

Classic Copy Structure

In a classic mail-order copy argument, a good lead should be visualized as the first step in a straight path of feeling and logic from the headline or display theme to the concluding call for action. In that all-important first step, the readers should be able to see clearly where the path is taking them. Otherwise they may not want to go. (This is the huge error of ads that seek to pique your curiosity with something irrelevant and then make a tie-in to the real point. Who's got time for satisfying that much curiosity these days?)

The sections of a classic copy argument may be labeled *problem, promise of solution, explanation of promise, proof, call to action*. However, if you're going to start with the problem, it seems like a good idea at least to hint right away at the forthcoming solution. Then the readers won't mind your not getting to the point right away, as long as they know where you're going. A generation ago, when the pace of life was slower, a brilliant copywriter could get away with spending the first third of his copy leisurely outlining

the problem before finally getting around to the solution. But in today's more hectic times, it's riskier.

Here is an ad seeking Duraclean dealers in which the problem lead contains the promise of solution:

> I found the easy way to escape from being a "wage slave."

> I kept my job while my customer list grew . . . then found myself in a high-profit business. Five years ago, I wouldn't have believed that I could be where I am today.

> I was deeply in debt. My self-confidence had been shaken by a disastrous business setback. Having nobody behind me, I had floundered and failed for lack of experience, help, and guidance.

The copy could have simply started out, "Five years ago, I was deeply in debt," and so on. But the promise of happier days to come provides a carrot on a stick, drawing us down the garden path. You could argue that the headline had already announced the promise. But in most cases good copy should be able to stand alone and make a complete argument even if all the display type were removed.

Here, from an ad for isometric exercises, is an example of the flashback technique referred to earlier:

[*Starts with the promise*]

> Imagine a 6-second exercise that helps you keep fit better than 24 push-ups. Or another that's capable of doubling muscular strength in 3 weeks!

> Both of these "quickie" exercises are part of a fantastically simple body-building method developed by Donald J. Salls, Alabama Doctor of Education, fitness expert, and coach. His own trim physique, his family's vigorous health and the nail-hard brawn of his teams are dramatic proof of the results he gets—not to mention the steady stream of reports from housewives, athletes, even school children who have discovered Dr. Salls' remarkable exercises.

[*Flashback to problem*]

> Most Americans find exercise a tedious chore. Yet we all recognize the urgent personal and social needs for keeping our bodies strong, shapely, and healthy. What man wouldn't take secret pride in displaying a more muscular figure?

> What woman doesn't long for a slimmer, more attractive figure? The endless time and trouble required to get such results has been a major, if not impossible hurdle for so many of us. But now [*return to the promise*] doctors, trainers, and physical educators are beginning to recommend the easy new approach to body fitness and contour control that Dr. Salls has distilled down to his wonderfully simple set of 10 exercises.

Of course, a really strong, exciting promise doesn't necessarily need a statement of the problem at all. If you're selling a "New Tree That Grows a Foot a Month," it could be argued that you don't actually have to spell out how frustrating it is to spend years waiting for ordinary trees to grow; this is well known and implied.

Other Ways to Structure Copy

There are as many different ways to structure a piece of advertising copy as there are to build a house.

But response advertising, whether in publication or direct mail, has special requirements. The general advertiser is satisfied with making an impression, but the response advertiser must stimulate immediate action. Your copy must pile up in your readers' minds argument after argument, sales point after sales point, until their resistance collapses under the sheer weight of your persuasiveness, and they do what you ask.

One of the greatest faults in the copy of writers who are not wise in the ways of response is failure to apply this steadily increasing pressure. This may sound like old-fashioned "hard sell," but, ideally, the impression your copy makes should be just the opposite. The best copy, like the best salesperson, does not appear to be selling at all, but simply to be sharing information or proposals of mutual benefit to the buyer and seller.

Of course, in selling certain kinds of staple merchandise, copy structuring may not be important. There the advertising may be compared to a painting in that the aim is to convey as much as possible at first glance and then convey more and more with each repeated look. You wouldn't sell a 35-piece electric drill set with a 1,000-word essay, but rather you would sell it by spreading out the set in glowing full-color illustrations richy studded with "feature call-outs."

But where you are engaged in selling intangibles, an idea or ideas instead of familiar merchandise, the way you structure your copy can be vitally important.

In addition to the classic form mentioned above, here are some other ways to structure copy.

With the "cluster-of-diamonds" technique, you assemble a great many precious details of what you are selling and present them to the reader in an appropriate setting. A good example is the "67 Reasons Why" subscription advertising of *U.S. News & World Report*, listing 67 capsule descriptions of typical recent news articles in the magazine. The "setting"—the surrounding copy containing general information and argumentation—is as important as the specific jewels in the cluster. Neither would be sufficiently attractive without the other.

The "string-of-pearls" technique is similar but not quite the same. Each "pearl" is a complete little gem of selling, and a number of them are simply strung together in almost any sequence to make a chain. David Ogilvy's

"Surprising Amsterdam" series of ads is like this. Each surprising fact about Amsterdam is like a small-space ad for the city, but only when all these little ads are strung together, do you feel compelled to get up from your easy chair and send for those KLM brochures. This technique is especially useful, by the way, when you have a vast subject like an encyclopedia to discuss. You have not one but many stories to tell. If you simply ramble on and on, most readers won't stay with you. So make a little list of stories you want to tell, write a tight little one-paragraph essay on each point, announce the subject of each essay in a boldface subhead, and then string them all together like pearls, with an appropriate beginning and ending.

The "fan dancers" technique is like a line of chorus girls equipped with Sally Rand fans. The dancers are always about to reveal their secret charms, but they never quite do. You've seen this kind of copy many times. One of the best examples is the circular received in answer to an irresistible classified ad in *Popular Mechanics*. The ad simply said "505 odd, successful enterprises. Expect something odd." The circular described the entire contents of a book of money-making ideas in maddening fashion. Something like: "No. 24. Here's an idea that requires nothing but old coat hangers. A retired couple on a Kansas farm nets $240 weekly with this one." "No. 25. All you need is a telephone—and you don't call them, they call you to give their orders. A bedridden woman in Montpelier nets $70 a week this way." And so on.

With the *machine gun* technique, you simply spray facts and arguments in the general direction of the reader, in the hope that at least some of them will hit. This may be called the no-structure structure, and it is the first refuge of the amateur. If you have a great product and manage to convey your enthusiasm for it through the sheer exuberance of your copy, you will succeed, not because of your technique, but despite it. And the higher the levels of taste and education of your readers, the less chance you will have.

Establishing the Uniqueness of Your Product or Service

What is the unique claim to fame of the product or service you are selling? This could be one of your strongest selling points. The word *only* is one of the greatest advertising words. If what you offer is "better" or "best," this is merely a claim in support of your argument that the reader *should* come to you for the product or services offered. But if what you are offering is the "only" one of its kind, then readers *must* come to you if they want the benefits that only you can offer.

Here are some ways in which you may be able to stake out a unique position in the marketplace for the product or service you are selling: "We're the largest." People respect bigness in a company or a sales total— they reason that, if a product leads the others in its field, it must be good. Thus "No. 1 Best-Seller" is always a potent phrase, for it is not just an airy claim but a hard fact that proves some kind of merit.

But what if you're *not* the largest? Perhaps you can still establish a unique position, as in "We're the largest of our kind." By simply defining your identity more sharply, you may still be able to claim some kind of size superiority. For example, there was the Trenton merchant who used to boast that he had "the largest clothing store in the world in a garage!"

A mail-order photo finisher decided that one benefit it had to sell was the sheer bigness of its operation. It wasn't the biggest—that distinction belonged, of course, to Eastman Kodak. But it was second. And Eastman Kodak was involved in selling a lot of other things, too, such as film and cameras and chemicals. Its photo-finishing service was only one of many divisions. So the advertiser was able to fashion a unique claim: "America's Largest *Independent* Photo Finisher."

"We're the fastest-growing." If you're on the way to *becoming* the largest, that's about as impressive a proof of merit as being the largest—in fact, it may be even *more* impressive, because it adds the excitement of the underdog coming up fast. *U.S. News & World Report* used this to good effect during the 1950s while its circulation was growing from approximately 400,000 to about three times that figure: "America's Fastest-Growing News-Magazine." Later, the same claim was used effectively for Capitol Record Club, "America's Fastest-Growing Record Club."

"We offer a unique combination of advantages." It may be that no one claim you can make is unique, but that none of your competitors is able to equal your claim that you have *all* of a certain number of advantages.

In the early 1960s, the Literary Guild began to compete in earnest with the Book-of-the-Month Club (BOMC). The Literary Guild started offering books that compared very favorably with those offered by BOMC. But the latter had a couple of unique claims that the Guild couldn't match—BOMC's distinguished board of judges and its book-dividend system, with a history of having distributed $375 million worth of books to members.

How to compete? The Guild couldn't claim the greatest savings; one of Doubleday's other clubs actually saved the subscriber more off the publisher's price. It couldn't claim that it had books offered by no other club; some of Doubleday's other clubs were offering some of the same books, and even BOMC would sometimes make special arrangements to offer a book being featured by the Guild.

But the Guild was able to feature a unique *set* of advantages that undoubtedly played a part in the success it has enjoyed: "Only the Literary Guild saves you 40 percent to 60 percent on books like these as soon as they are published." Other clubs could make either of these two claims, but only the Guild could claim both.

"We have a uniquely advantageous location." A classic of this was James Webb Young's great ad for "Old Jim Young's Mountain Grown Apples— Every Bite Crackles, and the Juice Runs Down Your Lips." In it Jim Young, trader, tells how the natives snickered when his pappy bought himself an abandoned homestead in a little valley high up in the Jemes Mountains. But "Pappy" Young, one of the slickest farmers ever to come out of Madison

Avenue, knew that "this little mountain valley is just a natural apple spot—as they say some hillsides are in France for certain wine grapes. The summer sun beats down into this valley all day, to color and ripen apples perfectly; but the cold mountain air drains down through it at night to make them crisp and firm. Then it turns out that the soil there is full of volcanic ash, and for some reason that seems to produce apples with a flavor that is really something."

Haband Ties used to make a big thing out of being located in Paterson, New Jersey, the silk center of the nation. Even though most of the company's ties and other apparel were made of synthetic fibers, somehow the idea of buying ties from the silk center made the reader feel he was buying ties at the very source. In the same way, maple syrup from Vermont should be a lot easier to sell than maple syrup from Arizona.

Finally, suppose you believe that you have something unique to sell, but you hesitate to start an argument with your competitors by making a flat claim that they may challenge. In that case you can *imply your uniqueness* by the way in which you word the claim. "Here's one mouthwash that keeps your mouth sweet and fresh all day long" doesn't flatly claim that it's the only one. It simply says, "at least *we've* got this desirable quality, whether any other product does or not." *Newsweek* identified itself as "the news magazine that separates fact from opinion"—a powerful use of that innocent word *the* which devastates the competition.

"Versatility" Campaign: Apple Computer

The computer market is huge, and the competition is fierce. Among the unquestioned leaders is Apple Macintosh Computer Systems.

Situation

The small-business market includes over 22 million desk workers. This group's aggregate expenditures for personal computers come to $12 billion. This market had generated sizable revenue prior to the "Versatility" campaign. However, Apple's position was eroding at the time.

Strategy

Apple developed a three-year plan, designed to capitalize on the small-business market opportunity. A direct response print ad was developed to qualify high-potential prospects (see Exhibit 17–4). The ad was directed to any small-business owner who might come upon it in general business publications. The same ad appeared in vertical publications directed to such fields as accounting, law, real estate, engineering and design, architecture, communications, advertising, and publishing.

Exhibit 17–4.   **Direct Response Ad**

General ad directed to small businesses in all categories.

Results

When Wunderman Worldwide, the agency, saw the results, it noted that the ad which appealed to all small businesses did very well in general business publications but not so well in vertical publications. So the agency developed a new strategy for vertical publications, *version copy to each category of business being pursued*. Responses doubled! (See Exhibit 17–5 for versioned copy targeted to the communications field.)

A final note: The lack of a coupon was purposeful. It was learned that specifying an 800 number as the only means to respond had a positive effect in qualifying leads. Dealers were sent only qualified leads—small businesses that indicated they were in a position to act immediately.

Effective Use of Testimonials

If you have a great product or service, you have an almost inexhaustible source of great copy practically free—written by your own customers. They will come up with selling phrases straight from the heart that no copywriter, no matter how brilliant, would ever think of. They will write with a depth of conviction that the best copywriters will find hard to equal.

The value of testimonials in mail-order advertising has been recognized for nearly 100 years, is generally taken for granted, and nonetheless is frequently overlooked. If a survey were conducted of companies dependent on responses by mail, the survey would undoubtedly reveal that a shockingly high percentage of those companies have no regular, methodical system of soliciting, filing, and using good testimonials. Yet a direct marketing enterprise may often stand or fall on whether it makes a good use of testimonials.

Many years ago the Merlite Company was founded to sell the Presto midget fire extinguisher, entirely through agents. The advertising job was to pull inquiries from prospective agents, who were then converted to active salespeople by the follow-up direct mail package. One of the first efforts for Merlite was the creation of a testimonials-soliciting letter. From this letter, which was mailed to a fair number of their best agents, came the story that formed the basis for a successful small-space ad that ran for years and resulted in the sale of thousands of units. The headline: "I'm Making $1,000 a Month—and Haven't Touched Bottom Yet!" In those days, $1,000 a month was big money—it represented just about the top limit of the wildest dreams of people of modest means. If the ad had claimed, "Make $1,000 a month selling this amazing little device," it would have sounded like a hard-to-believe get-rich-quick scheme. But the fact that an actual agent said it (his name and picture appeared in every ad) made the possibility a fact, not a claim. And the "haven't touched bottom yet" was a homey additional promise that probably no city slicker copywriter would have thought of if he or she were creating a fictional testimonial.

Many U.S. School of Music ads in the past were built around testimonials. Being able to play a musical instrument has a deep meaning for people that could best be expressed by the students themselves. One ad bore a headline

Exhibit 17–5.   **Category Direct Response Ad**

Versioned ad directed to the communications field.

extracted from an ecstatic student's comments: "I Can't Believe My Ears—
I'm Playing Music! My friends all think it's me, but I keep telling them it's
your wonderful course."

One of the most appealing and effective stories used in art school
advertising was that of a Florida mother who enrolled in the course and
became one of the state's best-known painters. Her story was filled with
more joy of fulfillment, credible praise for the course, and identification for
other women than could be used in the ad. For instance, the day her
textbooks arrived, she felt like a "child with a new toy." Her instructors were
"just wonderful. I actually came to feel they were my friends." But what if
you're a homemaker tied down with housework and babies? Isn't it hard to
find time to paint? "It's not as hard as it sounds. When you have something
exciting to look forward to, the housework flies. It's like when you're ex-
pecting a guest. You seem to get through the chores easily because you're
looking forward to the visit." But won't hubby and kids be resentful if Mom
spends a lot of time painting? Not her family. "They're so enthusiastic.
Everytime I complete a painting, it's like a wonderful family party at our
home." Isn't this reassuring? Isn't this what every creative woman would
enjoy? And doesn't she make it all sound wonderfully possible and attainable?

You may have received some unsolicited testimonials that you have
gotten permission to use and are already using. But if you expand this collection by setting up a methodical testimonial-soliciting program, you can
increase tenfold your effective use of testimonials. Because the quality and
usefulness of testimonials vary widely, the more testimonials you pull in, the
more pure gold you should be able to pan from the ore. Of course, it's
important to get the testimonial donor's signature on some kind of release
giving you permission to use his or her comments, name, and photo, if any.
The wording of the releases varies. Some companies are content with a very
simple "You have my permission" sentence; others use a more elaborately
foolproof legal form. You should consult your attorney about the kind you
choose to use.

Your testimonial-soliciting letter should drop a few gentle hints about
your interest in hearing of actual benefits and improvements from your
product. Otherwise you'll get too many customers writing similar lines of
empty praise such as "it's the greatest" and "it's the finest."

Justify the Price

"Why Such a Bargain? The Answer Is Simple." These eight magic words constitute one of the most important building blocks in the mail-order sale. They
have been expressed hundreds of different ways in the past, and will appear
in hundreds of new forms in the future. But whether in the mail-order ads of
magazines and direct mail yesterday and today, or the televised home-printed
facsimile transmission of tomorrow, the price justification argument will
always be with us. It does an important job of making the low price seem

believable and the high price not really so high.

Here are a number of examples of price justification from the past. As you read through them, ask yourself if it isn't likely that similar arguments will still be used in the year 2010.

Doubleday Subscription Service: "How can the Doubleday Subscription Service offer these extremely low prices? The answer is really quite simple. Not everyone wants the same magazines. By getting all the publishers to allow us to make their offers in one mailing, each subscriber has a chance to pick and choose; each magazine gets its most interested readers at the lowest possible cost. The savings are passed on to you in the lowest possible prices for new, introductory subscriptions."

Reader's Digest (Music of the World's Great Composers): "How is this low price possible? Without the great resources of RCA and the large 'audience' of *Reader's Digest*, such a collection would have to cost about $60.00. This sum would be needed to cover royalties to musicians, the cost of recording, transferring sound from tape to records, manufacturing and packaging. But because a single large pressing of records brings down the cost of manu-facturing, and because the entire edition is reserved in advance for *Digest* subscribers, you can have these luxury-class records now at a fraction of the usual price for records of such outstanding quality!"

Singer (socket wrench and tool set): "This set is not available in stores—but sets like these sell regularly in stores at a much higher price. You save the difference because—unlike the usual store which sells just a few sets at a time, we sell many hundreds, thus enabling us to purchase large quantities at big savings which we pass on to you."

American Heritage (History of the Civil War): "The post-publication price of the standard edition will be $19.95; it can be kept down to this level because of the exceptionally large first printing. But if you reserve a copy before publication (a great help with shipping, storage, inventory, etc.) we shall be glad to reduce the $19.95 price by 25 percent." (Notice the double whammy here. First, the value of the pre-publication edition is justified, and then the even greater value of the post-publication edition is justified.)

Book-of-the-Month Club (Pre-Publication Society): "Like the 'limited edition'—a very old custom in publishing—'pre-publication' offerings are designed to help underwrite the costs of any publishing project where there is an exceptionally high risk and heavy investment. Under modern printing conditions, if a publisher can be assured of a relatively large edition, the per-copy cost is reduced with almost every extra thousand copies printed. In recent years the usual procedure has been for the publisher to print an elaborate circular announcing the 'pre-publication offer' (similar to the one enclosed) and to permit booksellers, at a slight cost, to mail these announce-ments to select good customers. Rarely, however, do more than a few hundred booksellers over the country participate in this kind of promotion, with the result that comparatively few book lovers ever learn of it, and then usually only in large cities. The efforts of the Pre-Publication Society will be far more thorough and widespread."

Visual Reinforcement of Words and Ideas

Our powers of comprehension are largely built on our earliest sensations and associations. First comes touch, but that won't be much help to advertising until Aldous Huxley's "Feelvision" is invented. Next, when we are several months old, comes image, as we learn to associate Mama's smiling face with getting fed, burped, and changed. Then comes the spoken word, when we learn to call Mama by name. This early experience with the image and the spoken word is what makes television such a potent advertising force.

Our earliest experience with the printed word is usually in our heavily illustrated first reader (or preschool picture book). It is printed in large clear serif type, in lowercase—which is why serif body types seem more readable than sans serif, and lowercase more comfortable than upper. And when the book says, "Oh! See the boy!" sure enough, there is usually a picture of a boy. This makes it less likely that we would stand up in class and read aloud, "Oh! See the doy!"

Advertising has seized on this fact of human development and developed it into an astonishingly effective tool of communication. It has learned, probably far more than ever before in human history, to team words and pictures for greater impact than either alone can achieve. Sometimes it's a *rebus*, in which a picture is substituted for some of the words. For instance, instead of saying "(a summons, a will, a deed, a mortgage, a lease) are a few of the reasons why every family should have a lawyer," an ad for New York Life Insurance Company substituted pictures of documents, such as a will and a mortgage, for the words in parentheses.

Sometimes, it's a *pantomime*, with the words providing only the necessary minimum of explanation. An Itkin Brothers office furniture ad showed in four pictures what the subhead promised: "In less than 45 minutes you can have four new offices without changing your address, increasing rent, or interrupting work." The pictures were the headline, and the four captions under the photos of the partitions being installed simply read: "8:45 . . . 8:50 . . . 9:15 . . . and 9:25."

Sometimes, it's a *visual literalism*. For instance, our small-space ad for the U.S. School of Music, headed "Are You Missing Half the Fun of Playing the Guitar?" showed only half a guitar. The instrument was literally sawed in half.

Sometimes, it's an *abstract picture*. How can you picture the abstract concept "two," for instance? Avis made it literal with a photo of two fingers.

Also, the overall appearance of the ad provides visual reinforcement. Even if there are no illustrations, which is often the case, the typography and design can convey a great deal about the kind of company behind the advertising. For decades most mail-order advertising was notorious for being less attractive than general advertising; much of it still is. Whether this helps or hurts results is hotly debated. It may be that a certain homey or buckeye look adds an air of unsophisticated honesty and sincerity. But for any company involved in starting an ongoing relationship with a customer, the appearance of its direct marketing advertising should convey that it is a responsible, tasteful, and orderly company with which to do business.

The Response Device

Most direct response ads carry a reply coupon or card for ease of responding. The significant exception is small-space ads. A two-inch ad would have to be about twice as big to accommodate a coupon. Many advertisers find that it does not produce twice as many results.

A black-and-white page with an insert card (a postpaid reply postcard inserted next to the ad) costs about two and a half times more than a black-and-white page alone but usually pulls at least four times as much as a page without coupon. (Advantages of insert cards were explored in Chapter Ten.)

There are many variations of the postpaid reply envelope, depending upon cost and publication policy: oversize card insert, full-page insert with detachable card, four-page card stock insert with detachable card, eight-page newspaper advertising supplement with bound-in or stuck-on card or envelope, loose envelope (such as for film processing) inserted in Sunday newspapers, and so on.

The creative problem in preparing coupon or card copy is to summarize the message from the advertiser to the prospect as clearly, succinctly, and attractively as possible. Many readers tear out a card or coupon and leave it in a pocket or drawer for days or even weeks before deciding to send it in. At that point, the reader wants to know what this minicontract entails. It is important to provide as much resell and reassurance as possible.

If the advertiser is a club, the coupon copy should clearly spell out terms of membership.

Check boxes, numbers to be circled, and other aids to make completing the form easy should be provided wherever possible.

Any money-back guarantee, whether already mentioned in the adjoining copy or not, should be clearly stated.

Telescopic Testing

For many years it has been standard practice in direct mail to test simultaneously as many as five or six or even ten or twelve different copy appeals, formats, or offers. Giving each package equal exposure over a representative variety of lists is probably the most scientifically precise research method in advertising. But this practice has *not* been so common in publication advertising. There, for a long time, advertisers were limited to the simple *A/B split-run* test, in which every other copy of a given issue of a publication would contain Ad A and every other copy Ad B (separately keyed, of course). (See Exhibit 17–6.) This too is very precise. The main thing is to make sure that the circulation purchased is large enough to provide a statistically significant variation in results between the two ads. But for testing your way to a breakthrough, it can be slow.

If you test two ads, wait for the results; then test two more, and so on, a year or so may pass before you discover the "hot button." On the other hand,

Exhibit 17–6.   A/B Copy Test

The makers of Wynn's Friction Proofing Oil wanted to test two different sales appeals: (1) Get more power with less gas; (2) save one gallon of gas in every ten. These two "reader ads" were written to test the appeals. The second appeal brought twice as many sample requests as the first one.

ADD THIS PRODUCT TO ANY MOTOR OIL FOR MORE POWER WITH LESS GAS

Sluggish motors get a new lease on life with Wynn's Friction Proofing Oil. This new chemical compound added to your present brand of motor oil every 1000 miles, bonds a super-slick surface to engine parts. This virtually eliminates the friction drag that wastes up to half your car's power, and gives you so much extra mileage from gasoline that it's like getting one gallon free with every ten you buy. Besides paying for itself in gasoline savings, Wynn's cuts carbon and sludge, frees sticky valves, reduces wear and repairs. Try Wynn's for new pep, power, economy from your car. We're so sure you'll continue to use it that we make this special introductory offer of a regular 1000-mile size 95¢ can of Wynn's for only 10¢. Just send your name and address, enclosing 10¢ in coin or stamps. By return mail you'll get a certificate entitling you to a 95¢ can of Wynn's without additional charge at any Wynn dealer. Limit one. Offer expires April 30. Write today—Wynn Oil Company, Dept. A-4, Azusa California.

AT SERVICE STATIONS, GARAGES, NEW CAR DEALERS

CAR OWNERS! SAVE ONE GALLON OF GAS IN EVERY TEN

Sluggish motors get a new lease on life with Wynn's Friction Proofing Oil. This new chemical compound added to your present brand of motor oil every 1000 miles, bonds a super-slick surface to engine parts. This virtually eliminates the friction drag that wastes up to half your car's power, and gives you so much extra mileage from gasoline that it's like getting one gallon free with every ten you buy. Besides paying for itself in gasoline savings, Wynn's cuts carbon and sludge, frees sticky valves, reduces wear and repairs. Try Wynn's for new pep, power, economy from your car. We're so sure you'll continue to use it that we make this special introductory offer of a regular 1000-mile size 95¢ can of Wynn's for only 10¢. Just send your name and address, enclosing 10¢ in coin or stamps. By return mail you'll get a certificate entitling you to a 95¢ can of Wynn's without additional charge at any Wynn dealer. Limit one. Offer expires April 30. Write today—Wynn Oil Company, Dept. C-12, Azusa, California.

AT SERVICE STATIONS, GARAGES, NEW CAR DEALERS

if you test the control against one ad in Publication A and and another in Publication B (we often do), it is useful, but it does introduce another variable, the difference in the two publications. A truly scientific test has only one variable.

All our experience and common sense tell us that six or eight tests are far more likely to produce a hit than only two. To solve this problem, direct marketing advertisers are turning increasingly to multiple ad testing. We call it *telescopic testing*, because it permits the advertiser to telescope a year's testing experience into a single insertion. Telescopic testing simply applies the direct mail principle of multiple testing to publication advertising. But it requires publications or formats with the mechanical capability of running such tests. Perhaps the first magazine to offer this capability was *TV Guide*. Because television programs are different in each region, *TV Guide* publishes over 80 different regional editions. Theoretically, you could do over 80 different split-runs, one in each regional edition, in a single week. (But you wouldn't, because the circulation for each test would be too small.) By testing Ad A vs. Ad B in the first region, Ad A vs. Ad C in the next region, and so on, it is possible to test as many as 10 or 15 different ads or ad variations simultaneously. By assigning to Ad A results the numerical value of 100, we can give the other ad results proportionate numerical values and rank them accordingly.

An easier way to do multiple testing is by intermixed card stock inserts bound into a magazine so that Ad A appears in Copy 1, Ad B in Copy 2, Ad C in Copy 3, and so on.

Advertisers began testing new appeals and offers by doing A/B regional splits of black-and-white pages and even half-pages in the local program section of *TV Guide*. The following examples illustrate what can be done:

- A book series achieved at 252 percent improvement.

- A correspondence course inquiry ad was improved 209 percent.

- A name-getting giveaway program brought its advertising cost per coupon down to 19 cents!

The technique of applying telescopic testing is discussed in Chapter Twenty. Today there are three basic methods of running multiple tests:

1. Simultaneous split-runs in regional editions of a magazine that offers such a service, with one ad used as a control in all the splits

2. Free-standing stuffers or loose newspaper preprints, intermixed at the printing plant before being supplied to the publication

3. Full-page card inserts in magazines, intermixed at the printing plant

It's a rather expensive game to play, but major direct marketers today are playing for multimillion-dollar stakes. All it takes is one breakthrough to pay for all the necessary research in a very short time.

A dramatic example of the application of telescopic testing is provided by a series of six ads created for *Consumer Reports* and tested simultaneously against the control ad via intermixed bound-in inserts in *TV Guide*. Shown

in Exhibit 17–7 through 17–13 is the first page of each of the seven insert tests. Study each carefully and see if you can give ratings for Ads A through G.

Have you rated the ads? Now let's review the actual results by coupon count. Ranking Ad A—the control ad—as 100, here is the relative pull of each ad, courtesy of Joel Feldman, director of marketing/circulation for the magazine at the time:

Ad A—100 (control)	Ad E—65
Ad B—107	Ad F—61
Ad C—101	Ad G—33
Ad D—82	

While the 7 percent gain scored by the winner, Ad B, may not seem like a startling improvement, it is important to keep in mind that this 7 percent was on top of the impressive gains scored by Ad A, the winner in previous tests. And the circulation of 500,000 given to each ad resulted in a sufficiently large number of responses to make the results highly significant statistically. So thanks to this test, the client could be confident that future publication advertising would be 7 percent more efficient—a substantial gain when applied to millions of dollars worth of advertising.

Creating "Stopping Power" for Your Ads

As a final thrust toward getting more of your ads read and acted upon, let's explore some unique techniques for stopping the reader as he or she flips through a magazine or newspaper. These techniques were developed by creative directors of the far-flung Young & Rubicam network of agencies around the world.

The premise of "stopping power" is that if you can stop a person long enough to read an intriguing headline, your chances of getting the person to read and act upon the balance of the ad are greatly enhanced.

Hanley Norins, a former creative director at Young & Rubicam West, put the entire Y&R training program into perspective in a remarkable book, *The Young & Rubicam Traveling Creative Workshop*.[1] He devoted one chapter to direct marketing and direct response advertising. The seven principles of "stopping power" are detailed as follows:

1. Attracts the defined target audience, plus an audience beyond

2. Demands participation

3. Forces an emotional response by touching on a basic human want or need

[1] Prentice Hall, 1990.

Exhibit 17–7.   **Control Ad A in Insert Test**

Exhibit 17–8.   **Ad B in Insert Test**

Exhibit 17–9.   **Ad C in Insert Test**

Exhibit 17–10.   **Ad D in Insert Test**

Exhibit 17–11.   **Ad E in Insert Test**

Exhibit 17–12.   **Ad F in Insert Test**

Exhibit 17–13.   **Ad G in Insert Test**

4. Creates a desire to know more

5. Surprises the reader

6. Exposes expected information in an unexpected way

7. Breaks with the personality and rules of the product category

These seven principles give the creative person a "cafeteria list" of guidelines, any of which may be selected as appropriate for a given headline.

The techniques of applying "stopping power" give the creative person eight different options for applying the principles:

1. Open-minded narrative (picture or thought) in which the resolution is not presented

2. Ironic twists on ordinary behavior

3. Play on words in the headline

4. Incongruity of visual elements and/or words by unusual juxtaposition of elements

5. Exaggeration

6. Simplification

7. Shocking visual and/or headline

8. Participation visuals (e.g., tests, games, multiple visuals)

Self-Quiz

1. Good direct response advertising should make its strongest appeal to

_____

_____.

2. Who are the best prospects?

_____

_____

_____

3. In print advertising, advantages belong to the _____

_____.

Benefits belong to the _____

_____.

4. When are benefits more important?

_____

_____

5. When are advantages more important?

_____

_____

6. Fill in this list of ultimate benefits:

a. _____   j. _____

b. _____   k. _____

c. _____   l. _____

d. _____   m. _____

e. _____   n. _____

f. _____   o. _____

g. _____   p. _____

h. _____   q. _____

i. _____

7. Semantics is the hydrogen bomb of _____.

8. Most successful headlines have a "hook" to catch the reader and pull him or her in. The most common hooks are such words as:

a. _____   d. _____

b. _____   e. _____

c. _____   f. _____

9. A common error in writing leads is that the writer _____

_____.

10. A good writing principle is that body copy should _____

_____.

11. What labels may be applied to the sections of a classic copy argument?

a. _____

b. _____

c. _____

d. _____

e. _____

12. Name four other ways to structure copy.

    a. _____

    b. _____

    c. _____

    d. _____

13. What four-letter word is one of the greatest advertising words?

_____

14. Name five unique claims to fame that may prove to be the strongest selling points for a product or service.

    a. _____

    b. _____

    c. _____

    d. _____

    e. _____

15. What is the major advantage of using testimonials in direct response advertising?

_____

_____

_____

_____

16. Name one of the most important building blocks in the mail-order sale.

_____

_____

_____

17. Name four ways you can give visual reinforcement to words and ideas.

    a. _____

b. _____

c. _____

d. _____

18. When is a coupon not indicated for a direct response ad?

_____

_____

_____

_____

19. Define *telescopic testing*.

_____

_____

_____

_____

20. What are the three basic methods of running multiple tests?

a. _____

b. _____

c. _____

21. Define *stopping power*.

_____

_____

Pilot Project

You are a copywriter by profession. You have just been employed by a direct response advertising agency. The agency has been appointed by a home study school offering a course in accounting. Your copy supervisor has asked you to come up with headlines designed to get inquiries. Develop one headline for each of these ultimate benefits:

Health: _____

_____

Money: _____

_____

Security: _____

_____

Pride: _____

_____

Approval: _____

_____

Enjoyment: _____

_____

Excitement: _____

_____

Power: _____

_____

Fulfillment: _____

_____

Freedom: _____

_____

Identity: _____

_____

Relaxation: _____

_____

Escape: _____

_____

Curiosity: _____

_____

Possessions: _____

_____

Sex: _____

_____

Hunger: _____

_____

Managing Your Direct Marketing Operation

CHAPTER EIGHTEEN

Managing a Lead-Generation Program

Many products and services cannot be sold cost effectively through a one-step sales effort. A two-step, or multistep, program is usually necessary when a significant customer investment is required, or when personal interaction is necessary to complete a transaction. The two major uses of a lead-generation program are:

1. Identifying prospect/customer interest or potential prior to committing to the cost of a face-to-face sales visit

2. Generating interest and stimulating traffic into a local retail outlet

The first instance is *lead qualification* and the second is *lead* (or traffic) *generation*. If your needs can be met by either of these activities, you need a lead-generation program.

Types of Lead-Generation Programs

There are three general types of lead-generation programs. Although the principles that govern are the same, the needs that dictate the programs differ.

Business-to-Business

The primary objective in business-to-business lead generation is to get qualified leads from prospects who, in effect, raise their hands and say, "I'd like more information about your proposition." The thrust of the promotion can be as simple as encouraging prospects to request literature with an

inducement to order by mail. Telephone follow-ups of those who request literature is often an integral part of the lead-generation program. For more complex propositions, those requiring interaction with a live salesperson, the objective is to get a request for a salesperson to call. However, the cost of an industrial sales call being what it is today—McGraw-Hill estimates well in excess of $200—mail and phone follow-up is becoming the norm rather than the exception.

A recent development, in the office equipment field in particular, is the establishment of office equipment stores. In this case manufacturers like IBM and Xerox use direct marketing methods to induce qualified prospects to visit their stores to discuss their needs and to see live demonstrations.

Business-to-Consumer

The feasibility of lead-generation programs for consumer products is almost always dictated by price point and available channels of distribution. The unit of sale inherent in package goods, for example, obviates the practicality of a lead-generation program except in the case of a cents-off coupon co-op. (See Chapter 13, "Co-ops.")

However, lead-generation programs do make eminent sense for the likes of a lawn care service where the annual expenditure is in the area of $150. Or for electronic equipment like VHS. Or for refrigerators, or air-conditioning, or freezers, or insulation—each a considered purchase of magnitude for the consumer.

Some manufacturers sell major equipment directly to the consumer. Most sell through traditional retail channels. In the former, the objective is to get qualified leads and to complete the transaction by mail and/or telephone follow-up. In the latter, the objective is to drive a qualified prospect to a retail outlet.

Public Relations

A third type of lead-generation program uses public relations as the medium for getting leads. Done right, public relations is an extremely effective method of producing leads in both the consumer and business fields.

As a matter of fact, more often than not, editorial mention of a free booklet offer or a new product is likely to produce more leads than a space ad. The theory is that the reader puts more stock in editorial mentions than in ads. The other side of the coin is that conversions to orders are more likely from space ads than from editorial mentions.

The policies of publishers vary when it comes to giving free editorial mention. Some publishers give editorial mention only if an ad is placed; others give editorial mention irrespective of space advertising. Many firms prepare and distribute their own news releases to likely publications. However, there is no substitute for a good public relations agency in getting news releases placed.

Adjusting the Quality and Quantity of Leads

No matter what the type of lead-generation program, all marketers have an option to produce what are commonly referred to as "loose" or "tight" leads. Loose lead offers can be expected to produce a higher front-end response; tight lead offers can be expected to produce a lower front-end response, but a higher closure percentage. Listed below are ten lead "looseners" and ten lead "tighteners":

Looseners:
1. Tell less about the product.
2. Add convenience for replies.
3. Give away something.
4. Ask for only a little information.
5. Highlight the offer.
6. Make the ad "scream."
7. Don't ask for a phone number.
8. Increase the offer's value.
9. Offer a contest or sweeps.
10. Run in more general media.

Tighteners:
1. Mention a price.
2. Mention a phone or sales call.
3. Tell a lot about the product.
4. Ask for a lot of information.
5. Specify rules for the offer.
6. Ask for postage on the reply.
7. Bury the offer in the copy.
8. Tie the offer to a sales call.
9. Change the offer's value.
10. Ask for money.

The decision as to whether you want loose leads or tight leads must be dictated by experience. If salespeople close only one out of ten loose leads, for example, they may become discouraged and abandon the program. On the other hand, if salespeople close three out of ten loose leads vs. five out of ten tight leads with twice as many leads to draw from, they (and management too) might opt for the loose lead program.

Gathering Input from the Sales Force

When planning a promotion, marketers often overlook the most valuable tie to their customer base—the sales force. No source will be able to relate to the specific needs and product application for a market as well as the members of the sales force. They are on the "firing line." They know what is going on in the territory, who their competition is, the spheres of influence among their prospects. Even the message in your communications can be influenced in both tone and content by the sales force.

Setting the Objectives of the Program

The special need for objectives in a lead-generation program relates to the quality of leads. An abundance of leads can be meaningless if an insufficient number convert to sales. The key question is: What ratio of sales to inquiries

do we need to make this program profitable? This must be spelled out when setting objectives.

Determining the Promotion Strategy

Strategies should identify the steps required for accomplishing the program's objectives. They are the road map for getting from where you are to where you want to be. In addition, they should mesh with the strategies being applied by the sales force and other distribution channels. For example, if the sales force's strategy is soliciting the legal profession to sell word processors, then the promotion's strategy may be to develop a direct mail/lead-generation campaign directed at the legal profession. This, in turn, would provide qualified leads from the legal profession for the sales force to convert into sales.

Planning the Implementation Stage of the Program

Once objectives and strategies are established, the time to implement the program—make it come alive—arrives. Implementation involves consideration of the following areas:

- *Sales force involvement*. Any sales force can make or break a lead-generation program. Front-end involvement, as stated, is essential. So is foreknowledge of the full promotional effort, including media selection, samples of ads and/or mailing packages, and detailed explanations of any offers or incentives. Finally, a feedback loop should be established for a qualitative assessment of positive and negative results of the promotion.

- *Capacity and lead-flow planning*. Lead flow is not a faucet that can be turned on or off at will. Lead flow must be planned so that leads come in at a rate equal to the sales force's capacity to handle them. Although there will be more on this subject later in this chapter, the key point to remember is that either too few leads or too many leads will work to the detriment of the program.

- *Creative strategy*. Creative strategy for a lead-generation program should reflect the creative strategies applied for other advertising efforts, including general advertising, but the look and feel of the communication should be consistent with the overall image of the company to get the full benefits of an integrated campaign.

- *Media strategy*. The key question is: Given the target market and the product offering, what medium will most effectively accomplish the task? Whether it be mail, print, broadcast, cable—whatever the medium—key considerations such as penetration, key prospects reached, number of contacts, and so forth must be considered.

- *Fulfillment strategy*. As simple as it sounds, one must know exactly what will happen to a lead, once it's received. If there is to be a brochure, for

example, ample quantities must be in stock before the initial communication occurs. Measurement systems (covered later in this chapter) must be in place. Systems must be in place for scheduling sales calls, referring leads to the field, call-back programs, and so on. Failure to be ready to fulfill promptly can kill the best of promotions.

You've informed your sales force, planned capacity, made your offer, and then the leads start coming in. How do you manage this process to ensure the maximum effectiveness and efficiency for the entire program?

Capacity Planning

Let's begin by taking a closer look at capacity planning. We said that it was a critical component of the up-front planning process, but it is also key to managing on an ongoing basis. No matter how carefully planned, a program can change because of internal and external variables.

For instance, postal deliveries might be slower or faster than anticipated, a computerized customer file might malfunction, a new product could take twice as much time to sell to a lead as anticipated. The possibilities are endless, but the point is simple: Plan your capacity to be adaptable to change.

Let's look at a typical capacity-planning chart that indicates an optimum lead flow (see Table 18–1). Assuming a salesperson can average one cold prospect call a day, this table shows how many calls each office can make in a working month 20 days (20 calls per person). This information determines what quantity of mail is required at a 5 percent return to furnish leads for these calls, given that probably 20 percent of them will be qualified calls and the rest will be screened out prior to a sales call.

Thus control can be exercised over mailings so that the two salespersons in Denver, for example, will not be suddenly swamped by scores of sales leads. In their district, 4,000 mailing pieces would be needed to furnish them with 40 qualified leads, as many as the two salespersons can follow up in one month. ZIP code selectivity helps to target mailings within a district.

To keep a constant flow of leads moving to the field at an average of 3,500 a month would require 70,000 mailing pieces per month. A year's campaign (12 months multiplied by 70,000) requires 840,000 mailing pieces.

Of course, all of this up-front planning and development is directed toward providing the sales center with an even flow of qualified leads. In simple terms, the sales center is a centralized location that houses the telemarketing sales force. This subject is covered in detail in Chapter Fourteen, "Telemarketing."

Table 18–2 presents a sales center with a need for about 450 leads per week. Direct mail, television, radio, and print are all being utilized.

Table 18–1. Capacity-Planning Chart

District Offices	Number of Salespeople in Each	Total Qualified Calls Needed Each Month	Total Leads Required (at 20% Qualified)	Mailings Required (at 5% Return)
Indiana	10	200	1,000	20,000
Tennessee	14	280	1,400	28,000
Virginia	10	200	1,000	20,000
Michigan	10	200	1,000	20,000
Illinois	16	320	1,600	32,000
West Virginia	13	260	1,300	26,000
New Jersey	5	100	500	10,000
San Francisco	8	160	800	16,000
Maine	9	180	900	18,000
Seattle	9	180	900	18,000
New York City	10	200	1,000	20,000
Ohio	10	200	1,000	20,000
Texas	7	140	700	14,000
Utah	3	60	300	6,000
Connecticut	6	120	600	12,000
Pittsburgh	9	180	900	18,000
Philadelphia	11	220	1,100	22,000
Miami	3	60	300	6,000
Des Moines	7	140	700	14,000
Los Angeles	2	40	200	4,000
Denver	2	40	200	4,000
Atlanta	3	60	300	6,000
Totals	175	3,540	17,700	354,000

Lead Qualification

It is no secret that in any lead-generation program lead quality varies a great deal. In fact, generally speaking, about 20 percent of total leads result in about 80 percent of total sales revenue. It makes sense, therefore, to optimize time and effort with a good lead-qualification system. There are two good reasons for optimizing time and effort:

1. Time is money: Given the cost of an industrial sales call (over $200, by a McGraw-Hill estimate) it costs too much to have a salesperson call on unqualified prospects.

2. Good leads get "cold": While salespeople are pursuing low-quality leads, high-quality leads get "cold." Each day that a lead is not acted upon lessens the likelihood of sales conversion.

How can leads be qualified? The best way is to build screening devices into the up-front media selection.

Table 18–2.   Lead-Flow Report

	Program Code	D Map	Post Class	Drop Date	Resp. %	Drop Quant.	Resp. Quant.	1/02	1/09	1/16	1/23	1/30	2/06	2/13	2/20	2/27	3/06	3/13	3/20	3/27
Direct mail																				
Payroll—control pkg.	CB-85555-001	1	1	1/02	3.00	35,000	1050		74	179	273	263	53	53	53	53	32	21		
Payroll—test pkg.	CB-85556-T01	1	1	1/02	2.00	10,000	200		14	34	52	50	10	10	10	10	6	4		
	CB-85556-T02	1	1	1/02	2.00	10,000	200		14	34	52	50	10	10	10	10	6	4		
Accounting—control	CB-86666-002	2	1	2/06	1.50	50,000	750							53	128	195	188	38	38	38
Accounting—test	CB-86667-T03	2	1	2/06	1.00	10,000	100							7	17	26	25	5	5	5
	CB-86667-T04	2	1	2/06	1.00	10,000	100							7	17	26	25	5	5	5
	CB-86667-T05	2	1	2/06	1.00	10,000	100							7	17	26	25	5	5	5
	CB-86667-T06	2	1	2/06	1.00	10,000	100							7	17	26	25	5	5	5
Direct response:																				
T.V.								275	200	125			225	225				190	225	225
Radio								100	75				75		100		50	100	100	100
Print								75	75	75	75	75	75	75	75	75	75	75	75	75
Lead-Flow Totals								450	452	447	452	438	448	453	443	447	456	452	458	458

Note: This is a hypothetical case.

Lists in the business field, for example, can be selected by sales volume, number of employees, or net worth. If must be recognized, however, that while such selectivity can produce better-quality leads, it can also reduce the number of leads, sometimes significantly. If a product or service tends to have more of a mass application, this may not be desirable.

There are a number of ways to handle lead qualification after leads are received. The following is a prototype of a telephone script for lead qualification. A well-structured telephone script can help a telemarketing specialist to immediately "weed out" low-potential prospects prior to initiating a sales call.

Sales representative:	Thank you for calling us, Mr. Johnson. My name is Valerie Gelb. How can I help you?
Prospect:	Well, I saw your advertisement and I'm interested in your (product).
Sales representative:	I'm pleased to hear that, Mr. Johnson. You know we have several models. It would help me to recommend the most efficient one for your needs, if I knew a little more about your company. *Just what product or service do you offer?*
Customer response:	
Sales representative:	That's interesting. You know we have quite a few customers in the same business in (City) who find our (product) does an unusually good job for them. *Where are you located?*
Customer response:	
Sales representative:	Well, in a business like yours, with so many locations, you must have used products similar to ours before. *Just how did they work out for you?*
Sales representative:	*Did they do what you expected of them or did you have any particular problems?*
Customer response:	
Sales representative:	Well, I can assure you you won't have those kinds of problems with our product. Especially since we can offer you a model more suited for the way your company uses it. *By the way, is there more than one division in your company that might be using (product)?*

Customer response:

Sales representative: That means you will need a considerable quantity to begin with—and a continuing supply.
Just how many (products) do you regularly use each month?

With this series of six simple questions, a sales representative can qualify a prospect's sales potential in three important categories: the appropriateness of the product for the prospect's needs, the potential sales volume the prospect represents, and the ability of the company to fulfill the sale and service the account.

This questionnaire approach can also be an excellent means of capturing marketing information about prospects and customers. Demographic and psychographic information can be part of the feedback loop to the media selection and targeting of the initial "up-front" communication.

The most efficient way to sort leads is by degrees of potential. Table 18–3 shows how one very successful advertiser sorts leads.

Table 18–3. Lead-Sorting Form

Code	Lead Disposition	Analysis	Follow-up Action	Result
A	High potential	Refer to outside sales force		
B	Medium potential	Sell by telephone		
C	Low potential	Resurface at later date		
D	No potential	No potential-information seekers		

Lead-Flow Monitoring

As mentioned earlier in this chapter, the more quickly a lead is acted upon, the higher the likelihood of conversion. The theory behind this is that the interest is highest when a prospect has first responded to an offer. The longer that lead sits, the "colder" the prospect becomes. (Although it differs by offer, a rule of thumb is that a lead should be acted upon within ten days *maximum*. Sooner, if possible.)

But, as anyone who has worked with a lead-generation program will tell you, sometimes leads come in at a greater rate than anticipated, no matter how carefully planned. Or, sometimes less than anticipated. The latter will not cause "cold" leads, but they could have impact on sales personnel morale, overhead costs, and so on. Whether too high or too low, it pays to have contingency systems in place.

Contingency Planning

Let's look at a typical lead-flow planning model to see the normal distribution of leads into a sales center. The accompanying illustration indicates that we have learned over time that the response to mailings will almost always follow this response curve, with 50 percent of total response in the first four weeks and the balance over the next six weeks.

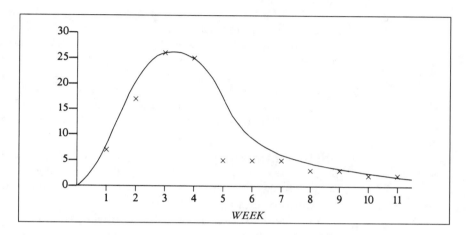

The next illustration below is simply a series of these response "waves," each representing mailings. If print or broadcast were being used, a different formula for each would have to be developed.

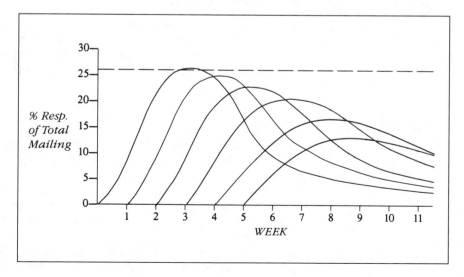

At best, our planning will keep us within 90 percent to 100 percent of the dotted line, our stated capacity. But what if some of the internal or external

events mentioned earlier should change our response curve and create a shortfall? Two basic systems that can be employed to effectively manage this occurrence are discussed below.

"In Queue" or "Lead Bank" System   Many companies create a "lead bank" system, which is a means of always being above capacity. When a lead enters the sales center, it first enters the lead bank before being dispatched for follow-up. If there is always an extra week's worth of leads, and they are handled first-in, first-out, no leads are penalized or allowed to get "cold." Naturally, the lead bank would be stocked with mail responses. You must handle phone responses immediately.

If and when there is an underdelivery of leads, the lead bank is drawn down until additional leads can be driven into the center. Or when an overdelivery occurs, the bank can be increased temporarily until the up-front solicitation can be decreased.

Shelf Contingency   It is always wise to have additional up-front communications "on the shelf"—that is, produced and ready to go—in the event of an underdelivery. If the lead-generation program is direct mail, for example, two weeks of additional mail packages in reserve will assure a timely response to an underdelivery problem. After normal capacity resumes, the lead bank can be replenished.

Tracking and Results Reporting

Tracking and results reporting are as important as management of leads in the sales center. These activities will result in quantification of the actual effort, relating the success of the program to its objectives, and making management aware of the degree of efficiency, market penetration, and revenue streams.

Tracking

Which information an advertiser decides to track is largely a function of individual needs. However, the following information data may be considered essential:

1. *Number of leads by effort.* Whether for a mailing, print ad, or broadcast spot, the number of leads responding to each effort should be captured. This is usually handled by a specific code for each.

    For instance, a mailing with a split copy test is actually two mailings. Therefore each response device should have a specific code, so that when it's received at the sales center, the proper mailing can be credited. If phone response is encouraged, as it should be, a specific phone extension

code should be given for each mailing, thus making it possible to credit the proper promotion effort.

By capturing information by code, the winning test promotions will emerge.

2. *Quality of lead/conversion information.* The best-pulling mailing or ad isn't always the most successful, for it is conversion to sales that is the true measure of success. The following comparison of two mailing packages illustrates the point:

	Number Mailed	Percent Response	Number of Responses	Percent Conversion	Number of Sales
Package A	20,000	2.0%	400	6%	24
Package B	20,000	1.0	200	15	30

As you can see, Package A would seem to be the more successful package. But when conversion is factored in, the greatest number of sales actually came from Package B. Other data captured might be list utilization, demographic information, sales volume, and number of employees.

Once these data are captured, it is critical that they be maintained on a system. The critical element of this system is the customer file. This file should include all information captured from various offers, as well as follow-up information such as calls made, time between provision of leads and sales calls, and cost per sale. The ideal is to be able to determine sales efficiency through cost per sale by office, individual salesperson, and source of lead.

Results Reporting

There's little question that an efficient lead-generation program will increase sales and cut sales costs. But it is important that results be measured and reported. Documentation of results is essential for three basic reasons: (1) to measure against original objectives of the lead-generation program, (2) to prove value to the sales force, and (3) to prove value to management.

Anatomy of a Business-to-Business Lead-Generation Program

At this point we have distilled the factors involved in building a lead-generation program. but knowing the factors is one thing; making the factors work is often quite another thing.

We must start with the realization that sales representatives in general loath and avoid paperwork. They often resent any intrusion in their territory

and scorn measurement and control. So the question is: Knowing the inherent resistance, is it possible to develop a model program that will really work?

For the answer to this question, we go to Bob Hutchings, former advertising advisor, IBM Corporate Advertising, White Plains, New York. In a career with IBM spanning almost four decades. Mr. Hutchings held many positions. He is renowned for the expertise he brought to IBM Instruments Inc. in the development of a computerized inquiry and sales lead-qualifying system. His system faces and solves the problems of lead generation. What follows is an explanation of the Hutchings system and, equally important, what is behind it.

Business-to-business buying, in general, is an evolutionary decision-making process and not an impulse process, as evidenced by consumer marketing. Many salespeople use the traditional AIDA formula in the persuasion process: they (1) create **A**ttention, (2) generate **I**nterest, (3) develop **D**esire, and (4) initiate **A**ction.

Advertising has accepted a similar model developed by researchers Lavidge and Steiner to explain how advertising works. Their model, like the AIDA formula, is based on a hierarchy of effects in the communication process. It is possible to borrow from this model and establish a hierarchy of effects for the selling process (Exhibit 18–1). The model assumes that before purchasing action occurs, an evolution takes place: Mentally, the prospect moves through a series of steps starting with awareness and ending in the purchase action.

There are a number of discrete steps in this process. It is here that the opportunities to increase the efficiency of personal selling efforts exist. It is here that advertising plays a more important role in the selling process.

Salespeople and advertising efforts both start at the information level. However, advertising can do a more cost-efficient job of creating awareness, developing knowledge, and generating interest. These are the areas of opportunity for advertising in the hierarchy of effects.

The attitude and behavioral levels of evaluation, conviction, and purchase are more appropriately handled by salespeople. These steps often require a face-to-face dialog or a product demonstration to facilitate the decision-making process.

To increase efficiency and cut costs, salespeople should do what they do best, and advertising should do what it does best. An effective inquiry system assigns specific roles to both.

Requirements for Success

Locate Computer in the Advertising Department   It is advisable to locate the computer for the inquiry system in the advertising department. Advertising people are good caretakers for the system; they have a natural interest in justifying advertising programs. The personal computer, with its easy-to-use inquiry-handling software makes the decision to install it in the advertising department a relatively easy one.

Exhibit 18–1.   **Hierarchy of Effects for Purchasing Decision Process**

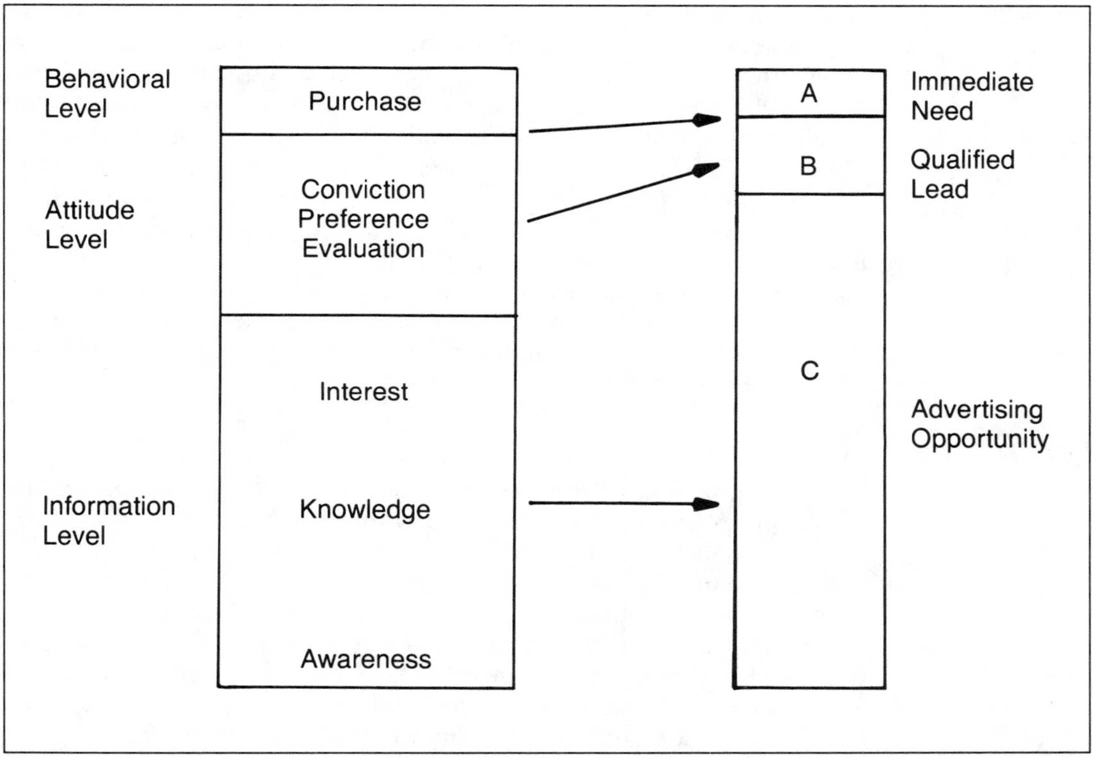

When the system resides in the advertising department, controls can be structured to eliminate delays in responding to inquiries. When inquiries are handled by other departments, delays are often experienced because of other priorities. Other departments often do not associate sales value with the inquiry handling, not understanding that with time the inquiries "cool." Thus sales opportunities are lost.

Sales representatives frequently believe that leads generated by headquarters are questionable. Cold inquiries sent for a follow-up contribute to that belief. An unfortunate reality is that salespeople often discard the entire bundle of sales leads when the first few are unproductive.

The inquiry system will survive if emphasis is placed on the ability of the system to measure the promotion and identify its contribution to sales.

Make Advertising Objectives Inquiry-Oriented.   Advertising objectives must be clearly defined as inquiry-driven advertising. The creation of advertising that employs known response techniques should be the mission of agency and/or staff copywriters and art directors. Their advertising should be measured against response-oriented goals. The inquiry system starts with the offer.

Employ Alternative Offers in Response-Oriented Advertising

Responses to hard offers, such as "Send a Salesperson," and soft offers, such as "Send Information," position the inquirer's interest in an obvious way. Requests to send a salesperson indicate an immediate need. Requests for information indicate a lower interest level. Frequently overlooked are additional offers that can position the inquirer within other steps of the buying-decision hierarchy. One such offer is "Put me on your mailing list." This type of offer identifies continuing interest in the product or subject presented in the advertising.

Responses to hard offers are associated with an immediate need and require no further qualification before they are sent as sales leads. Most inquiries, however, are responses to soft offers. Unfortunately, about 77 percent of such responses are not yet qualified for a personal follow-up. Respondents to soft offers must be investigated and qualified before the leads are released to the salespeople.

Qualifying Soft Offers

The mailing package that is used to fulfill an inquiry has more value than just supplying product information. It is a vehicle that can be used to gather information about the inquirer's level of interest in buying. The fulfillment package is often misused. It is frequently a haphazard collection of material assembled as an afterthought. Too often a response card with an offer similar to the original is used. It is unlikely that the same person will respond to the same offer twice. The fulfillment package must be an integral part of the initial creative planning process for the direct response advertising program.

A bounce-back card should be inserted with the mailing package. This card is the key to qualifying inquiries (Exhibit 18–2). This reply card differs from an inquiry business reply card. Its purpose is to get information about inquiries, their ability to buy, and their potential as prospects. The bounce-back card is not offer-oriented and therefore a reason must be given as to why it should be returned. Here is one way to position it:

> We hope your inquiry has been answered to your complete satisfaction. If it hasn't, we'd like to know about it. We would appreciate your taking a minute to respond to these few questions. This will help us to provide you with the thorough service we want you to have.

The bounce-back card questions are easily answered. A simple check mark does most of the job, and space for comments is provided.

From these questions a profile can be drawn that places the respondent in one of a series of follow-up categories (Exhibit 18–3).

Monitoring the Fulfillment Follow-Up

The computer monitors the time from the shipment date of the fulfillment package. If the bounce-back card is not returned within a specified time, a

Exhibit 18–2.   **Lead Qualifier**

BOUNCE BACK BRC

We hope your inquiry has been answered to your complete satisfaction. If it hasn't, we'd like to know about it and would appreciate your taking a minute to respond to these few questions. This will help us to provide you with the thorough service we want you to have.

1. Was the information you received adequate?
   ☐ Yes   ☐ No

2. If you need additional information, please specify.
   _____

3. Are you contemplating purchasing analytical instruments?   ☐ Yes   ☐ No   If yes, are your requirements   ☐ immediate   ☐ 3-6 months ☐ 6-12 months   ☐ over 12 months

4. What is your application? _____

5. Would you like an IBM Technical Marketing Representative to call?   ☐ Yes

   Phone No. _____

6. Do you wish to remain on our mailing list?
   ☐ Yes   ☐ No

7. Comments _____
   _____

If your address is incorrect,
please make corrections.

> Baker80208B NMR2
> B Baker
> Sr Research Physicist
> Denver University
> University Park
> Denver CO 80208

Please help us by completing this postage free card and returning it to us.

Exhibit 18–3.   **Inquiry Classification**

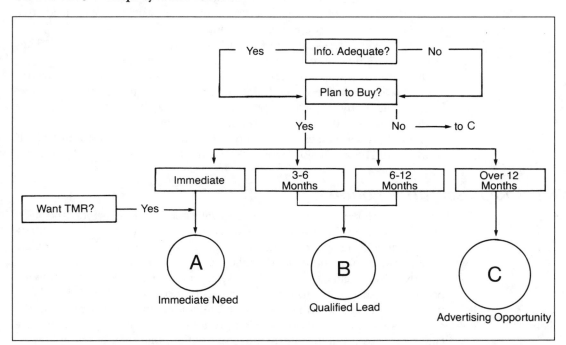

A and B leads are sent to TMR; C lead is placed in database for advance follow-up.

follow-up letter and another bounce-back card are sent. The letter appeals for response by asking, "Has your recent inquiry been answered properly?" If there is still no response, a second follow-up is sent within 30 days. This letter is more direct: "We're back again because we haven't heard from you." The envelope includes another bounce-back card.

The bounce-back card has now been exposed three times to the inquirer. Additional follow-up is usually nonproductive.

Data from the bounce-back cards are analyzed; it is the compilation of information drawn from the original inquiry card and the bounce-back card that identifies an inquirer as a qualified sales lead.

Some inquiry management systems use the telephone to qualify all inquiries. However, the telephone can prove costly when the volume of inquiries is extensive. Those systems managers who use the telephone to upgrade and further qualify promising bounce-back respondents consider this method to be more cost efficient.

Classifying Responses

When a sales representative is requested on either the inquiry card or the bounce-back card, the card is classified as "A" in the computer and sent for follow-up as "immediate need." The "A" will be used for forecasting sales potential and generating management reports.

Bounce-back cards that are analyzed as "continuing interest" are classified as "B." They are sent to the sales representative as qualified sales leads that need development through personal contact.

All other inquiries reside in the computer and are classified as "C." They are the emerging market and a very responsive mailing list.

It is the "C" group that represents the advertising opportunity. Advertising follow-up with direct mail programs drive the group up the purchasing-decision hierarchy at less cost than personal selling. When they arrive at the qualification level, the sales representative takes over.

Too often companies discard inquiry names if they are not immediately productive. This is a major error and a waste of excellent business potential.

Sales Representative Follow-Up

When unqualified inquiries are sent to salespeople, they are, for the most part, unproductive and tend to lower sales morale. With a qualification system a dramatic change in attitude can take place. Better sales leads stimulate a cooperative spirit and make the follow-up reports easier to obtain.

Advertising management and marketing management need to know the potential of sales leads to future business. In most companies, it is unlikely that an order is closed on the first call. The follow-up report is critical to the evaluation of the various advertising programs. Many inquiry systems have failed because accurate information was not supplied about the follow-up process.

Getting salespeople to report on the follow-up call is a problem. One way to overcome it is to design a simple, easy-to-use report form. The follow-up report form illustrated in Exhibit 18–4 is a self-mailer that requires only a check mark in a box in the "Excellent" or "Good" columns within the four categories. The four categories represent the segments for forecasting the closing of the order. Each box is assigned a number. These numbers become the basis for advertising evaluations and other management reports.

Exhibit 18–4.   Inquiry/Follow-Up Report Form

Sales Inquiry Information Record

Today's
Date: 04/6
Territory DANIEL SPARKS

INQUIRY
FROM: H. BARGER

GENERAL ELECTRIC COMPANY
175 Curtner Ave.
San Jose, CA 95125

Product Interest: CS
Fulfillment Sent: 03/15

Inquiry Classification: B

Special Requests:

SOURCE: CHEM & ENG NEWS

- -

Follow Up Report: BARGER95125H

Product Interest: CS

Contact Date:

Responded By: ☐ Phone   ☐ On Site   ☐ Other
Next Step Planned:
☐ Demonstration
☐ CSC Visit
☐ Sample Evaluation
☐ Price Quote
☐ Proposal

COMMENTS: _____
_____
_____
_____

Return Follow Up Report

Closing Potential
(check one box)

1-3 Months*	① Excellent	② Good
3-6 Months	③ Excellent	④ Good
6-12 Months	⑤ Excellent	⑥ Good
Over 12 Months	⑦ Excellent	⑧ Good
No Potential	☐ Excellent	

*Forecast? ☐ Yes ☐ No If Yes, $ _____ Revenue

Type of Funding
☐ Internal   ☐ Grant   Seeking funds
☐ No Funding   ☐ Don't Know
What competition if any? _____
_____

Marketing Rep. Sig. _____

Inquiry systems seldom have all follow-up reports returned for evaluation; a return of 75 percent is good. However, harassing salespeople for delinquent reports can do more damage to sales department support of the inquiry system that the missing data can.

Inquiry System Reports

The information collected provides a database from which a wealth of useful information is available. The computer summarizes the results of the advertising and sales effort. It can sort in countless ways and will produce printed reports or graphs.

This information can be put to work in many ways and can help provide advertising accountability. Reports prove useful in researching and evaluating new markets. They can evaluate publication effectiveness and provide insight into the value of various creative appeals. Some reports can be used to evaluate the effectiveness of sales follow-up activity, and even the equity of sales territory assignments. Reports can be generated as needed, but they should be prepared and circulated on a monthly basis.

Here are reports that are especially helpful to sales representatives:

1. *The company profile report* (Exhibit 18–5). This report documents a historical record of inquiries received from a single company. People who respond to the advertising are listed with their qualification rating, date of inquiry, and product interest. This report also has value in maintaining sales territory coverage when representatives change.

Exhibit 18–5.   **Company Profile Report**

```
REPORT UXM010                    ***COMPANY PROFILE***                      PAGE: 1
SPEC ID: 1047                                                               DATE:
-----------------------------------------------------------------------------------
WILLIAM H RORER INC                                                SIC: 283-DRUGS
500 VIRGINIA DRIVE                                                 REGION: NORTHEAST
PORT WASHINGTON PA 19034                                           TERRITORY JIM CIOBAN


-------------------------------INQUIRIES RECEIVED FROM: ---------------------------
                                              PROD     PROM/      DATE/       INQRY
NAME            PHONE           TITLE          INT     MEDIA      SOURCE*      CLASS
L M SATTLER     215/628-6388                   LO      12 PF    03/11'   TS     B
E KELLY         215/628-6621                   LO      12 PF    03/15    TS     B
L M SATTLER     215/628-6388    CHEMIST         LO      17 VG    09/22     S     A


--------------------------------- LAST INQUIRY FOLLOW UP RECORD --------------------
                  NAME:   L M SATTLER
          CONTACT DATE:   9/28/82
      PRODUCT INTEREST:   LO
                ACTION:   PROP PLANNED
           COMPETITION:
             POTENTIAL:   1
       TYPE OF FUNDING:   INTERNAL
          RESPONDED BY:   ON SITE

              COMMENTS:

*CODES:
(TS) TRADE SHOW — (S) SPACE — (L) LIT — (DM) DIR MAIL — (BB) BOUNCE BACK
```

2. *The trip-planning guide*. The inquiry data can be sorted in ZIP code sequence and supply a reference to the sales representative planning a more orderly coverage of territory. When appointments are scheduled in one ZIP code location, another nearby company can be called upon.

3. *Quarterly inquiry listing*. An inquiry report can be prepared that lists the total respondents by territory. Labels can be made and used for local mailing programs.

The following types of reports are useful to sales management:

1. *The purchase potential report* (Exhibit 18–6). The source of information for the purchase potential report is the sales lead follow-up card. The closing potential numbers assigned by the salespeople establish a ratio norm against which other programs are evaluated. This norm becomes a stronger management tool as the inquiry system database grows.

   Norms are useful in comparing current-month activity against previous-month activity and comparing achievements against year-to-date objectives. They are also useful in comparing sales region and sales representative effectiveness.

   The purchase potential identifies the volume of potential sales. This report is useful for manufacturing planning. The same report also helps sales managers plan for appropriate sales closing action. For instance, a potential rating of "1" may require only a special incentive to get the order, while a "3" may need more sales contact, including a product demonstration.

2. *The product inquiry report* (Exhibit 18–7). The product inquiry report maintains a running record of the numbers of inquiries for each product in the line. Quite often, there is a correlation between product inquiries and product sales volume. This report can highlight those areas where more advertising is needed to increase the number of inquiries.

3. *The regional inquiry report* (Exhibit 18–8). This report compares the effectiveness of one region with another in scoring inquiry potentials. A similar report compares sales representatives within a region on their record.

These types of reports are useful to advertising management:

1. *The daily flash report* (Exhibit 18–9). This report identifies the daily status of each promotion. The daily mail count is recorded by a bar chart. A trend line that records the total inquiries for the campaign is overlayed. As time progresses, the bar chart forms a bell-shaped curve that can be used to identify the halfway point of the inquiry returns. Identifying this point is useful in projecting the life of the promotion.

Exhibit 18–6.   **Purchase Potential Report**

NATIONAL POTENTIAL FOR LEAD CLOSING							DATE: JUNE PAGE: 1
NAME	COMPANY	CITY	ST	POT	PROD	TER	REG
R P SLOANE	HONEYWELL	PHOENIX	AZ	1	E2	RK	DW
A P MASINO	HANSENS LAB INC.	ROCHESTER	NY	1	VO	CD	PC
D HALPERN	EATON CORP	MURRAY HILL	NJ	1	U1	JK	PC
C A CHANG	WYETH LABS	TOLEDO	OH	1	I3	LL	HD
G LARSON	A W LYONS	RARITAN	NJ	1	LO	LC	PC
C K KIM	ORTHO PHARM CORP	SPRING HOUSE	PA	1	I9	JC	TM
J R BRECO	SHERWIN WILLIAMS	PHILADELPHIA	PA	2	NB	JC	TM
C T KITCHEN	KITCHEN MICROTECH	MORGAN TOWN	WV	2	L9	GC	HD
F RANDA	PARKER CORP	DES PLAINES	IL	2	G1	GO	HD
S G WEBER	PENNWALT CORP	AURORA	IL	2	VO	DC	TM
D JUNG	GENERAL GRAIN	CRANBURY	NJ	2	VO	JK	PC
R LA CORTE	SMITH KLINE & FRENCH	PITTSBURGH	PA	2	VO	DC	TM
B PEPPE	UNIV. PITTSBURG	PITTSBURGH	PA	2	VO	DC	TM
E N PLOSED	S C JOHNSON CO	RACINE	WI	2	I3	GO	HD
B SWARIN	CITY OF BARTLESVILLE	BARTLESVILLE	OK	3	E2	JB	JM
K P KOSITIO	GLYCO CHEMICALS	PASADENA	CA	3	I3	SB	DW
P LENAHAN	ELECTRONIC PROP. CO	ALBUQUERQUE	NM	3	RO	FH	JM
A C SHAIKI	AVACARE	PLANO	TX	3	VO	JB	JM
K NOMURA	UNIV. CALIFORNIA	PACIFIC PAL	CA	3	I3	JB	JM
H L WALDRAM	PROPELLANT LAB	WARREN	PA	3	N8	MF	HD
R E LIVINGS	GENERAL MOTORS	WILLIAMSPORT	PA	3	U9	DC	JM
M T LITTLE	NORTHROP CORP	IRVINE	CA	3	E2	FS	DW
C M OAKLEY	PARKER CHEMICAL CORP	LANCASTER	PA	3	VO	DC	TM
J F SHALLA	CARTER WALLACE CORP	GLENVILLE	IL	3	VO	GO	HD
R W CASE	RIVERFRONT MERTS	COVINGTON	KY	4	P2	GC	HD
M W KIRBY	FOOD MATERIALS	HAWTHORNE	CA	4	I3	FS	DW
F N FRY	ALLIED CHEMICAL	MIDLAND	MI	4	U9	LL	HD
G J BEYER	UPJOHN COMPANY	CRANBURY	NJ	4	VO	JK	PC
T C ALLEN	SQUARE DEAL CO	NEWARK	DE	4	U9	JC	TM
W E BRAKES	COOK COUNTY HOSPITAL	CHICAGO	IL	4	I3	GO	HD
R C BUTTERHOP	DUPONG CORP	NEWARK	NJ	4	VO	JK	PC
J R BOLANDS	ECHO SOUND CORP	CHICAGO	IL	4	VO	GO	HD
B N AMAND	US FDA	WASHINGTON	DC	4	U1	BG	TM
I SIEGE	ARMSTRONG WORK CORP	LEWISTOWN	PA	4	VO	DC	TM
J ROP	CARTER WALLACE	SANTA CLARA	CA	4	VO	DD	DW
T W ALLEN	DRAFT INC	NORWOOD	PA	4	I3	DC	TM
L GOLHY	ALLERGAN PHARM	INDIANAPOLIS	IN	4	VO	JV	HD
M JUHA	BTI CORPORATION	DUARTE	CA	4	VO	FS	DW
F LIPARI	GENERAL STORE COMPANY	PEORIA	IL	4	VO	GO	HD
W E BAKER	UNIV. CINCINNATI	CINCINNATI	OH	4	VO	GC	HD
J PARHUA	KEYSTONE CARBON CO	READING	PA	4	VI	DC	TM

2. *The publication effectiveness report* This report lists the various publications used and identifies the total exposure of a promotion. This is done by multiplying the circulation of the publication by the number of insertions. The report determines the comparative pulling power of each publication, while at the same time comparing the cost effectiveness of them all. Thus the groundwork is established for determining future use of each publication.

Exhibit 18–7.   **Product Inquiry Report**

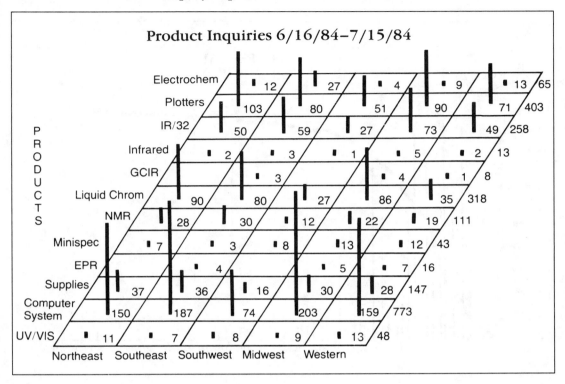

Exhibit 18–8.   **Regional Inquiry Report**

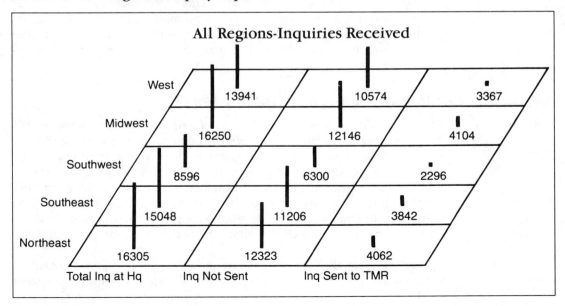

Exhibit 18–9.   **Daily Flash Report**

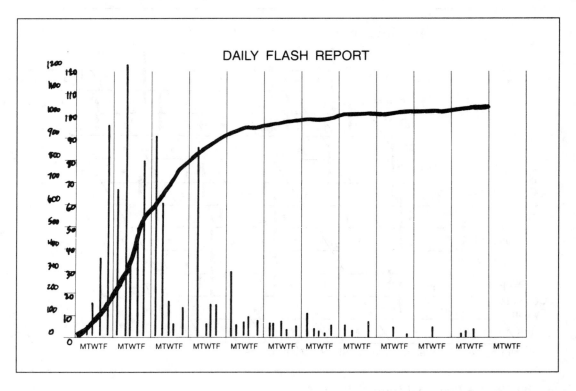

3. *The cost-to-potential-revenue report.* This report identifies the cost per thousand to reach the market with a promotion, the cost per inquiry, the percentage of qualified inquiries, the cost per qualified inquiry, the sales potential resulting from the inquiries, and the forecast revenue-to-advertising cost ratio.

Advantages of Reporting with Graphic Charts

Charts add a dimension to the meaning of a report. Managers who need to know the progress of inquiry promotion programs, and those responsible for support of the inquiry system, generally have limited time to review results. Submitting hard-copy reports loaded with columns of figures is a mistake.

Most managers manage by comparison. Graphic charts present easy-to-see relationships and encourage deeper involvement in the report. It is easier to compare a present position against a past position and the intended objective with a chart than it is a printout of hundreds of numbers.

In conclusion, the efficient handling and managing of inquiries in marketing is a major problem for many companies. An inquiry management system can be a solution, and it can also become a valuable company asset.

- An inquiry system helps advertising to become more accountable for its expenditures; it integrates the advertising and selling functions into a unified whole.
- The system can increase sales productivity by the elimination of unproductive follow-up calls; it is a position aid in finding prospects ready to buy.
- The application of an inquiry system to the advertising and marketing functions can become a valuable management tool, one that is useful in assessing progress toward objectives.

An inquiry management system works because it measures results—the ingredient most wanted in advertising and marketing activity today.

Case Histories

With an inquiry management system as a backdrop, let us now look at two case histories—the first involving consumer direct marketing and the second involving business-to-business direct marketing.

Launch of the 1992 Lexus SC400 Sport Coupe

Murray Bowes, chairman of Bowes Deutsu & Partners, Los Angeles, had this to say about the firm's exciting lead-generation program for the Lexus Sport Coupe: "There is a saying in the automotive industry: You only get to launch once"—meaning that when introducing a new car, one had better do it right the first time, because there won't be a second time.

Mr. Bowes went on to recount the history of the program:

"In the Fall of 1990 the agency began to be introduced to a top-secret car code-named the Lexus F2. This new car was to be a sport coupe designed to round out Lexus' highly successful line. The introduction of the F2 absolutely had to be successful so as to carry Lexus' momentum and image into 1992 and beyond.

"Through the Winter and Spring of 1991 the agency created what we hoped [would be], a highly predictive database using multiple regression analysis. Key predictors were thought to be present vehicle ownership, past behavior and a long list of demographic and physiographic factors. The database was completed in late Spring. The same week we got our first sneak viewing of the real car, now named the Lexus SC400 Sport Coupe.

"With the database complete and totalling 275,000 of what was believed to be the most likely prospects for this vehicle, creative went into its final stage. The strategy was to send the audience a communication prior to launch that would offer them a free teaser video of the vehicle. [See Exhibit 18–10.] The notion was to have the video in hand prior to the launch date as an exclusive. On the day of launch another mailing arrived to the same audience, whether or not they [had] ordered the video, revealing the total car and inviting a test drive. [See Exhibit 18–11.]

Exhibit 18–10. **Letter Offering Teaser Video**

LEXUS

J. Davis Illingworth, Jr.
Group Vice President and General Manager

19001 S. Western Avenue
Torrance, California 90509-2991

Mr. John Q. Sample
1234 Anystreet
Anytown, US 12345

June 19, 1991

Dear Mr. Sample,

You are invited to witness automotive history in the making -- the unveiling of the new Lexus Coupe.

Combining exceptional luxury with outstanding performance, the Lexus Coupe ignores the rules, sets new standards and excites on a purely emotional level.

Imagine refined luxury, serious performance and sporty styling all in one car. Then add the superb Lexus limited warranty*, excellent dealer support and outstanding customer service. The result is a commanding vehicle that rivals the world's finest motor cars and yet, is surprisingly affordable.

The new Lexus Coupe--the SC 400--is awaiting your test drive at;

Lexus of Anytown
123 Main Street
Anytown, US 12345
123-456-7890

We are sure you'll appreciate the excitement and design excellence of the Lexus Coupe.

Sincerely,

J. Davis Illingworth, Jr.
Group Vice President and
General Manager

P.S. If you prefer, simply return the enclosed response card or call 800-444-LEXUS (800-444-5398), and we will send you a complimentary video that introduces this extraordinary new automobile... The Lexus Coupe.

*For more information on the Lexus limited warranty, see your local Lexus dealer.

A DIVISION OF TOYOTA MOTOR SALES U.S.A., INC.

See the future of automotive excellence today.

We invite you to experience the brand new Lexus Coupe in an exciting video. The video is yours free simply by inserting this card into the postage-paid envelope and mailing it to us. Or, call toll-free:
800-444-LEXUS (800-444-5398).

(Please allow 3-4 weeks for delivery.)

Mr. John Q. Sample
1234 Anystreet
Anytown, US 12345
99999999-99999

Please help us better understand your automotive needs by completing the brief survey below:

1. Please list vehicles currently in your household

MAKE MODEL YEAR

A. __________
B. __________
C. __________

2. When do you plan to purchase your next vehicle?

☐ Less than 3 months ☐ 3-6 months ☐ 6-12 months ☐ Over 1 year

3. Which vehicles are you considering for your next purchase?

MAKE MODEL

A. __________
B. __________
C. __________

Lead-generation mailing consisted of a letter offering the free video, a brochure hinting at the features of the new Lexus Coupe, the response form, and a business reply envelope.

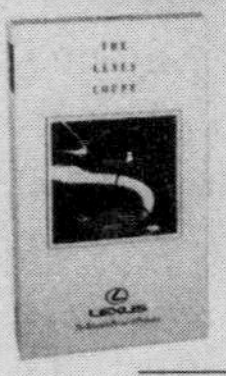

Exhibit 18–10 (*Continued*).   **Letter Offering Teaser Video**

INTRODUCING

THE LEXUS COUPE

Exhibit 18–11. **Letter Invitation to Test-Drive Car**

LEXUS

J. Davis Illingworth, Jr.
Group Vice President and General Manager

19001 S. Western Avenue
Torrance, California 90509-2991

Mr. John Q. Sample
1234 Anystreet
Anytown, US 12345

June 19, 1991

Dear Mr. Sample,

You are invited to witness automotive history in the making -- the unveiling of the new Lexus Coupe.

Combining exceptional luxury with outstanding performance, the Lexus Coupe ignores the rules, sets new standards and excites on a purely emotional level.

Imagine refined luxury, serious performance and sporty styling all in one car. Then add the superb Lexus limited warranty*, excellent dealer support and outstanding customer service. The result is a commanding vehicle that rivals the world's finest motor cars and yet, is surprisingly affordable.

The new Lexus Coupe--the SC 400--is awaiting your test drive at;

Lexus of Anytown
123 Main Street
Anytown, US 12345
123-456-7890

We are sure you'll appreciate the excitement and design excellence of the Lexus Coupe.

Sincerely,

J. Davis Illingworth, Jr.
Group Vice President and
General Manager

P.S. If you prefer, simply return the enclosed response card or call 800-444-LEXUS (800-444-5398), and we will send you a complimentary video that introduces this extraordinary new automobile...The Lexus Coupe.

*For more information on the Lexus limited warranty, see your local Lexus dealer.

A DIVISION OF TOYOTA MOTOR SALES U.S.A., INC.

See the future of automotive excellence today.

We invite you to experience the brand new Lexus Coupe in an exciting video. The video is yours free simply by inserting this card into the postage-paid envelope and mailing it to us. Or, call toll-free:
800-444-LEXUS (800-444-5398).

(Please allow 3-4 weeks for delivery.)

Mr. John Q. Sample
1234 Anystreet
Anytown, US 12345
99999999-99999

Please help us better understand your automotive needs by completing the brief survey below:

1. Please list vehicles currently in your household

MAKE MODEL YEAR
A. ______
B. ______
C. ______

2. When do you plan to purchase your next vehicle?

☐ Less than 3 months ☐ 3-6 months ☐ 6-12 months ☐ Over 1 year

3. Which vehicles are you considering for your next purchase?

MAKE MODEL
A. ______
B. ______
C. ______

Follow-up mailing, which arrived the day of the launch, included a letter giving the address of the nearest dealer, another response form offering the free video, a four-color fold-out booklet showing the new car and its special features, and another business reply envelope.

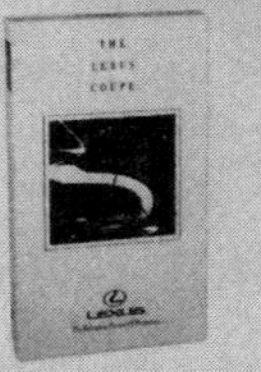

Exhibit 18–11 (*Continued*).   **Letter Invitation to Test-Drive Car**

"The results? Response to the video was a staggering 12 percent, and of those responders nearly 11 percent actually purchased an SC400!

"The launch of the SC400 Sport Coupe was not only one of the most successful new model introductions ever, [but] production was actually sold out for 6 months!"

Lead-Generation Program: National City Bank

A lead-generation program for the National City Bank, Cleveland, Ohio, was created by Yeck Brothers Company of Dayton, Ohio. The program consisted of five personal letters with impact enclosures. The details of the campaign were as follows:

Objective:	Qualify prospects for National City Bank representatives to get new corporate clients.
Prospects:	Key corporate executives responsible for financial operations in companies with sales between $25 million and $100 million.
Account officers:	Account officers direct this program to their top prospects.
Format:	Personal letter with impact enclosure.
Results:	Thirty-seven percent response after the first five mailings of a continuing series: 6 percent became new customers.

The five letters, along with illustrations of impact enclosures follows, are presented in Exhibits 18–12 to 18–16.

Exhibit 18–12.   **Letter No. 1**

National City Center
Post Office Box 5756
Cleveland OH 44101-0756
Phone 216/575-2000

Mr. Jack Dempsey
President
Dempsey Printing
23645 Mercantile Road
Beachwood, Ohio   44122

Dear Jack:

I'd like to tell you about these pennies.

They make a point about us.

They are all the same size. All the same color. I believe their
metal content is identical. But one stands out from the rest. A
coin dealer will tell you its value is over 100 times the others.

Yes, it has an "added value."

It is the same here at National City, where we are committed to
contributing an added value. I know it's true here in my office
where it's my job to make things happen fast for my clients.

I call it Responsiveness.

You might call it good service, or the ability to solve whatever
problem comes along...quickly.

At any rate, it is the way we perform. You could say we are
dedicated to it.

Of course, we are ready to serve you, however we can. Any time
you are interested to learn more, just try me at the number on
my card. I'll come a-running.

                              Sincerely,

                              Connie A. Greene

Encs.
P.S. You'll probably decide to spend the Lincoln head pennies
      even though they are bright, shiny and new. But you
      may want to hold on to that Indian head. It has an
      "added value," you know.

A MEMBER OF NATIONAL CITY CORPORATION

Exhibit 18–13.   Letter No. 2

NATIONAL
CITY BANK

National City Center
Post Office Box 5756
Cleveland OH 44101-0756
Phone   216/575-2000

One bank is not like all the rest

Mr. Phil Warner
President
Cherry Knoll Springwater Inc.
7130 Leavitt Road
Amherst, OH 44001

Dear Mr. Warner:

You'll remember I wrote you recently about the way I ...

... jump ...

when my clients call?

Well, you may want to try me at the number on my card. Whether you
want to talk about another line of credit, an equipment loan, or just
a checking account for a special project, well, as I told you before,
I'll come a-running.

But there is more to our good service than speed.

We really enjoy coming up with solutions. To little problems or bigger
ones. So if you have been looking for a better way - or any way - to
resolve a problem of yours, I'd be happy to talk it over.

I should also remind you that we have a lot of people around our place
who know a lot of answers. And they like to dig up those answers, just
as much as I do.

I'd like to be able to convince you that we are pretty good at coming
up with a better way of doing things.

When you have a need, I'd like to tell you more.

                          Sincerely,

                          Lisa N Barracini

Encs.
P.S. Yes, one of those stamps is not like all the rest. In fact,
      it will do the job of all the other five put together. It's
      just a matter of finding a better way of doing things. And
      we enjoy doing that.

A MEMBER OF NATIONAL CITY CORPORATION

Exhibit 18–14.   **Letter No. 3**

NATIONAL
CITY BANK

National City Center
Post Office Box 5756
Cleveland OH 44101-0756
Phone   216/575-2000

One bank is not like all the rest

Mr. Robert Lally
Norton brothers Company
4158 E. 131 St.
Cleveland, OH 44105

Dear Mr. Lally:

As they say, "There's more than one way to skin a cat."

To tell the truth, I've never learned what that alternate way might
be, and for that matter, I've never had any instructions on any way.

However, I do know that there are alternate ways to do things in
our business.

And you might say we specialize in them.

Yes, although we've been around since 1845, we're finding new solutions all the time. Ways to do things that help our clients.

The fact is you might think of us as your "alternative."

By that I mean your "alternative financing source," or your "alternative investment channel" or perhaps your "alternative bank." We
can serve you in lots of ways.

It's something to think about.

If you care to, then please consider what we can do for you, and
give me a call at the number on my card. I'll be there waiting.

                          Sincerely,

                          Gloria McDuffie

Enc.
P.S. I've enclosed your four-way "alternative" screwdriver. Carry
      it. You'll find it handy and quick to respond. It will "serve
      you in lots of ways." Just like us.

A MEMBER OF NATIONAL CITY CORPORATION

Exhibit 18–15.   Letter No. 4

NATIONAL CITY BANK

National City Center
Post Office Box 5756
Cleveland OH 44101-0756
Phone   216/575-2000

One bank is not like all the rest

Mr. Jack Dempsey
President
Dempsey Printing
23645 Mercantile Road
Beachwood, OH 44122

Dear Jack:

A while back I told you that we like to solve problems.

Credit lines, term loans, cash management, deposit accounts, whatever.

I must say we have a unique bunch of people around here. Being 145
years old, and being considered a "steady and stable institution,"
you wouldn't think that we would have a lot of young ideas. But
that's what we do have.

"Young ideas."

We get them because we've developed a positive attitude toward problem solving. We don't exactly have a "think tank," but maybe we do
in a way because we all have a positive attitude toward change.

"A positive attitude toward change."

Yes, we like to find new solutions.

We'd like to find one for you.

If you would care to talk about a need you have, or if you would just
like to talk and find out more about what makes us tick, my number is
still the same.

                              Sincerely,

                              Hugh

Encs.
P.S. I should explain about the lock. It is sort of a puzzle.
      The combination is 0-0-0. It will open when you set it
      this way, on 0-0-0. But naturally you'd like to set it
      for your own confidential combination. Can you figure it
      out? If not, just mail the card, and we'll tell you how.

A MEMBER OF NATIONAL CITY CORPORATION

Dear Jack,

Yes, I'd like to know how to set the combination.

☐ Please mail me instructions.
☐ O.K. Come on over and demonstrate how it works.
  And I suppose you'll also want to tell me all about
  National City and your "young ideas."

Signature _____

       Mr. Jack Dempsey
       President
       Dempsey Printing
       23645 Mercantile Road
       Beachwood, OH 44122

Exhibit 18–16.   **Letter No. 5**

NCB
NATIONAL
CITY BANK

National City Center
Post Office Box 5756
Cleveland OH 44101-0756
Phone   216/575-2000

One bank is not like all the rest

Mr. Tom Patrick
Vice President
Patrick Electric Co. Inc.
1181 N. Abbe Rd.
Sheffield Village, OH 44054

This is just

a quick note

to remind you ...

... we're willing to try about anything to find new ways to

handle your financing and banking requirements.

Sometimes you have to do things differently to open minds to

new ideas.

I'm ready if you are.

Call me ...

... anytime.

A MEMBER OF NATIONAL CITY CORPORATION

Self-Quiz

1. What are the three general types of lead-generation programs?

   a. _____

   b. _____

   c. _____

2. Names three ways to "loosen" a lead.

   a. _____

   b. _____

   c. _____

3. Names three ways to "tighten" a lead.

   a. _____

   b. _____

   c. _____

4. What are the four basic tasks that must be managed up front before any lead-generation program is introduced?

   a. _____

   b. _____

   c. _____

   d. _____

5. What is the best way to make certain that the sales force isn't oversupplied or undersupplied with leads?

   _____

   _____

   _____

   _____

6. Usually about 20 percent of total leads will result in about _____ percent of total sales revenue.

7. McGraw-Hill estimates the cost of an industrial sales call to be over

   $ _____.

8. The most efficient way to sort leads is by degrees of potential. With high potential as the very best, name the three remaining degrees of potential.

a. high potential   c. _____

b. _____   d. _____

9. Most lead-generation programs will produce _____ percent of total response over the first four weeks.

10. What are the two best systems that can be used to manage the problem of a shortfall in lead generation?

a. _____

b. _____

11. What are the two ways that leads should be tracked?

a. _____

b. _____

12. Salespeople seldom return all follow-up reports to headquarters. What is considered to be a *good* percentage?

☐ 25%   ☐ 50%   ☐ 75%

13. What is the value of a purchase potential report?

_____

_____

_____

_____

Pilot Project

You work for a firm that manufactures central air-conditioning systems for the home. A minimum sale comes to $5,000. All sales are handled through a sales force. The target market is home owners with a median income of $50,000.

Your firm has decided to test the viability of a lead-generation program and has selected Milwaukee, Wisconsin, as a test market. Your assignment is to develop a marketing plan for management review.

In preparation for actually writing the marketing plan, answer the following questions:

1. What information will you need from the sales force?
   Examples might be: (a) Who is the firm's major competitor? (b) Who is the decision maker in the home? (c) What are the major objections the sales force has to overcome?

2. What objectives will you set for the program?
   For example, how many leads per day would you propose to furnish each salesperson? How would you propose to screen leads so you could distinguish between high potential and low potential? What other objectives would you set?

3. What would your strategies be for obtaining highly qualified leads?
   One strategy, for example, might be an offer to conduct a free survey to determine the cost of central air-conditioning in a home. Another strategy might be a special promotion aimed at customers in Milwaukee, asking them to provide names of friends whom they consider most likely to have an interest in central air-conditioning. What other strategies might you employ?

4. How will you implement your lead-generation program? Here are some key questions you should answer in your marketing plan:
   a. Will you ask your sales force to provide names of key prospects? How else will you involve the sales force?
   b. What media strategies will you employ?
      - Will you use compiled lists of home owners? At what median income level?
      - Will you use direct response lists? If you will, what kinds of direct response lists? (Lawn care subscribers, for example?)
      - Will you use newspapers? Which ones?
      - Will you use magazines? Which ones?
      - Will you use radio? Which stations?
      - Will you use TV? Which stations?
      - Will you use cable TV? Which stations?

CHAPTER NINETEEN

Mathematics of Direct Marketing

Until 1967 there were not many places to turn for the development and application of advanced mathematical formulas to measure the many facets of direct marketing that go to make up its accountability and profitability. Indeed, many of the most successful practitioners of the period, in spite of their seemingly satisfactory profitability, were using only the most rudimentary of mathematical principles.

It was typical to be able to state that promotion of a *total* customer file was profitable but to be unable to identify profitability by segments based upon various criteria, including frequency of purchase, recency of purchase, amount of purchase, and type of merchandise purchased.

Seeing this void in the direct marketing field, Robert Kestnbaum launched a unique management consulting firm not only to serve existing direct marketing operations, but also to provide feasibility studies for major corporations that wished to explore direct marketing. Since 1967 Mr. Kestnbaum and his organization, Kestnbaum & Company, have served such distinguished firms as L.L. Bean, Sears Roebuck, American Express, IBM, Hewlett-Packard, Johnson & Johnson, Moore Business Forms, and AT&T. This chapter distills the mathematical formulas and principles developed by this unique management consulting firm.

(It is to be noted that monetary values used in some exhibits in this chapter have grown with inflation. The concepts and relationships, however, continue to be as valid today as they were when first established.)

Creativity in direct marketing brings recognition, awards, and applause. Unfortunately, profitability and success do not always accompany the recognition and the awards. Some of the attributes of direct marketing that appeal most to those who engage in it are the accuracy with which profitability can be evaluated and the careful way that a program can be expanded with predetermined financial risk. Accountability and analysis lie at the heart of successful direct marketing.

Profitability and Break-Even Analysis
Establishing Unit Profitability

The most convenient starting point for establishing the profitability of an activity is to determine the contribution associated with each unit sold or with the average order handled. This process begins with separation of costs into variable and fixed costs.

For our purpose here, variable costs are those that relate primarily to each order processed or each unit sold. They may be classified into merchandise costs, which include everything related to making, delivering, and packaging the product, and operating costs, which include order processing, warehousing, shipping, and the cost of computer processing.

It is a good idea to use a worksheet to help identify all revenue and the variable- and fixed-cost items that come into play. Try to think of every possible cost that could be incurred and document the sources or components of each for future reference. Exhibit 19–1 illustrates a simple worksheet that can be prepared easily. Exhibit 19–2 illustrates a more detailed analysis that can be programmed on any size computer. It has the advantage of forcing attention on smaller units of activity and the frequency with which each kind of activity occurs.

Regardless of the form used, the output of the first part of the analysis (Exhibit 19–1 or Exhibit 19–2) is the amount of money associated with each unit or each order that is available to pay for selling costs and other fixed costs. After the latter are recovered, the same amount of money becomes profit. This amount is labeled *order margin* by some people, or *contribution* to selling cost, overhead, and profit by others. Regardless of the label used, note two things about its composition:

1. Some companies may include an allocation to cover overhead, thus making it a contribution to selling cost and profit only. This is the way the figures are treated in these exhibits.

2. No advertising or selling costs are included. The reasons for this are dealt with in the next section.

Selling Costs

In direct marketing the costs of placing advertisements, making mailings, or using the telephone should be considered as selling expense rather than advertising. The messages delivered by whatever media are chosen are the salespeople of direct marketing. As we will see in a minute, it is convenient to consider these selling costs as a special kind of semifixed expense in that a commitment is made to a given program before any sales are obtained.

When catalogs or other mailed materials are being used, it is customary to express selling costs on the basis of each thousand pieces mailed or otherwise distributed. When an advertisement is placed in a magazine or a broadcast medium, the cost of each advertising appearance or group of appearances is used.

Often it is advisable to test variations in advertisements and/or mailing packages. Because variations are tested in small quantities, inordinate costs occur for printing and extra creative efforts. It would be misleading to include these one-time costs as part of the regular profitability calculation. (An exception would be the development expense of a catalog to be used only during a single selling season.) It is generally preferable to consider the added costs of creative and small printing quantities as part of overhead expense. Companies are encouraged to establish a separate budget for testing. The budget can be managed over time by comparing the costs of testing to the value of the lessons learned. Evaluation of potential profitability of a total direct marketing effort should be computed on the basis of selling costs one expects to encounter in an ongoing program of the size normally conducted for a roll-out.

Relationship between Contribution per Order, Selling Cost, and Response Rate

The break-even point and profitability are determined by the interrelationship between contribution to selling cost, overhead, and profit associated with an average order, the selling cost per thousand or per advertisement, and the response rate.

The total available contribution to selling cost, overhead, and profit may be viewed as a pie. Whatever portion of the pie is used to recover selling cost and overhead leaves the remainder for pretax profit. In the examples shown in Exhibits 19–1 and 19–2, an allocation to cover overhead has been included in the applicable costs. The contribution shown in Lines 16 and 240, respectively, need to be applied only to selling cost and profit. If the available contribution equals 35 percent of net sales, as in this case, then that 35 percent must be divided between selling cost and profit. Thus a selling cost of 20 percent, or $8 per order, leaves 15 percent, or $6 per order, for profit. Conversely, a selling cost of 25 percent, or $10 per order, leaves a 10 percent pretax profit equal to $4 per order.

The relationship between selling cost and required response rate can be seen quickly. Assuming that we are satisfied with a 25 percent selling cost and a 10 percent pretax profit, we have $10 per order to pay for whatever advertising medium is used. As is shown in the bottom portion of Exhibit 19–3, a statement insert costing $60 per thousand to print and place would produce the targeted profit if net sales equal 6 orders per thousand, or 0.6 percent, while a catalog or brochure costing $400 per thousand in the mail would require net sales of 40 orders per thousand, or 4 percent.

Note that these calculations are based on *net sales*. If returns are 2.1 percent, then 6 net orders per thousand will require 6.1 gross orders, or 0.61 percent response, and 40 net orders per thousand will require 49.9 gross orders, or 4.09 percent.

Exhibit 19–1.   **Direct Marketing Profitability Work Sheet**

Promotion *Sample Catalog Test Mailing*

Line

Line		Amount	Total
1	Selling Price	$ 35.40	
2	Plus Service Charge	$ 4.60	
3	Total Selling Price		$ 40.00
4		$ 40.00	
5			
6	Merchandise Cost	13.05	
7	Drop Shipping & Delivery	2.30	
8	*Goods Lost in Shipment*	.13	
9	*Processing, Credit Check, & Collection Cost	2.68	
10	*Cost of Returns	.06	
11	*Bad Debt	.31	
12	*Money Cost (Installment Receivable)	—	
13	*Exchange Handling*	.21	
14	*Overhead & Inventory Carrying Cost*	7.26	
15	*Total Cost*		26.00
16	*Net Order Contribution*		$ $14.00 (P)

This exhibit is a simple work sheet that can be used to calculate the profitability of a direct mail promotion. There are four primary calculations involved:

1. Contribution per net order to selling cost, overhead and profit (Line 16). Total selling price including shipping and handling or service charge revenue is shown in Line 3.

   All order-related variable costs are itemized in Lines 6 through 14 and summed in Line 15. These costs are calculated on a *net order* basis. If certain overhead/fixed costs are estimated as a percentage of sales, they can also be included, as has been done here in Line 14.

   The second part of the exhibit, on pages 000–000, provides the detailed calculations of those items marked with an asterisk. Order-processing and collection costs are derived by multiplying the unit costs by the appropriate base, assuming 100 gross orders. Order-processing unit costs are multiplied by gross orders. Credit card discount costs are applied to net orders. The total is then divided by net orders to obtain the cost per net order.

   Costs of returns are calculated in a similar fashion. Unit costs are summed and multiplied by the return percentage. The result is then divided by the net orders expressed as a percentage of gross orders.

   Bad debt is calculated by multiplying the estimated bad debt percentage of sales by the total selling price.

   Contribution per net order (Line 16) is derived by subtracting total variable cost (Line 15) from the total selling price (Line 3).

Exhibit 19–1 (*Continued*).   **Direct Marketing Profitability Work Sheet**

Circularization Costs per M

17	Circular	$_____
18	Inserts	_____
19	_____	_____
20	_____	_____
21	Letters	_____
22	Order Forms	_____
23	Envelopes	_____
24	_____	_____
25	_____	_____
26	List Rental	_____
27	Inserting, Addressing, Mailing	_____
28	_____	_____
29	*Catalog Printing & Mailing*	291
30	Postage	109
31	_____	_____
32	Total Circularization Cost	$ 400.00
33	Fixed Overhead per M	allocation incl. above
34	Total Circ. & Overhead	$400.00 (C)
35	Break-even Net Sales per M (C) ÷ (P)	2.86% 28.57 orders

2. Promotion and fixed-overhead cost per thousand (Line 34). This involves a summing of the costs of all relevant promotional components and an estimate of the fixed overhead per thousand pieces mailed (Lines 17 through 33). Total cost per thousand is summed in Line 34.

3. Net orders per thousand required to break even (Line 35). This is calculated by dividing the promotion and overhead cost per thousand (Line 34) by the net order contribution to selling cost, overhead, and profit (Line 16).

4. Total profit at various levels of response (top of page 524). Total profit at given response levels is calculated as follows:
    Convert the response level to a projected net orders per thousand (Line 37).
    Subtract the orders required to break even (Line 35) to obtain the unit sales per thousand earning full profit (Line 39).
    Multiply by net order contribution (Line 16) to obtain net profit per thousand (Line 41).
    Multiply this figure by the total circulation quantiiy in thousands (Line 42) to obtain total net profit (Line 43).
    Divide net pretax profit per thousand (Line 41) by net sales per thousand (Line 37) and multiply the quotient by 100 to obtain net pretax profit as a percentage of sales (Line 44).

(Continued)

Exhibit 19–1 (*Continued*).   **Direct Marketing Profitability Work Sheet**

Total Profit at Various Levels of Net Pull

36	Projected Net Sales per M (dollars)	1,200.00	1,600.00	1,800.00
37	Projected Net Sales per M (units)	30.00	40.00	45.00
38	Less: Break-even Net Sales (units) (Line 35)	28.57	28.57	28.57
39	Unit Sales per M Earning Full Profit	1.43	11.43	16.43
40	Net Order Contribution (Line 16)	× 14.00	14.00	14.00
41	Net Pretax Profit per M	$ 20.02	160.02	230.02
42	M Circulars Mailed	× 200.00	200.00	200.00
43	Total Net Profit	$ 4,004.00	32,004.00	46,004.00
44	Net Pretax Profit % to Sales	1.7%	10.0%	12.8%

Supporting Calculations and Assumptions

PROMOTION
TERMS
ASSUMPTIONS

Sample Catalog Test Mailing

1. No. Pieces Mailed		200	M
2. Credit Check	_____ Yes	X	No
3. Gross Orders Rejected		0	%
4. Gross Shipments Returned		2.1	%
5. Net Sales Uncollectable		.78	%

Order Processing and Collection Costs (Line 9)

a.	Gross Orders	100 ×	$ 2.54	=	$ 254[a]
	Less: Credit Rejects	___ ×	_____	=	_____
b.	Gross Sales	___ ×	$ _____	=	$ _____
	Less: Returns	___ ×	_____	=	_____
c.	Net Sales	(A)97.9 ×	$ .08	=	$ 8[b]
	Total				$ 262 (B)
	Cost Per Net Sale (B ÷ A)				$ 2.68

[a] Includes mail-order processing, phone-order processing, and order-picking/packing.
[b] Credit card discount of 2 percent applied to.

Exhibit 19–1 (*Continued*).   **Direct Marketing Profitability Work Sheet**

---

*Cost of Returns (Line 10)

Return Service Charge	$_____.68_____
_____	_____
Drop Shipment Charge	_____
Shipping Out	_____
Shipping Back	____2.25____
Missing Items	_____
Total	$____2.93____(A)
% Returns Projected	____2.1____%(B)
Return Cost per Net Sale (A × B) ÷ (100 − B)	$_____.06_____

---

*Bad Debts (Line 11)

Total Selling Price	$____40.00____(A)
% Reserve for Bad Debts	____.78____%(B)
Bad Debt Cost per Net Sale (A × B)	$_____.31_____

---

*Money Cost (Line 12)

Contract term plus _____ months	_____(A)
Times Sales Decimal (if A is 12 or under divide by 12; if 13 to 24 dived by 24; etc.) (A) ÷_____ =	_____(B)
Total Sales Price (Line 3)	$_____(C)
Money Employed (B × C)	$_____(D)
Effective Interest Rate	_____%(E)
Money Cost (D × E)	_____

Exhibit 19–2.   **Direct Marketing Profitability Analysis: Average Contribution per Order**

Line No.		Base Cost 1	Factor % 2	Weighted Cost/Unit 3[a]	Net Cost per Unit 4[b]
201.0	Selling Price	35.40	100.00	35.40	35.40
202.0	Installment Price	—	—	—	—
203.0	Shipping & Handling Revenue	4.60	100.00	4.60	4.60
204.0	Additional Options & Accessories	—	—	—	—
205.0	Total Average Sale	—	—	40.00	40.00
206.0					
207.0	Merchandise Cost	13.05	100.00	13.05	13.05
208.0	Premium for Purchase	—	—	—	—
209.0	Options or Accessories	—	—	—	—
210.0	Credit Card Discount	0.80	10.00	0.08	0.08
212.0	Sales Tax Not Collected	—	—	—	—
213.0	Bad Debt	40.00	0.78	0.31	0.31
214.0	Subtotal	—	—	13.44	13.44
215.0					
216.0	Order Card Postage	—	—	—	—
217.0	Order Processing	0.68	95.00	0.65	0.66
218.0	Order Picking/Packing	1.80	100.00	1.80	1.84
219.0	Shipping Cost	2.25	100.00	2.25	2.30
220.0	Premium for Examination	—	—	—	—
221.0	Credit Check	—	—	—	—
222.0	Return Handling	0.68	2.10	0.01	0.01
223.0	Return Refurbishing	—	2.10	—	—
224.0	Shipping Exchanges	4.73	3.00	0.14	0.14
225.0	Postage Refund, Return, & Exchange	2.25	5.10	0.11	0.12
226.0	Goods Lost in Shipment	13.05	1.00	0.13	0.13
227.0	Telephone Order Processing	1.75	5.00	0.09	0.09
228.0	Subtotal	—	—	5.18	5.30
229.0					
230.0	Total Direct Costs	—	—	18.63	18.74
231.0					

[a] Column 1 × Column 2.
[b] Based on returns of 2.1 percent.

This exhibit is part of the output of a computer-programmed profitability analysis, which is a more sophisticated counterpart to the work sheet in Exhibit 19–1. It involves much greater detail on the individual cost components and the frequency with which they occur.

Revenue components are itemized in Lines 201–205, and direct costs are itemized in Lines 207–230.

Lines 232–238 detail the overhead and indirect cost. Contribution per order is derived in Lines 240 and 242, while Lines 243 and 244 calculate different combinations of selling cost and pretax profit, which correspond to the 35 percent contribution to selling cost and profit (Line 240).

Column 1 lists the base cost for each component.

Column 2 displays the weighting factor that is applied to the base cost. This factor is expressed either in terms of: frequency of occurrence expressed as a percentage, as in Lines 201–230; or an interest rate, as in Lines 232–234; or a percentage of sales, as in Lines 235–244.

Exhibit 19–2 *(Continued)*.   **Direct Marketing Profitability Analysis: Average Contribution per Order**

Line No.		Base Cost 1	Rate % 2	Weighted Cost/Unit 3[a]	Net Cost per Unit 4[b]
232.0	Cost of Money—Installment Receivables	—	12.00	—	—
233.0	Cost of Money—Receivables	—	12.00	—	—
234.0	Product Inventory	2.17	12.00	0.26	0.26
235.0	Overhead—Departmental	40.00	—	—	—
236.0	Overhead—Corporate	40.00	17.50	7.00	7.00
237.0	Subtotal	—	—	7.26	7.26
237.5					
238.0	Total Cost	—	—	25.89	26.00
239.0					
240.0	Contribution to Selling Cost & Profit	—	35.00	14.11	14.00
241.0					
242.0	Contrib. to Selling Cost, OH & Profit	—	53.15	21.37	21.26
243.0	Selling Cost if Pretax Profit Target Is	10.00	25.00	—	10.00
244.0	Pretax Profit if Selling Target Is	20.00	15.00	—	6.00

Line No.	Supporting Calculations and Assumptions	Constant Assumptions
11.0	Selling Price	$35.40
13.0	Installment Terms: No. of Payments	—
14.0	Installment Terms: Amount of Payment	—
15.0	Total Installment Price	—
15.1	Implied Interest Charges	—
15.2	Simple Interest Rate "Reg Z"	—
16.0	Shipping & Handling Charge	$ 4.60
17.0	Additional Price of Option of Accessory	—
21.0	Merchandise Cost	$13.05
22.0	Cost of Premium, Free with Purchase	—
23.0	Cost of Option or Accessory	—
24.0	Cost of Premium, Free for Examination	—
25.0	Average Inventory Value	$ 2.17
31.0	Order Card Postage	—
32.0	Order Processing	$ 0.68
33.0	Order Picking/Packing	$ 1.80
34.0	Shipping Cost	$ 2.25
36.0	Telephone Order Processing	$ 1.75
41.0	Return Handling	$ 0.68
42.0	Return Refurbishing	—
43.0	Postage Refund on Returns & Exchanges	$ 2.25

Column 3 contains the weighted cost per gross unit obtained by multiplying Column 1 by Column 2.
Column 4 derives the cost per net unit by adjusting the values in Column 3 by the return rate factor.
The second part of this exhibit lists the input assumptions used to derive the profitability analysis report.
Lines 11–43 list the unit costs associated with each order, return, and exchange.

(Continued)

Exhibit 19–2 (*Continued*). **Direct Marketing Profitability Analysis: Average Contribution per Order**

Line No.		% Freq/% Rate 1	Discount /Uncollect 2
51.0	Cash with Order	90.00	0.87
52.0	Net 30 Days	—	—
61.0	Charge to American Express	—	4.10
62.0	Charge to Diners Club	—	—
63.0	Charge to MasterCard	5.00	2.00
64.0	Charge to Visa	5.00	2.00
65.0	Charge to Other Cards	—	—
67.0	Total Charge Cards	10.00	2.00
71.0	Installment Receivables	—	—
73.0	Sales Tax—Not Collected	—	—
81.0	Percent Purchased w/Option or Accessory	—	—
82.0	Percent Lost in Shipment	1.00	
83.0	Percent Returned Goods	2.10	—
84.0	Percent Exchanges	3.00	
85.0	Percent Paying Shipping & Handling	100.00	—
86.0	Percent Order Card Postage	—	
87.0	Percent Postage Refunds	100.00	
88.0	Percent Telephone Orders	5.00	
89.0	Percent Interest Paid	12.00	
91.0	Percent Corporate Overhead	17.50	
92.0	Percent Departmental Overhead	—	
92.5	OVHD=(0)%(Avg. Price+S&H) or (1)%Price	—	
93.0	Percent Selling Cost Target	20.00	
94.0	Percent Pretax Profit Target	10.00	

The first column of Lines 51–94 contains the weighting factors used in the profitability calculations: frequency of occurrence, in Lines 51–88; interest rate, in Line 89; percentage of sales, in Lines 91–94.

The second column contains the bad-debt rate and credit card discount rates that are applied to each application transaction (Lines 51–73).

Exhibit 19–3. **Break-Even and Profitability Analysis**

Average Order			$ 40.00
Contribution		35%	$ 14.00

	Statement Insert	Catalog
Promotion Cost Per 1000	$ 60.00	$ 400.00
Net Orders per 1000 Required to Break Even	4.30	28.60
Net Response %	.43%	2.86%
Net Sales Per 1000	172.00	$1,144.00

	Case A		Case B	
Target Profit	15%	$ 6.00	10%	$ 4.00
Promotion Cost Target	20%	$ 8.00	25%	$10.00

	Statement Insert	Catalog	Statement Insert	Catalog
Net Orders per 1000 Required to Make Target Profit	7.50	50.0	6.0	40.0
	.75%	5.0%	.6%	4.0%
Net Sales Per 1000	$ 300	$2,000	$ 240	$1,600

Break-even orders = Promotion cost per thousand ÷ contribution order.
Net orders per 1000 required to reach selling cost target = promotion cost per 1000 ÷ promotion cost target per order.
Net sales per 1000 = orders × $40.

This exhibit displays the calculation of the response required either to break even or to meet certain profitability targets.

The first part of the exhibit displays the contribution per net order, both as a percent of sales and as a dollar figure. This figure was calculated in Line 16 of Exhibit 19–1 and in Line 240, Column 4 of Exhibit 19–2.

The second part of the exhibit shows break-even calculations for two media: a statement insert and a catalog. For each medium:

The promotion cost per thousand is divided by the dollar contribution per order to obtain the net orders per thousand required to break even.

Response percentage is simply orders per thousand divided by 10.

Net sales per thousand are calculated by multiplying net orders per thousand by the average order size, which in this case is $40.

The third part of the exhibit presents similar calculations for response required to meet different profitability targets.

Targeted profit per order is first established. For example, when the average order is $40 and targeted pretax profit is 15 percent, then $6 per order must be set aside as profit.

Allowable promotion cost equals total contribution per order less the targeted profit per order.

The promotion cost per thousand is divided by this new allowable promotion cost per order to obtain net orders per thousand required, to achieve the targeted profit.

Net sales per thousand are obtained by multiplying the required net orders by the $40 average order size.

Profitability of a Continuity Program

The same calculation can be applied to determine the profitability of a continuity program. Suppose, for example, that a set of five $40 items is being sold, each successive item being shipped only when the preceding one is paid for. Exhibit 19–4 summarizes the figures for each shipment in the program individually as well as for the total program. Revenue and expenses are calculated for each shipment in exactly the same way as was illustrated in Exhibits 19–1 and 19–2, except that return and bad-debt rates are much higher for the continuity.

Exhibit 19–4.   **Direct Marketing Continuity Program Profitability Work Sheet: Average Contribution to Selling Cost and Profit per 100 Starters[a]**

| | Shipment Number | | | | | |
Line No.	1	2	3	4	5	Total
1 Starters/Gross Shipments	100.00	76.50	61.93	52.39	45.79	336.61
2 Returns %	10%	8%	6%	5%	5%	7.40%
3 Net Shipments	90.00	70.38	58.21	49.77	43.50	311.86
4 Bad Debt %	15%	12%	10%	8%	8%	11.30%
5 Units Bad Debt	13.50	8.45	5.82	3.98	3.48	35.23
6 Net Sales	$3,600	$2,815	$2,328	$1,991	$1,740	$12,474
7 Merch. Cost	1,175	918	760	650	568	4,070
8 Operating Costs	1,052	738	564	442	387	3,183
9 Fixed Costs	655	512	424	362	317	2,270
10 Contrib. to Selling Cost & Profit	$ 718	$ 646	$ 581	$ 537	$ 469	$2,951
11 Cum. Net Sales per Starter	36.00	64.15	87.43	107.34	124.74	
12 Cum. Contrib. per Starter	$ 7.18	$13.63	$19.44	$24.81	$29.51	

[a] Columns and rows may not foot exactly due to rounding.

This exhibit calculates the cumulative profit per starter for a five-shipment continuity program by tracing all activity associated with 100 starters and calculating a mini profit-and-loss for each shipment.

Line 1 contains the gross shipments for the previous item in the series. For each shipment after the first, the gross shipments equal the gross shipments for the previous item less returns and bad debt (Lines 2–5). In a typical continuity program there would also be voluntary cancellations, which would reduce subsequent shipments. These have been ignored here to simplify the example.

Lins 6 contains net sales, which are calculated by multiplying the net shipment by the $40 average-order size.

Costs for each shipment are summarized in Lines 7–9. Operating costs included bad debt. These costs are developed using the same cost factors illustrated in Exhibits 19–1 and 19–2. For example, fixed costs are calculated as 18.2 percent of net sales.

Contribution to selling cost and profit (Line 10) is obtained by subtracting operating and fixed costs from net sales. Cumulative net sales and profit are calculated in Lines 11 and 12, respectively.

When the figures, other than percentages, in the total column are divided by 100, the value per starter is obtained. Thus there are 3.37 gross shipments per starter, $124.74 net sales per starter, and $29.51 contributions per starter.

Results for the total program are the sum of transactions made to the average customer starting in the program. Total net sales per starter are $124.74 and, after applicable expenses, contribution to selling cost and profit per starter is $29.51. Again, the marketers in this example can target how much of this contribution they want to devote to acquiring a starter and how much they want to leave as pretax profit. Since the total value of the sale is higher, the *absolute* amount that can be spent to acquire a starter and the *absolute dollar profit* per starter are greater.

Arithmetic of Two-Step or Inquiry-Conversion Promotions

Up to this point we have assumed that the seller uses an individual mailing or ad to produce sales. Very often it is more profitable to generate inquiries with various low-cost methods and then convert those inquiries into sales by using special mailings, by telemarketing (Chapter Fourteen), or by a combination of these methods. In the example of the continuity offer, an average sale of $124.74 opens the possibility of using an inquiry-conversion approach.

Inquiries can be generated through any of the media available to the direct marketer. For example, if an advertisement costing $2,000 placed in a magazine produces 1,000 inquiries, the cost per inquiry would be $2. In addition, there will be a cost of perhaps $30 or $40 per thousand to process inquiries into a usable mailing list. As shown in the top portion of Exhibit 19–5, the seller must convert 14.4 percent of inquiries costing $2 each in order to generate a 10 percent pretax profit on sales.

Varying the media, kinds of advertisements, appeals, and offers will affect the cost of generating inquiries. Typically, the more highly qualified an inquiry, the more costly it will be to generate but the higher the conversion rate will be. The thoughtful direct marketer will experiment continuously with various ways of producing inquiries and various means of converting them in order to fine-tune a program and to maximize profits.

Most companies find that an inquiry list will support repeated conversion mailings. There is likely to be a fall-off in response to each successive effort, but it is profitable to continue making conversion mailings until the incremental cost of the last mailing is greater than the contribution it generates.

Part B of Exhibit 19–5 illustrates the results of a series of conversion mailings costing $225 per thousand to execute. Given the 10 percent objective for pretax profit, $17.04 is available from each order to pay for the order acquisition cost. This means in order to maximize short-term profit, a conversion series can be continued until the last mailing pulls 13.2 net orders or 14.3 gross orders per thousand, or 1.4 percent, assuming returns of 7.4 percent. Short-term profit is maximized after the third conversion mailing, since the actual selling cost for the fourth mailing exceeds the allowable cost. However, the total program would exceed the profit target until a fifth conversion mailing.

Exhibit 19–5. **Inquiry-Conversion Profitability**

A. REQUIRED RESPONSE RATE FOR ONE FOLLOW-UP MAILING

	$/Order	*%*
Net Sales	$ 124.74	100.0%
Contribution to Selling Cost and Profit	29.51	23.7
Pretax Profit at 10%	12.47	10.0
Allowable Selling Cost at 10% Profit	$ 17.04	13.7%

	Cost per 1,000 Inquires
Advertising Cost at $2.00 per Inquiry	$2,000
Processing Cost	40
Total Acquisition Cost	2,040
First Follow-up Mailing	225
Total Initial Investment	$2,265

Net orders required to generate 10% Profit = $2,265÷$17.04 = 132.9 or 13.3%
Gross orders required assuming 7.4% returns = 132.9÷92.6% = 143.5 or 14.4%

This exhibit highlights the profitability calculations of inquiry-conversion programs. It uses the net sales per starter and contribution per starter derived in Exhibit 19–4.

Part A displays the calculation of the required response rate for a single follow-up mailing to an inquiry-generation effort. The allowable selling cost at a 10 percent profit is calculated by subtracting the allocation for profit from the contribution to selling cost and profit per order. The initial investment per thousand inquiries is calculated by summing the advertising cost, the inquiry-processing cost, and the cost of first follow-up mailing.

Net orders required to generate the targeted profit are calculated by dividing the initial investment per thousand by the allowable selling cost per order.

Gross orders required per thousand are calculated by factoring up the net orders by a return rate assumption.

Improving the Figures

To improve the bottom line, the direct marketer must focus on at least one and preferably on all of the three factors affecting profitability: unit contribution, selling cost, and response rate. Unit contribution can be improved by raising the gross margin, perhaps by upgrading the product or offering sets or combinations of items. Opportunities for cost reduction in every aspect of the business should be explored continuously. Chapter Four deals with the importance of testing alternative advertisements, packages, appeals, and offers in order to improve response and performance.

A special kind of analysis can be applied by catalog marketers. Not only can overall result be analyzed, but also each item or category of products can

Exhibit 19–5 (*Continued*).   **Inquiry-Conversion Profitability**

B. CONVERSION SERIES PROFITABILITY FOR 1,000 INQUIRIES

	Acquisition	*Conversion Mailings*				
		#1	**#2**	**#3**	**#4**	**#5**
Quantity Mailed		1,000	880	838	822	815
Response Percent		12.0%	4.8%	1.9%	.8%	.3%
Orders		120	42	16	7	2
Less Returns		9	3	1	0	0
Net Orders		111	39	15	7	2
Cumulative Net Orders		111	150	165	172	174
Allowable Selling Cost at $17.04		$1,891	665	256	119	34
Cumulative Allowable Selling Cost		$1,891	2,556	2,812	2,931	2,965
Actual Selling Cost	$2,040	225	198	189	185	183
Cumulative Actual Selling Cost	2,040	2,265	2,463	2,652	2,837	3,020
Cum. Balance Available for Selling Cost	($2,040)	($ 374)	$ 93	$ 160	$ 94	($ 55)

Part B of this exhibit outlines the profitability calculation for a series of five conversion mailings subsequent to the inquiry-generation effort.

The quantity mailed on each subsequent mailing is equivalent to the previous quantity mailed less orders produced from the previous mailing. Often it is not practical to extract buyers, and most of the conversion series is mailed to all inquirers.

Net orders are derived by subtracting returns. The 7.4 percent return rate was calculated in Line 2 of Exhibit 19–4.

Allowable selling cost is calculated by multiplying the net orders by the allowable selling cost per order at a 10 percent profit, i.e., $17.04.

Actual selling cost includes the acquisition cost and the cost of each conversion mailing.

The cumulative balance available to spend on conversion mailings, taking into account the 10 percent profit target, is shown in the last row. A negative balance after the fifth conversion effort indicates that selling cost exceeds the allowable 13.7 percent by $55. Since total selling costs will equal $3,019.88 (total acquisition cost plus $225/M for conversion mailings), and total net sales are $21,704.76 (174 net orders × $124.74), the overall selling cost would be 13.9 percent if the last conversion effort were retained. Those last two orders, however, would cost $91.50 each to obtain ($183 ÷ 2) and would be very unprofitable.

be subjected to the same type of profitability analysis as well. When sales and profitability of items in a category or in a price range are aggregated, the performance of that group of items can be determined. Unprofitable individual items or categories of items can be eliminated, remerchandised, or given different amounts of space in order to improve their performance.

Return on Investment

Thus far we have looked at direct marketing programs as though they occur at one point in time. Actually, of course, the events associated with the program take place over a period of several months or even years. When we consider the timing of revenues and costs, we can begin to obtain a picture of cash flows, which are vital to the health of any business, as well as of return on investment, which may well be the best indicator of long-term business success.

Compared to other businesses, direct marketing does not have large investments in buildings and equipment. Often the most important considerations for direct marketers are the expenditure for inventory and the commitment that must be made to advertisements, catalogs, or other selling materials before any sales are received. For these reasons, several different ways of thinking about return on investment have been advanced. The more important ones will be reviewed here.

Return on Selling and Inventory Investment

For a company that is already in business, the major decisions that must be made in advance of each season or selling period are the size of the selling campaign to be undertaken and the amount of inventory to be purchased. Consider the case of a catalog marketer whose average order value is $40, including shipping and handling revenue, and whose profitability is identical to that shown in Exhibits 19–1 and 19–2. Assume that this company has two selling seasons a year and that it turns its inventory six times each year or three times each season. Its catalogs cost $400 per thousand, for which the bills are paid 30 days after mailing and from which most orders are received within 90 days of mailing.

Exhibit 19–6 shows a simplified profit and loss statement for 1,000 catalogs. The company is investing $400 in its catalogs, plus one-third of the $510 cost of goods, or a total of $570. Within a 90-day period it receives back this entire amount plus $148 in pretax profit. Some people calculate the return on the investment in inventory and selling cost as $148 ÷ $570, or 26 percent. However, this return is actually received within 90 days, and theoretically the investment could be rolled over 4 times each year. The actual return is closer to 4 times 26 percent, or 104 percent. While this calculation has the advantage of being quick and easy to make, it is not only imprecise, but it is also erroneous.

A better way to consider the mathematics of direct marketing and return on investment is to try to simulate revenues and expenses month by month as they are expected to occur. Exhibit 19–7 presents a simple financial model for the same catalog effort. Revenues flow in according to the historic response pattern that this cataloger has experienced. One-third of the needed inventory is purchased each month, beginning one month in advance of mail date, and catalogs are paid for 30 days after mail date. The total sales, costs, and pretax profit for the 9 months involved are the same as in Exhibit 19–6.

Exhibit 19–6.   Income and Expense Statement for 1,000 Catalogs

40 Orders at $40 per Order (including shipping and handling revenue)		Percent
Gross Sales	$1,600	
Returns	34	
Net Sales	1,566	100.0%
Merchandise Cost	510	32.6
Operating Cost	223	14.2
Fixed Cost	285	18.2
Contribution to Selling Cost & Profit	548	35.0
Selling Cost	400	25.5
Pretax Profit	$ 148	9.5%

This exhibit illustrates a mini profit-and-loss for 1,000 catalogs mailed, assuming 40 gross orders at $40 per order, returns at 2.1 percent of gross, and cost factors identical to those shown in Exhibits 19–1 and 19–2.

This analysis identifies a maximum monthly cash drain of $221 per thousand catalogs in the third month and a cumulative cash drain that peaks in the first and again in the third months. Cash flow will be an important consideration to the management of this company. The internal rate of return[1] on these cash flows is 303.6 percent, which is a much more accurate way of stating return on this company's investment and is very different from the 104 percent calculated by the simple method in the preceding paragraph.

Long-Term or Lifetime Value of a Customer

Most direct marketing businesses are based on the proposition that it may be worthwhile to spend money to acquire a new customer, because that customer will buy again from the company, at which time a profit will be generated. Since different customers will make repeat purchases at different times and different rates, how can we determine the long-term value of a customer or a group of buyers?

One could approach this problem historically. Suppose that a catalog marketer were able to track all activity from 1,000 customers who were acquired at the same time in January, five years ago. During the five-year period examined, the company did not change its distribution policy.

[1] Internal rate of return is the single rate at which the discounted value of all cash flows is zero. It is a good measure of the true rate of return on cash flows.

Exhibit 19–7. **Financial Model for 1,000 Catalogs**

					Month					
	1	**2**	**3**	**4**	**5**	**6**	**7**	**8**	**9**	**Total[a]**
Gross Sales	—	$608	$528	$208	$ 96	$ 80	$ 48	$ 16	$ 16	$1,600
Returns	—	13	11	4	2	2	1	0	0	34
Net Sales	—	595	517	204	94	78	47	16	16	1,566
Merchandise Cost	170	170	170	—	—	—	—	—	—	510
Operating Cost	—	85	74	29	13	11	7	2	2	223
Fixed Cost	—	108	94	37	17	14	9	3	3	285
Contribution to Selling Cost & Profit	(170)	232	179	138	64	53	32	11	11	548
Selling Cost	—	—	400	—	—	—	—	—	—	400
Cash Flow	($170)	$232	($221)	$138	$ 64	$ 53	$ 32	$ 11	$ 11	$ 148

[a] Columns may not total exactly due to rounding

Monthly internal rate of return (IRR) = 25.3%; annualized IRR = 303.7%.
This exhibit displays a simplified financial model corresponding to the situation shown in Exhibit 19–6. The difference is that this model displays the timing of the revenues, costs, and cash flows as they occur over nine months.
The monthly internal rate of return is the monthly rate at which the present value of the cash flows equates to zero.
The annualized internal rate of return is the monthly rate multiplied by 12.

Catalogs were sent to all customers who had purchased within three years. Although this simple catalog circulation policy has been used by many direct marketers, it is by no means recommended as the best or even a desirable approach. (See Chapter Two for a discussion of direct marketing databases and segmentation.)

The same technique illustrated in Exhibit 19–7 is applied to each individual catalog mailing. All the revenues, costs, and cash flows associated with this group of 1,000 customers are analyzed month-by-month for 120 months until there are so few active customers left from the original 1,000 that their additional purchases would have negligible impact.

Although this model is created on a monthly basis using a computer, Exhibit 19–8 summarizes the results for each year. Let us say that the owners

Exhibit 19–8.   **Lifetime Value of 1,000 New Buyers**

	Yr 1	Yr 2	Yr 3	Yr 4	Yr 5
Gross Sales	$11,086	$7,505	$6,173	$2,830	$1,739
Returns	233	158	130	59	37
Net Sales	10,854	7,348	6,044	2,770	1,703
Merchandise Cost	3,538	2,395	1,970	903	555
Operating Costs	1,541	1,043	858	393	242
Fixed Costs	1,975	1,337	1,100	504	310
Contribution to Selling Cost & Profit	3,799	2,572	2,115	970	596
Selling Cost	1,600	1,600	1,600	625	408
Cash Flow	2,199	972	515	345	188
Discounted at 25%	1,759	622	264	141	62
Present Value	2,848	—	—	—	—
Lifetime Value per Customer	2.85	—	—	—	—

This exhibit summarizes the long-term revenues, costs, and cash flows associated with a group of 1,000 new buyers to a catalog operation similar to that displayed in Exhibit 19–7. These values were derived using a financial model like that shown in Exhibit 19–9, with the following significant differences:

It is assumed that there are four catalog mailings each year to this group of 1,000 customers.

Response rates to the catalog mailings vary by the recency of purchase starting with 9 percent for customers who purchased in the most current 6-month season down to 3 percent for customers who have not purchased for 3 years.

The exhibit displays the annual totals resulting from the financial modeling technique applied to each catalog mailing.

The allowable investment to acquire a customer is derived by discounting each year's cash flow at 25 percent to obtain a present value for the 5-year stream of cash flows and dividing the present value by 1,000 to obtain a lifetime-value customer.

The average order and cost structure of the catalog mailings is identical to that displayed in Exhibit 19–7.

of this company have targeted a long-term return on their investment of at least 25 percent per year. If we discount the annual pretax profit shown in this schedule at a 25 percent rate, then the value in that first January of all future profits in excess of a 25 percent per year return is $2,848 per thousand customers, or $2.85 per customer. This means that, given the company's historic catalog circulation policy and actual sales results, the company could afford to have spent $2.85 in that first January to acquire each customer,

with the expectation of earning a 25 percent per year return on all such customers acquired.

Most companies are not in a position to track all of the sales and costs associated with each customer over an extended period of time. Moreover, companies change their policies with respect to the number and content of mailings sent and the rules used to determine who will receive each mailing. The sophisticated direct marketer today can build computer models that calculate the statistical probability of purchases in each season by customers having different profiles; can estimate the results of changing the nature, number, and effectiveness of mailings or other contacts; and can incorporate assumptions as to changes in order size, margins, and costs.

Building computer models to estimate the long-term value of customers is not a trivial matter. Models can range widely in detail and complexity.

These models usually are built on a personal computer using one of the popular spreadsheet software packages. A model typically will have three major sections. There are some important considerations applicable to each section:

1. *Assumptions and parameters*. It is convenient to group in one place all or most of the factors that the user would be likely to change. These may include cost assumptions and ratios; response rates to key list segments; the patterns by which orders, shipments, returns, and payments flow over time; and planned circulation quantities for each medium and/or campaign. Often it is convenient to include in many of these cells a scaler variable that permits changing a series of relationships or values by entering a single number.

    The level of detail incorporated in this section must be carefully determined. It should reflect all of the important drivers in the business, but the user must have a reasonable basis for determining the value of each parameter that is included. The more parameters and assumptions that are used, the more elegant the model will be and the more time will be needed to maintain it and use it to explore alternative "what-if" scenarios. A compromise appropriate to the business must be made.

2. *List cells and transitions*. This section defines the house list cells or segments, rented list groups, and other prospect groups that are reached by some promotional activity. These should be the basic building blocks of the company's circulation or marketing plan. Once again there should be enough groups so that significant changes to or variations in the circulation plan can be accurately reflected, but not so many groups that it becomes too difficult to maintain the model.

    Two major kinds of factors must be determined for each list cell that is defined in the model. First, the anticipated response rate and average-order size must be entered into the model for each cell and each promotion that members in that cell will receive. Second, the size of each cell at the time its members receive each promotion must be estimated.

Projecting the size of each cell can be a tricky proposition. Several methods can be used, including some new statistical methods that produce excellent estimates. The logic and programming in this section are likely to be the most complex in the model. Accuracy must be verified by seeding the model with actual figures that are several years old and checking that it produces a relatively good picture of today's population of each list cell.

3. *Profit and loss statement*. This section displays the end result of the model and is the part in which the user generally is most interested. It produces a cash flow income statement for each month, or each campaign or catalog, or each season, depending on how the model has been structured. When summarized, it might look somewhat like Exhibit 19–8. It should be a high-level statement showing only as much detail as is necessary to reflect key revenue and cost factors that are the typical focus of management.

This is also the section that proves the accuracy of the model. When constructing a model, always begin with one or two years of historical information and extend the model into the future as many years as may be desired. When the model calculates the cash flow statement for the years in which actual results are known, the income statement produced should be very close to the actual cash flow statement for the business in that period. Similarly, revenues, costs, and cash flow estimated by the model for the next one or two seasons should turn out to be very close to actual results. With this kind of proof, management can feel comfortable in using this model to develop estimates of the long-term value of customers.

Such computer models can then be used to simulate the consequences of changes in strategy or policy. Exhibit 19–9 illustrates the impact on return on investment of the pursuit of three different strategies to build a catalog mail-order business. The model assumes that the same amount of money is invested in each strategy. The strategies are to:

1. Mail more catalogs to rented lists to acquire more customers.

2. Expand the catalog by adding more products and increasing the number of pages.

3. Create an extra catalog to be mailed to better customers during the fall season.

Exhibit 19–9 illustrates that over the five-year horizon for which results are simulated, the company in question would invest most advantageously in expanding its product line. You will notice, however, that the customer acquisition strategy appears to be closing the gap quickly at the end of the period and might be expected to outperform the product line expansion

Exhibit 19–9. **Return on Investment**

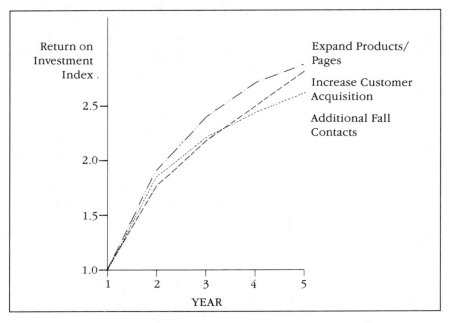

This exhibit displays the performance of three alternative growth strategies, as measured by return on investment.

The three strategies are:

1. Expand products or pages for each catalog.
2. Increase customer acquisition efforts by mailing to more rented lists and expanding the space-advertising budget.
3. Introduce an additional fall catalog each year.

The actual return on investment has been indexed to the return in the first year to disguise the actual figures.

strategy in the sixth or seventh year. Further study might indicate that this particular company could blend the two approaches by expanding the size of some of its catalogs and also enlarging its customer acquisition activities.

Measurements and Analysis

Calculating profitability. Determining lifetime value of customers. Developing long-range strategies for building businesses. Building models. These are the instruments sophisticated direct marketers use. But only well-planned and well-executed campaigns produce the desired results.

Direct marketers build on the strongest foundation if they plan each campaign around efforts that have been tested previously. (See Chapter Twenty for more discussion of the statistics and strategy of testing.) Of course, a company launching a new business has no prior testing experience to use as

the basis for its planning. Such a company must proceed cautiously, placing relatively few ads or mailing only the number of pieces required to determine whether a package, or an offer, or a list is successful.

Established direct marketers, however, plan their campaigns to achieve a predetermined balance between contacting former customers who would be expected to purchase at a high rate and seeking to acquire new customers. The balance that each company strikes is dependent on the relative profitability of each type of effort and its long-range growth strategy.

Exhibit 19–10 illustrates a mail plan for the same catalog marketer we have used as an example throughout this chapter. The total mail plan calls for sendiing 1 million catalogs, which produce a 4.63 percent gross response overall and an average order of $41. Prior experiencce with the company's own list of customers and rented lists ranges widely, as shown. Several new lists are included as tests. In order to keep expanding the business, it is wise for most direct marketers to utilize 10 percent to 15 percent of each campaign to test new lists, or packages, or offers.

Some aspects of this mail plan are worth pointing out. House lists totaling 200,000 former buyers are expected to produce approximately $3,200 sales per thousand. With an average order of $45, they are expected to produce a 7.25 percent gross response and a 24.5 percent pretax profit. In contrast, mailings to proven rented lists are expected to show an average order size of $38 to $42 and response rates of 3.73 percent to 4.45 percent and a 10 percent pretax profit. Test mailings of 5,000 to each of 20 new lists are expected to break even.

Using the same profitability calculation as is shown in Exhibits 19–1 and 19–2, the individual profitability of the mailing to each list is estimated. This is easy to do, since we know the selling cost associated with each list, namely catalog, postage, and mailing expense plus list rental where applicable. And we are estimating the response rate and average order size based on experience.

What is the actual profitability of this mailing? Exhibit 19–11 shows the actual results as of the report date and projected results at the end of the season. The company has been very careful to code its order forms to indicate the list to which each catalog was sent and has asked those customers placing their order by phone to look at the mailing label on the catalog and provide the list code shown thereon. By dint of these efforts, 80 percent of the orders received can be attributed to a specific list. The remaining 20 percent of orders that could not be coded by list must be allocated in the same proportion as attributed orders. This step is extremely important since one would otherwise underestimate the response from each list mailed and might be tempted to stop mailing lists that would then appear marginal.

Since this analysis is being prepared at a time when historic order response patterns indicate that the catalog is 80 percent done or that orders received to date represent 80 percent of all orders that will be received, the actual results for each list after allocation of uncoded orders are divided

Exhibit 19–10. Catalog Mail Plan[c]

1 Code	2 List Description	3 Mail Qty	4 Avg Order	5 Resp %	6 Gross Sales/M	7 Gross Sales	8 Net Sales/M	9 Selling Cost[a]	10 Sell Cost%[b]	11 Pretax Profit	12 Profit per M	13 Profit %[b]
1000	House List	200000	$45.00	7.25	$3262	$652400	$3193	$67000	10.49	$156544	$782	24.51
2010	Rollout List 1	70000	40.00	4.36	1744	122080	1707	28000	23.43	13830	197	11.57
2020	Rollout List 2	70000	40.00	4.27	1708	119560	1672	28000	23.92	12967	185	11.08
2030	Rollout List 3	70000	40.00	3.73	1492	104440	1460	28000	27.38	7786	111	7.61
2040	Rollout List 4	70000	42.00	4.09	1717	120190	1680	28000	23.80	13183	188	11.20
2050	Rollout List 5	70000	40.00	4.18	1672	117040	1636	28000	24.44	12103	172	10.56
2060	Rollout List 6	70000	38.00	4.09	1554	108780	1521	28000	26.29	9273	132	8.71
2070	Rollout List 7	70000	40.00	4.45	1780	124600	1742	28000	22.95	14694	209	12.05
2080	Rollout List 8	70000	40.00	3.82	1528	106960	1495	28000	26.74	8649	123	8.26
2090	Rollout List 9	70000	40.00	4.00	1600	112000	1566	28000	25.54	10376	148	9.46
2100	Rollout List 10	70000	40.00	3.91	1564	109480	1531	28000	26.12	9513	135	8.88
20	Subtotal	700,000	$40.00	4.09	1636	1,145,130	1602	280,000	25.00	112,374	161	10.02
3001	Test List 1	5000	37.00	3.25	1202	6010	1176	2000	34.00	59	11	1.00
3002	Test List 2	5000	37.00	3.07	1135	5675	1111	2000	36.00	−55	−11	−0.99
3003	Test List 3	5000	40.00	3.16	1264	6320	1237	2000	32.33	165	33	2.67
3004	Test List 4	5000	34.00	3.16	1074	5370	1051	2000	38.04	−160	−32	−3.04
3005	Test List 5	5000	37.00	3.16	1169	5845	1144	2000	34.95	2	0	0.03
3006	Test List 6	5000	37.00	3.16	1169	5845	1144	2000	34.95	2	0	0.03
3007	Test List 7	5000	37.00	3.21	1187	5935	1162	2000	34.42	33	6	0.57
3008	Test List 8	5000	37.00	3.11	1150	5750	1125	2000	35.53	−29	−5	−0.52
3009	Test List 9	5000	37.00	3.16	1169	5845	1144	2000	34.95	2	0	0.03
3010	Test List 10	5000	37.00	3.16	1169	5845	1144	2000	34.95	2	0	0.03
3011	Test List 11	5000	38.00	3.16	1200	6000	1174	2000	34.05	55	11	0.94
3012	Test List 12	5000	37.00	3.16	1169	5845	1144	2000	34.95	2	0	0.03
3013	Test List 13	5000	36.00	3.16	1137	5685	1113	2000	35.94	−52	−10	−0.93
3014	Test List 14	5000	37.00	3.16	1169	5845	1144	2000	34.95	2	0	0.03
3015	Test List 15	5000	37.00	3.26	1206	6030	1180	2000	33.88	66	13	1.12
3016	Test List 16	5000	37.00	3.06	1132	5660	1108	2000	36.09	−60	−12	−1.08
3017	Test List 17	5000	42.00	3.16	1327	6635	1299	2000	30.79	273	54	4.20
3018	Test List 18	5000	32.00	3.16	1011	5055	989	2000	40.42	−268	−53	−5.42
3019	Test List 19	5000	37.00	3.16	1169	5845	1144	2000	34.95	2	0	0.03
3020	Test List 20	5000	37.00	3.16	1169	5845	1144	2000	34.95	2	0	0.03
30	Subtotal	100,000	37.00	3.16	1169	116,885	1144	40,000	34.96	43	0	0.04
	Total/Average	1,000,000	$41.36	4.63	$1915	$1,914,415	$1874	$387,000	20.65	$268,961	$269	14.35%

[a] Assumes roll-out catalog cost of $335/M and list rental cost of $65/M.
[b] Percentage of net sales assuming a 2.1 percent return rate.
[c] See notes to exhibit on page 540.

by 0.8 to produce projected results at the end of the order cycle. Resulting profitability is based on projected results, not on orders received to date.

Basing the analysis simply on orders to date would again understate final sales and profitability significantly. Finally, this analysis calculates the statistical probability of exceeding the minimum 10 percent target for pretax profit. What a handy tool this final column provides. It synthesizes into a single number the likelihood of achieving the desired profit by mailing to that list again, assuming, of course, that all other conditions remain the same.

That last assumption should not be dismissed quickly. Conditions in the economy shift. Some companies make radical changes in the composition of their product line. Some companies whose lists you rent may have made important changes resulting in customers who behave differently. A direct marketer can make better use of statistics and arithmetic than can a person engaged in any other form of marketing. But it is not all science. The tools discussed in this chapter will help you, but they will not substitute for careful decision making based on good business judgment. Learn the tools well— and then apply your own good sense.

Exhibit 19–10 Notes Exhibit 19–10 shows a sample mail plan that would be put together before a mailing. The primary purpose of putting together such a plan is to build the sales and profits projection for the total mailing by estimating the performance of each list separately.

Column 1 contains the key code used on the response device to indicate the list from which each order is obtained.

Column 2 contains a written description of the list.

Column 3 shows the mail quantity of each list.

Columns 4–6 detail the expected average-order size, response rate, and resulting gross sales per thousand for each list. These results applied to the mail quantity provide the expected total gross sales for each list, which are displayed in Column 7.

Column 8 contains the expected net sales per thousand, which is estimated from the gross sales by applying a return factor.

Column 9 indicates the total catalog mailing cost, and Column 10 expresses that selling cost as a percentage of net sales.

Column 11 displays the expected pretax profix, which is derived by subtracting the merchandise cost, operating cost, fixed cost allocation, and selling cost from the expected net sales. All of these calculations can be approximated readily using the procedure shown in Exhibits 19–1 and 19–2.

Column 12 gives the resulting profit per thousand, and the final column shows profit as a percentage of net sales.

Exhibit 19–11. Catalog Mail Report[b]

Mail Date:
Percent Done: 80%

Catalog No:
Week Ending:

Code	List Description	Mail Qty	Cum Orders	Cum Sales	Avg Order	Adj Sales	Adj Sales/M	Sales	Sales/M	Projected Resp%	Projected Sell Cost%[a]	Projected Profit	Proj Prof/M	Prob of 10% Profit[a]
1000	House List	200000	8500	$385000	$45.29	$481249	$2406	$601561	$3007	6.64	11.38	$139124	695	100.00%
2010	Rollout List 1	70000	1899	74665	39.32	93331	1333	116663	1666	4.24	24.52	11974	171	83.12
2020	Rollout List 2	70000	2272	80000	35.21	100000	1428	125000	1785	5.07	22.89	14831	211	99.99
2030	Rollout List 3	70000	1735	73632	42.44	92040	1314	115050	1643	3.87	24.87	11421	163	57.69
2040	Rollout List 4	70000	2048	99225	48.45	124031	1771	155038	2214	4.57	18.45	25123	358	100.00
2050	Rollout List 5	70000	2028	70400	34.71	88000	1257	110000	1571	4.53	26.01	9691	138	5.27
2060	Rollout List 6	70000	2240	90880	40.57	113600	1622	142000	2028	5.00	20.15	20656	295	100.00
2070	Rollout List 7	70000	1822	85360	46.85	106700	1524	133375	1905	4.07	21.45	17700	252	100.00
2080	Rollout List 8	70000	1830	84825	46.35	106031	1514	132538	1893	4.08	21.58	17414	248	100.00
2090	Rollout List 9	70000	2311	87440	37.84	109300	1561	136625	1951	5.16	20.94	18814	268	100.00
2100	Rollout List 10	70000	2112	84748	40.13	105935	1513	132418	1891	4.71	21.61	17373	248	100.00
3001	Test List 1	5000	120	5500	45.83	6875	1375	8593	1718	3.75	23.78	944	188	74.13
3002	Test List 2	5000	80	3175	39.69	3968	793	4960	992	2.50	41.19	-300	-60	0.00
3003	Test List 3	5000	125	5550	44.40	6937	1387	8671	1734	3.90	23.56	971	194	78.12
3004	Test List 4	5000	96	3596	37.46	4495	899	5618	1123	3.00	36.38	-74	-14	0.00
3005	Test List 5	5010	140	4925	35.18	6156	1228	7695	1535	4.37	26.62	632	126	25.07
3006	Test List 6	5000	98	3877	39.56	4846	969	6057	1211	3.05	33.74	75	15	0.00
3007	Test List 7	5000	90	5575	61.94	6968	1393	8710	1742	2.80	23.45	984	196	74.62
3008	Test List 8	5000	79	3549	44.92	4436	887	5545	1109	2.45	36.84	-100	-20	0.00
3009	Test List 9	5015	130	4890	37.62	6112	1218	7640	1523	4.04	26.83	611	121	14.90
3010	Test List 10	5000	88	3765	42.78	4706	941	5882	1176	2.75	34.74	15	3	0.00
3011	Test List 11	5000	100	5590	55.90	6987	1397	8733	1746	3.13	23.40	992	198	79.50
3012	Test List 12	5000	89	3699	41.56	4623	924	5778	1155	2.77	35.37	-20	-4	0.00
3013	Test List 13	5000	150	6200	41.33	7750	1550	9687	1937	4.67	21.09	1319	263	99.01
3014	Test List 14	5000	134	5235	39.07	6543	1308	8178	1635	4.17	24.99	802	160	48.64
3015	Test List 15	5002	130	4325	33.27	5406	1080	6757	1350	4.05	30.27	314	62	0.15
3016	Test List 16	5000	135	4375	32.41	5468	1093	6835	1367	4.20	29.98	342	68	0.21
3017	Test List 17	5008	135	5440	40.30	6800	1357	8500	1697	4.19	24.08	909	181	67.12
3018	Test List 18	5000	98	3997	40.79	4996	999	6245	1249	3.05	32.71	139	27	0.01
3019	Test List 19	5000	155	6015	38.81	7518	1503	9397	1879	4.82	21.74	1219	243	97.41
3020	Test List 20	5000	85	5255	61.82	6568	1313	8210	1642	2.65	24.88	813	162	51.70
	Total/Average	1,000,035	31,054	$1,310,708	$42.20	$1,638,375	$1638	$2,047,959	2048	4.85	19.30	$314,708	$315	100.00%

[a] Based on net sales assuming a 2.1 percent return rate.
[b] See notes to exhibit on page 540.

Exhibit 19–11 Notes   Exhibit 19–11 shows a sample mail report that would be generated during the course of a mailing.

Columns 1–3 include the source code, list description, and actual mail quantity, respectively.

Columns 4 and 5 display the actual cumulative orders and sales as of the date of the report.

Column 6 contains the average-order size derived by dividing the cumulative sales by the cumulative orders.

Column 7 displays the adjusted sales, which are obtained by adding a pro-rata allocation of the uncoded sales to each list. The adjusted sales per thousand in Column 8 are derived by dividing the adjusted sales by the mail quantity.

Column 9 shows projected sales, which are derived by dividing the adjusted sales by the estimated percentage done for the catalog at the time of the report. Historical order response patterns are applied to the mail dates for each list to determine the percentage done. Column 10 divides Column 9 by the mail quantity in thousands.

Column 11 contains the projected response rate, which is obtained by projecting cumulative orders to completion in the same way that sales were projected, and dividing the projected orders by the mail quantity.

Column 12 contains the estimated selling cost percentage of net sales obtained by dividing the promotional cost by the projected net sales for each list.

The projected profit and profit per thousand in Columns 13 and 14 are derived by applying the relevant costs to the projected sales.

The last column contains the profitability of meeting the 10 percent profit target. This figure is derived by comparing the projected response rate with the response rate required to produce a 10 percent profit given the average-order size for each list. Taking the actual mail quantity into consideration, this figure represents the statistical probability that each list would achieve or exceed the target response rate when mailed again under similar conditions.

Self-Quiz

1. Contribution per unit or per average order is calculated by subtracting _____ from average unit selling price or from average order value.

2. Selling cost in direct marketing is the expense of _____ _____.

3. It is helpful to treat creative expense and the extra cost of _____ _____ by budgeting them as part of _____ expense.

4. Typically, the more highly qualified an inquiry is,

   ☐ the more costly it will be to generate.

   ☐ the less costly it will be to generate.

5. In the short run, it is profitable to continue making conversion mailings to an inquiry list until the _____ of the last mailing is _____ the contribution it generates.

6. What are the three factors that determine profitability?

a. _____

b. _____

c. _____

7. Catalog marketers should not only analyze overall results, but they should also analyze results for each _____ and _____ of items.

8. A practical way to compute return on investment is to try to simulate _____ and expenses _____ as they are expected to occur.

9. Name three strategies that might be applied to improving return on investment for a catalog operation.

a. _____

b. _____

c. _____

10. In order to expand an ongoing direct marketing program, it is wise to devote a portion of each campaign to _____.

11. When analyzing results of a campaign, uncoded response should be _____ to _____ in the same proportion as _____.

12. Making roll-out promotion decisions is greatly aided by calculating the statistical probability that each test will exceed _____.

Pilot Project

You have a mail-order item that sells for $45. Your total cost, including product cost, shipping and handling costs, estimated returned goods, and overhead is $29. Your mailing cost is $350 per thousand.

Considering your unit profit per sale and your cost per thousand mailed, perform the following calculations:

1. Number of orders required per thousand to break even.

2. Number of orders required per thousand to make a 10 percent profit.

CHAPTER TWENTY

Creativity and Testing

"We've got to develop ideas with breakthrough potential and test their validity" is an oft-repeated statement in direct marketing circles. The never-ending quest for the breakthrough is motivated by fantastic payoff potential. "Book-of-the-Month Club" was a breakthrough concept, leading to billions of dollars of book sales. Newspaper and magazine inserts. The "Gold Box" concept. TV support for other media. Ink-jet imaging. Each a gigantic breakthrough.

But how does one develop breakthrough ideas? Are there techniques to be applied? Yes.

Urgent Need for Creativity

The major breakthroughs of past decades all came about as a result of brilliant creativity. But, sad to say, a strong case can be made for the widespread belief that there is a dearth of breakthrough ideas today as compared to the recent past. Two reasons are given for this condition: (1) the tendency to "play it safe" to protect the bottom line, and (2) not enough way-out testing to lead to creative new breakthroughs. In short, creativity is deteriorating.

To illustrate what I mean by creativity, let me share the following story with you.

The Yamaha Piano Story

Situation Analysis

Yamaha had succeeded in capturing 40 percent of the global piano market. Unfortunatey, just when Yamaha became market leader, the overall demand for pianos started declining by 10 percent a year.

Around the world, in living rooms, dens, and concert halls, there are some 40 million pianos. For the most part, the pianos just sit and gather dust.

As head of Yamaha, what do you do?

Some American analysts would advise: "Get out of the piano business!"

Solution to the Problem

1. Yamaha's marketers determined that one possible way to solve the problem was to add value to the millions of pianos already out there.

2. In this exercise they remembered the old player piano—a pleasant idea with a not very pleasant sound.

3. Using a combination of sophisticated digital and optical technology, they developed a "player" program that can distinguish 92 degrees of speed and strength of key touch.

4. With this technology, piano owners could now record live performances by the pianists of their choice, or they could buy such recordings on a computer-like disk.

5. So now, for an expenditure of around $2,500, piano owners could retrofit their idle, untuned, dust-collecting pieces of oversized furniture so that great artists could play for them in the privacy of their homes.

End Result of the Value-Added Concept

1. Owners of 40 million more or less idle pianos became a vibrant market for $2,500 retrofitting sales.

2. Yamaha started marketing this technology in April 1988 and sales since then have been explosive.

3. This very technology has created a new interest in learning to play the piano.

After reading about Yamaha's success, we should all ask ourselves these questions:

1. Do we have products or services that have become obsolete?

2. By thinking in terms of "value added," can we create whole new markets?

It's been said that creativity is something everyone talks about but few can define. To determine your creative ability, I urge you to review these 16 traits of successful creative people:

- Curiosity
- Sense of humor
- Independence
- Observation
- Persistence
- Motivation
- Good imagination
- Energy
- Hard work
- Ambition
- Visual thinking
- Originality

- Eclectic taste
- Love for reading
- Self-confidence
- Awareness of the "big picture"

Rate yourself on a 1–10-point scale for each trait: 160 points—creative genius; 120–160—brilliant; 80–120—need counseling; under 80—stick to bean counting.

Regardless of what your score is, you can improve. Consider taking these steps to improve your personal creativity:

1. Block out the time.
2. Get comfortable.
3. Eat something healthful.
4. Stock up lots of background.
5. Experience the world.
6. Be ready when the ideas strike.
7. Use a "don't disturb" sign.
8. For "blue-sky" projects have a glass of wine.
9. Let your work rest before evaluation.
10. Enjoy the process.[1]

The Power of Group Dynamics

American businesspeople traditionally expect ideas to surface at meetings called by managers. But, as one who has sat in on literally thousands of meetings, I must say that I find most meetings to be dull, nonproductive, and idea-poor. No motivation. Little preparation. No group dynamics.

In a great little book entitled *Good Business in Bad Times*, written and published by Martin Edelston, founder of Boardroom Reports Inc., of New York, the author shows how easy it is to turn every meeting into an idea session.

As a mattter of fact, Edelston's system isn't new: It reinvents the employee suggestion system created at Eastman Kodak in 1898 and replicated by firms like GE, Westinghouse, and Bell Laboratories in the early 1900s. Unfortunately, most suggestion systems today are tired, producing ideas like "Turn the air-conditioning down" or "Turn the air-conditioning up." Edelston's plan, by contrast, leads to suggestions that increase sales and profits. It also cuts employee turnover because people feel they are important. These developments make it much easier for management to introduce changes.

[1] Susan K. Jones, *Creative Strategy in Direct Marketing*, Lincolnwood, IL: NTC Business Books, 1991.

The Boardroom system came about as a result of a suggestion by Peter Drucker, the famed marketing guru, who gave Edelston this suggestion about conducting meetings: "Have everyone who comes to a meeting be prepared to give two ideas for making his or her own work or department work more productive . . . ideas that will help the company as a whole."

Edelston couldn't wait to try the plan. He did make one change at the outset: He asked for three ideas instead of two for improving work, saving money, or making money. And he tried for a 50 percent productivity increase right away!

Searching for a name for the program, Boardroom Reports ran a company-wide contest. Many of the suggested names began with a word that started with the letter "i": Ideas, Innovation, Improvement, Incentive, Inventive, Intelligence, Ingenuity, Inspiration . . . and I. Thus the name for the program emerged as "I-Power."

What Makes the I-Power Program Work?

The technique that makes the program work is so simple that some MBAs might regard its application as too "childish" for their exalted stature. But it works!

Here's the technique. When Mr. Edelston or one of his managers runs a meeting, he walks around the table with a pocket full of bills. "We've learned by practice," says Mr. Edelston, "that the chief value of our small money awards is to create a bit of theater. To change the pace."

Amounts ranging from $1 to $10 are distributed at idea meetings and for monthly awards. To the person who contributes the greatest number of A-rated ideas in a given month, $50 is given. Also, two tickets to any show in town is awarded for the best idea of the month. This technique produces a continuous flow of ideas. The meetings foster both competition and a community feeling in the process.

But the modest rewards Boardroom Reports gives are not the real reason why the program works. The real reason is that Boardroom shows respect and appreciation for the thinking that goes into each idea. It does so by spending management time and money to keep track of the ideas—and by implementing them promptly.

Now two years into the I-Power program, Boardroom is getting more ideas per person than it ever did. The average at present is 70 ideas from each person over a 12-month period. And the numbers keep climbing.[2]

---

[2] Boardroom has developed a number of forms for guidance in making the I-Power program work smoothly. To obtain a free set of the forms, write to: Good Business, Boardroom Forms, Boardroom Reports Inc., 330 West 42nd Street, New York, NY 10036.

Brainstorming

Brainstorming, first popularized in the 1950s by Alex Osborne of BBD&O, continues to be one of the most effective methods of finding new creative solutions to difficult problems. Scores of examples could be cited of break-throughs that have resulted from brainstorming, but a few will suffice. But first, let's look at some rules for brainstorming.

Selecting a Leader

Select a leader, and have him or her take all responsibility for contact with reality; everyone else in the brainstorming meeting is to "think wild." In the brainstorming meeting, the leader plays a low-key role. It's important to avoid influencing the participants. The duties of the leader are:

- To see that detailed notes are taken on all ideas expressed
- To see that the agenda and time schedule are adhered to
- To admonish any critical thinkers in the group—no negative thinking is allowed during the brainstorming session
- To see that the group takes time to "build up" each idea
- To keep all participants involved and contributing

House Rules during Brainstorming

1. Suspend all critical judgment of your own—or other people's—ideas. Don't ask yourself if this is a *good idea* or a *bad idea*. Accept it and rack your brain for ways to improve the concept.

2. Welcome "freewheeling," off-the-wall thinking. Wild, crazy, funny, far-out ideas are important. Why? Because they frequently shock us into a totally new viewpoint of the problem.

3. Quantity, not quality, is the objective during the brainstorm session. This may sound contradictory. It's not. Remember, every member of the group has been briefed on the problem in advance. You have a carefully planned agenda of material to cover. Consequently, your group is well directed toward the right problem. Therefore we can say, "Go for quantity in the idea session."

4. Build up each idea. Here's where most brainstorming sessions fail. They just collect ideas as fast as they come and let it go at that. The leaders should carefully slow the group down so they stop with each idea and help build it up. Enhance each idea, no matter how crazy or offbeat it may seem.

It's the leader's responsibility to see that these four guidelines are adhered to in every meeting, but he or she should do this in a very low-key, informal manner. It is important that the leader not become a dominant, authority figure in meetings.

Brainstorming is part of a three-phase process:

1. Before starting, create an agenda and carefully define problem(s) in writing.

2. Set quotas for ideas and a time limit for each section of the agenda.

3. Review the house rules with participants before each brainstorming session.

When the session is over, then—and only then—use your normal everyday judgment to logically select ideas with the most potential from all of the available alternatives.

Brainstorming Examples

Example 1   *The problem*: Insurance companies are not allowed to give free gifts as an incentive for applying for an insurance policy. How can we offer a free gift and stay within the law? That was the brainstorming problem. Sounds like an impossible problem. Right? Wrong. Brainstorming participants broke through with a positive solution, a blockbuster.

The breakthrough: The brainstorming idea that hit pay dirt was to offer the free gift to everyone, whether they apply for the policy or not.

The result: A 38 percent increase in applications.

Example 2   *The problem*: How can we avoid paying postage for sending prizes to "no" entrants in an "everybody wins" sweepstakes? (Possible savings in postage to the marketer—if the problem could be solved—was about $250,000.)

The breakthrough: We asked "no" entrants to provide a stamped, self-addressed envelope. We included a prize in the shipping carton for those who said "yes." (The Post Office Department approved the requirement at the time.)

The result: This was the most successful sweepstakes contest the sponsor ever conducted. The sponsor also enjoyed savings of $250,000 in postage.

Example 3   *The problem*: We have 36 competitors selling to schools. They all promise "prompt shipment" of their pompons. How can we dramatize the fact that we ship our pompons in 24 hours and thus capture the bulk of the market?

The breakthrough: We inserted a Jiffy Order Card in the catalog, in addition to the regular order form, featuring Guaranteed Shipment Within 24 hours.

The result: Pompon sales increased a dramatic 40 percent!

Example 4 *The problem*: As a leading agricultural chemical company, we manufacture both a corn herbicide and corn insecticide. Each product has its own positioning in the farm market, and each product has a different share of market in various geographic areas across the nation. How can new users for each product be won over from the competition?

The breakthrough: We created a combination rebate program. Because the ratio of herbicide to insecticide remains relatively constant regardless of farm size, we offered a rebate on *both* products when purchased at the same time.

The result: A significant number of farmers who had planned to purchase the two products from different manufacturers took advantage of the rebate offer and purchased both products from the sponsor, with an average order of $25,000.

Fantasy Games

Of all the games creative people play, my favorites are fantasy games. These can be defined as games that enable one to reach out for satisfaction of his or her most fervent wishes. Here's a fantasy game anyone can play in a group or alone. The rules are simple: Before you charge into the solution to a direct marketing problem, write three words on the top of a piece of paper —"I wish that . . . ." Then complete the sentence with your most fervent wish. Let's take some examples:

Fantasy 1. Some time ago, someone probably said, "I wish I could find a way to spread my advertising sales cost over several books rather than one." Out of it came the negative option and the Book-of-the-Month Club. A marketing triumph.

Fantasy 2. A client recently expressed this wish: "I wish we could cut our bad debts in half." A fantasy? Not at all. Brainstorming provided a way to cut the client's bad debts by 80 percent!

Fantasy 3. "I wish that we could find a way to contact customers just one week before their suppliers are depleted." A unique computer system to accomplish exactly that came out of this wish.

Lateral Thinking

Recently I sent a memo to all of our writers, asking the question, "What do you do when your creative process turns blah?" Here is the reply of one of our senior writers: "I use the principles of random word technique and lateral thinking. I also like to use the Think Tank, a piece of gadgetry designed by Savo Bojicic of University of Ontario. It forces the user to break

the habit of logical, vertical thinking and opens the mind to creative, uninhibited lateral thought. Here's how I use the Think Tank:

> First, I twist the dials on the sides of the Think Tank to jumble up the words inside. Second, I copy down six random words that appear in the window of the Think Tank. Third, I spend at least five minutes with each word, using word associations and so forth, that relate to the problem I'm trying to solve. Usually one or more of the words will "trigger" an idea. Here's an example.
>
> My problem was to come up with some new ideas on how to get more credit card holders for Amoco. I twirled the dial on the Think Tank and the word "water" popped into the window. In a matter of milliseconds my free, stream-of-consciousness thinking was set in motion and led to a unique idea. Water made me think of boats. Boats need gasoline, just as cars do (a good-size cruiser may spend $75 to $100 or more for a fill-up). There are Amoco gas pumps at marinas on the water. Why not send our regular credit card solicitation package with a special letter and special appeal to a list of boat owners? Credit the lateral thinking process with this breakthrough idea.

Creative Stimulators

The degree of truly creative output is directly related to two factors: clear and specific definitions of problems to be solved and the right "atmosphere" for developing creative solutions.

Frank Daniels, a former creative director with Stone & Adler, has a system for stimulating creative people. Using a long-established technique for idea stimulating, he provides creative people with eight "stimulators" designed to expand their thinking. The examples that follow were applied to the Lanier Company, manufacturers of dictating equipment. Creativity was being stimulated for promoting a minirecorder, Lanier's Pocket Secretary. Each of the eight stimulators is accompanied by a key thought and a series of questions designed to promote creative solutions.

Can We Combine?

Combining two or more elements often results in new thought processes. The following questions are designed to encourage brainstorming participants to think in terms of combinations.

Key thought: Combine appropriate parts of well-known things to emphasize the benefits of our product. "Think of owning a Rolls-Royce the size of a Volkswagen" (Lanier Pocket Secretary).

- What can be combined physically or conceptually to emphasize product benefits?

- Can the product be combined with another so that both benefit?

- Where in the product offer would a combination of thoughts be of most help?

- What opposites can be combined to show a difference from competitive products?

- What can we combine with our product to make it more fun to own, use, look at?

- Can part of one of our benefits be combined with part of another to enhance both?

- Can newness be combined with tradition?

- Can a product benefit be combined with a specific audience need through visual devices? Copy devices?

- What can we combine from the advertising and sales program to the benefit of both? Can salespersons' efforts be combined into advertising?

- Can we demonstrate product advantages by using "misfit" combination demonstrations?

- Can we combine manufacturing information performance tests with advertising to demonstrate advantages?

Time Elements

Saving time and having extra time are conventional human wants. This series of questions is designed to expand one's thinking toward making time a plus factor in the product offer.

Key thought: Alter time factor(s) in present offer, present schedules, and present product positioning to motivate action.

- Does seasonal timing have an effect on individual benefits?

- Can present seasonal timing be reversed for special effect?

- Can limited offers be effective?

- Can early buyers be given special consideration?

- Can off-season offers be made?

- Are there better days, weeks, or months for our offers?

- Can we compress or extend present promotional sequencing?

- Can our price be keyed to selected times of the week, month, year?

- Can we feature no-time-limit offers?

- Can we feature limited-time offers?

- Can we feature fast delivery or follow-up?

Can We Add?

An axiom of selling is that the customer often unconsciously compares the added benefits of a competitor's product with those of your product. The products with the most added benefits traditionally sell better. These questions are designed to ferret out added benefits for a particular product.

Key thought: Look for ways to express benefits by relating functional advantages of unrelated products or things. "We've taken all the best cassette recorder features and added one from the toaster" (pop-out delivery).

- What has been added to our product that's missing from others?

- Do we have a deficiency due to excess that can be turned into advantage?

- Is our product usable in many different ways aside from the intended use?

- Is our product instantly noticeable? Is it unusual in terms of size, shape, color? What unrelated symbols can we use to emphasize this unique characteristic?

- Does our product make something easier? What have we added by taking this something away?

- Does our product make order out of chaos or meaningful chaos out of total chaos? What have we added by taking this something away?

- What does the purchase of our product add to the buyer's physical condition, mental condition, subconscious condition, present condition, future condition?

- Where will the buyer be if he or she does not purchase? What will be missing from the buyer's life?

- Does our product give its full benefit to the buyer immediately, or does the buyer build up (add to) his or her well-being through continued possession?

Can We Subtract?

Taking away can often be as appealing as adding to. Less weight, less complexity, less fuss, less bother are fundamental appeals. These questions steer brainstorming participants in that direction.

Key thought: Subtract from the obvious to focus attention on the benefits of our product or service. "We've weighed all the minirecorders and made ours lighter."

- What deficiencies does our product have competitively?

- What advantage do we have?

- What features are the newest? The most unusual?

- How can our product use/cost be "minimized" over time?

- Can a buyer use less of another product if he or she buys ours?
- Can the evidence of total lack of desire for our product be used to illustrate its benefits?
- Can the limitations of our benefits be used as an appeal?
- What does lack of our product in the buyer's living habits do to him or her?
- Does our product offer a chance to eliminate any common element in all competitive products?
- Does our product reduce or eliminate (subtract) anything in the process of performing its work?
- Will our product deflate (subtract from) a problem for the buyers?

Can We Make Associations?

Favorable associations are often the most effective way to emphasize product benefits. "Like Sterling on silver," a classic example of a favorable association, is an [observation] [saying] [remark] [comment] that accrues to the benefit of the product being compared with other products.

Key thought: Form a link with unrelated things or situations to emphasize benefits.

- Can we link our product to another, already successful product to emphasize benefits?
- Can we appeal to popular history, literature, poetry, or art to emphasize benefits?
- What does the potential buyer associate with our product? How can we use this association to advantage?
- When does the potential buyer associate our product with potential use?
- Can associations be drawn with present or future events?
- Can associations be made with abstractions that can be expressed visually, musically, with words, and so forth?
- Can funny, corny, challenging associations be made?
- Can associations be made with suppliers of component parts?
- Is our product so unique that it needs no associations?
- Can our product be associated with many different situations?

Can We Simplify?

What is the simple way to describe and illustrate our major product benefit? As sophisticated as our world is today, the truism persists that people relate

best to simple things. These questions urge participants to state benefits with dramatic simplicity.

Key thought: Dramatize benefits individually or collectively with childishly simple examples, symbols, images.

- Which of our appeals is strongest over our competition? How can we simplify to illustrate?
- Is there a way to simplify *all* our benefits for emphasis?
- Where is most of the confusion about our product in the buyer's mind?
- Can we illustrate by simplification?
- Is our appeal abstract? Can we substitute simple, real visualizations to emphasize?
- Could a familiar quotation or picture be used to make our appeal more understandable?
- Is our product complex? Can we break it up (literally) into more understandable pieces to emphasize benefits?
- Can we overlap one benefit with another to make product utility more understandable?
- Can we contrast an old way of doing something with the confusing part of our product to create understanding?
- Is product appeal rigidly directed at too small a segment of the market? Too broad a segment?
- Can we emphasize benefits by having an unskilled person or child make good use of the product in a completely out-of-context situation?

Can We Substitute?

The major product benefit for our product is often so similar to major product benefits of competitive products that it is difficult for the consumer to perceive the difference. Substituting another theme, such as Avis did when the company changed its theme to "We Try Harder," can often establish a point of difference. These questions inspire participants to think in terms of substitution.

Key thought: Substitute the familiar for another familiar theme for emphasis; substitute the unfamiliar for the familiar for emphasis.

- Can a well-known theme for another product be substituted for our theme, or can a well-known benefit for another product be substituted for our benefit?
- Can an incongruous situation be used to focus emphasis on our theme or benefits?

- Can a series of incongruous situations be found for every benefit we have? Can they be used in one ad? Can they form a continuity series of ads?

- What can be substituted for our product appeal that will emphasize the difference between us and our competitors?

- Can an obviously dissimilar object be substituted for the image of our product?

- Can a physical object be used to give more concrete representation of a product intangible?

- Is our product replacing a process rapidly becoming dated? Can we substitute the past for the present, or the future for the past or the present?

- Can we visualize our product where the competitor's product is normally expected to be?

- Can we visualize our product as the only one of its kind in the world, as if there were no other substitutes for our product?

Can We Make a Reversal?

The ordinary can become extraordinary as usual situations are reversed. A man wearing a tennis skirt. A woman wearing a football helmet. A trained bear pushing a power mower. These questions are designed to motivate participants to think in terms of reversing usual situations.

Key thought: Emphasize a benefit by completely reversing the usual situation.

- What are the diametrically opposed situations for each of our product benefits?

- For each copy point already established, make a complete reverse statement.

- How would a totally uniformed person describe our product?

- Can male- and female-oriented roles be reversed?

- Can art and copy be totally reversed to emphasize a point?

- How many incongruous product situations can be shown graphically? Verbally?

- Can we find humor in the complete reversal of anticipated product uses or benefits?

Test the Big Things

Whether testable ideas come out of pure research, brainstorming, or self-developed creativity, the same picture applies: *Test the big things*. Trivia

testing—for example, testing the tilt of a postage stamp or testing the effect of various colors of paper stock—are passé. Breakthroughs are possible only when you test the big things. Six big areas from which breakthroughs emerge are:

1. The products or services you offer
2. The media you use (lists, print, and broadcast)
3. The propositions you make
4. The copy platforms you use
5. The formats you use
6. The timing you choose

Five of the areas for testing appear on most published lists these days. But testing new products and new product features is rarely recommended. Yet everything starts with the product or service you offer.

Many direct marketers religiously test new ads, new mailing packages, new media, new copy approaches, new formats, and new timing schedules season after season with never a thought to testing new product features. Finally, the most imaginative of creative approaches fails to overcome the waning appeal of the same old product. And still another product bites the dust.

This need not happen. For example, consider the most commonplace of mail-order items, the address label. Scores of firms offer them in black ink on standard white stock. Competition is keen: Prices all run about the same. From this variety of competitive styles, however, a few emerge with the new product features: gold stock, colored ink, seasonal borders, and so forth. Tests are made to determine appeal. The new product features appeal to a bigger audience.

Projectable Mailing Sample Sizes

Determining mail sample sizes for testing purposes was covered thoroughly in Chapter Nine, "Mailing Lists." As we pointed out, a 5,000 test of a given list is usually adequate to get a "feel" of responsiveness, but continuations are almost certain to vary because of time lapse, seasonality, change in list sources, economics, weather conditions, consumer behavior, and a host of other factors.

Some direct marketers live by probability tables that tell the mailer what the sample size must be at various response levels within a specified error limit, such as 5 or 10 percent. No one argues the statistical validity of probability tables. Although probability tables can't be relied on too heavily because it is impossible to construct a truly scientific sample, such tables, within limits, can be helpful. Table 20–1 is based on a 95 percent confidence level at various limits of error.

Table 20–1. Test Sample Sizes Required for 95 Percent Confidence Level for Mailing Response Levels from 0.1 Percent to 4.0 Percent

R (Response)	Limits of Error (Expressed as Percentage Points)														
	.02	.04	.06	.08	.10	.12	.14	.16	.18	.20	.30	.40	.50	.60	.70
.1	95,929	23,982	10,659	5,995	3,837	2,665	1,957	1,499	1,184	959	426	240	153	106	78
.2	191,666	47,916	21,296	11,979	7,667	5,324	3,911	2,994	2,366	1,917	852	479	307	213	156
.3	287,211	71,803	31,912	17,951	11,488	7,978	5,861	4,487	3,546	2,872	1,276	718	459	319	234
.4	382,564	95,641	42,507	23,910	15,303	10,627	7,807	5,977	4,723	3,826	1,700	956	612	425	312
.5	477,724	119,431	53,080	29,858	19,109	13,270	9,749	7,464	5,987	4,777	2,123	1,194	764	530	390
.6	572,693	143,173	63,632	35,793	22,908	15,908	11,687	8,948	7,070	5,727	2,545	1,432	916	636	467
.7	667,470	166,867	74,163	41,717	26,699	18,541	13,622	10,429	8,240	6,675	2,966	1,669	1,068	741	545
.8	762,054	190,514	84,673	47,628	30,482	21,168	15,552	11,907	9,408	7,621	3,387	1,905	1,219	847	622
.9	856,447	214,112	95,160	53,528	34,258	23,790	17,478	13,382	10,573	8,564	3,806	2,141	1,370	951	699
1.0	950,648	237,662	105,628	59,415	38,026	26,407	19,401	14,854	11,736	9,506	4,225	2,376	1,521	1,056	776
1.1	1,044,656	261,164	116,072	65,291	41,786	29,018	21,319	16,322	12,897	10,446	4,643	2,611	1,671	1,160	853
1.2	1,138,472	284,618	126,496	71,155	45,539	31,624	23,234	17,788	14,055	11,385	5,060	2,846	1,821	1,265	929
1.3	1,232,097	308,024	136,899	77,006	49,284	34,225	25,145	19,251	15,211	12,321	5,476	3,080	1,971	1,369	1,006
1.4	1,325,529	331,382	147,280	82,845	53,021	36,820	27,051	20,711	16,364	13,255	5,891	3,314	2,121	1,473	1,082
1.5	1,418,769	354,692	157,640	88,673	56,751	39,410	28,954	22,168	17,515	14,188	6,305	3,547	2,270	1,576	1,158
1.6	1,511,818	377,954	167,980	94,489	60,473	41,995	30,853	23,622	18,664	15,118	6,719	3,780	2,419	1,680	1,234
1.7	1,604,674	401,168	178,297	100,292	64,187	44,574	32,748	25,073	19,811	16,047	7,132	4,012	2,567	1,783	1,310
1.8	1,697,338	424,334	188,592	106,083	67,894	47,148	34,639	26,521	20,955	16,973	7,543	4,243	2,716	1,886	1,385
1.9	1,789,810	447,452	198,868	111,863	71,592	49,717	36,526	27,966	22,096	17,898	7,955	4,474	2,863	1,988	1,461
2.0	1,882,090	470,523	209,121	117,631	75,284	52,280	38,410	29,407	23,235	18,821	8,365	4,705	3,011	2,091	1,536

(Continued)

Table 20-1 (Continued).   Test Sample Sizes Required for 95 Percent Confidence Level for Mailing Response Levels from 0.1 Percent to 4.0 Percent

R (Response)	Limits of Error (Expressed as Percentage Points)														
	.02	.04	.06	.08	.10	.12	.14	.16	.18	.20	.30	.40	.50	.60	.70
2.1	1,974,178	493,544	219,352	123,386	78,967	54,838	40,289	30,846	24,372	19,742	8,774	4,935	3,158	2,193	1,611
2.2	2,066,074	516,518	229,564	129,129	82,643	57,391	42,165	32,282	25,507	20,661	9,182	5,165	3,306	2,295	1,686
2.3	2,157,778	539,444	239,753	134,861	86,311	59,938	44,036	33,715	26,638	21,578	9,590	5,394	3,452	2,397	1,761
2.4	2,249,290	562,322	249,920	140,581	89,972	62,480	45,903	35,145	27,769	22,493	9,997	5,623	3,599	2,499	1,836
2.5	2,340,609	585,152	260,068	146,288	93,624	65,017	47,767	36,572	28,896	23,406	10,403	5,851	3,745	2,600	1,911
2.6	2,431,737	607,934	270,192	151,983	97,269	67,547	49,627	37,996	30,021	24,317	10,807	6,079	3,891	2,702	1,985
2.7	2,522,673	630,668	280,296	157,667	100,907	70,074	51,483	39,416	31,144	25,227	11,211	6,307	4,036	2,803	2,059
2.8	2,613,416	653,354	290,380	163,339	104,537	72,595	53,335	40,834	32,264	26,134	11,615	6,534	4,181	2,904	2,133
2.9	2,703,968	675,992	300,440	168,998	108,159	75,110	55,183	42,249	33,382	27,039	12,017	6,760	4,326	3,004	2,207
3.0	2,794,328	698,582	310,480	174,645	111,773	77,620	57,026	43,661	34,497	27,943	12,419	6,986	4,471	3,105	2,281
3.1	2,884,495	721,124	320,499	180,281	115,380	80,125	58,867	45,070	35,611	28,845	12,820	7,211	4,615	3,205	2,355
3.2	2,974,470	743,618	330,496	185,904	118,979	82,623	60,702	46,476	36,721	29,745	13,220	7,436	4,759	3,305	2,428
3.3	3,064,254	766,063	340,471	191,516	122,570	85,118	62,535	47,878	37,830	30,642	13,619	7,660	4,903	3,404	2,501
3.4	3,153,845	788,461	350,427	197,115	126,154	87,607	64,364	49,278	38,936	31,538	14,017	7,884	5,046	3,504	2,574
3.5	3,243,244	810,811	360,360	202,703	129,730	90,089	66,188	50,675	40,040	32,432	14,414	8,108	5,189	3,603	2,647
3.6	3,332,452	833,113	370,271	208,278	133,298	92,568	68,009	52,069	41,141	33,325	14,811	8,331	5,332	3,702	2,720
3.7	3,421,467	855,367	380,163	213,842	136,859	95,041	69,825	53,460	42,240	34,214	15,207	8,554	5,474	3,801	2,793
3.8	3,510,290	877,572	390,031	219,393	140,412	97,507	71,638	54,848	43,336	35,103	15,601	8,776	5,616	3,900	2,865
3.9	3,598,921	899,730	399,878	224,932	143,957	99,969	73,446	56,233	44,430	35,989	15,995	8,997	5,758	3,998	2,938
4.0	3,687,360	921,840	409,706	230,460	147,494	102,426	75,252	57,615	45,522	36,874	16,388	9,218	5,900	4,097	3,010

Testing Components vs. Testing Mailing Packages

In the endless search for breakthroughs, the question continually arises: In direct mail, should we test components or mailing packages? There are two schools of thought on this. The prevailing one is that the big breakthroughs come about through the testing of completely different mailing packages as opposed to testing individual components within a mailing package. Something can be learned from each procedure, of course. In my opinion, however, the more logical procedure is to first find the big difference in mailing packages and then follow with tests of individual components in the losing packages, which can often make the winning packages even better.

In package testing, one starts with a complete concept and builds all the components to fit the image of the concept. Consider the differences between these two package concepts:

	Package 1	Package 2
Envelope	9" × 12"	No. 10
Letter	Eight-page, stapled	Four-sheet (two sides) computer written
Circular	None	Four-page, illustrated
Order form	8½" × 11", perforated stub	8½" × 3⅔"

The differences between these two package concepts are considerable. Chances are great that there will be a substantial difference in response. Once the winning package evolves, component tests make excellent sense. Let us say the 9" × 12" package is the winner. A logical subsequent test would be to fold the same inserts into a 6" × 9" envelope. A reply envelope may be considered as an additional test. Computerizing the first page of the eight-page letter could be still another test.

How to Test Print Advertising

For direct marketing practitioners who are multimedia users, testing print advertising is just as important as testing direct mail. And, as with direct mail, it is important that the tests be constructed in such a way as to produce valid results.

Gerald Schreck, media director of Doubleday Advertising Company, New York, gave the following pointers on A/B split tests in an *Advertising Age* feature article.

The split helps you determine the relative strengths of different ads. For example, you can run two ads, A and B, in a specific issue or edition of a publication so that two portions of the total run are equally divided and identical in circulation. The only difference is that Ad A will run in half of the issue and Ad B will run in the other half. For measuring the strength of the ads, a split includes an offer requiring your reader to act by writing or

sending in a coupon. Then all you need do is compare the responses with the individual ads. If done properly, this method can be accurate to two decimal points. You also have the advantage of real-world testing to find out what people actually do, not just what they say they'll do. And because all factors are held equal, the difference in results can be attributed directly to your advertising (See Exhibit 20–1.)

Exhibit 20–1.   Variations in the Uses of Splits

A/B Split	Clump Split	Flip-Flop Split
A	A	A
B	A	B
A	A	B
B	B	A
	B	
	B	

A/B splits. In an ideal situation, an issue of a split-run publication will carry Ad A in every other copy and Ad B in the alternate copies.

Clump splits. Most often, however, publications cannot produce an exact A/B split. They will promise a clump. That is, every lift of 50 copies, for instance, will be evenly split, or even every lift of 25 or 10. The clump can be very accurate when the test is done in large circulations.

Flip-flops. For publications that offer no split at all, you can create your own. Take two comparable publications, X and Y. Run Ad A in X and Ad B in Y for the first phase. Then for the second phase, reverse the insertions: Ad B in X and Ad A in Y. Total the respective results for A and B and compare.

The split that isn't. We recently asked one magazine publisher if he ran splits. The production manager told us, "Oh, yes, we run a perfect split. Our circulation divides exactly—one-half east of the Mississippi and one-half west." Look out. That is not a valid split.

Although the A/B split can't tell you why individuals respond to your ad, the technique can tell you what they responded to. And a real bonus is that when you have completed your tests, you'll have a list of solid prospects.

In the A/B split, how can you compare one run against another run of the same ad? You can "key" coupons or response copy by:

1. *Dating.* On your coupons, try JA392NA for January 3, 1992, in *Newsweek* for Ad A and JA392NB for the same insertion of Ad B.

2. *Department numbers.* Use Dept. A for Ad A and Dept. B for Ad B in your company's address.

3. *Color of coupon.* One color for Ad A, another for Ad B.

4. *Color of ink.*

5. *Names.* In Ad A ask readers to send correspondence to Mr. Anderson; for Ad B, have them write to Mr. Brown.

6. *Telephone numbers.*

7. *Shape of coupon.*

8. *IBM punches.* You don't even need a computer. Just select a pattern you can read.

9. *The obvious.* Right on the coupon, use "For Readers of *Glamour*" in Ad A and "For *Glamour* Readers" in Ad B.

10. *Address information.* Mr., Mrs., Miss in Ad A; Mr., Ms., in Ad B.

11. *Abbreviations.* In your address, New York for Ad A, N.Y. for Ad B.

12. *Typeface.* In Coupon A, all caps for NAME, and so forth, and in Coupon B, upper-and lower-case for Name, and so on.

The possibilities are virtually unlimited. All you need is a code that's in keeping with your ad and the publication, one you find is easy to understand and use.

Telescopic Testing

Although it is certainly necessary to construct meaningful A/B split tests, they do have limitations. When marketers run an A/B split test, they don't know what would have happened if they had been able to run Ad C against Ads A and B and, additionally, Ads D, E, F, and G—all simultaneously, all in the same edition, all under measurable conditions.

Today, testing to find the best ad among a multiplicity of ads all tested under the same conditions is quite feasible. The method is widely known as *telescopic testing.* Telescopic testing is simply the process of telescoping an entire season of test ads into one master test program. (Examples of telescopic testing were given in Chapter Seventeen. Regional editions of publications and other developments make telescopic testing possible. Indeed, with regional editions you can telescopic a year's testing sequences into a single insertion, testing many ads simultaneously. *TV Guide* offers the best opportunity for telescopic testing: It publishes over 100 different editions. *Woman's Day* offers 26 regional editions. *Time*, with 8 regional editions, makes it possible to test 9 different ads or ad variations simultaneously.

Tom Collins, a pioneer in telescopic testing, has established a rule of thumb for estimating the minimum circulation you should buy for your ad tests to make results meaningful. First, start by assuming you need an average of 200 responses per appeal to be statistically valid. Then, multiply your allowable advertising cost per response by 200. Finally, multiply that figure

by the number of key numbers in the test. This will give you the total minimum expenditure required to get meaningful results.

To clarify the technique further, let's say you want to test four new ads against a control ad, which we will call Ad A. Your tests for the four new ads against the control ad will be structured as follows: A vs. B; A vs. C; A vs. D; A vs. E. Thus we have a total of five ads requiring eight different keys. (Ad A, the control ad, is being tested against a different ad in four separate instances and therefore requires four different keys.)

To read the results in this kind of test, we simply convert Ad A to 100 percent, depending on the results achieved. In this way, Ad C can be compared with Ad E, for instance, even though they are not directly tested against one another. Now, let's say we want to test the four new ads in *TV Guide* against the control ad. Further, using the Collins formula, let's assume we need a circulation of 2 million to get 200 or more replies for each side of each two-way split. The type of schedule that would be placed in *TV Guide* to accomplish this objective appears on page 567. Note that a careful review of the markets selected for each split (region) shows that all markets are balanced geographically.

Telescopic testing is not limited to regional editions of publications. Newspaper inserts serve as an ideal vehicle for such testing. The test pieces are intermixed at the printing plant before being shipped to the newspaper. All test pieces, however, must be exactly the same size. Otherwise, newspapers cannot handle them on their automatic inserting equipment.

Using full-page card inserts in magazines is still another way to test simultaneously a multiplicity of ads. Scores of magazines now accept such inserts. It is important to remember that in telescopic testing we are looking for breakthroughs, not small differences. As Collins puts it, "We are not merely testing ads, we are testing hypotheses. Then when a hypothesis appears to have been proved by the results, it is often possible to construct other, even more successful ads, on the same hypothesis."

Test hypotheses tend to fall into four main categories:

1. What is the best price and offer?

2. Who is the best prospect?

3. What is the most appealing product advantage?

4. What is the most important ultimate benefit? (By ultimate benefit we mean the satisfaction of such basic human needs as pride, admiration, safety, wealth, peace of mind, and so on.)

Idea development and testing are soul mates. The two things to keep uppermost in mind are: (1) strive for breakthrough ideas and (2) test the big things.

Split 1—Ad A vs. Ad B		Split 2—Ad A vs. Ad C	
Edition	Circulation	Edition	Circulation
San Francisco-Metro	750,000	Northern Wisconsin	170,000
Pittsburgh	225,000	Philadelphia	230,000
Detroit	225,000	Cleveland	55,000
South Georgia	67,000	Kansas City	230,000
Iowa	210,000	Western New England	175,000
Phoenix	275,000	North Carolina	272,000
Western Illinois	87,000	Colorado	139,000
Northern Illinois	186,000	Illinois/Wisconsin	225,000
	2,025,000	Gulf Coast	125,000
		Minneapolis/St. Paul	126,000
		Central California	115,000
		Southeast Texas	64,000
		West Virginia	165,000
			2,091,000

Split 3—Ad A vs. Ad D		Split 4—Ad A vs. Ad E	
Edition	Circulation	Edition	Circulation
Central Ohio	210,000	Eastern New England	665,000
Michigan State	309,000	Chicago Metro	475,000
Western New York State	65,000	Orlando	140,000
Central Indiana	230,000	Oklahoma State	184,000
San Diego	255,000	St. Louis	235,000
New Hampshire	141,000	Eastern Illinois	100,000
Portland	195,000	Missouri	141,000
Eastern Virginia	160,000	Eugene	45,000
Kansas State	92,000	Idaho	57,000
Tucson	70,000		2,042,000
North Dakota	65,000		
Eastern Washington St.	145,000		
Evansville-Paducah	104,000		
	2,041,000		

Self-Quiz

1. What strategy did Yamaha employ to solve the dormant piano market problem? _____

   _____

   _____

2. Name four traits of successful creative people.

   a. _____   c. _____

   b. _____   d. _____

3. Boardroom Reports gets an abundance of creative ideas from its employees through a program called the "I-Power Program." What is the technique that makes the program work? _____

_____

_____

_____

4. What are the duties of the leader in brainstorming?

   a. _____

   b. _____

   c. _____

   d. _____

   e. _____

5. What are the three phases of the brainstorming process?

   a. _____

   b. _____

   c. _____

6. One way to solve a difficult problem is to fantasize. The first three words of your expressed desire should be: _____

_____.

7. What is lateral thinking?

_____

_____

_____

8. What are the six big things to test in direct marketing?

   a. _____

   b. _____

   c. _____

   d. _____

   e. _____

   f. _____

9. What is the safest rule to follow in testing mailing lists?

   _____

   _____

   _____

10. In direct mail testing, which is preferable?

    ☐ Testing components   ☐ Testing complete mailing packages

11. Name six ways to key a print ad.

    a. _____

    b. _____

    c. _____

    d. _____

    e. _____

    f. _____

12. Define *telescopic testing*.

    _____

    _____

    _____

13. Name the four categories into which test hypotheses seem to fall.

    a. _____

    b. _____

    c. _____

    d. _____

Pilot Project

You are engaged in a fantasy game. Three wishes follow. Come up with at least three solutions for each of the wishes.

1. *I wish that* I could get all my customers to suggest friends who would likewise become customers.

2. *I wish that* I could get all my customers to pay their bills within 45 days.

3. *I wish that* I could reach all the people in this country who are over 6 feet tall.

Research for Direct Marketers

Overview

Since the inception of direct marketing, the primary method for assessing direct marketing programs has been the "in-market" or "in-mail" test.

What has made the direct marketing process particularly appealing to marketers is that the results produced by these tests have been *measurable, quantifiable*, and *predictable*. In other words, these results have provided a quantified measurement of *overt* response in terms of "making the sale," "producing a qualified sales lead," or "stimulating someone to request further information."

By overlaying this overt behavior with geodemographic data, it has been possible to build statistical models that can define high-propensity response groups, providing far more precise methods for marketing and prospecting.

Research and Testing the Big Things

The most important question concerning marketing research is: "When should I spend money on marketing research?" Yet direct marketers frequently treat research and testing as an either/or proposition, viewing the two activities as financial trade-offs and choosing to spend their money on either testing or marketing research. Such reasoning, however, overlooks the fact that testing is an integral part of the total marketing research process and that marketing research and testing are therefore not separate issues.

The question of when you should use marketing research was clearly answered in the last chapter. You should spend money on marketing research before testing "the big things."

Direct marketers who complain that research has not worked have frequently employed it to evaluate subtactical issues such as exposing to focus groups various offers or laundry lists of product attributes.

As shown in Exhibit 21–1, many direct marketers begin their testing considerations at this lower, subtactical level, which is where the test plan should be implemented, not researched. Thus overlay selections and specific offers are frequently considered before a new target audience is defined and selected, or headlines and product attributes are evaluated without first developing a strong, relevant product positioning for the new target-audience segment. Many research dollars are wasted on researching such subtactical issues.

Exhibit 21–1. **A Hierarchy of Test Variables**

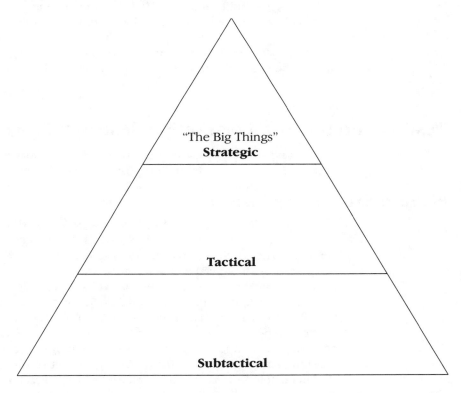

Strategic	**Tactical**	**Subtactical**
("The Big Things")	List Selection	Overlay Selection
Media Selection	End Benefits	Laundry List
Product Positioning	Headline/Copy	of Attributes
Communications	Offer/Pricing/	Specific Words
Platform	Premium	and Phrases
Motivation Strategy	Major Package	Offer Components
Package Format	Components	(99 Ways)
		Variations of
		Package Components

Marketing research dollars are most effectively spent on evaluating strategic issues—evaluating the big things to be sure they are worth spending the time and money for testing. The use of marketing research in testing the big things serves two functions. First, it provides the basis for the financial go/no-go testing decision. That is, the cost estimate of the research can be compared with the projected revenue and profits obtained if the test is successful (e.g.: Should we spend $20,000 on marketing research to evaluate our chances of making a million-dollar profit?).

Second, marketing research can serve as a valuable insurance policy against possible test failure if the strategic marketing variables to be tested turn out not to be "the big things." Thus the estimated cost of the research can be compared with the projected profit and time losses if the test is a failure (e.g.: Should we spend $30,000 on marketing research to help save a possible $20,000 loss as well as lose 6 months in developing a new test plan?).

In the balance of this chapter we show how marketing research has been and can be used to help in developing and testing the big things.

Testing and the Total Marketing Research Process

The testing process consists of four phases: (1) exploratory research, (2) pretest research, (3) tests, and (4) posttests. (See Exhibit 21–2.)

Phase 1: Exploratory Research

The *exploratory phase* of the testing process deals with defining and understanding your target audience as well as the marketplace in which you compete. The focal point of the exploratory phase is *situation analysis*, which deals with understanding the geodemographic characteristics of your target audience as well as its attitudes, habits, and needs—particularly those characteristics that are most influential on heavy, regular usage of your product or service. The situation analysis should also cover an understanding of the competition and market dynamics in terms of what attributes and benefits each competitive product or service brings to the market, and why consumers are attracted to them. The end result of this situation analysis should be points of maximum leverage on which a direct marketing program can be developed. Such leverage points usually center on special ways of segmenting a target audience, methods for reaching each specified target-audience segment, and special ways of segmenting products or services.

Phase 2: Pretesting

The *pretesting phase* consists of developing, assessing, and refining the marketing and creative products before in-market testing. There are several issues that should be addressed in this phase:

Exhibit 21–2.   The Total Marketing and Research Process

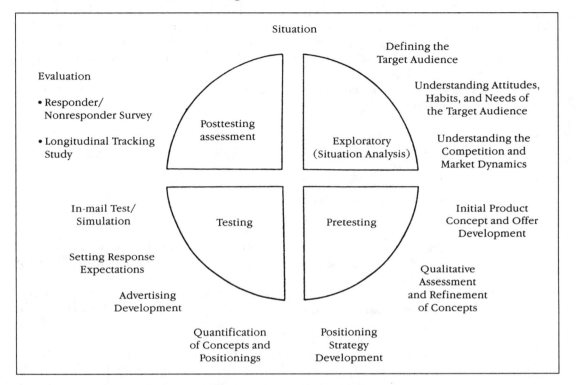

Situation

Defining the
Target Audience

Evaluation

- Responder/
Nonresponder Survey

Understanding Attitudes,
Habits, and Needs of
the Target Audience

- Longitudinal Tracking
Study

Posttesting
assessment

Exploratory
(Situation Analysis)

Understanding the
Competition and
Market Dynamics

In-mail Test/
Simulation

Testing

Pretesting

Initial Product
Concept and Offer
Development

Setting Response
Expectations

Advertising
Development

Qualitative
Assessment
and Refinement
of Concepts

Quantification
of Concepts and
Positionings

Positioning
Strategy
Development

- Determine that your product or service is offering an attribute or benefit that the consumer really wants—that is, something that is preemptive, setting it apart from the competition.

- Develop and refine the creative and the offer. In this area, qualitative research such as focus groups or in-depth individual interviews can help determine whether the creative approach is communicating information about the product or service and the offer in a manner that is clear, believable, and relevant to consumers in the target audience.

- Research usually referred to as copy testing can be used to assess alternative creative executions and offers. This research is usually quantitative in nature, that is, a survey, and is used to develop comparative profiles of the creative and the offer. Such research is useful in two ways. First, it helps to provide objective criteria for improving the creative or the offer, rather than giving them some subjective grade. Second and even of greater importance, however, is that this research can reduce the number of alternatives to be tested, thus greatly reducing test costs and increasing the accuracy of reading back-end results. Research done in the pretest phase can often help to uncover variables or clarify issues that should be addressed in the *testing phase*.

Phase 3: Testing

One of the first questions asked by those businesses new to direct marketing is: "When can we stop testing?" And the answer, of course, is: "Never!" The testing process is dynamic and continuous (which is why the diagram in Exhibit 21–2 is a circle). The main objective in all testing is to learn, modify, and improve.

The *testing phase* brings together five key variables for assessment in the market:

- The product or service
- The medium or method of accessing the defined target audience
- The time or season
- The advertising/communication
- The offer or promotion

The test plan consists of the combinations in which these variables will be tested as well as the determination of response expectations and financial objectives.

Although all of the elements of the test plan are crucial, the most important single variable in direct marketing is the medium, or the access to the consumer, since this access provides the strongest point of leverage for all other test variables. In fact, if the medium cannot provide access to qualified consumers in sufficient quantities, the remainder of the elements in the direct marketing mix become almost irrelevant by comparison. That is why testing is so critical to finding the lists that will access high-propensity prospects in sufficient quantities.

An alternative method of testing is simulation, which can be used in conjunction with live testing. Simulation systems such as STAR (Simulator Testing Advertising Response—a system developed by Direct Marketing Research Associates and Erard Moore Associates) predict response without running actual space advertising, package/statement inserts, or direct mail packages. Simulation can save time and costs by reducing the number of variables to be tested in-market and often by eliminating the need to address variables or issues that are of little importance to the direct marketing mix.

Simulation uses a close facsimile of an actual ad or direct mail package mailed to a sample of consumers with a questionnaire and letter. Separate packages are mailed to test and control cells. Data from the questionnaires are combined with actual responses to the simulated mailing to develop a prediction of relative response performance.

Phase 4: Posttesting Assessment

Posttesting assessment is potentially the area of greatest strength for direct marketing research. Assessment attempts both the analysis of test response

and the development of diagnostic information in order to determine *why* the response rate was achieved and *what* can be done to achieve higher response rates.

The analysis of response rates is a measurement of overt behavior in terms of making a sale, a request for more information, or qualifying a sales lead. Marketing research can also provide diagnostic insights that can help to measure the quality of the response. For example, responder/nonresponder surveys can help pinpoint these issues:

- *Incremental sales*: The degree to which new consummers were attracted to the offer vs. the sales' merely subsidizing current customers, particularly heavy or frequent buyers

- *Competitive conquest*: The degree to which competitive customers tried your product or service and were converted to regular customers

- *Attitudinal shifts*: The degree to which the brand image of your product or service was enhanced by direct advertising

In addition, questionnaires, which can help provide much added value to both the consumer and the marketer, can be included as an integral part of the mailing package.

- The response to relevant questions about the product or service helps to establish a vital two-way communication, or dialog, between the marketer and the consumer.

- The dialog can help establish a relationship with the consumer that can give the product or service a preemptive position in the mind of the consumer.

- The information provided by consumers can be used to qualify or segment them, giving the marketer valuable insights into subsequent positioning of products or services and more precisely targeting the appropriate message to the appropriate segment.

Marketing Research for Traditional and Nontraditional Direct Marketers

Let's begin by comparing the key direct marketing problems faced by traditional direct marketers vs. those confronting nontraditional direct marketers. Once these issues are comprehended, it will be easier to understand the role that marketing research needs to play in each of the two areas.

It has been said that in the land of the blind the one-eyed man is king. Traditional direct marketing today finds itself in exactly the opposite environment: How to compete when everyone has the eyesight of an eagle? Thus

traditional direct marketers today find themselves in a maturing industry in which the major competitors are experienced and sophisticated, many of the market segments are glutted with similar products and services, and everyone's mailbox is cluttered with very similar-looking pieces.

Within such an environment, marketing research should address such issues as:

- Developing mailing pieces that cut through the mailbox clutter by more discretely and relevantly being targeted to specific consumer segments in terms of the offer and the visual and message elements. This could certainly help to dramatically increase response rates and enhance the marketer's image while making the sale.

- More effectively prospecting for new customers by developing an in-depth understanding of the types and numbers of "high-propensity prospects" available, and translating these consumer segments into targetable groups that can be directly accessed. This could help reduce quantities mailed as well as mailng costs.

- Providing strategic direction of growing traditional direct marketing businesses in terms of identifying new product and service categories with high growth potential, assessing the most dynamic segments within each category, and screening for the most viable products and services within each segment.

Nontraditional direct marketers such as consumer goods manufacturers and retailers are just beginning to explore the many possible applications that direct marketers can offer their businesses. These applications include:

- Institutional direct marketing programs in which the use of major consumer brands can be extended from home consumption to include institutional consumption.

- The use of direct marketing for a direct distribution system as an alternative or supplement to retail distribution. A direct marketing distribution system can be quite effective for name brands of clothing and gourmet food items that may require an inordinate number of stock keeping units (SKUs) and a great deal of copy and illustration in order to sell successfully.

- The use of direct marketing as a vehicle for testing new positionings for a brand economically and discretely, without telling the media or competitors and without disturbing your current franchise.

- Targeted promotions that can be used by retailers and manufacturers to provide specific measurable, projectable promotional programs to selected prospects and customers.

- Customized communications that can be used by retailers and manufacturers to deliver discrete, measurable messages targeted to specific customer or prospect profiles.

- The use of direct marketing as a media vehicle to provide direct access to selected customers and prospects for retailers and manufacturers.

The role of marketing research as it relates to a number of nontraditional direct marketing approaches (see a description of the research process on pages 572–575) can include two broad areas: the front-end, or development of programs; and the back-end, which is concerned with the measurement and assessment of these programs.

Direct Marketing Research for Consumer Products
Front-End Research

Let us now examine some specific examples in which marketing research can support direct marketing efforts for consumer products and services.

The first example will demonstrate the use of research in the initial phases, the exploratory and pretest phases, by defining target-audience segments, providing an understanding of these segments, and translating this understanding into product/service positionings, an offer, and a relevant, believable, understandable message.

In the past, direct marketers centered their research activities on analyzing consumers' geodemographic characteristics and purchase behaviors. Direct marketers used these approaches because these two variables are most readily linked with list and prospect selection. Attitudinal, psychographic, and lifestyle data have been much underutilized by direct marketers because these factors are not readily translated to list or prospect selection.

To realistically define, understand, reach, and communicate with target audiences, however, it is imperative that research deal with consumers on all four relevant levels:

- Geodemographics
- Psychographics and lifestyles
- Attitudes
- Purchase behavior

All four factors must be dealt with. They must all be integrated to form pictures of "real" consumers, who they are and where they live (geodemographics); what their basic attitudes and values toward life are and how these attitudes are translated into the way these persons live (psychographics and lifestyles); their perceptions, attitudes, and values with respect to various product and service categories (attitudes); and how these perceptions, attitudes, and values translate into selection making in the marketplace (purchase behavior).

The *Stone & Adler Study of Consumer Behavior and Attitudes toward Direct Marketing* was the first attempt to perform such an interdisciplinary synthesis. The study was designed, fielded, and analyzed with the help of Goldring & Company Inc. and the Home Testing Institute. Once the data were collected within each of the four levels, they were integrated through a software program called PAG (Positive Attribute Group)[1].

PAG is a comprehensive analytical technique for determining the *combination* of purchase activities, demographics, psychographics and lifestyles, and attitudes toward direct marketing at work in the direct marketing environment. PAG enabled us to segment the direct marketing environment and identify the four variables and their combinatons that were active in each segment.

The PAG program subsequently produced six consumer clusters arrayed in an order (of importance) that breathed life into each of the clusters.

Cluster 1: Mailbox Gourmets

Let us begin with the most important cluster for direct marketers: "Mailbox Gourmets." If anyone wonders who the magical 20 percent to 30 percent that almost all direct marketers target are, the answer is the Mailbox Gourmets (26 percent of the population).

In terms of psychographics and lifestyles, Mailbox Gourmets perceive themselves to be sophisticated. They want more of everything—especially travel. They are extremely active and involved and perceive themselves as not having enough leisure time.

Mailbox Gourmets are affluent. Their demographics show them to be above average in education, and income and to be engaged in white-collar occupations. This cluster is also female-intensive. Although three-fourths are married, this percentage is slightly below marriage averages. The family structure is less traditional, with more two-paycheck families or single professionals, particularly women.

It is not surprising that their attitudes toward direct marketing are extremely positive. They enjoy it, and are comfortable with it, and although most people perceive themselves to be novices when transacting by mail or phone, these people perceive themselves to be experts.

All of this information translates into direct marketing purchasing behavior that earns this cluster its name: they spend a lot (significantly more than any other cluster) and they buy often.

Cluster 2: Young Turks

In terms of psychographics and lifestyles, the "Young Turks" are very trendy, as one would expect. They also consider themselves to be—whether they are, in fact, or not—sophisticated and worldly.

Demographically, this group accounts for 10 percent of the households and form a perfect yuppie profile: They are single and male-intensive, well educated, and economically aspiring.

[1] Goldring & Company, © 1986.

Although Young Turks are also very positive toward direct marketing, they tend to be cautious because they are emerging consumers. This makes them very "presentation sensitive." Because they are so active, they are more likely to order via an 800 number than any other cluster group. The Young Turks are the second highest group in terms of dollars spent and purchase frequency, but their expenditures are significantly less than those of the Mailbox Gourmets.

Cluster 3: Life Begins at 50   The "Life-Begins-at 50" cluster comprises 7 percent of households and is completely middle-of-the-road in terms of psychographics and lifestyle.

Demographics indicate that these older consumers are "empty nesters": Their children are grown and away at college or married. As a group they are engaged in a mixture of blue- and white-collar occupations.

Like the Young Turks, the Life-Begins-at-50 cluster is also quite positive but cautious toward direct marketing. The cautiousness, in this case, is due to the fact that these people are the experienced "old pros" who have been shopping direct for 20 to 30 years. This experience has been transformed into a demanding attitude. They know what they want and the marketer had better give it to them.

These data translate into direct marketing dollar expenditures and purchase frequencies just below those of the Young Turks; but the products this cluster is likely to buy are vastly different. The Life-Begins-at-50 cluster is more likely to buy higher-ticket items such as home furnishings or housewares. They are also more likely to buy vitamins and minerals, and to belong to a book club. Young Turks, on the other hand, are more likely to purchase products related to self-indulgence, such as electronic "toys" and sports equipment.

Cluster 4: Dear Occupant   Now we come to the great faceless, nameless masses that account for 14 percent of households—"Dear Occupant." Actually, they are the leftovers in the clustering process and therefore represent those who were:

- Neither too positive nor too negative in their attitudes

- Neither affluent nor destitute

- Neither the lightest nor the heaviest buyers

As such, they are truly the mundane, the moderate, the middle.

Cluster 5: Kitchen Patriots   When members of these households (23 percent of total) are not out shopping at their favorite shopping mall or mass merchandiser, they are likely to be home reading the daily newspaper, a magazine, or their mail at the kitchen table à la Archie and Edith Bunker.

In terms of lifestyles and psychographics, this cluster is the backbone of traditional American morality and values:

- They are extremely patriotic.

- Home, family, and community are extremely important to them.

- They have sufficient leisure time, which is one reason they shop so much. In fact, many of them have more time than money.

Demographically, this group is blue-collar intensive, average in income and education, and indexes highest among those 55 years old and older.

Although the Kitchen Patriots' attitudes toward direct marketing are basically negative, they like to browse through their mail, including direct mail pieces and catalogs. But because of their negative attitudes toward direct marketing, coupled with their propensity toward retail shopping, Kitchen Patriots tend to be non-direct-marketing buyers or light, selective buyers at best.

Cluster 6: Above-It-Alls   Finally, we have the most negative, the pro-retail cluster, the "Above-It-All." that account for 20 percent of all households. They are nearly a carbon copy of the Mailbox Gourmets with a major difference: While they are gourmets, they are antimailbox.

In terms of lifestyles and psychographics, this cluster is career-oriented, active, and involved in fads and causes, it perceives itself as taking a leadership position, and it is athletic.

Demographically, Above-It-Alls are somewhat more affluent than Mailbox Gourmets. They tend to be more traditional in household composition, wives are, more often than not, full-time homemakers—which, of course, gives them more time for retail shopping. This cluster also tends to be more strictly suburban than the Mailbox Gourmets, who are more split between suburbs and cities. The Above-It-Alls' attitude toward direct marketing is basically negative. In fact, not only do Above-It-Alls like mail, in general, much less than any other group, they don't like to browse, and, in particular, they don't see direct marketing as a convenience. Not surprisingly, this cluster rates as non-direct-marketing buyers or light, selective buyers at best. They want to *see* and *touch* the merchandise first, try it on, and obtain instant gratification both in purchasing and returning merchandise.

Putting Attitudinal Research to Work for Your Business

If information is to be useful to a business, it must be analyzed and interpreted for strategic implications that lead to specific actions. Let us now take a look at how attitudinal data can be directly applied to business in terms of:

1. Profiling target audiences and product categories

2. Segmenting customers for precise file selection, and developing highly targeted products, services, and creative appeals

Profiling Target Audiences and Categories

There are two major reasons why a business may want to use target-audience and category profiling:

1. For new-business development

2. For expanding an established business

For new-business development, it is important to know *who* are the users within a category. Not only is it important to know who they are geodemographically for the purpose of list selection, but it is also important to know who they are attitudinally. Attitudinal understanding leads to meaningful positioning to the target audience. Thus the target audience can be communicated with in the most relevant, believable, and understandable manner.

For expanding an established business,. profiling can provide an important perspective to the direct marketers by showing how high is up. Unfortunately, too many direct marketers are trapped by their house files; they don't have the necessary information to make the best strategic use of media when prospecting.

Profiling can provide these insights by allowing direct marketers to compare customers on their files against category users on a national basis. Thus direct marketers can then judge whether they are obtaining their fair share of the target-audience pie. If they are not, they can then fine-tune their demographics for media selection. Even more importantly, they can fine-tune their creative approach and offer so that they have a better chance of being seen and read by their target-audience prospect.

Let us briefly examine how such profiling and segmentation can be done. The first step is for the marketer to perform a buyer concentration analysis from its customer file, as shown in Exhibit 21–3. Such a buyer concentration study will segment the file into groups of heavy or frequent buyers, medium buyers, and light or infrequent buyers.

The second step consists of overlaying the buyer segments with attitudinal and lifestyle data, and then developing a second level of segmentation, as shown in Exhibit 21–4. This segmentation is accomplished by selecting a sample of names from the house file and administering a survey questionnaire containing attitudinal and lifestyle questions. By combining the answers to these questions with the geodemographic and purchase behavior data already on the file, PAG clusters can then be developed. At this stage, two analyses are critical: (1) the percentage of the customer file that comprises each of the six clusters and (2) the percentage of light, medium, and heavy buyers that comprised each of the six clusters.

Exhibit 21–3.   **Buyer Concentration Analysis**

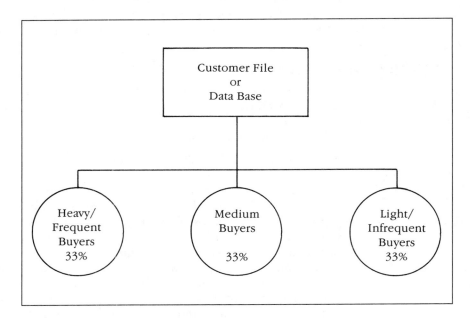

The third step consists of developing a profile comparing your customer file and a nationally representative sample of consumers (i.e., a consumer database). This comparison allows you to determine whether or not you are getting your fair share of such groups as:

- Affluent/upscale consumers

- Younger or emerging consumers entering the marketplace

- Transitional consumers who are changing their lifestyles and their purchasing habits.

For example, the comparative profile shown in Exhibit 21–5 points to a possible problem with the highest-propensity direct marketing consumers who are significantly under represented on the customer file. There could be similar problems if the buyer concentration analysis shows that a disproportionate number of Mailbox Gourmets, Young Turks, and Life-Begins-at-50 consumers are merely medium and light buyers.

The use of national consumer databases can bring additional strategic marketing insights to your business when applied across a variety of product and service categories as well as segments within these categories. (See Chapter Two, "Database Marketing.") Let us review some examples of such applications in three diverse categories: insurance, credit cards, and clothing catalogs.

Exhibit 21–4.   **Attitudinal and Lifestyle Overlay**

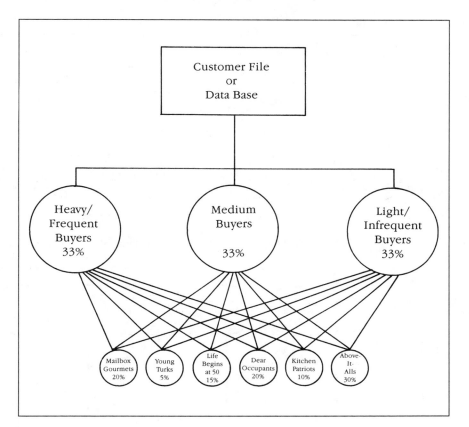

Insurance Profiles   The *Stone & Adler Study of Behavior and Attitudes toward Direct Marketing* examined both the incidence of insurance inquiries and insurance purchases (by mail or phone) during a preceding 12-month period. The total incidence of inquiries was higher than expected at 25.9 percent. When the incidence of inquiries was analyzed by individual consumer clusters, it was observed that inquiries were relatively flat across all six clusters (see Exhibit 21–6).[2]

Thus inquiries were not skewed toward those clusters that were direct mail responsive. In other words, of the total inquiries, the extremely direct-marketing-positive Mailbox Gourmets accounted for 26 percent of the inquiries, while the extremely direct-marketing-negative Above-It-Alls accounted for 20 percent of the inquiries, which is directly proportional to their representation in the general population. If the inquiries were indexed by cluster, therefore, each cluster would index at 100.

[2] Data for Exhibits 21–6 through 20–14 are from the Stone & Adler National Profile.

Exhibit 21–5.   **Comparative Consumer Profile**

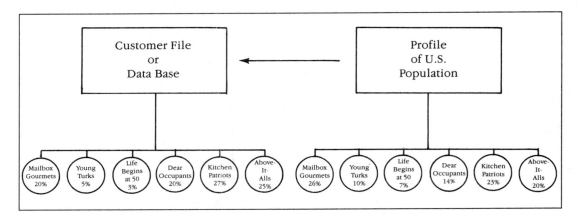

Exhibit 21–6.   **Insurance Inquiries by Consumer Cluster**

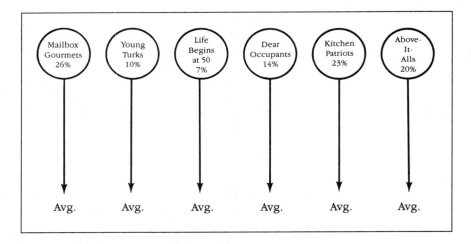

The incidence of insurance conversions by mail or phone totaled approximately 44 percent of the conversions, or 11 percent of the total sample (Exhibit 21–7). When the incidence of conversions was analyzed by individual consumer clusters, the same pattern emerged for conversions as for inquiries.

Conversions were also relatively flat across all six clusters. That is, conversions were not skewed toward those clusters that were the most direct mail responsive in other categories. Again, conversions were proportionate to each cluster's representation in the total U.S. population. All clusters would therefore index at or near 100.

The conclusion drawn was that insurance was one of the *least* direct marketing responsive of all the 26 product and service categories surveyed

Exhibit 21–7.   **Insurance Conversions by Consumer Cluster.**

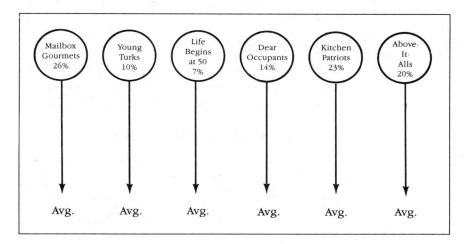

in the Stone & Adler study. However, the potential direct marketing audience for insurance is much larger than many other categories, because it has a less negative bias toward direct marketing.

But to take advantage of such an opportunity, direct marketers must strategically use research data of the type shown above to:

- Define the highest-propensity consumer segments for each type of insurance product

- Understand the needs for each type of insurance product from the perspective for each consumer segment

- Communicate the positioning, offer, and benefits of each insurance product in a manner that is understandable, relevant, and believable to the targeted consumer segments

Credit Card Acquisition Profiles   Credit card acquisition in the Stone & Adler study included only new credit cards from new credit card sources that were obtained within the past 12 months. Acquisition did not include any credit cards that had expired and for which the company sent a new one. Acquisitions were based upon either a solicitation received in the mail or a coupon sent in from a newspaper or magazine ad.

Acquisition profiles were developed for the four major categories of cards:

- Bank cards such as Visa and MasterCard

- Travel and entertainment cards such as American Express, Carte Blanche, and Diners Club

- Department store cards such as those from Sears, J.C. Penney, Wards, Neiman-Marcus, Saks Fifth Avenue, Bonwit Teller, and local department stores
- Gasoline cards such as Amoco, Shell, and Texaco

The total incidence of bank card acquisition was 20 percent. As you can see in Exhibit 21–8, the incidence by cluster was heavily skewed toward the clusters that are the most positive toward direct marketing.

Exhibit 21–8.   **Bank Card Acquisition Patterns**

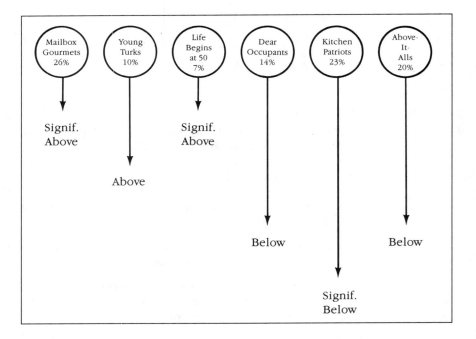

The total incidence of travel and entertainment card acquisition was 5 percent, which was the lowest of all four credit card market segments and a good indication of the maturity that this segment is displaying. Again, acquisition of travel and entertainment cards, for the most part, is skewed toward the most direct-marketing-positive clusters. (See Exhibit 21–9.)

The total incidence of department store card acquisition was 23 percent. This percentage was the highest of all four credit card segments. The same skewed pattern that we observed in bank and travel and entertainment cards persists, except that it is even more accentuated. (See Exhibit 21–10.)

The gasoline credit card segment also showed a degree of maturity similar to that of travel and entertainment cards, with an incidence of acquisition at 12 percent. The skewing of acquisition toward positive direct marketing clusters is the least pronounced in this market segment. (See Exhibit 21–11.)

Exhibit 21–9. **Travel and Entertainment Card Acquisition Patterns**

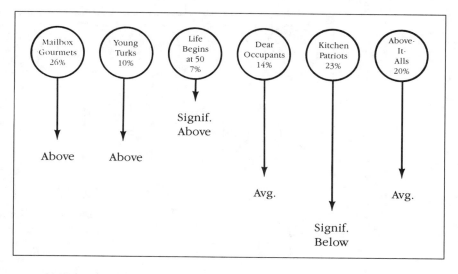

Exhibit 21–10. **Department Store Card Acquisition Patterns**

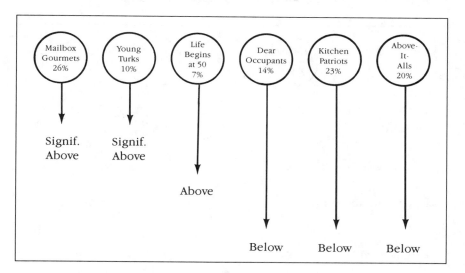

In summary, when above-average acquisition patterns are observed across all four credit card segments, clearly the most positive direct marketing clusters demonstrate the highest propensity to obtain credit cards. (See Exhibit 21–12.)

What are the implications of credit card acquisition being so heavily skewed toward positive direct marketing consumers? First, there is a general need for credit. Clearly, there is a new need for total credit in the form of multiple cards, not merely one card. But who are these high-propensity

Exhibit 21–11.   **Gasoline Card Acquisition Patterns**

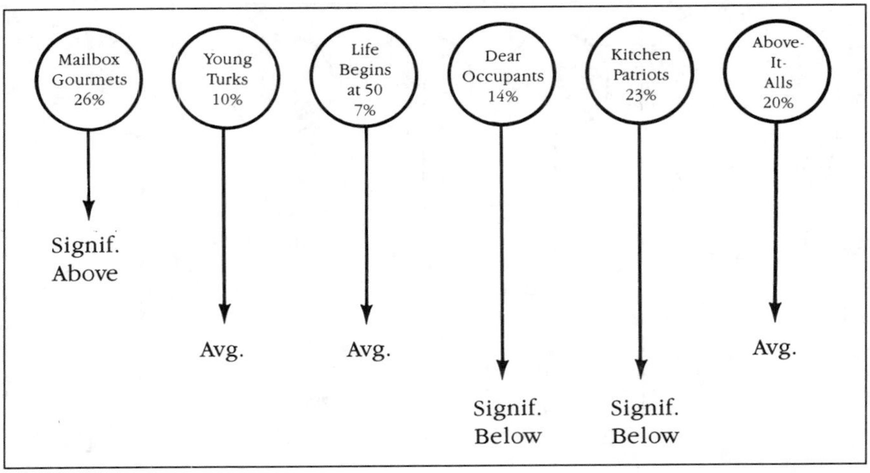

Exhibit 21–12.   **Above-Average Acquisition Patterns**

	Mailbox Gourmets 26%	Young Turks 10%	Life Begins at 50 7%	Dear Occupants 14%	Kitchen Patriots 23%	Above-It-Alls 20%
Bank cards	X	X	X			
T and E cards	X	X	X			
Department store cards	X	X	X			
Gasoline cards	X					

credit card acquirers? Supplementary work in this area shows that there are identifiable, targetable groups such as emerging and transitional consumers.

Emerging consumers can be found in the Young Turks cluster and among the younger Mailbox Gourmets. Demographically, these are recent college or technical school graduates, young aspiring professionals, newlyweds, and new parents (Full Nest I).

Transitional consumers can be most readily found in the Life-Begins-at-50 cluster and among the older Mailbox Gourmets. These people are undergoing major lifestyle changes such as divorce, remarriage, or a midlife career change, all of which affect credit needs.

Catalog Clothing Buyer Profiles   Respondents to the Stone & Adler study were asked whether they had purchased any clothing within the past *three* months either at retail outlets or through mail order (where "you sent in a mail order form or phoned in your order, and the item was delivered to your home, office, or elsewhere"). At 74 percent, the total incidence of purchasing clothing from all sources, both retail and direct, was the highest of all 26 categories measured in the Stone & Adler study.

As can be seen in Exhibit 21–13, the Mailbox Gourmets and Young Turks, the two most positive direct marketing clusters, demonstrated the highest incidence; the Kitchen Patriots and Above-It-Alls, the most negative direct marketing groups, showed the lowest incidence.

Exhibit 21–13.   Clothing Buyer Profiles—Retail and Direct

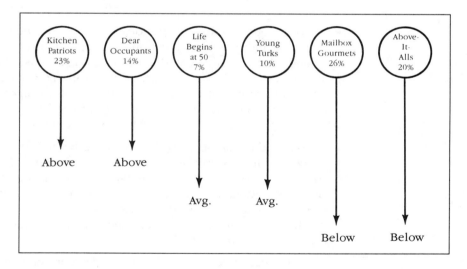

When we isolate catalog clothing purchases, a somewhat different pattern emerges (Exhibit 21–14). The incidence of purchase among Mailbox Gourmets registers significantly above average at 52 percent or an index of 200. Conversely, the incidence among Young Turks slips below average at 8 percent. And the incidence among Kitchen Patriots slips to under one half of their representation in the sample of 11 percent, while purchase incidence of Above-It-Alls registers a mere 5 percent or one-quarter of their representation in the sample.

Several strategic implications can be drawn from these data:

Exhibit 21–14.   **Catalog Clothing Buyer Profiles**

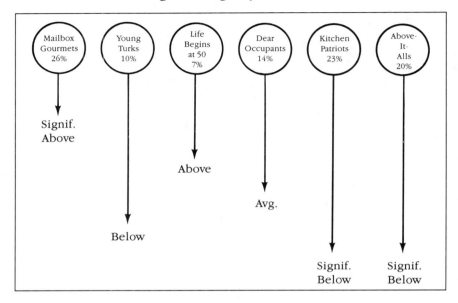

- Mailbox Gourmets are conspicuous consumers in the clothing category. They buy more at both retail and catalog. Unfortunately, the growing mailbox clutter is also centering on this group because Mailbox Gourmets are on "everyone's" mailing list. Research should be used, therefore, to develop intrusive catalogs and mass media advertising to break through the clutter, and to develop unique types or lines of merchandise that will continue to attract the loyalty of Mailbox Gourmets.

- Although the Life-Begins-at-50 cluster exhibited the second highest propensity to buy clothing from catalogs, their purchases tend to be concentrated on a much narrower range of merchandise than the Mailbox Gourmets. Research should be used, therefore, to develop creative messages that motivate this cluster to try products they have not purchased by mail before, and to select the merchandise with the highest propensity to generate trial.

- The underperformance by the Young Turks represents a major lost opportunity to clothing catalog marketers, particularly in terms of an extremely high net present value. Research could help by directing catalog marketers on the best ways of communicating with and reassuring them about the key issues of styling and fit.

- Although the Kitchen Patriots and Above-It-Alls do not represent a major opportunity for direct mail clothing sales, they should not be summarily dismissed by direct marketers. Since direct mail, particularly catalogs, are used by both of these groups as reference materials for retail shopping, direct marketing can be used effectively among both groups as a targeted advertising vehicle to increase retail traffic.

Direct Marketing Research for Business-to-Business Applications

Many people ask whether the principles of marketing and research are the same for business-to-business products and services as they are for consumer products and services. After all, this line of reasoning goes, the people making purchases for businesses are the same consumers who buy television sets, automobiles, and toothpaste, aren't they? The answer is: "Not exactly."

When John Q. Consumer begins buying products for a business, the situation becomes much more complicated than it is for consumer products. In a business environment, he is part of a much larger, more complex institutional hierarchy. Thus responsibility for the purchase decision, as well as the ultimate consumption of the products or services, is a much more involved process.

For example, regardless of the organization of the business, the target audience within a business will normally have at least three hierarchical levels (see Exhibit 21–15). The purchaser is the person responsible for recommending and making the purchase, whether he or she is the purchasing agent, office manager, or director of human resources. The gatekeeper is a CEO or chief financial officer from whom the purchaser must often obtain approval. The end user is often a department manager in the production, accounting, or marketing department whose department will actually be using the products or services purchased. In fact, either the gatekeeper or end user may originate the purchasing process as well as influence it.

Exhibit 21–15.   **Business-to-Business Purchasing Process**

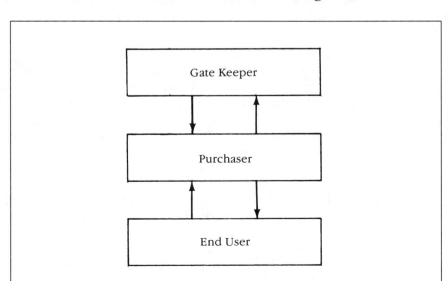

To make matters even more difficult, there are problems with finding qualified prospects on each of these three levels. First, we must understand that not everyone we contact is in the market for our products or services. At one extreme are those prospects who are simply not interested, either in our product or service category, or in the particular brand we are selling. Others may have recently purchased and made long-term commitments. Thus, although these prospects are in our category, they are not available to us for an extended period of time.

At the other extreme are those who are left, a group of prospects we call *active considerers*. And not even all of these prospects are available to us because they must first be converted from prospects to serious shoppers.

Thus when direct marketers approach business-to-business marketing problems by merely testing and retesting rather than carefully defining and thoroughly understanding each level of prospect audience being targeted, you can readily see why the odds of success are so often slight.

How can marketing research raise the odds of obtaining the highest-propensity prospects? Let's review a couple of examples.

Profiling

Business-to-business house files can be matched against a national database of businesses such as Dun & Bradstreet. This process will result in a more thorough knowledge of the current client base—a well-defined target market for future prospecting. With this knowledge comes a better understanding of the marketing and communications programs necessary to more effectively penetrate the desired segments.

The information and insights obtained through profiling can help the business-to-business marketer accomplish a number of objectives:

- *Marketing and creative objectives*: To define and target business segments of the highest propensity; to provide creative and marketing guidance in communicating with high-propensity target audience segments on a clearer, more relevant, and believable basis

- *Promotional*: To provide creative and marketing guidance in developing specific reactivation and increased activity programs to the current customer file

- *Sales*: To help increase the efficiency of the sales force, by directing them to concentrate their efforts on the highest-propensity segments of the prospect universe

- *Media*: To attain greater efficiency in direct mail and other media

Business-to-business profiling is usually developed on a three-phased basis:

- *Phase I: Account identification and matching.* This phase consists of linking the national database operations files to the business-to-business house file.

- *Phase II: Appending data from the national database to the business-to-business house file.* This phase utilizes the existing compiled business establishment data (e.g., geographic, type of business, size of business, and type of location) from the national database.

- *Phase III: Development of market segmentation profiles.* This phase consists of analyzing the business-to-business customer file on the basis of the distribution and concentration of customers within specific market segments (e.g., the extent to which your current best customers are concentrated within certain areas such as SIC codes, geographic areas, company size, and revenue contribution groups).

Another way of analyzing the activities of current customers and assessing their potential is by drawing maps or creating matrixes of current purchasing activities, as shown in Exhibit 21–16.

Based upon the purchase activity quadrant in which the customer falls, we are in a position to segment our customer file and target specific messages and offers to best leverage the different opportunities:

- *Quadrant 1* represents our best customers, those who spend the most dollars and purchase the most frequently. Clearly, the emphasis in this segment is on maintaining loyalty and providing rewards for continuity.

- *Quadrant 2* represents customers who spend a lot of dollars but spend infrequently. Large average-order sizes combined with low levels of purchase frequency indicate that they may be using us for a few specialized purchases. Supplementary research, such as in-depth personal interviews among a sample of customers in this quadrant, can help uncover the reasons we are being used on an infrequent, specialized basis. These issues can then be addressed in both the creative and offer to move them into Quadrant 1.

- *Quadrant 3* represents customers who spend just a few dollars but make purchases relatively frequently. Small average-order sizes combined with high levels of purchase frequency indicate that these customers are "cherry picking" our inventory, concentrating on the lowest-cost sales items. Again, supplementary research, such as in-depth personal interviews among a sample of customers in this quadrant, can help us uncover problems that can be addressed with both creative and offers to stimulate purchases of a wider range of merchandise, particularly higher-ticket items.

Exhibit 21-16.   **Purchase Activity Matrix**

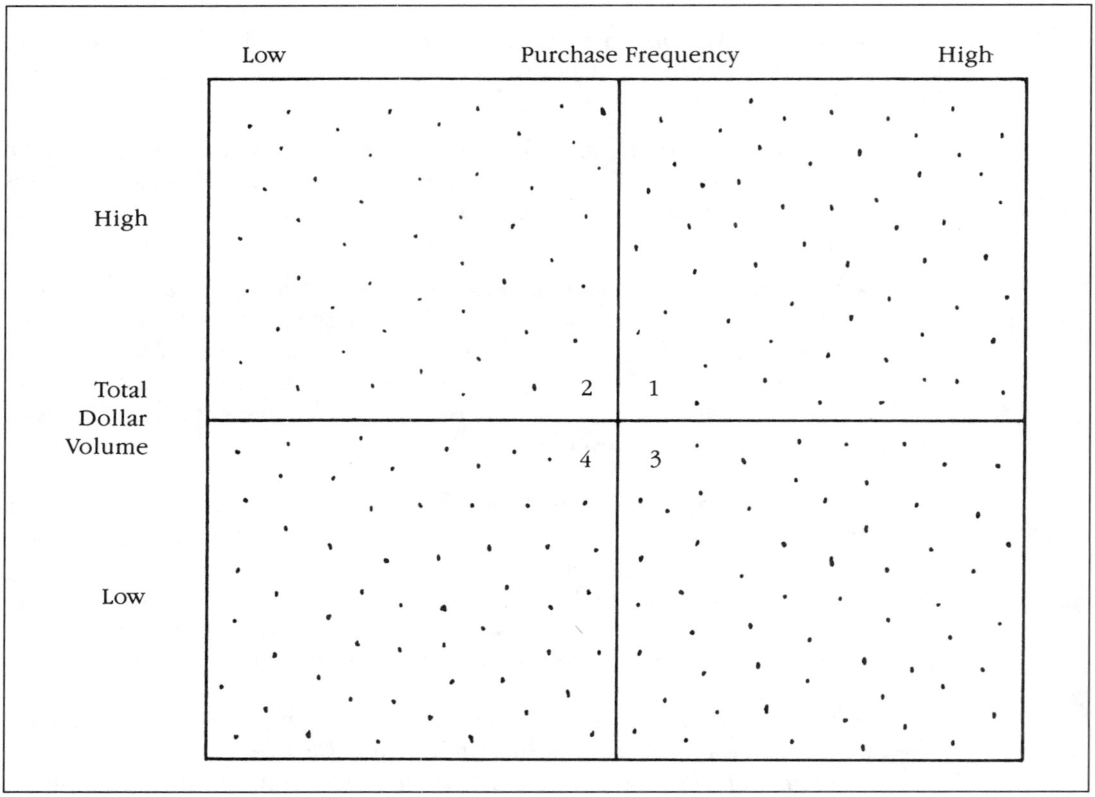

- *Quadrant 4* represents the worst of all possible worlds—the customer who doesn't spend very much or very often. The potential payoff in identifying such customers is in saving money by targeting a higher proportion of spending toward those customers in the first three quadrants.

We can further assess the potential of these customers by observing the degree to which companies with certain characteristics, such as SIC code, size, and geographic location, tend to be concentrated in certain quadrants. For example, if customers from four SIC codes are predominant within Quadrant 1 (highest sales volume, greatest purchase frequency), we should then analyze what our share of market or degree of penetration is in each of the four SIC codes. When this is done by comparing the customers in our house file against the total number of businesses within each SIC code on the national database, a profile of our market penetration can be drawn, as shown in Exhibit 21-17.

Exhibit 21–17.   **Company Penetration in Selected Market Segments**

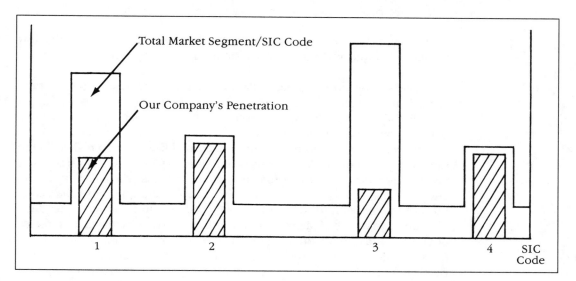

Primary Research for Marketing and Creative Development

Somtimes there is insufficient information available for profiling, particularly when a new market or segment is being entered. Such situations call for the marketer to obtain primary information directly from prospects in the form of qualitative information (focus groups or in-depth personal interviews) and/or quantitative data (surveys).

Research for a New Marketing Venture

The need for research relating to a new marketing venture arose when the Harris Corporation called on Stone & Adler to develop qualified leads for marketing a state-of-the-art office automation system. This unique system performed both word-processing and data-processing functions from a single workstation and could function as a compatible component of the current user's data-processing network.

Since this was a new marketing venture for Harris, research was needed to provide a basic understanding of the attitudes toward, and the decision-making process involved in, selecting office automation systems, such as:

- How the need for office automation systems is arrived at (i.e., how the purchase process is initiated)

- Who is involved in the decision-making process

- Criteria used in the decision-making process

- Informational sources used in the decision-making process

Research was also needed to understand what the effect of the low recognition level of Harris Corporation as an entrant in this market would have upon key prospects.

Since the proposed target audience for this system were the Fortune 1,000 companies, the research process began with focus groups consisting of "key decision makers" of office automation systems selected from a sample of these companies. A wide variety of industry groups were included.

To begin with, the exercise of finding the real key decision makers in the sample corporations became a survey unto itself. Often, three to five contacts had to be made before the actual decision maker was reached. This knowledge had major implications for our ultimate targeting because the actual titles of the decision makers varied widely. Some had traditional titles such as manager/director of Management Information Systems, manager/director of Office Automation Systems, or manager/director of Information Services. But the majority of decision makers had titles that appeared to be unique to each sample company and contained several functions under one hat, such as manager of Office Information Systems and Corporate Planning and Administration, manager of Office Automation Systems and Information Center, or director of Office Automation Systems and Information Technology.

Decision-Making Process Regardless of the decision maker's title, however, he or she (approximately 20 percent of the persons in our sample were female) formed one level within a three-level purchase process hierarchy (see Exhibit 21–18).

The purchase process centered around the manager/director of Management Information Systems or Office Automation Systems as the functional leader, the technical expert. The CEO or president's involvement in the decision-making process tended to revolve around the issue of financial considerations and the effect of the computer systems on the operating efficiencies of the departments obtaining the equipment. In some instances, however, the CEO or president was the originator of the purchasing process.

The perspective of the staff managers was specifically applications-oriented in terms of "What functions will the machine perform for my department?" "How easy is the equipment for my people to learn—since they aren't EDP experts?" "How compatible is the software with our current software?" "What happens if something breaks?" The purchase process frequently began from this perspective. Usually one of three scenarios occurs:

1. The department manager wishes to have an additional piece of equipment that is already in another department of the company.

2. The department manager wishes to have an additional piece of equipment from a "nonapproved" vendor.

Exhibit 21–18.   **Purchase Process Hierarchy**

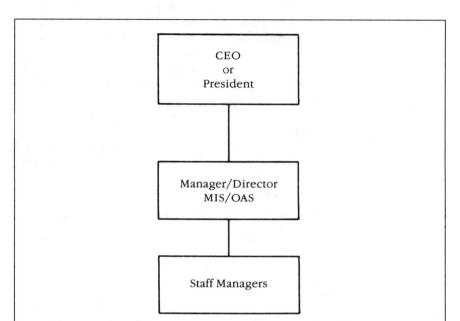

3. The department manager requests a major new system, which requires a system study to be conducted.

Scenarios 2 and 3 will require major involvement on the part of the MIS (Management Information Systems)/OAS (Office Automation Systems) director.

Current Marketing Environment   The Harris Corporation was facing a marketing environment in which much of the investment in major office automation equipment had already been made. Hence for the majority of target prospects the emphasis was on updating and refining the systems already in place. (Current systems were generally decentralized. Each division operated its own mainframe; a few were without mainframes.)

The procedures for purchasing this type of equipment appear to be ritualized and formal. Many corporations have ongoing equipment investigation committees. Purchases are often made based on an "approved vendor list" consisting of large well-known companies such as IBM, WANG, and DEC (Harris was not on approved vendor lists). Since these decisions are of such high visibility, most MIS and OAS key decision makers tend to be relatively conservative in terms of not looking to be "the first" to try a product or system. In the eloquent words of one battle-scarred OAS director, "I have no desire to be on the bleeding edge."

Major Criteria for Office Automation System Selection   A
major requirement when purchasing new equipment appears to be system
compatibility, for two basic reasons. First, a significant amount of money has
been spent on the current equipment, and additions must therefore be able
to interface with it. Second, most systems purchases involve software rather
than hardware and are being purchased for ordinary managers and clerical
workers rather than for data-processing people. Therefore new equipment
must require minimum training and run current software programs. The
second major requirement is for equipment and systems that satisfy basic
functional needs of the department.

Other key aspects of office automation equipment that decision makers
looked for during their last purchase of equipment included:

- Ease of use
- Ability to share the system among other operators
- Support with installation, software, and maintenance
- Communication with other equipment
- Staying power of the vendor company

Sources of Information in Decision Making   When looking for
information on new products, key decision makers tended to rely on:

- Word of mouth from peers in the field and other technical people at work,
  which was viewed as the most important souce of information
- Marketing representatives and their companies' literature
- Seminars
- Trade publications

Other Information Developed   A variety of other information was
developed from the study: reactions to concept statements describing the
proposed office automation system on a blind (nonbrand) basis, research
to determine which current competitors would most likely market such a
system, and reactions to Harris Corporation's marketing such a system.

Conclusions and Implications   The conclusions and implications
upon which the subsequent advertising strategy was developed revolved
around four issues:

- Credibility, or the ability to convince prospects that Harris Corporation's
  high level of experience and technical expertise in other markets was being
  transferred to the office automation equipment market

- Complexity of the decision-making process with multiple levels of target audiences, each having its own needs and points of view

- Conservatism on the part of key decision makers because of the high visibility of the decision, and the concomitant need for risk reduction through vendor approval lists

- Compatibility with current systems in terms of both hardware and software

The Future of Research in Direct Marketing

The future of research will be dictated by the problems that it is asked to address. For example, as traditional marketing categories continue to mature and competitors face increasing clutter in the mailbox, in print, and on TV, the problem of identifying, understanding, and reaching the highest-propensity prospects looms larger and larger.

Hence the major problem common to both traditional and nontraditional direct marketers, given the current environment, is *identifying and understanding key target audience segments*. This is particularly true in terms of focusing on points of greatest strategic leverage, and developing techniques to gain *direct access* to these segments. The problem is shared and must be jointly solved by research and media working in tandem. While this may, at first glance, seem to be a relatively simple, straightforward problem to solve, it isn't.

Consumer Insights and Delivery Process

As long as the disciplines of research and media are treated as separate functions, they will not be able to participate in the *consumer insights and delivery process* that is needed to address the problems of both traditional and nontraditional direct marketers.

As you can see by the integrated process shown in Exhibit 21–19, the process begins with research defining *who* the target audience is and *why* it behaves the way it does.

The primary purpose of this chapter has been to show direct marketers and would-be direct marketers the true value of research and the types of research that can identify target markets and lead to well-executed direct response advertising. Conducting the actual research is best left to professional researchers. For the direct marketer, knowing what should be researched is imperative.

Exhibit 21–19. **Consumer Insights and Delivery Process**

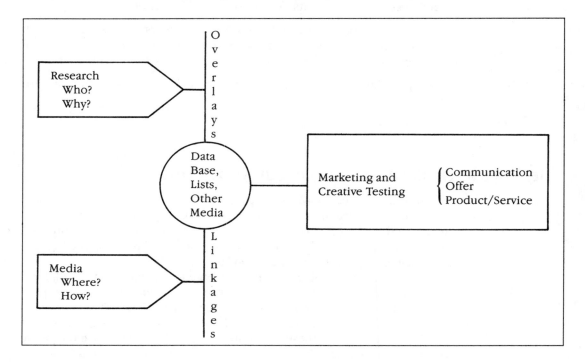

Research
Who?
Why?

O
v
e
r
l
a
y
s

Data
Base,
Lists,
Other
Media

Marketing and
Creative Testing

{ Communication
  Offer
  Product/Service

L
i
n
k
a
g
e
s

Media
Where?
How?

Self-Quiz

1. Name the last two of the four phases in the marketing research process.

   a. Exploratory research   c. _____

   b. Pretest   d. _____

2. The exploratory phase deals with defining and understanding the _____ audience.

3. The pretesting phase consists of developing, assessing, and refining the _____ and _____ products before in-market testing.

4. The testing phase consists of bringing together five key variables for assessment in the market:

   a. The product or service

   b. The media or method of accessing the defined target audience

    c. The time or season

    d. _____

    e. _____

5. Posttesting assesses reactions of both responders and nonresponders. Responder/nonresponder surveys can help pinpoint such issues as:

    a. Incremental sales

    b. Competitive conquest

    c. _____

6. Define *high-propensity prospects*:

_____

_____

_____

7. Define these terms:

Geodemographics _____

_____

Psychographics and lifestyles _____

_____

8. PAG identifies six consumer clusters:

    a. Mailbox Gourmets   d. _____

    b. Young Turks   e. _____

    c. Life Begins at 50   f. _____

9. Why is it important to profile a target audience?

_____

_____

_____

10. Research principles are the same for business-to-business products and services as they are for consumer products and services.

    ☐ True   ☐ False

Pilot Project

Suppose that your company acquired a product line in a category totally unfamiliar to you. No information exists as to who used such products or why. Consumer attitudes toward the line and competitive products are unknown.

Your assignment is to prepare a research plan that will provide the basic information necessary to market this product line. This plan should include a statement of research objectives for each project item and the specific type of technique best suited to meet the objectives.

Careers in Direct Marketing

What Is Direct Marketing?

Individuals who have read this book but who previously were unfamiliar with direct marketing will probably be very enthusiastic about the potential of the field and may be thinking about the career possibilities it offers.

Direct marketing, already a major force in business, continues to increase in scope, expenditure, and technology. A steady stream of fresh, newly trained talent will be required to fill positions not only in companies that are expanding their direct marketing efforts, but also in companies entering the direct marketing stream for the first time, whether exclusively or as an integrated function of their marketing and advertising mix.

Those who have taken a course in direct marketing or those who have a basic understanding of the principles and practices of direct marketing will have a chance to start a very exciting career. Those who are aware of specific position categories, where they are, and how to find them will have an edge in the competition for jobs.

Discussed in this appendix are some of the many career opportunities available, why a career in direct marketing is a good choice, how to get experience, where the jobs are and how to find them, and some basic tips for the marketing of the most important product—you!

Advantages of a Direct Marketing Career

As recently as a few years ago, most people entered direct marketing not by choice, but by chance. Once they got involved in direct marketing, they were here to stay. Direct marketing is growing daily and changing constantly. It offers challenges that are testable, measurable, and accountable. The constant emphasis on testing offers a chance to try new offers, new premiums,

new lists, and the like, along with a constant opportunity to learn. It's fun, it can be financially rewarding, and it is never dull.

Although almost every first job is difficult to get, because of lack of experience, direct marketing has an advantage that most other fields do not: It is testable, measurable, and accountable. Accountability is what leads to rapid advancement—much more so than in other fields. Direct marketers know almost immediately what's working. They can readily compute the return on their investment (ROI), and those who consistently add to the ROI are promoted quickly.

Direct marketing offers the opportunity to test new ideas quickly and relatively inexpensively. It's a chance for you to broaden your advertising and marketing experience. When you realize who's using direct marketing, you'll realize why a background in its techniques is advantageous and why it's a sound career choice.

Who's Using Direct Marketing?

Virtually any kind of organization can use direct marketing to sell its products and services, to raise funds, to generate inquiries, to call attention to issues, to elect candidates, to build store traffic, to generate leads for salespeople. The organization might be a consumer product manufacturer, a financial service organization (bank, savings and loan, personal credit, or insurance company), a consumer mail-order marketer, a business and industrial mail-order marketer, a publisher (newspaper, magazine, book), a book-and-tape club, an industrial manufacturer, a business equipment manufacturer, a retailer, a public utility, a travel and transportation company, a package-goods manufacturer and distributor, a fund raiser, a service organization (public relations firm, trade association, management consultant). Fortune 500 and 1000 companies are well represented in this list.

Even companies that have traditionally used image-building, general advertising are now integrating direct marketing into their marketing and advertising mix. Businesses now are becoming more customer-driven than market-driven. Direct marketing is "smart" marketing/advertising, and the database is key. Companies are using their marketing databases to target the right message to the right prospect at the right time, establishing *relationships* with their customers. That's why direct marketing is so attractive to an increasing number of firms and advertisers.

Direct marketing is being used more and more extensively not only in the United States, but throughout the world as well. Global opportunities—companies using direct marketing within other countries, as well as U.S. firms doing business directly in foreign countries—represent yet another example of expansion in the field, and suggest a good reason for you to be in it.

With the integration of direct marketing into the general marketing and advertising mix, the individual with a background in "direct," who is familiar with its "language" and techniques, will be an asset to any company.

Direct Marketing Careers

Because job functions often vary from company to company, standard job titles and descriptions are difficult to define. Also, new techniques, new segmentation methods, and new technology will over time probably add to the list of job titles. Nevertheless, some of the general career areas that presently offer great opportunities in direct marketing are described below.

Direct Response Advertising Agencies

In a speech at a major industry conference, David Ogilvy advised advertising agency leaders not to hire anyone unless he or she had direct response experience. "Direct marketers know what works!" he said. When he made this comment in the 1970s, there were only a handful of direct response agencies. Indicative of the growth of direct marketing is the fact that every major advertising agency has since formed or acquired a direct response division. In addition, there are several "independent" agencies that specialize in direct response. Also, more and more general agencies are hiring individuals with direct response knowledge in order to be able to offer their clients "integrated" advertising.

Job titles and departments in direct response agencies are similar to those in general advertising agencies, but the opportunity for advancement can be more rapid in direct response. Trends in integrated marketing and advertising, where direct response is often used in tandem with sales promotion, public relations, and media advertising, make the individual with knowledge of direct response advertising much more valuable.

Depending upon background, interests, and career goals, an individual can choose a direct response agency career in traffic, account management/client services, media, creative, or production. With their increased sophistication, many agencies now either have a research department or will form one shortly.

The new emphasis on more narrowly defined target audiences means new emphasis on database marketing. As a consequence, several agencies are developing database services for their clients. Many agencies have become what is called "full-service" agencies, with additional departments to service client needs in telemarketing, list consulting, and lettershop services. Job titles and departments in direct response advertising agencies are similar to those in general advertising agencies.

There are direct response agencies that deal solely with the consumer market or with the business-to-business market or with fund-raising, as well as agencies that are concerned only with catalog marketing. Obviously, an

understanding of these markets and of direct marketing techniques is critical to success in an agency career.

As an entry-level applicant, you should decide whether to begin on the agency side or the client side and/or whether to work for a large agency or a small agency. Obviously, there are pluses and minuses on both sides, but you will have to compare your goals, aspirations, and personality with the information gleaned from research about individual companies.

Traffic Coordinator Traffic is an excellent entry-level opportunity in that it offers a chance for an aspiring account executive or creative person to get a foot in the door and learn the agency business. The traffic coordinator is responsible for coordinating the component parts of a total advertising project with each of the agency's departments.

Account Executive An account executive is responsible for liaison with the client, involvement in marketing strategy, and coordination with various other departments involved in the creation of the advertising and its implementation. In general, the account executive should have a background in marketing, business, advertising, or communications. These are not necessarily prerequisites, but they are extremely helpful.

Creative The creative department of a direct response agency involves copywriters and graphic arts people. A course in copywriting is not a prerequisite for copywriters, but the individual must have a love of words and possess the proven ability to communicate with them clearly and concisely. The more you have written, the better.

Unlike general advertising, which seeks to create *awareness*, often through clever, creative ads, direct response advertising must *sell*. The copywriter, working closely with all departments of the agency, must have a thorough knowledge of the target audience—what it wants, why it buys, and how it reacts.

Direct response copywriters must always remember that they are first, last, and always *salespeople*. They must have a thorough knowledge of the product or service and be able to sell its *benefits*, rather than its features. They must tell what the product or service can do for the customer, rather than what it is. Their copy, along with the proper offer and media, is what does the selling. In order to gain experience, newcomers should write, write, and continue to write! Collecting samples of direct mail and direct response print advertising is good training. And, of course, a portfolio is a must.

An aspiring copywriter can begin as an assistant or junior, then advance to copywriter, senior copywriter, and copy supervisor/director. Often, copywriters become vice presidents/creative directors, supervising both copywriters and graphic arts people.

Art and Layout   Those persons with artistic talents can find jobs as artists, layout artists, or product photographers, working closely with the copywriters in developing the creative concept and "marrying" the copy to the graphics. Obviously, talent—as demonstrated by a portfolio and then through experience—is positively required in this department.

Media Buying and Production   There are many opportunities for entry-level positions in media buying. Media include mail, print, broadcast, new electronic media, and telephone.

There are several agencies that handle direct response broadcast production. When hiring, these departments generally look for people who have a background in direct response, broadcast, communications, and, sometimes, liberal arts. Knowledge of direct response broadcast techniques, either through actual experience or from reading the various books dealing solely with this topic, is helpful. Students who have worked in production or in the management of campus radio or TV stations will have had some valuable applicable experience. On-the-job training will have familiarized them with direct response details.

The advent of all the new electronic media, such as cable TV, shopping on home computers, and home-shopping TV channels means that the individual interested in the future technology will have to keep up with the constantly changing times by reading trade publications such as *Broadcasting*, *Cable Vision*, *Channel News*, *Electronic Media*, *Multichannel News*, *Television/Radio Age*, *Media Industry Newsletter*, and *Home Video Publisher*. Many of these new electronic media are in the experimental stage; there is a constant flux of corporate newcomers and much room for success—or failure.

The media personnel must coordinate with all departments. They are responsible not only for the selection of list, space, or time, but also for their purchase and for the analysis of the results. Media orders must be coordinated with brokers and publications and placed on a timely basis. Media people must be good negotiators when bargaining for print space or broadcast time, getting not only the lowest rates, but also the best positions or times. An analytical mind is critical, along with the ability to effectively communicate recommendations based on the results.

Production   Production staff must be detail-oriented, and they must be able to deal with change and to work under the pressure of deadlines. They are responsible for working with the various suppliers, such as printers and lettershops. They must see to it that the advertising message's component parts are complete, that the colors are correct, that there are no typographical errors (imagine what a misplaced decimal point could do to the client's bottom line!), and that postal regulations and size standards are adhered to.

Research   An aspiring researcher will begin at the assistant level in the research department and can work up to senior management. Because of the statistical nature of research, courses in research methodology, quantitative and behavioral statistics, psychology/sociology, and the like are obligatory. Unlike some other areas of direct response marketing, an MBA may be required for success in the research department.

A Final Word   A career at a direct response agency is exciting and challenging. The constant emphasis on testing means that there is always an opportunity to try new ways of getting that immediate response. A change in a word in the offer, a different premium or list, a change in the advertising medium, or any one of the many other variables can mean significant increases (or decreases!) in response rates. Those responsible know immediately what worked and what did not.

Yes, an agency career can be exciting, but it can also be extremely demanding. Only you can decide if this is the career for you. If you're a "nine-to-fiver," if you cannot work under the pressure of client demands and deadlines, if you are not a risk-taker and open to criticism, then an agency career is not for you.

Mailing Lists

Once the direct mail package or catalog has been completed in-house or by an outside agency, it must reach the right prospects. The most creative mailing will be a failure if it is not sent to the right target audience. That's where mailing lists come into the picture.

Depending upon an individual's qualifications, goals, and credentials, there are three (or possibly four) areas involved in the list business. An individual with a bent for numbers, research, computers, analysis, or sales can find a challenging and lucrative career as a broker, a manager, a compiler, or with a computer service bureau or database company.

List Brokers   Like brokers in other industries, the list broker serves both the list owner and the mailer (user). The list broker helps the marketer select the lists that will work best for the particular product or offer. The broker helps in the planning of the mailings, the analysis of the response, and the forecasting for future mailings, and is often involved in the clients' marketing strategy. Brokers are accountable too: They are measured by their client on the success of their recommendations.

List brokers must also be familiar with databases. They must know where they can be obtained and what they can do. They may make recommendations on when to overlay demographic and lifestyle data on "house" (the mailer's own) or rented lists.

Entry-level jobs in list brokerage are often at the level of either administrative assistant or assistant account manager (or executive); these positions can lead to a higher postion as senior account manager or vice president/

account supervisor. The successful account executive has a lot of client contact and must be ambitious and eager to learn about new lists, must pay attention to detail, and must have good oral and written communications skills.

List Managers Lists are rented to the broker or directly to the mailer by an internal or external manager. The manager performs a sales function for the list owner, and is also concerned with clerical and detail work and follow-up with the list owner (in the case of external list managers) and with the mailer. The manager must explain why the list should be tested or used, which companies have used it successfully in the past, and what its indications are for other clients.

For both manager and broker careers, a marketing and sales background is helpful. Also, strong communications skills are essential, even for those with marketing backgrounds.

List Compilers List compilers can specialize in business and professional markets or in consumer markets. Compilers "capture" data from a variety of commercial and public sources such as directories and from voter and automobile registration lists. They must have experience in developing sources for names and a methodology for producing lists having a high degree of accuracy. This end of the business tends to be more technical in nature, requiring the services of data processors, computer programmers, program analysts, software engineers, and the like. The very large compilers have databases with marketing-oriented information on millions of individuals and households.

Service Bureaus Service bureaus are connected with all of the list areas. The advent of ZIP codes, National Change of Address (NCOA), DMA's Mail Preference Service (MPS) and Telephone Preference Service (TPS), and customer information files has brought the list maintenance service bureau into prominence. Service bureaus perform sophisticated data-processing and data conversion tasks such as merge/purge, personalized computer letters, postal presorting, model development and analysis, and list rental fulfillment—all requiring the services of individuals with computer training and technical background. In addition, service bureaus employ salespeople to sell their services to brokers, managers, and mailers.

Lettershops

With the billions and billions of pieces of direct response advertising that go into the mail, lettershops perform an absolutely essential function for the direct mail field. They represent a sales area that is often ignored by job applicants. Lettershops, which can be either independently owned and operated or part of full-service direct response agencies, represent the last link in the direct mail process.

Although many of the jobs are mechanical or clerical in nature, letter-shops also require salespeople to sell the services of the company. The sales personnel give advice on exactly how names and addresses should be delivered to the lettershop. They specify the requirements for insertion and labeling and furnish mailers with written reports indicating receipt of materials and mailing costs. Because many salespeople work on a commission or salary-plus-commission basis, the more cost efficient they are to their clients, the more those clients will use their services and recommend them to others.

Catalogs

Catalogs are probably the most visible medium of direct response advertising. You have only to open your mailbox to realize the number of catalogs, that are published, and hence the number of job opportunities they offer. Those of you who are interested in catalogs may think first of *consumer* mail-order catalogs, but you should also consider *business-to-business* catalogs and those used by retailers.

Careers in catalogs include merchandising; marketing; lists, media, and database operations; production; forecasting; customer service; and inventory and logistics.

Some mail-order catalog companies produce their catalogs in-house, at agencies that specialize in catalog production, or at direct response agencies that create catalogs for some of their clients. Corporate research will tell you which catalogs are produced in-house and which ones utilize the services of outside agencies.

If you've studied retailing, a career with a retail catalog organization offers some exciting possibilities. In addition to merchandising, there's marketing and creative, production, testing, list maintenance and management, and database operations—all on the front end of this business.

There is also the fulfillment function of the catalog and mail-order business. The most beautiful catalog in the world will be a dismal failure if the inventory, delivery, and customer service departments are inadequate. These present some excellent entry-level training opportunities for newcomers who want to learn the catalog business. Customer service reps and inventory people are often in a position to make recommendations for improvement, thereby getting their name known to management, which makes promotion and hiring decisions. Moreover, with the emphasis on customer service being critical to the success of *all* businesses, job candidates with such experience will be a step ahead of their competition, and the experience will prove invaluable throughout any business career.

Jobs in catalog agencies are similar to those already discussed in direct response agencies. Some mail-order companies create their own marketing strategies, develop and rent their own lists, do their own testing, and so on. If they have only some of the agency capabilities, they then utilize the services of agencies that specialize in design and production for the rest.

Telemarketing

Telemarketing agencies are structured like advertising agencies, but their medium is the telephone. A client will hire a telemarketing agency to make or receive calls. A marketing representative or the executive responsible for new-business development will develop leads, make the "sales" presentation to the client, and formalize the "pitch" with a written marketing plan or proposal. The marketing rep is then responsible for client communications. Previous experience in telemarketing is helpful, but sales experience is certainly required.

A telemarketing account executive organizes and manages the client's program within the agency. Good written and oral communication, organizational, and analytical skills are required. The account executive coordinates script writing, testing, list preparation, and client reports.

Scriptwriters are the creative people of the telemarketing agency. Different copy skills are required in telemarketing because the script must be written to be heard, anticipating questions and preparing responses in advance to prospect questions. Journalism and creative writing are helpful backgrounds for this line of work.

Some direct marketing companies do their own telemarketing in-house; others utilize telemarketing agencies that have "centers." It is the telemarketing center manager's responsibility to supervise the making or receiving of calls based on the client's marketing strategy, lists, and script requirements. The center manager must recruit, train, schedule, and motivate the center's "communicators."

A center manager should have a background in business administration and human resources. Telemarketing operations experience is essential, along with people management skills, logistics, and scheduling. Due to the increased automation technology in telemarketing, a background in computer science is advantageous.

Telemarketing trainers instruct the communicators about the products or services. In addition, they teach listening skills and sales techniques. They may monitor the communicators during the sales calls to make sure all goes according to the script and marketing plan and make adjustments to the script if necessary.

An individual interested in sales will therefore get terrific training as a telephone communicator. Very often, communicators work part-time and come from all walks of life—students, homemakers, actors, and others who find part-time employment convenient. For this reason, telemarketing is a good entry-level job and provides excellent training for those wishing to advance. Good communications skills are essential, but a business or marketing background is not required.

Where Do You Go from Here?

Now that you are familiar with some of the many career choices in direct marketing, where do you go from here? How do you find out about the different companies? How can you gain the experience that every employer looks for?

First, anyone interested in this field should read specialty books on the various aspects of direct response. Become familiar with the "lingo" of direct marketing. Become acquainted with its techniques. Read the trade press and keep up with who's doing what, with mergers and acquisitions, with promotions and career changes. Make lists of people and companies. Do research on individual companies by contacting them for copies of their promotion pieces and annual reports.

To build your contact mailing list, refer to the *Direct Marketing Market Place* (National Register Publications). This directory lists hundreds of companies in the direct marketing field by business category. It lists key contacts, addresses, and phone numbers, and it gives a brief description of what the company does. The Direct Marketing Association (DMA) also publishes nine different service directories that list direct response agencies, list brokers, compilers, managers, research firms, international organizations, and other business segments. These directories are available for sale or they can be consulted in the DMA library.

The DMA's very extensive reference library and resource center is available *by appointment* (212–768–7277, extension 690) to DMA members (free of charge), to full-time students with ID (free of charge), and to individuals (charge for one-time use). The person interested in learning about direct marketing will find a wealth of information, including all books dealing with the subject, trade publications, business category files containing reprints of articles, company files, portfolios of DMA's award-winning ECHO campaigns, and much more.

You will find it helpful to join local direct marketing organizations. There are over 40 of these scattered throughout the country and the world. Most of these groups have local Direct Marketing Days, which often include trade shows. These events offer wonderful opportunities for you to expand your education and to make contacts.

Internships help you gain actual work experience in direct marketing—a chance to turn theory into practice. The Direct Marketing Educational Foundation and some of the local clubs sponsor internship programs with local members, and some positions can be obtained by writing individually to local companies.

Full-time students interested in gaining hands-on experience might want to enter the Leonard J. Raymond Collegiate ECHO Awards Competition. This is a direct response and/or integrated advertising competition in which student teams act as a direct response agency, plan the marketing and creative strategies, plan the campaign, construct the budget, and project the results for a major corporate sponsor. Valuable prizes aimed at furthering direct response education (through attendance at a DMA annual conference

or through a local Direct Marketing Day or reference books) are available for the winning teams and their faculty advisors. Honorable mention certificates are also awarded in the solo categories of creativity, marketing, budgeting, and most innovative campaign concept.

Full-time college seniors can apply for the Foundation's four-day Collegiate Institute, which includes the basics of direct marketing and direct response advertising. Included as part of the program is a session on résumé writing and interviewing. Résumés of Institute participants are made available upon request to companies that might wish to hire entry-level applicants.

In addition, the Direct Marketing Educational Foundation conducts other programs, for both students and professors, that are geared at expanding the scope of direct marketing education. It also has additional career information, course listings, sample course outlines, a bibliography of direct marketing texts and career resources, and a listing of local direct marketing clubs. For more information about the programs of the Direct Marketing Educational Foundation, contact DMEF, 6 East 43rd Street, New York, NY, 10017–4646; 212–768–7277, ext. 329.

Individuals interested in direct marketing should collect various forms of direct response ads. Pay attention to format, copy, order forms, positioning, and the like. These real-world examples are excellent educational tools. Of course, your own portfolio should be maintained in a highly professional manner.

Where Are the Jobs?

Although the majority of direct marketing firms are located in New York, Chicago, and Los Angeles, others can be found throughout the United States and abroad—and in increasing numbers. Local direct marketing clubs often list position openings in their newsletters. Many will print positions-wanted ads free of charge in the classified sections of their newsletters. Also, you can consult the *Direct Marketing Market Place*, local classifieds, and/or the trade press. There are several executive-recruiting firms that deal with direct response positions, but they rarely deal with entry-level openings.

A Word about Salaries

This appendix has deliberately avoided providing salary information. There are so many variables for each job function that it would be practically impossible to quote salary ranges. Salaries depend upon the location of the company, its size, the specific job responsibilities, benefits, and so on. Job seekers would be advised to consult local classified ads to determine the "going rate" or salary range for a particular job title.

Remember that entry-level salaries in direct marketing are competitive with salaries in other areas of marketing and advertising. However, due to direct marketing's testability, measurability, and accountability, the opportunities for advancement in this area are much greater. Although salary is an important consideration, it should never be the sole deciding factor. Your responsibilities, educational and training opportunities, and promise for future advancement are equal, if not more important, considerations.

Marketing Yourself

The various techniques you have learned throughout this book will help you with the most important job—marketing yourself.

Just as you would do research before marketing a product, you must do research about your own goals, likes and dislikes, and strengths and weaknesses. You must also do research about prospective employers. The information you glean from directories, annual reports, trade publications, and personal contacts will serve to make up your own personal database of prospects. The research will help you target your résumé to your best prospects rather than "blanketing the universe" with résumés!

Just as you would want your prospect to act immediately and buy your product or service, you want that employer to act—by calling you for an interview and then by hiring you.

Remember that your résumé is your ad, your cover letter is your sales pitch, your interview is your sales call, and your thank-you letter is your follow-up. Don't do anything in marketing yourself to a prospective employer that you wouldn't do in marketing a product or service. Remember to keep your résumé benefit-oriented, telling what *you* can do for the company, stressing accomplishments rather than responsibilities. List only relevant information—information that will help you get the job you are seeking.

Laurie Spar
Vice President
Direct Marketing Educational Foundation

Glossary

ABC Audit Bureau of Circulations.

ACORN A Classification of Residential Neighborhoods; a marketing segmentation system that enables consumers to be classified according to the type of area in which they live.

Accordion fold Two or more parallel folds which open like an accordion.

Account qualification matrix Scientific method of measuring each case as it is completed for potential future purchases.

Action devices Items and techniques used in direct mail to encourage positive response, e.g., tokens, scent strips.

Active buyer Customer whose latest purchase was made within the last 12 months. *See also* **Buyer** and **Actives**.

Active member Customer who is fulfilling the original commitment or who has fulfilled that commitment and has made one or more purchases in the last 12 months.

Active subscriber Customer who has committed for regular delivery of magazines, books, or goods or services for a period of time still in effect.

Actives Customers who have made purchases within a prescribed time period, usually one year; subscribers whose subscriptions have not expired.

Additions New names, either of individuals or companies, added to a mailing list.

Add-on service Service of the Direct Marketing Association that gives consumers an opportunity to request that their names be added to mailing lists.

Address Coding Guide (CG) List of beginning and ending house numbers, ZIP codes, and other geographic codes for all city delivery service and streets served by 31,540 post offices located within 6,601 ZIP codes.

Address Correction Requested Endorsement printed in the upper left-hand corner of the address portion of the mailing piece (below the return address), which authorizes the U.S. Postal Service, for a fee, to provide the known new address of a person no longer at the address on the mailing piece.

Advertisement rate card Printed card issued by the publishers of journals and newspapers detailing advertising cost, advertisement sizes, and the mechanical details of production.

Advertising schedule List of advertisements booked by media showing details of sizes, timing, and costs.

Against the grain Folding paper at right angles to the grain of the paper; a sheet of paper will fold easily along the grain but will possibly crack when folded against the grain.

A.I.D.A. Most popular formula for the preparation of direct mail copy. The letters stand for (get) Attention, (arouse) Interest, (stimulate) Desire, (ask for) Action.

Airbrush Small pressure gun shaped like a pencil that sprays paint by means of compressed air. Used to obtain tone or graduated tonal effects in artwork.

Airtime Jargon term denoting the amount of actual transmission time available for an advertisement on television and radio.

Alterations Changes made in the copy after it has been set in type.

American Standard Code of Information Interchange (ASCII) Widely used code adopted by the American Standards Association for transmission of information.

Antique paper Rough-surfaced paper which is only sightly calendered.

Art paper Paper coated with a mineral substance to produce a glossy surface.

Artwork Finished layout consisting of drawings, photographs, lettering, and copy.

Assigned mailing dates Dates by which the list user has to mail a specific list; no other date is acceptable without approval of the list owner.

Assumptive close Closing technique in which the salesperson offers the product or service with the assumption that the target has made the decision to buy.

Asterisk bills State laws that require telephone companies to advise subscribers that they can have an asterisk placed in front of their names if they do not want to receive telemarketing calls.

Audience Total number of individuals reached by a promotion or advertisement.

Audit Printed report of the counts involved in a particular list or file.

Automatic call distributor (ACD) Equipment that automatically manages and controls incoming calls, sends calls to the telephone representative who has been idle the longest, answers and queues calls during busy periods, and plays recorded messages for waiting callers. It automatically sends overflow calls to a second group and provides management reports on the call activity. It can stand alone or be integrated with a PBX. *See Also* **PBX**.

Automatic dialing recorded message player (ADRMP) Machine that dials preprogrammed telephone numbers, automatically plays a prerecorded message (normally a sales pitch), then records responses.

Automatic interaction detection (AID) Program for segmenting a list from a heterogeneous to a homogeneous market.

Automatic redial Telephone feature that permits the last number dialed to be automatically dialed again at the push of one button.

Automatic route selection (ARS) Switching system that chooses the least costly path from available owned or leased circuits. *See also* **LCR**.

Autotyped letters Individually prepared letters produced on a typewriter activated by a prepunched roll of paper similar to that used in a player piano.

Backbone Back of a bound book connecting the two covers; also known as spine.

Back-end Activities necessary to complete a mail-order transaction once an order has been received; measurement of a buyer's performance after he has ordered the first item in a series offering.

Bangtail Promotional envelope with a second flap that is perforated and designed for use as an order blank.

Banker Envelope Envelope with the flap on the long edge.

Batch Grouping of orders.

Batch processing Technique of executing a set of orders/selections in batches as opposed to executing each order/selection as it is received; batches can be created by computer programming or manually by date.

Benefits Features of a product or service. Benefits are what sells the product or services.

Bill enclosure Promotional piece or notice enclosed with a bill, invoice, or statement.

Bindery Place where final trimming, stitching/stapling, order-form insertion, and any necessary off-press folding is done.

Binding   Finishing process that glues, staples, or stitches the pages of a catalog to the cover.

Bingo cards   Reply card inserted in a publication and used by readers to request literature and samples from companies whose products and services are either advertised in the publication or mentioned in its editorial columns and feature articles.

Bleed   Extension of the printed image to the trim edge of a sheet or page.

Block   Metal, rubber, or plastic plate engraved, cast, or molded for printing.

Blocked calls   Calls that receive busy signals.

Blocking out   Operation of eliminating undesirable backgrounds and portions of a photographic negative by opaquing the image.

Blueprint   Sometimes called *blues* or *bluelines*, a prior-to-printing proof made from a photographic negative or positive, used for checking type/photo position.

Body type   Types used for the main body of the text as distinct from its headings.

Boiler room/bucket shop   Term to describe outbound phone rooms where facilities are less than ideal for the telephone sales representative and sometimes for the activity itself. High turnover of representatives and low overhead for the owners are trademarks of this kind of operation.

Boldface type   Type that is heavier than standard text type, often used for headlines and paragraph lead-ins, and to emphasize letters, word, or sentences.

Bond paper   Grade of writing or printing paper used when strength, durability, and permanence are essential.

Book   Catalog.

Booklet   Usually, a small flyer-type promotional piece.

Boom   In broadcasting, a semirigid tubelike apparatus that extends from the headset and positions the microphone close to the user's mouth.

Bounce-back   Offer enclosed with a mailing sent to a customer in fulfillment of an order.

Bringing up the color   Color correcting; intensifying color on press or in separations.

Broadcast media   Direct response source that includes radio, television, and cable television.

Broadside   Single sheet of paper, printed on one or two sides, folded for mailing or direct distribution, and opening into a single, large advertisement.

Brochure   Strictly defined, a high-quality pamphlet, with specially planned layout, typography, and illustrations; also used loosely to describe any promotional pamphlet or booklet.

Broker   Agent authorized to buy or sell for an organization or another individual.

Bromide   Photographic print made from a negative, or a positive used as a proof.

Bulk   Thickness of paper.

Bulk mail   Category of third-class mail involving a large quantity of identical pieces addressed to different names and specially processed for mailing before delivery to the post office.

Bulk rebate   Category of postage that allows rebate for second-class presorted mailing; delivery will normally be made within seven working days. Amount of rebate depends on the volume of mail.

Burnout   Exhaustion and lack of motivation often experienced by telephone sales representatives working long shifts without proper training or compensation.

Burst   To separate continuous-form paper into discrete sheets.

Business list   Any compilation of individuals or companies based on a business-associated interest, inquiry, membership, subscription, or purchase.

Business reply service   Reply-paid service in which postage for the respondent's reply is paid for by the advertiser.

Business-to-business telemarketing
Telemarketing to industry.

Buyer One who orders merchandise, books, records, information, or services.

C/A Change of address.

Call In telemarketing, this term encompasses uncompleted and completed connections, busys, temporarily disconnected, disconnected–no referral, disconnected but referred, and no-answers; does not include status of results such as sale/no-sale/follow-up.

Call-back Any contact required to follow up an activity.

Call card Record of details on prospects or customers; often arranged chronologically.

Call forcing Call distribution feature that automatically directs a waiting call to an available agent. The agent receives an audible tone burst that signals the call coming through. A button need not be pressed to receive this call.

Call guide Informal roster of points to be covered during a telephone sales presentation that allows for personalization.

Call management Process of selecting and managing the optimum mix of equipment, network services, and labor to achieve maximum productivity from a telemarketing center.

Call management system Equipment that gives detailed information on telephone activity and cost.

Call objective Clear reason for the call; the best calls are those that tend to have only one objective.

Call objective guideline Worksheet that allows preparation for the specific objective; often used in training and for new-product introductions.

Call queuing Placing incoming calls in a waiting line for access to an operator station.

Call restriction Procedure designed to limit the range of calling power given to employees, as when only selected personnel are able to make long-distance calls.

Carriers Transportation facilities suppliers.

Case Complete and measurable telephone sales cycle from beginning to end; e.g., 100 names on a list equals 100 cases.

Cash buyer Buyer who encloses payment with order.

Cash on delivery (COD) Expression meaning that a customer pays for an order when it is received.

Cash rider Also called *cash up* or *cash option*, an addition to an order form offering the option of full cash payment with the order, at some saving over the installment-payment price as an incentive.

Cash with order Requirement made by some list owners for full payment at the time an order is placed for the list.

Catalog Book or booklet displaying photos of merchandise, with descriptive details and prices.

Catalog buyer Person who has bought products or services from a catalog.

Catalog request Order for the catalog itself. The catalog may be free; there may be a nominal charge for postage and handling, or there may be a more substantial charge that is often refunded or credited on the first order.

Cell size Smallest unit or segment quantity of an individual variant within a test program.

Census tract Area within a ZIP code group denoting households with uniform social and economic characteristics.

CHAD Change of address; also called *C/A*.

Charge buyer Person who has charged merchandise ordered by mail; or a person who has paid for merchandise only after it has been delivered.

Cheshire label Specially prepared paper (rolls, fanfold, or accordion fold) used to reproduce names and addresses to be mechanically affixed to mailing pieces.

Chromalins One method of proofing a color separation. Four separate, extremely

thin plastic sheets (one for each color) are overlaid, producing a color reproduction of the separations.

Chromes Often misused term actually referring to color transparencies; also used as nickname for chromalins.

Circulars General term for printed advertising in any form, including printed matter sent out by direct mail.

Closed case Any case that has completed the sales cycle and has ended in a sale, no sale, or no potential.

Clustering Grouping names on a telemarketing list according to geographic, demographic, or psychographic characteristics.

Cluster selection Selection routine based on taking a group of names in a series; e.g., a cluster selection on an nth name basis might be the first 10 out of every 100 or the first 125 out of 175, etc.; a cluster selection using limited ZIP codes might be the first 200 names in each of the specified ZIP codes, etc.

COAM Customer owned and maintained equipment.

Coding (1) System for ascertaining from replies the mailing list or other source from which an address was obtained; (2) structure of letters and numbers used to classify characteristics of an address on a list.

Cold calls Sales calls to an audience unfamiliar to the caller.

Cold lists Lists that have no actual or arranged affinity with the advertiser, i.e., they have not bought from, belonged to, or inquired of the advertiser itself or of any particular affinity group.

Collate (1) To assemble individual elements of a mailing in sequence for inserting into a mailing envelope; (2) program that combines two or more ordered files to produce a single ordered file; also the act of combining such files. *See also* **Merge-purge**.

Collation Orderly assembly of sheets or signatures during the bindery process.

Color print Printed reproduction of a transparency or negative, inexpensive but not of top quality; also called a *"C" print*.

Commercial envelope Oblong envelope with a top flap.

Communicator call report (CCR) List identifying for each telephone sales representative what calls were handled during a shift, the date, the contact name, and all information pertaining to the details of each call made.

Compiled list Names and addresses derived from directories, newspapers, public records, retail sales slips, trade show registrations, and the like, to identify groups of people with something in common.

Compiler Organization that develops lists of names and addresses from directories, newspapers, public records, registrations, and other sources, identifying groups of people, companies, or institutions with something in common.

Completed cancel Person who has completed a specific commitment to buy products or services before cancelling.

Completed contact Any contact that finalizes a preplanned portion of a sales cycle.

Comprehensive Complete and detailed layout for a printed piece; also called *comp* or *compare*.

Computer letter Computer-printed message providing personalized, fill-in information from a source file in predesignated positions; full-printed letter with personalized insertions.

Computer personalization Printing of letters or other promotional pieces by a computer using names, addresses, special phrases, or other information based on data appearing in one or more computer records; the objective is to use the information in the computer record to tailor the promotional message to a specific individual.

Computer record All of the information about an individual, a company, or a trans-

action stored on a specific magnetic tape or disk.

Computer service bureau   Facility providing general or specific data-processing.

Consultative selling   Personalized method of sales that first identifies a customer's needs and then sells a product or service to meet those needs.

Consumer list   List of names (usually with home address) compiled or resulting from a common inquiry or buying activity indicating a general buying interest.

Consumer location system   Market identification system containing information derived from Target Group Index and ACORN.

Contact   Any conversation with a decision maker or any communication that advances a case toward completion.

Contact-to-closed-case ratio   Number of completed contacts required to complete a case; e.g., contact mail-contact would be a two-Contact-to-closed-Case ratio.

Continuity program   Products or services bought as a series of small purchases, rather than all at one time, generally based on a common theme and shipped at regular or specific time intervals.

Contributor list   Names and addresses of persons who have given to a specific fund-raising effort. *See also* **Donor list**.

Control   Last successful mailing package without any changes that allows a true measurement of the performance of each of the variants on test; generally used to test against new variants.

Controlled circulation   Distribution at no charge of a publication to individuals or companies on the basis of their titles or occupations; typically, recipients are asked from time to time to verify the information that qualifies them to receive the publication.

Controlled duplication   Method by which names and addresses from two or more lists are matched (usually by computer) in order to eliminate or limit extra mailings to the same name and address.

Conversion   (1) Process of reformatting, or changing from one data-processing system to another; (2) securing specific action such as a purchase or contribution from a name on a mailing list or as a result of an inquiry.

Conversion rate   Percentage of potential customers who, through a direct mail solicitation, become buyers.

Co-op mailing   Mailing of two or more offers included in the same envelope or other carrier, with each participating mailer sharing the mailing cost based on some predetermined formula.

Copy   Written material intended for inclusion in the various components of a mailing package or advertisement.

Copy date   Date by which advertising material ready for printing must reach a publishing house for inclusion in a particular issue.

Cost per inquiry (C.P.I.)   Simple arthmetical formula derived by dividing the total cost of a mailing or an advertisement by the number of inquiries received.

Cost per order (C.P.O.)   Similar to cost per inquiry but based on actual orders rather than inquiries.

Cost per thousand (C.P.M.)   Common rate for list rentals when fee is based on every 1,000 names rented to telemarketers.

Coupon   Part of an advertising promotion piece intended to be filled in by the inquirer or customer and returned to the advertiser; it often entitles the bearer to a discount on an item at time of purchase.

Coupon clipper   Person who has given evidence of responding to free or nominal-cost offers out of curiosity, with little or no serious interest or buying intent.

Creative   Preprinting aspects of catalog preparation: design, layout, copy writing, and photography; used as a noun in the catalog business.

Crop   To trim part of a photo or copy.

C.T.O. Contribution to overhead (profit).

Databank Information resources of an organization or business.

Database Collection of data to support the requirements and requests for information of a specific group of users.

Database definition The clear understanding between telemarketing management and database management as to what will be captured and displayed from the database.

Data capture/entry Any method of collecting and recording information.

Data processing Organization of data for the purpose of producing desired information; involves recording, classifying, sorting, summarizing, calculating, disseminating, and storing data.

Data sheet Leaflet containing factual information about a product or service.

Deadbeat Person who has ordered a product or service and, without just cause, hasn't paid for it.

Decoy Unique name especially inserted in a mailing list for verifying list usage.

De-dupe *See* **Duplication elimination**.

Delinquent Person who has fallen behind or has stopped scheduled payment for a product or service.

Delivery Method of oral presentation used, e.g., businesslike, informal, formal.

Delivery date Date a list user or designated representative of the list user receives a specific list order from the list owner.

Demographics Description of the vital statistics of an audience or population; includes personal characteristics, name, title, occupation, address, phone number, etc.

Direct mail Printed matter usually carrying a sales message or announcement designed to elicit a response from a carefully selected consumer or business market.

Direct mail advertising Any promotional effort using the Postal Service, or other direct delivery service, for distribution of the advertising message.

Direct Mail Order Action Line Service provided by the Direct Marketing Association that attempts to help consumers resolve problems they may have encountered when shopping by mail.

Direct Marketing Association (DMA) Organization representing special interests of those in the business of direct marketing.

Direct response Advertising through any medium inviting direct response by any measurable means (mail, telephone, walk-in, etc.)

DMA Mail Preference Service Service provided by the Direct Marketing Association that allows consumers to request that their names be added to or deleted from mailing lists.

Donor list List of persons who have given money to one or more charitable organizations. *See also* **Contributor list**.

Doubling day Point in time established by previous experience by which 50 percent of all returns to a mailing will normally have been received.

Drop closing Process of completing a sale by initially offering top-of-the-line items or services and then adjusting the offer to a lower range of prices.

Drop date *See* **Final date**.

Drop out Deletion of type from all four colors, resulting in "white" type.

Drop ship Fulfillment function whereby the manufacturer of the product does the actual shipping of the item to the customer.

Dummy (1) Mock-up giving a preview of a printed piece, showing placement of the material to be printed; (2) fictitious name with a mailable address inserted into a mailng list to verify usage of that list.

Dummy name Fictitious name and address inserted into a mailing list to verify usage of that list; also known as a *sleeper*.

Duplicate Two or more identical name-and-address records.

Duplication elimination Specific kind of controlled duplication providing that no

matter how many times a name and address is on a list or how many lists contain that name and address, it will be accepted for mailing only once by that mailer; also known as *dupe elimination*.

Dye transfer High-quality, four-color print made from a transparency; most often used when retouching is needed.

800 service Inbound long-distance service that is free to the caller, and paid for by the recipient.

Enamel Coated paper that has a glossy finish.

Envelope stuffer Any advertising or promotional material enclosed with business letters, statements, or invoices.

Ergonomics Study of the problems of people adjusting to their environment, especially seeking to adapt work or working conditions to suit the workers.

Exchange Arrangement whereby two mailers exchange equal numbers of mailing list names.

Exhibition list List of people who have registered as attendees at trade or consumer exhibitions.

Expire Former customer who is no longer an active buyer.

Expiration Subscription that is not renewed.

Expiration date Date on which a subscription expires.

File maintenance Activity of keeping a file up to date by adding, changing, or deleting data. *See also* **List maintenance** and **Update**.

Fill-in Name, address, or words added to a preprinted letter.

Film positive Photographic print on transparent film taken from artwork for use by the printer.

Final date Targeted date for mail to be in the hands of those to whom it is addressed.

Finished size Overall dimensions of a piece of printed matter after folding and other procedures have been completed.

First-class letter contract Post office service for mailers that consist of at least 5,000 identical items, can sort into towns, and require first-class service; offers discounts of up to 12 percent.

First-time buyer Person who buys a product or service from a specific company for the first time.

Fixed field Way of laying out, or formatting, list information in a computer file that puts every piece of data in a specific position relative to every other piece of data. If a piece of data is missing from an individual record, or if its assigned space is not completely used, that space is not filled. Any piece of data exceeding its assigned space limitation must be abbreviated or contracted.

Fixed lists Cost per sale including all other costs except promotions.

Flag Computerized means of identifying data added to a file; usage of a list segment by a given mailer.

Flat Paper industry's term for unprinted paper adopted by the direct mail industry to refer either to unprinted paper or, more particularly, to printed paper prior to folding.

Flat charge Fixed cost for the sum total of a rental list; usually applies to smaller lists.

Flight A given mailing, particularly when multiple drops are to be made on different days to reduce the number arriving at one company at one time.

Folio Page number as it appears on a printed page.

Follow-up contact Any contact required to finalize a previous commitment or to close a transaction.

Follow-up system Part of an automated telemarketing system which keeps track of calls that should be recycled into the outgoing program and rescheduled at a later time; its purpose is to trap information and release it to communicators at the appropriate time.

Foreign mail   Lists of householders and businesses outside the United States.

Format   Size, style, type page, margins, printing requirements, and the like that are characteristic of a publication.

Former buyer   Person who has bought one or more times from a company but has made no purchase in the last 12 months.

Fortune 1000   Thousand largest industrial companies in the United States, as published by *Fortune* magazine; almost all have sales volumes per year of over $1 billion.

Fortune 300   *Fortune* magazine's selection of the 50 largest companies in 6 classifications: banking, retailing, wholesaling, insurance, construction, and utilities.

Four-line address   Typical individual-name list with at-business addresses requires a minimum of four lines: name of individual, name of company, local address, city, state, and ZIP code.

Four-up, three-up, two-up   Number of similar items printed on one sheet of paper; e.g., four-up indicates the sheet will be guillotined to print four finished articles; (also *four-to-view*, *three-to-view*, etc.).

Fourth-class mail   Parcel post, the U.S. Postal Service delivery of mail parcels weighing over 16 ounces.

Free lancer   Independent artist, writer, or photographer who is not on staff but works on a per-project or hourly rate as the need arises.

Free-ride   *See* **Envelope stuffer** and **Piggy-back**.

Free sheet   Paper without mechanical wood pulp.

Free-standing insert   Promotional piece loosely inserted or nested in a newspaper or magazine.

Frequency   Number of times an individual has ordered within a specific period of time. *See also* **Monetary value** and **Recency**

Friend of a friend   Name of someone thought to be interested in a specific advertiser's product or service; submitted by a third party.

Front-end   Activities necessary, or the measurement of direct marketing activities, to obtain an order.

Fulfillment   Process of supplying goods after an order has been received.

Fund-raising list   List of individuals or companies based on a known contribution to one or more fund-raising appeals.

Galley listing or sheet list   Printout of list data on sheets, usually in ZIP or alphabetic order.

Galleys   Proofs of typesetting in column width taken before page make-up.

Gathering   Assembly of folded signatures into correct sequence.

Genderization   Program run to add gender to mailing lists (based on first names where available).

Geographics   Any method of subdividing a list based on geographic or political subdivisions (ZIP codes, sectional centers, cities, counties, states, regions).

Gift buyer   One who buys a product or service for another.

Giftees   List of individuals sent gifts or magazines by mail, by friends, donors, or business firms. Giftees are not truly mail-order buyers; rather they are mail-order recipients and beneficiaries.

Gimmick   Attention-getting device, usually dimensional, attached to a direct mail printed piece.

Gone-aways   *See* **Nixie**.

Governments   Often-overlooked source of lists, e.g.; lists of cars, homes, dogs, bankers, hairdressers, plumbers, veterinarians, buyers, subscribers, inquirers, TV stations, ham operators, and CBs, among others.

Grid test   Means of testing more than one variable at the same time; a useful method for testing different offers by different packages over a group of prospect lists.

Groundwood pulp   Paper that contains wood pulp.

Groups   Number of individuals having a unifying relationship, e.g., club, association, membership, church, fraternal order, political group, sporting group, collector group, travel group, singing group, etc.

Guarantee   Pledge of satisfaction made by the seller to the buyer and specifying the terms by which the seller will make good his pledge.

Gummed label   *See* **Label, gummed**.

Half-life   Formula for estimating the total response to be expected from a direct response effort shortly after the first responses are received; makes valid continuation decisions possible based on statistically valid partial data.

Halftone   Photograph or other tonal illustration reproduced by lines of small dots.

Handling charge   Fixed charge added per segment for special list requests; also shows up as part of shipping and handling charges for transportation of labels, cards, sheets, or tape.

Hard copy   Printout on a sheet list or galley of all data available on a magnetic source such as a tape, hard disk, or floppy disk.

Head of family   From telephone or car data, the name and sex of the individual on the registration file.

Headline   Primary wording utilized to induce a direct marketing recipient to read and react.

Heat transfer   Form of label that transfers reverse carbon images on the back of a sheet of mailing pieces by means of heat and pressure.

High-Potential/Immediate-Need   Any case that requires immediate contact by the outside sales force.

High school student list   Serveral compilers provide lists of high school juniors and seniors with their home addresses; original data, usually printed phone rosters, are not available for all schools or localities.

Hit   Name appearing on two or more mailing lists.

High-ticket buyer   Buyer who has purchased expensive items by mail.

Home office   For major businesses, the executive or home office location as differentiated from the location of branch offices or plants.

Homogenization   Unfortunate and misleading combination of responses from various sources; often the use of a single "average" response for a mailing made to customers and prospects alike.

Hot line   Most recent buyers on a list that undergoes periodic updating. (Those who have just purchased by mail are the most likely buyers of other products and services by mail.)

Hot-line list   The most recent names available on a specific list, but no older than three months; use of the term *hot line* should be modified by *weekly*, *monthly*, etc.

Households   Homes selectable on a demographic basis; householders (consumers) may be selectable on a psychographic basis.

House list   Any list of names owned by a company as a result of compilation, inquiry or buyer action, or acquisition, that is used to promote that company's products or services.

House list duplicate   Duplication of name-and-address records between the list user's own lists and any list being mailed by the list user on a one-time use arrangement.

ICSMA   International Customer Service Manager's Association.

Imposition   Way in which pages are positioned in order to print and fold correctly on a press.

In-house   Related to services or products that can be furnished by the advertiser himself; e.g., in-house lists, in-house print.

In-house telemarketing   Telemarketing done within a company as a primary or supplementary method of marketing and selling that company's own products.

Inactive buyer Buyer who has not placed an order or responded during a specified period of time.

Inbound calls Calls that come into a tele-marketing center.

Inbound telesales A department within a telemarketing operation devoted to the handling of incoming calls.

Income Perhaps the most important demographic selection factor on consumer files. Major compiled files provide surprisingly accurate individual family incomes up to about $40,000. Incomes can be selected in $1,000 increments; counts are available by income ranges for every ZIP code.

Incoming specialist Trained professional telephone specialist skilled at handling incoming order requests and cross-selling or up-selling to close a sale.

Indexing Creation of a standard, say, 100 percent of recovery of promotion cost, to allow comparison between mailings of different sizes.

Indicia The required indication in the area usually reserved for the postage stamp designating the type of mailing.

Individual Most mailings are made to individuals, although all occupant or resident mail is, in effect, to an address only. A portion of business mail is addressed to the establishment (by name and address) only, or to a title and not to an individual.

Influentials In business mail order, those executives who have decision-making power on what and when to buy; those who exercise clout in their business classification or community; in consumer mail, those individuals (executive, professionals, educators, clergy, etc.) who make a difference in their localities or workplaces.

Initial source code Code for the source that brought the name to the customer file for the first time.

Ink-jet Computer-generated ink droplets that apply ink through a small orifice to form characters; often used for purposes of personalization.

Input data Original data, usually in hard copy form, to be converted and added to a given file. Also, taped lists made ready for a merge-purge, or for a databank.

Inquiry (1) Request for literature or other information about a product or service; (2) response in the form of an inquiry for more information or for a copy of a catalog.

Insert Leaflet or other printed material inserted loose in a publication or mailing package.

Inset Leaflet or other printed material bound in with the pages of a publication rather than inserted loose.

Installment buyer Person who orders goods or services and pays for them in two or more periodic payments after their delivery.

Insurance lists Lists of people who have inquired about or purchased various forms of insurance; lists of insurance agents, brokers, adjustors, executives.

Intelpost Royal Mail electronic transmission service for copy, artwork, and other urgent documents.

International 800 service Telephone service allowing toll-free calls to another country.

Intralist duplication Duplication of name and address records within a given list.

Italic Sloping version of a typeface, usually used for emphasis.

Item In the selection process for a mail-order list, term denoting the type of goods or service purchased; in input terms, it is a part of a record to be converted.

Julian dating Three-digit numerical system for date-stamping a transaction by day: January 1 is 001, December 31 is 365.

Key code Means of identifying a given promotional effort so that responses can be identified and tracked.

Key code (generic) Form of hierarchal coding by which promotional vehicles can be analyzed within type of media—

newspapers, magazines, Sunday supplements, free-standing stuffers, mailing lists, radio promotion, TV promotion, takeovers, and so on.

Key code (key)   Group of letters and/or numbers, colors, or other markings, used to measure the specific effectiveness of media, lists, advertisements, offers, etc., or any parts thereof.

Keyline   Any of many partial or complete descriptions of past buying history codes to include name-and-address information and current status.

Keypunch   Means of converting hard copy to machine-readable form by punching holes in either cards or paper tape.

Keypunch/keystroke   Clerical means used to convert hard copy data, one character at a time, to magnetic form.

Keystroke   Means of converting hard copy to machine-readable form through a typewriter key or similar means. A good portion of keystroke conversion today goes directly to some electronic form, usually either on cassette or tape. When many key-to-tape machines are linked together, the data go directly to disk in the computer complex.

Key verifying   For 100 percent accuracy, having two operators at the data-entry stage keypunch the same data.

Kill   To delete a record from a file.

Label   Slip of paper containing the name and address of the recipient that is applied to a mailing for delivery.

Label, gummed   Perforated label form on paper stock which must be individually separated and moistened before being applied with hand pressure to the mailing piece.

Label, one-up   Conventional pressure-sensitive labels for computer addressing are four-across horizontal; one-up labels are in a vertical strip with center holes for machine affixing.

Label, peel off (pressure-sensitive)   Self-adhesive label form that can be peeled off its backing form and pressed onto a mailing piece.

Laid paper   Paper having parallel lines watermarked at equal distances, giving a ribbed effect.

Laser letters   Letters printed by the latest high-speed, computerized imaging method. The new lasers can print two letters side by side, each of 35 or 40 lines, in one second.

Late charge   Charge imposed by some list owners for list rental fees not paid within a specific period.

Layout   (1) Artist's sketch showing relative positioning of illustrations, headlines, and copy; (2) positioning of subject matter on a press sheet for most efficient production.

Lead generation   Mailing used to invite inquiries for sales follow-up.

Lead qualification   Determination, by telemarketing, of customer's level of interest in and willingness and ability to buy a product or service.

Length of line   The computer, which has the capacity to print 132 characters across a 14½" sheet, has forced discipline in the choice of line length. In four-across cheshiring, the longest line cannot be more than 30 characters; for five-across this limit is 23 characters. Capable data processors, utilizing all 8 lines available on a 1"-deep label, can provide two full lines, if need be, for the title line.

Length of residence   Major compilers who utilize telephone or car registration data maintain the number of years (up to 16) a given family has been at the same address, thereby providing another selection factor available from these stratified lists.

Letterhead   Printing on a letter that identifies the sender.

Lettershop   Business organization that handles the mechanical details of mailings such as addressing, imprinting, and collating; most offter some printing facilities and many offer some degree of creative direct

mail services.

Lifestyle selectivity Selectivity based on the lifestyle habits of segments of the population as revealed through lists indicating what people need, what they buy, what they own, what they join, and what they support; major lists based on consumer surveys provide data on hobbies, ownership, and interests.

Lifetime value In direct mail and marketing, the total profit or loss estimated or realized from a customer over the active life of that customer's record.

Lift letter Separate piece added to conventional solo mailings asking the reader to consider the offer just once more.

List acquisition (1) Lease or purchase of lists from external services; (2) use of internal corporate lists.

List affinity Correlation of a mailing offer to selected mailing list availabilities.

List bank Names held in inventory for future use.

List broker Specialist who makes all necessary arrangements for one company to use the list(s) of another company. A broker's services may include research, selection, recommendation, and subsequent evaluation.

List building Process of collecting and utilizing list data and transaction data for list purposes.

List bulletin Announcement of a new list or of a change in a list previously announced.

List buyer Technically, one who actually buys mailing lists; in practice, one who orders mailing lists for one-time use. *See* **List user** and **Mailer**.

List card Conventional 5" x 8" card used to provide essential data about a given list.

List catalog Directory of lists with counts prepared and distributed, usually free, by list managers and list compilers.

List cleaning List updating or the process of correcting a mailing list.

List compilation Business of creating lists from printed records.

List compiler One who develops lists of names and addresses from directories, newspapers, public records, sales slips, trade show registrations, and other sources for identifying groups of people or companies having something in common.

List count Number of names and addresses on a given segment of a mailing list; a count provided before printing tapes or labels; the universe of names available by segment or classification.

List criteria Factors on a mailing list that differentiate one segment from another; may be demographic, psychographic, or physical in nature.

List customer-compiled In prior year, list typed and prepared to customer order. Today, virtually all lists are precompiled on tape for any selection the user orders.

List, mailing Names and addresses of individuals and/or companies having in common a specific interest, characteristic, or activity.

List databank *See* **Databank**.

List enhancement Addition of data pertaining to each individual record that increases the value of a list.

List exchange Barter arrangement between two companies for the use of a mailing list; may be list for list, list for space, or list for comparable value other than money.

List franchise Provision by major compilers, on a franchise basis and usually for only a few years, of copies of all or parts of their files to list wholesalers and mailing shops.

List key *See* **Key code**.

List maintenance Any manual, mechanical, or electronic system for keeping name-and-address records (with or without other data) up to date at any specific point(s) in time.

List management system Database system that manages customer and prospect lists, used to merge and purge duplicates

between in-house lists and those obtained from outside sources and to select names for direct mail promotions and outgoing telemarketing programs.

List manager   Person who, as an employee of a list owner or as an outside agent, is responsible for the use, by others, of a specific mailing list(s), and who oversees list maintenance, list promotion and marketing, list clearance and record keeping, and collecting for use of the list by others.

List manager, in-house   Independent manager serving multiple lists. Some large list owners opt to manage the list rental activity through full-time in-house employees.

List monitoring   *See* **Monitoring.**

List owner   Person who, by promotional activity or compilation, has developed a list of names having something in common; or one who has purchased (as opposed to rented, reproduced, or used on a one-time basis) such a list from the list developer.

List performance   Response logged to a mailed list or list segment.

List protection   Safeguarding of a list through review of mailing and mailer, insertion of list seeds, and obtaining of a guarantee of one-time use only.

List ranking   Arranging list items in descending order on the basis of logged response and/or logged dollars of sales.

List rental   Arrangement whereby a list owner furnishes names to a mailer and receives a royalty from the mailer.

List rental history   Report showing tests and continuations by users of a given list.

List royalty   Payment to a list owner for use of a list on a one-time basis.

List sample   Group of names selected from a list in order to evaluate the responsiveness of that list.

List segmentation   *See* **List selection**.

List selection   Process of segregating smaller groups within a list, i.e., creating a list within a list.

List sequence   Order in which names and addresses appear in a list—by ZIP code, alphabetically, chronologically, etc.

List sort   Process of putting a list in a specific sequence.

List source   Original source used to generate names on a mailing list.

List test   Part of a list selected to try to determine the effectiveness of the entire list. *See* **List sample**.

List user   Mailer, on company that uses names and addresses on someone else's list as prospects for its product or service.

Load up   Process of offering a buyer the opportunity of buying an entire series at one time after the customer has purchased the first item in that series.

Logotype (logo)   Symbol or statement used consistently to identify a company or product.

Look-up service   Service organization that adds telephone numbers to lists.

Machine-coated paper   Paper coated on one or both sides during manufacture.

Machine-readable data   Imprinted alphanumeric data, including name and address, that can be read and converted to magnetic form by an optical character reader.

Magalogue   Mail-order catalog that includes paid advertisements and, in some cases, brief editorials, making it similar to a magazine in format.

Magnetic tape   Film for storing electronically recorded data, often in list format to allow computerized matching with other lists for purposes of appending phone numbers or eliminating duplications.

Magnetic tape charge   Charge made for the tape reel on which a list is furnished and which usually is not returnable for credit.

Mail Advertising Service Association (MASA)   Major trade association of mailing houses responsible for fulfillment in the United States; has some 500 members and over 6,000 lettershops and mailing houses.

Mail count   Amount of mail deposited with the Postal Service on a given date as reported on the certification form.

Mail date   Drop date planned for a mailing, usually as agreed upon by the mailing list owner and the list user.

Mailer   (1) Direct mail advertiser who promotes a product or service using outside lists or house lists or both; (2) printed direct mail advetising piece; (3) folding carton, wrapper, or tube used to protect materials in the mails.

Mailer's Technical Advisory Committee   A group of representatives from virtually all associations involved in any form of mailing and related services that meets periodically with Postal Service officials to provide advice, technical information, and recommendations on postal policies.

Mailgram   Combination telegram-letter, with the telegram transmitted to a postal facility close to the addressee and then delivered as first-class mail.

Mailing house   Direct mail service establishment that affixes labels, sorts, bags, and ties the mail, and delivers it in qualified ZIP code strings to the Postal Service for certification.

Mailing List/Users and Suppliers Association   Association founded in 1983, specifically targeted to mailing list uses and abuses.

Mailing machine   Machine that attaches labels to mailing pieces and otherwise prepares such pieces for deposit in the postal system.

Mailing package   The complete direct mail unit as it arrives in the consumer's mailbox.

Mail monitoring   Means of determining length of time required for individual pieces of mail to reach their destinations; also utilized to verify content and ascertain any unauthorized use.

Mail order   Method of conducting business wherein merchandise or services are promoted directly to the user, orders are re-ceived by mail or telephone, and merchandise is mailed to the purchaser.

Mail Order Action Line (MOAL)   Service of the Direct Marketing Association that assists consumers in resolving problems with mail-order purchases.

Mail-order buyer   Person who orders and pays for a product or service through the mail.

Mail Preference Service (MPS)   Service of the Direct Marketing Association for consumers who wish to have their names removed from national commercial mailing lists.

Make-up   Positioning of type and illustrations to conform to a layout; in lithography usually called a *paste-up*.

Makeready   In letterpress, the building up of the press form so that heavy and light areas print with the correct impression.

Management information system (MIS)   System, automated or manual, that provides sales support information for both the sales representative to enhance sales activity and management to evaluate sales performance.

Manual telephone sales center   Completely paper-driven telephone sales center.

Marginal list test   Test that almost, but not quite, qualifies for a continuation.

Market   Total of all individuals or organizations that represent potential buyers.

Market identification   Establishment of criteria to predetermine specific markets that will be primary targets of a telemarketing project.

Market penetration   Proportion of buyers on a list to the total list or to the total area. For business lists, penetration is usually analyzed by two-digit or four-digit Standard Industrial Classification codes.

Marketing mix   Various marketing elements and strategies that must be used together to achieve maximum effectiveness.

Markup   Details of the size and style of type

to be used; also known as *type specification*.

Marriage mail Form of co-op in which the offers of two or more disparate mailers are combined in one folder or envelope for delivery to the same address.

Master file File that is of a permanent nature, or regarded in a particular job as authoritative, or one that contains all sub files.

Match To cause the typing of addresses, salutations, or inserts into letters to agree with other copy that is already imprinted.

Match code Code determined by either the creator or the user of a file for matching records contained in another file.

Matched city pairs For testing purposes when individual markets must be utilized, a means to do A in City Y but not B, while doing both A and B in City X with the premise that the two cities are reasonably matched as to size, income spread, and lifestyles.

Matte finish Dull paper finish that has no gloss.

Maximum cost per order Lifetime value of each major cell of customers on a customer file; helps set a limit on the price to pay for a new customer.

Mechanical Finished artwork ready for printing production; generally includes type matter pasted in position.

Mechanical addressing systems System in which small lists are filed on cards or plates and addressing is done by mechanical means.

Media Plural of *medium*; the means of transmitting information or an advertising message (direct mail package, inserts, magazines, posters, television, etc.).

Media data form Established format for presenting comparative data on publications.

Media insert Insert, either loose or bound, generally in business and consumer publications.

Median demographic data Data based on medians rather than on individuals; e.g., a census age is the median for a group of householders.

Medium Channel or system of communication, e.g., a specific magazine, newspaper, TV station, or mailing list.

Member get member A promotion where existing members are offered a gift for enrolling new members.

Merge To combine two or more lists into a single list utilizing the same sequential order, and then to sort them together, usually by ZIP code.

Merge/purge To combine two or more lists for list enhancement, suppression, or duplication elimination by a computerized matching process.

Military lists Lists of persons in military service.

Minicatalog New prospecting device consisting of a fanfolded set of minipages 3" × 5" used as cardvertisers, billing stuffers, and package inserts; also utilized by some mailers as a bounce-back.

Minimum (1) Minimum billing applied to list rentals involving a small number of names; (2) minimum billing for given mailing and/or computerized sources.

Minimum order requirement Stipulation, irrespective of the quantity ordered, that payment of a given number of dollars will be expected.

MOAL *See* **Mail Order Action Line**.

Mobility rate Annual rate at which families move or businesses fail, change names, or are absorbed each year.

Modeling Process involving use of spreadsheets via a computer that provides reasonable answers to "what-if" scenarios.

Monetary value Total expenditures by a customer during a specific period of time, generally 12 months.

Monitoring Listening in on telephone conversations from extensions, usually for training of telephone sales representatives;

also known as a *service observing*.

Mono   In printing, printed in a single color.

MPS   *See* **Mail Preference Service**.

Multibuyers   Identification through a merge-purge of all records found on two or more lists.

Multifamily   *See* **Multiple dwelling**.

Multiple buyer   Person who has bought two or more times (not one who has bought two or more items at one time only); also known as *multibuyer* or *repeat buyer*.

Multiple contact case   Situation in which more than one contact with a prospect or customer is needed to complete or close a sale.

Multiple dwelling   Housing unit for three or more families at the same address.

Multiple regression   Statistical technique that measures the relationship between responses to a mailing with census demographics and list characteristics of one or more selected mailing lists; used to determine the best types of people/areas to mail to, and to analyze customers or subscribers.

Multiple regression analysis   Statistical procedure that studies multiple independent variables simultaneously to identify a pattern or patterns that can lead to an increase in response.

Multiple SICs   On major files of large businesses, the argmentation of the primary Standard Industrial Classification with up to three more four-digit SICs. Business merge-purges often disclose multiple SIC alignments unavailable on any single list source.

Name   Single entry on a mailing list.

Name acquisition   Technique of soliciting a response to obtain names and addresses for a mailing list.

Name drain   Loss, mainly by large businesses, of the names and addresses of prospective customers who write to them or visit their stores.

National change of address   Service of the U.S. Postal Service that provides national data on changes of address.

Negative   Photographic image on film in which black values in the original subject are transparent, white values are opaque, light greys are dark, and dark greys are light.

Negative option   Buying plan in which a customer or club member agrees to accept and pay for products or services announced in advance at regular intervals unless the individual notifies the company, within a reasonable time after announcement, not to ship the merchandise.

Nesting   Placing one enclosure within another before insertion into a mailing envelope.

Net name arrangement   Agreement, at the time of ordering or before, whereby a list owner agrees to accept adjusted payment for less than the total names shipped to the list user. Such arrangements can be for a percentage of names shipped or names actually mailed or for only those names actually mailed.

Net names   Actual number of names on a given list mailed after a merge-purge; the concept of paying only for such names.

Net-net names   Agreement made by a renter with a list owner to pay only for names that survive such screens as income, credit, house list duplicates, prior-list suppress names, and ZIP suppress programs; the surviving portion can be quite small.

Net unique name file   Resultant one-per-record unique unduplicated list, one of the chief outputs of a merge-purge operation.

New connects   New names added to the connected lines of telephone, gas and electric utilities.

New case   Telephone contact yet to be made.

New households   New connects by local phone companies; data on new names from one telephone book to another are over one year old.

Newspaper lists　List data on engagements, births, deaths, and newsmaking items and changes published in newspapers.

Nine-digit ZIP code　Postal Service system designed to provide an automated means of utilizing an extended ZIP code to sort mail down to small contiguous areas within a carrier route.

Nixie　Mailing piece returned to a mailer (under proper authorization) by the Postal Service because of an incorrect, or undeliverable, name and address.

Nonprofit rate　Preferential Postal Service rate extended to organizations that are not maintained for profit.

No-pay　Person who has not paid for goods or services ordered. Also known as an a *uncollectable*, a *deadbeat*, or a *delinquent*.

North/south labels　Mailing labels that read from top to bottom and that can be affixed with Cheshire equipment.

Novelty format　Attention-getting direct mail format.

*n*th **name or interval**　Statistical means of taking a given number of names equally selected over the full universe of the list segment being sampled. The *n*th number interval is derived by dividing the total names in the list by the sample number desired.

*n*th **name selection**　Method of selecting a portion of a mailing list for test mailings (e.g., every fifth, tenth, twentieth name).

Objective case　Each telemarketing project has a specific objective for each case, e.g., make a sale, reactivate an account, arrange for an appointment.

Occupant list　Mailing list that contains only addresses (no names of individuals and/or companies).

OCR (Optical Character Reader)　Automatic computer input process whereby the computer scanner is able to read printed characters and convert them to electronic data.

Offer　The terms promoting a specific product or service.

Offices　Compilations of businesses with telephones providing offices of professionals and of multiple professionals per office, where desired, brought together by their common telephone number.

Offset litho　Method of transferring the printing image from flat plate to paper via a covered cylinder.

One-off　*See* **One-time use of a list**.

One-shot mailing　Offer designed to make the sale in a single transaction.

One-stage mailing　Mailing designed to take orders directly without any follow-up process.

One-time buyer　Buyer who has not ordered a second time from a given company.

One-time use of a list　Intrinsic part of the normal list usage, list reproduction, or list exchange agreement in which it is understood that the mailer will not use the names on the list more than once without specific prior approval of the list owner.

One-year contract　Form of lease in which the renter is granted unlimited use for one year of a given set of compiled records; usually treated as a "sale for one year."

On-line availability　Linkup system in which an operator at a remote terminal can obtain list information from a data bank or database at another location.

Opacity　Property of a sheet of paper that minimizes the show-through of printing from the reverse side or from the next sheet.

Open account　Customer record that at a specific time reflects an unpaid balance for goods and services ordered without delinquency.

Operations review　Annual or semiannual review of the entire telephone sales center and strategic plan of a company.

Opportunity seeker　Class of mail-order buyer or prospect that seeks a new and different way to make an income; ranges

from people who look for ways to work at home, to expensive franchises.

Optical character reader (OCR) Electronic scanning device that can read characters, either typed with a special OCR font or computer created, and convert these characters to magnetic form.

Optical scanner Input device that optically reads a line of printed characters and converts each character to its electronic equivalent for processing.

"Or Current Resident" Line added by computer to a three-line consumer list in an attempt to obtain greater deliverability and readership in case of a change in residential occupants.

Order blank envelope Order form printed on one side of a sheet, with a mailing address on the reverse; the recipient simply fills in the order and folds and seals the form like an envelope.

Order card Reply card used to initiate an order by mail.

Order entry procedure Process of capturing the name, address, item, dollars, and key for a transaction, and connecting it to electronic data, which then trigger creation of a picking document, a billing document, and usually the effect of that transaction upon inventory and inventory control.

Order form Printed form on which a customer can provide information to initiate an order by mail.

Order margin Sum represented by the difference between all costs (except promotion) and the selling price (after returns).

Origination All the work needed to prepare a promotional package, e.g., copy, design, photography, typesetting, color separation.

Outbound calls Calls that are placed by the telemarketing center. *See also* **inbound**.

Outbound telesales Proactive approach to a given market by a planned program to develop leads and/or sales.

Outside list manager *See* **List manager**.

Overlay In artwork, a transparent or translucent covering over the copy where color breaks, instructions, or corrections are marked.

Overprinting Double printing; printing over an area that already has been printed.

Owners Owners of mail-order response lists and operators of mail response companies who "own" the customer and inquiry lists that they offer on the list rental market. All such proprietary lists much be "cleared" by such owners or their agents to be rented for one-time mailing by others.

Package insert Any promotional piece included in merchandise packages that advertises goods or services available from the same of different sellers.

Package test Test of part or all of the elements of one mailing piece against another.

Page proofs Proofs taken after make-up into pages, prior to printing.

Paid cancel Person who completes a basic buying commitment before canceling that commitment. *See also* **Completed cancel**.

Paid circulation Distribution of a publication to individuals or organizations that have paid for a subscription.

Paid during service Method of paying for magazine subscriptions in installments, usually weekly or monthly, and usually collected personally by the original salesperson or a representative of the publisher.

Pandering list List of individuals who have reported receipt of sexually offensive literature to the Postal Service to ensure that the same mailer cannot, except by facing criminal charges, mail to them again.

Panel Group of people having similar interests that is used for research purposes. *See also* **Focus research**.

Para sales force Sales team that works as a supplement to another sales team either on the telephone or in the field.

Pass (1) One run of the paper through the printing press; (2) to clear a page for a subscription.

Pass-along effect Additional readership acquired as executives forward particularly interesting mail to their associates. Business catalog mailers seek to harness this effect by printing a group of germane titles on the cover as a suggested routing for such pass-along readership.

Passing a File Process of reading a file sequentially by computer to select and/or copy specific data.

Past buyer *See* **Former buyer**.

Paste-up Process by which an artist puts together type copy and photographs into final artwork ready for photographic reproduction.

Payment, method of Record or tag showing how a customer paid for a purchase (by check or credit card or money order); available as a selection factor on a number of response lists.

Payment rate Percentage of respondents who buy on credit or takes a trial on credit and who then pay.

Peel-off label Self-adhesive label attached to a backing sheet that is attached to a mailing piece. The label is intended to be removed from the mailing piece and attached to an order blank or card.

Peg count Tally of the number of calls made or received over a set period of time.

Pending case Case in which an initial contact has been made and the communicator is waiting for a response or additional information.

Penetration Relationship of the number of individuals or families on a particular list (by state, ZIP code, SIC code, etc.) compared to the total number possible.

Penetration analysis Study made of the "share of market" held by a given mailer within various universes by classification or other demographic characteristics; for business mailers, the chief means to ascertain which markets by SIC and number of employees are most successfully penetrated in order to prospect more efficiently.

Performance evaluation Weekly or monthly review of a salesperson's performance by first-line supervision.

Periodical Publication issued at specific intervals.

Peripheral listing Creation of a variant kind of audience from that specified, e.g., addressing to the parents of College Student or High School Student X, titling to Mrs. X from a list of doctors by name and address at home, addressing a child by name to attract the eye of the parent, or inviting the new neighbors to view a new car at a given address.

Personalization Adding the name of the recipient to a mailing piece, or the use of a computer to input data about the psychographics of the customer being addressed.

Phone list Mailing list complied from names listed in telephone directories.

Photosetting Production of type matter in positive form on bromide or film by the use of electromechanical equipment that is usually computer-assisted.

Pick-up and delivery charges Charges relating to collection or delivery of outside lists or components involved in the mailing process.

Piece rate Third-class mail breaks into two main rate categories—third-class bulk rate (for discounts) and third-class piece rate. For the price of a first-class stamp, a piece weighing up to 3 1/2 ounces may be placed in the mail stream without any prior sortation, a charge that is currently over 40 percent greater than the unit charge for third-class bulk mail.

Piggy-Back Offer that hitches a free ride with another offer.

Pigment Powdered substance used to give color, body, or opacity to printing inks.

Pilot Trial program designed to test the feasibility of a possible telemarketing program.

Platemaking Process by which artwork is converted into letterpress or offset plates for printing.

Pocket envelope   Envelope with the flap on its short side.

Point   Measure used to describe type sizes.

Political lists   Mailing lists that break into two main categories—voter registration files mailed primarily during political campaigns, and fund-raising files of donors to various political causes.

Poly bag   Transparent polyethylene bag used as envelopes for mailings.

Pop-up   Printed piece containing a paper construction pasted inside a fold that, when the fold is opened, "pops up" to form a three-dimensional illustration.

Positive   Photographic image on film that corresponds to the original copy; the reverse of a negative.

Positive option   Method of distributing products and services incorporating the same advance notice techniques as a negative option but requiring a specific order each time from the member or subscriber, generally more costly and less predictable than negative option.

Postage refund   Sum returned to a mailer by an owner or manager for nondeliverables exceeding a stipulated guarantee.

Postcard   Single sheet self-mailer on card stock.

Postcard mailers   Booklet containing business reply cards that are individually perforated for selective return to order products or obtain information.

Post codes   Codes added to the addresses on a mailing list that define sales and distribution areas; a fully post-coded address list earns an additional discount when bulk mailing under the first- and second-class discount schemes.

Post-paid impression (PPI)   *See* **Printed postage impression**.

Precall planning   Preparation before a sales call to promote maximum effectiveness.

Preclearance   Act of getting clearance on a rental before sending in the order.

Premium   Item offered to a potential buyer, free or at a nominal price, as an inducement to purchase or obtain for trial a product or service offered via mail order.

Premium buyer   Person who buys a product or service in order to get another product or service (usually free or at a special price), or person who responds to an offer of a special premium on the package or label (or sometimes in the advertising) of another product.

Preprint   Advertising insert printed in advance for a newspaper or magazine.

Prerecorded message   Taped message, often recorded by a celebrity or authority figure that is played to inbound callers or included in an outbound call.

Presort   To prepare mail for direct delivery to post offices or to carriers at post offices. Over half of all for-profit third-class bulk mail is now mailed at carrier-route presort discount rates.

Press date   Date on which a publication goes to print.

Prestructured marketing   Marketing using computer software that provides a highly efficient system for annual fund-raising and capital drives, special events, and membership development by providing detailed information on specific target groups.

Price lining   Setting of prices by a seller in accordance with certain price points believed to be attractive to buyers.

Printed postage impression (PPI)   System enabling producers of bulk mailings to preprint "Postage Paid" on their envelopes; a wide range of designs is available allowing compatibility of style with other print detail on the envelope.

Printer's error   Error in printed copy that is the fault of the typesetter and corrected at the printer's expense.

Printout   Copy on a sheet of a list, or of some selected data on a list such as matched pairs indicating duplication from a merge-purge, or an array of largest buyers or donors.

Priority For a continuation, method of arranging the tested lists and list segments in descending order on the basis of number of responses or number of dollars of sales per thousand pieces mailed; for political mail, a special next-day delivery service offered by the Postal Service.

Prior list suppress Utilizaton of prior data to remove matching data from a new run and thus reduce the payment for the list data as used.

Private mail Mail handled by special arrangement outside the Postal Service.

Proactive telemarketing Seller-initiated or outbound calling.

Process colors Black and three primary colors—magenta (red), cyan (blue), and yellow—into which full-color artwork is separated before printing.

Product information cards Business reply cards bound in a booklet for selective return to order products or obtain information; also sometimes mailed loose in the form of a pack of cards.

Professional lists Direct marketing lists that break down into some 30 categories, from architects to veterinarians. For example, a new list on the market based on a classified list of doctors (MDs) with phones has verified addresses and phone numbers of over 100,000 of some 190,000 physicians in private practice.

Projected roll-out response Based on tests results, the response anticipated from a large continuation or program.

Prompt Form of sales presentation by a professional telesalesperson that is comprised of predetermined but unscripted steps in the telephone call that will be presented in every closed case.

Proof Impression taken from types, blocks, or plates for checking for errors and making amendments prior to printing.

Prospect Name on a mailing list considered to be that of a potential buyer for a given product or service who has not previously made such a purchase.

Prospecting Using mailings to get leads for further sales contacts rather than to make direct sales.

Protected mailing period Period of time, usually one or two weeks prior to and one or two weeks after the mail date for a large quantity of names, in which the list owner guarantees no competitor will be given access to the list.

Pseudocarrier routes The Postal Service Carrier Route (CRIS) tape lists millions of bits of data delineating 160,000 individual carrier routes. Major consumer compilers break up the areas not serviced by individual carriers into 240,000 extra pseudo-carrier routes for marketing penetration selection or omission.

Pseudo SICs Modifications of the U.S. Department of Commerce Standard Industrial Classification codes. By adding a fifth character to the SIC four-digit designations, major compilers now provide 4,600 SIC classifications with greater specificity. When the phone companies provide all of their classified listings, the number of different classifications for selection can total over 8,500. A six-digit SIC system is now under construction by Dun & Bradstreet and Data Base America.

Psychographics Characteristics or qualities used to denote the lifestyle or attitude of customers and prospective customers.

Publisher's letter Letter enclosed in a mailing package to stress a specific selling point.

Pull Proportion of response by mail or phone to a given promotional activity.

Purge Process of eliminating duplicates and/or unwanted names and addresses from one or more lists.

Pyramiding Method of testing mailing lists that starts with small numbers and, based on positive indications, follows with increasingly large numbers of the balance of the list until the entire list is mailed.

Qualification sortation Third-class bulk mail sorted to meet Postal Service qualifications for three different mail streams.

Qualified lead Potential customers that have been determined to need, want, and be able to purchase a specific product or service.

Quantity pricing Pricing, usually by compilers, offering price breaks for varying list quantities rented over a period of a year.

Queue A function of an automatic call distributor that holds all (incoming) calls in the order in which they arrive until the next available agent takes the first in line, moving the next call up in sequence.

Questionnaire Printed form presented to a specific audience to solicit answers to specific questions.

Quotation Price presented to a prospective mailer before running a list order requiring special processing.

Random access Access mode in which records are obtained from or placed into a mass storage file in a nonsequential manner so that any record can be rapidly accessed.

Rate of response *See* **Response rate**.

Rating points Method of measurement of TV or radio audience size.

Reactive telemarketing Customer-initiated buying by telephone (inbound calling).

Readership Number of people who read a publication as opposed to the number of people who receive it.

Rebate *See* **Bulk rebate**.

Recency Latest purchase or other activity recorded for an individual or company on a specific customer list. *See also* **Frequency** and **monetary value**.

Record Name-and-address entry on a file.

Record layout Description covering the entire record length to denote where on a tape each part (or field) of the record appears, such as name, local address, city, state, ZIP code, and other relevant data.

Record length Number of characters occupied by each record on a file.

Referral name *See* **Friend of a friend**.

Reformatting Changing a magnetic tape format from one arrangement to another, more usable format; also called *conversion*.

Refund (1) For a list, return of part of payment due to shortage in count or excessive nondeliverables (over the guarantee); (2) for a product sold by mail, a return of the purchase price if an item is returned in good condition.

Registration list List constructed from state or local political-division registration data.

Regression analysis Statistical means to improve the predictablility of response based on an analysis of multiple stratified relationships within a file.

Renewal Subscription that has been renewed prior to or at expiration time or within six months thereafter.

Rental *See* **List rental**.

Repeat buyer *See* **Multiple buyer**.

Repeat mailing Mailing of the same or very similar packages to the addresses on a list for the second time.

Reply card Sender-addressed card included in a mailing on which the recipient may indicate a response to the offer.

Reply-O-Letter One of a number of patented direct mail formats for facilitating replies from prospects, featuring a die-cut opening on the face of the letter and a pocket on the reverse; an addressed reply card is inserted in the pocket and the name and address thereon shows through the die-cut opening.

Reprint Special repeat printing of an individual article or advertisement from a publication.

Repro High-quality reproduction proof, usually intended to be used as artwork for printing.

Reproduction right Authorization by a list owner for a specific mailer to use that list on a one-time basis.

Request for proposal (RFP) Pro-forma device for outlining specific purchasing requirements that can be responded to in kind by vendors.

Response Incoming telephone contacts generated by media.

Response curve Anticipated incoming contact volume charting its peak and its decline, based on hours, days, weeks, or months.

Response rate Gross or net response received as a percentage of total promotions mailed or contacts made.

Return envelopes Addressed reply envelopes, either stamped or unstamped—as distinguished from business reply envelopes that carry a postage payment guarantee—included with a mailing.

Return postage guaranteed Legend imprinted on the address face of envelopes or other mailing pieces when the mailer wishes the Postal Service to return undeliverable third-class bulk mail. A charge equivalent to the single-piece, third-class rate is made for each piece returned. *See also* **List cleaning**.

Returns Responses to a direct mail program.

Reverse out To change printing areas so that the parts usually black or shaded are reversed and appear white or grey.

R. F. M. R. Acronym for recency-frequency-monetary value ratio, a formula used to evaluate the sales potential of names on a mailing list.

R. O. P. *See* **Run of paper**.

Roll-out Main or largest mailing in a direct mail campaign sent to the remaining names on the list after tests to sample portions of the list have shown positive results.

Rough Rough sketch or preliminary outline of a leaflet or advertisement; also known as *scamp*.

Royalty Sum paid per unit mailed or sold for the use of a list, an imprimatur, a patent or the like.

Running charge Price a list owner charges for names run or passed but not used by a specific mailer.

Run of Paper (1) Term applied to color printing on regular paper and presses, as distinct from separate sections printed on special color presses; also called *run of press*. (2) Term sometimes used to describe an advertisement positioned by publisher's choice—in other than a preferred position—for which a special charge is made.

Run-on price Price from a supplier for continuing to produce (generally print or envelopes) once an initial run is in process; includes only materials and ongoing charges, and not origination or machine makeready.

Saddle stitching Stapling a publication from the back to the center.

Sale Formal agreement to buy, make an appointment, or any other definition of a sale as determined by the objective of a specific case.

Sales conversion rate Number of sales in relation to number of calls initiated or received.

Sales message Description of the features and benefits of a product or service.

Sales presentation Structured anatomy of an offer describing how the product or service works.

Salting Deliberate placing of decoy or dummy names in a list for the purpose of tracing list usage and delivery. *See also* **Decoy** and **Dummy**.

Salting via seeds, dummies, or decoys Adding names with special characteristics to a list for protection and identification purposes.

Sample package (mailing piece) Example of the package to be mailed by the list user to a particular list. Such a mailing piece is submitted to the list owner for approval prior to commitment for one-time use of that list.

Scamp *See* **Rough**.

Scented ink   Printing ink to which a fragrance has been added.

Score   Impressing of an indent or a mark in the paper to make folding easier.

Scratch and sniff   *See* **Scented inks**.

Screen   (1) Use of an outside list (based on credit, income, deliverability, ZIP code selection) to suppress records on a list to be mailed; (2) halftone process in platemaking that reduces the density of color in an illustration.

Screen printing   Method of printing from stencils placed on a fine mesh tightly stretched on a frame, through which ink or paint is forced.

Script   Prepared text presentation used by sales personnel as a tool to convey a sales message in its entirety.

Seasonality   Selection of time of year; the influence of seasonal timing on response rates.

Second class   Second-class mail in the postal rate system; covers periodicals.

Sectional Center (SCF or SCF Center) Postal Service distribution unit comprising different post offices whose ZIP codes start with the same first three digits.

Sectional Center Facility (SCF) Geographic area designated by the first three digits of a ZIP code.

Seed   Dummy or decoy name inserted into a mailing list.

Seeding   Planting of dummy names in a mailing list to check usage, delivery, or unauthorized reuse.

Segment   Portion of a list or file selected on the basis of a special set of characteristics.

Segmentation   Process of separating characteristic groups within a list for target marketing.

Selection   Process of segregating or selecting specific records from a list according to specific criteria.

Selection charge   Fee above the basic cost of a list for a given selection.

Selection criteria   Characteristics that iden-

tify segments or subgroups within a list.

Self-cover   Cover printed on the same paper as the test pages.

Self-mailer   Direct mail piece mailed without an envelope.

Self-standing stuffers   Promotional printed pieces delivered as part of a daily or Sunday newspaper.

Senior citizen lists   Lists of older individuals past a specific age, available for over 50-, 55-, 60-, and 65-year-olds.

Separations   Color separations either prepared by an artist using separate overlays for each color or achieved photographically by use of filters.

Sequence   Arrangement of items according to a specified set of rules or instructions.

Series rate   Special rate offered by publications and other media for a series of advertisements as opposed to a single insertion.

Set-up charge   Flat charge assessed on some lists in addition to the cost per thousand.

Shared mailing   Mailing that promotes the products of two or more companies, with the participants sharing the mailing list and all other costs.

Sheet fed   Relating to a printing technique whereby paper is fed into the printing press in single sheets, as opposed to paper on a roll.

Shipping time   Approximate number of days required for production of a list order.

SIC (Standard Industrial Classification) Classification of businesses, as defined by the U.S. Department of Commerce.

SIC count   Count of the number of records available by two-, three-, four-, or five-digit Industrial Standard Classification.

Signature   In book, magazine, and catalog production, name given to a large printed sheet after it has been folded to the required size; a number of signatures make up a publication.

Significant difference   In mathematical terms, difference between tests of two or

more variables, which is similar differentiation. The significant difference varies with the confidence level desired. Most direct-mail penetration utilizes a 95 percent confidence level, wherein 95 times out of 100 the results found in the test will come close to duplicating on a retest or combination.

Single-family household Private home, housing only one household, as distinct from multiple-family residences.

Singles (1) One- or single-person household; (2) list of unmarried adults, usually for social linking.

Single-step See **One-stage mailing**.

Sleeper See **Dummy name**.

Solo mailing Mailing promoting a single product or a limited group of related products, and usually consisting of a letter, brochure, and reply device enclosed in an envelope.

Sorting (1) Computerized process of changing the given sequence of a list to a different sequence; (2) interfiling two or more lists.

Source count Number of names and addresses, in any given list, for the media (or list sources) from which the names and addresses were derived.

Space ads Mail-order ads in newspapers, magazines, and self-standing stuffers; one of the major media utilized for prospecting for new customers.

Space buyer Media buyer (usually in an advertising agency) who places print mail-order advertising.

Space-sold record Any record on a house file (customers, inquirers, catalog requests) that has been generated through advertising space placed in publications.

Spanish lists Lists based on surname selects available to reach the Hispanic market.

Special position Designated location in a publication ordered by the advertiser for his advertisement, usually at extra cost.

Specific list source Original source material for a compiled file.

Specific order decoy Seed or dummy inserted in the output of a list order for that order only. The specific seed, which identifies the order, is usually in addition to list protection decoys in the same list.

Specifier Individual who can specify or purchase a product or service, particularly at larger businesses; in many cases, this is not the individual who enters the order.

Spine See **Backbone**.

Split run Printing of two or more variants of a promotional ad run on an nth or A/B split through the entire printing: use of geographic segments of a publication for testing of variants.

Split test Two or more samples from the same list, each considered to be representative of the entire list and used for package tests or to test the homogeneity of the list.

Spot color Use of one additional color in printing.

SRDS Standard Rate & Data Service, which prints a rates and data book covering basic information on over 20,000 mailing lists.

Standard Industrial Classification (SIC) Classification of businesses as defined by the U.S. Department of Commerce, used to segment telephone calling lists and direct marketing mailing lists.

Standard Metropolitan Statistical Area (SMSA) U.S. Bureau of the Census term for an area consisting of one or more counties around a central urban area.

State count Number of names and addresses, in a given list, for each state.

Statement stuffer Small printed piece designed to be inserted in an envelope carrying a customer's statement of account.

Step up Use of special premiums to get mail-order buyers to increase their unit of purchase.

Stock art Art sold for use by a number of advertisers.

Stock cut Printing engravings kept in stock by the printer or publisher.

Stock format Direct mail format with pre-printed illustrations and/or headings to

which an advertiser adds its own copy.

Stopper Advertising slang for a striking headline or illustration intended to attract immediate attention.

Storage Data-processing term indicating the volume of name-and-address and attached data that can be stored for future use on a given computer system.

Stratification Capacity to offer demographic segmentation on a list; the addition of such demographics to a customer file.

Student lists Lists of college or high school students. For college students, both home and school addresses are available; for high school students, home addresses for junior and seniors are available.

Stuffers Printed advertising enclosures placed in other media, e.g., newspapers, merchandise packages, and mailings for other products.

Subblock Along with enumeration districts, the smallest geographic segment of the country for which the U.S. Census Bureau provides demographic data.

Subscriber Individual who has paid to receive a periodical.

Success model Set of logical steps followed by successful salespeople to sell a product or service and used as a training example for new salespeople.

Suppression Utilization of data on one or more files to remove any duplication of specific names before a mailing.

Suppression of previous usage Utilization of the previous usage or match codes of the records used as a suppress file. Unduplication can also be assured through fifth-digit pulls, first-digit-of-name pulls, or actual tagging of each prior record used.

Suppression of subscribers Utilization of the subscriber file to suppress a publication's current readers from rental lists prior to mailing.

Surname selection Ethnic selection based on surnames; a method for selection of such easily identifiable groups as Irish, Italian (and hence Catholic), Jewish, and Spanish. Specialists have extended this type of coding to groups such as German, English, Scotch, and Scandinavian.

Suspect (1) Prospect somewhat more likely to order than a cold prospect; (2) in some two-step operations, a name given the initial inquirer when only one in X can be expected to convert.

Swatching Attaching samples of material to a printed piece.

Sweepstakes list (Sweeps) List of responders, the majority of them nonbuyers, to a sweepstakes offer.

Syndicated mailing Mailing prepared for distribution by firms other than the manufacturer or syndicator.

Syndication (1) Selling or distributing mailing lists; (2) offering for sale the findings of a research company.

Syndicator Operation that makes available prepared direct mail promotions for specific products or services to a list owner for mailing to its own list; most syndicators also offer product fulfillment services.

Tabloid Preprinted advertising insert of four or more pages, usually about half the size of a regular newspaper page, designed for insertion into a newspaper.

Tagging (1) Process of adding information to a list; (2) transfer of data or control information for usage and unduplication.

Take-one Leaflet displayed at point of sale or in areas where potential consumers congregate, e.g., credit card recruitment leaflets, display and dispenser units at hotels and restaurants.

Tape Magnetic tape, the principal means of recording, storing, and retrieving data for computerized mailing list operations.

Tape conversion Conversion of hard-copy data to magnetic tape.

Tape format (layout) Location of each field, character by character, of each record on a list on tape.

Tape record All the information about an

individual or company contained on a specific magnetic tape.

Tape reel   Medium on which data for computer addressing or merge/purge are handled.

Target   Person to whom a sales call is directed.

Target Group Index (TGI)   Analysis of purchasing habits among consumers covering 4,500 brands/services in over 500 product fields.

Target market   Most likely group determined to have the highest potential for buying a product or service.

Tear sheet   Printed page cut from a publication; sometimes used in place of a complete voucher copy as evidence of publication. *See also* **Voucher copy**.

Teaser Advertisement or promotion planned to excite curiosity about a later advertisement or promotion.

Telco   Telephone-operating company.

Telecommunication   Any electrical transmission of voice or data from sender to receiver(s), including telegraphy, telephony, data transmission, and video-telephony.

Telecommuting   Practice of employees working in their homes while linked to their office by telephone and, in most cases, a computer; sometimes referred to as *telework*.

Telecomputer   Nontechnical term for an Automatic Dialing Recorded Message Player (ADRMP), a machine that automatically dials, plays a prerecorded message, and records responses.

Telemarketing   Use of the telephone as an interactive medium for promotion or promotion response; also known as *teleselling*.

Telemarketing-insensitive medium   Any medium used to advertise a product or service that does not properly highlight a telephone number.

Telemarketing service vendor   One who sells the service of conducting telemarketing calls; also known *telemarketing agency* or *telemarketing service bureau*.

Telephone household   Household with a listed phone number. (Random access calling can ring unlisted and nonpublished numbers.)

Telephone list   List of consumers or establishments compiled with phone numbers from published phone directories.

Telephone list appending   Adding of telephone numbers to mailing lists.

Telephone marketing   Any activity in direct marketing involving the telephone, e.g., list building or telephone follow-up to a lead-generation program.

Telephone Preference Service (TPS)   Program of the Direct Marketing Association that allows consumers who do not want telemarketing calls to have their names removed from a majority of telemarketers' lists with only one request.

Telephone sales   Implementation of the telemarketing plan.

Telephone sales representative (TSR)   Person who markets and sells by telephone; also known as a *telemarketer* or *agent*.

Telephone sales supervisor (TSS)   Person who oversees the performance of TSRs.

Telephone sales techniques   Formalized methods that structure the entire sales process.

Telephone service center   *See* **TSC**.

Teleprospecting   Cold canvassing of telephone households or telephone non-households by personal phone calls (not to be confused with telemarketing, which pertains to calls made to customers or inquirers).

Teleprospecting list   List of prospects with phones used for telephonic (cold calling) prospecting.

Telesales   Function dedicated to receiving or making outgoing contact by telephone.

Test   Period of time in which a minimum of 100 cases are completed for analysis and

management decisions as to whether or not a particular project or program is viable.

Test campaign Mailings of test pieces to a number of outside lists to establish a bank for continuation mailings; must not be to only one list, which is a "continuous series of one experiment."

Testing Preliminary mailing or distribution intended as a preview or pilot before a major campaign. Test mailings are used to determine probable acceptance of a product or service and are usually made to specially selected lists.

Test market Trial market for a new product or service offer.

Test panel List of the parts or samples in a split test.

Test quantity Test mailing to a sufficiently large number of names from a list to enable the mailer to evaluate the responsiveness of the list.

Test tape Selection of representative records within a mailing list that enables a list user or service bureau to prepare for reformatting or converting the list to a more efficient form for the user.

Text Body matter of a page or book as distinguished from the headings.

TGI *See* **Target Group Index**.

Third-class mail Bulk mail. The U.S. Postal Service delivery of direct-mail promotions weighing less than one pound.

Third-party endorsement In a mailing made for the joint benefit of an outside mailer and a company over the company's customer file, the imprimatur of the company; e.g., Britannica mailing the *Farm Journal* list with an offer ostensibly from the publication to its subscribers.

Third-Party unit Service bureau that makes calls for hire; also known as a *contract unit*.

Three-digit ZIP First three digits of a five-digit ZIP code denoting a given sectional center facility of the Postal Service.

Three-line address For consumer mail, a conventional home or household address of an individual; for business mail, the name and address of an establishment without the name of an individual.

Three-up *See* **Four-up**.

Throwaway Advertisement or promotional piece intended for widespread free distribution. Generally printed on inexpensive paper stock, it is most often distributed by hand to passersby or house to house.

Tie-in Cooperative mailing effort involving two or more advertisers.

Till forbid Order for service that is to continue until specifically canceled by the buyer; also known as TF.

Time Media buyer (usually at a specialized agency for direct response electronic) who "buys" time periods and spots for direct response radio or TV promotion.

Time zone sequencing Preparation of national telemarketing lists according to time zones so calls can be made at the most productive times.

Tint Light color, usually used for backgrounds.

Tip-on Item glued to a printed piece.

Title Designation before (prefix) or after (suffix) a name to accurately identify an individual (prefixes—Mr., Mrs., Dr., Sister, etc; suffixes—M.D., Jr., President, Sales etc.).

Title addressing Utilizing the title or function at a business; adding a title to a business address rather than addressing to a specific person by name.

Token Involvement device, often consisting of a perforated portion of an order card designed to be removed from its original position and placed in another designated area on the order card, to signify a desire to purchase the product or service offered.

Town marker Symbol used to identify the end of a mailing list's geographic unit; originated for towns but now used for ZIP codes and sectional centers.

Track record Accounting of what a given list or list segment has done for given mailers in the past.

Trade show registrants   (1) Persons who stopped at a given trade show booth and signed up to receive additional information or a sales call; (2) persons assigned by their companies to operate a trade show booth or booths.

Traffic   Number of calls made or received per hour, day, or month on a single line or trunk of a telephone system.

Traffic builder   Direct mail piece intended primarily to attract recipients to the mailer's place of business.

Transparency   Positive color film such as a slide.

Trial buyer   Person who buys a short-term supply of a product, or who buys the product with the understanding that it may be examined, used, or tested for a specified time before they need to decide whether to pay for it or to return it.

Trials   Individuals who ordered a short-term subscription to a magazine, newsletter, or continuity program. In list rental, trials are not equal to those who convert to customer status.

Trial subscriber   Person who orders a service or publication on a conditional basis, which may relate to delaying payment, the right to cancel, a shorter than normal term, or a special introductory price.

Truncation   Dropping the end of words or names to fit an address line into 30 characters for four-across Cheshire addressing.

TSC   Telephone sales center, the department that is responsible for making and receiving telemarketing sales contacts.

Turnover rate   Number of times within a year that a list is or can be rented.

Two-stage sell   Process that involves two mailings or approaches—the first inviting an inquiry and the second converting the inquiry to a sale.

Type and scan   Computerized data entry system that utilizes data typed by typewriter with a special font that is then optically scanned to magnetic tape.

Typeface   All printing type of a specific design.

Typesetting   Assembly of reading matter by the use of handpicked metal type, by keyboarding, and/or by casting or photo-typesetting.

Type specification   *See* **Mark-up**.

Uncollectible   One who hasn't paid for goods and services at the end of a normal series of collection efforts.

Undeliverable   Mailing piece returned as not being deliverable; also known as a *nixie*.

Unique ZIP code   Five-digit ZIP code assigned by the Postal Service to a company or organization to expedite delivery of its large volume of incoming letter mail. With the advent of ZIP + 4, a large number of businesses and institutions now have their own unique ZIP code.

Unit of sale   Average dollar amount spent by customers on a mailing list.

Universe   Total numbers of individuals that might be included on a mailing list; all of those fitting a single set of specifications.

Update   Addition of recent transactions and current information to the master (main) list to reflect the current status of each record on the list.

Up front   Securing payment for a product offered by mail order before the product is sent.

UPS   United Parcel Service, a major supplier of small-package delivery.

Up-scale list   Generic description of a list of affluents; can be mail-responsive or compiled.

Up-selling   Promotion of more expensive products or services over the product originally discussed.

Usage history   Record of the utilization of a given list by mailers, managers, or brokers.

U.S. Business Universe   Database containing the names and addresses of virtually every business, institution, and office of a professional in the United States.

User Firm that uses telemarketing in its overall marketing program, whether it is executed in-house or by a telemarketing service vendor.

Utilities One of the major groupings of business lists, public service industries (such as water, power, light), often included with mining, contracting, manufacturing, and transportation as part of the industrial complex.

Validation mailing Second modest mailing to confirm initial test results prior to making a large continuation or rollout.

Variable field Way of laying out list information for formatting that assigns a specific sequence to the data, but not specific positions.

Variable-length record Means of packing characters on a name and address record so as to eliminate blank spaces. For most rental work such lists must then be reformatted to fixed fields in which each field, whether filled or unfilled, occupies the same numerical positions on a tape.

Variables (criteria) Identifiable and selectable characteristics that can be tested for mailing purposes.

Vendor Supplier of any facet of direct response advertising: lists, creative, printing, marketing, computerization, merge/purge, fulfillment.

Verification Process of determining the validity of an order by sending a questionnaire to the customer.

Volume discount Scheduled discount for volume buyers of a given compiled list.

Voters registration list List utilized to add multiple family members as well as age data to compiled consumer files.

Voucher copy Free copy of a publication sent to an advertiser or organization as evidence that an advertisement has been published.

Wallet flap envelope Special business reply envelope that utilizes the inside of a large flap to serve as the order form.

Warranty list List of buyers who mail in warranty cards identifying the particular product and its type, with or without additional demographic data.

Weighting (1) For evaluation of customer lists, a means of applying values to the RF$UISM data for each cell. (For larger lists this is better done by a computer regression analysis); (2) for merge/purge, a means of applying a form of mathematical analysis to each component for unduplicating.

White mail Incoming mail that is not on a form sent out by the advertiser; all mail other than orders and payments.

Wholesaler (Reseller) Merchandiser of lists compiled or owned by others, usually working with compiled lists mainly covering a local area; differentiated from a broker by type of list and coverage.

Window envelope Envelope with a die-cut portion on the front that permits viewing the address printed on an enclosure; the die-cut window may or may not be covered with a transparent material.

Wing mailer Label-affixing device that uses strips of paper on which addresses have been printed.

With the grain When folding paper, parallel to the grain.

Word processor Typewriter with a memory utilized to produce individualized letters; also useful in updating and expanding smaller mailing lists.

Working women In direct mail, a relatively new selection factor. Lists may be either compiled (e.g., women executives of S&P major companies) or mail-order responsive (e.g., paid subscribers to *Working Woman* magazine).

Workstation Area where telephone reps perform their jobs; (2) integrated voice /data terminal.

Yield (1) Count anticipated from a computer inquiry; (2) responses received from a promotional effort; (3) mailable totals from a merge/purge.

Yuppies Young, upwardly mobile professional people.

ZIP code Registered trademark of the Postal Service; a five- or nine-digit code identifying regions in the United States.

ZIP code count In a list, the number of names and addresses within each ZIP code.

Zip code omission Loss of a ZIP code on a given mailing list.

ZIP + 4 code Designation by the Postal Service for the nine-digit ZIP-coding structure.

ZIP code sequence Arrangement of names and addresses on a list according to the numeric progression of the ZIP code in each record. This form of list formatting is mandatory for mailing at bulk third-class mail rates, based on the Postal Service sorting requirement.

Zip code string Merging of multiple selections into one ZIP code string to avoid minimums.

Index